SIPRI Yearbook 1987
World Armaments and Disarmament

sipri

Stockholm International Peace Research Institute

SIPRI is an independent institute for research into problems of peace and conflict, especially those of arms control and disarmament. It was established in 1966 to commemorate Sweden's 150 years of unbroken peace.

The Institute is financed mainly by the Swedish Parliament. The staff, the Governing Board and the Scientific Council are international.

The Governing Board and Scientific Council are not responsible for the views expressed in the publications of the Institute.

Governing Board

Ambassador Ernst Michanek, Chairman (Sweden)
Egon Bahr (Federal Republic of Germany)
Professor Francesco Calogero (Italy)
Dr Max Jakobson (Finland)
Professor Dr Karlheinz Lohs (German Democratic Republic)
Professor Emma Rothschild (United Kingdom)
Sir Brian Urquhart (United Kingdom)
The Director

Director

Dr Walther Stützle (Federal Republic of Germany)

sipri

Stockholm International Peace Research Institute
Pipers Väg 28, S-171 73 Solna, Sweden
Cable: PEACERESEARCH STOCKHOLM
Telephone: 46 8/55 97 00

SIPRI Yearbook 1987

World Armaments and Disarmament

FOR REFERENCE ONLY

sipri

Stockholm International Peace Research Institute

OXFORD UNIVERSITY PRESS
1987

Oxford University Press, Walton Street, Oxford OX2 6DP
Oxford New York Toronto
Delhi Bombay Calcutta Madras Karachi
Petaling Jaya Singapore Hong Kong Tokyo
Nairobi Dar es Salaam Cape Town
Melbourne Auckland
and associated companies in
Beirut Berlin Ibadan Nicosia

Oxford is a trade mark of Oxford University Press

Published in the United States
by Oxford University Press, New York

Previous Yearbooks published under title
'World Armaments and Disarmament:
SIPRI Yearbook [year of publication]'

British Library Cataloguing in Publication Data
SIPRI yearbook of world armaments and
disarmament.—1987–
1. Arms control—Periodicals 2. Disarmament—Periodicals
3. Arms and armour—
I. Stockholm International Peace Research Institute II. World armaments
and disarmament.
ISSN 0307–2205
327.1'74'05 JX1974
ISBN 0–19–829114–0

Library of Congress Cataloging in Publication Data
Data available

Set by Wyvern Typesetting, Bristol
Printed and bound in Great Britain by
Biddles Ltd., Guildford and King's Lynn

Contents

Part II. Military expenditure, the arms trade and armed conflicts

Part III. Developments in arms control

Preface

The eighteenth SIPRI Yearbook is a work of both change and continuity alike. It bears witness to the continuous efforts of an international and independent institute to document the development of an increasingly complex situation in the world of armaments and disarmament. And it continues to do so in the somewhat artificial framework of a calendar year, despite the fact that no year is an independent political entity in itself but is always tied in with the past and related to the future. The task is not made easier by the fact that the future slips into the present—from the completion of the manuscripts (at the end of 1986) to the publication date (June 1987). This difficulty is particularly felt when the international situation, especially the relation between East and West, is in a high state of flux. In early 1987 it became patently clear that, with General Secretary Mikhail Gorbachev firmly in charge of Soviet policy and boldly on the offensive in the area of arms control, and with the political authority of President Ronald Reagan seriously in question, the Yearbook task had become an even more difficult one for an observer of international security. Still, the Yearbook aim is as always: to serve the public with as objective a picture as possible of what has happened in the world politico-military affairs in the past year.

In the *SIPRI Yearbook 1987* the reader is offered a new format, designed to facilitate the endeavour to find a way through the facts, figures and analysis. From this year, the reader will find the Yearbook divided into four parts: I. Weapons and technology, II. Arms trade, military expenditure and armed conflicts, III. Developments in arms control and IV. Special features, focusing on important subjects that arise during the year, such as, this year, the Chernobyl disaster, or that re-emerge as crucial problems on the way to a less-armed world, such as the question of arms control verification.

Although generously supported by a grant from the Swedish Parliament, SIPRI is too small a research institute to cover all the relevant issues entirely on its own. This year we are proud to have secured the co-operation of several distinguished international researchers and experts outside the SIPRI staff, for whose contributions SIPRI is grateful: Dr Hans Blix, Dr Christoph Bertram, Dr Steven Canby, Dr Richard Darilek, Stephen Goose and Professor Allan Krass. But no Yearbook could appear if there were not a dedicated staff to carry the burden of designing, researching, writing and editing its contents. Richard Fieldhouse accepted the complex task of serving as the Yearbook Director, guiding the effort from conception to completion, pulling together many different issues which are difficult to co-ordinate in one book. Connie Wall and Billie Bielckus again shouldered the tremendous responsibility of editing the Yearbook and piloting it through all the thorny stages of production. No manuscript could, of course, be prepared for printing without the committed help of the secretaries, and special thanks are due this year to Marianne Lyons, Åsa Pihlstrand, Kerstin Sköldberg, Bella Kjellgren and Miyoko Suzuki. Gerd Hagmeyer-Gaverus, SIPRI's computer systems manager, performed the technical miracles that were needed for production of the Yearbook. I would like to extend my thanks to all of them, including Barbara Adams, who bravely accepted my request to help launch the introduction of the first Yearbook to appear during my service as SIPRI Director. All have met the challenge with a degree of devotion that testifies well to their commitment to the cause of peace.

Given the importance of the subjects covered by the Yearbook, SIPRI invites the readers to assist us in our endeavour to further improve its contents and format with any comment or suggestion they may care to offer. This invitation is extended in the spirit uniquely expressed by Albrecht Goes, the German poet and theologian. In his book *Tagwerk* he recalls the inscription on the Hiroshima memorial: 'Rest peacefully—it will not happen again.' He then adds: 'This may well be said there. Our thinking, however, must be guided by a somewhat different imperative: "Watch carefully; otherwise it will happen again".'

Dr Walther Stützle
Director of SIPRI
March 1987

GLOSSARY AND CONVENTIONS

Acronyms

AAM	Air-to-air missile	ERW	Enhanced radiation (neutron) weapon
AASM	Advanced air-to-surface missile	Eureka	European Research Co-ordination Agency
ABM	Anti-ballistic missile	FEBA	Forward edge of the battle area
ACM	Advanced cruise missile	FOFA	Follow-on forces attack
ADM	Atomic demolition munition	GLCM	Ground-launched cruise missile
ALCM	Air-launched cruise missile	IAEA	International Atomic Energy Agency
ASAT	Anti-satellite	ICBM	Intercontinental ballistic missile
ASM	Air-to-surface missile	INF	Intermediate-range nuclear force
ASW	Anti-submarine warfare		
ATBM	Anti-tactical ballistic missile	IOC	Initial operating capability
ATM	Anti-tank missile	IRBM	Intermediate-range ballistic missile
AWACS	Airborne warning and control system	ISMA	International Satellite Monitoring Agency
BMD	Ballistic missile defence		
BW	Biological weapon (warfare)	KEW	Kinetic-energy weapon
C³I	Command, control, communications and intelligence	Laser	Light amplification by simulated emission of radiation
CBM	Confidence-building measure	LRTNF	Long-range theatre nuclear forces
CBW	Chemical and biological warfare	MAD	Mutual assured destruction
CD	Conference on Disarmament (Geneva)	MARV	Manoeuvrable re-entry vehicle
		MFR	Mutual force reduction
CDE	Conference on Disarmament in Europe (Stockholm)	MBT	Main battle tank
CEP	Circular error probable	MHV	Miniature homing vehicle
CSBM	Confidence- and security-building measure	MIRV	Multiple independently targetable re-entry vehicle
CSCE	Conference on Security and Co-operation in Europe (Helsinki, Belgrade, Madrid, Vienna)	MLRS	Multiple-launch rocket system
		MoU	Memorandum of understanding
		MRV	Multiple (but not independently targetable) re-entry vehicle
CTB	Comprehensive test ban	MURFAAMCE	Mutual Reductions of Forces and Armaments and Associated Measures in Central Europe
CW	Chemical weapon (warfare)		
DC	Disarmament Commission		
DEW	Directed-energy weapon		
EDI	European Defence Initiative	NATO	North Atlantic Treaty Organization
EMP	Electromagnetic pulse	NNA	Neutral and non-aligned countries
Enmod	Environmental modification		

NPT	Non-Proliferation Treaty	SLBM	Submarine-launched ballistic missile
NST	Nuclear and Space Talks		
PNE(T)	Peaceful Nuclear Explosions (Treaty)	SLCM	Sea-launched cruise missile
		SRAM	Short-range attack missile
R&D	Research and development	SRBM	Short-range ballistic missile
RDT&E	Research, development, testing and evaluation	SSB	Non-nuclear-powered ballistic-missile submarine
RPV	Remotely piloted vehicle	SSBN	Nuclear-powered ballistic-missile submarine
RV	Re-entry vehicle	SSN	Nuclear-powered attack sub-marine
SALT	Strategic arms limitation talks		
SAM	Surface-to-air missile	START	Strategic arms reduction talks
SCC	Standing Consultative Commission (SALT)	TNF	Theatre nuclear forces
		TTB(T)	Threshold Test Ban (Treaty)
SDI	Strategic Defense Initiative (US)	WTO	Warsaw Treaty Organization (Warsaw Pact)
SICBM	Small ICBM		

Glossary

Anti-ballistic missile (ABM) system	Weapon system for intercepting and destroying ballistic missiles.
Binary chemical weapon	A shell or other device filled with two chemicals of relatively low toxicity which mix and react while the device is being delivered to the target, the reaction product being a supertoxic chemical warfare agent, such as nerve gas.
Biological weapon (BW)	Living organisms or infective material derived from them, which are intended for use in warfare to cause disease or death in man, animals or plants, and the means of their delivery.
Chemical weapon (CW)	Chemical substances—whether gaseous, liquid or solid—which might be employed as weapons in combat because of their direct toxic effects on man, animals or plants, and the means of their delivery.
Circular error probable (CEP)	A measure of missile accuracy: the radius of a circle, centred on the target, within which 50 per cent of the weapons aimed at the target are expected to fall.
Conference on Disarmament (CD)	Multilateral arms control negotiating body, based in Geneva, which is composed of 40 states, including all the nuclear weapon powers.
Conference on Disarmament in Europe (CDE)	Conference on Confidence- and Security-Building Measures and Disarmament in Europe, the first stage of which opened in Stockholm, Sweden, in January 1984, and concluded in September 1986. Part of the CSCE process. *See also*: Conference on Security and Co-operation in Europe.
Conference on Security and Co-operation in Europe (CSCE)	Conference of the NATO, WTO and European neutral and non-aligned states, which began in 1972 and in 1975 adopted a Final Act (also called the Helsinki Declaration) containing, among others, a Document on confidence-building measures and disarmament. The next follow-up meeting began in November 1986 in Vienna.

Conventional weapon	Weapon not having mass destruction effects. *See also*: Weapon of mass destruction.
Counterforce attack	Nuclear attack directed against military targets.
Countervalue attack	Nuclear attack directed against civilian targets.
Cruise missile	Unmanned, self-propelled, guided weapon-delivery vehicle which sustains flight through aerodynamic lift, generally flying at very low altitudes to avoid radar detection, sometimes following the contours of the terrain. It can be air-, ground- or sea-launched and deliver a conventional or nuclear warhead.
Disarmament Commission (DC)	A subsidiary, deliberative organ of the UN General Assembly for disarmament matters, composed of all UN members.
First-strike capability	Theoretical capability to launch a pre-emptive nuclear attack which would destroy all of an adversary's retaliatory nuclear forces.
Flexible response	The NATO doctrine for reaction to an attack with a full range of military options, including the use of nuclear weapons.
Helsinki Declaration	*See*: Conference on Security and Co-operation in Europe.
Initial operating capability (IOC)	Date by which a weapon system is first deployed, ready for use in the field.
Intercontinental ballistic missile (ICBM)	Ballistic missile with a range in excess of 5500 km.
Intermediate-range nuclear force (INF)	Theatre nuclear forces with a range between 1000 and 5500 km. *See also*: Theatre nuclear force.
Kiloton (kt)	Measure of the explosive yield of a nuclear weapon equivalent to 1000 tons of trinitrotoluene (TNT) high explosive. (The bomb detonated at Hiroshima in World War II had a yield of some 12–15 kilotons.)
Launcher	Equipment which launches a missile. ICBM launchers are land-based launchers which can be either fixed or mobile. SLBM launchers are missile tubes on submarines.
Launch-weight	Weight of a fully loaded ballistic missile at the time of launch.
Megaton (Mt)	Measure of the explosive yield of a nuclear weapon equivalent to one million tons of trinitrotoluene (TNT) high explosive.
Multiple independently targetable re-entry vehicle (MIRV)	Re-entry vehicles, carried by one missile, which can be directed to separate targets along separate trajectories (as distinct from MRVs).
Mutual Assured Destruction (MAD)	Concept of reciprocal deterrence which rests on the ability of the nuclear weapon powers to inflict intolerable damage on one another after surviving a nuclear attack. *See also*: Second-strike capability.
Mutual reduction of forces and armaments and associated measures in Central Europe (MURFAAMCE)	Subject of negotiations between NATO and the Warsaw Treaty Organization, which began in Vienna in 1973. Often referred to as mutual force reduction (MFR).
Nuclear and Space Talks (NST)	Negotiations between the USA and the USSR on strategic and intermediate-range nuclear weapons and on space weapon issues. Began in March 1985.
Peaceful nuclear explosion (PNE)	Application of a nuclear explosion for non-military purposes such as digging canals or harbours or creating underground cavities.
Re-entry vehicle (RV)	That part of a ballistic missile designed to carry a nuclear warhead and to re-enter the earth's atmosphere in the terminal phase of the missile's trajectory.

Second-strike capability	Ability to survive a nuclear attack and launch a retaliatory blow large enough to inflict intolerable damage on the opponent. *See also*: Mutual Assured Destruction.
Standing Consultative Commission (SCC)	US–Soviet consultative body established in accordance with the SALT agreements, to promote the objectives and implementation of the agreements.
Strategic arms limitation talks (SALT)	Negotiations between the Soviet Union and the United States, held from 1969 to 1979, which sought to limit the strategic nuclear forces, both offensive and defensive, of both sides.
Strategic arms reduction talks (START)	Negotiations between the Soviet Union and the United States, initiated in 1982, which sought to reduce the strategic nuclear forces of both sides. Terminated by the USSR in December 1983. The Nuclear and Space Talks that opened in Geneva in March 1985 include strategic arms reductions. *See also*: Nuclear and Space Talks.
Strategic nuclear weapons	ICBMs, SLBMs and bomber aircraft carrying nuclear weapons of intercontinental range (over 5500 km).
Terminal guidance	Guidance provided in the final, near-target phase of the flight of the missile.
Theatre nuclear force (TNF)	Nuclear weapons with ranges of less than 5500 km, sometimes divided into long-range (over 1000 km), medium-range (200–1000 km) and short-range (up to 200 km) theatre nuclear weapons.
Throw-weight	The sum of the weight of a ballistic missile's re-entry vehicle(s), dispensing mechanisms, penetration aids, and targeting and separation devices.
Toxins	Poisonous substances which are products of organisms but are inanimate and incapable of reproducing themselves. Some toxins may also be produced by chemical synthesis.
Warhead	That part of a weapon which contains the explosive or other material intended to inflict damage.
Weapon of mass destruction	Nuclear weapon and any other weapon which may produce comparable effects, such as chemical and biological weapons.
Yield	Released nuclear explosive energy expressed as the equivalent of the energy produced by a given number of tons of trinitrotoluene (TNT) high explosive. *See also*: Kiloton and Megaton.

Conventions

. .	Data not available or not applicable
—	Nil or a negligible figure
( )	Uncertain data
[ ]	Estimate with a high degree of uncertainty
m.	million
b.	billion (thousand million)
$	US $, unless otherwise indicated

SIPRI Yearbook 1987: World Armaments and Disarmament

Oxford University Press, Oxford, 1987, 495 pp.
(Stockholm International Peace Research Institute)
ISBN 0-19-829-114-0

ABSTRACTS

ARKIN, W. M., BURROWS, A. S., COCHRAN, T. B., FIELDHOUSE, R. W., NORRIS, R. S. & SANDS, J. I., 'Nuclear weapons', in *SIPRI Yearbook 1987*, pp. 3–43.

1986 was a year of extreme contrasts in the nuclear weapon field. On the one hand, the USA and the USSR agreed in principle to radically reduce and even abolish entire categories of nuclear weapons. On the other hand, all five nuclear weapon states continued with their significant nuclear weapon modernization programmes. The USA and the USSR each introduced at least one new strategic weapon system; Britain began construction of its first Trident Class submarine; France deployed the first of a new generation of nuclear air-to-surface missiles, and China conducted a series ·of missile tests apparently for MIRV applications, and revealed that its first SSBN is operational. As in the past, the nuclear weapon developments outpaced the arms control talks.

FIELDHOUSE, R. & NORRIS, R. S., 'Nuclear explosions', in *SIPRI Yearbook 1987*, pp. 45–55.

Nuclear weapon testing issues are again at the centre of the arms control and nuclear weapon debates. The great international interest in a comprehensive test ban and the current differences between the USA and the USSR on nuclear weapon testing issues have focused renewed attention on the subject. However, there is a disparity between the most basic information about how many nuclear explosions are conducted and the more difficult questions of why nations conduct nuclear explosions and whether they can agree to cease them. By improving and studying the available information on nuclear explosions a clearer understanding may permit movement towards the task of limiting and ceasing all nuclear explosions. If one knows the various sources of information on nuclear explosions and understands the problems and limitations of such information, it becomes clear that more and better information is necessary.

JASANI, B., 'Military use of outer space', in *SIPRI Yearbook 1987*, pp. 57–84.

Despite the spate of recent space launch failures both the USA and the USSR continue their military space programmes vigorously. The USA is reviving its expendable rocket programme and has conducted important SDI tests in space. These tests have raised important questions about the conflict between continued SDI tests and US compliance with the 1972 ABM Treaty. The USSR has entered a phase of launching sophisticated long-lived photoreconnaissance satellites. It seems unlikely that US-Soviet agreement on strategic defence research or deployment will materialize without understanding of the Soviet research programme. Without information from the Soviet Union, decision-makers and the general public are dependent on US sources. It is important that this situation be corrected before the 1987 ABM Treaty Review Conference, which is faced with a serious lack of information about research by the major space powers.

CANBY, S., 'Conventional weapon technologies', in *SIPRI Yearbook 1987*, pp. 85–95.

The need to strengthen conventional military forces is increasingly recognized. Many believe this can be done via standardization and advances in state-of-the-art technology. The nature of emerging technologies is leading to shifts in the way countries manage high technology, the manner in which technologies translate into weapon modernization and the impact of technology on ground and anti-tank warfare. Much modernization is driven by a 'deficiency race' between opponents. Much is an attempt by military and industry to improve the attributes of weapons simply because it can be done, with little thought as to how improvements translate into operational military value. Among the interesting developments was the fibre-optic guided missile. It is a rare example of technologies coming together to produce a novel application and expanded capabilities in a simple and inexpensive manner.

PERRY ROBINSON, J. P., 'Chemical and biological warfare: developments in 1986', in *SIPRI Yearbook 1987*, pp. 97–115.

The CBW arms control regime continued to be violated during 1986. Despite international condemnation, Iraq continued to use chemical weapons in its war ·with Iran and there were numerous allegations of violations by other states. Although CW talks proceeded at different levels throughout the year, the pace of arms control negotiation in this field was clearly outstripped by that of armament. The Reagan Administration finally gained authorization for CW-weapon production and, led by the USA and France, NATO finally committed itself to modernization and expansion of its CW forces. Western sources continued to report that the USSR was still increasing its CW weapon capabilities. Soviet statements made during the year stood in sharp contrast to Western reports of Soviet deployments of chemical weapons in East European countries and their supply to other governments.

OHLSON, T., & SKÖNS, E., 'The trade in major conventional weapons', in *SIPRI Yearbook 1987*, pp. 181–296.

Despite severe economic problems, Third World countries receive about two-thirds of the global flow of major weapons, of which almost half are accounted for by five countries—Iraq, Egypt, India, Syria and Saudi Arabia. The arms imports of all other Third World countries have declined by 25% between the periods 1977–81 and 1982–86. The USA and the USSR still dominate global arms sales, but their joint share in deliveries to the Third World is declining. More commercially oriented suppliers—particularly in Western Europe but also in China and the Third World—are increasing their shares. Fierce competition coincides with an overall reduction of global demand for weapons. The shift towards a buyer's market—in combination with the specific type of demand created by the Iraq–Iran War—has led to structural changes on the arms market. Numerous scandals during 1986 illustrate that commercial aspirations and political considerations frequently clash. The political will and ability to restrain arms flow are low.

TULLBERG, R. & HAGMEYER-GAVERUS, G., 'World military expenditure', in *SIPRI Yearbook 1987*, pp. 119–79.

Reasons behind the absence of estimates of Soviet or Chinese military expenditure and regional and world totals are explained. The trends in other countries are examined. For the second year running the US defence budget allocation showed a reduction in real terms. Whereas figures show Middle Eastern military expenditure to have fallen since 1984, there are few reliable data from countries involved in armed conflicts and much variation within the region. In India and Pakistan superpower patronage is fuelling a costly arms race; the Japanese military budget of December 1986 breached the 1% limit for the first time; military expenditure in Africa has declined since 1980; and despite conflicts in Central America there was little detectable increase in domestic military spending—the military activity is in part determined by security assistance from other governments and international organizations. A World Bank study on Argentine military spending is discussed. World spending on military R&D is estimated at $85–100 billion, and is heavily concentrated in a few countries.

GOOSE, S. D., 'Armed conflicts in 1986, and the Iraq–Iran War', in *SIPRI Yearbook 1987*, pp. 297–320.

War and armed conflict flourished in 1986, with 36 armed conflicts in progress. These conflicts involved some five and one-half million soldiers from 41 countries, one-quarter of the world's nations. Many other nations are involved in other ways, including arms transfers or other support for the combatants. Many of the conflicts are guerrilla struggles. All the conflicts pose an increasing threat to civilians near the fighting; many of the conflicts carry the risk of escalation and the possibility of involving the superpowers. Of all the armed conflicts during 1986, the Iraq–Iran War was the most violent and costly, and perhaps the most significant in terms of its effects on other nations. It is estimated that this war has caused one million casualties since it began. Iraq has used chemical weapons on several occasions and Iran uses 'human wave' tactics that result in huge casualties. There is no end of the war in sight, not least because many outside nations help keep the war going with their assistance. Neither side is able to win the war and neither can accept the other's terms for peace.

BERTRAM, C., 'US–Soviet nuclear arms control', in *SIPRI Yearbook 1987*, pp. 323–37.

1986 was an extraordinary year for East–West arms control. Never before have the positions of the USSR and the USA seemed so close. Much of the year witnessed the often encouraging diplomatic efforts towards compromise between the world's major powers. Yet, at the end of the year, the barriers blocking agreement proved insurmountable for the time being. Arms control once again seemed to have reached a dead end. However, a new if more modest alternative to traditional arms control—that of practised but not negotiated arms control based on unilateral restraint—might have a chance to evolve. This appears to be a distinct possibility with the US Congress and perhaps with Soviet decision-makers as well. Although not a replacement for negotiated and ratified treaties, unilateral restraint is preferable to the alternative of none.

DARILEK, R., 'The future of conventional arms control in Europe, A tale of two cities: Stockholm, Vienna', in *SIPRI Yearbook 1987*, pp. 339–81.

Conventional arms control in Europe has come to an important juncture. The conclusion of the Stockholm Conference in September 1986 represents the first arms control agreement involving the two superpowers since 1979, and the best effort yet at what are called confidence- and security-building measures in the CSCE process. At the same time, the NATO-WTO talks on Mutual and Balanced Force Reductions, which have been held in Vienna since 1973, have not produced any visible success. The question is what the future will hold for conventional arms control in Europe, whether on operations—as in Stockholm—or on forces—as in Vienna—or both. The Stockholm results chart new ground in several areas, particularly their binding nature, verification provisions and the inclusion of all of Europe 'from the Atlantic to the Urals' in the zone of application. Whether or not these concepts can be applied to conventional arms reduction efforts in Europe remains to be seen, although some lessons can be drawn now. The fundamentally different approaches of the two processes and the many different political imperatives they encompass diminish the possibility of simply merging CDE and MBFR.

GOLDBLAT, J., 'Multilateral arms control efforts', in *SIPRI Yearbook 1987*, pp. 383–408.

In 1986 the Conference on Disarmament again failed to reach agreement on any of its agenda items. There was slight progress towards a chemical weapons ban, but the draft treaty still contains considerable gaps. Talks on the cessation of nuclear weapon tests were conducted at cross purposes: the USSR insists on an immediate halt to testing, while the USA sees a test ban as a distant goal. Nevertheless, a few interesting proposals for verification of compliance may facilitate meaningful limitations on US and Soviet testing. The need to reinforce the legal regime of outer space is widely recognized and suggestions for confidence-building undertakings related to the protection of satellites were put forward. On the regional level, the Treaty of Rarotonga entered into force, establishing a nuclear-free zone in the South Pacific, thus strengthening the global non-proliferation regime. The USA refused to sign the additional protocols, while the USSR signed with reservations that have weakened the Treaty. The Contadora Act remains unsigned because of the continued conflict between the USA and Nicaragua.

GOLDBLAT, J., 'The review of the Biological Weapons Convention', in *SIPRI Yearbook 1987*, pp. 409–22.

The second Review Conference of the BW Convention, held in 1986, has strengthened the authority of the Convention. The parties reaffirmed their commitment to implement its provisions and upheld unreservedly its comprehensive scope which excludes loopholes for the use of biological science for other than peaceful purposes. Some procedures have been established to clarify controversial issues, while the agreed confidence-building measures creating greater openness in the field of biological research may help to reduce or remove suspicions of breaches. All this could add to the effectiveness of the Convention.

BLIX, H., 'The Chernobyl reactor accident: the international significance and results', in *SIPRI Yearbook 1987*, pp. 425–32.

The Chernobyl accident caught the world by surprise. The international community had not expected such an event since national governments are responsible for and presumed to apply strict safety and control standards to their nuclear reactor operations. The accident shocked many into realizing that the existing system of international co-operation on nuclear energy safety matters, resting largely with the International Atomic Energy Agency, was not sufficient to adequately handle such events. Consequently these nations agreed to several measures of further co-operation that will help to reduce the likelihood of similar disasters in the future or to minimize their dangers if they do occur. The impression made by Chernobyl reminded states that more needs to be done to improve nuclear safety and prevent future nuclear disasters.

KRASS, A., 'Recent developments in arms control verification technology', in *SIPRI Yearbook 1987*, pp. 433–46.

Two areas of verification technology are examined in which significant progress has recently been made. In seismology theoretical understanding of the seismic signals from earthquakes and explosions has increased, especially concerning the usefulness of high-frequency (greater than 10 Hz) body waves for discrimination at low yields. Both earthquake and noise signals are strongly suppressed at high frequencies, allowing the detection and identification of even strongly decoupled explosions with high confidence. With unmanned seismic monitoring stations a comprehensive test ban treaty would be highly verifiable. Progress in adaptive optics, synthetic aperture radar and very long baseline interferometry have opened significant new possibilities for earth-based observation and imaging of space objects. Successful tests of atmospheric compensation of both laser beams and radar signals have demonstrated the feasibility of relatively high resolutions, allowing the verification by national technical means of restrictions on a variety of space weapons.

Introduction: 1986—a year of peace?

WALTHER STÜTZLE

Superscript numbers refer to the list of notes and references at the end of the chapter.

I. 1986: An overview

1986 was not what the United Nations had proclaimed it to be: the International Year of Peace. It has been a year of both change and continuity. While the first is closely associated with one man in particular, Mikhail Gorbachev, the latter has to do with the fundamental problems of international security, not only within the East-West context.

The still new General Secretary of the Central Committee of the Communist Party of the Soviet Union (CPSU), at the helm for only a little more than two years now, has been presenting a new political style and new approaches to domestic and foreign policy issues at an almost breath-taking pace. With the new party programme accepted at the Twenty-Seventh Party Congress in February 1986, the thrust of Gorbachev's political plan has clearly emerged: foreign policy has been subordinated to the demands of the Soviet Union's domestic agenda. To the extent that foreign policy occupies the attention of the Soviet leadership, the emphasis is on relations with the United States, with arms control clearly enjoying priority.[1] Whether the new language used by Gorbachev can and will be translated into workable concepts still remains to be seen.[2] No doubt, the release of dissident Andrei Sakharov and Gorbachev's policy of 'Glasnost' (making public) have already earned him credit even in very critical Western circles.[3] Whether these quite new developments can evolve into an enduring policy depends on a number of factors: Will Gorbachev's desire to reform the Soviet system, without changing its basic nature, find support from within the system or will it be perceived as a change forced upon it, thus producing dangerous resistance? Can Gorbachev manage reform so as to anticipate and solve the resulting difficulties that will affect allied countries, such as the German Democratic Republic, Poland and Czechoslovakia, the control of which is of strategic importance to Soviet security? Will Gorbachev be able to reduce the distrust in and suspicion of the USSR, caused by his predecessors, in the West in general and in particular in the United States and among some of its major allies, such as the United Kingdom, France and the Federal Republic of Germany? And finally, will Gorbachev be skilful enough to overcome charges or the appearance of weakness if the West does not resist the temptation to claim that Soviet movement in foreign policy—for example, in arms control—is a result of Western pressure, rather than Gorbachev's plan to shield his domestic reform effort? No answers to these questions are available yet.

Turning to some of the elements of continuity in international security, 1986 has not produced a clearer picture either. True, the great disasters have not happened, but that does not mean that all is well.

At the end of 1986, there were 36 armed conflicts around the world, involving roughly five and a half million soldiers from 41 countries (see chapter 8).

It is also true that the strongest military powers, notably the five nuclear weapon countries—the USA, the USSR, the United Kingdom, France and China—were not engaged in war or military conflict against each other, and so their nuclear arsenals were not being actively used. Likewise, there was not the slightest danger that the dominant alliances of our time—the North Atlantic Treaty Organization (NATO) and the Warsaw Treaty Organization (WTO)— would lose political control over a Europe that looks excessively armed. Yet this situation is not one from which to take great comfort. Basically, two reasons account for this: First, political developments outside the established framework of East-West relations—such as the Iraq-Iran War, or the very serious debt crises—not only cause worries for the countries concerned, commonly referred to as the Third World. But also, as a result of these problems, the industrialized nations of the world may well find their own security affected, if not threatened, should they not produce policies that are more sensitive to the social and economic elements of international security. Second, though East and West dispose of vastly more weapons—nuclear, chemical and conventional—than are needed to ensure the right of self-defence, 1986 has not brought the two major alliances (NATO and the WTO) any closer to arms limitation agreements, let alone arms reductions or disarmament.

II. Continuing problems of international security

Although great attention is focused on East-West issues and arms control, it seems more likely that security crises will erupt in the Third World, thus drawing in the superpowers. One must keep in mind the complex and volatile problems in the developing nations. Three such cases are discussed below.

Iraq-Iran: a war of attrition

The Iraq-Iran War, now in its seventh year, has produced more than the tragedy of approximately one million casualties—350 000 dead and 650 000 wounded. 'The financial and economic costs of the war have been similarly staggering' (see chapter 8). Iraq has so far spent roughly $180 billion on it, and Iran around $220 billion. Measured in terms of oil revenues, on which both countries ultimately depend, they incurred war costs which far exceeded the oil revenues earned ever since the production of oil began in 1918 (in Iran) and in 1931 (in Iraq). What might be even more important for the future of peace is the fact that no external power seems to be able to exert influence on either of these two countries.

Considering the need to end the war and limit its adverse effects on international security, it is necessary to establish communication with the two countries at war. Surely this must be done with great skill and understanding of the nature of the conflict. It is here where the Reagan Administration's attempt to establish new channels of communication via arms sales with what it regarded as the 'more moderate' elements in Tehran seems to have suffered from bad judgement and a high degree of amateurism. This failure must, however, not distract from the remaining need to prevent the conflict from further escalation and possible geographic extension. Nor must the White House Iran fiasco obscure the fact that other governments have also failed, even if in a less visible manner, to exert a calming influence, for example, by limiting arms trade to the combatants, if not actually fuelling the war. Neither the Soviet Union nor, for that matter, the European Community should feel comfortable about their own lack of imagination and political skill in limiting the war. What the Tower Commission, formed in late 1986 to investigate the Iran affair, called 'a US policy that worked against itself'[4] may one day well be remembered as a symptom of the inability and/or unwillingness of most industrialized countries of the North, regardless of their social systems, to have understood in time the dangers of a war that is fought over a religious credo, and that threatens an area from Jordan and Egypt down to Oman, the stability of which is important to all nations, and not only for reasons of oil supply.

How wise are security policies that rely on the war-deterring effect of nuclear and conventional weapons in East-West relations without realizing that fire looms large in the backyard, fuelled by religious zeal?

South Africa: a political and human tragedy

Though of a very different nature, the conflict in South Africa also sheds light on the inability of nuclear weapon states and industrialized countries to act jointly in order to promote peaceful political change before the tragedy erupts into a civil war with even greater bloodshed.

Why is it that all industrialized countries do not apply sanctions against a regime that is founded on a racist philosophy, detains and even tortures children,[5] is involved in overt and/or covert military destabilizing operations against neighbouring majority-ruled states, and completely defies the entire body of the United Nations (UN), of which it has been a member since 1945? Surely one belittles the problem by referring to it as simply the irony of history that Israel, whose people once suffered most from the racist fanaticism of another people—namely, the Jews under the Nazi regime—is providing the South African Government with significant arms deliveries. If anything, this demonstrates what morality is worth in international politics. 1986 has brought South Africa again to the front pages because the cruelty of apartheid policy seems to have moved closer to a civil, perhaps even regional, war. Even if such an escalation can be averted, the seeds of hatred sown among the Blacks, in particular the young, will make it difficult, if not impossible, for other countries, such as those of the European Community, to influence positively South Africa's first and decisive steps into a post-apartheid period.

Debt crisis: the ticking debt bomb

There is a third area of immediate relevance to the security of northern industrial countries, the increasing negative effect of which cannot be influenced by the traditional means of a security policy, that is, weapons and diplomacy. The debt bomb, now ticking for quite a number of years, did not succeed in being defused in 1986 either.

In 1985 Brazil's balance of trade accounted for a surplus of $9.5 billion, but it dropped sharply to only $105 million in January 1986. A correct service on the entire burden of the debt of $108 billion would, however, have required Brazil to pay approximately $23 billion in 1986.[6] In February 1987 Brazil's President, José Sarney, suddenly suspended interest payments, initially for three months.

For a long time now, the debt burden has weighed heavily on the shoulders of Third World countries. President Sarney's recent announcement, however, marks a novelty in the relationship between Third World debtors and creditors. So far only Peru had applied a similar radical method when President Alan García, in August 1985, determined that his country would spend not more than 10 per cent of its export income on debt-servicing.

Whether Argentina, another large debtor country, will follow suit is still unclear as of March 1987. But here also the situation is serious, since the country has reached another decisive moment in fighting its economic deficiencies and is negotiating a new $2.15-billion financing package with its creditors.[7] Argentina's President Raúl Alfonsín has applauded Brazil's decision, and Finance Secretary Mario Brodersohn has announced that Argentina would act similarly should creditors not be forthcoming with new concessions. Brazil's action consequently has to be seen as a major step. Should Brazil's suspension measure succeed, similar concessions cannot easily be denied to other debtors. Should it fail, Brazil's economy is faced with a situation with which it can hardly cope: 'Whatever the outcome, Sarney's decision has turned a completely new page in the history of the debt crisis, so intensively marked by risky development'.[8]

It is by no means clear whether the world banking system could survive if a debtors' cartel emerged based on the philosophy that a breakdown of the world economy is to be preferred to bankruptcy of only the debtor countries. A senior London banker is reported to have likened the process of applying emergency measures to large developing country debtors (since August 1982 when Mexico first ran out of money) to a game of Monopoly: 'The debtor country passes "Go" and receives £200, but the money is scarcely adequate when he moves round the board and lands on Mayfair. Then it all begins again'.[9] Still, creditor countries have thus far proved unable to design a rescheduling of debts that would allow for both the prospect of a promising social and economic development of debtor countries and a lowering of the creditors' risk of economic failure that would occur should major countries default on their debts.

Of course, the solution of this widely underestimated problem cannot be achieved if Third World countries do not also help, for example, by substantially cutting back their military spending, which often amounts to many times the amount of financial development aid they receive.

III. East-West: impasse or movement?

No new arms reduction agreements were concluded in 1986. And yet, 1986 may be remembered as the year in which failure and success in this thorny area of international relations seemed closer to each other than ever before.

The Reykjavik meeting

Many observers hold the view that, at the Reykjavik meeting on 11 and 12 October 1986, General Secretary Mikhail Gorbachev and President Ronald Reagan missed a historic and unique opportunity for substantial progress in arms control. But did opportunities really exist? The question has to be asked: What was the principal interest of both leaders when they met at Reykjavik?

In order to make a success out of Reykjavik (which was supposed to be a preparatory meeting for a real summit meeting but which quickly developed into fully-fledged negotiations), no less was called for than consensus on whether or not to maintain the 1972 Anti-Ballistic Missile (ABM) Treaty. Thus the crucial question was whether or not both leaders would muster sufficient political resolve to preserve the Treaty, which is the cornerstone of the US-Soviet strategic relationship. After all, interpretation difficulties are not a new feature in the history of international treaties. The ABM Treaty is no exception in this respect. It is no surprise, therefore, that the negotiators of the ABM Treaty had foreseen that developments could emerge which would test the will of both parties to the Treaty regarding adherence to the political philosophy—equal security through mutual vulnerability.

It was this prudent attitude that brought the negotiators to enter provisions into the ABM Treaty that could be invoked should complicating new problems emerge. Article XIII provides for the creation of a 'Standing Consultative Commission', within the framework of which the parties pledged to 'consider questions concerning compliance with the obligations assumed and related *situations which may be considered ambiguous*' (emphasis added).[10] But as the history of the 1970s and early 1980s has shown, this co-operative arrangement did not prove to be strong enough to prevent large segments of US policymakers and public opinion from believing that Gorbachev's predecessors had cheated the United States by letting projects go ahead, such as the Krasnoyarsk radar station, which is regarded as a violation of the Treaty.[11]

Before going to Reykjavik, even when proposing the meeting, Gorbachev could and should have known that Ronald Reagan was elected (in 1980) and re-elected (in 1984) to the White House on a ticket that stood for re-establishing US self-confidence based on its own strength, rather than on co-operative arrangements with the Soviet Union. Gorbachev's advisers, among them Anatoly Dobrynin, who had been serving as the Soviet Ambassador to Washington for some 25 years (until 1986) could and should have explained to him how badly the security policy of his predecessors had affected political psychology in the West, first and foremost in the United States. The Soviet-Cuban intervention in Angola in 1975; the public rebuff in 1977 to Secretary of State Cyrus Vance, when he proposed deep cuts in strategic arms to the USSR; the relentless buildup of SS-20 missiles targeted against Western Europe, China and Japan; the disregard for human rights; and the invasion of Afghanistan in December 1979 had not been forgotten, and their damaging political consequences had not yet disappeared.

It can be debated whether the reasons that brought Ronald Reagan into the White House have been fully compatible with the political mandate into which he translated the election victory. None the less, before Gorbachev went to Reykjavik, a careful study of Reagan's position could have demonstrated to him that the President continued to believe in his own interpretation of the mandate and showed no signs of changing it.

Consequently, it was logical that, in 1986, the President confirmed his unwavering will not to let the Strategic Defense Initiative (SDI) become a 'bargaining chip',[12] and it was ill-founded hope for Gorbachev to expect Reagan to sacrifice the most important creation of his entire foreign policy programme. Thus, in order to tempt Reagan away from his 'broad' ABM interpretation, announced in 1985 and reinforced in 1986,[13] and entice him into an agreement to maintain the ABM Treaty along the principles upon which it had been agreed, it would have been necessary for Gorbachev to offer such radical changes in Soviet policy that Reagan would be able to drop publicly his deeply rooted reasons for distrust in the Soviet Union and thus give up the SDI insurance policy, as he calls it. For Gorbachev to corner Reagan in this way would have required far more than the announced withdrawal of only six regiments (roughly 8000 troops) out of more than 100 000 Soviet troops from Afghanistan.[14] Indeed, a pledge to withdraw completely and under international control was required, and so was a demonstrably liberalized emigration policy for Soviet Jews and a forthcoming solution of ABM compliance issues. In short, to promote arms control, more was required than openings in this important but not independent area of international affairs.

As the Reykjavik meeting clearly proved, none of the requirements existed to bring it to a successful outcome. Gorbachev did not feel in a position to concede to Reagan what the President needed in order to consider accepting the original ABM philosophy. And Reagan felt unable to grant Gorbachev what the General Secretary required to attempt to solve problems on non-SDI arms control subjects or on ABM non-compliance charges.

True, President Reagan has repeatedly stated his interest in 'more constructive relations with the Soviet Union'. But no design has been offered yet about how to turn this credo into a credible and workable policy. On the contrary, Reagan has only been specific when describing what he would not accept, and that is, in his own words, not to let the Soviet Union 'cripple our Strategic Defense Initiative'.[15]

What the President, however, regards as 'the most positive defense programme'[16] is perceived by his opposite number in the Kremlin as the major stumbling block on the road to any progress in arms control.[17]

The logic of Gorbachev's position on this very point cannot easily be disputed. With the offer, on the one hand, of major concessions from previously stated Soviet positions,[18] he could not really be expected to approve, on the other hand, of Ronald Reagan's SDI plans. Why should Gorbachev accept a rearrangement of the furniture in the house of common East-West security, based on mutual vulnerability, if his partner in the White House is at any rate about to destroy the roof?

And why should a Soviet leader, whose political priority clearly is to correct the severe shortcomings of his country's economic system, embark on a new and costly round of arms competition that at best would eat up the money desperately needed to make the necessary investment in a better economic administration? Gorbachev has boldly stated that 'the fundamental tasks of the country's economic and social development also determine the CPSU's international strategy'.[19]

Considering the burden of military expenditures on the Soviet economy (see chapter 6),[20] Gorbachev's statement should neither be surprising nor be misunderstood. When it comes to the principle of parity and of equal security with the USA (as enshrined in the 1972 ABM Treaty and the SALT [Strategic Arms Limitation Talks] agreements of 1972 and 1979), the new Soviet leader cannot settle for less than his predecessors have done, although he has criticized them heavily in other areas. Judging from the events of 1986, Ronald Reagan either fails to recognize the substance of Gorbachev's position—and the promises it may hold if met with a constructive and imaginative policy on the part of the West—or he refuses to accept the consequences, in the hope that superior US technology will provide a shield behind which the USA can enjoy invulnerability or a kind of hermetic seal to be put over the Soviet Union, impenetrable for every Soviet weapon of intercontinental reach.

In short: Reykjavik demonstrated one of the tragic features of current East-West relations, that is, the two superpowers are again not only out of step with each other but are marching in opposite directions.

Given the importance of the ABM Treaty, which is up for its third review conference in the autumn of 1987, this situation is unlikely to change fundamentally until both countries admit that there is simply no way for SDI and the ABM Treaty to live together in this world. In fact, what is at stake is an ever broader and more fundamental principle of international security in the nuclear age. Only if the two powers rediscover that, with the advent of the nuclear age, the tools for encouraging political change differ profoundly from those of the pre-nuclear age, will they find a way out of the impasse. To the degree that weapons—in particular nuclear weapons—can contribute to a situation of non-war, they are obviously already doing so. Consequently, a new ABM-violating arms race in space can at best end in a new sky-high level of deterrence. What, however, if something goes wrong on the way to this politically questionable and financially costly objective? The USA and the USSR must have felt the doubts themselves when, in January 1985, they agreed to do everything to 'end the arms race on earth and prevent one in space'.[21] Where and when, however, political improvements in the international system are intended, it must be recognized that weapons, at best, can preserve and defend, but they cannot help to bring about a transformation into a less hostile and mutually profitable relationship between the great powers. To accomplish that, other instruments are called for, such as economic co-operation, and technological and cultural exchange. The fact that this approach can only be successfully applied when the two powers exercise mutual restraint was already recognized in 1972 when Washington and Moscow agreed to abstain from 'trying to achieve indirect or direct advantages at the expense of each other' (translation supplied).[22]

1986 in general and the Reykjavik meeting in particular made it abundantly clear, however, that the United States and the Soviet Union are far away from reapplying these criteria to their relationship. Hence, if there is a fundamental disagreement on what the ABM Treaty says, it is pointless to discuss whether it would have helped had an agreement been reached in Iceland not to withdraw from the ABM Treaty for 20 years (as Gorbachev had originally suggested), for 8 years (as Reagan had offered), or for 10 years, upon which the two leaders verbally agreed in the end. After all, political solutions cannot emerge from technical proposals if a joint understanding is lacking as to whether or not to maintain the Treaty in its original meaning.

Of course, the argument can be made that SDI in all likelihood will not emerge in line with Reagan's hopes. Thus, one may argue, reasons to worry about Reagan's reinterpretation of the ABM Treaty should not be allowed to become the overriding concern. This is, however, both true and false. Seen through Western eyes, it is very unlikely that technology can provide an airtight shield against the opponent's strategic nuclear weapons. Whatever the likelihood or the doubts, the sheer intention on the part of the President will profoundly influence the perception in Soviet leaders' minds of the US policy and lead to decisions that one day may prove to be not easily changed. After all, those in the West who, for good reasons, have long maintained that stated Soviet intentions should be taken seriously must now also be expected to realize that the Soviet Union cannot be asked to do less *vis-à-vis* the United States.

This complex situation of interacting perceptions is further complicated by the difference in decision making in the two systems. While it seems possible and even very likely that Congress and, in two or three more years, a new President will cut back Reagan's SDI plans to a far more modest system of Ballistic Missile Defence (BMD), the Soviet political system, based on long-term, rather inflexible planning, may find it very difficult, if not impossible, to adjust decisions taken earlier.

The solution to this complicated constellation of problems will to a great extent depend on the attitude of the US Congress. Should Congress accept Reagan's redefinition of the ABM Treaty—the so-called 'broad interpretation'—US foreign policy is bound to become incalculable for the Soviet Union, and surely not for it alone. It was clear to the US Senate in 1972 that space-based BMD systems would not be permitted under the Treaty's provisions and that ABM systems should serve the sole purpose of safeguarding a second-strike capability, thus equal security through mutual vulnerability. Reagan's new 'broad interpretation' allowing for test and development of such systems that carry the risk of equipping the United States with a first-strike capability—at least during the period in which the Soviet Union is catching up—challenges not only the Soviet Union. At risk is also the foreign policy authority of the US Senate—a situation of far-reaching importance not only for the USA but also for its friends and opponents alike.

1986 has therefore not only left behind a President who is considerably weakened due to the failure of his Iran operation, his inability to control the US budget deficit (Reagan himself, in his 1987 State of the Union Message, calls it 'outrageous') and to deal with a new Soviet leader in a manner that allows for strategic compromises. It has also shifted the responsibility back to Congress for answering the troublesome question of when and how the two major nuclear weapon powers will find a way back to a co-operative approach to, first and foremost, arms control.

Hopes lie in the newly acquired majority of the Democratic Party in the Senate in 1986, thus in Congress and its ability to impose restraint on Reagan's SDI plans, which are risky to the degree that they go beyond the limits of the ABM Treaty. This programme also provides the military in the Soviet Union with a pretext to pressure Gorbachev beyond the current Soviet BMD programme into a fully-fledged arms race in space.

Woodrow Wilson, Democrat and US President from 1912 to 1920, in his famous doctoral thesis of 1884 castigated the US governmental system because it acted as a 'Congressional Government'. Looking at the security problems of our time, one cannot help but hope that Congress will again live up to the standard so heavily criticized 103 years ago. Comfort may come from the observation that Karl Löwenstein, a brilliant student of the US Constitution, once offered: 'It can be taken as an organic law of US policy that Congress will overrule the President and establish a congressional government once a weak President is confronted with a Congress dominated by the opposition' (translation supplied).[23]

Senator Sam Nunn's letter of 6 February 1987[24] to the President seems to confirm the functioning of this special feature of the US Constitution. Based on his unique experience in defence and international security matters and equipped with the newly acquired authority of the chairmanship of the powerful Armed Services Committee, the Democratic Senator from Georgia strongly warned Ronald Reagan not to terminate the US policy 'of observing the traditional, or so called "restrictive", interpretation of the ABM Treaty . . . pertaining to the development and testing of space-based or otherwise mobile ABM systems and components'. 'Were the Administration', the letter continues, 'now to decide to abandon the traditional ABM Treaty without having achieved a consensus with NATO and the Congress that such an action was warranted, it would have several extremely adverse consequences'. Senator Nunn unambiguously points out that a Reagan decision, in this respect, would be taken on Capitol Hill 'as the end of arms control under your administration—whether accurate or not', and would also be seen as a unilateral Executive Branch decision to disregard the interpretation of the Treaty which the Senate believed it had approved when the accord was ratified in 1972. Hence, it would 'provoke a Constitutional confrontation of profound dimensions'.

Though Nunn does not explicitly refer to consequences for the US-Soviet relationship, his concern may be seen as implied in the assessment that arms control may be irreparably damaged by the President's approach. Nor can the

President be in any doubt that Nunn's reference to NATO implicitly reminds the Administration that NATO allies have frequently asked for adherence to the restrictive interpretation of the Treaty[25] and that the President was thus about to damage his relationship not only with Congress, but also with his allies and his opponent in the Kremlin.

Nunn's letter is not just a document of carefully and decisively discharged congressional responsibility. It also strongly signals that the President is close to assembling a unique group of opponents in Congress, NATO and the Kremlin. It remains to be seen whether the President is able to realize that his Administration and personal reputation are on a stormy course which he can hardly weather from an isolated White House position without causing greater damage to more than just the memory of his own presidency.

A world free of nuclear weapons?

It is in the light of this rather sobering development that another important subject has to be judged. In his speech of 15 January 1986, Gorbachev outlined the prospect of a nuclear weapon-free world by the year 2000, thereby joining a vision that Ronald Reagan previously delineated in his famous speech of 23 March 1983, known as the starting shot for SDI.

Clearly, serious doubts concerning the established deterrence philosophy are not new. They have beleaguered the international community for more than three decades. In fact, great hopes that mankind would ultimately come to grips with the problem of nuclear weapons were associated with the Partial Test Ban Treaty (PTBT) of 1963, the Non-Proliferation Treaty (NPT) of 1968, the ABM Treaty of 1972, SALT I (1972) and SALT II (1979), to mention only the major events. Again, around the Soviet buildup of SS-20 missiles and NATO's ensuing two-track decision of 1979, an intensive debate developed on all aspects of nuclear weaponry—military, political and ethical. A design has not yet emerged through which the world could reach nuclear weapon-free status.

Yet, it is true that 1986 marks a new point of departure because it was the year when the two most powerful leaders in world politics verbally agreed that the world should be freed of nuclear weapons. Their numerous calls for eliminating all nuclear weapons raised several immediate questions: How credible is such a radical vision if its producers cannot even agree on comparatively simpler goals, such as limiting and reducing the existing weapon stockpiles? And why should anyone believe in the seriousness of the vision (though it may have been proffered seriously) if even existing arms control agreements (such as the ABM Treaty and SALT II) are either in grave danger or already no longer adhered to, as, in the latter case, had admittedly been true with the United States since November 1986?

But even if the United States and the Soviet Union could draw up and sign such an agreement, that is, to strive for a nuclear weapon-free world, a few large obstacles would nevertheless continue to exist:

1. The UK, France and China (the three other nuclear weapon powers) are

currently engaged in expanding and refining their respective inventory; the latter two are not even parties to the Non-Proliferation Treaty.

2. No agreement to make the world free from nuclear weapons can undo the knowledge about how to produce them.

3. Even if, by some miracle, all nuclear weapon states could be brought to accept an agreement to turn the world back to a nuclear weapon-free status and all threshold countries (such as Argentina, Brazil, India or Israel) would follow suit, the questions of verification and compliance would still exist. Is the international community ripe and ready to accept a verification scheme such as the one required to ensure not only the disbandment of all development and production facilities but also against the possibilities of cheating?

Certainly no arms control negotiations held thus far suggest that such an arrangement is currently within reach. This raises the question of whether an international system with a known and treaty-limited existence of nuclear weapons is safer than one in which potential opportunities to cheat remain a permanent source for distrust.

4. There is a general perception that, in the past, nuclear weapons have deterred war between nuclear powers and, to some degree, the use of military means for offensive political purposes between them. Among the examples often referred to, the Berlin crisis of 1961–62 stands out prominently. Of course, this conclusion can hardly be drawn on evidence; however, neither can the opposite. So, it is perception one deals with rather than facts, beliefs rather than truth. Thus, the task of scrutinizing some of the basic questions is a perennial one: To what degree does the past hold answers for the future? If a nuclear weapon-free world could be established and verified, would non-nuclear wars between great powers then become more likely? Or, does the devastating power of modern non-nuclear weaponry generate sufficient deterrence to rule out a war between the major powers? Is the nuclear Damocles-sword of total annihilation necessary to deter the nuclear weapon powers from war against each other in general and, should conflict erupt, to force them to cease fighting because the risk of escalation into nuclear holocaust is too great? We simply do not know how a world without nuclear weapons would work.

None of these questions will easily find answers. The search for them is not simplified either by the fact that the pursuit and preservation of peace also involve a great number of complex ethical problems, such as: Is it morally responsible to threaten with the destruction of the world in order to preserve its existence? And, is it really nuclear weapons that should occupy man's mind, or is it rather the need to preserve or establish freedom and justice? In view of these questions—and many more will emerge as the dilemma is fully investigated—there is only one observation that can already be offered with certainty: as of today, no answers exist, neither in political life nor in the area of research.

Therefore, it is hardly surprising that previous political leaders who espoused the vision of a nuclear weapon-free world have hitherto also failed to produce a design of how to turn the vision into a workable policy. Gorbachev and Reagan, before, during and after the Reykjavik meeting, have not managed to demonstrate that they are the decisive exception to the rule. Consequently, they have made it easy for people to accuse them of using the vision only as a propaganda ploy, even if they were both sincere in their intention. And the same is true for the argument that the vision has only been presented in order to blur the failure on the part of both superpowers to come to grips with solvable problems, such as deep cuts in strategic inventory, the destruction of all chemical weapons, the cessation of nuclear testing, and at least a considerable lowering of the testing thresholds.

Forces at work

Broadening the view beyond the bilateral US-Soviet relationship, there seems to be some room for hope although of a somewhat uncertain nature. The hope is connected with the results of the Stockholm Conference and deals with confidence- and security-building measures in Europe. There is also scepticism related to the influence of allies on the East-West policy of the Reagan Administration.

Stockholm: moderate progress

Based on what started with the Helsinki Final Act (1975), 33 European countries together with the United States and Canada agreed in September 1986 on politically binding measures designed to make military affairs in Europe more transparent and mutually calculable.[26]

For a variety of reasons the Stockholm Document is unique:

1. Though neither initialled by delegation leaders, signed by governments nor ratified by parliaments, all 35 parties to the Document consider the measures agreed upon as politically binding.

2. For the first time an agreement was reached that spells out important security arrangements for all of Europe, from the Atlantic to the Urals.

3. Equally new and of great importance was the preparedness of General Secretary Gorbachev to open for the first time Soviet territory to obligatory on-site inspections, a political breakthrough, limited as its actual military value may be.

4. In addition to repeating respective UN principles, the Document denounces the Brezhnev doctrine, invented to justify the occupation of Czechoslovakia in 1968, in stating that the parties 'will abide by their commitment to refrain from the threat or use of force in their relations with any State, regardless of that State's political, social, economic or cultural system and *irrespective of whether or not they maintain with the State relations of alliance*' (emphasis added).[27]

5. Despite the failure of the two superpowers to make progress in the field of nuclear arms control and notwithstanding a poor Soviet-US relationship, the Stockholm results manifest the ability of Europeans to pressure the two superpowers to agree to security-related agreements—provided all European countries work along the same principle and provided the agenda is not too ambitious.

6. Given the fundamental political differences between East and West, Stockholm has demonstrated that arms control stands a chance if the crucial problem is dealt with first, that is, to build confidence by curbing the forces producing distrust, such as uncertainties about military exercises and manoeuvres.

True, there is no reason to overrate the Stockholm success. Since the Helsinki Accords of 1975, it took 11 years to arrive at this result. Not a single soldier has been disarmed or relocated, nor has a single piece of military equipment been removed by simply agreeing to the Stockholm rules. And, because of WTO resistance, no agreement has been reached to exchange information about the deployment pattern of troops. The Document itself testifies to the continuing low level of confidence: 'the observers will be allowed to use their personal *binoculars*, which will be *subject to examination and approval by the host State*' (emphasis added).[28] No doubt, the tougher problem still remains to be solved, namely, to develop the Stockholm approach into something that deserves to be called conventional arms control in Europe. To achieve this will prove to be difficult not only for the NATO and the WTO countries. Difficult questions also face the neutral and non-aligned (NNA) countries. The Stockholm experience showed the NNA-countries that they have to be actively involved in European politico-military affairs and that neutrality in the future can rely on the principle of security through secrecy only to a lesser degree.

As of today, it is unclear when agreement will be reached on a mandate for a follow-up conference and whether the further development of confidence-building measures has to be dealt with in a forum separate from negotiations about genuine conventional arms control. It is likely, however, and even desirable, that the Mutual and Balanced Force Reduction (MBFR) negotiations, conducted since 1973 between NATO and the WTO, will be superseded by Stockholm II. Complex questions wait for answers that would allow a workable mandate: how to relate the necessary further refinement of confidence-building measures, procedurally and structurally, to initial, and presumably modest, arms control arrangements; how to secure the participation of the NNA-countries without impairing their status and security; and how to draw France into this arms control process in view of the fact that it once proposed the Stockholm approach not in order to promote arms control but rather to make MBFR (in which France has continuously refused to participate) disappear.

Last, but not least, the loss of the arms control initiative, in general, to the Soviet Union owing to President Reagan's deeply rooted distrust may at least impede and prolong the process of defining a new mandate. 1988 will be his last year in office, and he may feel no great need to bow to policies of which he has always been sceptical.

Distrust is still making itself felt at the chemical weapons (CW) negotiations in Geneva, in spite of some recent developments. Early in February 1987, the Soviet Ambassador to the 40-nation Geneva Conference on Disarmament (CD) signalled the readiness of his country to accept on-site, international inspection of declared chemical weapon stockpiles. This move on the part of the Soviet Union was interpreted by Western diplomats as Soviet readiness to accept Western proposals regarding the location of chemical weapon stockpiles as well. But the more difficult question of accepting mandatory, across-the-board inspection on challenge remained unsolved.[29]

Washington asked already in 1984 for mandatory inspection on challenge within 24 hours and with no possibility for the host country to refuse it. Accepting the possibility that a country may have a legitimate interest in refusing inspection, the UK offered a compromise in 1986 that would require the refusing state to provide alternative measures to satisfy the inspection request. The British formula also provided a mechanism to convince the reluctant state to make further efforts should it fail either to accept on-challenge inspection or to produce satisfactory alternative measures. The United States, however, has thus far not found it possible to accept the British compromise.[30]

Ignored allies

Looking at the Atlantic Alliance, 1986 again has not been a very encouraging year. In fact, with the experience of the Reykjavik meeting, allies have had to realize at last that Ronald Reagan does not care much about NATO when it comes to the subjects of strategic importance on the East-West agenda. While Reagan's offer to Gorbachev—a world free of nuclear weapons—literally amounted to turning NATO's strategy of flexible response upside down, the President saw no point in concerning himself with the views of his allies. His failure to inform and his negligence to consult his allies before going to the meeting with Gorbachev, or at least after the meeting, made it abundantly clear what rank NATO has in his mind. Although NATO's agreed strategy for dealing with the WTO rests on the principle of 'defence and détente', the President rejected Gorbachev's far-reaching offers without even considering to seek the advice of governments in NATO capitals. Thus, it came as no surprise that Ronald Reagan did not even find the Atlantic Alliance worth mentioning in his State of the Union Message in January 1987, three months after the Reykjavik encounter.

Of course, 1986 was not the first year in which the Reagan Administration failed to observe established intra-Alliance rules. Already in 1982 he rejected a compromise agreement on intermediate-range nuclear forces (INF)—known as the 'walk in the woods'—worked out by Paul Nitze and Soviet negotiator Youli Kvitsinsky without informing allies, not even the most concerned ones (Belgium, the FRG, Italy, the Netherlands and the UK), although a considerable limitation on long-range theatre nuclear forces in Europe was at stake and the deployment of Pershing II missiles could have been avoided.

Only a year later, in March 1983, the President caught his allies by complete surprise when he proclaimed his SDI philosophy, which implies a radical change in Western security policy. Leaving aside other comparatively smaller bones of contention in the Alliance—such as the attempt of the Reagan

Administration to thwart the West German gas pipeline deal with the Soviet Union in 1983, or the use of military force against Libya in April 1986—1986 has made it clear that to ignore allies' interests and views is a permanent feature of Reagan's NATO policy.

Of course, the situation would perhaps be different had Washington's European allies, in the meantime, managed to form a joint position on major subjects of security policy, such as arms control. But 1986 again has brought no change in the historical irony that Western Europe fails to come of age in international affairs though constantly being encouraged to do so by Washington, ever since 1962 when John F. Kennedy outlined the vision that NATO should rest on two pillars—Western Europe and the United States. For a major US ally to call publicly on the Alliance to take Gorbachev up on his new positions and to state that the West is 'in need of an active political strategy' (put forward by the West German Foreign Minister Hans-Dietrich Genscher on 1 February 1987 in a major speech to the World Economic Forum in Davos, Switzerland)[31] amounts to severe criticism of Washington as well as to an admission of insufficient, if any, European influence on the important subject of our time. In short, with Gorbachev in power, Lord Carrington's assessment of 1983 is even more relevant today: 'We do not lack the weapons or the will to deter or to defend. Nor should we lack the confidence in the future of Western democracies. But we do lack a positive political strategy for dealing with the Soviet Union. And it is this failure of concerted definition which causes the trouble'.[32]

Notes and references

[1] Meissner, B., 'Die Ergebnisse des XXVII Parteikongresses der KPdSU', *Europa Archiv*, no. 8 (1986), pp. 237–46.

[2] Richard Löwenthal speaks of 'the boldest and most promising overhaul of the system' in the Soviet Union in the 70 years of its history; see 'Den Enkeln ins Stammbuch', *Die Zeit*, 6 Mar. 1987, p. 17.

[3] See, e.g., the Chief Executive of the Deutsche Bank, FRG's largest bank, talking about the Gorbachev Peace Forum of Feb. 1987 in an interview in *Der Spiegel*, 23 Feb. 1987, pp. 143–46; see also FRG Foreign Minister Hans-Dietrich Genscher's speech to the World Economic Forum held in Davos, Switzerland in *Bulletin der Bundesregierung*, no. 13 (4 Feb. 1987), pp. 93–97.

[4] See *International Herald Tribune*, 27 Feb. 1987, p. 1.

[5] See *International Herald Tribune*, 15 Oct. 1986; see also Gräfin Dönhoff, M., 'Die Insel der Unseligen', *Die Zeit*, 6 Mar. 1987, p. 3.

[6] See 'Revolte der Schuldner', *Die Zeit*, 27 Feb. 1987, pp. 23 and 24.

[7] See *Financial Times*, 26 Feb. 1987, p. 1.

[8] *Neue Zürcher Zeitung*, 24 Feb. 1987, p. 13 (translation supplied).

[9] Noll, A., 'When the bankers become restive', *Financial Times*, 23 Feb. 1987, p. 14. Major debtors: Mexico $100 billion, Brazil $102 b., the Philippines $20 b., Argentina $50 b., Nigeria $22 b. and Peru $14 b. At the end of 1985, the debts of the 15 major debtor Third World countries amounted to approximately $442 b.; *Frankfurter Allgemeine Zeitung*, 20 Jan. 1987.

[10] Goldblat, J., *Agreements for Arms Control: A Critical Survey*, SIPRI (Taylor & Francis: London, 1982), pp. 107–201.

[11] See Haas, R., 'The ABM Treaty: verification and compliance issues', *The ABM Treaty: To Defend or Not to Defend?*, Strategic Issue Papers, SIPRI (Oxford University Press: Oxford, 1987, forthcoming).

[12] President Reagan in Aug. 1986; see McGeary, J., 'MIRVed mission to Moscow', *TIME*, 18 Aug. 1986, p. 18.

[13] On 6 Oct. 1985, Robert McFarlane stated in a television interview that it was the official policy to consider research, testing and development (but not deployment) of BMD systems and

components involving 'other physical principles' to be approved and authorized by the Treaty; see 'ABM: The shift that never was', *Newsweek*, 21 Oct. 1985, p. 55. See also, *Report to the Congress on the Strategic Defense Initiative*, US Department of Defense, June 1986, Washington, DC, Appendix C: 'This review led to the judgement by the President that a reading of the ABM Treaty that would allow the development and testing of such systems based on other physical principles, regardless of basing mode, is fully justified'; p. C1.

[14] Gorbachev announced the reduction of forces in Afghanistan in a major foreign policy speech delivered in Vladivostok on 28 July 1986; see *Europa Archiv*, no. 16 (1987), pp. D 457–66.

[15] See State of the Union Message, 27 Jan. 1987, reprinted in US Information Service *Wireless File*, 28 Jan. 1987, Stockholm, p. 3.

[16] State of the Union Message (note 15).

[17] See Gorbachev's Press Conference directly after the Reykjavik meeting, *Europa Archiv*, no. 24 (1986), pp. D 669–81. The point was also made in the Soviet offer of 1 Mar. 1987 to the United States to reach an INF agreement within six months; see text in *Frankfurter Allgemeine Zeitung*, 2 Mar. 1987, p. 2.

[18] The offer was to eliminate land-based INF missiles targeted on Europe with no compensation for British and French strategic systems in a bilateral US-Soviet agreement. Gorbachev also recognized the important distinction in the ABM Treaty between permitted research and prohibited testing with respect to components of strategic defence systems. For summaries of the proposals offered by both sides at the Reykjavik meeting, see Mendelsohn, J., 'Arms control back in Reagan's court', *Bulletin of the Atomic Scientists*, vol. 42 (10 Dec. 1986), pp. 8–10.

[19] See Gorbachev's speech to the Twenty-Seventh Party Congress of the CPSU, 25 Feb. 1986, *Europa Archiv*, no. 8 (1986), p. D 215.

[20] Harry Maier, a GDR economist who since May 1986 has been living in the FRG, reports that out of 10 roubles spent in the USSR on R&D, 8 are allocated to military programmes. See Maier, H., 'Ihr klatscht ja nicht, Genossen. Der sowjetische Parteichef Michail Gorbatschow stösst mit seinem Kurs auf Widerstand', *Die Zeit*, 21 Nov. 1986, pp. 33–34.

[21] From the joint US-Soviet communiqué, quoted in US Information Service Defense Policy Document '1985: Major US Arms Control Initiatives', 20 Dec. 1985, p. 5.

[22] See Agreement on Basic Principles of Relations between the USA and the USSR, signed at Moscow on 29 May 1972, in Goldblat (note 10).

[23] Löwenstein, K., *Verfassungsrecht und Verfassungspraxis der Vereinigten Staaten* (Springer: Berlin, Göttingen, Heidelberg, 1959), pp. 394–95.

[24] Reprinted in *Aerospace Daily*, 1 Feb. 1987, pp. 214–15.

[25] See, e.g., report about the talks between Foreign Minister Hans-Dietrich Genscher and Paul Nitze on the subject, *International Herald Tribune*, 27 Feb. 1987, p. 1; see also Gordon, M. R., 'US team is told not to discuss strict limits for ABM Treaty', *International Herald Tribune*, 23 Feb. 1987, p. 2.

[26] See Stockholm Conference Document in appendix 10A.

[27] See Stockholm Conference Document (note 26), para. 15.

[28] See Stockholm Conference Document (note 26), para. 53.2.

[29] See Netter, T., 'Soviet, in shift, accept international inspection of some chemical arms', *International Herald Tribune*, 28 Feb. 1987, p. 1.

[30] The British proposal is contained in Conference on Disarmament document CD 715, 'Chemical weapons convention: verification and compliance—the challenge element', 15 July 1986. US Assistant Secretary of Defense Richard Perle even went so far as to call the British compromise formula 'nonsense'; see Sommer, T. and Bertram, C., 'Kann man den Russen trauen?', *Die Zeit*, 13 Mar. 1987, p. 16.

[31] See Genscher (note 3).

[32] Lord Carrington, Alastair Buchan Memorial Lecture, 21 Apr. 1983, London in *Survival*, July/Aug. 1983, pp. 146–53.

Part I. Weapons and technology

Chapter 1. Nuclear weapons

Introduction / US nuclear weapon programmes / Soviet nuclear weapon programmes / British nuclear weapon programmes / French nuclear weapon programmes / Chinese nuclear weapon programmes

Chapter 2. Nuclear explosions

Nuclear explosions and the test debate / Information on nuclear explosions / Nuclear explosions and test-related issues in 1986

Chapter 3. Military use of outer space

Introduction / Military uses of satellites / Satellite launch failures / Collisions with debris in outer space / Anti-satellite programmes / Strategic defence / Conclusion

Chapter 4. Conventional weapon technologies

Resource management / New technologies / Military modernization / A revolutionary capability: fibre-optic guided missiles / In perspective

Chapter 5. Chemical and biological warfare: developments in 1986

The CBW arms control regime / Continued violation of the Geneva Protocol by Iraq / Allegations of non-compliance with the CBW treaties / The US binary munitions programme / 'The NATO chemical deterrent' / The Kohl-Reagan agreement / Chemical weapons and the Soviet Union / Proliferation of chemical weapons / Conclusion

1. Nuclear weapons

Prepared by the *Nuclear Weapons Databook* staff, Washington, DC, and SIPRI.*

Superscript numbers refer to the list of notes and references at the end of the chapter.

I. Introduction

Amidst sweeping proposals in 1986 by the United States and the Soviet Union to radically reduce and even abolish whole categories of nuclear weapons, both sides introduced at least one new strategic weapon system and continued to deploy a variety of existing nuclear weapon systems. After long research and development efforts the first MX intercontinental ballistic missiles (ICBMs) and B-1B bombers were declared operational and placed on 24-hour ('alert') duty in the USA, while the USSR fielded the SS-25 mobile ICBM and tested the new SS-NX-23 submarine-launched ballistic missile (SLBM). Deployments of nuclear weapons introduced in recent years continued at a steady pace. The USA and the USSR completed their deployment programmes for the Pershing II and SS-20 missile systems respectively, in late 1985; no more launchers were deployed, although additional missiles appear to be in production. In Britain, the keel of the first Trident Class submarine—the *Vanguard*—was laid. France deployed the first of a new generation of stand-off air-to-surface (ASMs), the ASMP, on Mirage IV aircraft. In addition France flight-tested an extended-range version of its M-4 SLBM, and placed orders for a new ballistic missile submarine and an aircraft-carrier. China conducted missile flight-tests during 1986 that appeared to be for developing multiple independently targetable re-entry vehicles (MIRVs) for China's ballistic missiles.

Directly bearing on current and future nuclear force structures were the year's developments in arms control. The USA and the USSR conducted three rounds of Nuclear and Space Talks in Geneva (see chapter 9), and a variety of other specially convened meetings took place. The most significant events were the US abrogation of the SALT II numerical limits, and the Reykjavik summit meeting in October. While some confusion still persists as to exactly what happened at Reykjavik there seemed to be, at least in principle, agreement between President Reagan and General Secretary Gorbachev to eliminate large categories of nuclear weapons. The translation of principle into reality remained a distant goal as the year ended.

In the United States, Congress took a more active role in influencing nuclear weapon and arms control policies. During the budget process, Congress cut funds for a number of nuclear systems, and the House of Representatives

* Robert S. Norris, Thomas B. Cochran, Jeffrey I. Sands and Andrew S. Burrows, Natural Resources Defense Council, Inc., Washington, DC; William M. Arkin, Institute for Policy Studies, Washington, DC; and Richard W. Fieldhouse, SIPRI.

passed binding legislation to cut off funding for nuclear weapons that would break the SALT II Treaty ceilings and mandated a testing moratorium for all but the smallest nuclear tests. In the November elections the Democrats regained control of the Senate, and with it the ability to set an agenda that will strengthen these trends in 1987.

Many other events occurred during the year which had, or will have, an influence on nuclear weapon programmes. A large number of serious accidents during the year raised questions about sophisticated technological systems. Parallels were drawn between the Challenger explosion in January, the Chernobyl disaster in April (see chapter 13) and the sinking of a Soviet submarine in October on the one hand and the complex nuclear offensive systems of today and the potential defensive systems of tomorrow on the other hand.

The USA continued its Strategic Defense Initiative (SDI) programme during the year, although Congress cut funding for the second year in a row, from $4.8 billion to $3.2 billion. During the year, a number of countries (including the Federal Republic of Germany and Israel) signed memoranda of understanding (MOU) with the USA on joint SDI research and development programmes. The SDI programme continues to be the major bone of contention in US–Soviet nuclear arms control negotiations.

This chapter examines the nuclear weapon developments of the five nuclear weapon states in 1986.

II. US nuclear weapon programmes

During the year the USA fielded approximately 800 new strategic weapons and almost 200 new theatre and tactical weapons (see tables 1.1 and 1.2). These included: 100 warheads for the first 10 MX missiles, 200 warheads for the seventh Trident submarine, 300 air-launched cruise missiles (ALCMs) for the first squadrons of B-52H bombers, 200 gravity bombs for the first squadron of B-1Bs, 50 sea-launched cruise missile (SLCM) warheads, 80 ground-launched cruise missile (GLCM) warheads and several dozen new 8-inch nuclear artillery shells.

ICBMs

After 12 years of research and development (R&D) the first MX (LGM-118A) ICBMs were placed on alert at the end of the year. On 22 December the first 10 MX missiles attained initial operational capability (IOC) with the 400th Strategic Missile Squadron of the 90th Strategic Missile Wing at F.E. Warren Air Force Base (AFB) in Wyoming. This is the first new US ICBM deployment in 16 years. To install the MXs, the Air Force removed Minuteman III missiles, modified their silos, assembled the MX ICBMs, emplaced the warheads and placed the missiles in the (empty Minuteman III) silos. The first Minuteman III was removed from its silo on 6 January, with 8 removed by early August and 14 by early October. By early August the first 2 MXs had been inserted in silos.[1]

The Air Force conducted MX flight-tests numbers 11–15 in 1986. The 12th flight was the first to carry 10 Mk 21 re-entry vehicles. The MX schedule calls for 16 R&D flight-tests before IOC and 4 afterwards. The first phase of Operational Testing and Evaluation (OT&E) will begin in the fall of 1988, testing 24 missiles over a three-year period. During the second phase of OT&E a total of 83 missiles, approximately seven missiles a year, will be fired from Vandenberg AFB.[2]

The search for survivable MX basing modes continued, even though more than 30 schemes have been rejected in the past. Throughout 1986 the Air Force revived some of the older ideas in an effort to find an acceptable basing mode to justify the purchase of a second batch of 50 missiles, as required by Congress.

On 19 December the President announced that funds would be requested in the FY 1988 budget to design a basing scheme for deploying MX missiles on trains. In peacetime the missiles would be kept on military bases. Upon warning they would be dispatched on the US railway system. The idea of using trains to base the MX was among the eight concepts examined but was not among the four leading ones[3] until late in the year, when the 'rail garrison' mode began to be seriously discussed.[4]

The small ICBM (SICBM) continued to be a controversial weapon programme throughout the year. Concern increased about the number of missiles required, and their cost, size and basing mode.[5]

The Senate cut in half the fiscal year (FY) 1987 SICBM funding request of $1.4 billion, noting that this would delay the scheduled IOC of late 1992. A House-Senate conference compromise resulted in $1.2 billion for the programme.[6]

The FY 1986 Department of Defense (DOD) Authorization Act called for an independent review of the SICBM and its basing options to be conducted by the Defense Science Board. Their March 1986 report recommended that the weight of the SICBM be increased from 13 636 kg to 16 818 kg. 'The recommended additional weight permits full target coverage, penetration aids, and the capacity for future payload variations—including a Maneuvering Re-entry Vehicle (MaRV), or two warheads of smaller size than the baseline configuration of a single MK 21.'[7]

A heavier SICBM would require a heavier mobile launcher. The projected gross weight of a mobile launcher with a missile has already increased from 68 182–79 545 kg to 81 818–88 636 kg for the standard 13 636-kg missile. Every extra kilogram of missile would add 2 kg to the launcher. Thus a 16 818-kg missile would increase the launcher weight to 88 181–95 000 kg.

During the year Congress tried but eventually failed to entwine the fates of the MX and the SICBM. Congressional advocates of the SICBM, particularly those in the House, continued to argue the missile's merits on strategic and cost grounds.[8] The 1987 budget limited MX procurement to 12 missiles—9 fewer than the Administration request. A House-Senate conference defeated an attempt to tie progress on the SICBM to actual deployment of more MXs.

The preferred method of SICBM basing consists of hardened mobile launchers (HMLs) randomly dispersed on DOD and Department of Energy (DOE) installations. This operational concept envisions a practice of periodic

Table 1.1. US strategic nuclear forces, 1987

| Weapon system | | | | Warheads | | No. in |
Type	No. deployed	Year deployed	Range (km)	Warhead × yield	Type	stockpile
ICBMs[a]						
Minuteman II	450	1966	11 300	1 × 1.2 Mt	W-56	480
Minuteman III (Mk 12)	240	1970	13 000	3 × 170 kt	W-62	750
Minuteman III (Mk 12A)	300	1979	13 000	3 × 335 kt	W-78	950
MX	10	1986	11 000	10 × 300 kt	W-87	110
Total	**1 000**					**2 290**
SLBMs						
Poseidon	256	1971	4 600	10 × 50 kt	W-68	2 750
Trident I	384	1979	7 400	8 × 100 kt	W-76	3 300
Total	**640**					**6 050**
Bombers						
B-1B	18	1986	9 800	8-24	b	250
B-52G/H	263	1955	16 000	8-24[b]	b	4 733
FB-111	61	1969	4 700	6[b]	b	360
Total	**339**					**5 343**
Refuelling aircraft						
KC-135	615	1957	..	..	..	..

[a] The four Titan II ICBMs remaining at Dec. 1986 are scheduled to be deactivated by mid-1987.
[b] Bomber weapons include six different nuclear bomb designs (B-83, B-61-0, -1, -7, B-57, B-53, B-43, B-28) with yields from sub-kt to 9 Mt, ALCMs with selectable yields from 5 to 150 kt, and SRAMs with a yield of 200 kt. FB-111s do not carry ALCMs or B-53 or B-28 bombs.

Sources: Cochran, T. B., Arkin, W. M. and Norris, R. S., *Nuclear Weapons Databook, Volume 1: US Forces and Capabilities*, 2nd edn (Ballinger: Cambridge, MA, forthcoming); Joint Chiefs of Staff, *United States Military Posture for FY 1988*; authors' estimates.

| Weapon system | No. | Year | Range | Warheads | | |
Type	deployed	deployed	(km)	Warhead × yield	Type	No. in stockpile
Land-based systems:						
Aircraft						
a	2 000	..	1 060–2 400	1-3 × bombs	a	2 800
Missiles						
Pershing II	108	1983	1 790	1 × 0.3–80 kt	W-85	125
GLCM	208	1983	2 500	1 × 0.2–150 kt	W-84	250
Pershing 1a	72	1962	740	1 × 60–400 kt	W-50	100
Lance	100	1972	125	1 × 1–100 kt	W-70	1 282
Honest John	24	1954	38	1 × 1–20 kt	W-31	132
Nike Hercules	27	1958	160	1 × 1–20 kt	W-31	75
Other systems						
Artillery[b]	4 300	1956	30	1 × 0.1–12 kt	b	2 022
ADM (special)	150	1964	..	1 × 0.01–1 kt	W-54	150
Naval systems:						
Carrier aircraft						
c	900	..	550–1 800	1–2 × bombs	c	1 000
Land-attack SLCMs						
Tomahawk	100	1984	2 500	1 × 5–150 kt	W-80-0	110
ASW systems						
ASROC	..	1961	10	1 × 5–10 kt	W-44	574
SUBROC	..	1965	60	1 × 5–10 kt	W-55	150
P-3/S-3/SH-3[d]	630	1964	2 500	1 × <20 kt	B-57	897
Naval SAMs						
Terrier	..	1956	35	1 × 1 kt	W-45	290

[a] Aircraft include Air Force F-4, F-16 and F-111, and NATO F-16, F-104 and Tornado. Bombs include four types (B-28, B-43, B-57 and B-61) with yields from sub-kt to 1.45 Mt.

[b] There are two types of nuclear artillery (155-mm and 203-mm) with four different warheads: a 0.1-kt W-48, 155-mm shell; a 1- to 12-kt W-33, 203-mm shell; a 0.8-kt W-79-1, enhanced-radiation, 203-mm shell; and a variable yield (up to 1.1 kt) W-79-0 fission warhead. The enhanced radiation warheads will be converted to standard fission weapons.

[c] Aircraft include Navy A-6, A-7, F/A-18 and Marine Corps A-4, A-6 and AV-8B. Bombs include three types with yields from 20 kt to 1 Mt.

[d] Some US B-57 nuclear depth bombs are allocated to British Nimrod, Italian Atlantique and Dutch P-3 aircraft.

Sources: Cochran, T. B., Arkin, W. M. and Norris, R. S., *Nuclear Weapons Databook, Volume 1: US Forces and Capabilities,* 2nd edn (Ballinger: Cambridge, MA, forthcoming); Joint Chiefs of Staff, *United States Military Posture for FY 1988;* authors' estimates.

random movement within a deployment area large enough to complicate enemy planning and targeting. During periods of increased tension the area of operation would double, and upon tactical warning of enemy attack the HMLs would disperse as far as possible. An average of eight square miles per missile would be needed for day-to-day operations, or 10 360 km^2 for a 500-missile force. A dispersed force would need 41 440 km^2.

A second basing concept is to put HMLs on alert at Minuteman missile bases where, upon tactical warning, they would disperse off site. A third concept combines the first two with some HMLs in random movement and some at Minuteman bases. A fourth alternative is the 'hard silo' in a patterned array basing mode, reminiscent of the 'dense pack' scheme for MX proposed in late 1982. During the year the number of candidate basing areas for possible SICBM deployment was reduced from 51 to 24, to be located in 14 states.[9]

By every account the SICBM programme will be costly. R&D costs (FY 1984–93) are estimated to be $12.7 billion. Total lifetime programme costs depend on which basing mode is chosen. Assuming 500 missiles are deployed, the costs range from $52.1 billion for the preferred random dispersal mode, to $44.8 for the Minuteman site option, to $47.0 for the mixed basing scheme.

Another SICBM development during the year was the apparent testing of an alternative candidate warhead to the baseline W-87 and W-88 warheads at the Nevada Test Site on 22 March (the Shot Glencoe test) sponsored by the Los Alamos National Laboratory.[10]

Deactivation of the Titan II missile force was almost completed during the year, with four missiles remaining at the end of the year and all Titan IIs expected to be deactivated by mid-1987.

Several new programmes have been initiated to enhance the targeting capabilities of US strategic nuclear forces against new Soviet mobile missiles and other 'strategic relocatable targets' (SRTs). The Air Force sought funding for a new R&D programme called Strategic Relocatable Target Capability in the amount of $985 000 for FY 1987 and $1.572 million for FY 1988. Two new Phase 1 warhead studies were initiated in March 1986 at the Los Alamos and Lawrence Livermore design laboratories to investigate warheads optimized for destroying such mobile targets. One design would use standard nuclear effects and the other advanced nuclear effects. Perhaps more complicated and more costly than the special warheads are the target acquisition problems associated with mobile missiles. The Air Force is considering special radars for this purpose for the Stealth and B-1B bombers.[11]

In a National Security Decision Directive, President Reagan ordered a study to investigate whether the USA should develop a MIRVed mobile missile about the size of the Minuteman, to augment or substitute for Midgetman.[12]

Strategic submarine programmes

Several strategic submarine programmes continued to be researched, purchased or deployed throughout the year. The FY 1987 budget authorized $1.52 billion for the 14th Ohio Class submarine (SSBN 739) and $1.124 billion for the first 21 Trident II missiles. On 16 August the *Nevada* (SSBN 733) was commissioned, and on 13 December the *Tennessee* (SSBN 734) was launched.

Prior to commissioning on 28 May the *Nevada*, the eighth Trident submarine, began its sea trials. This forced the Reagan Administration to decide whether to remain within the SALT II MIRVed missile ceiling of 1200. Throughout the first months of the year the battle intensified over whether to adhere to the unratified (and as of 31 December 1985 expired) SALT II Treaty. (In June 1985, in a similar situation, President Reagan ordered that the *Sam Rayburn* be dismantled to remain under the same ceiling to compensate for the introduction of the *Alaska*.)

White House announcements in late April indicated that a tentative decision had been made to stay within the SALT limits by ordering the dismantlement of the two submarines.[13] In many quarters that decision was seen as final. Advisers Paul Nitze and Edward Rowney were sent abroad to inform and consult certain other nations. The NATO allies strongly favoured continued US compliance with the SALT II Treaty.[14] On 9 April, 52 Senators (including 14 Republicans) wrote to the President encouraging him not to exceed the SALT limits.[15] Nevertheless on 27 May the White House announced that the United States would no longer be bound by the provisions of the SALT Treaty. At the same time it was announced that two Poseidon submarines would be dismantled, which would keep the USA within the limit, although the rationale given was that it was for budgetary reasons. The two submarines chosen for dismantlement were the *Nathan Hale* (SSBN 623) and the *Nathaniel Greene* (SSBN 636). The *Nathaniel Greene* had run aground in the Irish Sea on 1 April and sustained major damage.[16]

The Administration was taken by surprise by the storm of criticism that resulted. Congress involved itself in the issue almost immediately. On 19 June the House of Representatives approved a non-binding resolution (House Concurrent Resolution 350) by a vote of 256 to 145 with 37 Republicans voting for the majority, stating that 'the President shall continue to adhere to the numerical sublimits of the SALT agreement as long as the Soviet Union does likewise'.[17] Stronger binding legislation introduced by Representative Norman D. Dicks during House consideration of the DOD Authorization Bill (HR 4428) in August, prohibited any spending for deployment of nuclear weapons that would exceed the SALT numerical limits. This passed on 12 August by a vote of 225 to 186, with 19 Republicans voting with the majority.

The Senate took several actions as well. On 19 June the Armed Services Committee attached a non-binding resolution to the DOD Authorization Bill by a vote of 10 to 9. Stronger Senate legislation was introduced by Senators Joseph R. Biden, Jr, and William Cohen which would have prohibited funding of weapon systems that would exceed SALT, but this amendment did not pass. Instead the Senate agreed to a non-binding, 'sense of the Senate' provision urging that the United States voluntarily comply with the central numerical sublimits provided that the Soviet Union does likewise. The Senate language was adapted in a House-Senate conference.

According to a poll conducted by the *Washington Post* and ABC News in late June, 61 per cent of the respondents felt that the USA should abide by SALT II until a new accord is reached. Only 29 per cent agreed with Reagan's decision not to be bound by SALT.[18]

Strategic bomber programmes

After 16 years of development the first B-1B bombers were deployed. On 1 October 1986 the 337th Bombardment Squadron of the 96th Bombardment Wing reached IOC with the first B-1B placed on alert at Dyess AFB, Abilene, Texas. This is the first new heavy bomber for the USA since the Strategic Air Command (SAC) received its first B-52 in 1955. By the end of the year Dyess received the last of its allotted 29 aircraft, 14 of which will be used for training.[19] Ellsworth AFB, South Dakota, will have 35 aircraft in two squadrons by July 1987. One of the squadrons will be dedicated to conventional missions and one will maintain day-to-day nuclear alert.[20] Grand Forks AFB, North Dakota, and McConnell AFB, Kansas, will each get 17 aircraft by January and April 1988, respectively, if the schedule is met.

As the scheduled IOC approached, several problems developed, notably faulty electronic countermeasure equipment and leaky fuel tanks. It was also reported that the maximum altitude of the bomber with a full load of fuel and bombs was approximately 20 000 feet (about 6000 m).[21]

The B-1B will carry seven kinds of nuclear weapons: B-28, B-43, B-61 and B-83 gravity bombs, short-range attack missiles (SRAMs), ALCMs and eventually advanced cruise missiles (ACMs) in different combinations depending on the mission. The maximum payload capability is 56 818 kg. Internal loads can include up to 12 B-28 or B-43 bombs, 24 B-61 or B-83 bombs, and 24 SRAMS or 8 ALCMs on a rotary launcher. Externally the B-1B will be capable of carrying 14 additional ALCMs.

Some members of Congress continued to express concern about the growing number of classified military programmes that are not open to public scrutiny or discussion.[22] The Advanced Technology Bomber (ATB)—also called Stealth, under development by the Northrop Corporation—has long been in this category. On 3 June some cost estimates were released: research, development and procurement of 132 ATB aircraft are projected to cost $36.6 billion, or $277 million per aircraft (FY 1981 dollars).[23] In FY 1986 dollars the cost would be $50.3 billion or $381 million per aircraft. A secret DOD bomber study was delivered to Congress in the spring, affirming the Air Force position that it wants no more than 100 B-1Bs and 132 ATBs. No more B-52s are projected to be retired until after ATB deployment.[24]

With 98 B-52Gs already deployed with ALCMs, the Air Force began converting the B-52H force to carry ALCMs. By early January, 10 bombers had been modified. The pace and number of modifications were watched closely because the modification of the 131st B-52 would exceed the SALT II ceiling of 1320 MIRVed launchers and cruise missile-equipped bombers. The schedule changed over the year less for technical than for political reasons. In August it was reported that the Air Force schedule had slipped from the original date of 11 November to late December.[25] The 'delay' appeared to be an effort not to have the issue of breaching the SALT limit interfere with plans for a possible summit meeting. Just before the Reykjavik summit meeting the timing issue arose again, with some in the Reagan Administration arguing that violating the numerical ceiling would improve Reagan's bargaining leverage.[26] On 12 November the 131st modified bomber was pushed out of a hanger at Kelly AFB, San Antonio, Texas, putting the USA in technical violation of the SALT ceiling of 1320 MIRVed missiles and cruise missile-carrying bombers. The Administration interpretation was that the limit would be broken when the bomber joined its operational unit. On 28 November the 131st bomber arrived for deployment at Carswell AFB with SAC's 7th Bombardment Wing.[27]

The Soviet Union stated on 5 December that it would abide by the treaty 'for the time being', but added that the US decision gave the Soviet Union 'all grounds to regard itself free from its commitments'.[28]

There is little doubt that arms control issues will be high on Congress's agenda in 1987, especially since the Democrats recaptured the Senate. On 9 December a resolution was passed by House Democrats which commits the Democratic leadership of the House to move as early as possible in 1987 to pass legislation requiring that treaty limits be maintained. On 15 December 57 Senators (including 10 Republicans) sent a letter to President Reagan urging him to reverse his decision.[29]

The Air Force is currently working on a new solid-fuel, rocket-propelled, supersonic short-range attack missile (SRAM II, designated XAGM-131A) to replace the current AGM-69A SRAMs now carried on B-52 and FB-111A bombers.[30] The new SRAMs would be carried on the B-1B and the ATB. Flight-testing is planned for the summer of 1989 with an IOC in the second quarter of 1992.

SRAM II is planned to be faster and twice as accurate, with a smaller radar cross-section and three times the range of the current version. One of the new missions of SRAM II would be to target hardened facilities in the Soviet Union in addition to its defence suppression role for attacking Soviet air defence systems to allow US aircraft to fly across the Soviet borders. It will also be smaller. The original plan called for modifications to the single rotary launcher in the bomb-bay to make it capable of holding 12 of the missiles instead of 8, but this was dropped for budgetary reasons. The programme calls for purchasing 1633 missiles at a cost of $3.064 billion. The Administration requested $164.7 million for R&D for FY 1987. A House amendment had contained a provision to limit the Air Force to either the SRAM II or the ACM but not both. Eventually Congress cut the SRAM request to $70 million and requested a report from the Secretary of Defense detailing SRAM costs, effectiveness and warhead alternatives, which will delay the awarding of full-scale engineering contracts which had been scheduled for January 1987.[31]

Theatre nuclear forces

At the end of 1986, 208 of 464 planned GLCMs were deployed at bases in Belgium, Italy, the Federal Republic of Germany and the UK, 80 more missiles than at the end of 1985.[32] Deployment of the first GLCMs to Wüschheim Air Station in FR Germany began in March, preparation of the Netherlands base at

Woensdrecht continued, and construction of the second British base began. The full complement of 108 Pershing II missiles were deployed in FR Germany by the end of 1985.

Overall, the number of US nuclear warheads in Western Europe continued to decline, in response both to the agreement reached by NATO Ministers at Montebello, Canada, in October 1983 to reduce the numbers of nuclear warheads in Europe (see *SIPRI Yearbook 1986*) and political and fiscal decisions resulting in numerous retirement and reduction programmes.[33] By end 1986, about 4600 warheads (see table 1.3) were deployed in Europe.

Table 1.3. US nuclear warheads in Europe, 1965–95

Type	May 1965	Dec. 1981	Dec. 1986	End modernization[a] (1992–95)
Artillery				
8-inch	975	938	900 ⎫	
155-mm	0	732	732 ⎭	~500 total
Tactical SSMs				
Lance	0	692	692	692
Pershing I	200	293	100	100
Pershing II	0	0	108	108
Honest John	1 900	198	0	0
Sergeant	300	0	0	0
Nike Hercules SAMs	990	686	75	0
Bombs	1 240	1 929	1 629	1 329
B-57 NDB	–	192	192	192
ADMs	340	372	0	0
GLCMs	0	0	208	464
Total	**5 945**	**6 032**	**4 636**	**3 385**

[a] Assuming there are no further reductions of nuclear warheads because of future arms control agreements.

Source: Authors' estimates.

Reductions since the original NATO modernization decision in December 1979 have now included: (*a*) withdrawal of all atomic demolition munitions (ADMs) from Europe (1985); (*b*) phased retirement of all Nike Hercules missile warheads (began in 1981, to be completed by 1988–89); (*c*) retirement of nuclear warheads used to arm Greek and Turkish Honest John tactical missiles (1985); and (*d*) 'significant reductions in the total of tactical bombs' since 1981 with the deployment of new B-61 bombs replacing older B-28 and B-43 bombs on a less than one-for-one basis.[34]

After numerous delays, it appears that US nuclear artillery modernization in Europe is moving forward (see *SIPRI Yearbooks 1985* and *1986* for further discussion). In mid-1986, it was reported that non-enhanced radiation versions of the new W-79 8-inch nuclear artillery projectile had been deployed in FR

Germany.[35] These warheads will replace older W-33 warheads, which will be gradually retired as new weapons are introduced. The enhanced radiation (ER) warheads produced between August 1981 and October 1984 for the short-range Lance missile and 8-inch artillery will most likely remain stored in the USA until such time as they are converted to non-enhanced radiation versions. According to one report, only 40 enhanced radiation versions of the W-79 were produced.[36]

Production of the W-79 8-inch projectile was completed in August 1986. Cut-off of production was in keeping with the NATO Supreme Allied Commander, Europe (SACEUR) plans of 'making the 155mm the principal NATO nuclear artillery system'.[37] The new 155-mm projectile (W-82) continues in development (in a non-enhanced radiation version), was scheduled to enter production engineering in May 1986, and will begin deployment in the early 1990s.

Defence Ministry officials of FR Germany said on 8 November that the West German Pershing 1As and NATO nuclear aircraft were no longer on 'quick reaction alert' (QRA).

Naval nuclear weapons

Although the Reagan Administration has been successful in its drive to build a '600-ship Navy' its efforts to acquire new tactical nuclear weapons for the Navy have largely failed.[38] Although the first nuclear-armed Tomahawk SLCM was deployed in June 1984, numerous anti-submarine, anti-air and anti-ship nuclear warhead programmes have been delayed or cancelled as a result of congressional actions. These actions include: (a) denial of funds by Congress for development of nuclear warheads for the Sea Lance, a submarine-launched anti-submarine rocket to replace SUBROC; (b) slowdown of the surface ship-launched anti-submarine version of Sea Lance to replace ASROC; (c) cancellation of the new nuclear-armed surface-to-air Standard missile (SM-2(N)) to replace the Terrier; (d) slowdown of the anti-submarine warfare stand-off weapon nuclear depth bomb (ASW SOW/NDB) to replace the B-57 depth bomb; and (e) cancellation of potential nuclear warhead development programmes for the Phoenix air-to-air missile, 'supersonic anti-ship missile', vertical-launch ASROC (VLA), and Harpoon anti-ship missile.

In spite of the production and deployment problems associated with the new warheads, the Navy is continuing to work on the nuclear anti-submarine and anti-aircraft systems. Operational improvements are being incorporated into Navy ships and submarines to increase launcher flexibility and reaction time. The Vertical Launch System (VLS/MK45) on board surface ships is undergoing Operational Evaluation and is planned to become operational in the spring of 1987. The first test vertical launch of a Tomahawk SLCM from a ship was in May 1985, from the *Norton Sound* (AVM-1).[39] The *Bunker Hill* (CG-52), the first VLS-equipped cruiser, was commissioned into active service on 20 September. The Capsule Launch System (CLS/MK45) on Los Angeles Class attack submarines (commencing with the *Providence* (SSN-719)) is undergoing full-scale development.[40] The *Pittsburgh* (SSN-720) has been fitted with the CLS and is the test submarine for submerged testing of the Tomahawk SLCM.[41]

Deployment continues of the nuclear-armed version of the Tomahawk (TLAM/N). By the end of 1986, some 100 SLCMs had been deployed. According to the DOD, 'Tomahawk equipped submarines are now routinely deploying to several operational areas worldwide . . .'[42] The programme retains its goal of 3994 SLCMs, of which 758 will be the nuclear TLAM/N.

By the end of 1985, the Navy had certified 8 surface ships and 15 attack submarines to carry the Tomahawk, and had converted seven submarine tenders and three shore facilities to support submarine operations.[43] Six additional surface ships and 10 attack submarines are planned for SLCM certification in 1986, and the Naval Magazine, Guam will be upgraded to support SLCM operations.[44] As of March 1986, the planned Tomahawk platforms included 4 battleships, 5 nuclear-powered guided missile cruisers, 22 guided missile cruisers, 31 destroyers, and 29 guided missile destroyers for a total of 91 surface ships; and 68 Los Angeles Class and 39 Sturgeon Class attack submarines, for a total of 107 submarines.[45]

Operationally, Tomahawk SLCMs have been integrated into both the US Atlantic and Pacific Fleets. Its versatility and range (2400 km) allow it to be used to support tactical, theatre and strategic operations and contribute to what the Pentagon calls 'the Nuclear Reserve Force'.[46]

The Navy has begun phasing out the SUBROC submarine-launched anti-submarine stand-off weapon. Navy plans were approved by the DOD in January 1980 for a new Anti-Submarine Warfare Stand-Off Weapon (ASWSOW), now named Sea Lance, to replace the ageing SUBROC. Even though the development of a new missile was approved partly because it would emphasize a conventional warhead, in 1982 the Navy decided to pursue a nuclear depth bomb as the primary warhead and to deploy a conventional warhead two years after the initial deployment of a nuclear variant.[47] The ASWSOW, which has experienced numerous delays and funding cutbacks, was slated to begin full-scale engineering development in mid-1986,[48] but Congress eliminated funding for the weapon in the FY 1987 budget and decided to further delay the Sea Lance.

The Navy requested $1.6 million in the FY 1987 budget to begin development of an airborne ASW nuclear weapon—called the Nuclear Depth/Strike Bomb (NDSB)—to replace the B-57 nuclear bomb for delivery from patrol or carrier-based aircraft.[49] This weapon, which will serve both anti-submarine and tactical strike roles, will also replace B-43, B-61-2 and B-61-5 tactical strike bombs in the Navy.[50]

In May 1984, the Navy terminated its nuclear Standard Missile programme (SM-2(N)) owing to budget constraints. Four months later the Navy changed its mind, requesting reinstatement of funding based on the assessment that SM-2(N) 'is an essential part of the Navy's air defense capability for the 1990's'.[51] In FY 1986 the Navy requested $9.2 million for the programme, and Congress appropriated $3 million. In the FY 1987 budget, the Navy reduced the programme request itself from $23.9 to $9.2 million owing to 'program restructuring'. Congress deleted funds for the programme. Prior to congressional action on the FY 1987 budget, the Navy estimated that the total research, development, test and evaluation (RDT&E) costs for the SM-2(N) would be $257.8 million.[52]

SDI and the new 'Strategic Concept'

Over the past two years some of the most important weapon and arms control developments concerned a system that does not yet exist. The US Strategic Defense Initiative influenced budget, treaty interpretation, strategic doctrine, domestic political and international geopolitical issues during 1986.

Funding for SDI comes from DOD and DOE budgets. For FY 1987 the Administration requested $4.8 billion and $603 million respectively. Final congressional action cut the budgets, to $3.2 billion and $317 million respectively, a 34 per cent cut. This decision indicates that SDI will not grow by billions of dollars a year as the Administration had planned, but rather by a few hundred millions of dollars a year.

The issue of what kind of research, development and testing can be done under the terms of the Anti-Ballistic Missile (ABM) Treaty continued to be disputed among different parts of the Reagan Administration and proved to be the central cause of the stalemate between President Reagan and General Secretary Gorbachev at their October Reykjavik summit meeting.

Memoranda of understanding about the nature and amount of SDI research to be done in various countries were signed during the year: on 6 December 1985 with the United Kingdom, on 27 March 1986 with the Federal Republic of Germany and on 6 May 1986 with Israel. The issue of SDI involvement has become an important and sometimes politically difficult one for certain allied governments, especially those which support continued compliance with the ABM Treaty.

SDI remained the major obstacle to progress at the Geneva negotiations. The Reagan Administration stuck firmly to the belief that the SDI programme offered promise and should continue. For the Soviet Union the issues of defensive and offensive forces are clearly linked, and any progress on reducing strategic arms could only be achieved if there were continued restrictions on defensive programmes.

After the Reykjavik summit meeting the disagreement over SDI focused on the issue of how long a period of time there could be before any deployment begins and what kind of research could be permitted during this period.

Although the goal of a non-nuclear defence has been stated often by President Reagan and Secretary of Defense Weinberger, the SDI programme has a rather large nuclear weapon component. The Reagan Administration has accelerated funding to examine five Nuclear-Driven Directed Energy Weapon (NDEW) concepts by the national laboratories at Los Alamos and Livermore. These concepts are: the X-ray laser, hypervelocity pellets, directed microwaves, particle beams and the optical laser.[53] Most attention has gone to the X-ray laser.[54] At least five nuclear tests from 1980–85 at the Nevada Test Site have involved the X-ray laser. One X-ray laser test was scheduled for 1986 and two are scheduled for 1987.[55]

The impact of the concept of defence in general and of SDI in particular is taking hold among Administration policy makers and analysts and nuclear war planners. This evolving idea is labelled the new 'Strategic Concept' or new 'Strategic Policy'.[56] It was drafted by Paul Nitze in mid-1984 and given official approval in National Security Decision Directive (NSDD) 153, signed by President Reagan in January 1985. It was also included in NSDD 165, which was the set of instructions given to the US negotiators before their negotiations at Geneva which began on 12 March 1985. The strategic policy is intended to be the basis for future military doctrine and a goal for arms control objectives. It envisions a shift from a national strategy based on offensive deterrence to one based on both offensive and defensive weapon systems.

III. Soviet nuclear weapon programmes

Like the United States, the Soviet Union continued to field new nuclear weapon systems and pursue a variety of R&D programmes during 1986. Additional systems were deployed in all three legs of the Soviet nuclear triad: ICBMs, SLBMs and bombers (see table 1.4). Although SS-20 deployments appear to have completed, shorter-range theatre nuclear forces proceeded with modernization and deployment in Eastern Europe (see table 1.5).

ICBMs

The year saw the continuing deployment of mobile ICBMs. SS-11 Mod. 1 missiles were deactivated and SS-25 (Soviet designation RS-12M[57]) were deployed. By October 1986, 72 SS-25s had been deployed in a road-mobile configuration similar to that of the SS-20 in 8 regiments of 9 missile launchers each, with a compensating reduction of 72 in the number of SS-11 Mod. 1 missiles. The SS-25 is thought to have a refire capability.[58]

Early in the year US intelligence estimates posited that the first 10 rail-mobile 10-warhead SS-X-24 (Scalpel) ICBMs could conceivably be deployed as early as late 1986, to be followed by a silo-based version.[59] Evidence that the first deployments would be rail-mobile rather than silo-based came from monitoring the Soviet test programme over the period 1985–86.[60] The information monitored apparently caused the USA to reassess the missile, estimating that it is less accurate than originally believed.[61] Preparations for the deployment of the SS-X-24 were under way at the beginning of the year at two locations in the European USSR. However, it had not been deployed by the end of the year.

The SS-18 (designated Satan by NATO) Mod. 4 modernization programme was finally completed during 1986. Some single-warhead SS-17 Mod. 2 and SS-19 Mod. 2 missiles and 8- or 10-warhead MIRVed SS-18 Mod. 2 missiles may still be deployed.[62]

Soviet R&D on future ICBMs continues. Activity at the Soviet ICBM test ranges indicates that three new or modified ICBMs have entered the engineering and flight-testing state of development.[63] A new liquid-fuelled, silo-based heavy ICBM to replace the SS-18[64] was reportedly flight-tested three times in 1986. The first two tests were both failures. In the 2 April test the missile reportedly exploded shortly after emerging from its silo[65] at Tyuratam. During the second flight-test, conducted in mid-August, the missile exploded in mid-flight, perhaps as the first stage finished firing or when the second stage ignited. The failure was acknowledged by a Soviet Foreign Ministry spokesman, Boris D. Pyadyshev, at a news briefing—a new development in itself.[66] It was reported that the first successful flight-test of this SS-18 follow-on, which is expected to be designated SS-X-26 by NATO, took place from Tyuratam in mid-December.[67]

Other Soviet ICBM developments are mentioned in US documents, but with very little detail.[68] A possibly larger version of the SS-X-24 may 'begin flight-testing in the next few years'. There also could be a new version of the SS-25 with a MIRVed payload option. Modifications of the SS-18 and SS-19 will probably continue. According to an unofficial report, the USA expects the USSR to begin flight-testing an operational MaRV vehicle for its ballistic missiles, possibly by the end of the decade.[69]

Strategic submarine programmes

The Soviet Union continued its strategic submarine and SLBM programmes during the year. The SS-N-20 (Sturgeon) SLBM is now carried on four Typhoon submarines, of which as many as four more may be deployed by the early 1990s.[70] According to the Pentagon, developmental or prototype production of newer SLBMs is under way.[71] SS-N-20 production has reportedly been affected by a massive explosion at a Soviet missile fuel plant at Biysk, 80 km south-east of Novosibirsk.[72] It is possible that the Soviet Navy has begun using a two-crew system for the Typhoon Class submarine to reduce turnaround time between deployments.[73] Typhoon submarines, too large for existing strategic submarine base facilities at Polyarnyi, are reportedly based at Gremikha, some 300 km east of Severomorsk on the northern coast of the Kola Peninsula. According to these reports this base, in the final phases of completion, contains piers to specifically accommodate the Typhoon, and has hardened docking facilities in the surrounding granite cliffs.[74] Similar tunnels are also reported to be under construction at the Polyarnyi base and at the base near Vladivostok.[75]

The first two Delta IV Class submarines, each fitted with 16 of the long-range SS-N-23 (Skiff) missiles, are now in service. A third is probably on sea trials, and more are expected. The large, 10-warhead liquid-fuelled SS-N-23 has greater throw-weight, carries more warheads and is more accurate than the SS-N-18 (Stingray) currently carried on the Delta III submarines. After conversion Delta IIIs will probably carry the new missile as well.[76] Given past Soviet practice, it is likely that both the SS-N-20 and the SS-N-23 will be modified and improved.[77]

The USSR experienced a major nuclear weapon accident at sea in 1986. On the morning of 3 October a Yankee I submarine suffered an accident, killing at least three of the 120-man crew. The submarine was on routine patrol 880 km

Table 1.4. Soviet strategic nuclear forces, 1987

Weapon system		No. deployed	Year deployed	Range (km)	Warheads	No. in stockpile[a]
Type	NATO code-name				Warhead × yield	
ICBMs						
SS-11 Mod. 1	Sego	28	1966	11 000	1 × 1 Mt	29 – 56
Mod. 2		360	1973	13 000	1 × 1 Mt	380 – 720
Mod. 3		60	1973	10 600	3 × 250–350 kt (MRV)	190 – 360
SS-13 Mod. 2	Savage	60	1972	9 400	1 × 600–750 kt	63 – 120
SS-17 Mod. 2	Spanker	150	1979	10 000	4 × 750 kt (MIRV)	630 – 1 200
SS-18 Mod. 4	Satan	308	1979	11 000	10 × 550 kt (MIRV)	3 200 – 6 200
SS-19 Mod. 3	Stiletto	360	1979	10 000	6 × 550 kt (MIRV)	2 300 – 4 300
SS-X-24	Scalpel	..	1987?	10 000	7–10 × 100 kt (MIRV)	.. – ..
SS-25	Sickle	72	1985	10 500	1 × 550 kt	76 – 140
Total		**1 398**				**6 900 –13 000**
SLBMs						
SS-N-5	Sark	39	1963	1 400	1 × 1 Mt	41 – 47
SS-N-6 Mod. 1/2	Serb	288[b]	1967	2 400	1 × 1 Mt	450 – 520
Mod. 3			1973	3 000	2 × 200–350 kt (MRV)	
SS-N-8	Sawfly	292	1973	7 800	1 × 800 kt–1 Mt	310 – 350
SS-N-17	Snipe	12	1977	3 900	1 × 1 Mt	13 – 14
SS-N-18 Mod. 1/3	Stingray	224	1978	6 500	3–7 × 200–500 kt	710 – 1 900
Mod. 2			1978	8 000	1 × 450 kt–1 Mt	
SS-N-20[c]	Sturgeon	80	1983	8 300	6–9 × 350–500 kt	500 – 860
SS-N-23[c]	Skiff	32	1986	7 240	10 × 350–500 kt	340 – 380
Total		**967**				**2 400 – 4 100**
Bombers						
Tu-95	Bear A/B/C/G	100	1956	8 300	2–4 × bombs/ASMs	280 – 560
Tu-95	Bear H[d]	40	1984	8 300	8 × AS-15 ALCMs	320 – 640
Total[e]		**140**				**600 – 1 200**
Refuelling aircraft		140–170				

ABMs		1986	320	1 × unknown	32 – 64
ABM-1B	Galosh Mod.	1985	320	1 × unknown	32 – 64
ABM-3	Gazelle	68	70	1 × low yield	68 – 140
Total		**100**			**100 – 200**

a Figures for numbers of warheads are low and high estimates of possible force loadings (including reloads). Reloads for ICBMs are 5 per cent and 100 per cent; and for SLBMs 5 per cent and 20 per cent extra missiles and associated warheads. Half the SS-N-6s are assumed to be Mod. 3s, and SS-N-18 warheads are assumed to be 3 or 7 warheads. Bomber warheads are force loadings and force loadings plus 100 per cent reloads. It is assumed that 40 Bear Gs are now deployed (4 warheads each). All warhead total estimates have been rounded to two significant digits. Warhead estimates do not include downloading for single-warhead SS-17 Mod. 2, SS-19 Mod. 2 or SS-18 Mod. 1/3 missiles, which could be deployed, nor lower estimates for the SS-18 force, which could still include some Mod. 2 missiles with 8 or 10 warheads.

b It is not known whether the Soviet Union has already removed—or is planning to remove—from operational service an additional one or two Yankee Is during 1986 to make room for additional Typhoon and Delta IV Class submarines which may have entered sea trials. Alternatively, the USSR may have decided to wait to make these withdrawals until the USA exceeds the SALT limits.

c An additional Typhoon (20 SS-N-20 missiles) and Delta IV (16 SS-N-23 missiles) may be on sea trials and are thus included in the force totals. See note *b*.

d It is believed that, as of mid-1986, three squadrons of 12 Bear H aircraft each were in service. An additional squadron may have entered the operational force by the end of 1986.

e Excludes 30 MYA-4 Bison bombers which are under dispute. The USA believes that they remain SALT-accountable, while the USSR claims that they have been converted to refuelling tankers. Here they are included in the refuelling aircraft totals.

f Includes Badger and Bison A bombers converted to aerial refuelling and 15 confirmed new Bison conversions, with 30 possible new Bison conversions claimed by the USSR.

Sources: Authors' estimates derived from: Cochran, T. B., Arkin, W. M. and Sands, J. I., *Nuclear Weapons Databook, Volume IV, Soviet Nuclear Weapons* (Ballinger: Cambridge, MA, forthcoming); Arkin, W. M. and Sands, J. I., 'The Soviet nuclear stockpile', *Arms Control Today*, June 1984, pp. 1–7; Department of Defense, *Soviet Military Power*, 1st, 2nd, 3rd, 4th, 5th edns; NATO, *NATO–Warsaw Pact Force Comparisons*, 1st, 2nd edns; Berman, R. P. and Baker, J. C., *Soviet Strategic Forces: Requirements and Responses* (Brookings Institution: Washington, DC, 1982); Defense Intelligence Agency, *Unclassified Communist Naval Orders of Battle*, DDB-1200-124-85, Dec. 1985; Congressional Budget Office, *Trident II Missiles: Capability, Costs, and Alternatives*, July 1986; Collins, J. M. and Cronin, P. M., *U.S./Soviet Military Balance*, Library of Congress/Congressional Research Service, Report No. 85–83 F, 15 Apr. 1985; Background briefing on *SMP, 1986*, 24 Mar. 1986; SASC/SAC, *Soviet Strategic Force Developments*, S. *Hrg.* 99–335, June 1985; Polmar, N., *Guide to the Soviet Navy*, 4th edn (US Naval Institute: Annapolis, MD, 1986); Joint Chiefs of Staff, *United States Military Posture for FY 1988*.

Table 1.5. Soviet theatre nuclear forces, 1987

Weapon system		No. deployed	Year deployed	Range (km)	Warheads Warhead × yield	No. in stockpile[a]
Type	NATO code-name					
Land-based systems:						
Aircraft						
Tu-26	Backfire	144	1974	3 700	2–3 × bombs or ASMs	288
Tu-16	Badger	287[b]	1955	4 800	2 × bombs or ASMs	480
Tu-22	Blinder	136[b]	1962	2 200	1 × bombs or ASMs	136
Tactical aircraft[c]		2 885	..	700–1 000	1–2 × bombs	2 885
Missiles						
SS-20	Saber	441	1977	5 000	3 × 250 kt	1 323–2 200[a]
SS-4	Sandal	112	1959	2 000	1 × 1 Mt	112
SS-12 Mod. 1/2	Scaleboard	~130	1969/78	800–900	1 × 200 kt–1 Mt	130
SS-1C	Scud B	690	1965	280	1 × 100–500 kt	690–1 400
SS-23	Spider		1985	350	1 × 100 kt	
..	FROG 7	890	1965	70	1 × 10–200 kt	890–3 600
SS-21	Scarab		1978	120	1 × 20–100 kt	
SS-C-1B[e]		100	1962	450	1 × 50–200 kt	100
SAMs[f]		n.a.	1956	40–300	1 × low kt	n.a.
Other systems						
Artillery[g]		<7 700	1974	10–30	1 × low kt	n.a.
ADMs		n.a.	n.a.	–	n.a.	n.a.
Naval systems:						
Aircraft						
Tu-26	Backfire	132	1974	3 700	2–3 × bombs or ASMs	264
Tu-16	Badger	220	1961	4 800	1–2 × bombs or ASMs	480
Tu-22	Blinder	35	1962	2 200	1 × bombs	35
ASW aircraft[h]		204	1965	..	1 × depth bombs	204
Anti-ship cruise missiles						
SS-N-3	Shaddock/Sepal	264	1962	450	1 × 350 kt	264
SS-N-7	..	96	1968	56	1 × 200 kt	96
SS-N-9	Siren	224	1969	111	1 × 200 kt	224
SS-N-12	Sandbox	120	1976	500	1 × 350 kt	120
SS-N-19	..	112	1980	460	1 × 500 kt	112
SS-N-22	..	44	1981	111	1 × 200 kt	44

Land-attack cruise missiles						
SS-N-21	..	?	1986	3 000	1 × n.a.	n.a.
SS-NX-24	..	12?	1986?	<3 000	1 × n.a.	n.a.
ASW missiles and torpedoes						
SS-N-14	Silex	314	1968	50	1 × low kt	314
SS-N-15	..	n.a.	1972	40	1 × 10 kt	n.a.
SUW-N-1/FRAS-1	..	10	1967	30	1 × 5 kt	10
Torpedoes	..	n.a.	1957	16	1 × low kt	n.a.
Naval SAMs[i]						
SA-N-1	Goa	65	1961	22–32	1 × 10 kt	65
SA-N-3	Goblet	43	1967	37–56	1 × 10 kt	43
SA-N-6	..	33	1981	65	1 × 10 kt	33
SA-N-7	..	9	1981	28–52	1 × 10 kt	9

[a] Estimates of total warheads are based on minimal loadings of delivery systems plus reloads for launchers which are deployed with reload weapons. Since many systems are dual-capable, these figures should not be viewed as precise. As a consequence, all figures (with exceptions for SS-20 and SS-4 missile force loading estimates since these systems only carry nuclear warheads) are rounded to two significant figures.

[b] There are some 360 Badger and Blinder strike variants, approximately two-thirds of which are Badgers.

[c] Nuclear-capable tactical aircraft models include MiG-21 Fishbed L, MiG-27 Flogger D/J, Su-7 Fitter A, Su-17 Fitter C/D/H, Su-24 Fencer and Su-25 Frogfoot.

[d] The number of reload missiles available for each regiment is a matter of dispute. It is estimated that there is one missile reload available for two-thirds of the launchers in each regiment.

[e] Land-based anti-ship missile.

[f] Nuclear-capable land-based surface-to-air missiles probably include SA-1 Guild, SA-2 Guideline, SA-3 Goa, SA-5 Gammon, SA-10 Grumble and SA-12 Gladiator.

[g] Artillery include some 3700 M-1981 2S5 152-mm SP guns, M-1976 152-mm T guns, M-1975 2S7* 203-mm SP guns and M-1975 2S4* 240-mm SP mortars. An additional 4000 M-1973 2S3 152-mm SP howitzers and older 152-mm towed guns may be nuclear-capable, although the status of crew certification for these systems is unknown. The 152-mm guns deployed on Sverdlov cruisers could also be nuclear-capable, although the status of the cruisers themselves is unclear.

[h] Includes 94 Be-12 Mail, 50 Il-38 May and 60 Tu-142 Bear F. Land- and sea-based helicopters—including the Ka-25 Hormone, Ka-27 Helix and the Mi-14 Haze—could also have a nuclear delivery capability.

[i] The SA-N-1, SA-N-3 and SA-N-6 are believed to have a definite nuclear capability and the SA-N-7 a possible nuclear capability. Number deployed is the number of launch arms (e.g., two twin launchers equal four launch arms) deployed on ships. Overall, there are more than 3300 SAMs of these four types deployed on 70 ships of 11 classes.

Sources: Cochran, T. B., Arkin, W. M. and Sands, J. I., *Nuclear Weapons Databook, Volume IV, Soviet Nuclear Weapons* (Ballinger: Cambridge, MA, forthcoming); Arkin, W. M. and Sands, J. I., 'The Soviet nuclear stockpile', *Arms Control Today*, June 1984, pp. 1–7; Polmar, N., *Guide to the Soviet Navy*, 4th edn (US Naval Institute: Annapolis, MD, 1986); Department of Defense, *Soviet Military Power*, 1st, 2nd, 3rd, 4th, 5th edns; NATO, *NATO–Warsaw Pact Force Comparisons*, 1st, 2nd edns; Joint Chiefs of Staff, *United States Military Posture for FY 1988*; interviews with US DOD officials, Apr. and Oct. 1986; 'More self-propelled gun designations', *Jane's Defence Weekly*, 7 June 1986, p. 1003.

east of Bermuda and some 1914 km east of Cape Hatteras, North Carolina (31°11′N latitude, 55°14′W longitude) in the Atlantic patrol zone (a rectangular area some 1000–2000 km off the US east coast, known as 'The Box'). The accident apparently resulted from a fire and an explosion of the liquid-fuel propellant of the SS-N-6 (Serb) missile in the third port launch tube. The explosion blew off the missile door bending it back 'like a pretzel' and tore holes elsewhere in the hull which resulted in flooding.

After two attempts to move on its auxiliary diesel-electric engines, the submarine was taken in tow by one of the three Soviet merchant ships that had come to its rescue. These efforts did not succeed, and the submarine started to sink at about 12:20 hrs Eastern Daylight Time on 6 October and by 04:00 hrs had fully sunk.[78] The submarine remains Soviet property unless they declare it abandoned. Salvage attempts by either the USA or the USSR are unlikely given that it sank to a depth of 5625 m.

In another significant accident, on 11 September a SS-N-8 (Sawfly) SLBM fired from a Delta II submarine in the Barents Sea misfired and landed near the Amur river 290 km west of the Soviet city of Khabarovsk. The missile, more than 2400 km off course from its planned impact site on the Kamchatka Peninsula, carried a single dummy warhead weighing about half a ton. Missiles which malfunction are usually destroyed in flight, but a short circuit of the missile's electronic guidance system may have blocked the flight centre's destruction command. It is not known whether the missile landed on Chinese or Soviet territory.[79]

Strategic bomber programmes

There are some 140 Tu-95 Bear long-range bombers of five types assigned to the 36th (or Moscow) Strategic Air Army under the direct operational control of the Soviet High Command. All of the Bear bombers are capable of delivering a variety of conventional and nuclear gravity bombs. Three-quarters of the force were built in the 1950s, and two-thirds of these aircraft are configured to carry nuclear-capable air-to-surface missiles. The remaining one-quarter are new aircraft built in the 1980s to carry the new, nuclear-armed AS-15 air-launched cruise missile.

Bear H bombers can carry at least 8 and possibly as many as 12 AS-15 ALCMs internally in the bomb-bay and externally on pylons mounted under the wings. Integration of the ALCM into the Soviet bomber force is still progressing at a slow rate, with only three Bear H squadrons (approximately 40 aircraft) reportedly in service.[80] The Soviet Strategic Aviation forces have been increasingly simulating strategic stand-off cruise missile strikes against the Western continental land-mass with the Bear H in training and orientation flights. Soviet Bear H flights intercepted by the USAF Alaskan Air Command appear to indicate that some of the new aircraft are deployed in the Far East.[81]

The Soviet Union continues to reconfigure older Bear Bs and Cs to carry the supersonic AS-4 (Kitchen) missile instead of the subsonic AS-3 (Kangaroo). Several of these aircraft, known as Bear Gs, are operational.[82]

Five Blackjack A developmental aircraft are now reportedly in advanced flight-testing. A Pentagon official has said that the new bomber could be operational 'as early as 1988'.[83] The Blackjack is expected to carry AS-15 cruise missiles and nuclear gravity bombs.[84] The Blackjack will probably first replace Bear As, then Bear Gs, with all older Bear bombers replaced by the middle of the 1990s.[85]

A new, large air base under construction in the southern part of the Kola Peninsula may be used as an additional operating base in the region, supplementing the base at Olenegorsk. The length of the runway is 4600 metres (some 600 metres longer than Olenegorsk) and may be intended for the Blackjack bomber.[86]

A potentially significant development in 1986 was a specific statement made by Army General V. Shabanov, a Soviet deputy defence minister, about the 'chief component of our Armed Forces' combat might . . . the Strategic Missile Forces and the Strategic forces of the Navy and Air Force, which are in constant readiness to immediately inflict a retaliatory strike' as '*[t]his triad of strategic nuclear forces*' (emphasis added).[87] This statement, the first to use the word 'triad', could suggest that long-range bombers of the Strategic Aviation Armies may now be considered by the USSR to be on equal footing with the ballistic missile forces.

Strategic defence developments

The exact status and nature of the Soviet strategic defence programme continue to be an issue of some disagreement and contention in the West. Numerous Western reports gave few details of Soviet programmes involving lasers presumed to be for ASAT or strategic defence research purposes (see chapter 3).

The Moscow ABM system is now nearing the end of its modernization with updated Galosh missiles and new, dual-capable endo-atmospheric Gazelle missiles scheduled to begin operation in 1987.[88] The ranges of the new interceptor missiles are now estimated at 320 km and 70 km, respectively.[89] There is a report of Soviet stockpiling of Gazelle missiles. To some this is indicative of the Soviet tendency to overproduce, to others evidence of an intent for a more widespread ABM system.[90]

The supporting system of radars for detection, early warning, and target tracking and battle management is also being expanded and improved. Three Steelwork over-the-horizon backscatter (OTH-B) radars, in operation since the late 1970s, supplement the satellite-borne missile-launch detection network to provide about 30 minutes' warning of US or Chinese ICBM launches and determine the general origin of the missiles. Construction has begun on what appear to be three modern large phased-array radars (LPARs) of the type previously reported under construction at six other sites in the USSR, including the much-discussed LPAR at Abalakova near Krasnoyarsk. These three new sites would provide upgraded coverage against a missile attack from the Mediterranean and European approaches to Soviet territory.[91] By the end of the year it was reported that construction of buildings to house a large new radar operations centre had been completed at Abalakova and that it could be operating within a year.[92]

Theatre nuclear forces

Little change occurred in Soviet intermediate-range nuclear forces (INF) during 1986. SS-20 (Saber) deployments remained at 441 launchers, and SS-4 (Sandal) missiles remained at 112, the same figures as for 1985.[93] The SS-20 production and deployment programme may be completed, as the number of launchers has remained the same since September 1985, and SS-25 deployments continue at bases previously associated with the SS-20. No reports were received in 1986 that indicated the continued retirement of the SS-4s, although it is assumed that they are being dismantled.

Contrary to US Government predictions, the USSR did not deploy a prototype SSC-X-4 ground-launched cruise missile during 1986, nor a ground-launched variant of the SS-NX-24 sea-launched cruise missile.[94]

Among theatre forces the most interesting developments occurred in short-range weapons—designated 'operational-tactical' and 'tactical' by the Soviet Union. The SS-12M (SS-12 Mod. 2), SS-23 and SS-21 continued to be deployed, replacing and augmenting older SS-12, Scud-B and FROG-7 missiles (see table 1.5, and see *SIPRI Yearbook 1986*, pages 57–8, for descriptions of the missiles). During 1986, the SS-23 was deployed with Soviet forces in Eastern Europe, and Syria became the first non-Warsaw Pact country to receive the non-nuclear version of the missile.[95] The SS-21 and SS-12M continued to be deployed in Eastern Europe as well. A larger number of the older missiles are being retained outside the USSR and on active duty than had been previously expected. A portion are being used for training or as foreign military transfer weapons.

With respect to nuclear artillery, it is reported that all 152-mm, 203-mm and 240-mm systems now in service have the capability to fire nuclear projectiles (see table 1.5, note g). When fully deployed, the current generation of large calibre guns is expected to exceed 10 000, all with a nominal nuclear capability.[96] However, it is doubtful whether older towed guns would be given any nuclear capability. It also seems questionable whether the USSR has actually produced and deployed three different sizes of nuclear artillery projectiles.

IV. British nuclear weapon programmes

Of all the developments in British nuclear forces during 1986 (see table 1.6), the one which will have the greatest future effect was the start of the Trident submarine programme. The UK has embarked on a course that is planned to result in four submarines that will carry as many as 512 highly accurate MIRVed warheads. No final cost estimates for the programmes have yet been made, but it is certain to cost well over £10 billion. The arms control impact of Britain's most ambitious nuclear modernization effort remains to be seen.

Table 1.6. British nuclear forces, 1987[a]

| Weapon system | | | | Warheads | | |
Type	No. deployed	Year deployed	Range (km)[b]	Warhead × yield	Type	Max. no. in stockpile[c]
Aircraft						
Buccaneer S2	25[d]	1962	1 700	1 × bombs	WE-177[e]	30
Tornado GR-1	190[f]	1982	1 300	1 × bombs	WE-177	195
SLBMs						
Polaris A3-TK	64	1982[g]	4 700	2 × 40 kt	MRV	128
Carrier aircraft						
Sea Harrier	23	1980	450	1 × bombs	WE-177	25
ASW helicopters						
Sea King HAS 2/5	61	1976	–	1 × depth bombs	?[h]	61
Wasp HAS 1	22	1963	–	1 × depth bombs	?	22
Lynx HAS 2/5	75	1976	–	1 × depth bombs	?	75

[a] British systems certified to use US nuclear weapons include 31 Nimrod ASW aircraft based in Britain, and 20 Lance launchers (one regiment of 12 launchers, plus spares), and 136 artillery guns in five regiments (120 M109 and 15 M110 howitzers) based in FR Germany.

[b] Range for aircraft indicates combat radius, without refuelling.

[c] Some sources put the total number of nuclear warheads in the British stockpile as low as 185 warheads, comprised of: 80 WE-177 gravity bombs, 25 nuclear depth bombs and 80 Chevaline A3-TK warheads.

[d] Plus 18 in reserve and 9 undergoing conversion, probably the remainder from FR Germany.

[e] The WE-177 is thought to be a tactical 'lay-down' type bomb, with a variable yield between 5 and 200 kt.

[f] Some Buccaneer and Jaguar aircraft already withdrawn from bases in FR Germany, and already replaced by Tornado GR-1, may still be assigned nuclear roles in the UK. Upon full deployment in the UK and FR Germany, there will be 220 British Tornado GR-1 aircraft available for the nuclear strike/attack role.

[g] The Polaris A3-TK (Chevaline) was first deployed in 1982, and has now completely replaced the original Polaris A-3 missile (which was first deployed in 1968).

[h] The RN nuclear depth bomb is believed to be a low-yield variation of the RAF tactical bomb.

Sources: UK Ministry of Defence, *Statement on the Defence Estimates*, 1980 through 1986 (Her Majesty's Stationery Office: London, annual); Rogers, P., *Guide to Nuclear Weapons 1984–85* (University of Bradford: Bradford, 1984); Campbell, D., 'Too few bombs to go round', *New Statesman*, 29 Nov. 1985, pp. 10–12; US Defense Intelligence Agency, *Ground Order of Battle: United Kingdom*, DDB-1100-UK-85 (secret, partially declassified), Oct. 1985; Nott, J., 'Decisions to modernise U.K.'s nuclear contribution to NATO strengthen deterrence', *NATO Review*, vol. 29, no. 2 (Apr. 1981); International Institute for Strategic Studies, *The Military Balance 1986–87* (IISS: London, 1986); authors' estimates.

However, political developments in 1986 place questions of British nuclear forces in a new context. Opposition political parties in the UK have all opposed the Trident programme, and the Labour Party is campaigning for a strictly non-nuclear British defence and has pledged to rid Britain of all nuclear forces, US and British, if elected. Therefore, a political change in the UK could bring major changes in Britain's nuclear forces.

Submarine forces

On 30 April the British Government signed a contract with Vickers Shipbuilding and Engineering Limited (VSEL) for its first Trident ballistic missile submarine. The keel of the first submarine, to be named *Vanguard* (SSBN 05), was laid in September. The British Ministry of Defence (MOD) also asked VSEL to bid for the construction of the second Trident submarine. The other SSBNs in this V-Class are to be called *Vengeance, Victorious* and *Venerable. Vanguard* is scheduled to enter service in the mid- to late 1990s. Vanguard Class submarines are expected to have a submerged displacement of 15 500 tons (twice that of the current Resolution Class SSBNs), a length of 152 metres, and room for 16 missile tubes. It is believed that each missile will carry a maximum of 8 British-designed and -built warheads dispensed from a US-supplied MIRVed bus.

The British Vanguard/Trident programme provides a good example of the close nuclear co-operation between the UK and the USA. Although the submarines and the warheads themselves will be essentially designed and built by the UK, many of the components will come from and depend on the USA, including: Trident II/D-5 missiles; launch tubes (for the Vanguard) and all missile compartments; fire control systems; navigation sub-systems; and guidance and targeting data for the missiles.

British dependence on US systems and technology requires close co-ordination between the two countries. To expedite the exchange of information about and to purchase products for the Polaris, Chevaline and Trident systems, the British Navy maintains 33 personnel permanently assigned to the US Navy Strategic Systems Project Office (SSPO), operating at locations throughout the continental USA. The staff is responsible for the following subjects: navigation and training equipment, weapon system operations, strategic communications, support/spares/logistics, submarine design and electrical installation.[97] Regular training is provided to British Royal Navy technicians, field engineers and officers by the SSPO and contractors at Dam Neck, Virginia, and Charleston Naval Base, South Carolina, on all aspects of SSBN operations.[98] Co-operation between British and US scientists is also accomplished through established Joint Working Groups (JWGs) for various technical areas. There are nine current JWGs between the SSPO and the British MOD,[99] and a number of JWGs between the MOD and other US Federal agencies, such as the Department of Energy and the Defense Nuclear Agency. Of the total expected cost of the Trident D-5 programme (roughly £10 billion, according to one official estimate), the British Government has spent or is contractually committed to spending £3 billion as of December 1986. Of this amount, some £400 million has been spent on a new warhead production facility at Aldermaston.

All of Britain's four Resolution Class submarines have now been equipped with Polaris missiles incorporating the new Chevaline 'front end'. The last submarine to be equipped with Chevaline missiles, the *HMS Repulse*, is scheduled to go on operational patrol following the four Demonstration and Shakedown Operation (DASO) test launches expected in April and May of 1987. This modernization programme was started in 1974, with the first Chevaline-equipped submarine going on patrol in 1982. The Chevaline-equipped missiles, designated Polaris A3-TK, are intended to enable the Polaris missile system to penetrate Soviet ABM defences until the Trident D-5 missile system replaces Polaris in the mid-1990s.

The British Royal Navy is expected to complete installation of new engines on its Polaris missiles in 1987, at a total programme cost of £437 million.[100] The original engines for Britain's Polaris missiles were manufactured in 1967–68, so the missiles needed to be re-engined to enable the Polaris/Chevaline missiles to remain in working condition until they are replaced by the US Trident II D-5 missile system.

The US Naval Weapons Center (NWC) at China Lake, California, is responsible for static firings of the British Polaris A-3 Restart (A-3R) first- and second-stage engines. In February 1986 the last qualification test of the A-3R was conducted, and the performance evaluation test stage began a month later. As of January 1987 NWC China Lake has conducted 26 static tests in support of the British Polaris A-3R programme.[101] It is believed that the A-3R programme resulted in enough motors to equip no more than 80 operational missiles, which, following further tests, may result in insufficient missiles to equip all four Resolution Class SSBNs.[102]

The first submerged test launches of Polaris Production Evaluation Missiles fitted with the new engines took place in July 1986. The performance of the engines during the four launches over the US Eastern Space and Missile Center (ESMC) range met their specifications. Although one missile missed its intended target, it is believed to be because of guidance problems rather than engine malfunction.[103] If the schedule is kept, there will have been 48 test launches of British Polaris missiles over the ESMC range by mid-1987.[104]

Air Force

The Royal Air Force's (RAF) largest Tornado Wing was completed with the arrival at RAF Brüggen in FR Germany of Squadron 9 from RAF Honington on 1 October 1986.[105] This wing now comprises four squadrons of the nuclear-capable Tornado aircraft. Nine Tornado squadrons are now in service, of which seven are forward deployed in FR Germany. In addition, the Tornado Weapons Conversion Unit has 22 Tornados and in time of war would operate its aircraft as Squadron 45.

RAF Harrier GR5 aircraft are scheduled to enter service in 1987 with Harrier squadrons in FR Germany. The British MOD revealed in 1986 that there are no plans to provide GR5 aircraft with a nuclear strike role.[106] Until this revelation, the Harrier GR5 had been assumed to be nuclear-capable, like its US counterpart the AV-8B.

The RAF expressed interest in a new nuclear air-to-surface missile to replace the ageing WE-177 gravity bomb.[107] This new missile would enable Tornado aircraft to perform stand-off missions from outside enemy territory, thus avoiding the risks of trying to penetrate heavily defended airspace. However, the British requirement for a long-range stand-off missile, documented in the Naval, General and Air Staff Target 1236, does not at present include a nuclear option.[108] No firm decision has yet been made on the design, warhead or production of this missile.

Future nuclear choices

All British nuclear weapon programmes, including Trident, must be seen in the context of opposition political party pledges against various aspects of the present Conservative Government's nuclear force policies. A general election is expected no later than mid-1988, and possibly as early as the autumn of 1987. The Labour Party has called for a non-nuclear defence policy and has pledged to dismantle all British nuclear weapons and to remove all US nuclear forces from Britain within three years of taking office.[109] Although some of the opposition political parties do not advocate the complete removal of British and US nuclear forces from the UK, all are firmly committed to terminating the Trident programme. The Trident programme thus appears to have a future only with a Conservative Government.

V. French nuclear weapon programmes

There were a number of important developments in French nuclear forces during 1986 (see table 1.7) that will have a profound effect on the character and composition of these forces until the end of the century. Among these developments were the deployment of the first in a family of aircraft-delivered nuclear missiles (ASMP), the preparation for the deployment of an improved SLBM in 1987, and the definition of the parameters of future nuclear systems.

The development in 1986 that will cause the most severe changes in the outlay and composition of the nuclear forces in 1987 and beyond was the introduction of the new five-year military programming law. Under this new law the majority of previously planned nuclear-related programmes have been accelerated, while the conception and development of new systems have been speeded up. However, this may result in slowing down deployment schedules, owing to financial pressures exerted on the entire French budget.

The defence budget

A review of French defence spending by the coalition government which took office in 1986 led to several changes in key procurement programmes. Defence Minister Giraud accused the previous Socialist Government of underfunding in its 1983–88 defence plan, which, he claimed, led to serious procurement delays. As a result the government drew up a new five-year military programme act for the 1987–91 period, and on 13 November the National Assembly approved the budget. In the first year military expenditures are scheduled to rise by nearly 7 per cent (twice that of the previous year), with the capital budget rising by nearly 14 per cent.[110]

The strategic submarine force remains the highest priority, and the programme is apparently strengthened by the change of government. Plans include refitting improved M-4 SLBMs into the existing SSBNs, and developing a new generation of SSBNs to be equipped with two new types of SLBMs for the 1990s.

The new French Government, unlike its predecessor, favours the development of a mobile land-based strategic missile, planned for 1996. This missile system, the S4, previously known as the SX, would replace the last of the Mirage IVP aircraft and the S3 IRBMs.

Army

The Hadès tactical missile programme remains on schedule to be deployed in 1992, with a neutron warhead. In July 1986 the coalition government stated that it will not manufacture a neutron bomb now. On many occasions France has declared that it has mastered the complexities of the neutron bomb and has tested it several times. A decision to produce the warhead may be made as the Hadès deployment date approaches. The total number of launchers is still unclear but is believed to be between 90 and 120.

Following a meeting with West German Chancellor Kohl in February 1986, President Mitterrand stated, for the first time, that France would be willing to use tactical nuclear weapons to defend FR Germany. If time permitted, France would consult the Chancellor before using these 'prestrategic' weapons on West German soil.

Like NATO, France believes in coupling the use of conventional forces with the threat of resorting to nuclear weapons. France intends to deliver a nuclear warning to a potential aggressor 'at a place and time that will depend on the way the conflict develops'. This 'nuclear warning' will be designed not only to send an unequivocal sign to the aggressor but also to 'check the momentum of the aggressor', and will be 'diversified and graduated in strength'.[111] The nuclear hardware available for this 'unequivocal sign' includes 70 Pluton warheads (to be replaced by several hundred enhanced radiation warheads as part of the Hadès missile programme) as well as some 125 warheads assigned to aircraft of the tactical air force (FATAC) and the naval air arm.

Air Force

The first of two squadrons of Mirage IVP aircraft armed with the Air-Sol-Moyenne-Portée (ASMP) thermonuclear air-to-surface missile was declared operational at Mont-de-Marsan AB in France on 1 May 1986, followed by the second squadron at Cazeux AB on 1 December. Both

Table 1.7. French nuclear forces, 1987

| Weapon system | No. | Year | Range | Warheads | | No. in |
Type	deployed	deployed	(km)[a]	Warhead × yield	Type	stockpile
Aircraft						
Mirage IVP/ASMP[b]	18	1986	1 500[c]	1 × 300 kt	TN 80[d]	18
Jaguar A	45	1974[e]	750	1 × 6-8/30 kt	ANT-52[f]	50
Mirage IIIE	30	1972[e]	600	1 × 6-8/30 kt	ANT-52[f]	35
Refuelling aircraft						
C-135F/FR	11	1965	..	..	..	..
Land-based missiles						
S3D[g]	18	1980	3 500	1 × 1 Mt	TN-61	18
Pluton	44	1974	120	1 × 10/25 kt	ANT-51[h]	70
Submarine-based missiles						
M-20	64	1977	3 000	1 × 1 Mt	TN-61	64
M-4A	16	1985	4 000-5 000	6 × 150 kt (MIRV)	TN-70[i]	96
M-4 (modified)	16	1987	6 000	1-6 × 150 kt (MIRV)	TN-71[i]	<96
Carrier aircraft						
Super Etendard	36	1978	650	1 × 6-8/30 kt	ANT-52[f]	40

a Range for aircraft indicates combat radius, without refuelling.

b It is assumed that the remaining Mirage IVA aircraft (those not converted to IVPs) will no longer operate in a nuclear strike/attack mode (see text).

c Range does not include the 80- to 250-km range of the ASMP air-to-surface missile.

d The TN-81, an improved warhead for the ASMP, is presently under development by the CEA. If deployed, this warhead will first be operational aboard the Mirage 2000N and Super Etendard aircraft in 1988. In addition, Aérospatiale is working on a longer-range supersonic variant of the missile itself.

e The Mirage IIIE and Jaguar A aircraft were first deployed in 1964 and 1973, respectively, although they did not carry nuclear weapons until 1972 and 1974, respectively.

f Gravity bombs for these aircraft include: the ANT-52 (incorporating the same basic MR 50 charge as that used for the Pluton SSM), reported as being of 25- and 30-kt by CEA and DIA, respectively; and an alternate low-yield gravity bomb of 6-8 kt.

g S3D ('Durcie') is the designation for the recently completed hardening of the S3 missile. The original S3 missile was deployed in 1980.

h Warheads for the Pluton include the ANT-51 (incorporating the same basic MR 50 charge as the ANT-52) with a yield of 25 kt, and a specially designed alternate warhead of 10 kt.

i The *Inflexible* will be the only SSBN to receive the TN-70. All subsequent refits of the M-4 into Redoutable Class SSBNs will incorporate the improved TN-71 warhead. The M-4As of the *Inflexible* will eventually also be changed to hold the TN-71, dockyard space and budgets permitting.

j To be deployed starting on the SSBN *Le Tonnant* in the latter half of 1987. The TN-71 warhead configuration has an improved range of 6000 km maximum. It is unclear how many warheads are involved, but it is expected to be less than or equal to the standard six. The TN-71 is known to be lighter and have a smaller 'surface-equivalent-radar' image than the original TN-70.

Sources: Commissariat à l'Energie Atomique (CEA), 'Informations non classifiées sur l'armement nucléaire Français', 26 June 1986; CEA, 'Regard sur l'avenir du CEA', *Notes d'Information*, Jan.–Feb. 1986, p. 7; CEA, *Rapport Annuel 1985*, pp. 77–79; US Defense Intelligence Agency (DIA), *A Guide to Foreign Tactical Nuclear Weapon Systems under the Control of Ground Force Commanders*, DST-1040S-541-83, 9 Sep. 1983, with CHG 1 and 2 (secret, partially declassified), 17 Aug. 1984 and 9 Aug. 1985; DIA, *Air Forces Intelligence Study (AFIS): France*, DDI-1300-FR-77 (secret, partially declassified), Apr. 1977; DIA, *Military Capability Study of NATO Countries*, DDB-2680-15-85 (secret, partially declassified), Sep. 1985 and Dec. 1977; Laird, R. F., 'French nuclear forces in the 1980s and the 1990s', *Comparative Strategy*, vol. 4, no. 4 (1984), pp. 387–412; International Institute for Strategic Studies, *The Military Balance 1986/87* (IISS: London, 1986); authors' estimates.

squadrons will rotate aircraft on detachment to Istres and Orange Air Bases. Eighteen Mirage IVA aircraft have been modified (to IVP) to carry the ASMP missile, completing the programme. A few of these aircraft are used for training personnel at the Centre d'instruction des Forces aériennes stratégiques (CIFAS 328) at Bordeaux.[112]

The remaining unmodified Mirage IVA aircraft will probably be restricted to a training or reconnaissance role. The aircraft's nuclear strike/attack role derived chiefly from the AN-22 gravity bomb, which is due for retirement.[113]

The ASMP is a first for French nuclear forces and for French industry. It is the first French aircraft-delivered nuclear missile and the first missile powered by a ramjet using a solid-propellant booster.[114]

The 300-kt thermonuclear ASMP is designed to serve both strategic and so-called 'préstratégique' (tactical) purposes. In its strategic role it is deployed on Mirage IVP's, replacing the single 60-kt fission AN-22 gravity bomb.[115] In its 'préstratégique' role it will be deployed on Mirage 2000N and Super Etendard aircraft in 1988 replacing the ANT-52 gravity bomb. The first qualification flight of the ASMP from a Super Etendard aircraft was due at the end of 1986. All 53 aircraft are expected to carry the missile, some operating from France's two aircraft-carriers and others operating from land bases.

Operational evaluation of the ASMP for Mirage 2000N aircraft (to replace Jaguar and Mirage III aircraft), will begin in 1987 at the Centre d'Essais des Landes (CEL) test range.[116] The ASMP will be deployed on 75 Mirage 2000N aircraft (with 37 more in reserve). The planned IOC of the first squadron is mid-1988.[117]

Force Océanique Stratégique

On 4 March 1986 an improved M-4 SLBM with a new warhead was launched from a submarine submerged off the coast of Brittany. The announced range of the missile was 6000 km, 1600–2000 km longer than that of the first M-4As put on board the *Inflexible* in 1985.

This MIRVed M-4 SLBM was equipped with lighter, smaller warheads (the TN-71) than the deployed TN-70. The TN-71 warhead is said to be comparable to those of the better US ballistic missiles in terms of survival and penetration capability,[118] whereas the presently deployed TN-70 is comparable in terms of the weight/yield ratio.[119] The TN-71 version of the M-4 will first enter service in mid-1987 aboard the SSBN *Le Tonnant*. All M-4 SLBMs will eventually be fitted with these new warheads.

This particular M-4 was launched from the *Gymnote* experimental test submarine. It was the *Gymnote*'s 136th launch since it first began service test-firing the M-1 SLBM.[120] The *Gymnote* has been retired since October and will not be kept as a reserve SSBN, as was once believed.[121] It is not known which test submarine will be used for future SLBM flight-testing.

At the end of February the SSBN *Le Terrible* left on its 42nd operational patrol since entering active service in 1972. This was the 172nd patrol of the Force Océanique Stratégique (FOST) submarine force.[122] *Le Terrible* is third in line to be retrofitted with the improved M-4 SLBMs.

France and SDI

The French Government's Délégation générale pour l'Armement (DGA) armament agency recently sent a high-level delegation to the USA to discuss France's potential role in the US Strategic Defense Initiative programme.[123] The visit signals an increasing official interest in SDI by the French Government, which, in contrast to the governments of Britain and FR Germany, has not signed any SDI participation agreements.

Prior to this visit, President Mitterrand consistently opposed French participation in SDI on the grounds that it might compromise France's traditionally independent foreign policy. On the other hand, Prime Minister Chirac claims that France cannot afford not to be associated with SDI research, with the concomitant risk of being 'left on the sidelines of technological progress'.[124]

However, the French Government, although at odds over its official involvement, has never been opposed to participation in the programme by French companies, and has indicated that French and US industrialists should increase their co-operation in military high-technology fields.[125]

Executives of France's nationalized aerospace company Aérospatiale met in April 1986 with Strategic Defense Initiative Organization (SDIO) and US Army Strategic Defense Command officials in Washington. Discussions focused on the European anti-tactical ballistic missile (ATBM) programme and the potential role for an Aérospatiale weapon system in an ATBM segment of SDI. The French ATBM system would be directed at protecting France's strategic nuclear arsenal from Soviet intermediate-range ballistic missiles based in Eastern Europe.[126] Aérospatiale, in a joint venture with the French electronics firm Thomson-CSF and a US company, was selected as one of the seven industrial teams to participate in the architecture study of the ATBM programme.

Regardless of whatever strategic defences might emerge from the current US and Soviet research programmes, France has no intention of giving up its nuclear forces for defensive systems, as the United States has claimed as a long-term goal. In view of the possible reinforcement of terminal defence, the French reaction has been to 'increase without delay the capacity for penetration and destruction of our strategic missiles'.[127] Aérospatiale is currently designing effective countermeasures to enable France's M5 and S4 ballistic missiles to hit their targets once they are deployed and to remain operational through the early decades of the 21st century.[128]

Future nuclear choices

The first of a new class of French SSBN is expected to be ordered in early 1987[129] to enter service in approximately 1994. The 'New Generation' (NG) SSBN will use a new nuclear propulsion reactor, designated the K-15, which will enable the boat to be quieter and dive deeper than the present French submarines.

The development of yet another version of the M-4 SLBM was initiated during 1986. The 'almost invisible' TN-75 warhead will be employed on the M-4 missiles of the first NG SSBN.[130] The M-4s on the NG SSBNs will in turn be replaced before the end of the century by the M-5 SLBM, equipped with 8–12[131] very light and compact[132] TN-76 warheads.[133]

The first of two nuclear-powered aircraft-carriers planned for the French Navy will be named the *Richelieu*. The 35 000-ton ship was ordered on 4 February 1986. The keel will be laid at Brest at the end of 1987, and the ship is expected to start sea trials during the first half of 1995. The *Richelieu* is scheduled to replace the *Clémenceau* at the end of 1996.[134] It too will use the new K-15 nuclear reactor. A decision to build the second carrier will not be made until about 1990.[135]

Funding for development of the new lightweight mobile S4 land-based ballistic missile will start in 1987. Weighing about 9 tons, the S4 is expected to carry multiple nuclear warheads and have a range of at least that of the present S3 IRBMs, or 3500 km.[136] The initial operational capability date is set for 1996, with a total of 30 truck-mounted missiles eventually replacing the current 18 S3 missiles based in silos on the Plateau d'Albion.[137]

The S4 is also to be based on the Plateau d'Albion, either at St Christol Air Base or, more likely, spread out over the same land now taken up by the S3s. This encompasses some 170 km² of the plateau and surrounding hillside. In time of crisis, however, the S4s could be dispersed further afield, by land or by air[138] to other military bases, such as the Mirage aircraft bases.[139]

VI. Chinese nuclear weapon programmes

Available evidence suggests that, with one notable exception, changes to China's nuclear forces in 1986 were qualitative rather than quantitative (see table 1.8). China's first SSBN, the most recent element of China's triad, was declared operational during 1986, although it was launched in 1981 and has been training since then. The Chinese military conducted missile tests that were reportedly intended to extend the range of its nuclear missiles and, for the first time, to develop missiles with multiple and/or MIRVed warheads. China continued its programme of military reform and modernization during 1986 and centralized several nuclear weapon activities of its military, the People's Liberation Army (PLA). In an important development, in March China became the last of the five nuclear weapon states to renounce atmospheric testing of nuclear weapons.

Missile forces

Perhaps the most important development for Chinese nuclear forces was the series of missile tests conducted from the autumn of 1985 until early 1986. It is believed that several CSS-2 IRBMs and at least one SLBM were tested.[140] If these tests were as successful as they were reported to be, China could be proceeding towards a small force of MIRVed ballistic missiles, particularly longer-range missiles such as IRBMs, ICBMs and SLBMs. The tests were also

Table 1.8. Chinese nuclear forces, 1987

Weapon system	No. deployed	Year deployed	Range (km)	Warheads	No. in stockpile
Type				Warhead × yield	
Aircraft[a]					
Il-28 Beagle (B-5)	15-30	1974	1 850	1 × bombs[b]	15-30
Tu-16 Badger (B-6)	100	1966	5 900	1-3 × bombs	100-130
Land-based missiles					
CSS-1 (DF-2)	40-60	1966	1 100	1 × 20 kt	40-60
CSS-2 (DF-3)	85-125	1972	2 600	1 × 2-3 Mt	85-125
CSS-3 (DF-4)	~ 10	1978	7 000	1 × 1-3 Mt	20
CSS-4 (DF-5)	~ 10	1980	12 000	1 × 4-5 Mt	20
Submarine-based missiles[c]					
CSS-N-3	26	1983	3 300	1 × 200 kt-1 Mt	26-38

[a] All figures for these bomber aircraft refer to nuclear-capable versions only. Hundreds of these aircraft are also deployed in non-nuclear versions.
[b] Yields of bombs are estimated to range from below 20 kt to 3 Mt.
[c] Two missiles are presumed to be available for rapid deployment on the Golf Class submarine (SSB). Additional missiles are being built for new Xia submarines.

Sources: Joint Chiefs of Staff, *Military Posture (annual report) FY 1978, 1982, 1983*; Department of Defense, *Annual Report for 1982*; Defense Intelligence Agency, *Handbook on the Chinese Armed Forces*, Apr. 1976; Defense Intelligence Agency, 'A guide to foreign tactical nuclear weapon systems under the control of ground force commanders', DST-1040S-541-83-CHG 1 (secret, partially declassified), 17 Aug. 1984; Godwin, P. H., *The Chinese Tactical Airforces and Strategic Weapons Program: Development, Doctrine, and Strategy* (Air University: Maxwell AFB, AL, 1978); Washburn, T. D., *The People's Republic of China and Nuclear Weapons: Effects of China's Evolving Arsenal*, ADA 067350 (NTIS, 1979); US Congress, Joint Economic Committee, *Allocation of Resources in the Soviet Union and China* (annual hearing) 1976, 1981, 1982, 1983; Anderson, J., 'China shows confidence in its missiles', *Washington Post*, 19 Dec. 1984, p. F11.

meant to increase the ranges of ballistic missiles.[141] Deng Xiaoping, Chairman of the Central Military Commission, is reported to have commended the SLBM test personnel, saying that their work had 'led to increases in flying range, multiple targeting ability and operational flexibility' and that 'their work could be adapted to other strategic weapons'.[142] If China decides to develop MIRVed missiles, this would be a major change in force structure and could be one of the most significant Chinese nuclear weapon developments. MIRVed missiles would permit a rapid increase in the number of Chinese nuclear warheads without expanding the size of the missile force. They would also complicate any attempt by an adversary at ballistic missile defence against China's missiles. Furthermore, if ballistic missiles are given increased ranges, they will be able to operate from locations farther inland in China, away from the border with the Soviet Union.

On various occasions in 1986, official Chinese sources reported that China's only indigenously designed and -built nuclear-powered submarine had completed its training programme and had begun active operations. These were the first official confirmations, the latest of which included a photograph,[143] that China's Xia Class SSBN was in active service after five years of preparation. Two Xia Class submarines have been launched, and it has been assumed that both of them would be available in a crisis, although it was unclear if or when the submarines had become operational. The Xia Class submarines have 12 launch tubes for the CSS-N-3 SLBM, which is estimated to have a maximum range of 3300 km and a warhead yield between 200 kt and 1 Mt.[144] Similar official statements about Chinese submarines had been made in the past, without specifying what type of submarine was involved.[145] This led to some confusion since China has designed and built two types of nuclear-powered submarines—Han Class SSNs and Xia Class SSBNs. As a result, foreign news organizations did not initially report that it was an SSBN that had become operational until Chinese sources published a picture of the Xia Class submarine.

In accordance with its military modernization efforts, China opened several new training facilities during 1986. Two important institutions are the new National Defence University and a training academy for the Second Artillery Corps, the nuclear weapon command. Both these training facilities will be used to teach combined arms concepts and practices that will integrate nuclear weapons into the general training programme for officers. The new emphasis on joint operations and combined arms training that includes nuclear weapon planning is exemplified by China's Antichemical Warfare Corps, which is responsible for defence against nuclear and chemical attacks. According to an official Chinese news report, a military officer indicated that combined arms units have been given priority for nuclear and chemical defence.[146] The Corps has gained experience by participating in 'each of China's nuclear tests', and by 'handling radioactive and chemical leak accidents on many occasions'.[147]

Numerous details of China's nuclear weapon programme were reported for the first time in a series of articles about Deng Jiaxian, the nuclear physicist responsible for designing, building and testing China's nuclear weapons.[148] His identity as the director of the nuclear weapon effort was kept secret for nearly

30 years. Three new details are noteworthy. According to several articles, the Soviet Union explicitly promised in a 1957 agreement to supply China with a 'teaching model' of a nuclear weapon but failed to keep its pledge.[149] This appears to be the first specific public explanation of the broken promise. Another point of interest is a reference about how China was able to design a fusion warhead only 32 months after its first test of a fission weapon, less than half the time it took the USA, the USSR or France. According to the report, while Deng and his colleagues were having difficulty with the calculations for a theoretical design of a thermonuclear warhead, a group of nuclear scientists in Shanghai discovered some form of design 'shortcut' which allowed the project to proceed quickly. It no doubt helped China to know that four other nations had already exploded hydrogen bombs. The third new detail was the statement that China has conducted 32 nuclear tests since 1964, 3 more than available data indicate. It is believed that this figure is quoted from foreign sources; it is not an official figure.[150]

On 21 March 1986 Premier Zhao Ziyang announced China's decision to renounce atmospheric testing of nuclear weapons. Since 1975, when France ceased its above-ground tests, China had been the only nuclear weapon state to conduct tests in the atmosphere. Although not a signatory to the 1963 Partial Test Ban Treaty, China has decided to implement its main provision. China conducted its last atmospheric nuclear test in 1980.

Notes and references

[1] Smith, B. A., 'Air force installs first MX missiles in Minuteman silos', *Aviation Week & Space Technology*, 11 Aug. 1986, p. 25; Rhodes, J. P., 'The first Peacekeeper', *Air Force Magazine*, June 1986, pp. 82–4.

[2] Congressional Budget Office, *The MX Missile Test Program and Alternatives*, Staff Working Paper, Feb. 1986.

[3] The four leading concepts were Superhard Silos, Superhard Silos with Concealment, Carry Hard and Shallow Tunnel. The other four were Hardened Minuteman Silos, Rail Mobile, Ground Mobile and Deep Basing; see General Accounting Office (GAO), *ICBM Modernization: Status, Survivable Basing Issues, and Need to Reestablish a National Consensus*, GAO/NSIAD-86-200, Sep. 1986, p. 34; and US Congress, House Appropriations Committee (HAC), *Hearings on Department of Defense Appropriations for 1987*, Part 6, p. 380 (hereafter cited as HAC, *FY 1987 DOD*). The other three regular congressional hearing series are abbreviated similarly—HASC: House Armed Services Committee; SAC: Senate Appropriations Committee; and SASC; Senate Armed Services Committee.

[4] Halloran, R., 'Air force commander seeks to place MX missiles on trains', *New York Times*, 27 Oct. 1986, p. A18; Lynch, D. J. 'Air force favors MX on trains', *Defense Week*, 17 Nov. 1986, p. 1; Lynch, D. J., 'Reagan decision on Midgetman and MX expected', *Defense Week*, 15 Dec. 1986, p. 1.

[5] Smith, R. J., 'Midgetman missile plans generate political debate', *Science*, 6 June 1986, pp. 1186–8; Smith, R. J., 'Mobile missile design generates controversy', *Science*, 27 June 1986, pp. 1590–3; Smith, R. J., 'Proposal to ban mobile missiles favors targeting over arms control', *Science*, 22 Aug. 1986, pp. 831–3; Morrison, D. C., 'Missile gridlock', *National Journal*, 7 June 1986, pp. 1366–70; Walker, P. F. and Wentworth, J. A., 'Midgetman: missile in search of a mission', *Bulletin of the Atomic Scientists*, Nov. 1986, pp. 20–6; GAO, *DOD Acquisition, Case Study of the Air Force Small Intercontinental Ballistic Missile*, GAO/NSIAD-86-45S-16, 31 July 1986; GAO, *ICBM Modernization: Status, Survivable Basing Issues, and Need to Reestablish a National Consensus*, GAO/NSIAD-86-200, Sep. 1986.

[6] *Department of Defense Appropriation Bill, 1987*, Senate Report 99-446, pp. 312–15; *National Defense Authorization Act for Fiscal Year 1987*, Senate Report 99-331, pp. 168–70.

[7] DOD, Undersecretary of Defense for Research and Engineering (USDRE), *Report of the*

Defense Science Board Task Force on Small Intercontinental Ballistic Missile Modernization, Mar. 1986, p. v.

[8] Les Aspin, Chairman of the HASC, argued that of the $840 billion in costs for developing and operating strategic weapons over a more than 20-year basis, the Midgetman would be 5.3 per cent of the total. HASC, *Midgetman: Sliding Shut the Window of Vulnerability*, 10 Feb. 1986.

[9] DOD, Office of the Assistant Secretary of Defense for Public Affairs (OASD-PA), News Release No. 75–86, 28 Feb. 1986; USAF, *Legislative Environmental Impact Statement: Small Intercontinental Ballistic Missile Program*, Nov. 1986.

[10] Pincus, W., 'Nuclear test brings criticism by Soviets', *Washington Post*, 23 Mar. 1986, p. A1.

[11] Smith, R. J., 'Proposal to ban mobile missiles favors targeting over arms control', *Science*, 22 Aug. 1986, pp. 831–3; Lynch, D. J., 'Soviet targets slipping from view as US planners try to keep pace', *Defense Week*, 30 June 1986, p. 1.

[12] Gordon, M. R., 'Reagan orders a study to decide if US should build new missile', *New York Times*, 25 Apr. 1986, p. A1.

[13] Gordon, M. R. 'Reagan reported to favor keeping 1979 limit on arms', *New York Times*, 22 Apr. 1986, p. A1; Pincus, W. and Oberdorfer, D., '2 subs to be dismantled', *Washington Post*, 22 Apr. 1986, p. A20.

[14] Sloan, S. R., *The NATO Allies and the Issue of Continued US Observance of SALT II Limits*, Study Prepared for Senate Democratic Leader Robert C. Byrd by the Congressional Research Service (CRS), 4 Apr. 1986.

[15] *Congressional Record*, 10 Apr. 1986, p. S4026.

[16] Two other US submarine accidents were reported during the year. The *Atlanta* (SSN 712) ran aground in the Strait of Gibraltar on 29 April. Sometime around 20 October, somewhere in the Atlantic the *Augusta* (SSN 710) 'struck something underwater', possibly colliding with a Soviet submarine, and sustaining $1.5 million in damage.

[17] See House Foreign Affairs Committee, Report 99–643, 17 June 1986.

[18] Sussman, B., 'Public would preserve SALT II treaty, not help Nicaraguan contras', *Washington Post*, 25 June 1986, p. A16.

[19] Kenny, Maj. M., USAF, 'Pilot report: B-1B', *Air Force Magazine*, June 1986, pp. 58–62; Coyne, J. P., 'Bringing on the B-1B', *Air Force Magazine*, June 1986, pp. 63–9.

[20] 'B-1B readies for service', *Aviation Week & Space Technology*, 2 June 1986, pp. 46–62.

[21] North, D. M., 'Development problems delay full B-1B operational capability', *Aviation Week & Space Technology*, 3 Nov. 1986, pp. 34–5; Stewart, J., 'Flaws slow new fleet of planes', *Atlanta Journal and Constitution*, 9 Nov. 1986, p. 1.

[22] According to the HASC, black programmes have grown eight-fold in the past five years. See *Aviation Week & Space Technology*, 19 May 1986, p. 15; and Morrison, D. C., 'Pentagon's top secret "black" budget has skyrocketed during Reagan years', *National Journal*, 1 Mar. 1986, pp. 492–8.

[23] *Aviation Week & Space Technology*, 9 June 1986, p. 25.

[24] HAC, *FY 1986 DOD*, Part 2, p. 490.

[25] White House, Office of the Press Secretary, Presidential Statement on Interim Restraint, 27 May 1986; White House, Fact Sheet, US Interim Restraint Policy: Responding to Soviet Arms Control Violations, 27 May 1986; Gordon, M. R., 'Air force delay said to keep US to '79 arms limit', *New York Times*, 29 Aug. 1986, p. A1.

[26] Gordon, M. R., 'US might hasten breach of treaty', *New York Times*, 6 Oct. 1986, p. A12.

[27] Smith, R. J., '131st cruise B52 rolled out; treaty implications disputed', *Washington Post*, 18 Nov. 1986, p. A3; Smith, R. J., 'US poised to exceed SALT limit', *Washington Post*, 9 Nov. 1986, p. A1; Wilson G. C. and Smith, R. J., 'US to break SALT II limits Friday', *Washington Post*, 27 Nov. 1986, p. A9; Gordon, M. R., 'US exceeds limit set in 1979 accord on strategic arms', *New York Times*, 29 Nov. 1986, p. 1.

[28] Taubman, P., 'Soviet to abide by arms treaty "for time being"', *New York Times*, 6 Dec. 1986, p. 1.

[29] Fuerbringer, J., 'House Democrats press arms limits', *New York Times*, 11 Dec. 1986, p. A15; Gordon, M. R., '57 Senators ask Reagan in a letter to observe '79 arms pact', *New York Times*, 16 Dec. 1986, p. A12.

[30] *Aviation Week & Space Technology*, 9 Sep. 1985, p. 29; 'SRAM II Phase 2 Study', *Energy and Technology Review*, June–July 1986, pp. 2–3.

[31] *National Defense Authorization Act for Fiscal Year 1987*, Conference Report, House Report 99–1001, p. 442; Lynch, D. J., 'SRAM II still favored by AF', *Defense Week*, 10 Nov. 1986, p. 6.

[32] US DOD, *Annual Report of the Secretary of Defense to the Congress, FY 1988* (hereafter cited as *DOD, FY 1988*).

[33] Arkin, W. M., 'Fewer warheads in Europe', *Bulletin of the Atomic Scientists*, Aug./Sep. 1986, pp. 4–5.

[34] SAC, *Energy and Water Development Appropriations for 1987*, Part 2, p. 1258 (hereafter cited as SAC, *FY 1987 EWDA*).

[35] Fouquet, D., 'No plans for neutron bomb, says NATO', *Jane's Defence Weekly*, 16 Aug. 1986, p. 231.

[36] Manners, G., 'SACEUR's plans for nuclear stockpile', *Jane's Defence Weekly*, 25 Oct. 1986, p. 948.

[37] SAC, *FY 1987 EWDA*, Part 2, p. 1261.

[38] See, e. g., Morrison, D. C., 'The Navy's vanishing nuclear arsenal', *National Journal*, 13 Sep. 1986; Polmar, N., 'Tactical nuclear weapons', *US Naval Institute Proceedings*, July 1983.

[39] HAC, *FY 1987 DOD*, Part 4, p. 156.

[40] HAC, *FY 1987 DOD*, Part 4, p. 132.

[41] HAC, *FY 1987 DOD*, Part 4, p. 156.

[42] HAC, *FY 1987 DOD*, Part 4, p. 156.

[43] HAC, *FY 1987 DOD*, Part 4, pp. 132, 156.

[44] HAC, *FY 1987 DOD*, Part 4, pp. 132, 156.

[45] HAC, *FY 1987 DOD*, Part 4, p. 164.

[46] HAC, *FY 1987 DOD*, Part 4, p. 155.

[47] HAC, *FY 1987 DOD*, Part 5, pp. 513–14.

[48] HAC, *FY 1987 DOD*, Part 5, pp. 479, 558.

[49] HAC, *FY 1987 DOD*, Part 5, p. 560.

[50] SAC, *FY 1987 EWDA*, Part 2, p. 1270.

[51] HAC, *FY 1987 DOD*, Part 5, p. 555.

[52] HAC, *FY 1987 DOD*, Part 5, p. 555.

[53] HAC, *FY 1987 EWDA*, Part 4, p. 79; HAC, *FY 1987 EWDA*, Part 6, p. 1505–6. See also Hiatt, F. and Atkinson, R., 'Lab creating a new generation of nuclear arms', *Washington Post*, 9 June 1986, p. A1; Taylor, T. B. 'Endless generations of nuclear weapons', *Bulletin of the Atomic Scientists*, Nov. 1986, pp. 12–15; and Taylor, T. B., 'Nuclear testing is a Pandora's Box', *Federation of American Scientists Public Interest Report*, Dec. 1986.

[54] Smith, R. J., 'X-ray laser budget grows as public information declines', *Science*, 11 Apr. 1986, pp. 152–3.

[55] *TechTrends International*, 11 Aug. 1986, p. 6.

[56] The policy was first made public in a speech to the Foreign Policy Association by Deputy Secretary of State Kenneth W. Dam on 14 January 1985. (Department of State, *Current Policy No. 647*.) Subsequent speeches on 20 February 1985 and 28 March 1985 by Ambassador Nitze repeated the essential points (Department of State, *Current Policy No. 657* and *677*). See also Jackson, R. L., *The New Strategic Policy: Issues for Congressional Consideration*, CRS Report no. 85-134F, Congressional Research Service, 18 Apr. 1985; and Arkin, W. M., 'The new mix of defense and deterrence', *Bulletin of the Atomic Scientists*, June/July 1986, pp. 4–5.

[57] This designation and other information were released by the USSR to bolster its argument that the missile is a modification of the SS-13. (Foreign Ministry Press Conference with Chief of Staff Akhromeyev and Deputy Foreign Minister Bessmertnykh, cited by Melor Sturua in *Izvestiya*, FBIS-SU, 6 June 1986.) For a discussion of the SS-13/SS-25 issue, see Mendelsohn, J. 'Proportionate response: sense or nonsense?', *Arms Control Today*, Jan./Feb. 1986, p. 8.

[58] DOD, *Soviet Military Power* 1986 (hereafter cited as *SMP, 1986*), p. 26; US Arms Control and Disarmament Agency (ACDA), *Fiscal Year 1987 Arms Control Impact Statements* (hereafter cited as *ACIS, FY 1987*), p. 26. The transporter-erecter-launcher for the SS-25 had been previously described as off-road capable; see *SMP, 1984*, p. 24.

[59] Background briefing by senior Administration official, 24 Mar. 1986; *SMP, 1986*, pp. 26–7. The ICBM RV figure given in *SMP, 1986*, p. 25, includes 10 SS-X-24 missiles by the end of 1986.

[60] Background briefing by senior Administration official, 24 Mar. 1986.

[61] Gordon, M. R., 'Second Soviet missile mishap is reported by US officials', *New York Times*, 18 Sep. 1986, pp. A1, A18; Pincus, W., 'Officials debate threat of new Soviet missile', *Washington Post*, 12 Aug. 1986, p. A14.

[62] An interview with DOD officials in May 1984 indicated that the number of single-warhead SS-17 and SS-19 missiles deployed at that time was 'too few to matter'. The Joint Chiefs of Staff refer to 'the most accurate versions of the SS-18 and SS-19 missiles'; see *United States Military Posture for FY 1987* (hereafter cited as *JCS, FY 1987*), p. 21. *SMP, 1986*, preface, indicates that, as of the end of 1985, the Mod. 4 SS-18 modernization programme was 'reaching completion'.

[63] DOD, *FY 1988*.

[64] *SMP, 1985*, p. 31; *SMP, 1986*, p. 28; SASC/SAC, *Soviet Strategic Force Developments, Joint Hearings*, S. Hrg. 99-335, 26 June 1985, p. 9 (hereafter cited as SASC/SAC, *S. Hrg. 99/335*).

[65] The silos are reportedly larger than those used by the SS-18; see Gertz, B., 'Soviet test of SS-18 may violate SALT II', *Washington Times*, 13 Apr. 1986, p. 13.

[66] Gordon, M. R., 'US reports failure in recent Soviet test of big new missile', *New York Times*, 15 Apr. 1986, pp. A1, A8; Gordon, M. R., 'Second Soviet missile mishap is reported by US officials', *New York Times*, 18 Sep. 1986, pp. A1, A18; 'Soviet acknowledges explosion of a missile', *New York Times*, 19 Sep. 1986, p. A7.

[67] Gertz, B., 'Soviet successfully test missile that will be largest in arsenal', *Washington Times*, 7 Jan. 1987, p. 3.

[68] See, for example, *SMP, 1985*, p. 31; *SMP, 1986*, p. 28; *DOD, FY 1987*, p. 59; *ACIS, FY 1987*, p. 26; SASC/SAC, *S. Hearing 99-335*, pp. 6–9.

[69] Lucas, H., 'Soviet MARV to begin flight tests', *Jane's Defence Weekly*, 19 Jan. 1985, p. 96.

[70] *SMP, 1986*, p. 29.

[71] *SMP, 1986*, p. 121.

[72] *Jane's Defence Weekly*, 15 Feb. 1986, p. 223.

[73] Jordan, J., 'Leviathan of the deep', *Jane's Defence Weekly*, 1 Mar. 1986, p. 381. See also SIPRI, *World Armaments and Disarmament: SIPRI Yearbook 1986* (Oxford University Press: Oxford, 1986), p. 55.

[74] Details of the new submarine base, based on US Landsat photographs, were reported in August by the Oslo-based Norwegian Foreign Policy Research Institute; see 'Kola unveiled', *Jane's Defence Weekly*, 13 Sep. 1986, pp. 538–40; and 'Soviets building bases in Arctic, Norway says', *Washington Post*, 23 Aug. 1986, p. A18.

[75] A depiction of the base at Polyarnyy, with piers and two tunnels for Delta and Yankee Class submarines and other cruise missile and attack submarines, appears in *SMP, 1986*, pp. 20–1. Two tunnels are reported under construction at the base near Vladivostok; see *Sankei*, 31 Mar. 1986, cited in *Arms Control Reporter*, p. 611.B.304.

[76] *SMP, 1986*, p. 30.

[77] *SMP, 1986*, pp. 30–1. The missiles that are expected to be flight-tested before the end of the decade have also been described as replacements or follow-ons; see SASC/SAC, *S. Hrg. 99–335*, pp. 7, 11.

[78] Among the numerous articles on the incident see: Gwertzman, B., 'Moscow reports fire on atomic sub in North Atlantic', *New York Times*, 5 Oct. 1986, p. 1; Bohlen, C., 'Soviet A-sub blaze off Bermuda kills 3', *Washington Post*, 5 Oct. 1986, p. A1; Rosenthal, A., 'Soviet nuclear sub catches fire; 3 die', *Boston Globe*, 5 Oct. 1986, p. 1; Gwertzman, B., 'Soviet submarine, crippled by fire, on its way home', *New York Times*, 6 Oct. 1986, p. A1; Rensberger, B., 'Soviet sub fire seems to be out', *Washington Post*, 6 Oct. 1986, p. A1; 'Soviet sub under tow after blaze is put out', *Boston Globe*, 6 Oct. 1986, p. 1; Gwertzman, B., 'Soviet atomic sub sinks in Atlantic 3 days after fire', *New York Times*, 7 Oct. 1986, p. A1; Wilson, G. C. and Smith, R. J., 'Crippled Soviet sub sinks in Atlantic, no nuclear contamination expected', *Washington Post*, 7 Oct. 1986, p. A1; 'Moscow's new policy reflected in sub report', *New York Times*, 5 Oct. 1986, p. 14; Preston, A., 'Political consequences of the Soviet "Yankee" SSBN sinking', *Jane's Defence Weekly*, 18 Oct. 1986, pp. 876–7.

[79] Cannon, L. 'Missile test by Soviets goes astray', *Washington Post*, 16 Sep. 1986, p. 5; Berke, R. L., 'Unarmed Soviet test missile is reported to land in China', *New York Times*, 17 Sep. 1986, p. A4; 'Soviet SS-N-8 goes astray during test', *Jane's Defence Weekly*, 27 Sep. 1986, p. 658.

[80] *SMP, 1986* is not clear on the number of Bear H bombers. The document notes that there are 150 Bear bombers (pp. 8, 23), thus implying that about 50 Bear Hs are deployed, given the number of older Bear airframes, but also specifies that there are about 40 Bear Hs now in the inventory (p. 32).

[81] 'On the trail of the Soviet Bear-H', *Jane's Defence Weekly*, 11 Oct. 1986, p. 796. According to the Joint Chiefs of Staff, routine intercontinental training flights are conducted to points off both the North American coasts; see *JCS, FY 1987*, p. 31.

[82] *SMP, 1986*, p. 32; *SMP, 1985*, p. 33; *SMP, 1984*, p. 28.

[83] Background briefing by a senior defence official, 24 Mar. 1986. See also *SMP, 1986*, pp. 4, 33; SAC-SASC, *S. Hrg, 99–335*, p. 12. The expected introduction date for the Blackjack has been pushed back from 1986–87 in *SMP, 1983* (p. 26), to 1987 in *SMP, 1984* (p. 29) and to 1988 in *SMP, 1985* (p. 34).

[84] SASC/SAC, *S. Hrg. 99–335*, p. 12; *SMP, 1983*, p. 26; *SMP, 1984*, p. 29; *SMP, 1985*, p. 34; *SMP, 1986*, p. 33.

[85] *SMP, 1986*, p. 33.

[86] 'Kola unveiled', *Jane's Defence Weekly*, 13 Sep. 1986, pp. 538–40; 'Soviets building bases in Arctic, Norway says', *Washington Post*, 24 Aug. 1986, p. A18.

[87] *FBIS Daily Report*, USSR, FBIS-SU-86-164, vol. 3, no. 164 (25 Aug. 1986), p. V3, a translation of Army General V. Shabanov, USSR Deputy Defence Minister, under rubric 'Combat potential: technical equipment: the material basis of defense might', *Red Star*, 15 Aug. 1986, 2nd edn. pp. 2–3.

[88] *SMP, 1986*, pp. 41–4.

[89] Admiral Crowe testified that the Soviet Union has 'The world's only operational ABM system featuring interceptor missiles with both conventional and nuclear warheads'; see Statement of Admiral William J. Crowe, Jr, USN, Chairman of the JCS on Nuclear Testing before the Senate Foreign Relations Committee, 8 May 1986, p. 2. It is not clear whether he was referring to the Galosh or modified Galosh missile or the new Gazelle missile. The older ABM-1B Galosh was believed to be dual-capable. See *JCS, FY 1978*, p. 28; Collins, J. M. and Cronin, P. M., *U.S./Soviet Military Balance*, Congressional Research Service, Report No. 85–83F, 15 Apr. 1985, p. 22.

[90] 'White House assesses reports of Soviet Asat laser facilities', *Aviation Week & Space Technology*, 15 Sep. 1986, p. 21.

[91] Pincus, W., 'Soviet believed building radar sites', *Washington Post*, 16 Aug. 1986, p. A19; Gordon, M. R. 'U.S. is debating role of 3 new Soviet radars', *New York Times*, 19 Dec. 1986, p. A11; Morrison, D. C., 'Radar diplomacy', *National Journal*, 3 Jan. 1987, pp. 17–21. The sites are in Skrunda, in western Latvia; Mukachevo, in the Ukraine, near the Czechoslovakian border; and Baranovichi, 160 km south-west of Minsk.

[92] Gordon, M. R., 'Soviet finishing large radar center in Siberia', *New York Times*, 23 Nov. 1986, p. 8.

[93] Manners, G., 'SACEUR's plans for nuclear stockpile', *Jane's Defence Weekly*, 25 Oct. 1986, p. 948.

[94] *JCS, FY 1987*, p. 32; *SMP, 1986*, p. 33.

[95] 'Syria has SS-23 long-range missile site', *Jane's Defence Weekly*, 26 July 1986, p. 92; 'Soviet SS-23s in Europe', *Jane's Defence Weekly*, 25 Oct. 1986, p. 927.

[96] *SMP, 1986*, p. 39.

[97] Correspondence between US Navy SSPO and authors, Apr. 1986.

[98] Correspondence between US Navy SSPO and authors, Apr. 1986.

[99] The JWGs are: 1. Joint Systems Performance and Analysis; 2. Polaris Joint Reentry System Working Group; 3. Trident Joint Reentry System Working Group; 4. Joint Motor Life Study Coordination Group; 5. Joint Steering Task Group; 6. Strategic Weapon System Test Group; 7. UK Test Documentation Group; 8. Strategic Weapon Test Group; and 9. Joint US/UK Polaris Program Financial Management Working Group.

[100] 'Polaris remotoring near completion', *Jane's Defence Weekly*, 12 July 1986, p. 8.

[101] 'NWC Polaris Test Schedule', documents received in 1986 under the US Freedom of Information Act.

[102] Periodic static testing at NWC China Lake will further deplete the 80 sets of motors available, as will DASO flight-tests and A-3TK follow-on testing at ESMC. Eight sets of motors are expected to be expended in flight-tests during 1986–87.

[103] Hutchinson, R., 'Guidance system fault causes Polaris test failure', *Jane's Defence Weekly*, 16 Aug. 1986, p. 228.

[104] US Navy, SSPO, 'Polaris/Poseidon/Trident Flight Test History and Forecast-U', (secret, partially declassified), 17 Apr. 1986; and Freedman, L., *Britain and Nuclear Weapons* (Macmillan: London, 1980), p. 147.

[105] 'Full house at Brüggen', *RAF News*, 17–30 Oct. 1986, p. 1.

[106] *Hansard*, 107 (21), 9 Dec. 1986, col. 147.

[107] Urban, M., 'RAF seeks new missile to beat Soviet air defences', *The Independent*, 10 Nov. 1986.

[108] *Hansard*, 107 (21), 9 Dec. 1986, col. 146.

[109] Roberts, J., 'Kinnock would take 3 years to eliminate nuclear forces', *Defense Week*, 8 Dec. 1986, p. 3.

[110] 'Speech of M. Jacques Chirac, Prime Minister, at the Institute of Higher National Defence Studies (IHEDN)', 12 Sep. 1986, translated in *Speeches and Statements*, Sp.St/LON/126/86, by the French Embassy in London.

[111] See note 110.

[112] 'Une plus-value pour les FAS: Le Mirage IVP, Le missile air-sol moyenne portée (ASMP)', *Air Actualite*, no. 390 (May 1986), pp. 29–32.

[113] However, one source credits the Mirage IVA as being able to accommodate tactical nuclear gravity bombs; thus this aircraft could still have a reserve tactical nuclear role even after the

withdrawal of the strategic AN-22. See DIA, 'A guide to foreign tactical nuclear weapon systems under the control of ground force commanders', DST-1040S-541-83, 9 Sep. 1983, with CHG 1, 17 Aug. 1984 and 2, 9 Aug. 1985 (secret, partially declassified). In either case these aircraft will be phased out, as the first of 75 Mirage 2000Ns armed with the ASMP take on the nuclear role in 1988.

[114] See note 112.

[115] Commissariat à l'Energie Atomique (CEA), *Informations non classifiées sur l'armement nucléaire français*, 26 June 1986.

[116] Langereux, P., 'La France met en service le missile air-sol nucléaire ASMP', *Air et cosmos*, no. 1087 (15 Mar. 1986), p. 45.

[117] See note 116, p. 44.

[118] CEA, *Rapport Annuel 1985*, pp. 77–9.

[119] CEA, *Informations non classifiées sur l'armament nucléaire français*, 26 June 1986; and, CEA, 'Regard sur l'avenir du CEA', *Notes d'Information*, Jan.–Feb. 1986, p. 7.

[120] '136 missiles one été tirés par le "Gymnote"', *Air et cosmos*, no. 1090 (5 Apr. 1986), p. 26.

[121] Interviews with officials of the French Embassy, Washington, DC.

[122] 'Visite Ministerielle à bord du Terrible', *Air et cosmos*, no. 1087 (15 Mar. 1986), p. 28.

[123] 'French signals', *Aviation Week & Space Technology*, 3 Nov. 1986, p. 31.

[124] 'Speech of M. Jacques Chirac, Prime Minister, at the Institute of Higher National Defence Studies (IHEDN) (12 Sep. 1986)', translated in *Speeches and Statements*, Sp.St/LON/126/86, by the French Embassy in London.

[125] *France* magazine, French Embassy, Washington, DC.

[126] 'French in discussions with SDIO on ATBMs', *Defense Electronics*, Jun. 1986, p. 24.

[127] 'Excerpts from the Speech of M. Jacques Chirac, Prime Minister, Before the National Assembly', 9 Apr. 1986, *Speeches and Statements*, Sp.St/LON/44/86, French Embassy, London.

[128] 'Strategic and space systems', *Revue Aerospatiale*, no. 34 (Nov. 1986), pp. 32–4.

[129] *Air et cosmos*, 15 Mar. 1986, said it would be ordered by the end of the year. As of 6 November it had not yet been ordered.

[130] Assemblée Nationale, *Rapport no. 393, sur le projet de loi de finances pour 1987*, au nom de la commission des finances, de l'économie général et du plan, Annexe no. 39; Défense, Titres V et VI, 12 Nov. 1986, p. 38.

[131] *News from France*, 24 Nov. 1986, p. 2. *Jane's Defence Weekly*, 15 Nov. 1986, p. 1143, gives a figure of nine warheads; 'Missiles', *Air et cosmos*, 15 Nov. 1986, p. 9, gives 8–12 warheads.

[132] Ferrari, A., 'Regard sur l'avenir du CEA,' *Notes d'Information* (CEA: Paris, Jan.–Feb. 1986), p. 8.

[133] 'Défense 1987: un projet de budget lié à la Loi de programmation', *Air et cosmos*, 4 Oct. 1986, p. 27.

[134] 'Le future P.A.N. "Richelieu" de la Marine nationale,' *Air et cosmos*, no. 1083 (15 Feb. 1986), p. 53.

[135] 'L'Armee de Terre aura son "Leclerc" et la Marine son "Richelieu" et l'Armee de l'Air?', *Air et cosmos*, no. 1082 (8 Feb. 1986), p. 31.

[136] 'French five-year budget proposal includes funding for new missiles, ships, reconnaissance satellites', *Aviation Week & Space Technology*, 17 Nov. 1986, p. 25. Another source credits the S4 with only a single warhead; see 'Military program bill for 1987–1991 adopted', *News from France* from the French Embassy Press and Information Service, Washington, DC vol. 86.22 (24 Nov. 1986), p. 2.

[137] de Galard, J., 'L'Assemblée nationale a adopté le budget 1987 de la Défense', *Air et cosmos*, 22 Nov. 1986, p. 7; and 'Military program bill for 1987–1991 adopted', *News from France*, French Embassy Press and Information Service, Washington, DC, vol. 86.22 (24 Nov. 1986), p. 2.

[138] 'Military program bill for 1987–1991 adopted' (note 137).

[139] Speech to the French National Assembly by Defence Minister Giraud on 12 November, reprinted in *Journal Officiel*, 12 Nov. 1986.

[140] See 'Chinese flight test new missile version', *Aviation Week & Space Technology*, 30 June 1986, p. 16; 'Missile range increases', *Jane's Defence Weekly*, 15 Feb. 1986, p. 233; and *Asian Security 1986* (Research Institute for Peace and Security: Tokyo, 1986), p. 84.

[141] See *China Daily*, 28 Jan. 1986, translated in Institute for Defense and Strategic Analysis (IDSA) *News Review on China, Mongolia, the Koreas*, Feb. 1986, p. 77; 'Chinese flight test new missile version', *Aviation Week & Space Technology*, 30 June 1986, p. 16.

[142] Quotation from *People's Daily*, 25 Jan. 1986, reported in British Broadcasting Corporation (BBC), *Summary of World Broadcasts*, Part 3, 28 Jan. 1986, cited in Institute for Defense and Strategic Analysis (IDSA), *News Review on China, Mongolia, the Koreas*, Feb. 1986, p. 77.

[143] The photograph appeared in the Chinese and the English versions of *Xinhua* on 31 December.

[144] For background on China's SSBN programme, see Fieldhouse, R. W., 'Chinese nuclear weapons: an overview', in SIPRI, *World Armaments and Disarmament: SIPRI Yearbook 1986* (Oxford University Press: Oxford, 1986), pp. 97–113.

[145] See, for example, Ebata, K., 'Chinese SSNs "now in operation"', *Jane's Defence Weekly*, 13 Oct. 1984, p. 603.

[146] Li Yuezhu and Xiong Zhengyan, 'Antichemical warfare corps embody modernization', *Xinhua*, 1 Aug. 1986, translated in US Department of Defense, *Current News*, Foreign Media Edition, 12 Sep. 1986, p. 53.

[147] Li Yeuzhu and Xiong Zhengyan (note 146).

[148] See Ku Mainan, 'Deng Jiaxian: China's father of A-bomb', *Beijing Review*, vol. 29, no. 32 (11 Aug. 1986), pp. 20–2; *Outlook Weekly*, 26 June 1986 (in Chinese).

[149] Ku Mainan (note 148), p. 21; Davies, H., 'Russia "broke A-bomb promise to Chinese"', *Daily Telegraph*, 23 June 1986.

[150] Correspondence with the Chinese Military Attaché, Embassy of the People's Republic of China, Stockholm, Sweden, Jan. 1987.

2. Nuclear explosions

RICHARD W. FIELDHOUSE and ROBERT S. NORRIS;
appendix prepared by RAGNHILD FERM

Superscript numbers refer to the list of notes and references at the end of the chapter.

I. Nuclear explosions and the test debate

Nuclear weapon testing issues have been thrust once more to the front of the arms control and nuclear weapon debates in recent years. This is due to the widespread international interest in a comprehensive test ban (CTB) and to the current differences between the USA and the USSR on nuclear weapon testing. Since the USSR began its moratorium on nuclear tests in August 1985, the USA has come under increasing pressure, both domestic and international, to stop testing or, at a minimum, to resume negotiations with the Soviet Union on a CTB. Unfortunately, the large amount of attention paid to nuclear testing has not brought with it an equal amount of reliable factual information on which to debate the issues. Numerous questions are currently disputed, such as: Are nuclear explosions necessary to maintain existing stockpiles, to develop new nuclear weapon designs, or not at all? Is it possible, as posited by previous US Administrations, to maintain nuclear weapons under a CTB regime? Is it possible to verify compliance with a CTB?

   Although both the USA and the USSR have made scores of official public statements about nuclear testing and test limitations, neither government has done much to clarify these issues. On the contrary, both governments have presented information in such a way as to confuse the issues. Nor have the other three nuclear testing nations contributed to clarity: the UK sides with the USA; France is opposed to any test limitations and China has generally remained aloof from the debate. This leaves the public as confused today as it was before nuclear testing issues regained their current prominence.

   Each year since 1969, the *SIPRI Yearbook* has provided fundamental information about nuclear explosions: which nations have detonated which number of nuclear explosions, where and when they have taken place and, whenever possible, an estimate of the size, or yield, of the explosions. Most explosions are tests of nuclear weapons; the USSR has conducted some explosions for non-military purposes, the so-called peaceful nuclear explosions (PNEs), as recently as 1985. Although it is possible to detect all underground nuclear explosions above a certain yield, it is almost impossible to learn more than a few basic facts about each test: the time, place and relative magnitude of each event. The nuclear weapon states conduct their nuclear weapon activities with utmost secrecy to prevent others from learning details of their nuclear warheads and weapon systems. These are among the most closely guarded military secrets in the world. Consequently one does not know the exact yield of an explosion, for what purpose it was conducted, or what relation it has, if any, to weapons in a nation's stockpile or in development. Thus, while the public has a good record of the number of nuclear explosions, it has almost no knowledge of the most important details: What is the significance of the tests and can they be stopped? By improving and studying the available information on nuclear tests a clear understanding could be gained and used to move forward on the task of limiting and ceasing nuclear explosions.

This chapter discusses the most important sources of information on nuclear explosions, and explains the problems and limitations of such information and, therefore, the need to revise the data as new information becomes available. It concludes with a review of the nuclear explosions and related issues of 1986.

II. Information on nuclear explosions

The five nuclear weapon states (the USA, the USSR, France, the UK and China) are currently capable of conducting explosions for nuclear weapon tests. The USA, the USSR and the UK are signatories of the Partial Test Ban Treaty (PTBT) of 1963, prohibiting nuclear explosions in environments other than underground. Although France and China have not signed the PTBT, both nations have announced that they intend not to test nuclear weapons in the atmosphere. The Chinese announcement that they 'will no longer conduct atmospheric tests in the future' was made by Premier Zhao Ziyang on 21 March 1986. Thus it is possible that the Chinese atmospheric nuclear test conducted in 1980 was the last of its kind by any nation.

The simplest way to obtain information about nuclear tests would be for the five nuclear weapon states to announce their own tests, as recommended by a 1986 UN General Assembly resolution.[1] However, each of these five nations has its own different policy regarding information about its nuclear testing programme; all of them employ secrecy to a greater or lesser extent. Although the USA is the most open with information about its tests, it has not publicly announced every US test and has adopted an explicit policy not to announce some of its lower-yield tests.[2] It has now made public all tests conducted before the signing of the PTBT in 1963, although at the time many were not announced. According to the US Department of Energy, 'Some tests conducted underground since the signing of the treaty [PTBT] and designed to be contained completely have not been announced. Information concerning these events is classified'.[3]

The USSR generally has not made public any information about its nuclear tests, except for some peaceful nuclear explosions and some of its early atmospheric tests. In 1986, the USSR publicly stated for the first time the number of nuclear explosions it conducted during the year—nine—in a comparison of the US and Soviet testing programmes.[4] In another unusual move, the USSR has reported on the number of US tests during the Soviet moratorium period. On 19 December, *Pravda* reported that the USA had conducted 24 tests, 4 of which the USA had not announced.

Since 1962, the UK has conducted all its nuclear tests jointly with the USA at the US Nevada Test Site (NTS) and all have apparently been reported afterwards by the UK and the USA. France has occasionally discussed its tests, but has not done so regularly. The current French policy is not to announce any tests; French tests are usually reported afterwards by seismologists in New Zealand. China publicly discussed only a few of its atmospheric nuclear tests between 1964 and 1980, especially those successful tests that represented development milestones in the Chinese nuclear weapon programme. The Chinese Government has the policy of neither confirming nor denying its nuclear explosions. In 1986 several official Chinese publications stated that China had conducted 32 nuclear tests since 1964, 3 more than available data suggest.[5] It seems likely that this figure is quoted from foreign sources.

On those occasions when a government has provided public information about a test, the information has been limited, usually to only the date of the explosion, its general location and (less frequently) the general explosive yield or yield range. The current US yield range estimates are rarely useful: either less than 20 kt or 20–150 kt. The USA also usually provides the names and the general purpose of its announced tests, that is, to test weapon effects, designs, safety, reliability, and so on. No government provides details about the specific purposes of its tests, or their exact size; these matters are considered by all countries to be military secrets. Thus, information provided by the testing nations about their tests leaves the picture incomplete. A most revealing fact about the difficulty of obtaining reliable information is that the total number of nuclear tests by the five countries is still not known.

Sources of information

When a nuclear explosive is detonated it releases energy in forms that can often be detected from long distances. Nuclear explosions that take place underground cause seismic shocks much like small earthquakes. It is essentially the same phenomenon of ground motion for both events, but with measurably different characteristics. Since the five nuclear weapon states now conduct their nuclear explosions underground, seismic recording devices can measure the ground shocks and thus detect nuclear explosions and earthquakes alike at intercontinental distances. Seismic detection is the chief means by which underground nuclear explosions can be detected and identified. Numerous government- or university-affiliated seismic observatories gather and share data on seismic shocks from nuclear tests. From these data it is possible to assemble a fair picture of the nuclear testing activities of all five nuclear weapon nations. Some governments operate seismic detection networks for intelligence purposes; their information is not usually made public.

A number of seismic observatories offer their information for public and scientific use, to contribute to better knowledge of nuclear testing. Most prominent among these institutions is the Hagfors Observatory of the Swedish National Defence Research Institute, known by its Swedish initials as FOA. FOA produces the most regular and complete lists available from any government of known and presumed nuclear explosions world-wide. FOA uses data from its own seismic network and those from other observatories, comparing data and updating its lists. Numerous other institutions, such as those in New Zealand and Norway and the Australian Seismological Centre which opened in September 1986, are co-operating in efforts to establish a world-wide seismic monitoring system. Most of the seismic data exchanged by such institutions are incomprehensible to the nonspecialist, although several institutions translate these data into understandable lists of nuclear explosions or seismic events.

Among the other primary sources of information are the US Department of Energy (DOE), the US Defense Nuclear Agency (DNA) and the US Geological Survey (USGS). DOE, and its predecessor agencies (the Atomic Energy Commission and the Energy Research and Development Administration), have been the largest single source of information on nuclear tests. DOE is the US agency responsible for the US nuclear weapon test programme and, along with other agencies, for intelligence about other nations' nuclear weapon and test programmes. DOE obtains information on non-US nuclear explosions through the Atomic Energy Detection System (AEDS), a network of sensors operated by the Air Force Technical Applications Center (AFTAC) across and above the earth.[6] Through DOE, the USA has produced information about most US nuclear tests and a large portion of non-US nuclear explosions.[7] DNA is the US Department of Defense agency responsible for research on nuclear weapon effects. It recently published 42 volumes on US nuclear tests from the 1940s to the 1960s for its Nuclear Test Personnel Review programme.[8] The USGS is part of the US Department of the Interior and is concerned with, among other things, recording seismic activity for an understanding of earthquake behaviour. The USGS publishes a monthly report called 'Preliminary Determination of Epicenters' which lists records of world-wide seismic activity. Using this information it is possible to study potential nuclear explosions.

As a result of these and other sources, scientific evidence is available to provide additional information about nuclear tests. However, this seismic information is still not enough to provide a complete picture of nuclear testing; the current system cannot fill some of the gaps.

Problems with information

Even today's world-wide seismic detection capabilities can only provide a limited amount of information about nuclear explosions: the location, time and usually the approximate size of the event. It is not possible to know the precise yield of nuclear explosions (estimates are made), and seismic means cannot distinguish between a large chemical explosion and a very small nuclear one. Thus some nuclear tests may escape detection or may be too ambiguous to be classified as nuclear explosions. Several recent examples are illustrative.

On 11 July 1985, weak seismic signals were recorded coming from the area of the Soviet nuclear weapon test site at Semipalatinsk. The USA reported that the signals were proof of a very low yield (sub-kiloton) Soviet nuclear explosion that was only detectable by a new seismic array located near enough to the test site to receive high-frequency seismic signals. High-frequency signals are best able to discriminate between earthquakes and man-made explosions, but can only be accurately recorded at regional distances—up to 3000 km, depending on the geological conditions. The USA had information from such a system, the Norwegian Regional Seismic Array System (NORESS), that is operated by Norway in co-operation with the USA as part of a joint US–Norwegian seismic detection system.[9] The Hagfors Observatory did not detect or report the signals as having come from a nuclear explosion, reportedly because of problems with their computer equipment.[10] Consequently, there were differences in the estimates of Soviet nuclear explosions for 1985. Breaking with past practice, the USSR reported on 2 April 1986 that it had conducted nine nuclear explosions in 1985, thus confirming that more explosions had occurred than were agreed within the seismological community. The standard seismic networks had not properly identified the explosion.

In addition to questions about the exact number of tests there is also uncertainty as to their size. It is difficult, if not impossible, to know the exact yield of a nuclear explosion because of the problems involved in measuring precisely the energy released. Governments have a variety of methods for measuring and estimating their own nuclear tests; the problem is compounded when estimating the yields of foreign nuclear explosions. For example, the US Government, even with its sophisticated technology, is unsure of the exact size of Soviet nuclear explosions. This is because of uncertainties about the geologic formation of the primary Soviet nuclear weapon test site. If this were known in better detail more accurate estimates of the size of Soviet nuclear weapon tests could be made. The USA used a yield-estimating formula for many years that many experts said inflated the true yield. That formula was changed in 1986 (see below).

III. Nuclear explosions and test-related issues in 1986

According to available information, there were 23 nuclear test explosions in 1986. This is the lowest number of nuclear tests since 1960. The USSR did not conduct any tests during the year, as General Secretary Gorbachev extended the Soviet test moratorium four times, until 1 January 1987. The United States conducted 14 tests, France 8 and the United Kingdom 1 jointly with the USA. China did not conduct any nuclear tests during 1986.

During 1986, the issues surrounding nuclear testing remained prominent and contentious. The two superpowers mostly talked past one another as they pursued and presented their agendas. The USA focused its proposals on enhanced verification measures to the unratified 1974 Threshold Test Ban Treaty (TTBT) and the unratified 1976 Peaceful Nuclear Explosions Treaty (PNET) and showed no interest in a CTB. The Soviet Union initially rejected US proposals linked to the TTBT, but then agreed at the Reykjavik summit meeting to discuss all testing issues with the USA.

As part of a set of broad proposals to eliminate nuclear weapons by the year 2000, General Secretary Gorbachev extended the Soviet unilateral test moratorium on 15 January 1986 until the end of March. On 26 February the US House of Representatives passed a non-binding resolution by a vote of 268 to

148 calling on President Reagan to submit the TTBT and the PNET to the Senate for ratification.

On 13 March, Gorbachev announced, in a response to the leaders of the Six-Nation Peace Initiative (Argentina, Greece, India, Mexico, Sweden and Tanzania), that the Soviet moratorium would continue past 31 March for as long as the USA refrained from testing. On the following day President Reagan repeated a previous proposal to begin bilateral negotiations with the USSR to improve verification of the TTBT and the PNET. He also renewed his offer to have Soviet scientists observe and measure a US test at the Nevada Test Site in late April.

The USA conducted its first nuclear test of 1986 on 22 March, bringing an immediate protest from the USSR. Attention then focused on the next US test after 31 March, since it was expected to trigger the end of the Soviet moratorium. After being postponed twice, the test (code-named Mighty Oak) was finally conducted on 10 April. The initial Soviet response declared on 11 April 'that from now on it [the USSR] is free from the unilateral commitment made by it to refrain from conducting any nuclear explosions'.[11] But in a television speech on 14 May concerning the Chernobyl nuclear reactor accident of 26 April, Gorbachev extended the test moratorium a third time, to 6 August. In a television address on 18 August, Gorbachev extended the moratorium a fourth time, until 1 January 1987, emphasizing that an agreement ending nuclear tests could be signed at a US–Soviet summit meeting, and thus be the prologue to further progress in other arms control areas. On 18 December, the Soviet news agency TASS reported that the Soviet Union would abandon its moratorium after the first US test of 1987, reportedly scheduled for 29 January.

During the year the United States and the Soviet Union held three meetings of experts in Geneva to discuss the full range of US–Soviet testing issues, including verification measures and a CTB. The first session was held from 25 July to 1 August. A second session was held from 4 to 18 September and the third from 2 to 25 November. Because of the wide differences between the two countries on nuclear testing little progress was made.

In a surprising development, on 8 August the US House of Representatives passed by a 234–155 vote a binding amendment to the DOD Authorization Bill which would impose a one-year moratorium on all US nuclear tests larger than 1 kt beginning on 1 January 1987, contingent upon Soviet agreement to on-site inspection.[12] The day before, the US Senate had passed a non-binding resolution by a 64–35 vote calling for a resumption of CTB negotiations.[13] In a letter to Senator Goldwater on 10 October, the President pledged to ask for Senate ratification of the TTBT and the PNET if the Soviet Union would agree to 'essential' verification procedures before ratification proceedings begin. However, even if the Soviet Union fails to agree to such procedures, the President pledged still to make ratification a first order of business with the new Senate, but with the proviso that the treaties would not take effect until they are 'effectively verifiable'.[14]

As a result of congressional and public pressure to make progress towards test limitations, the Reagan Administration responded with numerous arguments for the need to continue testing.[15] The arguments often contradicted long-held assessments of the impact of a CTB. For example, for years a basic assumption about a CTB had been that it would help prevent or slow down the horizontal proliferation of nuclear weapons. The Administration argues the opposite, stating that if doubts were raised about US nuclear guarantees to its allies under a CTB, it would encourage the proliferation of nuclear weapons. According to Administration officials, another adverse effect of a CTB would be an increase in the number of warheads and the megatonnage in the US stockpile. This would occur, they argue, to compensate for the uncertainties surrounding their reliability. Such arguments were not subject to proper public debate because the US Government limited itself to making the assertions but not substantiating them, on the grounds that such details are classified.

On 21 January 1986, William J. Casey, then Director of Central Intelligence, formally approved changes in the procedures used to estimate the yields of large Soviet tests.[16] For several years an intense debate has occurred among seismologists and government intelligence officials over whether the most accurate formula was being used to calculate the yields of Soviet tests. Because of insufficient knowlede of the geologic composition of the Soviet test sites, various assumptions have been made which have led to different conclusions about the size of the tests. The calculation formula includes an 'adjustment factor' to account for the geology near Soviet test sites. This factor has been disputed for years and was increased to reflect revised assumptions about the geology in question. The change may reduce earlier yield estimates by some 20 per cent.[17] The issue is important because the Reagan Administration has frequently alleged that the Soviet Union has violated the TTBT by conducting tests above the 150-kt yield limit set by the TTBT.

In early July US seismologists began to install three seismic monitoring stations near the main Soviet test site south-west of Semipalatinsk. This came about as a result of an agreement between the private US Natural Resources Defense Council and the Soviet Academy of Sciences, signed on 28 May.[18] The seismic equipment began operating on 10 July and continuously provided information on seismic activity in the area throughout the rest of the year. (This information should be of great interest whether or not the USSR conducts any nuclear explosions, because so little is known outside the Soviet Union about the geology around the test site.) Such seismic information may improve US understanding of the geology to the extent that it can resolve the US allegation that the USSR has violated the 150-kt yield limit of the TTBT.

Notes and references

[1] United Nations, General Assembly, Resolution 41/59N, 'Notification of nuclear tests'.

[2] Cochran, T. B., Norris, R. S., Arkin, W. M. and Hoenig, M. M., 'Unannounced US nuclear weapons tests: 1980–1984', *Nuclear Weapons Databook*, Working Paper 86-1 (Natural Resources Defense Council: Washington, DC, Jan. 1986), p. 1.

[3] US Department of Energy, *Announced United States Nuclear Tests, July 1945 through December 1984*, Report Number NVO-209 (Rev. 5), (DOE Nevada Operations Office: Las Vegas, NV, 1985), p. i.

[4] 'The USA is seeking nuclear superiority', TASS, 2 Apr. 1986, English transcript dated 4 Apr.

[5] Previously, 29 tests had been identified with specific dates (see *SIPRI Yearbook 1986*, p. 102) and a 30th test was reported to have taken place. See Ku, M., 'Deng Jiaxiang: China's father of A-Bomb', *Beijing Review*, vol. 29, no. 32 (11 Aug. 1986), p. 22.

[6] For a description of the AEDS and the intelligence network that supports it, see Richelson, J. R., *The US Intelligence Community* (Ballinger: Cambridge, MA, 1985), pp. 56–8, 156–62.

[7] See US Department of Energy, *Announced United States Nuclear Tests, July 1945 through December 1985*, Report Number NVO-209 (Rev. 6), (DOE Nevada Operations Office: Las Vegas, NV, 1986); and 'Foreign nuclear detonations through December 31 1984', computer printout from DOE Nevada Operations Office dated 22 May 1985. The DOE Nevada Operations Office stated in a letter of November 1985 that 'this office no longer maintains lists or records in any form of foreign nuclear detonations'.

[8] For a list of these reports, see Norris, R. S., Cochran, T. B. and Arkin, W. M., 'Known US nuclear tests July 1945 to 16 October 1986', *Nuclear Weapons Databook*, Working Paper 86-2 (Rev. 1) (Natural Resources Defense Council: Washington, DC, Oct. 1986), p. 49.

[9] See SIPRI, *World Armaments and Disarmament: SIPRI Yearbook 1986* (Oxford University Press: Oxford, 1986), p. 123; 'NORSAR: Norwegian Seismic Array', undated brochure; 'Norwegian Regional Seismic Array System: NORESS', brochure dated 5 June 1985 from NORSAR.

[10] Swedish Foreign Affairs Minister Sten Andersson reported that the Hagfors Observatory 'observed an explosion on that day but the information necessary for registering and analysing it was not available on account of the computer breakdown. We can almost certainly say that we would have reported the test if the computer had functioned'. Swedish Ministry for Foreign Affairs, Interpellation No. 1985/86:167, Press Release, 20 May 1986.

[11] Soviet Embassy, Washington, DC, Press Release, 14 Apr. 1986, Soviet Government Statement.

[12] US Congress, *Congressional Record*, 8 Aug. 1986, pp. H5738–56.

[13] US Congress, *Congressional Record*, 7 Aug. 1986, pp. S10714–36.

[14] US Congress, *National Defense Authorization Act for Fiscal Year 1987*, Conference Report, House Report 99–1001, pp. 516–17.

[15] See, for example, Senate Foreign Relations Committee hearings of 8 May, 19 and 26 June 1986, and Senate Armed Services Committee hearings of 29–30 Apr. 1986; Wagner, R., letter to the *Washington Post*, 22 Mar. 1986, p. A26; and US Department of State, 'US policy regarding limitations on nuclear testing', *Special Report No. 150* (State Department: Washington, DC, Aug. 1986).

[16] Gordon, M. R., 'CIA changes way that it measures Soviet atom tests', *New York Times*, 2 Apr. 1986, p. A1.

[17] 'CIA lowers estimates of Soviet test yields', *Arms Control Today*, Apr. 1986, p. 21.

[18] Broad, W. J., 'US group checks Soviet atom site', *New York Times*, 14 July 1986, p. A1; and 'Monitoring nuke tests', *Newsweek*, 28 July 1986, p. 33.

Appendix 2A. Nuclear explosions, 1945–86

Table 2A.1 Nuclear explosions in 1986 (preliminary data)

Date[a]	Latitude (deg)	Longitude (deg)	Region	Body wave magnitude[b]
USA				
22 Mar.	37.083 N	116.066 W	Nevada	5.7
10 Apr.	37.218 N	116.183 W	Nevada	5.3
20 Apr.	37. N	116. W	Nevada	
22 Apr.	37.264 N	116.440 W	Nevada	5.4
21 May	37.125 N	116.060 W	Nevada	
5 June	37.098 N	116.016 W	Nevada	5.5
17 July	37.279 N	116.356 W	Nevada	
24 July	37.143 N	116.071 W	Nevada	
4 Sep.	37. N	116. W	Nevada	
11 Sep.	37.069 N	116.050 W	Nevada	
30 Sep.	37.300 N	116.307 W	Nevada	
16 Oct.	37.220 N	116.462 W	Nevada	5.6
14 Nov.	37.100 N	116.048 W	Nevada	5.8
13 Dec.	37.263 N	116.412 W	Nevada	5.7
UK				
25 June	37.265 N	116.499 W	Nevada	5.5
France				
26 Apr.	22.15 S	139.12 W	Mururoa	4.8
6 May	22. S	139. W	Mururoa	4.8
27 May	22. S	139. W	Mururoa	4.7
30 May	21.898 S	139.026 W	Mururoa	5.4
10 Nov.	22. S	139. W	Mururoa	4.9
12 Nov.	21.860 S	139.080 W	Mururoa	5.3
6 Dec.	22. S	139. W	Mururoa	5.0
10 Dec.	21.899 S	138.934 W	Mururoa	5.5

[a] The dates are all according to Greenwich Mean Time.

[b] Body wave magnitude (m_b) indicates the size of the event. m_b data for the US and British tests were provided by the Hagfors Observatory of the Swedish National Defence Research Institute (FOA); data for the French tests were provided by the New Zealand Seismological Observatory.

Table 2A.2. Estimated number of nuclear explosions 16 July 1945–5 August 1963 (the signing of the Partial Test Ban Treaty)

a = atmospheric
u = underground

Year	USA a	USA u	USSR a	USSR u	UK a	UK u	France a	France u	Total
1945	3	0							**3**
1946	2[a]	0							**2**
1947	0	0							**0**
1948	3	0							**3**
1949	0	0	1	0					**1**
1950	0	0	0	0					**0**
1951	15	1	2	0					**18**
1952	10	0	0	0	1	0			**11**
1953	11	0	4	0	2	0			**17**
1954	6	0	7	0	0	0			**13**
1955	17[a]	1	5[a]	0	0	0			**23**
1956	18	0	9	0	6	0			**33**
1957	27	5	15[a]	0	7	0			**54**
1958	62[b]	15	29	0	5	0			**111**
1949–58, exact years unknown			18						**18**
1959	0	0	0	0	0	0			**0**
1960	0	0	0	0	0	0	3	0	**3**
1961	0	10	50[a]	1	0	0	1	1	**63**
1962	38[a]	58	43	1	0	2	0	1	**143**
1 Jan.– 5 Aug. 1963	4	25	0	0	0	0	0	2	**31**
Total	**216**	**115**	**183[c]**	**2**	**21**	**2**	**4**	**4**	**547**

[a] At least one of these tests was carried out under water.

[b] Two of these tests were carried out under water.

[c] The total figure for Soviet atmospheric tests includes the 18 additional tests conducted in the period 1949–58, for which exact years are not available.

Table 2A.3. Estimated number of nuclear explosions 6 August 1963–31 December 1986

a = atmospheric
u = underground

Year	USA[a]		USSR		UK[a]		France		China		India		Total
	a	u	a	u	a	u	a	u	a	u	a	u	
6 Aug.–31 Dec. 1963	0	14	0	0	0	0	0	1					15
1964	0	29	0	6	0	1	0	3	1	0			40
1965	0	29	0	9	0	1	0	4	1	0			44
1966	0	40	0	15	0	0	5	1	3	0			64
1967	0	29	0	17	0	0	3	0	2	0			51
1968	0	39[b]	0	13	0	0	5	0	1	0			58
1969	0	29	0	16	0	0	0	0	1	1			47
1970	0	33	0	17	0	0	8	0	1	0			59
1971	0	15	0	19	0	0	5	0	1	0			40
1972	0	15	0	22	0	0	3	0	2	0			42
1973	0	12[c]	0	14	0	0	5	0	1	0			32
1974	0	12	0	19	0	1	7	0	1	0	0	1	41
1975	0	17	0	15	0	0	0	2	0	1	0	0	35
1976	0	15	0	17	0	1	0	1	3	1	0	0	38
1977	0	12	0	18	0	0	0	6	1	0	0	0	37
1978	0	16	0	28	0	2	0	7	2	1	0	0	56
1979	0	15	0	29	0	1	0	9	0	0	0	0	54
1980	0	14	0	21	0	3	0	11	1	0	0	0	50
1981	0	16	0	22	0	1	0	10	0	0	0	0	49
1982	0	18	0	31	0	1	0	5	0	0	0	0	55
1983	0	17	0	27	0	1	0	7	0	1	0	0	53
1984	0	17	0	28	0	2	0	8	0	2	0	0	57
1985	0	17	0	9	0	1	0	8	0	0	0	0	35
1986	0	14	0	0	0	1	0	8	0	0			23[d]
Total	**0**	**484**	**0**	**412**	**0**	**17**	**41**	**91**	**22**	**7**	**0**	**1**	**1075**

[a] See note a below.
[b] Five devices used simultaneously in the same test are counted here as one explosion.
[c] Three devices used simultaneously in the same test are counted here as one explosion.
[d] The data for 1986 are preliminary.

Table 2A.4. Estimated number of nuclear explosions 16 July 1945–31 December 1986

USA[a]	USSR	UK[a]	France	China	India	Total
815	597	40	140	29	1	**1622**

[a] All British tests from 1962 have been conducted jointly with the United States at the Nevada Test Site. Therefore, the number of US tests is actually higher than indicated here.

Sources for tables 2A.1–2A.4

Swedish National Defence Research Institute (FOA), various estimates; Norris, R. S., Cochran, T. B. and Arkin, W. M., 'Known US nuclear tests July 1945 to 16 October 1986', *Nuclear Weapons Databook*, Working Paper no. 86–2 (Rev. 1) (Natural Resources Defense Council: Washington, DC, Oct. 1986); Sands, J. I., Norris, R. S. and Cochran, T. B., 'Known Soviet nuclear explosions, 1949–1985', *Nuclear Weapons Databook*, Working Paper no. 86–3 (Rev. 2 June 1986) (Natural Resources Defense Council: Washington, DC, Feb. 1986); Department of Scientific and Industrial Research (DSIR), Geophysics Division, New Zealand, various estimates; and US Geological Survey.

3. Military use of outer space

BHUPENDRA JASANI

Superscript numbers refer to the list of notes and references at the end of the chapter.

I. Introduction

The summit meeting in Reykjavik in October 1986 between President Reagan and General Secretary Gorbachev again signalled the importance of military activities in outer space—the current military use of satellites, and the future development, testing and deployment of space weapons.

The past year showed that space activities are also subject to serious failures. Although 100 military-oriented artificial earth satellites were launched during the year by the USA, the USSR and China, satellite launch failures and accidents involving orbiting satellites have had considerable consequences for the satellite programmes of several countries and during the year raised new concerns about future satellite activities. Programmes have been cut back or delayed, and safety aspects of peaceful activities in outer space have been raised.

One important new development was the French civilian earth resources observation satellite, SPOT, which will offer new and improved photographic images of activities on earth to civilian and military interests alike.

The Soviet Union refrained from testing anti-satellite (ASAT) systems against a satellite. However, the USSR is reported by Western sources to be pursuing a number of laser programmes for ASAT purposes, although this has been denied by Soviet sources. Under a scaled-down programme, the USA conducted two ASAT tests aimed at stars, which did not violate the ASAT test ban imposed by the Congress.

In strategic defence efforts, the United States continued its Strategic Defense Initiative (SDI) tests in space and its work on ground-based directed-energy weapons. The USA reported that the USSR is also engaged in a large strategic defence research and development programme, but the Soviet Union has contributed no information on its activities to the public debate.

Section II describes the military satellite programmes of 1986, followed by discussions of the satellite launch failures and their impact on space programmes, and the incidents of satellite collisions in outer space. The anti-satellite and the strategic defence activities of the United States and the Soviet Union are dealt with in sections V and VI.

II. Military uses of satellites

Photographic reconnaissance satellites

An average of about 100 spacecraft have been launched per year since about 1967, and about one-third of them have been photoreconnaissance satellites

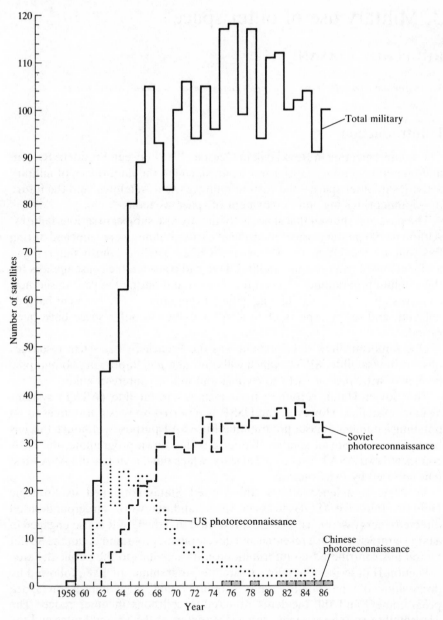

Figure 3.1. Total military satellites and photographic reconnaissance satellites launched 1958–86

(see figure 3.1).[1] Only the USSR and China launched this type of satellite in 1986, but the USA still had one previously launched photoreconnaissance satellite in orbit at the end of the year.

It is of interest to note that the Soviet Union launches more satellites for photoreconnaissance purposes than does the United States, owing to the fact that the lifetime of Soviet satellites has been much shorter—usually about 14 days, compared to three years for US satellites. Since 1982 the lifetime of Soviet photoreconnaissance satellites has greatly increased: first from 14 to 50 days, and then to 205 days for a satellite launched in 1985, and to 238 days for the Cosmos 1731 satellite launched in 1986 (see figure 3.2).

The USA launched its current KH-11 photoreconnaissance satellite in 1984 and was to have launched the follow-on, new-generation KH-12 satellite on a space shuttle in 1986. After the shuttle accident early in the year, this launch was postponed until about 1988, when it is planned to deploy a constellation of three KH-12 satellites for complete coverage. (An attempt to launch a US photoreconnaissance satellite was made in April 1986, but a failure in the rocket booster destroyed the satellite and the launcher.)

In October 1986 China successfully recovered its eighth photographic satellite. It is reported that the spacecraft, which was launched with the Long March 2 rocket, performed a resource survey mission.[2] This was China's 19th successful satellite since 1970, and it may have been on a photographic reconnaissance mission.

France, the fourth nation to carry out a photoreconnaissance satellite programme, in February 1986 decided to develop the Helios military reconnaissance satellite. A similar programme, for the SAMRO satellite (Satellite Militaire de Reconnaissance Optique),[3] was suspended in 1982. The Helios programme is expected to cost $550–700 million and includes four satellites, ground receiving stations and quick image-processing facilities.[4] The first satellite is planned to be orbited in 1992 in an 800- to 900-km sun-synchronous orbit; tests of the Helios sensors have already been conducted. Compared to the resolution obtained from the much publicized French civilian satellite, SPOT 1, that obtained from Helios military satellites is expected to be much better: SPOT 1 images have 10-m resolution and the new-generation SPOT 4 and 5 satellite images will have 2.5-m resolution, while those obtained from Helios will have 1-m resolution.

In 1986 it was reported that the French military obtains and processes images from the SPOT 1 satellite. In addition, the French space agency CNES (Centre National d'Etudes Spatiales) recently proposed merging the production programmes for the Helios and SPOT 4 and 5 satellites.[5]

France is consulting with Italy about possible Italian participation in the Helios programme; consultations with the Federal Republic of Germany have so far not resulted in any collaboration. (France is also preparing to negotiate with FR Germany for co-operation in developing radar reconnaissance satellites.[6])

Other military missions

The United States launched a total of only 5 satellites with military missions in 1986 (see appendix 3A), compared with 11 in 1985. In September an Atlas E launcher successfully orbited the NOAA 10 weather satellite.[7] It replaced the NOAA 6 which had been reactivated when NOAA 8 failed in 1985. The NOAA 10 weather satellite also carries the new search and rescue satellite

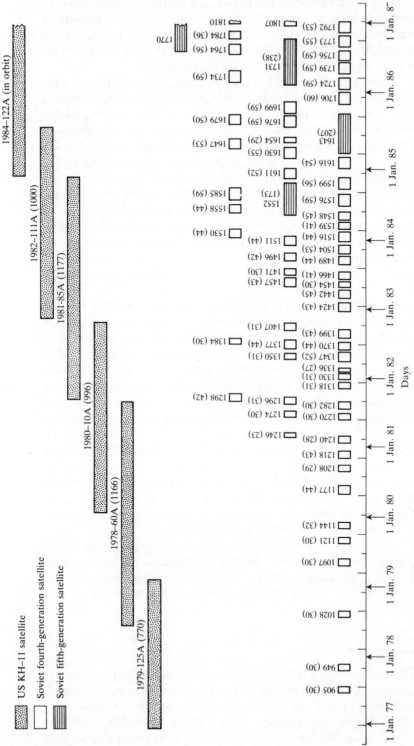

Figure 3.2. Lifetimes of the US KH-11 and the Soviet fourth- and fifth-generation photographic reconnaissance satellites, 1977–86.

The USA has had very long-lived satellites in orbit during the entire period. The USSR began to increase the lifetime of its satellites in 1977: in 1982 they orbited for over 50 days, in 1984 over 100 days and in 1985 over 200 days. Each block represents the lifetime of the satellite (given in days, in brackets). The identification numbers for Soviet satellites represent the Cosmos serial number. In 1986 the USA had only one photographic reconnaissance satellite in orbit.

(SARSAT) equipment which can, for example, detect emergency radio beacons from aircraft and ships in distress.

In November a $13 million US scientific satellite was launched from Vandenberg Air Force Base, using a Scout launcher.[8] This Polar Beacon Experiment and Auroral Research satellite (known as Polar Bear) was designed to facilitate interference-free functioning of both communications and weather satellites. Such interference is usually caused by the aurora borealis, which distorts radio signals sent to and from satellites in polar orbits, especially those on military missions. Auroral interference is also similar to interference that an atmospheric nuclear explosion would cause; the military studies auroral interference to improve the ability of satellites to communicate during a nuclear war. The Polar Bear satellite is able to determine the frequencies that can be used to avoid auroral interference.

In December the sixth US Navy FltSatCom (Fleet Satellite Communications) satellite was launched into a geosynchronous orbit by an Atlas Centaur launcher.[9] The satellite carries an extremely high-frequency (EHF) experimental communications package to test the electronics equipment on board and the ground facilities for the Military Strategic and Tactical Relay System (Milstar) satellite system, the next generation of satellites specialized for military communications.

The use of EHF systems has several advantages: for example, EHF radio waves have a large data-carrying capacity; antennas for such a system could be made smaller; it is easier to protect EHF links against deliberate interference; and EHF radio waves suffer fewer distortions (from auroral activities or an atmospheric nuclear explosion) in passing through the ionosphere.

The FltSatCom satellite, designated number 7 even though number 6 had not been launched by then, was launched on 4 December 1986. FltSatCom 6 and FltSatCom 8 will probably both have been launched by May 1987, and the three satellites will be placed in parking orbits to replace other satellites as required. Although these satellites are designed for lifetimes of five years, the four which are presently in orbit have already been in orbit for longer than five years.[10] Four FltSatCom satellites are required to obtain the desired coverage of regions located 70° north and 70° south of the equator.

The USA did not launch any navigation satellites in 1986. The last Navstar GPS (Global Positioning System) satellite was launched in October 1985 as the 11th in a network of 18 satellites. The GPS system is designed to provide extremely accurate data in three dimensions on the position of US military forces world-wide. Less accurate information will be available for commercial users, although it has been reported that improved data, from 25 m to 10 m, will become commercially available.[11]

France did not launch any military-oriented satellites in 1986. Its satellite programme has been affected by a number of past launch failures. In its Telecom communications satellite series, the next satellite to be launched is planned to carry military transponders for communications re-relay. France is also planning to launch a dedicated military communications satellite called the SYRACUSE (Système Radio Communications Utilisant Satellite).[12]

III. Satellite launch failures

The first accident in 1986 involving a US spacecraft occurred in January, and it was the most tragic since it caused the death of seven astronauts, including a private citizen. The space shuttle exploded soon after launch. It would have been the 25th shuttle flight.

In April 1986 the USA attempted to launch a Titan 34D rocket carrying a photoreconnaissance satellite.[13] According to reports, the problem occurred in the second of the two solid-fuel boosters. Before the first stage of the liquid-fuel core vehicle was ignited, the solid-fuel booster ruptured, causing an explosion only 8.5 seconds after take-off. A number of explanations have been advanced. Unlike in the shuttle accident, the seals between the booster joints were not suspected of being faulty. It is believed that there was a weak bond between the insulation material and the inside of a steel case on one of the motor segments; this may have eroded the case and ruptured the sidewall. Two launch pads were damaged, but they were repaired by the end of the year, and it is expected that a Titan 34D will be ready for launch in February 1987.[14]

A third US launch failure occurred in May 1986, this time with a Delta launcher. It was apparently caused by an electrical fault which caused the main engine to shut off.[15] Range safety officers deliberately destroyed the Delta booster and its payload, a GEOS (Global Earth Observation Satellite) weather satellite.

France also suffered satellite launch failures in 1986. In May, the Ariane V18 rocket failed to launch an Intelsat VR14 civilian communications satellite into orbit, owing to a failure in the third-stage engine.[16] Two other failures occurred with Ariane rockets in 1982[17] and 1985. In 1986 the Ariane programme was temporarily suspended.

Much less is known about Soviet launch failures. However, on 3 October 1986 it was reported that the Cosmos 1783 satellite, which was launched on an early-warning mission, failed to achieve the intended orbit: the apogee height was less than 20 000 km rather than the intended 40 000 km.[18] This effectively reduced its coverage time over the northern hemisphere by less than half, or 300 min. On 15 October, the Cosmos 1785 satellite was launched into the correct orbit, giving the intended 600-min. coverage.

Impact of launch failures

These satellite launch failures have resulted in changes and setbacks to those nations' space programmes. It is impossible to predict what the long-term consequences will be for either civilian or military space programmes.

In the USA, as a result of the shuttle failures and consequent setback of the scheduled programme, the US Air Force has stepped up its interest in expendable launch vehicles (ELVs) to ensure the continuation of the military-related programmes and to reduce reliance on the shuttle for military missions. In 1986, 7 Titan 34D, several Titan III, 15 Atlas, 9 Delta and 11 small Scout ELVs were available for military launches.[19] Military satellites are also being designed to be launched either by the shuttle or by complementary expendable launch vehicles (CELVs) such as the Titan IV. It therefore appears that US military activities in outer space may be gathering momentum again.

Launch failures prior to 1986 and during the year resulted in a disproportionate military use of the shuttle. The new shuttle schedule allocates fully 40 per cent of its capacity to the US Department of Defense (DOD), 50 per cent to NASA (National Aeronautics and Space Administration) missions, and only about 10 per cent to commercial, foreign and other US Government requirements (see table 3.1).[20] By comparison, in the schedule announced in June 1985, only 20 per cent of the payload belonged to the DOD.

Another development that is at least in part a result of these incidents are the invitations extended by a number of countries to launch the satellites of other countries.

China has offered to launch satellites on commercial terms; its first invitation was made in 1985—to use the Chinese Long March 3 launcher at a price about 15 per cent lower than for the use of US or West European launchers. In response, the Swedish Space Corporation signed an agreement with China to reserve space for its Mailstar electronic mail satellite.[21] China has also signed a memorandum of understanding with a US firm to launch two civilian communications satellites. All the agreements with China are either for civilian communications satellites or for those that carry basic scientific instrument packages.

It is claimed that China could produce and launch up to 12 boosters per year. It is too early to judge the feasibility of these prospective transactions, for one reason because China's launching services will not become available until the 1990s.

France has also offered to launch satellites for other countries. After the US shuttle accident in early 1986, the USA diverted some of its scientific shuttle payloads to the Ariane, and 19 European satellites are planned for launch by Ariane, one of which—Skynet 4B—was originally scheduled for launch by the US space shuttle. Five US satellites are planned for the Ariane, one of which was originally planned for the shuttle.[22] In addition to these, the Australian Aussat 3, the Japanese Superbird SCS 1A and 1B, and the Indian Insat 1C satellites are to be launched by the Ariane. The Japanese satellites were to have been launched by the US shuttle, and the Indian spacecraft carrying an Indian astronaut was scheduled to fly on board the shuttle in 1986.

The Soviet Union has also signalled its intention to enter the commercial launcher business. It will presumably employ its Proton D-1-e and D-1-h launchers, which are still in use. This D class is used to orbit satellites in geostationary orbit. The D-1-h series have been used to launch Soviet Salyut space stations.

The Soviet Union is developing a reuseable launch vehicle (RLV), similar to the US space shuttle, but, for example, with jet engines in its tail which increase its flexibility during launch;[23] the RLV launch engines are not re-usable.

Given its strong capability to launch large, heavy satellites, it is not surprising that the USSR has offered its launch services to other nations. The launch failures of other countries have perhaps not been the only impetus. As early as

Table 3.1. The US space shuttle schedules in 1985 and 1986

Planned in June 1985

Flight no. & orbiter	Date of launch	Payload	Flight no. & orbiter	Date of launch	Payload
1985			71 B Challenger	26 Nov.	DOD
61 A Challenger	30 Oct.	Space D1 (FRG)	71 C Atlantis	15 Dec.	DOD PAM-2
61 B Atlantis	27 Nov.	Morelos B (Mexico)			STC DBS-B
		Satcom Ku-1			Skynet 4 B (UK)
		Aussat 2 (Australia)			
		EASE[a]	**1987**		
61 C Columbia	20 Dec.	Satcom Ku-2	71 D Columbia	7 Jan.	EOS 2
		Syncom 4–5 (US Navy)			MSL 6
		MSL-2[b]			VOLT A[k]
					Intelsat 6–2
			71 E Challenger	9 Feb.	TDRS C[s]
1986					Opportunity
51 L Challenger	22 Jan.	Spartan[c]	72 A Discovery	15 Feb.	SRL 2[l]
			71 F Atlantis	25 Feb.	SLS 2[m]
61 E Columbia	6 Mar.	Astro 1[d]	71 G Columbia	3 Mar.	MSL 7
		Westar 7			DOD PAM-38-4
62 A Discovery	20 Mar.	DOD	71 H Challenger	2 Apr.	DOD PAM-5
61 F Challenger	15 May	Ulysses[e]			Satcom Ku-4
					Gstar
61 G Atlantis	21 May	Galileo[f]	71 I Atlantis	1 May	DOD
			71 J Columbia	11 May	IML 1[n]
61 H Columbia	24 June	EOS[g]			Spartan 205
		MSL 1			(USA)
		Skynet 4A[h]	71 K Challenger	27 May	LDEF-2
		Palapa B3	71 L Atlantis	29 June	MSL 8
		(Indonesia)			DOD PAM-
61 M Challenger	15 July	TDRS-D[s]			6 & 7
		Insat 1C (India)	71 M Columbia	16 July	Astro 3
61 J Atlantis	8 Aug.	Space Telescope			CRRES[o]
			71 N Challenger	27 July	MSL 9
61 K Columbia	3 Sep.	EOM 1/2			DOD PAM-9
					Spartan 206UH
61 I Challenger	24 Sep.	LDEF 1[i]			Opportunity
		Intelsat 6–1	71 O Atlantis	11 Sep.	DOD
61 L Atlantis	22 Oct.	MSL 5	71 P Columbia	17 Sep.	Sunlab 1[p]
		SHEAL 1[j]			Rosat[q]
		STC DBS-A	81 A Challenger	8 Oct.	DOD
		ASC-2			
		DOD			
71 A Columbia	30 Oct.	Spartan 2			
		HS 376-R			

1967 the USSR offered the services of the Proton launcher,[24] and in the late 1970s the Proton was offered to the European Space Agency (ESA) to launch Europe's first maritime satellite, MARECS-A. In 1983 an attempt was made to attract the launch of the Inmarsat, again with the Proton. In 1985 the USSR established the Glavcosmos Agency to organize and handle international marketing of Soviet launch services. It has been reported that the USSR has offered to launch spacecraft for a total cost of $20 million.[25] In 1986 the Glavcosmos Agency signed an agreement with India to launch its IRS-1A remote sensing satellite in 1987, using the Proton.[26] The satellite will weigh 900

Planned in October 1986

Orbiter	Date of launch	Payload	Orbiter	Date of launch	Payload
	1988				
Discovery	18 Feb.	TDRS-C[s]	Columbia	21 June	GRS 1 & 2
Atlantis	26 May	DOD			MSL 3
			. .	July	DOD
Columbia	28 July	DOD			
Discovery	22 Sep.	TDRS-D[s]			
Atlantis	17 Nov.	Hubble Space Telescope	. .	Aug.	DOD
			. .	Aug.	GPS 3 & 4 MSL 4
	1989		. .	Nov.	Planetary mission
Columbia	19 Jan.	Astro-1 TDRS-B[s]			
Discovery	2 Mar.	DOD			
			. .	Dec.	SLS
Atlantis	25 Apr.	Magellan[r]			
Discovery	2 June	DOD Spacelab			

[a] Test for assembling large structures.
[b] Materials Science Laboratory.
[c] Spartan is the small free-flying astronomical observatory.
[d] To obtain ultraviolet data on astronomical objects.
[e] European solar probe.
[f] US Jupiter orbiter and atmospheric probe.
[g] Electrophoresis Operation in space to produce pharmaceuticals.
[h] British Military Communications Satellite.
[i] Long Duration Exposure Facility; still in orbit after being released by 41C in Apr. 1984; supposed to be retrieved by 61J.
[j] SHEAL = Shuttle High Energy Astrophysics Laboratory for studying X-ray sources.
[k] A test of plasma interactions with solar arrays for Space Station studies.
[l] Shuttle Radar Laboratory.
[m] Spacelab Life Science flights.
[n] International Microgravity Laboratory.
[o] Will release metal vapours into the ionosphere and upper atmosphere.
[p] Will study the sun (the Spacelab 2 solar telescope).
[q] The West German X-ray astronomical satellite.
[r] Venus radar mapper.
[s] Payload also for DOD use.

kg and will be orbited in a 900-km polar orbit. Unlike previous such launches for India, the cost will be borne by India.

Finally, the Soviet Union offered in 1986 to launch commercial satellites for Japan,[27] and a communications satellite for Thailand[28] which would be built by the USA, but no completed deals have been reported.

All these ventures raise a number of problems that will have to be considered. There may be serious launcher-satellite compatibility problems in any attempt to launch one country's satellite from the launcher of another country. A second important consideration is that of the transfer of sensitive technology among countries: it seems reasonable to doubt whether any country would launch its spacecraft from abroad without rigid controls of both the release of information about its satellite and that obtained by its satellite. There is certain to be much discussion about these issues before any commercial deals are completed.

IV. Collisions with debris in outer space

On 13 November 1986 a spent booster of the Ariane V16 launcher (which had launched the SPOT 1 and the Swedish Viking scientific satellite) exploded while in orbit.[29] An accident in June 1983—in which the third stage collided with a small sub-satellite—also involved an Ariane launcher.[30] Both these accidents have highlighted the urgency of studying the question of collisions in outer space. The 1986 accident reportedly produced about 200 pieces of orbiting debris, and some of these may be in orbits close to that of the US KH-11 satellite. Since they are too small to be tracked, this cannot be determined exactly. Moreover, debris has been generated from explosions caused by seven US Delta rockets, and this debris is also orbiting in the vicinity of the KH-11 orbit.[31] Thus the United States may be particularly concerned about space debris which may be in the path of its only photoreconnaissance satellite presently in orbit.

A number of serious accidents involving Soviet satellites may have been caused by debris in outer space. Cosmos 954, which carried a nuclear reactor, fell to the earth in January 1978, contaminating the atmosphere and Canadian territory with radioactive materials.[32] It has been suggested that this was caused by a collision in outer space which damaged the satellite.[33] In 1984, Cosmos 1275, a Soviet navigation satellite, broke up over Alaska, an accident also possibly caused by a collision with space debris.[34] In July 1983, the US space shuttle Challenger was hit by something that chipped a window; it was later determined to be a tiny, 0.2-mm flake of white paint, probably from a spent rocket.[35] After the April 1984 shuttle mission, electronic boxes from the Solar Max satellite were recovered and found to have 160 holes in them, made by orbiting chips of paint.

More than 5600 orbiting objects are being tracked today. Of these, 5 per cent are operational payloads, about 20 per cent are non-operational payloads, 25 per cent are mission-related debris, and some 50 per cent are debris from satellite break-ups.[36] Of this space debris, 57 per cent comes from the USA and 40 per cent from the Soviet Union; another 3 per cent is from China, the ESA,

India and Japan.[37] In addition, there are now tens of thousands of small, untrackable fragments (perhaps 40 000, up to about 1 cm in size), and billions of flakes of paint. Because some of the larger pieces of debris further break up into smaller pieces, the debris population is increasing at the rate of 300–500 more pieces per year.[38] Since the space age began in 1957, man-made objects have fully doubled the number of microscopic particles in space compared to the natural background particles that existed at that time.[39]

As a measure of the damage debris can inflict, a 0.5-mm metal chip travelling at an average relative speed of about 10 km/s could puncture a space suit and kill an astronaut or a cosmonaut working outside a spacecraft. A particle of 1–10 mm could damage or even destroy an orbiting spacecraft. Thus the probability of serious accidents occurring in outer space is growing. And with continued satellite launches, and ASAT and defensive weapon-related tests involving collisions with targets, the risk will be further increased. A very serious consequence would be the mistaken identification of, for example, a collision with debris as the deliberate use of an anti-satellite weapon.

V. Anti-satellite programmes

USSR

The Soviet Union unilaterally proclaimed a moratorium on the testing of ASAT weapons in 1983. Nevertheless, in 1985 for the first time, and again in 1986, it admitted the existence of a Soviet ASAT programme.[40] Reports from the USA have also indicated the existence of a second generation of Soviet ASAT weapons. One report is based on information that in May or June 1986 a Soviet airborne laser laboratory (ALL) was destroyed in a fire near Moscow;[41] the laser was built to be carried on board an Ilyushin I1-76 transport aircraft. (The US Air Force had an ALL which could have had an ASAT application, but it was cancelled in 1984. It was mainly intended to damage and destroy missiles and aircraft in the atmosphere, for experimental purposes.)

The more significant report is about the existence of a ground-based laser ASAT weapon in the Soviet Union. US reports in 1986 suggest that the USSR has begun construction of two ground-based ASAT laser weapon facilities on mountain tops near the Soviet-Afghan border. One is located near the town of Dushanbe (38°38'N, 68°51'E), and there may be another at a second site in the same region.[42] The reports are not clear about whether these are operational, developmental or only research facilities. The Dushanbe site is reported to have a laser and a microwave facility. It is also believed that a large new radar is being constructed in the Caucasus Mountain region. The USSR has been constructing a radio telescope, in collaboration with an international group of scientists, near the small town of Zoamin (39°56'N, 68°25'E), directly north of Dushanbe.

The Dushanbe site is an appropriate location for a laser weapon: it is perhaps the closest location in the USSR to the equator, which would facilitate reaching vital US satellites in geostationary orbit. A mountain top is a good location for minimizing atmospheric absorption and other problems encountered by a laser beam as it travels through the atmosphere. There are two main ways of overcoming these problems. In one, the beam distortions are automatically corrected by use of so-called phase-conjugate mirrors. The other method is to use a pulsed laser beam rather than a continuous one, with durations of the pulse such that the laser light has little time to heat the atmosphere through which it travels, thus reducing its distortion.[43]

While it has been reported that Soviet officials acknowledge the development of such ground-based lasers, they claim that the lasers are intended for pointing and tracking experiments and that they are weak lasers that do not have ASAT applications.[44]

USA

ASAT activities in the United States have for several years focused on conventional kinetic-energy weapons or impact weapons, with non-nuclear warheads. The last US test against a target was conducted in September 1985; the following month, Congress imposed a one-year ban on testing against targets, subject to the USSR adhering to its ASAT test moratorium. At the end of 1986, the Soviet moratorium was still in force, and the United States had conducted no further tests against targets.

However, on 22 August 1986, the US Air Force successfully tested its miniature homing vehicle (MHV) ASAT against a distant star, used as a weak infra-red source.[45] This was the fourth MHV ASAT test. The fifth test was conducted on 30 September 1986: the MHV was launched from an F-15 aircraft at the Flight Test Center, Edwards Air Force Base.[46] In this test the ASAT MHV was launched against a star that was closer to the earth's horizon.

The US MHV ASAT programme has been cut back considerably: for example, the original procurement figure of 112 missiles has been reduced to 35, and the Air Force will operate only out of Langley Air Force Base rather than from a west coast base as well.[47] A 1986 classified report by the US General Accounting Office gives a programme cost of $5.3 billion—an increase of about 50 per cent over the original cost estimate.[48] In addition, in anticipation of possible Soviet countermeasures, the MHV would need to carry a larger amount of fuel to intercept a manoeuvring Soviet satellite; this would entail upgrading the F-15 aircraft engines to carry a larger ASAT payload, which would further increase the cost. The programme has since been reorganized to reduce the cost to $3.9 billion.

This programme has also encountered technical difficulties. The missile engines have exploded and the cryogenic cooling system for the infra-red sensor has malfunctioned many times. On one occasion a space test had to be terminated when the ASAT warhead failed to separate from the booster.

The trend in the United States is now to focus on ground-based lasers and in particular to draw upon the technology being developed under the SDI programme for ASAT applications.

VI. Strategic defence

Strategic defence—that is, defence against incoming intercontinental-range nuclear forces—is being investigated by the United States and the Soviet Union. Many of the technologies, even such 'exotic' systems as laser weapons, are based on programmes of a decade or two ago. What is different today are the concentrated efforts being pursued by both superpowers for research on strategic defence (SD) technologies and many of the new advances that have been made.

USA

In the United States, research and funding for defensive weapons are concentrated under one organization, the Strategic Defense Initiative Organization (SDIO). The budget request of the SDIO has increased more than five-fold over the period 1984–89 (see figure 3.3). However, if the current deceleration of appropriations by the US Congress continues, funding may slow down considerably. It has been suggested that budgetary constraints and satellite launch failures will slow down or change SDIO programmes from actual testing to programmes for theoretical and basic experimental physics research.

In the US SDI programme, a large and expensive effort is directed at exploiting technology for ballistic missile defence (BMD) based on land, in the air and in space. BMD weapons based in space would intercept ballistic missiles during their boost phase and their nuclear warheads in space, as they travel to their intended targets. The ground-based BMD weapons would intercept the warheads in space or in the atmosphere as they approach their targets. 'Defensive weapons' can be grouped into two basic types: kinetic-energy weapons (KEWs) and directed-energy weapons (DEWs) such as high-energy lasers. The USA is pursuing both types of system.

Two types of KEW are being investigated today: those that use electromagnetic forces for their propulsion and those that use chemical rockets. The latter type is undergoing field-testing. The US Army has initiated the development of the Exo-atmospheric Reentry-vehicle Intercept Sub-system (ERIS),[49] intended to destroy re-entry vehicles (RVs) at altitudes of about 100–160 km. In the High Endo-atmospheric Defense Interceptor (HEDI) programmes, the missile would intercept RVs within the atmosphere, at a maximum altitude of about 90 km.[50] Both these programmes are designed to test the feasibility of the weapons.

On 27 June 1986, in the Flexible Lightweight Agile Guided Experiment (FLAGE), a 3.6-m long ground-launched missile struck a target travelling at a speed of just under 1 km a second. The target was a metal cone launched from an F-4J fighter aircraft at a height of 13.2 km and was destroyed at an altitude of 3.6 km.[51] It was powered by a rocket engine, and its speed was 0.86 km/sec, so that the relative velocity was just under 2 km/sec.[52] The interceptor was launched 22 seconds after the target was released and crashed into it about eight seconds later. This was the sixth of a series of nine planned tests. The

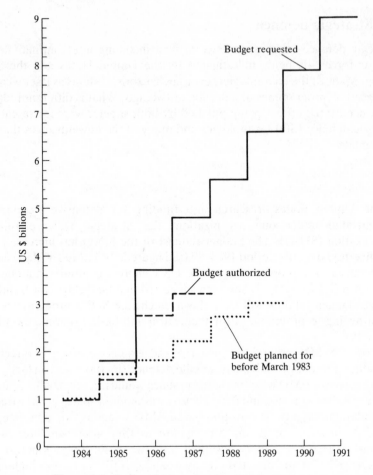

Figure 3.3. Budget history for the SDIO, 1983–91

purpose of these experiments is to test the new missile guidance and control systems: homing radar on board the missile generated data for the missile's guidance control system.

While these experiments apply to a system that might be deployed against short-range missiles, the basic technology is the same as that for ICBM interception. (FLAGE is a new name given to the former SRHIT—Small Radar Homing Interceptor Technology—programme.)

Another test was conducted on 5 September 1986, when the US National Aeronautics and Space Administration (NASA) successfully launched a Delta booster rocket which carried a classified SDI-related experiment.[53] In this test the Delta rocket was launched from Cape Canaveral with two vehicles on board to test the ability to detect rocket exhaust plumes and to demonstrate the capability of the guidance systems to aid in attacking a target. These two vehicles were the second stage of the Delta launcher, and an SDI-programme target satellite. The target satellite was observed by sensors on board the Delta. (The satellite had a liquid-propulsion unit and a large mast carrying a radar similar to that used on the Phoenix missile.) The Delta second stage contained several sensors: four to assess the rocket plume of a second vehicle, and four others to assess the plume characteristics of the Delta engine. The second stage also carried an infra-red imaging system—that used by the Maverick missile—and a laser radar which was orbited for the first time.

In the test the Delta booster placed its second stage into orbit, and the target satellite separated about 45 minutes after launch. As the satellite separated from the Delta, the Delta sensors measured the characteristics of the satellite against space and various backgrounds of the earth horizon and terrain. The satellite simulated the characteristics of an RV in orbit.

After 92 minutes of flight, as the two craft passed south of the White Sands missile range in New Mexico, a Minuteman missile second stage was launched. The Maverick infra-red sensor on the orbiting Delta launcher picked up the infra-red signature of the Minuteman's hot exhaust. The two orbiting vehicles then manoeuvred to face each other so that the Delta rocket could be set on a guided, head-on collision course with the manoeuvring satellite. The two spacecraft collided over Kwajalein Atoll in the Pacific Ocean.

The next experiment is planned to be conducted from a Delta launcher in 1987, when 80 per cent of the 9–12 flights using expendable launchers will be related to the US SDI programme.[54]

While there appears to be progress in the field of KEWs based on chemical-rocket propulsion techniques, there is also considerable interest in those with electromagnetic forces, such as electromagnetic railguns. In 1986 it was reported that important advances were made in the US Army and the Defense Advanced Research Projects Agency (DARPA) railgun programme. In one test, a projectile weighing up to 500 g was accelerated to a velocity of more than 4.2 km/sec.[55] The SDIO plans to carry out tests in 1988 in the Thunderbolt series which are designed to demonstrate high velocities and high repetition rates of fire,[56] aiming at desired velocities in excess of 10 km/sec for 'smart' projectiles[57] weighing up to 1 kg, and repetition rates of one shot per second.[58] (Chemical rockets can only achieve velocities of about 7 km/sec.) new SDIO facility, called Checkmate (compact high-energy capacitor module, advanced technology experiment), can fire two shots per day, designed to accelerate plastic cubes weighing 100 g to velocities of up to 4 km/sec.[59] The overall efficiency—that is, the ratio of the energy of the particle to that of the initial electrical energy put into the device—is about 20 per cent and is expected to increase to about 50 per cent. However, these goals are still a long way away.

In the field of directed-energy weapons, the US SDIO has concentrated research on developing a ground-based free-electron laser (FEL) in which a beam of electrons is injected through a magnetic field and the resulting laser light is focused to achieve energies capable of damaging or destroying ballistic missiles or their warheads. (For a description of the technology, see *SIPRI Yearbook 1986*, pages 139–40.) The research is being conducted primarily at the Lawrence Livermore and the Los Alamos national laboratories, and the current objectives are to achieve greatly improved efficiencies and to reduce dramatically the size of the FEL devices. While these technological obstacles are enormous, the efforts produced certain achievements in 1986.

At Lawrence Livermore, the reported DEW advance was in energy efficiency; this FEL demonstrated the ability to convert electron-beam energy into laser output energy at 40 per cent efficiency.[60] Although the overall efficiency—that is, the ratio of laser output energy to input electrical energy—is about 20 per cent, this compares favourably with the 2 per cent efficiency of conventional lasers.[61] However, the Livermore FEL output energy had a wavelength of 8.8 mm,[62] which is considered too long to damage a hardened target such as a warhead, although it could, in theory, damage a missile in its boost phase of flight. Wavelengths of about 1 μm are believed to be necessary to damage hardened targets, but at present this would require too large a laser system (perhaps 900 m long) to be manageable for deployment. In the planned Palladin experiment, attempts will be made to reduce both the size of the FEL and its output energy (to a wavelength of about 10 μm).[63]

At Los Alamos, the reported achievement was in the compact size of the laser. This was accomplished by using the radio-frequency quadruple (RFQ) technique—first developed in the USSR and refined at Los Alamos—in the FEL device. However, its efficiency is only 2 per cent. One effort to overcome this low efficiency is to re-design the magnetic system so that the electrons do not lose as much of their energy as in standard designs. The second is to recycle the unused electrons to power the system. Los Alamos has succeeded in amplifying the laser light as it passes through such a device. One problem with a high-power laser device is that the beam could cause damage to the optics of the system. One way to overcome this is to arrange the necessary mirrors in such a way as to reduce the chance of damaging them, but this again requires a large apparatus. These experiments are still at an early stage, and there appear to be no prospects for near-term applications.

Other concepts for SD systems, even more theoretical and futuristic than lasers, are being investigated. The US Air Force has identified a potential new source of energy for propulsion and possibly weapon applications. By causing the reaction between the proton (a subatomic particle) and an anti-proton[64] (a particle of equal mass but opposite charge), one could produce an energy release several orders of magnitude greater than known energy sources. For example, it is estimated that 1 milligram of anti-matter would release the energy of 6000 kg of rocket fuel or 44 tons of TNT.[65] Although it would require about 4 GW of energy to produce a militarily useable amount of anti-protons (10 mg), this is less than the 6 GW required to produce weapon-grade uranium-235.

While the potential of such energy sources holds great interest, the technological problems are enormous. The production of anti-matter is very complex, and the amount that can currently be produced is very small—of the order of 10^{11} anti-protons, or 100–10 millionths of a milligram per day. Storage problems also present extraordinary challenges today because of the difficulty of isolating anti-matter in storage. At the European Organization for Nuclear Research (CERN) in Switzerland, 10^{11} anti-protons per cm^3 have been stored.

While research will undoubtedly continue on these and other exotic weapon concepts, practical results seem to be very far in the future.

USSR

Much less is known about Soviet research and development of SD technologies and systems than about those of the USA. This is because the Soviet Union does not provide information about its work on such programmes, except for limited discussions of the modernization of the Moscow ABM system. As a result, the picture of Soviet work on strategic defences comes almost exclusively from the USA, which has expressed concerns that the USSR is conducting a massive strategic defence research programme and may be preparing a rapidly deployable nation-wide ABM defence system. The true situation is not known, and the nature and status of the Soviet SD programme continue to be contentious issues.

In two areas of strategic defence, the USSR is known to have modern systems deployed: air defences and the ABM system around Moscow. Soviet air defences are deployed widely across the USSR and include thousands of radars and surface-to-air missiles (SAMs) to counter enemy air forces, especially bombers and possibly cruise missiles. There have been suggestions from the West that certain Soviet SAMs may have a capability to destroy ballistic missiles in flight, particularly those based in Western Europe—such as the Pershing II. Such an anti-tactical ballistic missile (ATBM) capability is not prohibited by the ABM Treaty, but the technologies involved are virtually the same as those for ABM systems.

Modernization of the Moscow ABM system has been under way for several years and, when complete, will include a combination of updated long-range Galosh missiles and new, dual-capable endo-atmospheric Gazelle missiles that are expected to begin operation in 1987 (see also chapter 1). There will be 100 launchers, as permitted by the ABM Treaty.

The main Soviet ABM research and test facility is located at the Sary Shagan Missile Test Centre on Lake Balkash in south-central USSR. (A photograph of the test site taken by the French SPOT 1 satellite—see figure 3.4—shows the positions of some of the missile launch facilities and radars there.)

It is reported by the USA that the USSR is also conducting research on other types of technology at Sary Shagan, particularly laser facilities that are believed to be for strategic defence purposes. According to some reports, the USSR used a laser at Sary Shagan in tests in 1982 involving manned Soviet spacecraft.[66] The Pentagon has reported that the USSR already has ground-based lasers with a limited capability to blind satellites.[67] If such systems exist, they may also have a role in SD research programmes.

The USA has maintained that the USSR has been conducting research on advanced lasers for some time. To support this view, the USA has reported a few details on Soviet facilities such as Sary Shagan, or those near Dushanbe or Moscow. Very little is known in the West about what is actually taking place at these research centres or whether the work actually relates to strategic defence. Although a few Soviet scientific publications have made reference to laser

Figure 3.4. SPOT 1 satellite photograph of a major Soviet ABM test facility near Sary Shagan, Kazakhstan.

The main facility (A) with a large radar is located at 45°46′N, 72°35′E. Missile launch areas (B) can be seen around the main radar. There are very few permanent roads in this complex, so large vehicles make fresh tracks as shown in the photograph.

*Photograph by courtesy of Space
Media Network, Stockholm, Sweden*

research with space weapon applications or to high-power microwave and radio frequency generators, since 1981 no such information has appeared in the Soviet literature.

VII. Conclusion

While the failures of US and French satellite launchers have given impetus to other nations to enter the competition for launching satellites, this will by and large remain in the field of launching commercial satellites. Whether this will become a new trend will depend on which country is going to launch the satellite, which has built it and under which conditions it is to be launched. For example, if there is any risk that a launching country could gain access to sensitive technical data about the other country's spacecraft, the country which owns or has built the satellite may not wish to buy such launch services. Agreements signed by China for launching satellites are either for civilian communications satellites or for satellites that will carry basic research instrument packages. The USA is considering using the French Ariane launcher, but only for satellites with scientific missions.

The USA is also reviving its Atlas, Titan and Delta expendable launch vehicles. In addition, military satellites are being designed to be launched either by the space shuttle or by complementary ELVs such as the Titan IV. Also, some of the old US ICBMs (the Titan II) are being converted to space launchers. US military activities in outer space will be stepped up again: for example, a US Air Force research satellite was launched on 13 November 1986.

Nonetheless, the USA is a long way from its original plan of one shuttle launch per week by December 1986. The current shortage of military launch capabilities and reduced budgets for SDI have already slowed down some of the previously planned SDI demonstration tests.

Even so, some of the tests already conducted have brought up important questions about the conflict between continued SDI tests and US compliance with the ABM Treaty. Some observers have noted that the tests are coming closer to the limit of the permissible. Examples of these are the Homing Overlay Experiment of 10 June 1984 and the Delta rocket test of 5 September 1986. Although the Delta test used a satellite in orbit instead of a missile and an RV in ballistic trajectory, the test nonetheless served as a BMD test, in pursuit of SDI objectives. While the technique is not prohibited by the ABM Treaty, the eventual goal would be. Given the US re-interpretation of the ABM Treaty in 1985, and seeming confusion about what it permits and prohibits, the future of such space tests will be vigorously debated.

It seems unlikely that any US–Soviet agreement on strategic defence research or deployment will materialize without a better understanding in the West of the Soviet research programme. Otherwise the public will be left with the impressions given by Western accounts and will not provide political support for efforts to limit both programmes within the confines of the ABM Treaty. The ABM Treaty Review Conference that will convene in 1987 provides a badly needed opportunity for both superpowers to discuss these issues fully and reaffirm their mutual commitment to a treaty that has served their interests well.

Notes and references

1 Jasani, B., 'The military use of outer space', in SIPRI, *World Armaments and Disarmament: SIPRI Yearbook 1986* (Oxford University Press: Oxford, 1986), pp. 149–57.

2 'New satellite returns to earth', *Beijing Review*, vol. 29, no. 42 (20 Oct. 1986), pp. 6–7.

3 'L'utilisation militaire de l'espace', *Assemblée Nationale*, vol. 5, no. 398 (9 Oct. 1986), pp. 17–29.

4 'France tests spy sensor', *Flight International*, vol. 129, no. 4010 (10 May 1986), p. 25.

5 'CNES proposes merging Helios, SPOT programs', *Aviation Week & Space Technology*, vol. 125, no. 10 (8 Sep. 1986), p. 38.

6 Note 3.

7 'NOAA G boosts US confidence', *Flight International*, vol. 130, no. 4030 (27 Sep. 1986), p. 16;

'NOAA weather satellite launched on Atlas E', *Aviation Week & Space Technology*, vol. 125, no. 12 (22 Sep. 1986), p. 18.

[8] 'Scout puts "Polar Bear" in orbit', *Spaceflight*, vol. 29, no. 1 (Jan. 1987), p. 11.

[9] 'Military communications satellite launched on Atlas Centaur', *Aviation Week & Space Technology*, vol. 125, no. 22 (8 Dec. 1986), p. 28; 'FltSatCom drifts towards assigned position', *Aviation Week & Space Technology*, vol. 125, no. 24 (15 Dec. 1986), p. 21.

[10] 'Fltsatcom drifts towards assigned position', *Aviation Week & Space Technology*, vol. 125, no. 24 (15 Dec. 1980), p. 21.

[11] *Aviation Week & Space Technology*, vol. 125, no. 22 (8 Dec. 1986), p. 79.

[12] Note 3.

[13] 'Titan solid booster failure causes Vandenberg accident', *Aviation Week & Space Technology*, vol. 124, no. 18 (5 May 1986), pp. 24–5.

[14] 'Titan pads repaired', *Spaceflight*, vol. 28, no. 12 (Dec. 1986), p. 421.

[15] Turk, P. and Lopez, R., 'US expendable launchers', *Space Markets*, no. 2 (summer 1986), pp. 90–4.

[16] 'Next Ariane launch', *Spaceflight*, vol. 28, no. 9/10 (Sep./Oct. 1986), p. 334.

[17] Furniss, T., 'Ariane's big fix', *Flight International*, vol. 130, no. 29 (20 Sep. 1986), pp. 48–52.

[18] Covault, C., 'Soviet military space flight fails, warning satellite placed in wrong orbit', *Aviation Week & Space Technology*, vol. 125, no. 17 (27 Oct. 1967), p. 24.

[19] Lopez, R., Bulloch, C. and Rhea, J., 'Impact of Challenger loss', *Space Markets*, no. 1 (spring 1986), pp. 40–5.

[20] 'NASA unveils shuttle manifest for resumed flights', *Interavia AirLetter*, no. 11098 (6 Oct. 1986), p. 6; and Palca, J., 'Space shuttle programme for 1988 announced', *Nature*, vol. 323, no. 6088 (9 Oct. 1986), p. 481.

[21] *Aviation Week & Space Technology*, vol. 124, no. 12 (24 Feb. 1986), p. 21.

[22] Furniss, T., 'Ariane's big fix', *Flight International*, vol. 130, no. 4029 (20 Sep. 1986), pp. 48–52.

[23] Covault, C., 'Soviets begin Orbiter tests following engine installation', *Aviation Week & Space Technology*, vol. 124, no. 15 (14 Apr. 1986), pp. 16–18.

[24] Parfitt, J., 'The Soviet Proton launcher—a genuine commercial competitor?', *Space Market*, no. 2 (summer 1986), pp. 96–101.

[25] 'Proton "commercially viable"', *Flight International*, vol. 130, no. 4020 (19 July 1986), p. 36.

[26] 'Russians to launch India's IRS-1A', *Interavia AirLetter*, no. 11093 (29 Sep. 1986), p. 7.

[27] 'Soviets offer to launch Japanese commercial satellites', *Defense Daily*, vol. 145, no. 38 (23 Apr. 1986), p. 300.

[28] Butler, S. B., 'Soviet Union willing to launch Thai satellite', *Financial Times*, 11 Nov. 1986, p. 5.

[29] 'Used Ariane stage explodes, creating space debris hazards', *Aviation Week & Space Technology*, vol. 125, no. 22 (1 Dec. 1986), p. 34.

[30] Note 22.

[31] Note 29.

[32] Jasani, B., 'Ocean surveillance by earth satellites', *Ocean Yearbook 2*, E. M. Borgese and N. Ginsburg (eds), (University of Chicago Press: Chicago, 1980), pp. 250–69.

[33] Sedov, L., quoted in *Spaceflight*, vol. 20, no. 5 (5 May 1978), p. 184; and see note 29.

[34] Johnson, N. L., 'History and consequences of on-orbit break-ups', paper presented at the COSPAR Congress Graz, Austria, 1984; and see note 29.

[35] Marshall, E., 'Space junk grows with weapons tests', *Science*, vol. 230, no. 4724 (25 Oct. 1985), pp. 424–25.

[36] Kessler, D. J., 'Orbital debris issues', paper presented at the COSPAR Congress, Graz, Austria, 1984.

[37] Note 35.

[38] Note 35.

[39] Laurance, M. R. and Brownleed, D. E., 'The flux of meteoroids and orbital space debris striking satellites in low earth orbit', *Nature*, vol. 323, no. 6084 (11 Sep. 1986), pp. 136–38.

[40] 'Parallel restraints in the testing of anti-satellite weapons: a step towards preventing an arms race in outer space', Joint Papers, Lawyers Alliance for Nuclear Arms Control and the Association of Soviet Lawyers, 24–31 Mar. 1986 (Lawyers Alliance for Nuclear Arms Control, Inc.: Boston, MA, 1986).

[41] Gordon, M. R., 'US aids report Soviet lost airborne laser lab in a fire', *New York Times*, 24 Aug. 1986; and Hoffmann, H., 'Moscow's secret strategic defence initiative', *Military Technology*, vol. 10, no. 11 (Nov. 1986), pp. 38–44.

[42] 'White House assesses reports of Soviet ASAT laser facilities', *Aviation Week & Space*

Technology, vol. 125, no. 11 (15 Sep. 1986), p. 21; 'Are Soviets zapping US milsats?', *Military Space*, 10 Nov. 1986, p. 1.

43 'Soviet pulsed GBL threat to US satellites', *Defense Daily*, vol. 138, no. 3 (4 Jan. 1986), p. 20.

44 'Are Soviets zapping US milsats?', *Military Space*, 10 Nov. 1986, pp. 1–3.

45 'Fourth ASAT test', *Interavia AirLetter*, no. 11069 (25 Aug. 1986), p. 5.

46 'ASAT weapon strikes target successfully', *Defense News*, vol. 1, no. 38 (6 Oct. 1986), p. 14; and 'ASAT test', *Interavia AirLetter*, no. 11097 (3 Oct. 1986), p. 7.

47 'ASAT decisions hinge on test restrictions, technology advances', *Aerospace Daily*, vol. 139, no. 28 (8 Aug. 1986), pp. 219–20.

48 Marcus, D. J., 'ASAT debate', *Signal*, vol. 40, no. 10 (June 1986), p. 7; and Smith, R. J., 'Pentagon plans new anti-satellite tests', *Science*, vol. 233, no. 4762 (25 July 1986), pp. 409–10.

49 'Lockheed McDonnell Douglas with SDI contracts', *Military Technology*, vol. 10, no. 1 (Jan. 1986), p. 140.

50 'Hughes studies high endo-atmospheric kill vehicle', *Aviation Week & Space Technology*, vol. 124, no. 21 (26 May 1986), p. 101.

51 'Weinberger announces successful SDI-related experiment', *Wireless File*, US Information Service, 1 July 1986.

52 Gilmartin, T., 'FLAGE Project homes in on success, destroys moving target during test flight', *Defense News*, vol. 1, no. 25 (7 July 1986), p. 28; and 'Army/LTV missile intercepts reentry vehicle', *Aviation Week & Space Technology*, vol. 125, no. 2 (14 July 1986), p. 119.

53 Note 26.

54 Covault, C., 'Next SDI Delta launch to carry multiple research payload', *Aviation Week & Space Technology*, vol. 125, no. 20 (17 Nov. 1986), p. 20.

55 Aubin, F. M., 'Electromagnetic propulsion: the wave of the future', *Field Artillery Journal*, July–Aug. 1986, p. 31.

56 'Railgun experiments strive for high velocity repetition', *Aviation Week & Space Technology*, vol. 124, no. 4 (27 Jan. 1986), p. 21.

57 Smart projectiles have sensor and guide systems that enable them to home on to a target.

58 *Report to the Congress on the Strategic Defense Initiative*, June 1986 (Strategic Defense Initiative, Department of Defense: Washington, DC, 1986).

59 'Electromagnetic launcher facility begins operations in California', *Aviation Week & Space Technology*, vol. 124, no. 4 (27 Jan. 1986), p. 92.

60 Speser, P., 'The Strategic Defense Initiative—a lesson for technology-push strategies', *Laser Focus*, vol. 22, no. 9 (Sep. 1986), pp. 18–24.

61 'In the realm of the possible: the work on Strategic Defense', *Insight*, 10 Nov. 1986, p. 56.

62 'Introduction-type laser faces critical tests', *Aviation Week & Space Technology*, vol. 125, no. 7 (18 Aug. 1986), p. 54.

63 'Free-electron-laser development', *Energy & Technology Review*, Lawrence Livermore National Laboratory Report no. UCRL–52000–86–6/7, June–July 1986, p. 53.

64 Gordon, J. K., 'Air Force identifies technologies to improve defense capabilities', *Aviation Week & Space Technologies*, vol. 124, no. 24 (16 June 1986), pp. 63–4; Sanger, E., 'The proton rocket and the weapon beam', *New Scientist*, vol. 6, no. 147 (10 Sep. 1959), pp. 383–84.

65 Walgate, R., 'Defense lobby eyes anti-matter', *Nature*, vol. 322, no. 6081 (21 Aug. 1986), p. 678.

66 'White House assesses reports of Soviet Asat laser facilities', *Aviation Week & Space Technology*, 15 Sep. 1986, p. 21.

67 US DOD, *Soviet Military Power, 1986*, preface; conversation with DOD official, Apr. 1986.

Appendix 3A. Tables of satellites launched in 1986

Tables 3A.1-3A.10 were prepared in collaboration with G. E. Perry, MBE, and members of the Kettering Group.

Table 3A.1. Photographic reconnaissance satellites launched during 1986

Country, satellite name and designation	Launch date and time (GMT)	Orbital inclination (deg) and period (min)	Perigee and apogee heights (km)	Comments
USA				
USAF T-34D	18 Apr. —	— —	— —	Possible KH-11 failure; launcher exploded 5 seconds after launch; only one satellite, 1984–122A, in orbit at the end of Dec. 1986
USSR				
Cosmos 1715 (1986–01A)	8 Jan. 1131	73 90	237 283	Lifetime 14 days; high resolution
Cosmos 1724 (1986–04A)	15 Jan. 1424	67 90	168 233	Lifetime 59 days; high resolution; fourth generation
Cosmos 1728 (1986–09A)	28 Jan. 0824	70 90	225 274	Lifetime 14 days; high resolution
Cosmos 1730 (1986–12A)	4 Feb. 1117	73 90	228 307	Lifetime 9 days; high resolution
Cosmos 1731 (1986–13A)	7 Feb. 0838	65 89	179 259	Lifetime 238 days; fifth generation; fourth satellite in the series; previous ones were Cosmos 1552 launched in 1984 and Cosmos 1643 and 1654 launched in 1985; the latter might have been a fifth-generation spacecraft, which exploded 29 days after launch
Cosmos 1734 (1986–20A)	26 Feb. 1341	67 90	162 347	Lifetime 59 days; fourth generation; high resolution
Cosmos 1739 (1986–28A)	9 Apr. 0755	65 90	173 329	Lifetime 59 days; fourth generation; high resolution
Cosmos 1740 (1986–29A)	15 Apr. 1146	73 90	197 365	Lifetime 13 days; medium resolution; TF
Cosmos 1742 (1986–33A)	14 May 1243	73 90	198 361	Lifetime 14 days; medium resolution; TF
Cosmos 1746 (1986–40A)	28 May 0755	82 89	180 280	Lifetime 14 days; high resolution; Earth resources; data received by Priroda (Nature) Station
Cosmos 1747 (1986–41A)	29 May 0922	70 90	208 396	Lifetime 14 days; high resolution
Cosmos 1756 (1986–43A)	6 June 1243	65 90	173 344	Lifetime 59 days; fourth generation; high resolution
Cosmos 1757 (1986–45A)	11 June 0741	82 89	180 224	Lifetime 14 days; Earth resources; data received by Priroda (Nature) Station
Cosmos 1760 (1986–48A)	19 June 1034	70 91	208 398	Lifetime 14 days; medium resolution; TF
Cosmos 1762 (1986–51A)	10 July 0755	83 89	184 294	Lifetime 14 days; medium resolution; Earth resources; change of inclination from 82.3° to 82.6°

Table 3A.1 *cont.*

Country, satellite name and designation	Launch date and time (GMT)	Orbital inclination (deg) and period (min)	Perigee and apogee heights (km)	Comments
Cosmos 1764 (1986–53A)	17 July 1229	65 90	174 337	Lifetime 56 days; fourth generation; high resolution
Cosmos 1765 (1986–54A)	24 July 1229	73 90	196 369	Lifetime 14 days; medium resolution; TT
Cosmos 1768 (1986–58A)	2 Aug. 0922	83 89	183 276	Lifetime 14 days; high resolution; Earth resources; data received by Priroda (Nature) Station
Cosmos 1770 (1986–60A)	6 Aug. 1326	65 90	209 303	Lifetime 180 days; high resolution; fifth generation
Cosmos 1772 (1986–63A)	21 Aug. 1102	73 90	197 244	Lifetime 13 days; medium resolution
Cosmos 1773 (1986–64A)	27 Aug. 1146	65 90	173 345	Lifetime 55 days; fourth generation; high resolution
Cosmos 1775 (1986–66A)	3 Sep. 0755	70 90	207 380	Lifetime 14 days; medium resolution
Cosmos 1781 (1986–72A)	17 Sep. 0755	70 91	207 383	Lifetime 14 days; medium resolution
Cosmos 1784 (1986–77A)	6 Oct. 0735	65 89	211 281	Lifetime 36 days; fourth generation; high resolution
Cosmos 1787 (1986–81A)	22 Oct. 0907	70 90	230 281	Lifetime 13 days; high resolution
Cosmos 1789 (1986–84A)	31 Oct. 0755	83 89	182 287	Lifetime 14 days; medium resolution; Earth resources
Cosmos 1790 (1986–85A)	4 Nov. 1200	73 90	195 288	Lifetime 14 days; high resolution
Cosmos 1792 (1986–87A)	13 Nov. 1102	65 90	173 335	Lifetime 53 days; high resolution; fourth generation
Cosmos 1804 (1986–95A)	4 Dec. 1019	70 92	347 415	Lifetime 14 days; medium resolution
Cosmos 1807 (1986–99A)	16 Dec. 1410	67 90	166 338	Lifetime 180 days; fourth generation; high resolution
Cosmos 1810 (1986–102A)	26 Dec. 1102	65 89	182 297	In orbit at the end of Dec. 1986; fourth or fifth generation
China				
China 19 (1986–76A)	6 Oct. 0546	57 90	172 387	Lifetime 5 days; hemispherical capsule weighing 1850 kg with a radius of 0.7 m, recovered on 11 Oct.

Table 3A.2. Possible electronic reconnaissance satellites launched during 1986

Country, satellite name and designation	Launch date and time (GMT)	Orbital inclination (deg) and period (min)	Perigee and apogee heights (km)	Comments
USSR				
Cosmos 1726	17 Jan.	83	632	Lifetime 60 years; in the same plane[a]
(1986–06A)	0726	98	663	as Cosmos 1606
Cosmos 1733	19 Feb.	83	633	Lifetime 60 years; in the same plane
(1986–18A)	2302	98	662	as Cosmos 1544
Cosmos 1743	15 May	83	633	Lifetime 60 years; in the same plane
(1986–34A)	0434	98	665	as Cosmos 1626
Cosmos 1758	12 June	83	631	Lifetime 60 years; in the same plane
(1986–46A)	0448	98	669	as Cosmos 1666
Cosmos 1782	30 Sep.	83	636	Lifetime 60 years; in the same plane
(1986–74A)	1843	98	664	as Cosmos 1733
Cosmos 1805	10 Dec.	83	635	Lifetime 60 years; possible orbital
(1986–97A)	0726	98	662	plane mid-way between the 6 planes of established constellation

[a] Ranft and Perry have shown that more than one satellite can be operational in each plane so it is therefore no longer advisable to speak of direct replacement. Ranft, C. and Perry, G. E., 'Capability of Soviet spy satellite', *Jane's Defence Weekly*, vol. 5, no. 17 (3 May 1986), p. 815.

Table 3A.3. Ocean surveillance and oceanographic satellites launched during 1986

Country, satellite name and designation	Launch date and time (GMT)	Orbital inclination (deg) and period (min)	Perigee and apogee heights (km)	Comments
USA				
USA 15,[a] Noss-7	9 Feb.	—	—	
(1986–14A)	1005	—	—	
USA 16	9 Feb.	—	—	Three associated sub-satellites
(1986–14E)	1005	—	—	
USA 17	9 Feb.	—	—	Three associated sub-satellites
(1986–14F)	1005	—	—	
USA 18	9 Feb.	—	—	Three associated sub-satellites
(1986–14H)	1005	—	—	
USSR				
Cosmos 1735	27 Feb.	65	406	EOSAT; functioning on 31 Dec. 1986
(1986–21A)	0141	93	416	
Cosmos 1736	21 Mar.	65	250	RORSAT moved to higher orbit on 21
(1986–24A)	1005	90	264	June; fragment 1986–24E is probably the uranium fuel core ejected from the nuclear reactor of 1986–24A
Cosmos 1737	25 Mar.	73	416	New type of EOSAT at different inclina-
(1986–25A)	1926	93	431	tion; de-orbited after 253 days
Cosmos 1766	28 June	83	635	Lifetime 60 years; oceanographic
(1986–55A)	2107	98	666	satellite; similar to Cosmos 1500 and 1602
Cosmos 1769	4 Aug.	65	429	EOSAT; functioning on 31 Dec. 1986
(1986–59A)	0502	93	444	
Cosmos 1771	20 Aug.	65	751	RORSAT moved into 104-min. higher
(1986–62A)	1258	90	263	orbit on 15 Oct.

[a] Orbital data similar to NOSS-6 (1983–56A).

Table 3A.4. Possible early-warning satellites launched during 1986

Country, satellite name and designation	Launch date and time (GMT)	Orbital inclination (deg) and period (min)	Perigee and apogee heights (km)	Comments
USSR				
Cosmos 1729 (1986–11A)	1 Feb. 1814	63 718	633 39733	Lifetime 100 years; replaced Cosmos 1569
Cosmos 1761 (1986–50A)	5 July 0176	63 717	599 39747	Lifetime 100 years; replaced Cosmos 1698
Cosmos 1774 (1986–65A)	28 Aug. 0755	63 707	599 39236	Lifetime 100 years; replaced Cosmos 1547
Cosmos 1783 (1986–75A)	3 Oct. 1258	63 358	598 20057	Failure to replace Cosmos 1661? but orbital period exactly half the normal one
Cosmos 1785 (1986–78A)	15 Oct. 0922	63 717	595 39741	Lifetime 100 years; replaced Cosmos 1596
Cosmos 1793 (1986–91A)	20 Nov. 1200	63 709	584 39337	Lifetime 100 years; replaced Cosmos 1687
Cosmos 1806 (1986–98A)	12 Dec. 1829	63 718	617 39730	Lifetime 100 years; replaced Cosmos 1729[a]

[a] Relocated on replacement by Cosmos 1806.

Table 3A.5. Meteorological satellites launched during 1986

Country, satellite name and designation	Launch date and time (GMT)	Orbital inclination (deg) and period (min)	Perigee and apogee heights (km)	Comments
USA				
GEOS	3 May	—	—	Delta rocket failed
—	—	—	—	
NOAA 10/ Atlas E (1986–73A)	17 Sep. 1550	99 101	808 826	Satellite also carried SARSAT payload
USSR				
Meteor 2–14 (1986–39A)	27 May 0936	83 104	941 960	Lifetime 1200 years

Table 3A.6. Communications satellites launched during 1986

Country, satellite name and designation	Launch date and time (GMT)	Orbital inclination (deg) and period (min)	Perigee and apogee heights (km)	Comments
USA				
TDRS	28 Jan.	—	—	Failed in space shuttle accident
—	1638	—	—	
USA 20				
FltSatCom 7	5 Dec.	5	35551	Will serve as a spare for two existing
(1986–96A)	0224	1436	36023	satellites; carried Milstar test payload
USSR				
Cosmos				
1716–1723	9 Jan.	74	1484	Octuple launch
(1986–2A–H)	0253	115	1484	
Cosmos 1741	17 Apr.	74	782	Store-dump communications satellite;
(1986–30A)	2107	101	811	in same plane[a] as Cosmos 1503
Cosmos				
1748–1755	6 June	74	1454	Octuple launch
(1986–42A–H)	0405	115	1470	
Cosmos 1763	16 July	74	757	Store-dump communications satellite;
(1986–52A)	0434	101	806	in same plane as Cosmos 1741, but orbital period of 100.5 min. rather than 100.8 min.
Molniya 1–67	30 July	63	623	Replaces Molniya 1–59
(1986–57A)	1507	736	40621	
Molniya 1–68	5 Sep.	63	638	Replaces Molniya 1–57; lifetime 15
(1986–68A)	0907	735	40547	years
Cosmos 1777	10 Sep.	74	777	Store-dump communications satellite;
(1986–70A)	0141	101	812	in same plane as Cosmos 1570
Molinya 1–69	15 Nov.	63	462	Replaces Molniya 1–60
(1986–89A)	2136	718	39898	
Cosmos				
1794–1801	20 Nov.	63	585	Octuple launch
(1986–92A–H)	1200	706	1480	
Molniya 1–70	26 Dec.	63	538	Replaces Molniya 1–62
(1986–103A)	1522	718	39578	

[a] Ranft and Perry have shown that more than one satellite could be operational in each plane so it is therefore no longer advisable to speak of direct replacement. 'Soviet satellite longevity', *Aviation Week & Space Technology*, vol. 125, no. 16 (20 Oct. 1986), p. 160.

Table 3A.7. Navigation satellites launched during 1986[a]

Country, satellite name and designation	Launch date and time (GMT)	Orbital inclination (deg) and period (min)	Perigee and apogee heights (km)	Comments
USSR				
Cosmos 1725	16 Jan.	83	972	Replaced Cosmos 1577; no. 5
(1986–5A)	1146	105	1003	
Cosmos 1727	23 Jan.	83	962	Replaced Cosmos 1506; no. 12
(1986–8A)	1858	105	1016	
Cosmos 1745	23 May	83	966	Replaced Cosmos 1627; no. 1
(1986–37A)	1258	105	1011	
Cosmos 1759	18 June	83	969	Replaced Cosmos 1634; no. 6
(1986–47A)	2010	105	1003	
Cosmos 1791	13 Nov.	83	953	Replaced Cosmos 1553; no. 11
(1986–86A)	0614	105	1014	
Cosmos 1802	24 Nov.	83	963	Replaced Cosmos 1605; no. 4
(1986–93A)	2150	105	1025	
Cosmos 1808	17 Dec.	83	973	Replaced Cosmos 1598; no. 3; Cosmos
(1986–100A)	1702	105	1020	1704 never actually replaced Cosmos 1598

[a] In 1986, the triple GLONAS satellites Cosmos 1778–1780 all stabilized their ground tracks and transmitted.

Table 3A.8. Possible geodetic satellites launched during 1986

Country, satellite name and designation	Launch date and time (GMT)	Orbital inclination (deg) and period (min)	Perigee and apogee heights (km)	Comments
USSR				
Cosmos 1732	11 Feb.	74	1480	Same as Cosmos 1589
(1986–15A)	0658	116	1526	
Cosmos 1803	2 Dec.	83	1496	Transmitted on 150.30 MHz like
(1986–94A)	0658	116	1500	Cosmos 1589 and Cosmos 1660

Table 3A.9. Possible interceptor/destructor or SDI-related satellites launched during 1986

Country, satellite name and designation	Launch date and time (GMT)	Orbital inclination (deg) and period (min)	Perigee and apogee heights (km)	Comments
USA				
USA 19	5 Sep.	29 (39)	206 (211)	SDI-related launch; satellite payloads
USAF/Thor	1507	89 (94)	228 (747)	separated into two which observed a
Delta				launch of Aries rocket from White
(1986–69A)				Sands, New Mexico, and then manoeuvred into collision courses destroying each other; the collision resulted in two clouds of debris, one in orbit and the other not (given in brackets)

Table 3A.10. Manned space flights during 1986

Country, satellite name and designation	Launch date and time (GMT)	Orbital inclination (deg) and period (min)	Perigee and apogee heights (km)	Comments
USA				
STS-61C (1986–03A)	12 Jan. 1155	28 91	324 346	Seventh flight of Columbia; carried a crew of seven including US Congressman Nelson; deployed SatCom K1 (1986–03B); lasted 5 days, 23 hours, 4 min.
STS-51L —	28 Jan. —	— —	— —	Crew of seven; exploded 72 seconds after launch, killing all the crew; carried TDRS-B
USSR				
Mir (1986–17A)	19 Feb. 2136	52 91	324 340	Manned space station module with 6 docking ports
Soyuz T15 (1986–22A)	13 Mar. 1229	52 90	239 289	Soyuz T15 docked with Mir with crew, Leonid Kizim and Vladimir Solovyev; it separated from Mir on 5 May and docked with Salyut 7 space station on 6 May; it left Salyut on 25 June and redocked with Mir on 26 June; Soyuz T15 was recovered on 16 July after 125 days, 1 min.
Soyuz TM1 (1986–35A)	21 May 0822	52 91	328 359	Test of new manned spacecraft; docked with Mir while the crew were in Soyuz; 9 days

4. Conventional weapon technologies

STEVEN L. CANBY, C & L Associates, Potomac, MD

Superscript numbers refer to the list of notes and references at the end of the chapter.

The Reykjavik summit meeting in October 1986 focused renewed attention on conventional forces. In its aftermath, reductions in central nuclear weapon systems were for the first time tied to the notion of stronger Western conventional forces in Europe and to conventional arms control. The West has a definite advantage *vis-à-vis* the East in conventional weapon technology. In recent years, this advantage has clearly grown and many in the West believe that technological superiority in weaponry can offset the East's several-fold advantage in *combat* numbers, active and mobilized.[1]

I. Resource management

Many also believe that equipment standardization and interoperability can yield major budgetary savings and flexibility in the upkeep of NATO forces. In the past decade this belief has led to a policy initiative that has been second only to the continued quest to *couple* US central strategic nuclear systems to the defence of Europe.

The Quayle and Nunn-Roth-Warner amendments to the fiscal year (FY) 1986 US budget were meant to stimulate weapon harmonization. The first amendment eased constraints on Pentagon structuring of co-operative programmes. The second earmarked $200 million for NATO co-operative programmes in research and development (R&D) projects and an additional $50 million for parallel testing of Allied and US systems. This initiative led NATO armaments directors to sponsor six multinational development projects:

(*a*) a system to demonstrate stand-off airborne radar for surveillance and target acquisition;

(*b*) a 'fire and forget' terminally guided 155-mm shell;

(*c*) question and answer components for the NATO Identification System;

(*d*) a multi-function information distribution system;

(*e*) a modular stand-off weapon programme; and

(*f*) a support environment for the Ada high-level computer language.

The FY 1987 US budget gives these initiatives new status (e.g., the Senate's Balanced Technology Initiative, the House's Conventional Defense Initiative, and a Senate proposal to earmark $50 million in Strategic Defense Initiative (SDI) funds for exploration of anti-tactical ballistic missile systems on a co-operative basis with US allies).[2] Overall the USA has budgeted $2.9 billion until the end of 1992 on its NATO Armaments Cooperation Initiative, and reciprocal commitments are expected from European allies.

The 1986 initiatives moved technology and weapon modernization forward on familiar paths. The 1987 initiatives by contrast reflect the dynamism in emerging technologies and a shift in national approaches to the development and military application of high technology. Increasingly industry is setting the pace. Change has become so rapid that the military has become a follower rather than an initiator, and is criticized for being too slow and unable to capitalize on kaleidoscopic developments. In the USA the pace is set by competitive forces in research parks such as Silicon Valley near Palo Alto, California, Highway 128 in Boston, and the Research Triangle in Durham-Raleigh, North Carolina. In Europe, reflecting a perceived technology lag behind the USA and Japan, governments have been active. The European Economic Community is sponsoring ESPRIT (European Strategic Program for Research in Information Technology), RACE (Research into Advanced Communications Technologies in Europe) and BRITE (Basic Research in Industrial Technologies for Europe). France is separately sponsoring Eureka (a European research programme).

This new approach to R&D was crystallized by the US Strategic Defense Initiative and the subsequent European Air Defense (EAD) programme. Even if SDI and EAD do not bear fruit directly, there will be many spin-offs, both civilian and military. Rather than sponsoring its own research programmes the military is increasingly gathering and integrating the many developments occurring in diverse fields into updated components for familiar weapon systems—for example, the US Army's LHX helicopter family and the various NATO advanced tactical fighter aircraft—and occasionally into new systems of novel application, such as the Osprey tiltrotor Advanced Vertical Lift Aircraft programme which combines the essential features of helicopters and fixed-wing aircraft in one vehicle.

II. New technologies

The logic behind this shift derives from several general characteristics of modern technologies:[3]

1. Though diverse, they are nevertheless closely interrelated. Breakthroughs occur simultaneously over a broad front of applications and overlap in ways that are largely unanticipated, thus reinforcing each other and making cross-fertilization by interaction and information exchange a vital part of the process. To a large extent the new technologies are component-oriented, making the innovation process less rigid and more entrepreneurial and blurring ever more the distinction between civilian and military technologies.[4]

2. They tend to be highly fragmented. Because a better understanding of small parts of a larger process, or the availability of higher-performance materials for a particular function in a large ensemble, often gives a decisive edge over competitors, speciality knowledge is in demand.

3. They tend towards finite, comparatively short lifetimes. End products evolve continuously as new techniques are developed, recognized and incorporated. Most change is evolutionary, though revolutionary end products such as the fibre-optic guided missile (see below) occasionally appear.

These general characteristics of modern high technologies have two closely related consequences: (*a*) they are not necessarily produced and used within the same company, group or nation; and (*b*) they are by their very nature highly tradeable. There is an international market for them, and their ease of trade makes them difficult to secure.

III. Military modernization

Modern civilian and military technologies blend together into military applications. A short list includes:

(*a*) advanced composite materials for various desirable properties;

(*b*) genetic engineering for vaccines, casualty treatment and chemical/biological warfare;

(*c*) sensors of various types for target detection, identification and terminal homing under diverse conditions;

(*d*) very high speed integrated circuits (VHSIC) for data processing, with improved performance as a result of advances in materials such as gallium arsenide;

(*e*) artificial intelligence/robotic intelligence-management systems to analyse data as well as to undertake hazardous tasks.

Such applications of developing technology are the basis for the continual upgrading and modernization of specific military equipment, in both East and West. Each tank, fighter aircraft and ship can be viewed as a composite of attributes such as weight, range, rate of fire, and so on. The aim of modernization is to improve each attribute, sometimes by updating old platforms with new subsystems and components and sometimes by introducing new designs of old systems with the same set of attributes. Only occasionally is a revolutionary system with novel attributes developed. Such developments lead to large initial pay-offs, which eventually diminish as tactical and technological countermeasures are developed. As deficiencies emerge the developments are updated, but subsequent pay-offs are inevitably marginal.

Modern military forces are constantly updating their equipment. Part of this modernization is from 'technology push' to incorporate capabilities that become available. Most is from specific calls for technology to overcome identified deficiencies, creating the kind of action/reaction arms race that has been popularized in air warfare and is perhaps best typified today in anti-submarine and anti-tank warfare.

Ground and anti-tank warfare

The primary potential targets within the Soviet ground force array are hard mobile targets, some 53 000 tanks and 87 000 armoured fighting and self-propelled artillery vehicles. There are another 22 000 armoured vehicles in the East German, Polish and Czechoslovakian forces.[5] Because NATO's combat numbers are far smaller, anti-tank capabilities have always been a prime NATO concern.

A decade ago it looked as if NATO's anti-tank problem might be solved by the introduction of an improved generation of precision-guided munitions (PGMs). PGMs gave high-performance aircraft and artillery a point-kill potential rather than just an area fire capability, and PGMs of various ranges and lethality provided the infantry with a qualitative and quantitative anti-tank capability it lacked. However, terminally guided single-warhead systems, such as the Maverick missile for the Air Force and Copperhead shells for artillery forces, have not always worked well. The first proved technically poor, while the second has suffered from operational hurdles.

The driving forces behind the development of precision-guided munitions are the need to minimize exposure of the launcher and, where infra-red (IR) seekers are used, to replace them by less easily countered systems. The most appropriate technologies are imaging infra-red (IIR), millimetre-wave radar (MMW) and active laser seekers. Active lasers provide an imaging system which also gives information about the range and velocity of targets. MMW technology is faced with problems of ground clutter and detecting non-moving targets, and of reducing seeker diameter. Because there are countermeasures against seekers, some effort is being directed to the development of 'dual' seekers which combine the best features of both technologies in a single unit. Irrespective of the guidance system used, it is still necessary to develop algorithms able to process the vast amount of information available from the seeker in real time. VHSIC technology will increasingly allow more sophisticated and discriminating algorithms, making autonomous munitions more feasible.

Close combat weapons

Western infantry weapons were simple and robust and worked well initially. They are now threatened by Soviet technical advances in armour plating and weapons with stand-off ranges and greater use of suppressive fire. These same advances have also reduced the effectiveness of Western tank gunnery, forcing new Abrams, Challenger, LeClerk and Leopard tanks to mount more powerful 120-mm main guns instead of 105-mm guns which permit higher rates of fire and more on-board ammunition than the larger guns.

For ground weapons (including new West German mast-mounted PGMs), the difficulty in attacking tanks head-on is the pacing deficiency; tank guns lack the necessary kinetic energy, and the shaped-charge warheads of anti-tank missiles lack the requisite penetrating power. On Soviet tanks the frontal armour (which is slanted to add strength) has been enhanced by greater thickness and improved metallurgy against kinetic-energy penetrators and by new armouring techniques (applique and reactive armour) against shaped charges. These latter features have also been added to older tanks and some infantry fighting vehicles, giving them considerably more protection at manageable cost in weight against shaped charges.

A second pacing deficiency is the vulnerability of PGM crews during the time of missile flight. This is most pronounced for tripod-mounted and shoulder-fired missiles of the TOW, Milan and Dragon variety. Although some crew-protection measures have been taken—such as separating the launch system from the operator—the crews are still too vulnerable to indirect enemy fire and to direct counterfire during the many seconds of missile flight. Indirect fire remains a problem; the effect of direct counterfire has been reduced by improved propellants to reduce launch and flight signatures and to shorten flight times. The vulnerability of light armoured vehicles firing PGMs has largely been reduced by elevating the PGM launch pods above the vehicle. The US Army raises the launch pods by a few feet whereas the West German Army now has special vehicles with extended masts, which raise the launch pods above the trees and buildings behind which the crews are shielded.

The technological problem for tanks and PGM-firing infantry is warhead lethality against the frontal armour. For kinetic-energy penetrators, the technical objectives are ever higher velocities, flight stability and still denser penetrator cores such as depleted uranium for better impact energy. For shaped charges the technical objectives are more refined design, more even detonation pressure, and denser metal liners for improved penetration.

Artillery

Artillery has long been the primary weapon for attacking targets immediately beyond the close battle. Artillery is by nature an area fire system. Its effectiveness against armoured formations lies in incapacitating the less-protected support vehicles and in restricting tank visibility and ease of movement. Terminally guided warheads give artillery, rockets and large mortars an accuracy suitable for attacking armour on an individual round basis.

The Copperhead laser-guided round gives artillery an important additional capability. But the rounds have proved expensive to produce because it is difficult to make them rugged enough to be fired from a cannon, and there are hidden costs and difficulties. Incapacitating tanks with artillery is a convoluted process: the tank must be lased (illuminated) by a line-of-sight observer, the sighting must be processed through the artillery fire control centre and finally the shell guided to the target. During the minutes this requires under the best of circumstances, the observer's line-of-sight may be broken and the target may move beyond the shell's 'footprint' or cone of impact. If the area is obscured by smoke or dust, or is overcast, the Copperhead shell may not sense the laser reflection and guidance will fail.

The driving consideration in this programme has been to lower the unit cost of the guided shell to below $25 000 from the present unit cost (after considerable production) of $50 000. Projects under way seek to shorten the time lags between target detection by the observer and gun firing. Sightings by forward observers are now automated by lasers, which gives greater range estimation accuracy and speeds data transmission. A small computer—the Battlefield Computing System (BCS)—has also been developed so that individual guns can be 'dedicated' to Copperhead shells in order to speed firing and to reduce the disruptive effects of dedication upon the remainder of the gun battery. From a technological perspective, the important initiatives are artillery tube and rocket submunitions for potential multiple kills and fire-and-forget terminal guidance (e.g., the Sense and Destroy Armor (SADARM) system which disperses several submunitions per shell). The latter permits removing a line-of-sight forward observer from the loop and adding sensors capable of locking on to targets in conditions too obscured for lasers. Such automation is not cheap, however, and increases their vulnerability to countermeasures.

Interdiction

The classic function of tactical air forces has been interdiction. The US Air Force (USAF) has been oriented to close air support of battlefield forces and deep interdiction of enemy supply lines. European air forces have been oriented to battlefield interdiction between these ranges (roughly 10 to 100 km) with a focus on enemy reserves along key axes. This distinction underlays the differences in US and European perceptions of the deep-strike or follow-on-forces attack (FOFA) concept launched in 1982 by NATO's Supreme Allied Commander, Europe (SACEUR).[6]

Europeans have a focused concept of FOFA along key axes both to conserve expensive assets (whether aircraft or missiles) and to affect the centre of gravity (*Schwerpunkt*) of enemy operations. From the European viewpoint, the purpose of airpower is to isolate enemy forces, particularly reserves, so that they can be defeated piecemeal by manoeuvre and counter-attack. In contrast, SACEUR and the US Defense Science Board community would choose to target reinforcing Warsaw Pact formations (second echelons) while they are still several hundred kilometres from the battlefield, thus seeking to control the ratio of forces in actual contact. Theirs is a firepower/attrition concept of war, often confused with the US Army's new doctrine of AirLand Battle which is more in accordance with the European view. More than 100 km beyond the front line of battle there can be no discernible *Schwerpunkt* because of the density of the European road network. Deep FOFA would therefore waste expensive long-range missiles on targets of varied value.

The European approach calls for *emerged* technology, that is, technology in hand, tested and readily produced in Europe. The demands on target acquisition for European FOFA are relatively modest. Man stays 'in the loop' and the use of remotely piloted vehicles (RPVs) flying along identified axes is the preferred method of acquisition. It is relatively cheap and robust. Deep FOFA on the other hand requires *emerging* technology. Because of the distances involved and the time needed for launching and missile flight, data processing must be carried out in near real time and guidance can be provided to the missile in flight. This means that the process must be automated and that pre-packaged algorithms must be provided for interpreting data. This technology is not cheap, it can be readily spoofed and countered, and it is mostly of US origin. Examples of emerging technology, mostly associated with target acquisition and data processing, include:

1. The Advanced Synthetic Aperture Radar System II (ASARS II): a USAF high-resolution ground surveillance imagery radar system, which can locate and classify stationary objects.

2. The Precision Location Strike System (PLSS): an airborne surveillance

and control system intended to detect, identify and accurately locate enemy radar transmitters and some types of radar jammer very rapidly and to guide weapons or aircraft with sufficient accuracy to destroy them.

3. The Joint Surveillance and Target Attack Radar System (JSTARS): an airborne radar system intended to locate fixed or moving targets on the ground and to control attacks against such targets using aircraft or guided munitions.

4. The Joint Tactical Fusion programme: a data processing system designed to collect, combine, correlate, interpret and display an unfolding battle instantaneously so commanders can select the optimum response to a specific class of targets.

In other respects the technologies for the European and SACEUR versions of FOFA are similar. The delivery medium for FOFA in the immediate future will be existing aircraft and missiles. For aircraft the emphasis is on stand-off missiles like the Franco-German inertial-guided Apache (fitted with various warheads) to avoid local air defences. For missiles, which will be preferred in the future, the principal delivery means today is the US Multiple Launch Rocket System (MLRS), which European countries are procuring. The MLRS will be updated by the US Army to fire the Army Tactical Missile System (ATACMS), a larger and longer-range missile with one missile per canister instead of the present six. Subsequent upgrading may include a mechanism for receiving target course corrections while in flight.[7]

Terminal-guided submunitions are also similar. The principal warhead will be the Terminal Guided Submunition (TGSM) which is about the size of a 105-mm howitzer shell. Smaller submunitions like Skeet (a small, puck-sized, terminally fired, shaped charge-like self-forging penetrator) have proved insufficiently powerful against thin top armour when armoured vehicles are moving in non-combat circumstances far from the line of battle and can mount simple countermeasures. In addition the Skeet's small diameter and the need to deploy large numbers make sensors more sophisticated than simple IR and MMW impractical. (As a rule of thumb, 70–80 per cent of any guided missile's cost is in its seeker and guidance system. Sensor-fused weapons like self-forging fragments do not require sensing conversions to mechanical linkages for steering to the target. On the other hand their footprint is orders of magnitude smaller and their lethality is less. A Skeet submunition accordingly costs $1000 as compared to $20 000-50 000 for a TGSM.)[8]

Mines

Mines have traditionally been valued more for their barrier than their casualty potential. In the past minefields have been placed on the immediate battlefield or behind its front line principally for slowing or channelling an advance. With progress in dispensing mines remotely—by aircraft, rockets and artillery—and with advances in fusing and lethality, minefields can now be surreptitiously created behind enemy lines. Because even mixed (anti-tank and anti-personnel with diverse fusings) minefields can be readily cleared when they are not covered by gunfire, remotely delivered minefields are likely to assume a new form and purpose. Since their purpose is no longer as a barrier, they will be seeded for low density in order to produce casualties and to induce fear by their omnipresence. That is, while large minefields may be thrown up remotely as barriers across penetration fronts or for delaying and dividing immediate reinforcements, deeper minefields are likely to be of the nature of many small low-density patches which enemy combat and supply columns will repeatedly trigger unless areas are continuously swept by engineer units.

The latest in mine development is the Extended Range Antiarmor Mine (ERAM), which indicates the direction in which mine technology is heading: ability to control a wide area (and thus the ability to command a road from a concealed position to one side), to discriminate between tanks and lower-value targets, and to attack the tops of tanks. A single ERAM dispenser of nine mines places them in a ground pattern typically 200 to 300 metres long. ERAM uses a seismic sensor to switch on three acoustic sensors. Together, these can determine the location of the tank and its speed and direction, and can distinguish between tanks and other vehicles. ERAM fires a Skeet submunition with an IR warhead.[9]

Attack helicopters

In the past decade, first with wire-guided PGMs and more recently with laser-guided fire-and-forget PGMs (Hellfire), attack helicopters have become major anti-tank weapons, as well as platforms for attacking area targets. The latest demand on Western helicopter weaponry is to meet the need for self-defence against other helicopters, the Soviet Hind models in particular. This deficiency is being met by mounting air-to-air heat-seeking Sidewinder and Stinger missiles on to existing helicopters.

The US Army remains the technological leader in helicopters (with the USSR close behind, though on a somewhat different track). The current US helicopter undergoing modernization, the Apache (AH-64), is significantly superior to the US Cobra (AH-1) in all-weather operations, target acquisition and general lethality.

The US Army's proposed new $40 billion light helicopter family (LHX), its scout/attack (SCAT) version in particular, illustrates the modernization process and the way advances in diverse technologies are pulled together: better engines, especially engine controls; better aerodynamics, especially blade design; composite materials; much improved flight controls and information displays; greatly improved navigation, sensors and processing capability; much better simulators for design and training; and on-board maintenance techniques.[10] As in most modernizations, sponsors also claim drastic reductions in operations and maintenance (O&M) costs, in this case by half.

Perhaps untypical is the criticism engendered by the LHX programme from within the Defense Science Board community itself. First, many see it as a push for modernization for the sake of modernization, whether the need exists or not. Second, they doubt if the touted O&M savings will materialize because of the complexity of the new technologies, the SCAT in particular. Third, they note that the LHX programme is driven by questionable requirements like (a) an ability to fly themselves (instead of being transported) along a southern route from the USA to Europe, (b) a small radar cross-section in a combat environment in which radar-directed enemy systems are not the primary predator, and (c) a fully Automatic Target Recognition (ATR) capability.[11]

Indeed with ATR, the attack helicopters have come full circle from being low cost and high (military) value to high cost and redundant usefulness. Why mount an ATR in a manned, state-of-the-art helicopter platform merely for shooting a fire-and-forget missile? Fibre optics allow virtually the same capability to be incorporated in a kamikaze RPV no larger than a long Copperhead shell with stubby wings and extended fins.

IV. A revolutionary capability: fibre-optic guided missiles

The FOG-M fibre-optic guided missile was the most significant technological development to come to the fore in 1986. A similar missile (POLYPHEM) is under joint development by the West German MBB and French Aérospatiale companies; and Sweden is developing a mortar projectile with a fibre optic link. The US FOG-M and the West German-French POLYPHEM are essentially video-equipped RPVs with a zoom lens suitable for reconnaissance and attacking tanks and helicopters up to distances of 10 km and possibly more if the fibre's tensile strength is increased. They cost $20 000, weigh 50 kg and fly at speeds of more than 700 km per hour at an altitude of 200 m. The Swedish version amounts to a visually guided Copperhead, eliminating the need for a forward observer to lase the target.

FOG-Ms have many advantageous (even unique) features:

1. *Logistically*, they are very cheap, operators are easy to train, they can be proliferated, and they can be easily transported and supported.

2. *Tactically*, they can be fired inconspicuously from protected positions well to the rear (e.g., from within towns and forests), they can be used for (slow flying) reconnaissance and target search, and they can find and be steered to hit enemy targets themselves in supposedly safe positions.

3. *Operationally*, they can be readily concentrated and deployed along key axes to support attack or defence (which is the flexibility argument underlying much of the rationale for tactical airpower and the attack helicopter). They can also be used to bolster the firepower of specific sectors. As reinforcements in the midst of battle, their use is easy to co-ordinate with forces already in position because their range allows them to engage 'follow-on-forces' (in this case to help in 'force-ratio' management along critical axes). Their use in this regard releases tactical aviation and artillery for other tasks such as attacking enemy artillery and infantry.

4. *Technically*, they are robust (i.e., jam-proof and difficult to counter), they attack the tank at its weakest point—the top—with a relatively large warhead, and they have considerable growth potential. They can mount more sophisticated seekers without undue cost penalties because data processing and required decisions can be fed to the ground control station via an extraordinarily cheap and secure fibre-optic data link. For example, the system can be expanded to all-weather configurations to control several missiles in the

air simultaneously. And as automatic target-recognition technology matures, the system could accommodate a target-recognition capability allowing faster missiles than those currently limited by human reaction time.

FOG-M is thus an example of that rare blending of new technologies that produces novel applications. In so doing, it greatly simplifies many tasks, some of which could not otherwise be done regardless of cost and complexity. Indeed FOG-M was earlier rejected because of its threatening characteristics to the tank and engineering communities. It came to the fore because of an urgent need to correct a deficiency: the DIVAD Air Defense Gun proved unable to detect and attack helicopters hovering and flying close to the ground in the presence of jamming countermeasures. Its pulse-doppler radar, with moving-target-indicator processing, had excellent track-while-scan characteristics. The radar could not, however, handle the combination of jamming and multi-path returns that the practical (and cluttered) battlefield produced. Moreover, even if this had not occurred, the DIVAD would have been an operational failure because its gun and radar were collocated. That is, enemy helicopters could detect the DIVAD and attack forward tanks from areas in their line-of-sight while themselves remaining in safe spaces, shielded by terrain from the DIVAD's radar.[12] In addition because of the cost and vulnerability of radars, DIVAD systems were few in number and operated from overwatch positions to the rear of forward armour. Attack helicopters could accordingly stand-off and destroy exposed armour with impunity.

The search for a system to fill the resulting void led to the selection of the FOG-M missile, then in advanced development for anti-tank application. FOG-M is designed to fly with enough of a vertical trajectory to attack tanks from the top where the armour gains no effective thickness from the effects of obliquity. This trajectory matched that needed for attacking the hovering, masked helicopter.

If armies can overcome the problem of service branch conflict (the air-defence soldier cannot fire at tanks, and the infantry soldier cannot fire at aircraft), FOG-M can help meet both air defence and anti-armour require-ments. It is a weapon which favours the defender: it makes (tank) movement increasingly vulnerable on the modern battlefield. FOG-M is to the tank as the machine-gun bullet was to the infantry of 1914.

V. In perspective

With a few exceptions such as the FOG-M, conventional modernization continued in 1986 along the familiar lines of the past decade. During these years, Western modernization has sought to offset Eastern quantitative superiority with qualitative technological superiority. The empirical result has been a relative growth of Eastern conventional strength and a greater numerical imbalance of forces. In the West too, a new term has gained currency: structural disarmament. This occurs when force structure is cut in order to pay for ever costlier weapons. In the past decade this effect has been mostly offset by NATO's 3 per cent annual real increase in defence budgets. This goal is now falling by the wayside. In addition, countries like the Federal

Republic of Germany have been forced to reduce their active duty strengths according to the realities of their demographic situations.

Barring major budgetary increases or sharp departures in type of weaponry, technology is unlikely to redress the East-West conventional imbalance. Nor are the much touted Alliance co-operative programmes likely to save much either. The first is apparent from the nature of Lanchester's formulation: quality has the nature of a linear parameter, while quantity is squared. Given that the East obtains several times more combat equipment for the same overall strength as the West, the West's technology would have to be nearly an order of magnitude better in order to offset its *organizational* deficiency. That is clearly a tall order. Second, weapon standardization cannot lead to major savings. So far, it has *increased* costs. In principle, scale economies could lower costs by as much as 20 per cent of Alliance weapon investments. Given that these investments average about 20 per cent of national defence budgets, standardization in production can only obtain a *one-time* lowering of the level of Alliance costs by 4 per cent, and a similar amount from co-operative R&D. Clearly if 3 per cent annual growth was insufficient to arrest structural disarmament, *a fortiori* for standardization and the touted co-operative programmes. NATO must ask itself how the USSR can produce so much more equipment on a smaller budget (dollars or roubles) than the Alliance. The answer lies not in the productivity of their capital and labour. The answer lies in the comparative organization of the production process.

Notes and references

[1] The Eastern advantage lies only in combat numbers. In all other respects NATO, including French forces, is quantitatively superior to the Warsaw Pact, i.e., in terms of total resources and even peacetime military budgets and military strengths.

[2] Delpech, J-F., *New Technologies, the United States and Europe: Implications for Western Security and Economic Growth* (Woodrow Wilson International Center for Scholars, Smithsonian Institution: Washington, DC, Dec. 1986), pp. 19–20.

[3] For a detailed discussion of these points, see Delpech (note 2), pp. 3–9.

[4] Before 1935 most military applications of technology were from civilian systems. See van Creveld, M., *Technology and War* (C & L Associates: Potomac, MD, 1987, forthcoming).

[5] IISS, *The Military Balance 1986–1987* (IISS: London, 1986).

[6] For an examination of these issues see Canby, S. L., *Follow-on Forces Attack: European Perceptions* (C & L Associates: Potomac, MD, Aug. 1986). For details of the technical issues, see Canby, S. L., *New Conventional Force Technology and the Warsaw Pact Balance: The Operational Limits of Emerging Technology*, Adelphi Paper No. 198 (IISS: London, Summer 1985).

[7] For an unclassified discussion of technological programmes in support of FOFA, see Office of Technology Assessment (OTA), *Technologies for NATO's Follow-On Forces Attack Concept*, A Special Report of OTA's Assessment on Improving NATO's Defense Response, Office of Technology Assessment, US Congress, Washington, DC, July 1986.

[8] OTA (note 7), pp. 31–32.

[9] OTA (note 7), pp. 33–34.

[10] *Report of the Defense Science Board Task Force on LHX Requirements*, Office of the Under Secretary of Defense for Research and Engineering, Washington, DC, Aug. 1986, p. 7.

[11] Note 10, pp. 8 and 17–20.

[12] For a discussion of this and other operational limitations of the DIVAD system, see Canby, S. L., 'High-tech, high-fail defense: US military loses sight of real combat and laws of physics', *Los Angeles Times*, 16 Sep. 1985, Op Ed page.

5. Chemical and biological warfare: developments in 1986

J. P. PERRY ROBINSON, Science Policy Research Unit, University of Sussex, UK

Superscript numbers refer to the list of notes and references at the end of the chapter.

The field of chemical and biological warfare (CBW) was unusually active during 1986. Some of the developments of 1986 are recorded briefly here.[1] The chapter begins with a recapitulation of the current CBW arms control regime, for its underlying theme is of that regime coming under increasing threat.

I. The CBW arms control regime

Use of CBW weapons is prohibited by international law, principally the 1925 Geneva Protocol. Most states are parties to this treaty, although about a quarter of them, including the USSR and the USA, have reserved the right to retaliate in kind against violators. Efforts have long been continuing to broaden the prohibition of use into a universal ban on the weapons themselves. In the 1972 Biological Weapons Convention (BWC), these efforts succeeded insofar as weapons based on infective agents and a group of toxic agents[2] were concerned. Still under negotiation is the projected 'chemical weapons convention' (CWC), a treaty whose effect would be to extend the disarmament regime established by the BWC to the remaining weapons covered by the use-prohibition, strengthening the regime in the process with additional verification machinery.

The chemical talks proceeded at several different levels during the year: multilateral (within the Conference on Disarmament (CD) in Geneva), trilateral[3] and bilateral. There was real progress. A part of it is registered in the draft CWC set out in the annual report of the CD *Ad Hoc* Committee on Chemical Weapons,[4] described in chapter 11 below. Much of the progress remains undisclosed, however, forming the basis for the more private negotiating efforts that underpinned the work of the CD and which will presumably continue during 1987; the bilateral US-Soviet 'consultations',[5] for example, and such other activities as the Anglo-Soviet contacts on challenge inspection. In terms of yielding a CWC to which all governments would be prepared to commit themselves, this diplomacy still has a long way to go. Given their present momentum, the negotiations seem set to take at least another two or three years to resolve all the component issues. The possibility of interim measures, such as an agreement in principle[6] or the establishment of chemical weapon-free zones,[7] is being increasingly discussed.

II. Continued violation of the Geneva Protocol by Iraq

Iraq continued to use chemical warfare (CW) in its war with Iran, despite international condemnation. What appears to have been a new peak of intensity was reached during the second week of February 1986, when around 10 per cent of a large Iranian force attacking Faw fell casualty to CW weapons; some 2000 people are said to have been burned with mustard gas on 13 February alone.[8] Once again the United Nations Secretary-General sent in a team of investigators, which once again provided conclusive verification.[9] And once again reports of Iraqi use continued to be heard after the investigators had left and after the UN Security Council had uttered a rebuke.

The British Government has said that it believes there to have been at least 10 000 Iranian CW casualties in the war thus far.[10] Despite such devastation, there is as yet little clear evidence of Iraq's CW weapons in fact having bought significant military benefit, even as a counter to 'human wave' assaults.

III. Allegations of non-compliance with the CBW treaties

Allegations of states violating or failing to comply with their commitments under the treaties dealing with CBW and CBW weapons were as numerous in 1986 as in previous years. A summary is presented in table 5.1. Only in the case of the Iraqi chemical warfare was there conclusive international verification.

In contrast to earlier years, the accusations which the superpowers directed at each other were muted. It is true that during the first part of the year there had been a noticeable crescendo in statements by US officials alleging Soviet non-compliance with the BWC, reaching its peak in testimony submitted to a congressional committee (apparently unsolicited) from the Office of Assistant Defense Secretary Richard Perle in August,[11] during the run-up to the Second BWC Review Conference. But the equally noticeable diminuendo thereafter suggested that there had been private US-Soviet contacts on the matter prior to the review conference.

It is now widely held that the evidence underlying Washington's past accusations of Soviet CBW-treaty non-compliance is far less reliable than had originally been asserted. This is so for the evidence concerning the Sverdlovsk anthrax outbreak of 1979 and the equation of the South-East Asian 'yellow rain' with Soviet-supported mycotoxin warfare. It was reported during 1986 that the evidence which Washington says it has of Soviet toxic warfare in Afghanistan had recently been called into question after scrutiny by a panel of the Defense Science Board.[12]

IV. The US binary munitions programme

On 14 November 1986, when President Reagan signed into law a 1987 Defense Authorization Act that had been successfully defended against certain arms control amendments, his Administration finally gained the authority which it had been seeking since 1982 to commit US taxpayers' money to quantity production of CW weapons, abandoning a *de facto* US moratorium that had been in place since the summer of 1969. The Administration had long been maintaining that the existing US stockpile of CW weapons did not provide sufficient in-kind deterrence to a Soviet threat which it had been portraying as large and growing. Two types of binary munition were to be bought: the M687 artillery projectile, which is a 155-mm howitzer round for spreading agent GB (sarin), a non-persistent nerve gas, and Bigeye, which is a 500-lb class aircraft bomb for spraying agent VX, a persistent nerve gas.

US chemical-warfare rearmament is thus set to commence rather soon. According to the 1987 Act, 'final assembly of complete' Bigeyes may not take place before 1 October 1988, while any such production of complete M687 munitions prior to 1 October 1987 is precluded by the 1986 Act (strictures that had been portrayed as inducements to accelerate the CWC negotiations). But what is to be understood by 'final assembly' is not at all clear. If it means no more than the final insertion of the second binary-reactant container into the munition, those two dates have little practical significance: the whole point of a binary munition, so the US Army has been saying, is that it enhances safety by allowing its chemical components to be stored separately until immediately before use. Presumably something more is indeed meant, for the Congress had been informed well before it acted on the Fiscal Year 1986 defence budget that the M687 production line then ready in Louisiana would be turning out projectiles loaded with canisters containing OPA (one of the two binary chemicals),[13] in other words, virtually complete munitions. The canisters filled with DF—the other binary chemical—will be produced in Arkansas. The data in table 5.2 indicate that quantity production of M687 rounds could begin well before 1 October 1987, but that quantity production of the Bigeye would probably be impossible before 1 October 1988.

By the end of 1986, the US Congress had effectively abandoned its opposition in principle to chemical rearmament. For the first of the binary munitions, the M687, congressional support of the Administration's programme was now complete, and opposition to the second, the Bigeye, persisted less because it was a poison-gas weapon than because it seemed to be an inefficient and unreliable one. In fact this acquiescence had actually come in December 1985, when initial production funding for the M687 had been appropriated but—in a device designed to minimize the vote against the appropriation—fenced until the President could certify that, among other things, NATO had signified support for the programme by adopting an appropriate 'force goal'. Since such an action on the part of NATO was effectively under the control of the US Administration (unless the government of one of the European allies chose to make an issue of it), this stipulation was most unlikely to mean more than a short delay, however much its wording suggested that European political leaders, and therefore parliaments too, would be involving themselves in the matter. On 29 July 1986, President Reagan duly made the requisite certification to the Congress that the NATO requirements had been fulfilled.

By that time the Congress was nearing the stage of definitive action on the 1987 defence budget. As is shown in table 5.3, the funding sought in the budget for initial production of binary munitions was five times greater than the fenced appropriation of the previous year. There were moves within the Congress to delete the 1987 binary funding and to de-appropriate the 1986 funding. In attenuated form this resistance persisted into the House-Senate conference on the Defence Authorization bills, but there it finally ran foul of the politics associated with the suddenly imminent Reagan-Gorbachev meeting in Reykjavik.[14] More than 80 per cent of the initial production funding of some $117 million was eventually approved.

So by the end of 1986 the Pentagon had both the production capacity and the funding for manufacturing at least 100 000 rounds of new nerve-gas artillery ammunition,[15] a quantity comparable to the existing non-binary stockpile in FR Germany. It also had funding, albeit fenced (see table 5.3), for maybe 500 rounds of Bigeye—an asset, however, of uncertain value, given the uncomplimentary evaluation of the performance of the weapon in developmental testing which issued from the General Accounting Office (GAO) in May.[16] The Pentagon subsequently accepted much of the GAO criticism but maintained its position that the test results were nonetheless good enough to justify the decision in favour of low-rate initial production. A decision on full-rate production would not be taken until operational testing had been completed using low-rate production rounds. The GAO will be continuing to monitor the test programme.

V. 'The NATO chemical deterrent'

The 'force goal' on which the 1986 US Defense Authorization Act had made the future of the binary-munitions programme dependent was, in the words of the Act, to be one 'stating the requirement for modernization of the United States proportional share of the NATO chemical deterrent with binary munitions'. In fact there was no such thing as a 'NATO chemical deterrent', except on paper. There is a passage in the Alliance's (well-known though classified) 'forward defense, flexible response' strategy document (MC 14/3 of 1967) which states that NATO is to keep open an option for limited retaliation in kind as a means subsidiary to conventional and nuclear forces for deterring enemy chemical-warfare attack. But this option has remained unimplemented, not least because no member state has committed CW forces to NATO:[17] that is, French and US chemical agents are under exclusively national control.

Since about 1980, pressure for implementation had been growing within the NATO bureaucracy, apparently stimulated by the US Army. Its effects were largely confined to the military side prior to 1986, although General Rogers as Supreme Allied Commander, Europe (SACEUR) had initiated formal procedures whereby the political authorities would eventually be compelled to consider CW weapons. Implementation would involve action on all sorts of politically most delicate matters: not only the supply of CW weapons, but also their deployment and storage in Europe, as well as release procedures for them. The European politicians who, together with their transatlantic counterparts, comprise the political authorities of NATO have, understandably, long been reluctant to expose themselves and their staffs to all this. But the 'force goal' language in the US legislation, with its provocative talk of a 'NATO chemical deterrent', now compelled them to do so.

General Rogers put a draft force goal before his colleagues on the NATO Military Committee, which approved it on 13 February 1986. Over the next several weeks, the draft was revised until the international staff had found a form of words which would be acceptable to the defence ministers sitting on the NATO Defence Planning Committee. The ministers formally took note of it on 22 May as one of 1500-odd NATO *Force Goals for 1987–92*, their ambassadors having approved it on 15 May. The text is secret, but the account that has been published by the British Government suggests that it says nothing about a 'NATO chemical deterrent', still less a 'US proportional share' of such a thing; it merely invites the United States to modernize its CW-weapon stocks with binary munitions. The text does, however, refer to the CW provisions of MC 14/3, provisions which the force goal thereby reaffirms. It speaks of binary-munitions capability for short-, medium- and long-range systems in all regions of NATO, in accordance with the provisions of MC 14/3.

It is very clear from numerous official statements that the force goal is in no sense an endorsement of US stockpiling of CW weapons in Europe. On the contrary: West German support necessitated prior agreement between Bonn and Washington that the existing US stockpile in Europe, on Federal German soil, would be withdrawn before the period covered by the force goal had ended; and NATO adoption of the force goal appears to have been conditional, further, upon the text stating explicitly that the new binary munitions were to be stored in the USA for the time being. Subsequent movement of binaries into Europe was not excluded but prerequisites were specified as regards host-country assent and alliance-wide consultation. Several NATO governments were, nevertheless, declaring that they would never admit CW weapons on to their territories, even in time of war. They included the governments of Denmark, Greece, Iceland, Luxembourg, the Netherlands and Norway. Others, notably the governments of FR Germany, Italy and Britain, indicated varying degrees of readiness to consider crisis or even peacetime deployment, but insisted on veto rights. In Belgium the matter precipitated an awkward constitutional problem, the legislature espousing a policy similar to that of the Netherlands, but the executive a policy similar to that of Britain.

It is doubtful whether quite so many NATO governments would have adopted and then publicly declared policies on the basing of CW weapons and related matters if the force-goal issue had not arisen in the way it did. Although the matter of implementing the MC 14/3 CW provisions is now firmly on the political agenda of the Alliance, and will no doubt surface again by the time the next *Ministerial Guidance* comes up for approval by the Defence Planning Committee (May 1987), these policy declarations have hardly brought a 'NATO chemical deterrent' any nearer. Indeed, unqualified denial of wartime basing rights for CW might be regarded as tantamount to repudiation of the MC 14/3 retaliatory option.

But at the national level of NATO, the existing CW retaliatory capabilities are now set to increase. The US binary programme is going ahead; and France, according to the new five-year defence plan disclosed in November 1986, will soon be manufacturing CW weapons as well.[18]

VI. The Kohl-Reagan agreement

The undertaking by the Reagan Administration to withdraw the US stockpile of CW weapons from FR Germany by 1992 was widely depicted in the United States as an act of unilateral disarmament. The House of Representatives amended its Defense Authorization Bill to prohibit the withdrawal unless the stockpile were replaced with binaries (a stipulation which did not, however, survive the subseqent House-Senate conference). There was not a little commentary on the contrast between the Administration's willingness to remove chemical weapons from Europe and its refusal to enter negotiations for the establishment of a chemical weapon-free zone in Europe.[19]

For the Federal Republic, however, the undertaking had an altogether greater political significance, for it formed part of a package that could be portrayed as extending the sovereignty of the state. Early in 1986 a dialogue had opened at the official level between Bonn and Washington aimed at defining the terms under which the Federal Government could support a NATO force goal on binary munitions. By early May such an agreement had come within reach, and the occasion of the Western economic summit in Tokyo was used to finalize it. This happened during a meeting on 6 May between President Reagan, Chancellor Kohl and their foreign ministers. It is reported in the press that the 'gentleman's agreement' from Tokyo was then formalized over the next two weeks in an exchange of documents between Bonn and Washington.[20] No such documents have yet been released to the public.

According to statements made by the Federal defence and foreign ministers in the Bundestag on 15 May 1986, the main matters of agreement had been as follows:

(a) Withdrawal of US stocks of CW weapons from the Federal Republic by 1992.

(b) No deployment of binaries to NATO Europe during peacetime, 'not even within the scope of contingency planning', unless specifically requested and agreed by the countries concerned.

(c) Full political consultations to be held in NATO 'prior to the deployment of binary munitions in a contingency'.

(d) The Federal Republic 'will no longer be singled out' as the only location in Europe for deployment of CW weapons.

(e) 'In all contingencies the Federal Republic will be able to look after its interests on the basis of its unrestricted sovereignty'.

The agreement thus amounted to a waiver by the United States of certain rights under the 1954 Treaty Concerning the Presence of Foreign Defence Forces in the Federal Republic—in other words an effective increase of West German sovereignty. The troop-stationing treaty permits the USA to maintain its forces in the Federal Republic at the 'same effective strength' as they were when the treaty was signed. This allows the United States to modernize its forces, but not to increase them; the latter would require the express prior approval of Bonn. The case could no doubt have been made that replacement of the existing CW-weapon stockpile with binaries would be just such an act of modernization—always supposing that the existing stockpile, or a predecessor, had been there since 1954.

Alongside the binary-munition force goal, the Kohl-Reagan agreement appears to have staked out an outline for future intra-NATO relationships on CW weapons: relationships which, as they develop further, are bound to influence the manner in which CW deterrence doctrine is incorporated into evolving Alliance defence strategy—if it is incorporated at all.

VII. Chemical weapons and the Soviet Union

There were Western sources which continued during 1986 to report that the USSR was still increasing its CW-weapon capabilities.[21] Whether they were true or false the present author is in no position to say. As for public Western commentary during the year on Soviet CBW employment doctrine, there was little new beyond an increased preoccupation with the possible clandestine applications of CBW weapons by Soviet *spetsnaz* units. Notable, however, was the publication by a West German specialist of a comprehensive new review of perceived Soviet CW capabilities and intentions.[22] It included, in German translation, excerpts on CBW doctrine from a basic Soviet army field manual of 1962, hitherto classified, though often referred to, in the West.

In January, when General Secretary Gorbachev proposed an agreement on a multilateral basis 'not to transfer chemical weapons to anyone and not to deploy them in the territories of other states', he went on to say that the Soviet Union had 'always strictly abided by those principles in its practical policies'. In May, after the NATO force-goal decision, a TASS release from Moscow stated: 'The USSR . . . has always strictly followed in its practical policy the principle of non-transfer of chemical weapons to any state and their non-deployment in the territories of other countries'. These statements stood in sharp contrast to continuing Western reports of Soviet deployments of chemical weapons in East European countries and their supply to client governments in more distant countries.

Other aspects of Soviet CW capability were touched upon in other official Soviet releases during the year. An unprecedented TASS release from Moscow shortly before the one just quoted said: 'The USSR does not hold large-scale tests of chemical weapons and does not stockpile these weapons'.[23] It was reporting a Foreign Ministry press conference. The Soviet embassy in Washington has said that the *Pravda* account of the press conference did not repeat the statement.[24]

VIII. Proliferation of chemical weapons

Publicity continued to be given during 1986 to reports that more and more states were moving to acquire CW weapons. As in all matters where the purveyors of information are, ultimately, secret-intelligence services, interpretation of the reports requires caution; by and large, secret intelligence is not released into the public domain unless its controllers are seeking to influence public opinion. Stories about chemical proliferation can serve several different ends other than, for example, the stimulation of arms control; and not all of them require accuracy in the information that is disseminated.

In a Soviet commentary released by TASS from Moscow on 9 April 1986, it was stated that 13–15 countries now possess CW weapons. Later that month, a senior US Defense Department official told a congressional committee: 'We are looking now at 16 countries with chemical weapons. Six more are probable'. On 15 July, the CD was told by a minister of the British crown that 'there may be more than 20 nations which now either possess chemical weapons or are looking at the option of acquiring them'. In none of these statements were the supposed possessor countries identified.

A search of the literature, summarized in table 5.4, reveals that at least 37 countries have since 1980 been identified as possessors, nearly all of them on purportedly excellent authority. For how many of them are the reports in fact worthy of belief? As many as 22? Or as few as 4?

That some degree of proliferation has been happening is clear from the fact of large-scale Iraqi use of CW weapons. And the possibility of this use stimulating other countries to acquire the weapons, especially countries in the same general region, cannot be denied. This, together with the persuasive evidence that private industry in Europe has, perhaps unwittingly, been crucial to Iraq's acquisition of its weapons,[25] has stimulated intergovernmental efforts additional to CWC-negotiation to create obstacles to any further proliferation.

Such a measure was given as an example of the 'interim steps' which General Secretary Gorbachev proposed on 15 January 1986 pending the conclusion of a global chemical disarmament treaty. The Western response has been to reject the idea of any sort of CW equivalent to the Treaty on the Non-Proliferation of Nuclear Weapons (NPT), but to point instead to the approach which the Organization for Economic Co-operation and Development (OECD) countries have been following since 1984: that of controlling and monitoring exports of particular chemicals in a concerted fashion, for example through the activities of the so-called 'Brussels Club'.[26] In the spring, the Brussels Club, by then enlarged to 18 countries (the European 12 plus Australia, Canada, Japan, New Zealand, Norway and the USA), agreed on a warning-list of 35 chemicals that was to be circulated so as to enable private chemical industry to take action on a voluntary basis. This voluntary arrangement would supplement the formal export controls which the participating governments had already imposed in respect of shorter (and varying) lists of chemicals. In February, *Pravda* reported that *Regulations on Exports from the USSR of Chemicals of Dual Use* had been promulgated from the Soviet Union during the previous month.[27] There were, in addition, two rounds of US-Soviet 'bilateral discussions on spread of chemical weapons' which took place in Berne during March and September; but, if any bilateral measures were agreed, they have yet to be announced.

IX. Conclusion

The pace of arms control negotiation in the CBW field was clearly outstripped by the pace of armament during 1986. The West, led by the United States and France, finally committed itself to modernization and expansion of its CW forces—actions which, however, Western leaders claimed merely to be reciprocatory of Soviet actions. The USSR continued to maintain a near-silence on its own CBW armament.

Under these circumstances, the prospects for the projected chemical weapons convention appear less promising than in earlier years. And the existing CBW arms control regime continues to be flouted, most conspicuously in Iraq's violation of the 1925 Geneva Protocol.

Table 5.1. Allegations of CBW arms control violations during 1986

Implicated state	Activity alleged	Source of allegation
(a) *Activities outlawed by the 1972 Biological Weapons Convention*		
Soviet Union	Continuing to maintain 'an offensive biological warfare program and capability'—including acquisition of 'state-of-the-art developments in biotechnology', production of 'BW agents' and testing and evaluating 'delivery and dissemination systems for these agents'	US Government;[a] as with similar allegations in 1985, purported details were disclosed via press leaks of secret governmental papers[b]
United States	Preparation for bacteriological war against Nicaragua	Nicaraguan Ministers of Defence[c] and Health[d]
(b) *Use of CBW weapons*		
Ethiopia	Continuing use of chemical weapons by government forces during 1985 against Eritrean secessionists	A missionary physician in Eritrea[e]
. .	Use of 'chemical weapons' by the Sudanese Peoples Liberation Army during Jan. (?) 1986 in the Upper Nile region of the Sudan	Sudanese Government[f]
Iraq	In the Gulf War, the use of mustard gas and tabun on many occasions during Jan.-May, Sep. and Dec. 1986	Iranian Government;[g] episodes during Feb. 1986 were verified by the UN[h]
Iran	In the Gulf War, the use of mortar-fired mustard gas during Feb. 1986	Iraqi officials[i]
Soviet Union	In Afghanistan, use by Soviet forces of artillery and air-delivered gas near Paghman during Sep.-Oct. 1986	'Western diplomatic sources'[j]
. .	In Afghanistan, use of gas shell by *mujahideen* in the Nazian border district during Oct. 1986; more than 60 civilians injured	Kabul domestic radio[k]
Viet Nam	Poisoning of water supplies during Feb. 1986 by Vietnamese forces in Kampuchea, and, in Nov. 1986, a 'chemical attack' that killed 43 people and injured 'hundreds'	Voice of the National Army of Democratic Kampuchea[l]
Angola	Use by government forces of air- and ground-delivered toxic agents against UNITA infantry in Angola on three occasions during June-Aug. 1986, the agents causing 'quick death', blindness or dizziness	UNITA[m]
Chad	In the Chadian civil war, use of chemical weapons by government forces during Apr. (?) 1986	GUNT[n]

Implicated state	Activity alleged	Source of allegation
Libya	The use of poison gas by Libyan forces in northern Chad during Dec. 1986	Chadian Government[o]
Nicaragua	Use of 'toxic chemicals' against anti-Sandinistas in Nicaragua during Feb. (?) and Aug. (?) 1986	Contra groups[p]

[a] US Arms Control and Disarmament Agency, *Soviet Noncompliance*, 1 Feb. 1986, pp. 13–15; Department of Defense, *Soviet Military Power 1986*, Mar. 1986, pp. 76, 145; and Defense Intelligence Agency, report DST-1610F-057-86, *Soviet Biological Warfare Threat*, released Nov. 1986.

[b] For example, Gertz, B., 'Moscow perfecting "genetic" weapons, secret study warns', *Washington Times*, 17 Feb. 1986, p. 1; this quotes from 1984 and 1985 National Security Council reports.

[c] TASS from Managua, 2 Feb. 1986, as translated and quoted (WA061521) in *FBIS-SU* of 10 Feb. 1986.

[d] TASS, 3 July 1986, as quoted via *FBIS-SU* of 8 July in *Arms Control Reporter*, July 1986, p. 704.B.191.

[e] *NBC Defense & Technology International* (Apr. 1986), p. 15.

[f] SUNA, presumably from Khartoum, 6 Feb. 1986, as translated and quoted (JN061818) in *FBIS*.

[g] Statements to the CD in plenary session on 18 Feb. 1986 by the Permanent Representative of Iran to the UN Office at Geneva (CD/PV.340, pp. 30–31) and on 14 Aug. 1986 by the Minister of Foreign Affairs (CD/PV.379, pp. 3–5); IRNA from Hajj 'Umran, 4 Sep. 1986; and IRNA as quoted by Reuter for Bahrain, as in *Independent* (London), 'Thousands die in Iranian attack on southern front', 27 Dec. 1986, p. 6.

. [h] 'Report of the mission dispatched by the Secretary-General to investigate allegations of the use of chemical weapons in the conflict betwen Iran and Iraq', 6 Mar. 1986, in UN document S/17911 of 12 Mar. 1986.

[i] Minister of Information, as quoted by Fisk, R., 'The Gulf War flare-up', *Times* (London), 14 Feb. 1986; Rashid, Maj-Gen. M. A. as quoted by Kifner, J., *New York Times*, 23 Feb. 1986.

[j] A.P. from Islamabad, as in *Tehran Times*, 'Soviet forces using toxic bomb in Afghanistan', 12 Nov. 1986, p. 1; *Jane's Defence Weekly*, 22 Nov. 1986, p. 1206.

[k] Kabul domestic radio, 31 Oct. 1986, as quoted via *FBIS-SA* of 3 Dec. in *Arms Control Reporter*, Nov. 1986, p. 704.B.204.

[l] Voice of the National Army of Democratic Kampuchea, broadcasts on 7 Mar. 1986 (as translated and quoted—BK080756—by *FBIS*) and as quoted in *Jane's Defence Weekly*, 29 Nov. 1986, p. 1261.

[m] UNITA officers, as quoted by AP from Jamba, as in *Philadephia Inquirer*, 'Angola accused of chemical warfare', 23 Aug. 1986, p. 10, and by Moorcroft, P., 'A new heart for the UNITA army', *Jane's Defence Weekly*, 13 Sep. 1986, p. 537.

[n] TASS, 21 Apr. 1986, as quoted via *FBIS-SU* of 25 Apr. in *Arms Control Reporter*, May 1986, p. 704.B.172.

[o] Reuter from Ndjamena, as in *International Herald Tribune*, 'Battle reported in Chad's rebel north', 13 Dec. 1986, and as in *Independent* (London), 'Libyans "using napalm"', 23 Dec. 1986, p. 5; *New York Times* (J. Brooke from Ndjamena, 22 Dec.), 'US weapons begin to reach Chad', 23 Dec. 1986, p. 3.

[p] Kisan, as quoted by ACAN (Panama City) (A. Cerrato), 16 Feb. 1986, as quoted via *FBIS-LA* of 18 Feb. in *Arms Control Reporter,* Mar. 1986, p. 705.B.167; Nicaraguan Unity, as quoted by ACAN, 2 Sep. 1986, as quoted via *FBIS-LA* of 4 Sep. in *Arms Control Reporter*, Sep. 1986, p. 704.B.195.

Table 5.2. The US binary-munitions programme: status of production facilities, 1986

Facility	Plans, as of April 1986[a]		Funding status, as of Dec. 1986
	Award contract	Begin prove-out[b]	
M687 metal-parts facility,[c] Louisiana Army Ammunition Plant, Shreveport, LA	[Completed, June 1984[d]]		[FY 1982 funding]
Expanded M687 metal-parts facility	Jan. 1987	May 1988	Funded (FY 1987)
Bigeye metal-parts facility, Marquardt Co, Van Nuys, CA	Sep. 1986	Nov. 1987	Funding (FY 1986) still blocked by Congress[e]
Second-source Bigeye metal-parts facility	Apr. 1987	Sep. 1988	Unfunded
DF[f] facility, Pine Bluff Arsenal, AR	[Completed, June 1985[g]]		[FY 1981 and FY 1982 funding]
Dichlor[h] facility, undisclosed site	Apr. 1987	July 1988	Funded (FY 1987)
QL[i] facility, undisclosed site	Aug. 1986	July 1988	Funding (FY 1986) still blocked by Congress[e]
Bigeye fill and load-assemble-pack facility, Pine Bluff Arsenal, AR	Oct. 1986	June 1988	Funding (FY 1986) still blocked by Congress[e]

[a] Department of Defense, written submission for the record of the House Defense Appropriations Subcommittee after a hearing on 22 Apr. 1986. *FY 1987 Hearings*, part 3, pp. 780–83.

[b] 'Prove-out' comprises the trial production-runs conducted immediately after the contractor has finished building the facility.

[c] The Shreveport facility will also be used to load M687 155-mm casings with commercial-source canisters of OPA, the alcohol-amine binary reactant needed for this GB2 munition. See Department of Defense, written submission for the record of the House Defense Appropriations Subcommittee after a hearing on 2 May 1985, *FY 1986 Hearings*, part 5, p. 460.

[d] *Report of the President's Chemical Warfare Committee* (the Stoessel Report) (US Government Printing Office: Washington, DC, June 1985).

[e] See table 5.3, note a.

[f] DF is the organophosphorus binary reactant needed for the M687 155-mm GB projectile and the XM135 MLRS warhead.

[g] *New York Times* (B. Keller from Pine Bluff Arsenal), 'US preparing new production of nerve gases', 11 Aug. 1985, p. 1.

[h] Dichlor is the precursor from which DF is to be made at the Pine Bluff Arsenal Integrated Binary Production Facility. The US Army has a stockpile of dichlor sufficient to sustain at least one year's production of M687 155-mm GB2 projectiles: see GAO/NSIAD-85-141 of Sep. 1985, p. 82.

[i] QL is the organophosphorus binary reactant needed for Bigeye. It seems that the US Army has a significant stockpile of QL, sufficient to support some low-rate initial production of Bigeye.

Table 5.3. Recent US budgets and appropriations for CW

Figures are in US $m.

Item	Fiscal year 1986		Fiscal year 1987	
	Budget	Appro-priation	Budget	Appro-priation
Anti-chemical protection				
Research, development, test and evaluation	391	. .	395	. .
Equipment and construction	545	. .	420	. .
Current CW weapon stockpile				
Maintenance and security	64	. .	. .	. .
Demilitarization of items for disposal	132	. .	120.1	120.1
Binary munitions programme				
Completion of Bigeye production facilities	109.1	109.1ᵃ	0	−8.1
Initial production of Bigeye spraybombs	43.7	0	56.9	35.0ᶜ
Expansion of Bigeye production capacity	0	0	15.5	0
Initial production of M687 155-mm projectiles	21.7	21.7ᵇ	60.6	60.6
Expansion of production capacity for M687 and other DF-based binaries	0	0	25.7	25.7
Further development of MLRS binary warhead	20.4	20.4	25.3	. .
Further development of follow-on and other systems	12.5	18.5	11.9	. .

Sources: Congressional Research Service (Bowman, S. R.), Issue Brief order code IB85212, 'Binary chemical weapons production: issues for Congress', 14 Mar. 1986; and, for the FY 1987 Appropriations, the House-Senate conference report on *National Defense Authorization Act for Fiscal Year 1987*, House report no. 99-1001, 14 Oct. 1986.

ᵃ Section 1411(b) of the 1986 Defense Authorization Act precluded any use of this funding before the President had certified to Congress that certain stipulations regarding NATO had been fulfilled; this certification was made on 29 July 1986. Section 152(c) of the 1987 Act, which passed into law on 14 Nov. 1986, stipulated further that none of this funding might be used until the President had certified to Congress that '(1) production of the Bigeye binary chemical bomb is in the national security interests of the United States; and (2) the design, planning, and environmental requirements for such facilities have been satisfied'. No Bigeye facilitation contract seems likely to be awarded, therefore, until well into 1987.

ᵇ Section 1411(c) of the 1986 Defense Authorization Act precluded any use of this funding for final assembly of complete 155-mm binary munitions prior to 1 Oct. 1987. After that date, the funding might be so used if 60 days had elapsed from a Presidential certification to Congress that, *inter alia*, such assembly was 'necessitated by the national security interests of the United States and the interests of other NATO member nations' and that the plan for the destruction of the current (non-binary) stockpile was 'ready to be implemented'. But there are currently no restrictions on the use of this funding for procurement for components for the 155-mm GB2 round.

ᶜ Section 152(a) of the 1987 Defense Authorization Act provides that none of this funding may be used prior to 1 Oct. 1987, and that none of it may be used for final assembly of complete Bigeye munitions prior to 1 Oct. 1988.

Table 5.4. CW-weapons possessor states and alleged possessor states [1]

[Square-bracketed numbers cite footnotes to the table.]

State	Comments
Present [2] possessor states	
France	Current stocks are in the order of hundreds of agent tons; large quantitites had been disposed of during the 1960s.
United States	Current stocks are around 30 500 agent tons of which just under 7 per cent are deployed overseas (435 agent tons in FR Germany and 1610 agent tons on Johnston Atoll in the Pacific).
Soviet Union	Western estimates size the Soviet stockpile at 50 000–100 000 agent tons give or take a factor of around 5. The evidence as to whether and, if so, where the USSR has deployed CW weapons abroad is apparently ambiguous.
Iraq	Although its use of CW weapons in the Gulf War has been denied by the Iraqi Government, the evidence is that such use has been proceeding at a rate of several tens of agent tons per year.
States reportedly said by US officials to be possessors [3]	
Egypt	Said to have been the first Middle Eastern possessor, initially, some think, by recommissioning stocks that British forces had abandoned upon their departure from Egypt in 1952.
Syria [5]	Weapons said to have been imported initially—from the USSR, according to one report [6], from Egypt according to another [7]; but indigenous production capacity is now said to exist [6] at two new factories, including capacity for arming Soviet-supplied SS-21 missiles with CW warheads [7].
Israel	Indigenous production of nerve and mustard gases is said to have begun during the 1970s [8].
Libya [9]	But a 1984 Israeli source [10] stated that the Libyan stockpile was 'unconfirmed'.
Ethiopia	But the Ethiopian Government declared in 1982 that it neither manufactured nor used CW weapons [11].
Afghanistan [12]	. .
Pakistan [13]	But in Feb. 1986 the Pakistani Government declared that it did not possess CW weapons [14].
Burma	Said to be producing mustard gas using plant and chemicals imported from Italy and FR Germany.
Thailand	But other US officials are quoted as not believing Thailand to possess CW weapons [15].
Viet Nam	But the published evidence that Vietnamese forces have been using toxic weapons in Laos and Cambodia, especially the 'yellow rain' evidence, has been shown to be unreliable [16].
China	. .
Taiwan	Stocks said in 1984 to comprise some 50 tons of mustard gas, with plans for nerve gas as well [8].
North Korea [17]	Up to 250 agent tons now stockpiled according to the South Korean defence minister in June 1985 [18].
Cuba [19]	But in May 1984 the Pentagon stated that the CW threat had not yet spread to the western hemisphere [20].
Nicaragua [21]	But this particular report was subsequently denied by the Pentagon [22].
Romania [23]	. .
States reportedly said by US officials to be seeking possession [4]	
South Korea	. .
Iran	Apparent confirmation during Iranian parliamentary debate on the 1986/87 budget bill [24].
Other states said to be possessors	
East Germany [25]	But, according to an unofficial commentary published in mid-1985 that
Czechoslovakia [26]	probably reflects at least some of the US intelligence assessments, 'none of
Poland [27]	the East European countries deploys a stockpile of chemical munitions
Hungary [28]	under national control' [20].
Bulgaria [29]	

State	Comments
Argentina [31]	. .
Chile [32]	. .
Peru [33]	But in 1985 the Peruvian Government protested strongly against Peru being described as a possessor [34].
El Salvador [35]	. .
Guatemala [36]	. .
India [37]	But the Indian Government has several times declared its abjuration of CW weapons [38].
Philippines [39]	But possession of CW weapons by the Philippines was denied by its Washington embassy in Nov. 1984 [40].
South Africa [41]	But in Sep. 1983 the South African Defence Force denied ever having used any form of CW against SWAPO [42].
Angola [43]	. .
Chad [44]	. .

Notes and sources for table 5.4

[1] For most of the reports quoted here, it is not known what degree of capability actually to use CW weapons for military purposes was supposedly involved. Clearly there would be little sense in designating a country as a possessor state if all it possessed was a supply of unweaponized CW agent; and many states will have such supplies for research purposes, as, for example, in the study of anti-CW protective measures. Presumably states which have armed their police or internal-security forces with chemical-irritant (e.g., tear-gas) weapons are not, for that reason alone, designated as CW-weapon possessors.

[2] Past CW-weapon possessor states reportedly include: Canada, Czechoslovakia, Greece, Hungary, Indonesia (by succession to bulk stocks of mustard gas that had been manufactured by the government of the former Dutch East Indies), Italy, Japan, Poland, South Africa, Spain, Turkey, the United Kingdom and Yugoslavia.

[3] Unless indicated otherwise, the unofficial US Government assertions noted here are as reported by Ember (see note 4 below).

[4] Ember, L. R., 'Worldwide spread of chemical arms receiving increased attention', *Chemical & Engineering News*, vol. 64, no. 15 (14 Apr. 1986), pp. 8–16, p. 9.

[5] Since July 1986, Israeli sources have been giving increasing publicity to reports of Syrian CW weapons.

[6] US officials are quoted on this in Shaw, G., 'Syria reported to be making chemical arms', *Los Angeles Times*, 26 Mar. 1986, p. 1.

[7] According to 'Arab sources in the Middle East' quoted in *Jane's Defence Weekly*, 29 Nov. 1986, p. 1255, 'Syria "is producing chemical weapons"'.

[8] According, purportedly, to a CIA assessment: *Economist Foreign Report*, 12 July 1984, pp. 5–6, 'China and Israel'.

[9] In Aug. 1986 an unidentified US official was quoted as saying that Libya's acquisition of CW weapons had been assisted by exports from Western Europe; see Gordon, M. R., 'US and Soviet to meet again on curbing chemical weapons', *New York Times*, 26 Aug. 1986, p. 4. Press reports later in the year, attributing British intelligence sources, spoke of Libyan possession of Soviet-supplied nerve-gas warheads for Scud-B missiles; see O'Dwyer-Russell, S., 'Gaddafi arms Syria with gas warheads', *Sunday Telegraph*, 23 Nov. 1986, p. 1.

[10] Jaffee Center for Strategic Studies, *The Middle East Military Balance 1984* (Tel Aviv, 1984), p. 148.

[11] Statement by the Ethiopian representative in the First Committee of the UN General Assembly, 9 Dec. 1982.

[12] The 'Haig Report' speaks of 'some evidence that Afghan Government forces may have used Soviet supplied chemical weapons against the *mujahidin* even before the Soviet invasion': US State Department Special Report no. 98, *Chemical Warfare in South-East Asia and Afghanistan*, 22 Mar. 1982, p. 6.

[13] According, purportedly, to a Joint Chiefs of Staff paper which stated that Pakistan appeared to have CW-weapon capability: Anderson, J., 'Powderkeg fuse on our planet burning shorter', *Washington Post*, 3 Dec. 1981.

[14] Statement at the Conference on Disarmament by the representative of Pakistan: CD/PV.339 of 13 Feb. 1986.

Notes and sources *Cont.*

[15] Oberdorfer, D., 'Chemical arms curbs are sought', *Washington Post*, 9 Sep. 1985, p. 1.

[16] A major source on the still-continuing collapse of the US government's case in support of its 'yellow rain' charges against the Soviet Union and Viet Nam is: Seeley, T. D., Nowicke, J. W. Miselson, M., Guilleman, J. and Pongthep A., 'Yellow rain', *Scientific American*, vol. 254, no. 1 (Jan. 1986), pp. 128–37, and the two letters to the Editor published in the February issue of that journal. See also the annual reviews of the case published by the present author in SIPRI, *World Armaments and Disarmament: SIPRI Yearbook 1982*, pp. 339–43; *Yearbook 1983*, pp. 392–400; *Yearbook 1984*, pp. 331–40; *Yearbook 1985*, pp. 183–87, *Yearbook 1986*, pp. 161–64.

[17] In testimony before the House Defense Appropriations Subcommittee on 25 February 1986, the Chief of Staff of the US Army stated that North Korea stockpiled 'lethal offensive chemical weapons'.

[18] As quoted in: Howarth, H. M. F., 'Republic of Korea: black security perspectives', *International Defense Review*, vol. 18, no. 12 (1985), pp. 1977–78.

[19] Soon after Secretary of State Alexander Haig had initiated the 'yellow rain' accusations against Viet Nam and the Soviet Union in September 1981, reports began to appear in the press, with attribution to unidentified officials or to classified intelligence documents, to the effect that a Soviet supply of weapons similar to one implicated in the yellow-rain reporting had existed in Cuba since 1970. See, for example: Anderson, J., 'Top secret: Cuba has death rain chemical', *New York Post*, 16 Sep. 1981, p. 2; Lathem, N., 'Soviet nuke war bases in Cuba', *New York Post*, 11 Mar. 1982, p. 4; and Beecher, W., 'Toxic weapon used on Chinese?', *Boston Globe*, 30 July 1982, p. 15.

[20] At a Pentagon briefing, as reported in: Halloran, R., 'U.S. finds 14 nations now have chemical arms', *New York Times*, 20 May 1984, p. 22.

[21] 'Disturbing rumours that Soviet chemical weapons have been sent to Nicaragua' referred to in: Anderson, J., 'Upgrading germ-warfare intelligence', *Washington Post*, 30 Nov. 1984, p. E7.

[22] Those rumours (note 21) apparently originated in State Department reports of shipments of military *matériel* to Nicaragua from Cuba and the Soviet Union; Pentagon officials disclosed an intelligence assessment to the effect that the CW *matériel* included in those shipments comprised antichemical protective equipments, not CW weapons. See Wood, D. (Newhouse News Service), 'Nicaragua has gear for waging chemical war, Pentagon says', *New Orleans Times-Picayune*, 5 Dec. 1984, p. 19.

[23] Toth, R. C., 'Germ, chemical arms reported proliferating', *Los Angeles Times*, 27 May 1986, p. 1. Indigenous Romanian CW-weapons production capacity is also alleged in West German press reports. See, for example, the anonymous and unsourced report in *Bild Zeitung* (Hamburg), 10 June 1985, p. 4, and, based on a briefing from the Federal Ministry of Defence, Feldmeyer, K., *Frankfurter Allgemeine Zeitung*, 19 Aug. 1985, pp. 1–2.

[24] According to *Jane's Defence Weekly*, vol. 5, no. 22 (7 June 1986), pp. 1024–25 quoting the Iranian resistance newspaper *Iran Liberation*.

[25] CW-weapon production in the GDR has been alleged by several West German commentators, though it is not clear how closely they are reflecting governmental appraisals. See, for example, the *Bild Zeitung* and Feldmeyer articles cited in note 23 above. See also: Urban, I., *Die Welt* (Bonn), 11 June 1985, p. 1; the statement by J. Todenhöfer (the CDU/CSU disarmament spokesman) disseminated via DPA from Bonn at 1208 hrs, 12 Aug. 1985; Bensch, G., 'C-Waffenproduktion in der DDR', *Deutscher Ostdienst*, 3 Oct. 1985; and the report datelined Brussels, quoting unidentified NATO officials, in *Welt am Sonntag* (Hamburg), 2 Mar. 1986.

[26] According to West German reports. See, for example, *Bild Zeitung* [23]. See also the Todenhöfer statement and the *Welt am Sonntag* article cited in note 25.

[27] According to West German reports. See, for example, *Bild Zeitung* [23] and the Todenhöfer statement [25].

[28] According to West German reports. See, for example, the *Bild Zeitung* and Feldmeyer articles cited in note 23 above and the Todenhöfer statement [25].

[29] According to West German reports. See, for example, *Bild Zeitung* [23] and the Todenhöfer statement [25].

[30] Hamm, M. R., 'Deterrence, chemical warfare, and arms control', *Orbis*, vol. 29, no. 1 (Spring 1985), pp. 119–63.

[31] Unconfirmed press reports exist of British forces having encountered stocks of Argentinian CW weapons in the Falklands in 1982, e.g., *Daily Telegraph* (London), 18 Aug. 1982, p. 5, 'Argentine "gas shells" found in Falklands'. (This particular press report—apparently the source of more recent press commentary on the subject, as in Toth [23]—was almost certainly referring to smoke shell.)

[32] The existence in 1976 of indigenous capacity for small-scale production of nerve gas in Chile was purportedly confirmed in a confidential FBI memorandum; see Shribman, D., 'FBI learns

Chilean plot to kill Letelier in '76 involved nerve gas', *New York Times*, 14 Dec. 1981, p. D11. Chilean production capacity for 'bombs with nerve-paralyzing gas' is alleged in a Novosti release carried in *Krasnaya Zvezda*, 18 Aug. 1984.

[33] The CW-possessor status of Peru is alleged in an unpublished article dated October 1984 by Anderson, J. and Van Atta, D., cited in: Brauch, H. G., 'Chemical weapons: arsenals and recent developments', a paper presented at the Conference on Non Nuclear War in Europe, Groningen, 28 Nov.–1 Dec. 1984.

[34] Embassy of Peru, Stockholm, letter dated 25 June 1985 addressed to the Director of SIPRI.

[35] There have been several press and other reports alleging use of CW weapons by Salvadorean forces. One of the earliest was contained in the report of 11 Aug. 1981 by the Commission for the Defense of Human Rights in Central America (based in Costa Rica); see AP from San Jose, 12 Aug. 1981, as in *New York Times*, 13 Aug. 1981, p. A5, 'Rights group charges massacre by El Salvador'.

[36] There have been sporadic media reports of Guatemalan counterinsurgency use of CW weapons, e.g., a broadcast on 6 July 1982 over Havana international radio.

[37] Simonitsch, P., in *Frankfurter Rundschau*, 29 Aug. 1982, '[Chemical weapons: everyone has stocks, despite treaty)', spoke of Indian CW weapons as though they were well known to everyone; which they are not. However, still remaining today in India are some of the World War II lend-lease shipments to China of US CW munitions that went in by way of Assam.

[38] For example, statements at the Committee on Disarmament by the representative of India, CD/PV.31 of 26 Apr. 1979 and CD/PV.101 of 3 Feb. 1981.

[39] During Aug./Sep. 1984 there were reports of the Philippine Air Force using napalm and toxic bombs against the Moro National Liberation Front in Mindanao; see, for example, Dalton, K., from Manila, *Times* (London), 26 Sep. 1984, p. 4, 'Manila investigation into napalm bombing claim'; and the editorial 'Now established' in *Ang Pahayagang Malaya* (Quezon City), 27 Sep. 1984, p. 4.

[40] *Arms Control Reporter*, no. 11 (1984), p. 704.B.108.

[41] South African production of CW weapons is alleged in *Fireforce Exposed* (Anti-Apartheid Movement: London, 1979), p. 39, quoting an article in *Zimbabwe Peoples Voice*, 30 Sep. 1973. Use of such weapons during the May 1978 raid on Kassinga, Angola, was referred to in a joint UNHCR/WHO investigatory report dated 1 June 1978 (in UN Security Council document S/13473 of 27 July 1979).

[42] Letter from the Chief of Staff Operations dated 14 Sep. 1983 addressed to the editor of *Brassey's Defence Yearbook 1983*.

[43] UNITA has several times accused the Luanda Government of using toxic bombs against UNITA positions; see, for example, *Jane's Defence Weekly*, 5 Oct. 1985, p. 728.

[44] See the use-allegation noted in table 5.1.

Notes and references

1 A systematic and fully documented review will be provided in a forthcoming SIPRI publication. It will supplement SIPRI reviews of earlier years, for which see: SIPRI, *World Armaments and Disarmament: SIPRI Yearbooks 1982–85* (Taylor & Francis: London, 1982–85)—*1982*: pp. 317–61; *1983*: pp. 391–426; *1984*: pp. 319–49; *1985*: pp. 159–219; and Perry Robinson, J. P., *Chemical and Biological Warfare Developments: 1985*, SIPRI CBW Studies no. 6 (Oxford University Press: Oxford, 1986).

2 The toxic agents that are subsumed within the BWC are those labelled 'toxins'—a term which, however, has no single scientific connotation. As used in the BWC, the *travaux préparatoires* indicate that the term extends to all toxic agents of biological origin ('ABOs' in a US military parlance) including synthetic ones, as well as homologues and congeners. Examples of once-standardized toxic-warfare agents to which the BWC might be held to apply include botulin, shellfish poison and hydrogen cyanide. See, further, SIPRI, *The Prevention of CBW*, Vol. 5 of *The Problem of Chemical and Biological Warfare* (Almqvist & Wiksell: Stockholm, 1971), p. 110, and Geissler, E. (ed.), SIPRI, *Biological and Toxin Weapons Today* (Oxford University Press: Oxford, 1986).

3 In February, June and September 1986, representatives of the two German states and Czechoslovakia met together in Geneva to discuss CW, as had been agreed at the end of 1985.

4 Conference on Disarmament document CD/727, 21 Aug. 1986. The draft treaty, despite all its many gaps, occupies 52 pages of the report.

5 These private US–Soviet CW 'consultations' had begun, within the Geneva CD framework, during 1984. There was mention in the press of four rounds during 1986: in February, April, July and August. Another series of US–Soviet CW contacts took place in Berne.

[6] See, for example, the statements by Ambassador Imai of Japan before the CD in plenary session on 3 Apr. and 17 July 1986: Conference on Disarmament documents CD/PV. 353, pp. 14–19 and CD/PV. 371, pp. 12–14.

[7] For detailed discussion of such regional approaches, see Trapp, R. (ed.), *Chemical Weapon Free Zones?*, SIPRI CBW Studies no. 7 (Oxford University Press: Oxford, 1987).

[8] IRNA from Khatam al-Anbiya HQ, 0820 GMT, 13 Feb. 1986, as in FBIS-SA of 13 Feb. 1986 at LD130824; '8500 Iranians fall victim to renewed Iraqi use of chemical weapons', *Kayhan International* (Tehran), 23 Feb. 1986, p. 6; and Balali-Mood, M., Farhoodi, M. and Panjavni, F. K., 'Report of three fatal cases of war gas poisoning', a paper presented at the 'Second World Congress: New Compounds in Biological and Toxicological Warfare' (Chairman: A. Heyndrickx), Ghent, 24–27 Aug. 1986.

[9] 'Report of the mission dispatched by the Secretary-General to investigate allegations of the use of chemical weapons in the conflict between Iran and Iraq', 6 Mar. 1986, in UN document S/17911 of 12 Mar. 1986. See, further, Dunn, P., 'The chemical war: Iran revisited—1986', *NBC Defense & Technology International*, vol. 1, no. 3 (June 1986), pp. 32–39.

[10] Statement by Minister T. Renton at the CD in plenary session on 15 July 1986: CD/PV. 370, p. 3.

[11] Feith, D. J. (Deputy Assistant Secretary of Defense for Negotiations Policy), 'Testimony on biological and toxin weapons', a submission to the Subcommittee on Oversight and Evaluation, Permanent Select Committee on Intelligence, US House of Representatives, 8 Aug. 1986.

[12] Ember, L. E., 'New data weaken US yellow rain case', *Chemical & Engineering News*, 9 June 1986, pp. 23 and 99.

[13] Written submission of Brigadier J. C. Harrison (Deputy Director of Combat Support Systems, US Army) to the House Defense Appropriations Subcommittee in response to questions after a hearing on 2 May 1985: US Congress, House Appropriations Committee, *Hearings on Department of Defense Appropriations 1987*, part 5, pp. 460–61.

[14] Isaacs, J., 'Using summitry to thwart Congress', *Bulletin of the Atomic Scientists*, vol. 42, no. 10 (Dec. 1986), pp. 4–5.

[15] Bowman, S. R., 'Issue brief: binary chemical weapons production: issues for Congress', IB85212, Congressional Research Service, Library of Congress, Foreign Affairs and National Defense Division, Washington, DC, update of 14 Mar. 1986; Perry Robinson, J. P., 'Chemical and biological warfare: developments in 1985', SIPRI, *World Armaments and Disarmament: SIPRI Yearbook 1986* (Oxford University Press: Oxford, 1986), chapter 8.

[16] General Accounting Office (GAO), *Bigeye Bomb: An Evaluation of DOD's Chemical and Development Tests*, GAO/PEMD-86-12BR, May 1986.

[17] See, further, Perry Robinson, J., 'NATO chemical weapons: policy and posture', *ADIU Occasional Paper No. 4* (Armament & Disarmament Information Unit: University of Sussex, UK, Sep. 1986).

[18] The military spending programme for 1987–91 which the French Cabinet adopted on 5 Nov. 1986 specified that France 'should possess an appropriate deterrent capacity' in chemical weapons; see 'Innovation dans la loi de programmation militaire: les armes chimiques sont sur le gaz', *Le Monde*, 8 Nov. 1986. See, further, the comments on the programme made to the press by Prime Minister Chirac's security adviser, Jean Pig, as in 'Paris denkt an chemische Waffen', *Stuttgarter Zeitung*, 7 Nov. 1986, and 'Paris will Giftgas herstellen', *Frankfurter Rundschau*, 7 Nov. 1986, and those by Foreign Minister Raimond as in 'Paris sees need for chemical deterrent' *Times* (London), 8 Nov. 1986. Defence Minister Giraud told the National Assembly on 12 Nov. that production of CW weapons would begin in 1987.

[19] See, for example, the report from the workshop on 'Chemical Weapons and Western Security Policy' that was held at the Aspen Institute Berlin in June 1986, released in Washington on 21 Nov. 1986 as the first in a series of joint studies undertaken by the Aspen Strategy Group and the European Strategy Group under the co-chairmanship of Joseph Nye and Uwe Norlich. See also Hamm, M. R., 'Will binaries founder on allied rocks?,' *NBC Defense & Technology International*, vol. 2, no. 1 (1987), p. 8.

[20] See Perry Robinson (note 17).

[21] See, for example, US Defense Department, *Soviet Military Power 1986*, released Mar. 1986, p. 73; the statement by the British defence secretary to the House of Commons on 13 May 1986, as in *Hansard*, vol. 97, no. 112, col. 552; and the speech by the West German defence minister to the Bundestag on 15 May 1986.

[22] Krause, J., *Optionen chemischer Kriegführung in der Strategie des Warschauer Pakts*, Stiftung Wissenschaft und Politik, Ebenhausen, report no. SWP-AZ 2481, Aug. 1986.

[23] TASS in English from Moscow, 1635 hrs GMT, 20 May 1986, as excerpted in BBC *Summary of World Broadcasts*, SU/8265/A1/2-3, 22 May 1986.

[24] *Arms Control Reporter*, June 1986, p. 704.B.181.

[25] Among the 1986 disclosures see especially: Roberts, G., 'Deserter pinponts Iraqi gas war plant', *The Independent* (London), 27 Oct. 1986; Harris, R. and Woolwich, P., 'The secrets of Samarra', a 40-minute BBC *Panorama* television documentary screened in Britain on 27 Oct. 1986 at 2130 hrs; and Krosney, H., 'Iraq making deadly form of nerve agent', *Jerusalem Post*, 24 Nov. 1986, pp. 1, 4.

[26] SIPRI CBW Studies no. 6 (note 1), p. 52.

[27] The text of the Regulations, including the list of specific chemicals to which they apply, is printed in *International Affairs* (Moscow), Apr. 1986, pp. 151–52.

Part II. Military expenditure, the arms trade and armed conflicts

6. World military expenditure*

RITA TULLBERG and GERD HAGMEYER-GAVERUS

Superscript numbers refer to the list of notes and references at the end of the chapter.

I. Introduction

The publication of accurate and detailed estimates of military spending is important for a number of reasons. First, without such data there can be no domestic, informed debate on military issues. Second, these data provide a rough idea of the amount of military activity in a country. Examined over a number of years, they gave an indication of whether the overall size of the military establishment and the quantity of resources it absorbs are rising or falling. Such information is also of interest to other countries. Combined with other known facts about a country's economy it can be of assistance when assessing: (*a*) the extent to which economic constraints will affect the growth of military spending; and (*b*) the extent to which economic factors may figure in a country's attitude towards measures for arms control and disarmament. In addition, the international community has an interest in promoting comprehensive, open and verifiable bookkeeping since these are prerequisites for any disarmament measure which incorporates limitations on military spending.

The presentation of SIPRI's military expenditure data this year involves several changes: first, no figures are given for the USSR or China; second, regional and world totals of military spending have not been calculated. There are two basic reasons for these changes: first, the information currently available on Soviet and Chinese military spending is not sufficient to make accurate estimates, although it is known that it is a significant portion of the world total; and second, the data on military spending are not homogeneous and should not be aggregated for countries simply on geographical grounds.

SIPRI estimates of military spending for individual countries and years vary greatly in quality. For some countries no hard information is available, particularly for the most recent years. In order to produce regional and world totals, the missing data must be estimated by statistical methods. For the smaller countries, these estimation procedures have little impact on the totals. However, major uncertainty surrounds the estimates of military outlays for *all* years for two of the biggest spenders, China and the USSR. Speculation concerning the military budgets of these two countries has produced a wide spectrum of possible estimates whose impact on regional and world totals is very significant. For reasons discussed below, SIPRI is not giving estimates of Chinese and Soviet spending this year and thus cannot offer a figure for total current military spending.

* The section on research and development was written by MARY ACLAND-HOOD. Material for the section on the USA was contributed by ALEXIS CAIN, Defense Budget Project, Center on Budget and Policy Priorities, Washington, DC.

Military spending data expressed in local currency are largely of domestic interest. Military spending in constant prices is an indicator of the growth or decline of the military sector in a country; equally, military spending as a percentage of gross domestic product (GDP—the production of resources) measures the share of a country's resources taken by the military. However, putting a uniform money value on this spending by expressing it in US dollars, and then adding these dollar values for a region or the whole world, assumes a degree of comparability which the data do not possess.

One of the misleading aspects of such an exercise is that exchange-rates tend to be fixed by national governments and rarely reflect the true purchasing power of US $1 in another currency. Thus, military spending expressed in dollars may give a false picture of its size for purposes of comparison. Using an exchange-rate known as a purchasing-power parity rate would partially solve this problem—but appropriate rates are not available for all countries and for all years. It is also the case when calculating constant dollar series that, while changing the base year for the dollar exchange-rate leaves the trend in any one country unaltered, it alters the trend for the aggregate spending of two or more countries. That is, the trend of an aggregate military expenditure series is dependent on the base year chosen.

A bigger problem is that arising from the assumption that money prices are a true measure of value in all economies and in all circumstances. Money is only a correct measure of value when prices are not distorted by interference in the market. In a planned or *command economy*, resource allocation (the distribution of labour, raw materials, etc.) is carried out by a centralized administrative process as opposed to a price mechanism which balances supply and demand in a *market economy*. It follows that money prices do not reflect values in the same way in both systems.

Imagine a country where the servicemen are conscripts. They are housed and fed but receive no salary—simply a small allowance. Imagine then that, without making any other changes, it was agreed that these servicemen each be paid a salary at the going market rate for his skills. Military expenditure would almost certainly rise (by just how much depends on many factors). There has been no change in military preparedness but, in this example, military expenditure was lower when servicemen's compensation was decided by a central authority and higher when decided by the market. This is because the allowance (money) the authorities paid the conscripts was not a true measure of the value they placed on their services and which they were prepared to pay when they hired them in the market place. Comparing the two amounts of money spent tells us nothing about military capacity in either situation.

Most of us live in economies that are mixtures of these two systems of command and market prices and manage quite well to make comparisons— even if such comparisons are not strictly legitimate. But the world's two biggest military spenders lie at the opposite extremes of the command price–market price spectrum, and their spending in money terms cannot reasonably be compared or aggregated.[1]

Failure to understand this fact has caused a lot of confusion, especially with regard to Soviet and Chinese expenditure estimates. Since total military spending in the USSR expressed in roubles is not known—for reasons given in section III—attempts have been made to estimate it. There is a tendency to give the estimate a high dollar value in order to make it roughly equivalent to US spending. 'Common sense' says this must be the case: the USSR clearly has a powerful and extensive military machine and Soviet leaders admit that the military sector is a heavy burden on the economy and would like to give it fewer resources, while the US military sector is not so much an economic as a fiscal burden on the US economy and the Administration talks about spending more. It therefore does not seem to make sense if Soviet spending turns out to be significantly smaller than US spending. And yet this may very well be the case; the problem is that amounts of money do not measure value in the same way in both economies.

Similar theoretical and practical problems are involved in the estimation of military spending data for China. Here the official budget figure covers only a portion of total spending—perhaps only personnel costs or possibly personnel costs plus some items of investment. This lack of exact information makes it difficult to analyse the current military reforms in China, in particular the reduction in the size of the People's Liberation Army. The economic impact of this reform, which involves a switching from quantity to quality, cannot be followed without more accurate budget data.[2]

SIPRI military expenditure data are not published for the purpose of comparison. Their primary function is to provide standardized information in local currency on the military spending of individual countries (table 6A.1), much of which is not otherwise readily available. Military expenditure is also expressed as a share of GDP, giving an indication of the burden of this spending on the economy as a whole (table 6A.3). It may show, for example, that while military expenditure is falling in real or even nominal terms, the military sector is taking a growing share of a country's limited resources. A third table (table 6A.2) gives military expenditure in constant dollars; this illustrates the trend in spending for each country and permits comparisons and aggregation among countries with similar economies, bearing in mind the caveats discussed above.

In this chapter, military expenditure is examined within the context of central government spending for a number of countries throughout the world. Three special problems are highlighted: the public accountability of military spending; problems facing civilian governments in controlling military expenditure; and foreign assistance as a source of military expenditure.

II. NATO

In the final communiqué of the Defence Planning Committee issued in December 1986, the NATO ministers reiterated their determination to improve conventional forces so as to avoid an undue reliance on the early use of nuclear weapons. Emphasis was placed on the Conventional Defence Improvements (CDI) action plan with its two main preconditions: first, the provision of adequate resources in accordance with the 1985 Ministerial Guidance which recommended a 3 per cent real increase in military spending each year; and second, the more efficient use of these resources.

Table 6.1. NATO countries: estimated real growth of military expenditure, 1978–86[a]

Figures are percentages.

Country	1978	1979	1980	1981	1982	1983	1984	1985	1986[b]
North America									
Canada	9.8	−2.1	2.6	3.7	4.3	7.3	6.6	2.9	3.1
USA	0.8	1.0	2.1	5.0	4.6	5.8	5.4	2.4	3.2
Europe									
Belgium	6.6	2.2	2.0	0.9	−3.3	−4.0	−4.3	−2.9	(0.0)[c]
Denmark	3.9	0.6	0.9	1.1	2.9	0.8	−2.4	−2.4	−0.4
France	5.8	2.3	1.8	2.4	2.1	1.7	−0.3	−0.1	2.9
FR Germany	4.2	1.3	1.4	1.2	−1.3	0.8	−1.0	0.2	3.7
Greece	2.1	−3.1	−13.5	18.3	2.0	−8.8	18.8	−0.8	−6.8
Italy	4.3	6.3	4.6	2.1	7.0	2.2	3.0	3.6	3.0
Luxembourg	8.7	3.0	16.4	3.4	0.9	2.2	0.5	−2.5	11.5
Netherlands	−3.4	6.0	−2.7	1.1	−0.4	−0.9	1.7	−1.2	2.6
Norway	7.0	2.4	1.1	1.0	3.9	4.3	−3.7	15.2	−4.7
Portugal	1.0	1.5	8.4	−0.5	0.1	−3.8	−7.0	1.2	11.0
Spain	..	..	..	..	..	2.2	1.8	3.2	−5.8
Turkey	−8.4	−11.3	3.6	12.8	9.3	−3.7	−4.5	4.8	14.6
UK	1.7	5.5	5.9	4.0	4.3	3.2	4.5	0.1	0.7
Total									
NATO Europe	3.3	2.7	2.3	2.9	8.4[d]	1.2	1.2	0.7	1.9
Total NATO	**1.9**	**1.6**	**2.2**	**4.2**	**6.0[e]**	**4.0**	**3.8**	**1.8**	**2.7**

[a] Information in this table is based on NATO-defined military expenditure adjusted to calendar years and differs from the material taken from domestic sources.

[b] Data for 1986 are uncertain. NATO normally revises latest-year data extensively after one year.

[c] SIPRI estimate.

[d] Spain became a member of NATO in May 1982. The NATO Europe growth rate for 1982 *excluding* Spain would be 2.1 per cent and for total NATO, 3.7 per cent.

Source: Appendix 6A, table 6A.1. Spanish data from 1982 are taken from table 6.4.

First introduced in 1978, the 3 per cent spending goal was followed with some consistency by only four NATO countries: Canada, Italy, the UK and the USA. The latter two have now, in practice, abandoned it (table 6.1). The proposed peacetime transfer of real resources on this scale year after year into the military sector was a policy which could only hope to succeed in democratic societies during periods of high overall growth and general economic bouyancy. In a time of economic stagnation it was particularly unrealistic. The only NATO country to achieve real economic growth exceeding 3 per cent in the years 1979–84 was Turkey (3.9 per cent); only one other NATO country, oil-rich Norway, achieved growth exceeding 2 per cent in the same period. Annual economic growth in the other NATO countries was less than 2 per cent.[3] The continued call for 3 per cent real growth of military spending when there is no evidence of any long-term economic recovery among NATO countries is unrealistic.[4]

Another approach to the question of conventional weapon modernization involves greater efforts to reduce costs through armaments collaboration. Such schemes have rarely been an economic success and have been troubled by suspicion and rivalry between the participants. Letters of intent were signed during 1986 for the initial stages of work on seven joint US-European projects. Some NATO officials believed that this demonstrated a real change in attitude to transatlantic weapon collaboration. But the amount of US money to be put into such projects is small; the US willingness to co-operate on a small scale may not represent a genuine change of heart regarding US self-sufficiency in arms production. For example, two 'buy American' proposals brought before Congress during 1986 would have placed major obstacles in the way of collaboration had they been adopted.[5] Technology security—the prevention of the transfer of high-technology items and even low-level know-how to the Eastern bloc—is also a sensitive issue; the USA is ultra-cautious and Europeans feel they do not have full access to US technical information.[6]

The fate of the Rolling Airframe Missile (RAM) illustrates some of the problems involved in transatlantic armaments collaboration. The RAM is a joint US-West German venture. On the basis of critical reports concerning reliability and quality, the House and Senate Armed Services Committee voted to delete the RAM from the fiscal year (FY) 1987 budget. Funding was eventually restored after pressure from European NATO countries which pointed out that cancellation would have devastating consequences for transatlantic armaments co-operation. The unilateral action to terminate the project was deeply resented in Europe.[7]

Three NATO countries—the UK, FR Germany and Italy—have reached agreement with the USA on participation in the Strategic Defense Initiative (SDI) programme. The British and US governments had signed a memorandum of understanding (MoU) in December 1985 defining the terms for British participation. So far, contracts worth approximately $30 million have been allocated to the UK where the amount is felt to be disappointingly small compared to the hundreds of millions of dollars which had been suggested previously.[8]

The Government of FR Germany formally endorsed the participation of its scientists and corporations in SDI in March 1986. Italy became in September 1986 the third European government to sign an MoU permitting its industry and research groups to participate in SDI. Canada, Denmark, Greece, Norway and the Netherlands have declined to take part in SDI at a government-to-government level but will not prevent their domestic industries and research groups from seeking contracts under the programme.[9]

The USA

The FY 1987 budget

Congress appropriated $289.6 billion for national defence in fiscal year 1987—which runs from 1 October 1986 to 30 September 1987. Of the appropriation, $281.6 billion were for the Department of Defense (DOD), $7.5 billion were for military-related atomic energy activities in the Department of Energy (DOE) and the remainder were for other defence-related programmes. The appropriation for the previous year, FY 1986, had been $286.1 billion, so that after allowing for inflation, the defence vote for FY 1987 was 3.5 per cent less than the FY 1986 allocation. This was the second consecutive year of real reductions in the amount earmarked for military spending.

The Reagan Administration had originally asked for $320.3 billion but Congress, acutely aware of the need to reduce the overall budget deficit, pared over $30 billion from the request. The Republican-controlled Senate was prepared to be more generous than the Democrat-controlled House, but when the Administration rejected a plan to trade tax increases for a higher military budget, the stage was set for a real cut in spending. (Details of US defence budgets 1980–87 are given in table 6.2.)

The largest cuts from the Administration's budget request came in the investment accounts (procurement, research and development (R&D), military construction and DOE military-related activities), with more cuts coming from the procurement account than any other. Overall, $10.8 billion

Table 6.2. US Administration budget estimates for fiscal years 1980–87 (as of January 1987)

Figures are in US $b.

	1980	1981	1982	1983	1984	1985	1986	1987
Total budget authority								
Total national defence,[a]								
current prices	143.9	180.0	216.5	245.0	265.2	294.7	289.1	289.6
Total Department of								
Defense, current prices	140.7	176.0	211.6	238.7	258.2	286.8	281.4	281.6
Total national defence,								
constant (1987) prices[b]	202.2	227.8	255.7	279.0	293.4	314.4	299.0	289.6
Percentage change	*1.9*	*12.7*	*12.2*	*9.1*	*5.2*	*7.2*	*−4.9*	*−3.2*
Outlays[c]								
Total national defence,								
current prices	134.0	157.5	185.3	209.9	227.4	252.7	273.4	279.5
Total Department of								
Defense, current prices	131.0	153.8	180.7	204.4	220.8	245.4	265.6	270.2
Total national defence,								
constant (1987) prices	195.5	204.8	220.8	240.2	251.7	269.7	283.4	279.5
Percentage change	*2.9*	*4.8*	*7.8*	*8.8*	*4.8*	*7.2*	*5.1*	*−1.4*

[a] *National defence*: A broader concept than Department of Defense activities, including military activities financed outside the DOD budget, mainly the design, testing and production of nuclear weapons (budgeted for under the Department of Energy) and military construction.

[b] The inflation factors used to calculate 1987 constant dollars come from the Office of the Assistant Secretary of Defense (Comptroller), *National Defence Budget Estimates for FY 1987* (US Government Printing Office: Washington, DC, May 1986).

[c] *Outlays*: The actual spending of money in cash or cheques during a given year. Includes net lending. Outlays are seldom identical to *budget authority* in any fiscal year because outlays spent during a year may be drawn partly from the budget authority conferred in previous years and budget authority includes funds which will be spent in future years.

Source: *National Defense Budget Estimates for FY 1987* (US Government Printing Office: Washington, DC, May 1986).

were cut from the Administration's request for weapon procurement. However, this did not result in the cancellation of any major weapon systems, but rather in the procurement of fewer weapons than the Administration had requested. For example, the purchase of 12 MX missiles was authorized, rather than the 21 requested, and reductions were made in the Administration's request for F/A-18 fighters (from 120 to 84), F-16 fighters (from 216 to 180), F-15 fighters (from 48 to 42), AMRAAM missiles (from 260 to 180), Bradley fighting vehicles (from 870 to 720), and DDG-51 destroyers (from 3 to 2). The largest savings ($818 million) resulted from the elimination of one DDG-51 destroyer.

Procurement by the US Army, Navy and Air Force was cut by 14 per cent, 13.3 per cent and 10.3 per cent respectively. The readiness-related accounts— operations and maintenance (O&M) and personnel—were both increased over the FY 1986 level, though not by as much as had been requested.

As a result of congressional action, actual military spending (outlays) during FY 1987 is estimated at $279.5 billion, a decline in real terms for the first time since 1976. It remains to be seen whether spending can be held within the projected limit; this was not the case in FY 1986 when projected outlays were exceeded by $12 billion.

Containing military spending

Congress was particularly concerned with the question of defence outlays since they, not budget authority, determine the impact of military spending on the overall budget deficit in any one year. Congress authorizes the value of contracts or spending obligation that may be entered into each year but the actual amount paid out—outlays—on these contracts will be less than the amount authorized. Different categories of expenditure have different outlay rates (see table 6.3). Whereas most of the money authorized for personnel will

Table 6.3. US defence outlay rates by appropriation heading

Figures are percentages of first-year budget authority. Figures may not add up due to rounding.

Appropriation heading	Year					
	1	2	3	4	5	6[a]
Military personnel	98	1	0	0	0	0
O&M	73	21	3	0	0	0
Procurement	15	31	27	13	7	0
RDT&E	47	40	8	2	0	0
Military construction	13	36	26	10	8	3
Family housing	46	30	13	4	2	1

[a] Sixth-year 'spendout' rates are not given for the 1986 fiscal year in the *Financial Summary Tables*, though they are given for the preceding year. For FY 1987 procurement, military construction, and family housing, the sixth-year outlay rates are estimated assuming the same sixth-year total lapsed-funding percentage (cents on the dollar not spent) as exhibited by the six-year outlay rates beginning in FY 1986, which are given in the *Financial Summary Tables* for FY 1987.

Source: Epstein, J., *The 1987 Defense Budget*, Studies in Defense Policy (The Brookings Institution: Washington, DC, 1986), table 3, p. 5, based on Department of Defense, *Financial Summary Tables, Fiscal Year 1987*, table M. Outlay rates for special foreign currency programme and defence-wide contingencies are not shown.

be used in the same year as authorization, of every dollar authorized for buying weapons only 15 cents will be spent in the first year.

Procurement cuts will clearly have less impact on total outlays in the first fiscal year than cuts in the military personnel or O&M budgets. Trimming these latter budgets has been popular with Congress in recent years as it has sought to control military spending. The method has had serious consequences for force readiness and little long-term impact on the budget imbalance. In the FY 1987 budget deliberations, Congress made a more serious effort to come to terms with the endemic deficit problem: first, by slowing down procurement programmes with the effects mentioned above; and, second, by rescinding $5.3 billion of excess funds authorized under the FYs 1984–86 budgets. The impact of this latter action on spending in FY 1987 was estimated at $1.5 billion. Congress also made some minor alterations of an accounting nature which will reduce FY 1987 outlays but have almost no long-term impact on spending.

It remains clear, however, that effective cuts are hard to make. The real reason why military spending is difficult to control is the enormous growth in investment during the Reagan Administration. This has led to the rapid accumulation of unexpended funds which will be spent in future years on the programmes for which they were appropriated. The backlog represents almost 40 per cent of total current outlays and about 80 per cent of the procurement budget. Rescinding previously allocated funds is not a very fruitful exercise since in many cases cancellation penalties are incurred. Congress has had some small success in identifying and cutting inflationary padding from some weapon programmes, but in general the only way to cut these programmes is by stretching them out, slowing the rate at which weapons are produced and finally paid for; the long-term effect of such a policy is normally that of raising unit costs. Personnel numbers have already been reduced, and pay and conditions must be kept attractive if trained personnel are to be retained. As a result, only one-third of the budget remains over which Congress can exercise control and this is largely in the area of O&M.

The question of congressional control is the crucial one. Irrespective of its constitutionality, the Balanced Budget and Emergency Deficit Control Act of December 1985 (the Gramm-Rudman-Hollings Bill) is regarded by some critics as inefficient, even dangerous, since it enjoins equal percentage cuts in all programmes without reference to security needs.[10] The law may, however, force Congress to a more rational analysis of military goals and the means to achieve them, given limited resources.

One alternative remains, and that is to increase taxation. Not only is such a policy opposed by the President, but raising taxes to cover military spending is unlikely at this time to find favour with the US public. At the beginning of the decade, public concern about the Soviet invasion of Afghanistan and the revolution in Iran, combined with the belief that US defence had been neglected during the 1970s, produced considerable popular and legislative support for the Reagan buildup. According to a 1980 Gallup public opinion poll, 58 per cent of Americans believed that US spending for national defence was inadequate, 25 per cent thought that it was at about the right level, and only 11 per cent thought it was excessive. A Gallup poll taken in 1986, however, shows a reversal of public attitudes since 1980: 47 per cent thought that US defence spending was excessive, 36 per cent thought it was about right and only 13 per cent thought that it was inadequate.[11] This shift has been reflected in Congress' treatment of the Administration's budget requests. From FY 1981 to FY 1985, Congress appropriated 95 per cent of the funds requested by the Reagan Administration. In FY 1986 the share dropped to 88.8 per cent and in FY 1987 it was 90.4 per cent.

Spain

An event of importance for NATO in 1986 was Spain's decision to remain within the Alliance though without participation in the NATO military structure. Although Spain has been a member of NATO since 1982, its military expenditure data are not yet included in *Financial and Economic Data Relating to NATO Defence* published annually by NATO.[12] Recent research suggests that Spain's military expenditure classified by function rather than by ministry is over 50 per cent higher than the amount commonly presented as the 'defence budget'[13] (see table 6.4). This functional classification is close to the NATO definition of military spending and includes such items as central administration, pensions and paramilitary forces. As a result of this revision, Spanish military spending as a share of GDP is something more than 3 per cent rather than 2 per cent and is seen to be in the same class as that of its NATO partners Belgium, FR Germany, the Netherlands and Norway.

Table 6.4. Spanish military expenditure 1980–87: a comparison of two definitions

Figures are in billion pesetas, at current prices.

	1980	1981	1982	1983	1984	1985	1986	1987
Ministry of Defence	287.0	337.5	409.3	478.3	552.8	618.6	631.0	704.1
Defence (functional classification)	471.9	551.0	649.3	743.9	846.8	947.7	966.7	1077.4

Source: Fisas Armengol, V., 'Los presupuestos de defensa para 1987' [The defence budgets for 1987], Centre d'informació i documentació internacionals a Barcelona (CIDOB), 1986 manuscript.

III. The WTO

One of the difficulties involved in the estimation of military expenditure by the Warsaw Treaty Organization (WTO) is mentioned in the introduction to this chapter (section I). Since the economies of the WTO countries are essentially centrally planned, the monetary value of their military effort cannot be compared with military spending in market economies. This was an important consideration in relation to the aggregation of the military expenditure of individual countries to give regional or world totals. It remains worthwhile to attempt to estimate WTO military spending by country since it can then be compared with other economic variables for those countries.

The accurate estimation of WTO military spending estimates presents special problems. The single 'defence' figure given in WTO budgets only partially covers the military expenditure concept on which SIPRI seeks to standardize its data.[14] This is, of course, true for the majority of countries in the world; the deficiency can often be remedied by a close examination of a country's itemized accounts. Such accounts are not currently available for WTO countries; in the case of Poland, Hungary and Romania, which are now members of the International Monetary Fund (IMF), it is possible that their accounting procedures will be adjusted to comply with Fund recommendations.[15] For the remaining WTO countries, there are currently no prospects of being able to penetrate their budget data.

Estimating Soviet military expenditure

Soviet budget statistics are among the most impenetrable. Unlike other major industrial countries where budget data are presented in some detail, the USSR announces a single aggregate figure for its military budget and provides no breakdown of the expenditures covered. Nor is it possible to identify military spending under the budgets of other ministries. This has the unfortunate result of leaving the field open for a variety of estimates of Soviet military spending to be made, each based on different assumptions and serving different purposes.[16] For example, some of these estimates, given in dollar terms, have been used to justify the rapid growth of US spending in recent years. A Congressional Research Service report has observed: 'CIA estimates of Soviet defense spending are among the most frequently cited numbers in the public debate over the size of the US defense budget. For many, they succinctly summarize the Soviet threat in easily understandable terms.'[17]

In the following brief survey, two of the most common methods of estimating Soviet military spending are described. Only rouble estimates are discussed, for two reasons. When military spending data are given in dollars, there is an unfortunate tendency to use the estimates as a measure of relative military strength. Estimating a dollar figure for Soviet military expenditure does not imply that the overall military capacity of, for example, the USA and the USSR can be assessed through a comparison of these data. Second, bad rouble estimates are not improved by converting them into dollars—they simply deteriorate further.

The official Soviet budget

There is considerable evidence indicating that the official Soviet figure for 'defence spending' does not cover all military-related expenditure:

1. The USSR has an observably large and powerful military machine.
2. Even allowing for differences in the pricing system, it seems unlikely that Soviet spending could have been held at the same (and sometimes falling) nominal level for the period 1970–84. That is, the official figure lacks credibility.
3. Occasional references in Soviet sources to the content of the budget allocation to defence suggest that its coverage is less broad than the concept of

total military expenditure employed by SIPRI. For example, a 1965 Soviet source gives the following description:

The estimate of the Ministry of Defense anticipates expenditures for:

Payments for armaments, ammunitions, equipment, fuel and lubricant supplies, food, clothing, personal equipment, and other articles needed to ensure the battle and political training and battle readiness of troops;

maintenance and personal support (*khozyaystvennobytovoye ustroyastvo*) of military units (*chasti*);

maintenance of military educational institutions (Suvorov and Nakhimov schools, secondary and higher educational institutions, and military academies), networks of hospitals, other medical institutions and sanatoria, officers' homes, clubs, sports installations, etc.;

issuance of monetary allowances (*devol'stviye*) to servicemen and wages to workers and employees of military units and commands (*soyedineniya*);

financing capital construction and industrial enterprises of the Ministry of Defense USSR.[18]

This description is now over 20 years old and no information is available as to its current relevance. It must be emphasized that accounting practices differ widely between countries and that the above type of definition is quite normal. Most countries finance some military expenditure from other budgets—the problem is to identify and quantify the additional spending. In the Soviet case this is extremely difficult, perhaps impossible.

4. Known to be missing from the defence budget are allocations for R&D, atomic energy, stockpiling and military aid. Other missing items may include the KGB border guards who have many clearly military duties; internal troops of the Ministry of Internal Affairs (MVD); construction and billeting troops; railroad and road troops.[19]

5. Some categories of expenditure, such as weapon production, although included in the defence budget, must also be financed under other budget headings. For example, if costs of personnel, O&M and construction are added and the total is subtracted from the official defence budget, very little would be left to cover procurement in full, although this is itemized in the above definition.

Some items covered by the defence budget are non-military and should be deducted. Military industries produce some goods for civilian consumption, military construction troops build roads, bridges and buildings, and soldiers help with the harvest. This is normal procedure in countries where the armed forces are integrated into the economic and social fabric of the nation.

Methods of estimation

Two approaches are usually employed when estimating Soviet military spending: the expenditure residual and the building-block approaches.

The expenditure residual approach. Every year the Soviet state budget contains large sums of money that are unitemized or unaccounted for. Given the hypothesis that the defence budget is incomplete, these residuals have attracted attention as potential sources of military expenditure. The total budget has been examined for internal consistency and the following residuals are felt to be of particular interest:

1. The budgetary expenditure (BE) residual: expenditures specified in the central government budget are less than total outlays. Three forms of expenditure are financed from the remainder: (*a*) internal security, (*b*) loan service and (*c*) grants to investment banks. When these three items are subtracted there remains a residual, some or all of which might be spent for military purposes. (Some of the internal security allocation should also be included in military spending.)

2. The national economy (NE) residual: the main budget heading 'financing the national economy' contains a significant amount of expenditure in addition to that accounted for under the various sub-headings.

3. The same is true of the industry and construction residual. Under the budget heading 'financing the national economy' there is a sub-heading for 'industry and construction'. Adding individual line items and subtracting them from the total leaves a considerable residual.

Military R&D presents a separate problem. Its size is often estimated from the total science budget which it is assumed includes military R&D. This is supported by the following Soviet-source comment: 'The overall expenditures for "science" can be obtained from the Central Statistics Board of the USSR. However, not all these expenditures go to the development of science and technology. Thus only a part of the defence-related research is related to scientific and technical development'.[20] The actual share of military R&D in the total science budget is sometimes estimated with reference to the ratio of military to total R&D spending in Western countries which design and manufacture a full range of major armaments. Other methods involve an analysis of the overall R&D budget to determine its military content. R&D has been identified by analysts as the most imprecise element in the estimates of total Soviet military expenditure.[21]

All these methods of estimating total military spending are crude and often arbitrary. However, they have been widely employed by Western scholars who have no access to the results of intelligence monitoring. Painstaking research might lead to further refinement of estimation techniques but the results may still only be sophisticated guesswork.

The building-block approach. The second main method used to estimate Soviet military activity is the building-block approach. This method relies on the establishment of an accurate detailed inventory of the nature, size and content of Soviet defence programmes. Prices, measured in roubles, are then assigned to individual components of the inventory and these are then added together. In 1985, the CIA's costing model contained over 1100 defence components. However, few rouble prices are available for these items. Until 1977 the CIA had just 10. Although more are now known, precise values can still only be attached to a small fraction of military products and services. This means that CIA rouble costs rely to a very great extent on inappropriate extrapolations from US cost patterns.[22] Furthermore the accuracy of 'building-block' estimates cannot be independently evaluated because of the highly classified status of the CIA's data base and estimating procedures.[23]

The most commonly quoted and used estimates of Soviet military spending are those presented by the CIA (and the 'rival' DIA estimates), often without any of the detailed CIA caveats concerning their accuracy and possible usefulness. The fact that they are the product of intelligence agencies gives them credibility in the minds of the public which cannot be matched by the painstaking analysis of academics researching into the complexity of Soviet accounting principles.

The Congressional Research Service report concludes that, at best, CIA and DIA estimates provide only a gross picture of the size and trends of Soviet defence costs. Estimates of recent-year spending should be considered highly provisional.[24] It will be possible to evaluate estimates coming from these intelligence agencies only when the material on which they are based is open to independent assessment. All serious researchers are at pains to emphasize the degree of uncertainty involved in some of their own fundamental assumptions concerning the Soviet economy in general and military spending in particular. Only greater openness by the USSR concerning its defence expenditures can remedy the confusion currently surrounding Soviet spending estimates and prevent their illegitimate use as propaganda in the arms race.

At a SIPRI workshop held in 1986 on the estimation of Soviet military expenditure and the defence burden, new and existing approaches to the problem were closely examined by a diverse group of specialists.[25] SIPRI will continue the exercise of trying to improve the understanding of Soviet defence spending. Estimates made at the workshop of current Soviet spending ranged from 10 to 15 per cent of GNP. However, in the absence of a satisfactory series of spending data which could be used in an overall assessment of Soviet economic issues, SIRPI has chosen not to publish any Soviet series this year.

Estimating the military expenditure of non-Soviet WTO countries

SIPRI's estimates for the non-Soviet WTO military expenditure are taken from domestic sources. It is known that these do not give the full picture of military spending. There are items under other budget headings which should be classified as military, as well as some non-military spending included in the defence budget. To correct some of these deficiencies, estimates of military R&D should be included in the military budgets of Czechoslovakia, the German Democratic Republic (GDR) and Poland. In the case of the GDR, amounts should be added to cover border, transport and construction troops, and subtracted to exclude the civilian element of 'internal security' where this has been included in the defence budget. Other important items often covered by the budgets of other ministries have proved impossible to estimate; these include industrial investment relating to arms production and special benefits to military personnel and their families.[26] The extent to which East European countries meet the cost of Soviet troops stationed on their soil is not known.

Despite these problems, it is believed that the non-Soviet WTO data taken from domestic sources are adequate for the purpose of estimating trends in the

Table 6.5. Eastern Europe: average annual or annual percentage real growth in economic activity and military expenditure, 1975–85

Figures are percentage changes.

	1975–80	1980–85	1981	1982	1983	1984	1985
Bulgaria							
NMP[a]	6.1	3.7	5.0	4.2	3.0	4.6	1.8
Military expenditure	4.0	..	5.6	3.2	2.0	..	..
Czechoslovakia							
NMP	3.7	1.8	−0.1	0.2	2.3	3.5	3.1[b]
Military expenditure	1.0	..	−0.7	1.8	1.9	3.1	..
GDR							
NMP	4.1	4.5	4.8	2.6	4.6	5.5	4.8
Military expenditure	5.5	5.6	8.2	5.7	5.6	6.9	1.6
Hungary							
NMP	2.8	1.4	2.5	2.6	0.3	2.5	−1.0
Military expenditure	2.0	−0.8	3.0	−1.6	−7.5	−4.9	7.8
Poland							
NMP	1.2	−0.8[c]	−12.0	−5.0	6.0	5.6	3.0
Military expenditure	0.5	−0.7	−6.6	9.9	−9.6	−9.3	14.7
Romania							
NMP	7.2	4.4	2.2	2.7	3.7	7.7	5.9
Military expenditure	0.1	−2.6	−1.3	−7.5	−2.3	0.1	−2.6

[a] NMP—net material product.
[b] Estimate made by the secretariat of the UN Economic Commission for Europe.
[c] Average annual performance 1983–85, 4.9 per cent.

Source: *Economic Survey in Europe, 1985–86* (UN Economic Commission for Europe: New York, 1986), table 3.1.1., p. 114 and table 3.1.12, p. 132; SIPRI military expenditure data base.

spending of individual countries. This view is confirmed by an expert study submitted to the Joint Economic Committee of the US Congress:

Even if non-Soviet WTO defence budgets probably also exclude some outlays, the long-term growth in these figures is consistent with observed developments in defense programs and with general inflation rates apparent in the economy, thus suggesting that the official data roughly reflect actual trends in total military spending by the Ministries of Defense.[27]

Unlike the USSR, where official data on military spending remained unconvincingly the same for 15 years, the countries of Eastern Europe have exhibited patterns of growth and decline which reflect their economic fortunes in recent years. The most prosperous member of the group, the GDR, has maintained an exceptionally high rate of growth of military spending. This is also the case with Bulgaria, though the pattern there is more uneven (table 6.5).

The economic impact of military expenditure in the WTO

Irrespective of the special accounting problems involved in estimating Soviet military expenditure, it remains clear that military spending is a heavy burden on the Soviet economy and one which the current leadership is anxious to reduce. In many senses, SDI is a bigger economic threat to the USSR than it is a military challenge. If the USSR chooses to match the US SDI programme in full, including the development and deployment of space-based systems, the effort could in the long run damage General Secretary Gorbachev's plans to raise real incomes significantly by the end of the century.

There are two reasons for this: first, large-scale resources would have to be diverted from the private consumption sector into open-ended R&D in the new technologies associated with SDI; second, this very re-direction of additional resources to the military is incompatible with the economic liberalization which is an essential element of Gorbachev's economic drive. Fundamental to the programme of economic renewal is the replacement of centralized detailed planning of all industrial activity with a degree of planning, decision taking, financing and profit sharing at the local level. The successful model of privately formed co-operatives responsible for pricing and marketing their goods will be extended to the whole economy where it will form a special sector. From May 1987, small-scale private enterprise will be permitted, primarily within the service sector. Within a decade it is expected that the private co-operative sector will contribute 10–12 per cent to the national income and the private sector a further 4 per cent. Major investment is planned in industries producing consumer goods and in housing in an attempt to raise living standards.[28] These ambitious schemes for economic renewal and growth cannot be achieved unless the USSR, like China, reorders its priorities and gives less prominence to its military sector.

The Soviet economic reform programme has been greeted with a certain reserve by the leaders of the satellite states. There are some fears that Soviet economic expansion will be at their expense. Schemes to extend co-production and R&D collaboration are seen as a Soviet attempt to pick the raisins out of the already meagre East European cake, as well as presenting a further opportunity for Soviet domination and control. It may also be feared that a cut-back in the Soviet military effort will result in demands on the East Europeans to make a bigger contribution to their own defence at a time when they too are looking for ways out of economic stagnation. During 1986, Hungary argued for the more effective use of military spending, rather than its constant expansion.[29] In Romania another call was made for a reduction in military spending, this time in the form of a referendum which voted for total spending cuts of 25 per cent by 1990 and the reduction of armed forces personnel by 10 000. In 1983, Romania pledged to hold its military expenditure at the 1982 level until 1985, a pledge which it appears to have maintained.[30]

IV. Other Europe

All the countries in the SIPRI classification 'Other Europe' describe themselves as non-aligned and in most cases neutral. Questions are sometimes raised as to the economic cost of non-alignment and neutrality. A neutral country, in the terms set out in the Hague Convention of 1907, must be prepared to repel all attempts to invade its territory, airspace or territorial waters as well as attempts to use these for belligerent purposes. It must therefore be prepared to face attack by all other countries. An allied country,

Table 6.6. European countries: military expenditure in relation to other variables

Country	Military expenditure (average 1983–85) as:					
	$ per capita	Rank order	$ per sq. km	Rank order	As % of GDP[a]	Rank order
NNA[b]						
Austria	126	17	11 409	14	1.2	24
Finland	237	12	3 451	25	2.0	20
Ireland	94	20	4 695	23	1.7	22
Sweden	420	5	7 745	20	2.7	15
Switzerland	323	9	50 472	6	1.8	21
Yugoslavia	109	19	9 783	16	5.0	3
NATO						
Belgium	360	7	115 097	3	3.1	12
Denmark	325	8	38 527	8	2.3	18
France	511	2	51 237	5	4.1	6
FR Germany	437	4	107 316	4	3.3	8
Greece	284	11	21 293	11	6.9	1
Italy	194	13	36 654	9	2.7	15
Luxembourg	139	16	18 556	12	1.1	25
Netherlands	368	6	129 260	1	3.2	11
Norway	457	3	5 779	21	3.0	14
Portugal	78	21	8 656	18	3.3	8
Spain	185	14	14 162	13	3.3	8
Turkey	64	24	3 951	24	4.6	4
UK	521	1	119 914	2	5.3	2
WTO						
Bulgaria	125[c]	18	10 162[c]	15	3.1[c]	12
Czechoslovakia	178	15	21 599	10	3.5	7
German DR	317	10	48 978	7	4.6	4
Hungary	70	23	8 029	19	2.3	18
Poland	75	22	8 815	17	2.6[d]	17
Romania	49	25	4 720	22	1.4	23

[a] For Bulgaria, Czechoslovakia, German DR, Poland and Romania, military expenditure is given as a percentage of GNP.

[b] Neutral and non-aligned.

[c] 1982–84.

[d] 1983 only.

Sources: Population and area: *World Development Report* (Oxford University Press for World Bank: New York, 1986), table 1, pp. 180–81; military expenditure as a percentage of GDP/GNP: table 6A.3.

on the other hand, can depend on its allies not to attack it and can also expect help from them in the case of external aggression.

   A priori reasoning suggests it must be expensive for a European nation to face alone the same security threat which other European nations choose to meet as members of an alliance. On a more pragmatic level, there is a widely held opinion that non-alliance results in lower military spending. This view is held both by those who believe that alliance membership *per se* raises the level of military expenditure as well as by those who hold that the neutral nations of Western Europe are benefiting from the NATO military 'shield' without helping to pay for it.

   The factors which determine military spending are not simply geopolitical but reflect a country's history, culture, domestic politics and such current economic problems as unemployment, inflation or a balance-of-payments deficit. For these reasons and for those described in the introduction to this chapter relating to comparisons of military spending, it is neither possible nor relevant to isolate and measure the costs of alliance versus non-alliance membership. However, rank ordering of certain variables for all European countries will illustrate the importance they attach to certain relevant issues. The variables chosen are military expenditure in relation to population, land mass and GDP (see table 6.6).

V. The Middle East

Middle Eastern military spending has fallen since 1984. Two important qualifications must be made to this statement: there is a lack of reliable data from the countries involved in armed conflicts, and the pictures for sub-regions in the Middle East look very different.

The Gulf region is dominated by the expensive war of attrition between Iran and Iraq, which has since 1980 claimed the lives of between 350 000 and more than one million people according to different sources (see chapter 8).[31] Consequently, the Gulf states of Kuwait, Bahrain, Oman and the United Arab Emirates have shown a sharp increase in their military expenditures since the beginning of the Gulf War (figure 6.1a) until declining oil revenues forced them to cut expenditures in 1986. The trend for Saudi Arabia is different: falling defence expenditures in 1982–85 and increasing expenditure in 1986 (figure 6.1b).

Egypt, Israel, Jordan and Syria, however, have not significantly increased their expenditures in this decade, but have remained at about the same level since 1980 (figure 6.1c).[32]

In US FY 1986, Israel received $2.9 billion in US security assistance[33] (see figure 6.2). For US FY 1987 the figure will be $3 billion.[34] The Israeli Lavi fighter aircraft development programme now costs Israel about $550 million per year, some $300 million of which is taken from US security assistance. The United States criticizes these expenditures, arguing that it would be cheaper for Israel to purchase US aircraft (F-16s or F-18s) than to develop its own fighter.[35] Since the Lavi takes a substantial part of US Foreign Military Sales (FMS) funds to Israel, the 'Israeli Army is being starved of appropriations for its own programmes to upgrade its tanks and artillery, as well as being unable to modernise its helicopter forces'.[36] Financing the development of a domestic weapon system with Foreign Military Sales funds is a special arrangement which the US Government has with Israel, but a high percentage of the fighter components are US products. On 21 July 1986 the first prototype of the multi-mission fighter rolled out.[37] However, it is estimated that Israel will need close to $1 billion more to complete development of the Lavi.[38] Although the Israeli Treasury has warned of an economic decline for 1987 owing to a drop in tax revenues of nearly $700 million, the Defence Ministry asked for an additional $200 million for the FY 1987 budget.[39]

Egypt, the second largest recipient of US security assistance—absorbing

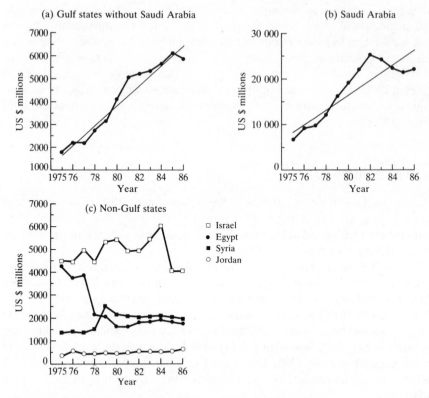

Figure 6.1. Middle Eastern military expenditure, 1975–86
Values are US $m. at constant (1980) prices. Linear regression lines in figures a and b show the 10-year trend.

Source: SIPRI military expenditure data base.

some 20 per cent of all US security funds—received $2.02 billion for US FY 1986 and $2.12 billion for 1987.[40] The IMF estimates Egypt's external debts today at about $38.6 billion.[41] Debt service consumes about 35 per cent of Egyptian foreign currency revenues,[42] and the shortage of hard currency has become acute.[43] Egyptian military debts to the West amount to about $8 billion, of which $5 billion is for US Foreign Military Sales purchases.[44] Egypt is already behind with $500 million in its repayment of military debts. The current economic crisis and falling oil revenues will make it even more difficult for Egypt to catch up with its debt payments.

Saudi Arabia experienced an enormous economic boom in the 1970s, owing to its oil earnings. However, in the spring of 1986 the Saudi Arabian Government, for the first time in its history, was unable to present a state budget, because it was impossible to calculate oil revenues in a situation of falling oil prices.[45] Although Saudi Arabia cannot keep up with its past level of state expenditures and has had to cut them drastically, military expenditure will

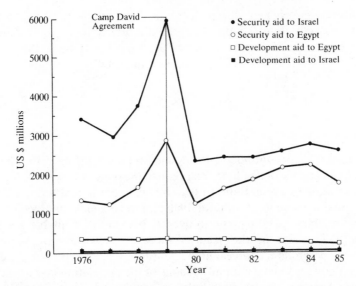

Figure 6.2. US economic and security aid to Egypt and Israel, 1976–85
Values are in US $m. at constant (1980) prices.

Source: *US Overseas Loans and Grants and Assistance from International Organizations, Obligations and Loan Authorizations, 1 July 1945–30 September 1985* (Agency for International Development: Washington, DC).

not be affected: it will rather increase, mainly because of the Iraq-Iran War, military aid and arms imports.[46]

Declining oil revenues and a down-swing in the Gulf economy also affected Kuwait, Bahrain and the United Arab Emirates. Bahrain for the first time issued treasury bills and borrowed from the local market to finance its state budget.[47] The United Arab Emirates faced a budget cut of at least 30 per cent in 1986.[48] In April 1986 Kuwait presented its fourth deficit budget, for FY 1987, anticipating a 41 per cent decrease in oil income compared with 1985.[49] Despite this difficult economic situation all the countries in the Gulf region tend to spend increasing resources on defence in order to meet the threat of the Gulf War spreading.

A violent *coup d'état* took place in South Yemen on 13 January 1986, taking the lives of between 2000 and 10 000 people according to various sources.[50] Rival tribes still dominate the political picture in South Yemen, causing several armed power struggles since its independence in 1969. For the Soviet Union the country has strategic importance: it is situated at the entrance to the Red Sea, and the Soviet Navy uses the port facilities of Aden to resupply its ships patrolling in the Indian Ocean. In the course of the internal conflict, the USSR made it clear to all neighbouring states that it would not accept any outside interference in the conflict. After almost a month of fighting, a new government came to power on 9 February 1986. South Yemen's military expenditure—showing a sharp increase from 1976 to 1981 and then declining—is only about 0.5–0.6 per cent of the total military expenditure in the Gulf region. However, it represents a heavy burden for the economy, absorbing on average about 17 per cent of the GDP.

VI. South Asia

Sri Lanka

Ethnic disturbances continued unabated in Sri Lanka during 1986. The central government's policy of a military response to the domestic violence has led to a growth of military expenditure of over 500 per cent in real terms since 1981. The original defence allocation for 1986 had to be almost doubled during the year and military spending rose to over 20 per cent of available government revenue.[51] The size of the security forces has grown rapidly, including auxiliaries, paramilitary forces, home guards and reservists. The government has taken powers to conscript all sections of the population and to establish a National Auxiliary Force of youth and young adults responsible to the President which would prevent or suppress 'any rebellion or insurrection or other civil disturbance'.[52] The police force has reportedly been expanded by 30 per cent during the year.[53] Mobilization on such a scale not only involves the government in direct costs but also disrupts the normal economic life of the country. Recent weapon purchases have included small arms, field artillery, helicopter gunships, light aircraft, patrol boats, landing craft and troop carriers. Many of these items have been bought urgently and it can be assumed that the terms of purchase have often been unfavourable.

In presenting the 1986 budget, the Minister of Finance and Planning repeated his comment of the previous year that for a poor country like Sri Lanka such a military buildup was not possible without accompanying sacrifices in growth, employment and living standards.[54] A continued military response to the violence would involve either a cut-back in development to accommodate escalating defence expenditures or the continuation of the development programme, causing a big government deficit which would have to be financed by domestic and foreign loans. This would seriously threaten the internal and external financial stability of the country. However, the President has made his viewpoint clear: 'I shall have a military solution to what I believe is a military problem. After doing so I shall tackle the political side'.[55]

Because of the collapse of world market prices for Sri Lanka's three main exports—tea, rubber and coconuts—and the disastrous fall-off in the numbers of tourists in the light of the civil disturbances, balance-of-payments and debt repayment prospects are bleak. Gains from declining oil prices have been balanced out by falling remittances from Sri Lankan workers in the Middle East. Government and guerrilla military activities are also disrupting domestic production and damaging the country's economic infrastructure.

Other nations in the region are being drawn into the conflict. India has been acting as a mediator between the majority Sinhalese and the minority Tamils in Sri Lanka. At the same time, many Tamils have taken refuge in southern India where there is a Tamil population of 50 million. They have received the support of the local population and camps have reportedly been set up in Tamil Nadu to train Tamil guerrillas.[56] Though forming a majority in Sri Lanka, the Sinhalese regard themselves as a minority within the region with no other homeland than Sri Lanka. They have turned to India's arch-rival, Pakistan, to train government commando forces and some pilots for counter-insurgency (COIN) operations.[57]

India

India is also experiencing internal tension on a serious scale. The claims of Sikh autonomy are leading to violent confrontations with government forces, particularly in the Punjab. To meet these and similar disturbances, a bill was passed in August to provide for a National Security Guard, an élite military corps, to combat internal disturbances and terrorism. The commando force would be trained in anti-terrorist tactics and adequately provided with weaponry and equipment.[58] It is not clear whether funds for this force are included in the defence budget.

The annual defence report for 1985–86 assumed multiple threats to India's security; most prominent were those from China and Pakistan. According to Indian perceptions, China's modernization programme 'with military over-tones' had security implications, as did any normalization of Sino-Soviet relations which might allow China to redeploy its forces from the Soviet border to Tibet. Pakistan is felt to pose a major threat for two reasons: first, the possible interaction of external forces with 'internal forces of dissent in the political and socio-economic spheres'; second, the flow into Pakistan of sophisticated arms from the USA which bear no relation to the situation in Afghanistan but which are interpreted as a buildup of forces threatening India.[59]

To contain these and other perceived threats, India continued to implement its ambitious 1985–90 Defence Plan. The emphasis is on the modernization and replacement of equipment to secure greater firepower, mobility and more modern means of communication, and on self-reliance in the production of weapons and import substitution. Resources earmarked for the military programme in the central government budget for FY 1986 grew by a nominal 11 per cent. In real terms, Indian military expenditure has grown by 5.6 per cent annually since 1981, the year in which Pakistan began receiving US security assistance.

Pakistan

The military budget for FY 1986, 10 per cent more than the previous year, was 38.6 billion rupees ($2.2 billion), that is, 38.5 per cent of total current government expenditure. Military expenditure and debt servicing together take 67.9 per cent of total current expenditure and 44.8 per cent of the total budget.[60] Other budget programmes included Rs 13.4 billion ($0.8 billion) for rural development, Rs 1.0 billion ($0.06 billion) for housing improvement and a total allocation of Rs 15.2 billon ($0.95 billion) for education.[61]

Some opposition parties and individuals have publicly questioned the growing defence budget in the light of the modest allocation to social welfare programmes. The leader of the opposition in the National Assembly demanded, without success, that the military allocations be discussed in the House.[62] Debate on the defence budget has been taboo since 1958: budget details are known only to the armed forces and public discussion is regarded as a 'security risk'.[63] Though the country is no longer under martial law, the elected assembly has had to move cautiously to assert itself against the extensive powers of the President.[64] The military remain a powerful political force with total control over national security issues. In this they are supported by the religious leaders and their followers who feel the need to maintain Pakistan's geographical and ideological frontiers.[65]

Aid to India and Pakistan

Superpower patronage of each of these two hostile nations is fuelling a costly arms race in a region where large sections of the population lack basic economic and social necessities.

The USA, which since 1981 has been giving security assistance to Pakistan, sought to balance its influence on the sub-continent by offering aid to India in 1986. It was exploiting what was seen as a loosening of ties between the USSR and India, following Soviet attempts to normalize its relations with China. The new US policy included an offer to assist India in modernizing its defence industry. Although agreement was reached in November 1986 on the sale of some US military equipment, negotiations for the supply of advanced material, including a supercomputer, were inconclusive. Problems arose over safeguards which would prevent its use by India in building nuclear weapons.

The following month, the Soviet Union offered India access to its top computer technology. A new trade and credit agreement was reached which is likely to result in even closer economic relations between the two countries than in the past. The Soviet Union has also offered India military assistance which goes some way towards balancing US aid to Pakistan. The early delivery of 40 MiG-29 fighter aircraft has been promised as well as assistance with the development of an airborne radar system.[66]

Pakistan is the fourth largest recipient of US aid, after Israel, Egypt and Turkey, having been pledged $3.2 billion in a six-year military and economic aid package beginning in 1981.[67] FMS assistance under the 1981 aid terms consisted of guaranteed loans at 10–14 per cent interest with a three-year grace period. As a result of these tough terms, debt repayments on the current package amount to $2 billion and a further $1.5 billion, it was claimed, was eaten up by inflation.[68] For the period 1987–93, Pakistan sought $6.5 billion, more than double the amount pledged in 1981, and on far better terms and conditions.

With the new aid negotiations imminent, a high-level group was appointed to study Pakistan's future procurement policy in the light of past experience, regional developments and the new economic and technological possibilities. It was held that US aid was too 'expensive' and not cost effective. The USA was reluctant to part with technology and combat efficiency, and might be even more so in the future. Pakistan should therefore seek alternative suppliers and less exacting patrons. Technological advances in Pakistan were making retrofits and updating possible without loss of efficiency. They reduced costs and dependence on outside sources while optimizing the use of domestically available technologies and personnel. Furthermore, as a result of its close ties with the USA, there had been political repercussions for Pakistan, particularly among its Islamic friends. There was also friction with the USA itself over Pakistan's nuclear programme, its anti-Zionist stance and its hostility towards India.[69]

Despite this flirting with alternatives, Pakistan accepted a new US aid agreement, announced in March 1986. The USA stressed that it would continue to play an important role in Pakistan's defence modernization. Pakistan will receive $4.02 billion in military and economic aid for the period 1987–93, a 35 per cent increase over the current agreement.[70] The new package will be on highly concessional (favourable) terms and include a $1.5 billion security assistance grant and long-term loans at an annual interest rate of 5 per cent. Net inflow of aid from the new package is put at $820 million.[71]

VII. The Far East

Japan

In December 1986, the Japanese Government decided to put forward a military budget for the coming fiscal year which would breach the so-called 1 per cent limit. The policy originally agreed upon by the ruling Liberal Democratic Party and the National Defense Council in November 1976 was that 'for the time being' the 'target' would be for defence spending not to exceed 1 per cent of GNP. Thus the limit has never been either legally or constitutionally binding (it could not be—Article 9 of the constitution forbids the maintenance of military forces, as well as any other war potential) nor has it ever placed a permanent and inflexible restraint on Japanese military spending. The decision was originally taken for political reasons at a time when Japan's national income was growing fast and there was public concern over the growth of military spending. It was of symbolic importance on two grounds: first, expressing the wish of the majority of Japanese not to participate in the East-West arms race; second, reassuring Japan's neighbours of its peaceful intentions. The current increases in spending reflect higher salaries, rising unit costs and increased cost-sharing for US forces in Japan.

In 1976, military expenditure was 0.9 per cent of GNP. Between 1976 and 1986, nominal GNP grew by 100 per cent and military expenditure by 140 per cent. The military expenditure share of GNP has therefore, inevitably, grown. Statistically, the data presented by the National Defense Agency have always been inadequate for any *exact* calculation of shares. The Agency publishes *budgeted* military expenditure figures for a fiscal year and compares them to *initial forecast* figures of GNP for a calendar year.[72] The more usual statistical exercise of comparing actual spending and income both on a calendar-year basis shows that the 1 per cent target level was reached in 1983. It should also be noted that if Japanese military spending were to be calculated on the basis of the NATO definition so as to include pensions, it would already take an estimated 1.6 per cent of GNP.[73]

The Philippines

Although the overall Philippine budget for 1986 was revised in June 1986, it is unclear whether increases in the military budget planned by the Marcos Government were adjusted. Among the many problems facing President Corazon Aquino in re-establishing democracy in the Philippines after the overthrow of Ferdinand Marcos is the reform of the armed forces. The size of the military establishment reportedly quadrupled during the Marcos era,[74] but the efficiency and morale of the forces were destroyed through politicization and inadequate training and procurement. It will not be easy for the President to keep her election promise to reduce military spending and to pass the savings on to education.[75]

Incompetence and indiscipline within the Civilian Home Defense Force will be dealt with through mass dismissal[76] but transforming the armed forces into an efficient, professional and apolitical body will be a costly process and a heavy burden on the troubled national economy.[77] Furthermore, groups both inside and outside the country are urging President Aquino to seek a 'military solution' to the country's insurgency problems. To this end, the US Congress approved a minimum of $200 million in security-related economic aid for the year beginning October 1986.[78]

North and South Korea

North and South Korea continue to be divided on ideological grounds more than 30 years after the truce which brought an end to open hostilities on the peninsula. Military spending takes a reported 31 per cent of government expenditure in the South and 14 per cent in the North (1986). The share of the national income devoted to military purposes is 6 and 12 per cent respectively. South Korean sources, however, estimate that the North's military spending accounts for about 30 per cent of total government expenditure and a massive 24 per cent of national income, since military outlays are to be found under other budget headings, such as the 'people's economic sector'.[79] Each side is patronized by a superpower. As well as having 42 000 US troops stationed on its soil, South Korea received $232 million in security assistance from the USA in US FY 1985 and $163 million in US FY 1986. North Korea reportedly has received 10 MiG-23 fighter bombers, Scud-B ground-to-ground and SAM-3 ground-to-air missiles from the USSR since summer 1985.

Military spending is not open to debate in either country. In North Korea, the budget is rubber-stamped by the Supreme People's Assembly following a speech by the Finance Minister during which few budget details are revealed. In South Korea, discussion on the size and composition of the military budget is at all times severely curtailed by the provisions of the National Security Law.[80]

In both countries the high level of military spending involves sacrifices in living standards. In the North, a strong military sector is as important a policy objective as more familiar economic and social goals. Ideologically, a strengthening of military power is held to be the equivalent of an improvement of living standards. At a more pragmatic level, it is clear that heavy military spending is a burden on the economy and a brake on social development. In the South, military spending has delayed the extension of the welfare schemes which have become essential as modern economic behaviour destroys older living patterns.[81]

The construction by North Korea of a dam for a hydroelectric power station just 10 km north of the demilitarized zone at a reported cost of $1.6 billion is causing great concern in the South. Experts disagree as to North Korea's need to expand its electricity-generating capacity on the scale planned or at the chosen site; South Korean officials are convinced of an ulterior military motive behind the project. The Kŭmgangsan Dam on the upper Han river is projected to hold back 20 billion tonnes of water. If the dam were breached, by accident or design, the water would flood large areas of South Korea including Seoul and the Han river valley, isolate units of the armed forces deployed north of the Han and damage five power stations along the lower Han river. After repeated calls to the North to halt the Mt Kŭmgangsan project, the Seoul Government has announced plans to build an effective counter-dam 'as a rightful means of self-defence'. The projected cost of the South Korean 'peace dam' is 600 billion won ($700 million). This is being raised partly by private subscription but will mainly be government financed. Despite their character as military installa-tions, it is doubtful whether the costs for either dam will be included in the respective military budgets of the two countries.

VIII. Oceania

New Zealand and Australia

In July 1986, the USA made it known that it would renounce its obligations towards New Zealand under the 1951 tripartite ANZUS Treaty following the ban by New Zealand on visits by nuclear-powered or -armed vessels to its ports.[82] So far no major changes have been made in New Zealand defence policy as a result of this change. There are probably two reasons for this: first, New Zealand emphasizes that it has not withdrawn from the ANZUS Pact; therefore, logically, no changes are needed. Second, New Zealand is currently struggling with a heavy public debt; tax revenues fell following zero economic growth in FY 1986 and resources were therefore not available to execute policy changes. Military spending was not, however, subject to the cuts experienced in other areas of public spending.

The increase in nominal gross military expenditure by New Zealand in FY 1986 was 22 per cent or about 4 per cent above inflation, 2 percentage points higher than the overall budget growth. Over 40 per cent of the rise was due to increases in salaries which affected all Defence Ministry programmes. There were few real increases in other items, a notable exception being a 150 per cent rise in capital expenditure under the heading 'Defence Science' for refit and maintenance work on a naval research vessel and the purchase of unspecified scientific equipment. Air force procurement spending fell as a result of the rephasing of the Skyhawk fighter aircraft modernization project. The army procurement programme included the purchase of small arms and vehicles, while the navy was given resources to buy a tanker. Earlier plans to introduce submarines into the service were dropped. The Defence Minister expressed concern over the amount and cost of the modern defence technology held necessary to maintain effective armed forces.

New Zealand fears US economic retaliation as a result of its nuclear policy.[83] Both Australia and New Zealand are dissatisfied with current US trade policy, especially the sale of low-price wheat and butter on the world market to the detriment of traditional Australian and New Zealand exports. The Australian Foreign Minister made the connection between US trade policy and Australian strategic capabilities quite specific, saying that income lost through US wheat sales meant less money for Australia to buy and operate military equipment and to participate in exercises.[84] Australia tried to exploit its 'loyalty' to the ANZUS Pact to gain reassurances from the USA over trade, but while a reference to such problems was made in the final communiqué from the August 1986 council meeting of ANZUS, Australia was given no guarantees regarding changes in US export policy.

Australian defence policies and the structure of the armed forces were examined in a special report published in May 1986 (the Dibb Report). Its main proposal was a movement away from the concept of 'forward defence' through military alliances with countries of South-East Asia to one of self-reliance and greater emphasis on local defence. The report found that Australia faced no foreseeable armed threat. Nevertheless a minimum 3 per cent annual real increase in military spending for at least 10 years was called for, since the local defence concept would involve a considerable amount of new weapon procurement. Spending on weapons was expected to increase from 28 per cent of the military budget in FY 1986 to 31 per cent in FY 1990 while spending on personnel would fall from 42 per cent to 36 per cent.

However, when the budget was announced at the end of August 1986, military expenditures were restricted to a 1 per cent growth and the procurement programme was cut. Even so, military spending had received favourable treatment. In a major effort to reduce the government deficit and halt the decline in the value of the Australian dollar, the budget provided for no real increase overall in public spending for FY 1986. The depreciation of the Australian currency by 40 per cent against the US dollar in less than two years had placed great strains on the procurement programme. Economies and rationalization were being sought and it was felt that more equipment could be produced locally. At the same time it was admitted that productivity in the heavily-subsidized government defence industries needed to be radically improved.[85]

In some cases, the issue of jobs for the home market versus foreign weapons bought with a depreciating currency overshadowed more fundamental discussions of a weapon's strategic worth. Work was begun on the development of the Australian-designed Jindalee system to provide over-the-horizon monitoring of aircraft and ship movements in the northern approaches to Australia. The system had been strongly recommended in the Dibb Report and given the highest defence priority. Total cost is currently estimated at A $500 million (US $310 million).[86] Critics of Jindalee claim that the system cannot provide complete surveillance and that existing AEW aircraft could do the job better.[87]

IX. Africa

Military spending in Africa has been declining since 1980 (figure 6.3) as have arms imports, which take a significant part of defence spending (figure 6.4). Even the oil-exporting countries with strong economies (Algeria, Congo, Gabon, Libya, Nigeria and Tunisia) were forced to cut their military expenditures on average by 9 per cent a year for the period 1981–85, mainly because of reduced oil revenues. There was an average overall decline of GDP per capita in Africa for the period 1980–85: −2 per cent a year compared with 1.7 per cent growth for the industrial countries and 1.3 per cent growth for the developing countries.[88] Drought, famine, falling export revenues, external debt in excess of $125 billion,[89] a massive trade deficit, natural and economic disasters as well as internal and external conflicts[90] have shattered African economies in the early 1980s and forced the governments to cut military expenditures, although their burden on most of the African economies remains the same or has increased.

A closer analysis of the African sub-regions shows different pictures over the period 1977–86. North Africa, including Algeria, Libya, Morocco and Tunisia, had a rising military expenditure curve until the end of 1982, after which a sharp drop occurred, mainly owing to falling income from oil exports (figure 6.5a). This region alone accounts for about 60 per cent of Africa's total arms imports in the period, with Libya as the biggest importer. However, Libya's income from oil is estimated to have been $4 billion in 1986 compared with $20 billion in 1978, that is, hardly enough to finance even food imports. A minimum of foreign reserves of $2–3 billion and a payment delay of about $9 billion on military and civil contracts are other aspects of the current Libyan economy. Its arms debts to the Soviet Union are estimated at about $4 billion, which are paid with oil at spot market prices.[91]

West and Central Africa, including all the countries from Mauritania in the north-west to Zaire in the south, show declining defence expenditures since 1976, with small increases in 1977 and 1980 (figure 6.5b). This represents a trend in several African countries which are not involved in internal and external conflicts.[92] Nigeria, a major economy in this region, accounts for most of this trend. Nigeria had to cut expenditures after experiencing a fall in annual oil earnings from $25 billion in the early 1980s to about $6.5 billion in 1986,[93] causing a severe economic crisis. The opposite is true for Chad and Uganda, with relatively high military costs for fighting internal conflicts. In the case of Chad, where Libyan troops still occupy parts of northern Chad and Libyan-supported guerrillas are fighting the government in the south, support

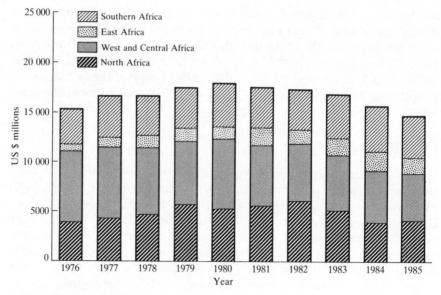

Figure 6.3. African military expenditure, 1976–85
Values are US $m., at constant (1980) prices.

Source: SIPRI military expenditure data base.

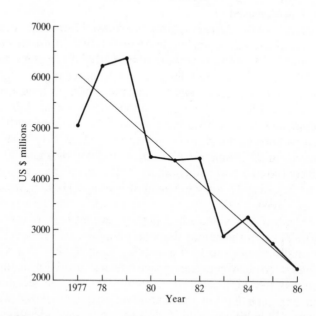

Figure 6.4. African arms imports, 1977–86
Values are US $m., at constant (1985) prices. Linear regression line shows the 10-year trend.

Source: SIPRI arms trade data base.

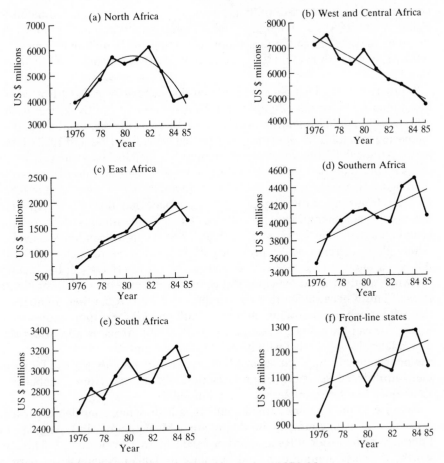

Figure 6.5. African military expenditure, by region, 1976–85
Values are US $m., at constant (1980) prices. Second-degree polynomial curve and linear regression lines show the 10-year trend.

Source: SIPRI military expenditure data base.

in the form of foreign aid came from both the USA, which has sent $10 million in emergency help,[94] and from France, which has sent troops to its former colony,[95] in response to a Libyan air raid on Chad in February 1986.

East Africa, including Ethiopia, Kenya, Malawi, Somalia, Sudan and Uganda, is a region with several recent and ongoing conflicts: in Sudan, Uganda, Somalia and Ethiopia. In this region military expenditure has increased over the past 10 years mainly because of these conflicts (figure 6.5c) Sudan is still engaged in a war that costs about $2.5 million a day,[96] against the 25 000-man Sudan People's Liberation Army (SPLA).[97] In the course of the conflict the SPLA rebels[98] stopped famine aid to southern Sudan, and starvation now threatens 2 million people. Egypt provided an estimated $6 million in military aid to Sudan in 1986.[99] Egyptian military aid up until 1986 amounts to some $52 million, including weapons for $28 million and material left by Egyptian troops sent to the country in 1983 in response to a Libyan air raid.[100]

Southern Africa, including the six front-line states—Angola,[101] Botswana, Mozambique, Tanzania, Zambia and Zimbabwe—and South Africa, is the other major conflict region in Africa.[102] Southern Africa also had a trend of increasing expenditures over the past 10 years, excluding 1981 and 1982 (figure 6.5d). Although South Africa's level of military expenditures is on average 2.5 times higher than that of the front-line states and therefore dominant in the total figure, the same trend is visible in both South Africa alone (figure 6.5e) and the front-line states (figure 6.5f). Economic sanctions,[103] 17 per cent inflation, high unemployment and the lack of investments describe the economic situation in South Africa,[104] which is financing a big military machine. Although an increase in the price of gold brought some relief to the South African economy, forecasts are pessimistic. Negative effects will be seen for the whole of the region, which is still economically very dependent on South Africa. This is because South Africa employs workers from other countries in the region, exports petroleum and food, and provides transport routes from South African harbours for their exports.[105] South Africa is now using this dependency in the conflict with its neighbouring countries, and in response to the international campaign against South Africa, the South African Government introduced sanctions against them. Trade to and from Zambia and Zimbabwe has for example been very limited.[106]

Because of the ongoing armed conflicts, a high defence burden is present especially in two countries in the region—Mozambique and Angola. In February 1986 President Reagan ordered the CIA to provide up to $15 million worth of arms, ammunition and supplies to União Nacional de para a Independência Total de Angola (UNITA) in Angola to back their conflict with Angola's MPLA government.[107] Having fought a war against UNITA for the past 11 years, Angola now faces a severe economic situation with a predominantly black-market economy,[108] although oil production by US companies in the far north props up the shattered economy.[109] Angola, once one of Africa's richest countries, has spent on average about 40 per cent of its government revenue on defence from 1983 to 1985.[110] Mozambique, a front-line state with a 15 per cent average increase of military expenditure over the past five years, is fighting a war with some 10 000 South African-supported insurgents and is facing a difficult economic situation. The last year of economic growth was 1981, and since then domestic production has fallen by about 40 per cent. The government estimates that about 30 per cent of the rural population now faces a serious food shortage.[111] The war continues to stop not only agricultural production but also the exploitation of coal, titanium, tantalum, copper and other natural resources in Mozambique,[112] worth billions of dollars.

Multilateral and unilateral assistance programmes for Africa provided both short-term emergency help and long-term aid for economic recovery programmes. The United States, for example, has increased both its development and its security assistance since 1979 (figure 6.6) the turning-point in most African economies, with the objective to 'encourage market oriented policies'[113] on the economic side and to guard security interests on the military side, that is, to limit or diminish Soviet/Libyan/Cuban influence in Africa. The main recipients of US security assistance in the form of loans and grants are Botswana, Chad, Kenya, Liberia, Somalia, Sudan and Zaire. However, African countries receive a minor share of total US security assistance, about 8 per cent during the years 1981–85.

Although the USSR has directed a significant portion of its foreign policy efforts towards Africa since the 1960s, its influence on the continent seems to be declining.[114] Nonetheless, Africa is still a major market for Soviet arms sales (see chapter 7).

X. Central America

There was little detectable increase in military expenditure in Central America in 1986 despite the lack of success in finding a solution to the conflicts which beset the region. Military activity, however, is not only determined by the military spending of the governments concerned but also by the security assistance received from other governments and international organizations. Security assistance comprises military loans and grants, economic loans and grants to cover fiscal and balance-of-payments deficits, and price support.[115]

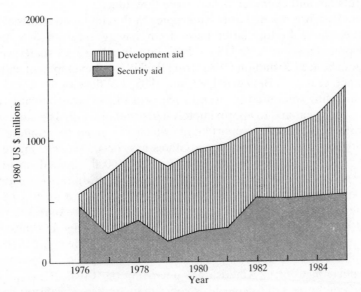

Figure 6.6. US aid to Africa, 1976–85

Source: US Overseas Loans and Grants and Assistance from International Organizations, Obligations and Loan Authorizations, 1 July 1945–30 September 1985 (Agency for International Development: Washington, DC).

These forms of economic assistance have been growing in recent years, as countries have found it impossible to adjust and restructure their economies in accordance with the rapidly changing patterns of world supply and demand.[116] Many economies in Central America are currently suffering from the effects of low commodity prices and heavy foreign debts; vital new investment is discouraged by the protracted domestic and intra-regional conflicts. Economic adjustment assistance has therefore become a powerful political tool in the hands of those countries and organizations able to distribute it.

The political and economic allegiance of most of the countries in the Central America region has already been secured along East–West lines. The major exceptions to this firm polarization are Mexico and, until recently, Costa Rica. This latter country deserves particular attention since its 37-year-old policy of unarmed neutrality is currently coming under pressure.

Costa Rica

During the 1960s and early 1970s, Costa Rica experienced a period of expansion, during which it developed into a relatively prosperous and democratically stable state providing adequately for the needs of its population. When the oil crisis of 1973 slowed growth, the government resorted to increased public spending and borrowing in order to maintain living standards. The economic situation deteriorated dramatically in 1980–81 as a result of both long- and short-term adjustment problems in the face of a $4 billion foreign debt. Living standards were falling and it was feared that the welfare state and even democracy were threatened.

Costa Rica was rescued from bankruptcy by the combined efforts of the IMF and the USA. In this latter case, from having received $16 million in development assistance for US FY 1980, largely in loans, Costa Rica currently receives about $120 million (1986) from the USA as development and security assistance grants.[117] Between 1983 and 1985, US development and security assistance has amounted to over 15 per cent of the government's recurrent budget each year and to approximately 6 per cent of GDP. The aid is mostly in the form of economic support funds which are given to promote political stability in areas where the United States has special security interests.

Costa Rican security forces number over 10 000, divided into the Civil Guard and the Rural Guard and supporting services. Military expenditure as a share of the central government budget is around 4 per cent, tiny by isthmus standards, though larger than the amount usually cited.[118] In recent years, the forces have received training and equipment from Israel and the USA. US military aid to Costa Rican security forces rose from nothing in US FY 1980 to $11 million in US FY 1985.

Conflicts in Central America are polarizing the Costa Rican population. Staunch supporters of Costa Rica's policy of unarmed neutrality see economic growth, social welfare and democracy as sufficient protection against the spread of revolution from their northern neighbour, Nicaragua. They are opposed by groups who favour privatization of the economy and a more belligerent approach to the Nicaragua problem, including militarization of the border area. The 1986 presidential election was a victory for the Social Democratic candidate, who holds the view that Costa Rica should be a welfare state rather than a garrison state.[119]

XI. South America

In real terms, military spending is falling in South America, though not as quickly as the decline in resource production (GDP). With all but two of the governments of the region now in civilian hands, it has proved possible to restrain military expansion. However, this is probably a reflection of economic rather than political realities.

Argentina and Brazil reached a number of agreements on economic integration during 1986. One of the aims of this 'mini common market' is to help bring about 'peace, democracy, security and development'.[120] The two countries failed, however, to reach agreement on two significant proposals: first, Argentina's request for mutual inspections of nuclear sites was not granted by Brazil; and second, the presidents could not agree on a proposed defence co-operation plan, the military establishments of the two countries preferring more informal arrangements.

Current emphasis on the role of the military in Argentina, Brazil and other South American countries as defenders of national territorial integrity rather than as guardians of domestic order has revived intra-regional rivalry. The Argentine military complain that their manpower situation is weak compared to those of Brazil and Chile. Improvements in recruitment and training cannot be made if budgets are cut. The Brazilian military are engaged in an expensive project to defend their long western and northern borders[121] as well as a further expansion of their military industries. The Peruvian military are concerned about long-standing border disputes with Chile and Ecuador.

The medium-term prospects for a genuine reduction in military spending are therefore not good. If the military institutions of these countries are to become the servants of society rather than its masters, it is necessary for the public to have full and correct information as to the money allocated to the military and how they spend it. In the case of Argentina, new standards of public accountability have made it possible to study how the country's resources have been used by the military in the past and how resources are being allocated to them under the current government.

Argentina

In 1985, the World Bank examined Argentine central government accounts for the period 1961–82 and found that military-related expenditures during the years 1970–82 were about 50 per cent higher than indicated by the official data.[122] Government figures did not include military construction and equipment purchases (which were mostly classified under economic development expenditures), the cost of military housing, nor the Treasury transfers which covered the 70 per cent deficit in the military retirement fund. Other personnel costs such as health care for the military and their dependents were classified as social expenditures.[123] When some of these additional costs were included by the World Bank in its calculations, the share of military expenditure in the total budget was between 21 and 30 per cent, rather than the 14 to 21 per cent suggested by the official Argentine data.[124]

In addition to budgeted expenditure, the military built installations and purchased weapons using off-budget funds directed through their own military-industrial complex, Fabricaciones Militares, through other special off-budget funds and foreign loans.[125]

The World Bank investigators were particularly concerned over the rapid growth of the deficit in the military pension fund. This is a typical budget problem for many countries where the promise of a good pension at an early age is, together with other welfare schemes, the major bonus of service life. In Argentina, the military pension fund deficit had increased by almost 10 per cent annually between 1971 and 1982. Although certain changes had been introduced, retirement benefits for military personnel were still generous— average pensions were up to four times higher than those paid to members of major civilian funds—and it was possible to retire after a relatively short period of service. Pension contributions were also far below the civilian norm. Many officiers were retired early for political or other reasons with full pension rights. As a result, as many military personnel had retired from the services and were drawing benefits as were still active in the service and paying contributions.[126]

It has not proved easy for the Alfonsín Government to keep the military out of the political arena and at the same time to accommodate them within the framework of the *Plan Austral*, the blueprint for Argentina's economic revival. During 1986, President Alfonsín was forced to give the armed forces special treatment over salaries, despite a strict wage control policy operating in both the public and private sectors and an already serious budget deficit. Officers in the armed forces were awarded a 25 per cent pay increase early in 1986, although the ceiling for salary rises under Phase 2 of the *Plan Austral* was 5 per cent. Officers were awarded a further 35 per cent pay rise in September 1986.[127]

Reform of the Argentine armed forces with the aim of producing a professional, efficient and apolitical body entails reorganization, retirement, retraining and, to a certain extent, re-equipment. Such reforms can only be achieved by additional spending, at least in the short run. The 1986 budget increased the allocation to the Ministry of Defence by 5 per cent, far in excess of the overall budget rise of 0.5 per cent. Final expenditure can, however, only be guessed at, since the 1986 budget was drawn up on the assumption of a 28 per cent inflation rate; average inflation for the year was, however, over 80 per cent. In 1985, 170 per cent more was spent than had originally been budgeted.[128]

President Alfonsín sought to gain control over the military establishment in a number of ways. Plans were announced to strip the armed forces of some of their independent economic power through the sale of the military-owned Fabricaciones Militares major share-holdings in a number of important petrochemical and other plants.[129] On the political front, he introduced a Defence Bill which would allow the armed forces to take action solely in the event of external aggression. This would replace a National Security Law, passed in 1966, which had been interpreted as giving the military the right to intervene in the country's internal politics, including combating domestic dissent.[130]

XII. Military research and development

World spending on military research and development (R&D) is roughly a quarter of world spending on all R&D and in 1986 was approximately $85–100 billion a year at current prices. (Current price estimates can vary considerably, depending on the exchange-rates and price indices used to construct them.) Spending in real terms seems to have been rising fairly fast in the 1980s, and was probably at least one-third as high again in 1986 as in 1980. During the 1970s it had stayed fairly constant, possibly dipping a little in the mid-1970s. US spending on military R&D fell in real terms and then rose again, but was probably roughly balanced by rising Soviet expenditure and, to a much lesser extent, by increased spending by the UK and some other countries.

Military R&D is concentrated very heavily in a few countries, which therefore overwhelmingly influence world trends. Total R&D—both civil and military R&D—is also heavily concentrated in a few countries, but less so than military R&D. The six biggest spenders account for some 80 per cent of world expenditure on total R&D (table 6.7), while for military R&D they account for some 90–95 per cent of world expenditure (table 6.8).

The USA and the USSR spend the most, both on total and on military R&D. They also have bigger shares of world military R&D than of world total R&D spending. Although they have been losing some of their share of total R&D—mainly to Japan, but also to FR Germany, France and the UK—they still account for about half the total. The USA and the USSR seem to have lost some of their share of military R&D during the 1970s. However, it is unlikely to have fallen below three-quarters of the world total, has since recovered and is probably still rising.

It is not possible to be precise about total world military R&D expenditure because of the lack of hard information about many countries. The most significant of these are the USSR—one of the two overwhelmingly large spenders—and China, which is one of the six largest.

The world estimates given here include some necessarily very rough estimates of Soviet dollar spending. These are based on the range of rouble estimates resulting mainly from estimation of the military share of R&D sector by sector for the most recent years for which disaggregated data are available.[131] There are major problems in converting Soviet expenditure into dollars—and these problems would still exist even if the level of expenditure in roubles were accurately known. For R&D, particularly military R&D, not enough is known about the composition of inputs or the conversion rates that should be used.[132]

Estimates of the dollar cost of Chinese military R&D expenditure are subject to the same problems and uncertainties as Soviet R&D spending. However, Chinese military R&D probably lies within the range US $750–1250 million.[133] Estimates of spending by the other countries for which data are not

Table 6.7. The six biggest spenders' shares of world total R&D expenditure

Country	Late 1960s	1980s
USA[a] ⎱ USSR ⎰	3/5	1/2
FR Germany ⎱ France ⎰ UK	1/6	1/5
Japan	1/20	1/10

[a] Of the two, US spending is probably the larger.

Sources are given in Acland-Hood, M., *Military R&D Resource Use and Arms Control*, SIPRI (Oxford University Press: Oxford, forthcoming), chapter 2 and appendix 2.

Table 6.8. The six biggest spenders' shares of world military R&D expenditure

Countries	Late 1960s	1980	Mid-1980s
USA ⎱ USSR ⎰	4/5	3/4–4/5	4/5–5/6
UK ⎱ France China ⎰ FR Germany	1/6	1/6	1/7

Sources are given in Acland-Hood, M., *Military R&D Resource Use and Arms Control*, SIPRI (Oxford University Press: Oxford, forthcoming), chapter 2 and appendix 2.

readily available are based on an assessment of each country's total R&D spending and of the probable military share of it, supplemented by a similar assessment of R&D employment.[134] Time series are not given for any of these countries, nor for the USSR or China.

Tables 6.9 and 6.10 give expenditure figures over the past 10 years for the 22 countries for which reasonably reliable data for a number of years are available and which do have some military R&D. These countries account for half or more of total military R&D expenditure, and represent all the spending size groups into which the significant military R&D spenders fall. Table 6.9 shows fiscal year expenditures in national currencies at current prices; table 6.10 shows them adjusted to calendar years and converted to constant 1980 US dollars. These tables indicate the level and trends in spending on military R&D. The amounts spent on research are important determinants of its results, even though they do not lead directly to measures of research output. It is clear that the USA, spending about seven times as much as the next biggest spender, the UK, would have to be enormously inefficient not to get many more results.

Not surprisingly, military R&D employment is also dominated by the big military R&D spenders. Two-thirds to three-quarters of all military R&D scientists and engineers are either in the USA or the USSR; more are found in the USSR, where research is more labour-intensive. Of the world's 4 million R&D scientists and engineers, probably over three-quarters of a million are engaged in military R&D. If support people are included, there are probably at least one and a half million people in the world working on military R&D.[135]

Table 6.9. Military R&D in 22 countries, current prices, fiscal years 1977–86

Country	Currency	Fiscal year[a] begins	1977	1978	1979	1980	1981	1982	1983	1984	1985	1986
Australia	m. dollars	1 July	..	87	94 ƒ	100	105	115	121	131*	..	..
Austria	m. schillings	1 Jan.	..	..	8	19	..	22	..	..	..	..
Belgium	m. francs	1 Jan.	68	50	77	58	64	129	67	59	59	..
Canada	m. dollars	1 Apr.	79	83	86	101	116	143	159	206	230	..
Denmark	m. kroner	[b]	8	8	4	5	5	6	6	22	22	19*
Finland	m. markaa	1 Jan.	15	17	19	20	24	29	32	37	40	42*
France	m. francs	1 Jan.	6 100	7 500	9 350	11 350	15 700	16 700	18 100	20 840	21 100	..
FR Germany	m. marks	1 Jan.	1 596	1 732	1 848	1 730	1 572	1 647	1 835	1 937	2 509	..
Greece	m. drachmas	1 Jan.	53	82	95	194	221	—	24	308	360	..
India[c]	m. rupees	1 Apr.	(864)	(1 082)	(1 386)	(1 347)	(1 768)	(2 052)	(2 500*)	(3 000*)	..	..
Italy	b. lire	1 Jan.	31.9	36.7	32.8	41.7ʲ	168.1 d	142.6	216.0	387.2	527.8	..
Japan	b. yen	1 Apr.	22.0	24.2	26.7	29.1	32.3	35.6	40.4	(45.8*)	(60.5*)	..
Netherlands	m. guilders	1 Jan.	74	84	91	91	107	124	109	120	(120*)	(109*)
New Zealand[e]	m. dollars	1 Apr.	2	2	4	3	4	4	(4)	(6*)	..	..
Norway	m. kroner	1 Jan.	92	96	96	102	161	220	304	335	383	305
Spain	m. pesetas	1 Jan.	285	409	759	1 746	2 354	3 506	3 829	..	..	..
Sweden	m. kronor	1 July	1 143	1 097	992	942	1 055	1 482	2 010	2 338	2 606	..
Switzerland	m. francs	1 Jan.	83	93	126	84	69	..	..	67	..	..
Thailand	m. baht	1 Oct.	..	..	..	..	..	134ᵍ	..	..	..	..
Turkey	m. lire	[f]	..	..	..	54	134	..	59	154	..	..
UK[h]	m. pounds	1 Apr.	(902)	(1 063)	(1 350)	(1 683)	1 739	1 758	1 977	2 169	(2 379*)	(2 510*)
USA[i]	m. dollars	1 Oct.ʲ	11 864	12 583	13 594	15 075	17 841	22 102	(24 500)ʲ	28 300 i	34 510* i	(41 680*)ʲ

[a] Fiscal years are entered under the calendar years in which they begin, with the exception of Thailand and the USA, for which they are entered under the calendar year in which they end. This ensures that the fiscal years are entered under the calendar year in which the greater part of them falls.

[b] 1977, 1 Apr.; 1978 onwards, 1 Jan.; 1978 data grossed up to a full year basis by the national authorities.

[c] The SIPRI estimates are military R&D (which does not include space), plus 75 per cent of space R&D, since 'the Department of Space . . . [is] engaged in research primarily orientated towards the achievement of strategic/defence objectives' (*R&D Planning in the Framework of National Plans*, Centre for the Study of Science, Technology and Development, Council of Scientific and Industrial Research: New Delhi, 1978), p. 2). If space is not included, the figures are about one-third smaller.

[d] Figures for years before 1981 have major omissions, including classified R&D.

[e] Expenditures of the Ministry of Defence, which are included in R&D objectives other than defence.

[f] 1977–81, 1 Mar.; 1983 onwards, 1 Jan. For 1982, 1 Mar.–31 Dec.

[g] 1 Mar. 1982–31 Dec. 1982.

[h] 1977–80 adjusted upwards to make them consistent with later years, which have fuller coverage because of improved reporting methods.

[i] 1977 outlays; 1978 onwards, obligations.

[j] Revised downwards from 1983. Previously, all space spending was classified as R&D or R&D support. From 1983 some has been reclassified as non-R&D.

Sources are given in Acland-Hood, M., SIPRI, *Military R&D: Resource Use and Arms Control* (Oxford University Press: Oxford, forthcoming), appendix 1.

Table 6.10. Military R&D in 22 countries, calendar years 1977–86.
Figures are in US $m., at constant (1980) prices and exchange-rates.

Country	1977	1978	1979	1980	1981	1982	1983	1984	1985	1986
Australia	125.6[a]	..	115.0 /	110.2	106.1	102.3	100.1	103.1*	..	..
Austria	..	..	0.7	1.5	..	1.5	..	..	..	..
Belgium	2.7	1.9	2.8	2.0	2.0	3.8	1.8	1.5	1.4	..
Canada	86.3	84.3	80.4	83.2	85.4	93.5	100.6	120.8	133.0	..
Denmark	1.8	1.8	0.8	0.8	0.8	0.8	0.9	2.8	2.7	(2.2*)
Finland	5.2	5.4	5.4	5.4	5.7	6.3	6.5	7.0	7.1	(7.2*)
France	1 982.8	2 235.2	2 517.1	2 685.8	3 276.1	3 116.5	3 081.3	3 303.0	3 152.1	..
FR Germany	991.1	1 047.0	1 072.3	951.8	813.7	809.6	873.1	899.9	1 139.8	..
Greece	2.1	2.8	2.8	4.5	4.2	—	0.3	3.4	(3.8)	..
India	(133.8)	(154.8)	(185.7)	(172.5)	(187.1)	(206.7)	(222.8)	(247.6)	..	..
Italy	58.1	59.5	46.4	48.7 /	166.6	121.4	160.3	259.4	325.2	..
Japan	108.8	116.6	124.2	125.6	132.3	142.4	157.8	(174.9*)	(218.4*)	..
Netherlands	43.0	46.9	48.7	45.8	50.4	55.2	47.2	50.3	(49.2*)	(43.5*)
New Zealand	2.5	3.0	4.4	3.3	2.9	2.7	(2.9)	(3.6*)	..	..
Norway	23.4	22.6	21.5	20.6	28.7	35.2	44.8	46.5	(50.7*)	(38.6*)
Spain	6.4	7.6	12.2	24.3	28.6	37.3	36.3	..	..	..
Sweden	..	323.0	281.0	228.6	210.6	246.4	311.3	358.9	387.1	..
Switzerland	53.8	60.1	77.9	50.4	38.8	..	..	..	..	..
Thailand	..	..	..	..	..	..	2.4	..	..	..
Turkey	..	..	..	(0.7)	1.2	1.2	0.9	..	..	..
UK	(2 936.8)	(3 181.8)	(3 503.9)	(3 718.7)	(3 583.3)	3 354.0	3 514.1	(3 695.2*)	(3 814.2*)	..
USA	16 363.6	16 206.8	15 850.5	15 766.5	17 125.2	19 386.4	21 050.5	23 673.7	27 796.7*	..

[a] Fiscal year 1976–77.

Sources are given in Acland-Hood, M., SIPRI, *Military R&D Resource Use and Arms Control* (Oxford University Press: Oxford, forthcoming), appendix 1.

Conventions for tables 6.9 and 6.10:
— Nil
.. Information not available
* Provisional figure
( ) SIPRI estimate
/ Break in series

(All these figures are approximate—definitions of scientists, engineers and technicians differ significantly from country to country, and data are not uniform or easily adjustable to approximate to uniformity.) Despite all the uncertainties and problems of arriving at estimates of world military R&D, it is clear that a great deal of money is spent and a great many highly educated people are working on devising new weapons and military techologies, and that these are large shares of the world total R&D effort. There seems little evidence to suggest that all this effort has increased security.

It is undoubtedly the USA and the USSR that dominate military R&D and set the overall pace. Most other countries' military R&D efforts only cover a few of the possible research areas. Many are far from being in the forefront or even 'state of the art' in the areas they do cover; they are mainly trying to catch up with technological changes made by the leaders years or even decades before. However, the technologically advanced countries do produce some research results superior to those of the USA and the USSR in some militarily useable areas. The USA contracts for some military R&D to be performed abroad partly because it is economical to use cheap foreign research labour and partly in order to gain political support abroad for the purposes of the research: but it also wants to exploit comparative research strengths in other countries.

Even so, the actions of the USA and the USSR are the overwhelming influence on the speed of military technological change in particular and on the particular directions it takes: what sort of new weapons are developed and how fast. Moreover, the particular combination of technological and institutional asymmetry that exists between them is probably the scenario most likely to lead to the fastest race for new armaments. The USA is the technological leader in most areas and is open about the broad lines of what it is doing. It therefore sets the pace for most military R&D. However, the USSR, its only real competitor overall, while in very many areas lagging in technology, by its extreme secretiveness successfully creates enough uncertainty about how advanced its military R&D is to maintain US fear of technological surprise. The USA assumes the worst—the most inflated views of what the USSR might conceivably be doing—and seeks to compensate for this uncertainty by keeping a very large technological lead. This apparent prudence speeds up the pace of the arms competition. The faster this becomes, the greater are the financial constraints on other countries' choices of what military R&D they can engage in; in the research areas they undertake they have to run faster and faster to stay in the same relative position.

It is therefore intelligent control of US and Soviet military R&D that could moderate the pace of military technological change. However, this does not mean that it is only these two countries that can and should act. Other countries do have some possible ways in which they can seek to influence the decisions on US and Soviet research that increasingly affect their security. One is to seek to influence the USA and the USSR politically. Another is to ensure that decisions on their own military R&D—including decisions on participation in international military research projects—are really always based on long-term security considerations and are not, even in part, a reaction to the latest development or made in the confused attempt to achieve unspecified and unlikely economic benefits hopefully labelled 'spin-off'. The increasing specialization of military technology makes the probability of civil spin-off less and less likely. Moreover, what spin-offs there are occur not only from military to civil uses, but also *vice versa*.[136]

Sources, methods and definitions

Military R&D is the effort to extend knowledge and technical expertise wherever there are thought to be military applications, existing or potential, in order to create more effective weapons, more effective means of using them and more effective ways of making weapons used by an adversary ineffective.

It is the objective of this R&D rather than the institutional sources of funds for it that distinguishes it as military. Therefore the military R&D expenditure data *preferred* are government funds used for the objective 'defence'. (The great bulk of military R&D is government funded.) The preferred definitions of the R&D figures are those of the Organisation for Economic Co-operation and Development (OECD) *Frascati Manual*.[137] Table 6.9 is on the basis of the fiscal years (defined in the table) for which the data were originally reported. For table 6.10 the data were adjusted where necessary to calendar years, assuming an even spread of expenditure throughout the year. Consumer prices were used as deflators, since they are available over the whole period covered for all the countries included, and their use results in reasonable indications of trends in resources used. This is also consistent with the calculation of the table on military expenditure in constant price figures (table 6A.2) in appendix 6A.

Notes and references

[1] To the extent that the Pentagon is a monopsonist (a single buyer in a market), it can determine price, but it cannot (in peacetime) command production.

[2] For a longer discussion on China, see SIPRI, *World Armaments and Disarmament: SIPRI Yearbook 1986* (Oxford University Press: Oxford, 1986), chapter 11, pp. 217–19.

[3] OECD, *Historical Statistics 1969–84* (OECD: Paris, 1986), table 3.1, p. 44.

[4] Although 1984 had been a good year for a number of NATO countries, the upswing was recognized as temporary. See OECD, *Economic Outlook* (OECD: Paris, Dec. 1985).

[5] Senator Glenn's amendment forbidding funds to foreign contractors unless US contractors cannot do the work was rejected, but it expressed a popular sentiment and may be taken up again. Another proposal, known after its sponsor as the Traficant Amendment, stipulates that where US and foreign suppliers are competing for a contract to provide equipment to the US armed forces and the price differential is less than 5 per cent, the contract must go to the US supplier unless the US Defense Secretary certifies that this is against the interest of national security.

[6] *Interim Report of the Sub-committee on Defence Co-operation*, North Atlantic Assembly, Military Committee, AD 181 MC/EG (86)2, International Secretariat, Nov. 1986, pp. 11–14.

[7] Note 6, pp. 21–22.

[8] Gen. James Abrahamson, summer 1985. Quoted in *Interim Report of the Sub-committee on Defence Co-operation* (note 6), p. 3.

[9] Note 6, pp. 1–10.

[10] SIPRI (note 2), chapter 11, p. 215 and chapter 12, section VII; Epstein, J., *The 1987 Defense Budget, Studies in Defense Policy* (The Brookings Institution: Washington, DC, 1986), p. 2.

[11] *Gallup Report* (Apr. 1986).

[12] The data are published by the NATO Press Service early in Dec. each year and thereafter published in *NATO Review*.

[13] See, for example, the presentation of the central government budget for 1986 in *El País*, 30 Oct. 1985, p. 136. For the calculation of the functional defence spending, see Fisas Armengol, V.,

'Los presupuestos de defensa para 1987' [The 1987 defence budgets], Centre d'informació i documentació internacionals a Barcelona (CIDOB), 1986 manuscript; and Fisas Armengol, V., 'Los presupuestos de defensa para 1986' [The 1986 defence budgets], in Aguirre, M., *et al.* (eds), *Anuario sobre armamentismo en España 1986* (Editorial Fontamara: Barcelona, May 1986), chapter 2, pp. 31–52.

[14] For the NATO definition of military expenditure, see appendix 6A, Definitions and sources, p. 178.

[15] The IMF has recently issued a manual describing the classification system to be used when reporting data for the IMF *Government Finance Statistics*. This classification system is also recommended for domestic use: IMF, *Manual of Government Statistics* (IMF: Washington, DC, 1986). The IMF does not yet publish data for these East European countries on a regular basis.

[16] This section is based on material to be found in SIPRI, *World Armaments and Disarmament: SIPRI Yearbook 1974* (Taylor & Francis: London, 1974), appendix 8B, 'Estimating Soviet military expenditure', pp. 172–204; Foelber, R. E., assisted by Donahue, S., *Estimates of Soviet Defense Expenditures: Methodological Issues and Policy Implications*, Congressional Research Service, (CRS) Report no. 85–131 F, 5 July 1986; Jacobsen, C. G., 'Soviet military expenditure and the Soviet defence burden' in SIPRI (note 2), chapter 13, pp. 263–74.

[17] CRS (note 16), p. CRS-viii.

[18] Gallik, D., *et al.*, *The Soviet Financial System* (US Department of Commerce, Bureau of the Census: Washington, DC, June 1968), pp. 174–75.

[19] CRS (note 16), p. CRS-23.

[20] *SIPRI Yearbook 1974* (note 16), p. 181.

[21] Acland-Hood, M., SIPRI, *Military R&D Resource Use and Arms Control* (Oxford University Press: Oxford, forthcoming).

[22] Jacobsen (note 16), p. 266.

[23] Jacobsen (note 16), p. 266.

[24] CRS (note 16), p. CRS-ix.

[25] The result of a SIPRI workshop on Soviet military spending estimates will be published in Jacobsen, C. G. (ed.), *The Soviet Defence Enigma* (Oxford University Press: Oxford, forthcoming).

[25] CRS (note 16), p. CRS-ix.

[26] For a study of these problems, see Alton, T. P., Lazaricik, G., Bass, E. M. and Znayenko, W., 'East European defense expenditures, 1965–78', in *East European Assessment*, Part 2, a compendium of papers submitted to the Joint Economic Committee, US Congress (US Government Printing Office: Washington, DC, 1981).

[27] Hardt, J. and Gold, D., 'The defence sector, Eastern European economies: slow growth in the 80's', Selected papers submitted to the Joint Economic Committee, US Congress (US Government Printing Office: Washington, DC, 28 Mar. 1986), vol. 1, p. 457.

[28] *Svenska Dagbladet* (Stockholm), 29 Dec. 1986.

[29] *The Times*, 22 Nov. 1986.

[30] *International Herald Tribune*, 8 Dec. 1986; SIPRI, *World Armaments and Disarmament: SIPRI Yearbook 1984* (Taylor & Francis: London, 1984), chapter 3, p. 88.

[31] *The Times*, 22 Sep. 1986.

[32] Syrian arms imports have risen sharply since 1982, but are not yet reflected in the official military expenditure figures. In case the deals are made on a loan basis, there can be a time-lag before the investments show up in the budget figures.

[33] See also SIPRI (note 2), chapter 11, p. 220, and for the definition of US security assistance, chapter 16, p. 312 in the same volume.

[34] *Foreign Assistance and Related Programs Appropriations for 1987*, Hearings before a Subcommittee of the Committee on Appropriations, House of Representatives, 99th Congress, Second Session (US Government Printing Office: Washington, DC, 1986), pp. 514–20.

[35] *Defense & Foreign Affairs Daily*, vol. 15, no. 114 (16 June 1986).

[36] *Milavnews*, vol. 25, no. 297 (July 1986), p. 18.

[37] *Defense & Foreign Affairs Daily*, vol. 15, no. 143 (25 July 1986).

[38] *Boston Globe*, 24 Aug., 1986, p. 18.

[39] *Financial Times*, 22 Oct. 1986.

[40] See note 34.

[41] *Neue Zürcher Zeitung*, 18 Sep. 1986.

[42] *Frankfurter Allgemeine Zeitung*, 18 July 1986.

[43] *Financial Times*, 4 June 1986.

[44] *Milavnews*, vol. 25, no. 298 (Aug. 1986), p. 7.

[45] *Neue Zürcher Zeitung*, 4–5 May 1986.

⁴⁶ See note 45. In 1986, Saudi Arabia took delivery of its first five AWACS aircraft, purchased in 1981; *Congressional Quarterly*, 21 June 1986, p. 1389.

⁴⁷ *Economic Times*, 19 Mar. 1986, quoted in *IDSA News Review of West Asia* (New Delhi), vol. 17, no. 4 (Apr. 1986), p. 171.

⁴⁸ *Financial Times* 17 Apr. 1986.

⁴⁹ *Financial Times*, 25 Apr. 1986.

⁵⁰ Hottinger, A., 'Der Bürgerkrieg in Südjemen', *Europa-Archiv*, no. 11, 1986, p. 316.

⁵¹ Almost half the total budget of 67 billion rupees was deficit-financed. *Far Eastern Economic Review*, vol. 132, no. 24 (12 June 1986), pp. 27–31.

⁵² *Emergency: Sri Lanka 1986* (International Alert: London, 1986), p. 31.

⁵³ *Far Eastern Economic Review* (note 51), pp. 27–31.

⁵⁴ *Far Eastern Economic Review*, vol. 130, no. 47 (28 Nov. 1985), p. 68 and vol. 134, no. 48 (27 Nov. 1986), p. 59.

⁵⁵ President Jayawardene in *The Times*, 27 Jan. 1986.

⁵⁶ *Emergency: Sri Lanka 1986* (note 52), pp. 27 and 29.

⁵⁷ *AMN* (Karachi), 30 Jan. 1986; *Far Eastern Economic Review* (note 51), pp. 26–31. Beyond South Asia, Sri Lankan security forces are receiving advice and assistance from Israeli experts and there are reports of British mercenaries manning COIN helicopter gunships. *AMN*, 30 Jan. 1986; *Emergency: Sri Lanka* (note 52), p. 30; *Hindu* (Madras), 1 Mar. 1986; *Milavnews*, vol. 25, no. 296 (June 1986).

⁵⁸ *Indian Express* (no date), quoted in *Asian Recorder* (New Delhi), 1–7 Oct. 1986. A National Security Force had been established in 1984 but it was then under the command of a senior police officer.

⁵⁹ *The Statesman* (New Delhi) and *Times of India* (New Delhi) in *Asian Recorder* (New Delhi), 4–6 June 1986.

⁶⁰ *Times of India* (New Delhi), no date, quoted in *Asian Recorder* (16–22 July 1986).

⁶¹ *Far Eastern Economic Review* (note 51), pp. 116–18.

⁶² *Dawn* (Karachi), 20 June 1986.

⁶³ *Amrita Bazar Patrika* (Calcutta), 9 July 1986, quoting *Dawn* (Karachi), no date.

⁶⁴ Martial law was lifted on 30 Dec. 1985 but the government retains extensive powers to curb opposition and dissent. Cronin, R. P., 'US assistance to Pakistan: foreign aid facts updated 20–3–1986' in *Defence Journal* (Karachi), vol. 12, no. 7 (1986).

⁶⁵ *Far Eastern Economic Review*, vol. 131, no. 2 (9 Jan. 1986), p. 24.

⁶⁶ *Milavnews*, vol. 25, no. 301 (Nov. 1986); *Far Eastern Economic Review*, vol. 134, no. 11 (11 Dec. 1986), p. 19.

⁶⁷ According to Secretary of State Shultz, this assistance is given Pakistan 'out of loyalty to a staunch ally that faces a direct Soviet threat and to maintain the pressure on the Soviets to move towards a negotiated settlement in Afghanistan'. It was also felt vital to support Pakistan as it 'enters a new era of democratisation which began with the lifting of martial law at the end of 1985'; *Pakistan Times* (Lahore), 9 Mar. 1986.

⁶⁸ *Business Recorder* (Karachi), 9, 25 and 27 Mar. 1986.

⁶⁹ *Muslim* (Islamabad), 19 Feb. 1986.

⁷⁰ Subject to US deficit limitation budget cuts.

⁷¹ *Statesman* (New Delhi), 25 Mar. 1986; *Muslim* (Islamabad), 25 Mar. 1986.

⁷² The percentage share is then given to two and sometimes three places of decimals. Old data are never adjusted. See, for example, *Defense of Japan 1984* (National Defense Agency: Tokyo, 1984), table 37, p. 266.

⁷³ *Financial Times*, 15 Dec. 1986; for the NATO definition, see appendix 6A, pp. 178–79, Definitions and sources.

⁷⁴ Kessler, R. J., *US Policy towards the Philippines after Marcus*, Policy Paper 37, June 1986 (The Stanley Foundation: Muscatine, IA, 1986), p. 11.

⁷⁵ SIPRI (note 2), chapter 11, p. 223.

⁷⁶ Orders have reportedly been issued by General Ramos to cut the size of the militia by approximately 35 000 men (*Indonesian Times*, 29 Mar. 1986). The exact current strength of the force is not known but estimates put it at between 40 000 and 65 000 full-time personnel.

⁷⁷ See note 75.

⁷⁸ *Congressional Quarterly*, vol. 44, no. 43 (25 Oct. 1986).

⁷⁹ *Vantage Point* (Seoul), vol. 9, no. 5 (May 1986).

⁸⁰ Other political considerations can usurp the parliamentary right to a full budget debate. This was the case in Dec. 1986 when the ruling party pressed through the budget bill in a few minutes behind locked doors.

⁸¹ A national pension system and minimum wage programme are planned for introduction in

1988 as well as a gradual expansion of the medical insurance system. *Korea Herald*, 31 Aug.-1 Sep. 1986.

[82] SIPRI (note 2), chapter 11, p. 225. The USA officially announced its decision in Aug. 1986 and New Zealand did not attend the ANZUS council meeting that month.

[83] *DMS International Defense Intellience*, vol. 8, no. 34 (25 Aug. 1986).

[84] *Defense and Economy World Report*, no. 1021 (3 Nov. 1986).

[85] *Milavnews*, vol. 25, nos. 299 and 300 (Oct. 1986).

[86] *Milavnews* (note 85).

[87] *Financial Times*, 12 Nov. 1986.

[88] *World Development Report 1986*, World Bank (Oxford University Press: New York, 1986), p. 45.

[89] *Foreign Assistance and Related Programs Appropriations for 1987* (note 34), p. 177.

[90] In the case of conflicts, the economies suffered from the lack of investments, damaged infrastructure, restrictions in trade and increased defence expenditures.

[91] Miller, J., 'Die Ausdehnung des libyschen Einflusses in Africa', *Europa Archiv*, no. 14, 1986, pp. 425–31.

[92] With the exception of the conflicts in Chad and the Western Sahara.

[93] *Financial Times*, 18 Nov. 1986.

[94] *Milavnews* (note 57), p. 7.

[95] *Neue Zürcher Zeitung*, 27 Feb. 1986.

[96] *Frankfurter Rundschau*, 4 Nov. 1986.

[97] *Christian Science Monitor*, 21 Aug. 1986.

[98] *Neue Zürcher Zeitung*, 4 Oct. 1986.

[99] *Milavnews* (note 36), p. 23.

[100] *African Defence*, May 1986, p. 11.

[101] Because no inflation data are available for Angola, a constant dollar series derived from Angola's current defence expenditures could not be used. Therefore constant 1980 US dollar figures have been estimated using SIPRI data on Angola's arms imports and adding 20 per cent for recurrent expenditures on troops. The assumption was that most of the Angolan expenditures are spent on arms imports. A comparison of available constant dollar expenditure estimates for the years 1977 to 1983 show that these and SIPRI's estimates are almost identical.

[102] Aside from the West Sahara conflict area.

[103] The effects the European sanctions on imports of South African goods will have on the apartheid regime will be limited because coal imports have so far been excluded from the bans. For South Africa, Europe and Japan are big markets, and as long as their sanctions are limited, this also limits the effects of the US boycott. See *Der Spiegel*, vol. 40, no. 42 (13 Oct. 1986), pp. 198–200.

[104] *Frankfurter Rundschau*, 10 Sep. 1986.

[105] *Africa Research Bulletin*, 31 Aug. 1986, pp. 8306–308.

[106] *Frankfurter Rundschau*, 8 Aug. 1986.

[107] *Congressional Quarterly*, 6 Sep. 1986, p. 2065.

[108] *Der Spiegel*, vol. 40, no. 41 (6 Oct. 1986), pp. 174–84.

[109] *Financial Times*, 30 Sep. 1986.

[110] Hodges, T., 'Angola to the 1990s: The potential for recovery', *The Economist Intelligence Unit*, Special Report no. 1079, Jan. 1987.

[111] *Financial Times*, 3 Dec. 1986.

[112] *Times*, 4 Nov. 1986.

[113] *Foreign Assistance and Related Programs Appropriations for 1987* (note 34), p. 188.

[114] Former allies such as Ghana, Guinea, Mali, Sudan, Egypt and Somalia have opened towards the West. Of the remaining countries—Angola, Ethiopia and Mozambique—only Ethiopia can be regarded politically as a strong ally. See: Kühne, W., 'Sowjetische Afrikapolitik in der "Aera Gorbatschow"', *Stiftung Wissenschaft und Politik* (SWP-S329/Fo. Pl. IV. 3f/86), May 1986, p. 5.

[115] Development funds are normally tied to specific projects. In those cases where projects would have been undertaken even if foreign funds had not been available, development aid frees domestic resources for other uses—such as military spending.

[116] SIPRI (note 2), chapter 16.

[117] *US Overseas Loans and Grants and Assistance from International Organizations, Obligations and Loan Authorizations, July 1 1945-September 30 1984* (Agency for International Development (AID): Washington, DC).

[118] This includes the budget of the Ministry of Public Security and that of the Rural Assistance Guards which in 1982 and 1983 took over 40 per cent of the budget of the Ministry of Government

and Police. *Ley de Presupuesto 1983: Ordinario y Extraordinario de la República* [Budget Law for 1983], San José, Costa Rica, 28 Dec. 1982.

¹¹⁹ *Latin American Regional Report Mexico & Central America*, RM-86-04, 2 May 1986, p. 6.

¹²⁰ Statement signed by Argentina, Brazil and Uruguay in Brasilia in Dec. 1986. It is intended that Uruguay will participate in the integration process in the future. *Latin American Regional Report Brazil*, RB-87-01, 8 Jan. 1987.

¹²¹ *Latin American Regional Report Brazil*, RB-86-01, 3 Jan. 1986 and RB-87-01, 8 Jan. 1987.

¹²² World Bank Country Study, *Argentina Economic Memorandum*, vol. 1, Main Report (World Bank: Washington DC, 1985), p. xxviii, para. xxi.

¹²³ World Bank (note 122), pp. 46–50.

¹²⁴ The military pension fund deficit which was covered by the Treasury is not included in this calculation. See World Bank (note 122), table II.11, p. 48.

¹²⁵ World Bank (note 122), p. 46.

¹²⁶ World Bank (note 122), pp. 47–9.

¹²⁷ *Latin American Weekly Report*, WR-86-06 (7 Feb. 1986), 'Postscript'; WR-86-07 (14 Feb. 1986), p. 2; and WR-86-36 (18 Sep. 1986), 'Postscript'. The same situation has arisen in Brazil. The Armed Forces have secured a 25 per cent wage increase while civilians are subject to a government policy of wage restraint.

¹²⁸ Presupuesto General para el ejercicio 1985, 27 Sep. 1985, Buenos Aires; Ley de Presupuesto General 1986, Camara de Diputados de la Nación: 1. Sesiones Extraordinarias 1985, Orden del Día no. 38, Sumario, printed 8 Apr. 1986, and 2. *Trámite Parlamentario*, no. 120, 10 Feb. 1986, Aprobación; *Latin American Weekly Report*, WR-86-08 (21 Feb. 1986), 'Postscript' and WR-87-03 (22 Jan. 1987), p. 7. Inflation in 1985 was 670 per cent.

¹²⁹ *Latin American Weekly Report*, WR-87-02 (15 Jan. 1987), p. 8.

¹³⁰ *Latin American Weekly Report*, WR-86-34 (4 Sep. 1986), p. 8, and WR-86-44 (13 Nov. 1986). Groups within the armed forces and the Chamber of Deputies fought to maintain the possibility of military intervention against certain acts of internal aggression and to retain the armed forces domestic intelligence duties, but by the end of 1986 the original bill had become law.

¹³¹ These rouble estimates are described in Acland-Hood (note 21), chapter 4.

¹³² The rouble-to-dollar research exchange-rates available are very shaky and the dollar-to-rouble rates are even worse.

¹³³ Note 21, chapter 5.

¹³⁴ Note 21, chapter 2.

¹³⁵ Note 21, chapter 2.

¹³⁶ Note 21, chapter 6.

¹³⁷ 'The socio-economic objectives of government R&D funding', *The Measurement of Scientific and Technical Activities: Proposed Standard Practice for Surveys of Research and Experimental Development, Frascati Manual 1980* (OECD: Paris, 1981), chapter 8.

Appendix 6A. Tables of world military expenditure, 1977–86

Notes, definitions, sources and conventions for the military expenditure tables can be found on pp. 177–79.

Table 6A.1. World military expenditure, in current price figures

Figures are in local currency, current prices.

		1977	1978	1979	1980	1981	1982	1983	1984	1985	1986
NATO											
North America											
Canada	m. dollars	4 228	4 635	4 948	5 596	6 525	7 544	8 562	9 519	10 185	10 919
USA	m. dollars	120 050	130 238	146 350	169 525	196 582	218 084	238 135	261 748	277 310	292 633
Europe											
Belgium	m. francs	89 480	99 726	106 472	115 754	125 689	132 127	136 615	139 113	141 582	(143 347)
Denmark	m. kroner	6 382	7 294	8 045	9 117	10 301	11 669	12 574	13 045	13 344	13 750
France	m. francs	73 779	85 175	96 439	111 672	129 708	148 021	165 029	176 638	186 715	196 465
FR Germany	m. marks	40 184	43 019	45 415	48 518	52 193	54 234	·56 496	57 274	58 650	60 378
Greece	m. drachmas	67 738	77 861	89 791	96 975	142 865	176 270	193 340	271 922	321 981	366 632
Italy	b. lire	4 533	5 301	6 468	8 203	9 868	12 294	14 400	16 433	18 584	20 332
Luxembourg	m. francs	1 029	1 154	1 242	1 534	1 715	1 893	2 104	2 234	2 265	2 533
Netherlands	m. guilders	9 092	9 146	10 106	10 476	11 296	11 921	12 149	12 765	12 901	13 244
Norway	m. kroner	5 934	6 854	7 362	8 242	9 468	10 956	12 395	12 688	15 446	15 788
Portugal	m. escudos	22 082	27 354	34 343	43 440	51 917	63 817	76 765	92 009	111 375	138 479
Spain[a]	m. pesetas	253 709	302 566	367 042	471 850	551 019	649 262	743 917	846 844	947 656	966 703
Turkey	m. lira	49 790	66 239	93 268	203 172	313 067	447 790	556 738	803 044	1 234 547	1 867 990
UK	m. pounds	6 650	7 325	8 775	10 957	12 754	14 442	15 590	17 091	18 142	18 998

		1977	1978	1979	1980	1981	1982	1983	1984	1985	1986
WTO											
Bulgaria	m. leva	(614)	[650]	[700]	[820]	[870]	[901]	[932]	[969]	[1 010]	. .
Czechoslovakia	m. korunas	20 130	20 808	21 380	22 900	23 099	24 560	25 261	26 276	(27 500)	[28 800]
German DR	m. marks	8 261	8 674	9 110	9 875	10 705	11 315	11 970	12 830	(13 041)	[14 045]
Hungary	m. forints	12 607	14 983	16 200	17 700	19 060	20 050	21 900	(22 700)	(23 300)	[25 500]
Poland	m. zlotys	63 315	65 653	70 780	74 285	84 450	191 100	210 900	(250 900)	[315 000]	[347 000]
Romania	m. lei	10 963	11 713	11 835	10 394	10 490	11 340	(11 660)	(11 888)	(12 113)	[12 208]
Other Europe											
Albania	m. leks	805	818	885	915	940	935	910	1 010	1 700	[2 300]
Austria	m. schillings	9 515	10 767	11 828	12 317	13 021	13 334	13 857	14 823	16 786	18 745
Finland[b]	m. markkaa	2 400	2 700	3 100	3 700	4 200	5 300	5 700	6 150	6 600	7 300
Ireland	m. punt	98.0	116	142	176	203	241	250	263	294	301
Sweden[c]	m. kronor	11 508	13 011	14 493	15 977	17 515	18 553	19 603	21 204	22 506	23 735
Switzerland[d]	m. francs	2 687	2 678	2 982	3 152	3 349	3 727	3 862	4 009	4 576	4 341
Yugoslavia	m. new dinars	38 766	43 379	56 330	76 100	99 800	116 822	152 689	244 308	(456 749)	[764 972]
Middle East											
Bahrain	m. dinars	14.3	40.5	53.9	59.2	80.7	106	(62.3)	[55.6]	[59.0]	[60.0]
Cyprus	m. pounds	10.4	8.9	12.6	10.3	14.7	[17.3]	[18.4]	[19.1]	[21.0]	. .
Egypt	m. pounds	[1 845]	[1 150]	[1 200]	[1 135]	(1 273)	[1 615]	(1 950)	[2 370]	[2 575]	[2 750]
Iran	m. rials	565 925	586 800	386 650	363 625	[488 500]	[641 250]	[657 500]	. .	. .	. .
Iraq	m. dinars	593	587	(788)	[990]	[1 350]	[2 400]	[3 200]	[4 300]	[4 000]	. .
Israel	t. new shekels	(4 067)	(5 493)	(11 793)	(27 846)	(54 823)	(120 500)	(329 294)	(720 364)	(654 865)	(814 928)
Jordan	m. dinars	96.5	102	133	136	160	179	196	197	(219)	[243]
Kuwait	m. dinars	203	244	257	291	(370)	(416)	[455]	[515]		
Lebanon	m. pounds	255	491	738	980	(654)	1 215	3 554	2 004	2 178	1 798
Oman	m. riyals	237	265	269	407	522	581	671	736	[745]	[601]
Saudi Arabia	m. riyals	[31 685]	(38 684)	(52 388)	(64 076)	(75 723)	(87 695)	(84 311)	(77 817)	(72 000)	[14 220]
Syria	m. pounds	4 160	4 740	8 287	8 415	9 646	10 703	11 309	(12 601)	13 673	[6 900]
United Arab Emirates	m. dirhams	1 928	3 019	4 394	6 330	7 672	7 268	7 042	[6 911]	[7 500]	. .
Yemen Arab Republic	m. rials	656	1 691	2 297	[2 400]	2 677	3 701	3 146	2 665	2 660	. .
Yemen, People's Democratic Rep. of	m. dinars	20.0	30.8	36.1	42.6	56.0	[57.5]	[65.8]	[66.1]	[65.3]	. .

Country	Unit										
South Asia											
Afghanistan	m. afghanis	2 617	2 919	5 472	[7 667]	..	3 661	4 805	(5 765)	(6 950)	(7 700)
Bangladesh	m. taka	1 917	2 038	2 409	2 891						
India	m. rupees	31 339	32 508	36 648	44 283	53 450	62 625	73 008	83 503	92 283	105 138
Nepal	m. rupees	165	190	217	244	274	342	432	(496)	635	909
Pakistan	m. rupees	9 047	10 436	12 163	14 181	17 545	21 488	24 323	27 653	32 503	36 865
Sri Lanka	m. rupees	478	560	804	971	1 051	1 500	1 800	2 600	(4 280)	10 700
Far East											
Brunei	m. dollars	175	203	372	410	416	(480)	(530)	[534]	[650]	[700]
Burma	m. kyats	1 251	1 247	1 324	(1 417)	(1 590)	(1 610)	(1 630)	(1 760)	(1 973)	[1 858]
Hong Kong	m. dollars	349	536	628	1 353	1 521	1 478	1 537	1 523	1 459	[1 530]
Indonesia	b. new rupiahs	(968)	(1 130)	(1 300)	(1 708)	(2 153)	(2 613)	[2 858]	(3 106)	[2 856]	[3 089]
Japan	b. yen	1 653	1 822	2 010	2 214	2 388	2 532	2 712	2 911	3 118	3 308
Korea, North	m. won	2 096	2 344	2 563	2 750	3 009	3 242	3 530	3 819	3 935	4 020
Korea, South	b. won	1 008	1 438	1 597	2 252	2 831	3 163	3 406	3 452	3 826	4 309
Malaysia	m. ringgits	1 987	2 183	2 547	3 389	4 693	4 896	4 819	(4 370)	(4 323)	4 215
Mongolia	m. tughriks	(405)	(421)	(480)	(426)	(630)	(716)	(726)	[795]	[849]	..
Philippines	m. pesos	4 924	4 863	5 240	5 829	6 746	7 778	(8 554)			
Singapore	m. dollars	1 007	987	1 051	1 305	1 540	1 655	1 575	2 280	2 503	2 307
Taiwan	m. dollars	58 500	70 000	80 500	96 500	135 500	135 500	138 500	137 500	151 650	160 650
Thailand	m. baht	(17 304)	(22 877)	24 165	27 700	32 000	35 500	49 000	53 000	52 000	55 300
Oceania											
Australia	m. dollars	2 365	2 590	2 911	3 388	3 962	4 603	5 241	5 965	6 790	7 490
Fiji	m. dollars	3.0	3.2	3.9	4.3	3.6	4.2	4.7	4.5	4.5	4.5
New Zealand	m. dollars	243	288	334	421	557	638	668	735	842	1 013
Africa											
Algeria	m. dinars	1 956	2 490	2 742	3 417	3 481	3 893	4 477	4 631	4 793	(5 459)
Angola	m. kwanzas	..	..	(15 150)	(15 060)	(15 060)	(15 060)	(23 370)	(29 520)	(34 410)	[38 000]
Benin	m. francs	2 112	1 997	3 680	(4 700)	(5 400)	(6 800)	(9 300)			
Botswana	m. pulas	6.5	17.1	24.0	27.9	28.7	24.0	29.6	[27.0]	[31.0]	[17.0]
Burkina Faso	m. francs	5 627	7 305	6 814	7 470	9 216	10 800	11 172	11 312	11 709	..
Burundi	m. francs	1 256	(1 533)	(1 800)	(2 500)	[2 700]	[3 300]	[3 200]	[3 900]	[4 200]	..
Cameroon	m. francs	12 769	13 700	14 876	18 816	22 860	26 645	32 216	(40 373)	(47 449)	[50 339]

		1977	1978	1979	1980	1981	1982	1983	1984	1985	1986
Central African Republic	m. francs	1 880	2 289	3 061	2 816	4 029	[5 000]	[6 500]	..	..	..
Chad	m. francs	5 255	5 186	5 890	..	..	..	..	(17 496)	[20 000]	[32 000]
Congo	m. francs	9 000	10 000	9 450	10 050	[11 250]	[16 500]	[18 600]	(21 596)	[25 000]	[25 000]
Côte d'Ivoire	m. francs	12 640	19 579	21 854	26 643	[25 000]	[28 400]	[29 057]	(31 807)	[35 560]	[39 400]
Ethiopia	m. birr	280	519	722	744	[789]	[811]	[816]	(915)	[990]	..
Gabon	m. francs	7 107	[12 160]	[12 036]	[18 600]	[25 600]	[29 100]	[33 000]	[35 100]	[42 400]	..
Ghana	m. cedis	140	179	(182)	[332]	538	526	(673)	(1 605)	[1 850]	..
Kenya	m. pounds	61.2	92.6	109	101	109	133	124	(110)	[132]	[150]
Liberia	m. dollars	8.3	9.5	9.3	16.8	37.4	65.8	27.3	22.6	[26.0]	..
Libya	m. dinars	[495]	[810]	[995]	[970]	[1 130]	[1 270]	[1 010]	[900]	..	..
Madagascar	m. francs	10 800	11 775	17 420	(19 315)	(23 500)	[27 200]	[29 600]	(31 730)	[33 520]	..
Malawi	m. kwachas	12.3	21.6	35.2	43.1	35.0	(29.0)	(34.3)	(42.1)	[44.4]	[58.0]
Mali	m. francs	12 751	14 080	15 331	16 295	17 217	19 302	20 486	(26 000)	[12 500]	(12 900)
Mauritania	m. ouguiyas	4 350	3 605	4 301	3 700	3 541	3 238	2 639	2 660	[2 740]	[2 850]
Mauritius	m. rupees	9.4	10.8	15.7	42.6	47.7	30.8	34.4	36.0	[37.0]	[46.0]
Morocco	m. dirhams	3 294	3 219	3 495	4 400	5 047	5 814	4 675	4 679	(5 245)	[6 817]
Mozambique	m. meticais	1 900	3 650	3 733	4 754	5 595	6 188	[8 300]	(10 200)	(10 300)	[11 214]
Niger	m. francs	2 143	2 862	3 509	4 103	4 286	4 232	[4 389]	[4 775]	..	..
Nigeria	m. nairas	1 266	1 202	1 122	1 429	1 372	1 164	1 162	[991]	[895]	[907]
Rwanda	m. francs	1 541	1 288	1 702	2 027	2 500	2 622	2 693	[2 500]	[2 650]	..
Senegal	m. francs	16 600	18 800	20 150	19 870	21 565	23 505	25 110	(27 046)	(28 235)	[28 490]
Sierra Leone	m. leones	7.4	8.3	10.0	14.1	17.5	17.9	18.6	[22.4]	[28.5]	..
Somalia	m. shillings	200	513	552	601	843	846	1 325	(1 831)	[1 807]	..
South Africa[e]	m. rands	(1 548)	(1 654)	(2 018)	(2 419)	(2 615)	[2 967]	[3 615]	[4 158]	[4 409]	[5 257]
Sudan	m. pounds	68.9	70.9	84.7	108	131	162	[248]	[385]	[460]	..
Tanzania	m. shillings	1 490	3 086	2 771	1 688	[2 848]	[3 287]	[2 920]	3 630	[3 500]	..
Togo	m. francs	4 268	4 615	4 661	5 155	6 202	6 138	6 328	6 872	7 670	..
Tunisia	m. dinars	52.2	61.8	65.4	78.6	113	(284)	(364)	(296)	(357)	[413]
Uganda	m. shillings	1 089	1 174	1 548	2 958	5 413	8 228	14 420	[26 000]	[45 000]	..
Zaire	m. zaires	97.9	[81.0]	[191]	[286]	[385]	[596]	713	[1 250]	[1 500]	..
Zambia	m. kwachas	[54.0]	[62.0]	[128]	[106]	[140]	[100]	[120]	[123]	[200]	..
Zimbabwe	m. dollars	135	156	186	300	267	325	382	(403)	(436)	548

Central America

Country	Unit										
Costa Rica	m. colones	211	207	242	275	318	711	902	1 114	1 239	1 460
Cuba	m. pesos	700	784	814	759	931	1 109	1 133	1 386	1 335	1 307
Dominican Republic	m. pesos	75.8	87.1	109	99.4	[126]	[128]	129	164	[200]	..
El Salvador	m. colones	143	159	175	254	322	395	442	574	[900]	[1 070]
Guatemala	m. quetzales	83.2	103	118	143	161	[208]	(231)	(270)	[400]	..
Haiti	m. gourdes	60.9	73.7	94.1	101	105	104	102	110	(132)	..
Honduras	m. lempiras	63.6	86.2	99.1	158	(198)	(216)	240	318	(317)	404
Jamaica	m. dollars	76.5	108	126	137	167	[175]	[200]	(228)	[278]	(400)
Mexico	m. pesos	10 500	12 214	17 779	24 000	37 890	52 212	[128 000]	[186 000]	[279 230]	[543 315]
Nicaragua	m. cordobas	363	459	(456)	(961)	(1 300)	(1 760)	(3 420)	[5 550]	[17 800]	..
Panama	m. balboas	[32.0]	[36.0]	[41.0]	[42.2]	[46.5]	[55.0]	[60.0]	88.0	(92.0)	[94.0]
Trinidad and Tobago	m. dollars	108	195	208	296	371	563	(545)	(490)	[465]	[465]

South America

Country	Unit										
Argentina	m. australes	0.1	0.1	0.4	0.7	1.6	[8.8]	(28.9)	181	1 649	2 820
Bolivia	b. pesos	2.1	2.7	3.2	4.8	8.0	(19.0)	(58.0)	[805]	[105 707]	[203 965]
Brazil/	m. cruzados	27.5	35.2	48.0	68.7	147	329	(988)	[2 874]	[10 071]	..
Chile	m. pesos	19 860	31 301	49 807	67 997	89 523	110 840	124 901	152 659	[174 999]	[219 000]
Colombia	m. pesos	..	..	20 530	29 030	35 830	44 330	69 800	100 870	[113 790]	[219 000]
Ecuador	m. sucres	5 116	4 097	4 638	5 539	6 639	6 870	9 540	13 900	..	..
Guyana	m. dollars	67.0	67.0	67.2	98.0	96.0	108	(142)	(156)	(192)	[276]
Paraguay	m. guaranies	4 204	4 892	5 793	7 644	10 581	11 687	[15 000]	[9 480]	15 790	21 360
Peru	m. intis	77.2	92.5	121	(283)	(613)	(1 014)	(2 274)	[4 770]	12 200	[17 000]
Uruguay	m. new pesos	464	697	1 361	2 693	4 770	5 168	..	..	..	..
Venezuela	m. bolivares	3 400	3 500	4 991	6 899	8 952	9 905	8 488	(9 800)	[11 200]	12 720

Table 6A.2. World military expenditure, in constant price figures

Figures are in US $m., at 1980 prices and exchange-rates. Totals may not add up due to rounding.

	1977	1978	1979	1980	1981	1982	1983	1984	1985	1986
NATO										
North America										
Canada	4 739	4 765	4 666	4 786	4 965	5 178	5 556	5 921	6 092	6 279
USA	163 111	164 442	166 118	169 525	178 063	186 237	196 969	207 572	212 498	219 299
Europe										
Belgium	3 562	3 798	3 882	3 959	3 995	3 862	3 708	3 550	3 446	(3 446)
Denmark	1 534	1 594	1 604	1 618	1 636	1 683	1 697	1 656	1 617	1 610
France	23 984	25 387	25 964	26 427	27 069	27 626	28 097	27 999	27 984	28 798
FR Germany	24 923	25 979	26 328	26 692	27 012	26 664	26 887	26 612	26 666	27 660
Greece	2 658	2 715	2 630	2 276	2 693	2 746	2 505	2 975	2 952	2 750
Italy	8 257	8 608	9 154	9 578	9 781	10 463	10 689	11 008	11 402	11 741
Luxembourg	40.3	43.8	45.1	52.5	54.3	54.8	56.0	56.3	54.9	61.2
Netherlands	5 287	5 106	5 413	5 269	5 325	5 306	5 259	5 351	5 289	5 429
Norway	1 507	1 612	1 651	1 669	1 686	1 752	1 828	1 761	2 028	1 933
Portugal	781	788	800	868	864	865	832	774	783	869
Spain[a]	5 661	5 641	5 918	6 581	6 706	6 907	7 058	7 184	7 413	6 986
Turkey	3 173	2 906	2 578	2 672	3 015	3 296	3 083	2 997	3 178	3 643
UK	22 413	22 804	24 065	25 481	26 506	27 643	28 525	29 795	29 817	30 023
WTO[g]										
Bulgaria	(902)	[946]	[971]	[1 000]	[1 056]	[1 090]	[1 112]	[1 144]	..	[2 917]
Czechoslovakia	2 475	2 519	2 493	2 593	2 595	2 624	(2 676)	(2 759)	(2 859)	(5 885)
German DR	3 507	3 686	3 859	4 167	4 508	4 765	(5 030)	(5 375)	(5 464)	(726)
Hungary	668	760	754	755	778	765	779	(746)	(715)	[2 890]
Poland	3 089	2 964	2 984	2 863	2 673	2 938	(2 656)	(2 762)	[3 013]	[1 083]
Romania	1 405	1 472	1 460	1 263	1 247	1 153	(1 127)	(1 136)	(1 107)	
Other Europe										
Albania[h]	115	117	126	131	134	134	130	144	243	[329]
Austria	840	918	973	952	942	915	921	932	1 022	966

Finland[b]	832	868	928	992	1 005	1 161	1 152	1 161	1 176	1 255
Ireland	290	319	344	362	347	351	329	319	338	333
Sweden[c]	3 647	3 751	3 898	3 777	3 694	3 604	3 495	3 501	3 460	3 501
Switzerland[d]	1 747	1 722	1 852	1 881	1 877	1 977	1 989	2 005	2 214	2 086
Yugoslavia	2 815	2 773	2 969	3 089	2 899	2 553	2 398	2 469	2 646	[2 772]
Middle East										
Bahrain	46.6	114	148	157	192	231	(132)	[118]	[128]	[127]
Cyprus	39.3	31.3	40.5	29.2	37.6	[41.6]	[42.1]	[41.3]	[43.2]	..
Egypt	[3 882]	[2 179]	[2 068]	[1 621]	[1 647]	[1 820]	[1 892]	[1 965]	[1 885]	[1 746]
Iran	11 944	11 080	6 605	5 149	5 570	[6 161]	[5 275]	[8 607]	[6 405]	..
Iraq	2 700	2 556	(3 235)	[3 353]	[3 815]	[5 981]	[7 791]	..	..	..
Israel	(4 929)	(4 412)	(5 315)	(5 434)	(4 935)	(4 922)	(5 476)	(6 038)	(4 038)	(4 030)
Jordan	440	436	496	457	499	519	542	524	(565)	[613]
Kuwait	934	1 031	1 017	1 075	1 275	(1 329)	(1 389)	(1 554)	..	..
Lebanon	121	195	266	285	164	268	730	296	..	..
Oman[h]	686	767	779	1 178	1 511	1 682	1 943	2 131	[2 157]	[1 740]
Saudi Arabia	[9 901]	[12 279]	[16 336]	[19 261]	22 164	25 396	24 183	22 557	21 429	..
Syria	1 388	1 505	2 511	2 144	2 076	2 015	2 009	(2 050)	[2 053]	[1 980]
United Arab Emirates	520	814	1 185	1 707	2 069	1 960	1 899	[1 864]	[2 023]	[1 861]
Yemen Arab Republic	215	492	530	[526]	559	752	605	456	445	..
Yemen, People's Democratic Rep. of	74.6	112	115	123	156	[146]	[151]	[144]	[135]	..
South Asia										
Afghanistan	81.5	83.9	125	[174]	..	..	..	(236)	(257)	(257)
Bangladesh	170	171	177	187	204	222	217	..	..	..
India	4 843	4 898	5 196	5 632	6 016	6 534	6 812	7 190	7 528	7 912
Nepal	17.5	18.8	20.8	20.3	20.5	23.0	25.8	28.8	[34.1]	42.6
Pakistan	1 175	1 278	1 375	1 432	1 584	1 832	1 953	2 083	2 314	2 533
Sri Lanka	45.3	47.3	61.3	58.7	53.9	69.4	73.1	90.5	(147)	346
Far East										
Brunei	96.1	106	189	191	180	(200)	(217)	[213]	[249]	[268]
Burma	189	201	202	(215)	(240)	(231)	(221)	(228)	(239)	[188]
Hong Kong	96.2	139	147	272	269	236	224	205	(190)	(194)

	1977	1978	1979	1980	1981	1982	1983	1984	1985	1986
Indonesia	(2 384)	(2 576)	(2 458)	(2 723)	(3 059)	[3 391]	[3 318]	(3 265)	[2 867]	(2 986)
Japan	8 467	8 987	9 573	9 767	10 042	10 370	10 915	11 454	12 019	12 627
Korea, North[h]	1 168	1 307	1 429	1 533	1 677	1 807	1 968	2 129	2 193	2 241
Korea, South	2 891	3 603	3 384	3 707	3 843	4 003	4 168	4 131	4 467	4 961
Malaysia	1 059	1 108	1 249	1 557	1 965	1 937	1 839	(1 605)	(1 582)	(1 559)
Mongolia[h]	(177)	(184)	(209)	(186)	(275)	(312)	(316)	[347]	[370]	:
Philippines	980	899	825	776	794	831	(831)	912	997	919
Singapore	556	520	532	609	664	688	646	:	:	:
Taiwan	2 244	2 538	2 662	2 681	(2 794)	3 142	3 169	3 146	3 477	3 683
Thailand	(1 200)	(1 470)	1 413	1 353	1 387	1 462	1 946	2 086	1 998	2 094
Oceania										
Australia	3 495	3 542	3 652	3 860	4 115	4 303	4 450	4 869	5 193	5 243
Fiji	4.8	4.8	5.5	5.3	4.0	4.3	4.5	4.1	3.9	:
New Zealand	353	373	382	410	471	463	452	469	465	503
Africa										
Algeria	729	792	783	890	792	829	855	885	799	(862)
Angola[i]	:	(343)	(505)	(502)	(502)	(502)	(779)	(984)	(1 147)	[1 267]
Benin[i]	10.0	9.5	17.4	(22.2)	[22.9]	[25.6]	[32.4]	[22.6]	[23.1]	[14.6]
Botswana	11.6	27.9	35.2	35.9	31.8	23.8	26.7	[39.1]	[37.9]	:
Burkina Faso	37.2	44.6	36.2	35.4	40.5	42.4	40.5	[29.5]	[30.7]	:
Burundi	25.8	(25.5)	(21.9)	[27.8]	[26.8]	[31.0]	[27.7]	[29.5]	(136)	:
Cameroon	79.3	75.8	77.1	89.1	97.7	101	104	(82.8)	(94.7)	[134]
Central African Rep.	12.5	(13.9)	(17.0)	[13.3]	[16.9]	(18.6)	[21.3]	[63.8]	[69.6]	[151]
Chad[h]	11.7	24.5	27.9	47.6	[45.5]	[59.2]	[71.0]	[117]	[128]	[133]
Congo	54.4	54.9	48.0	126	[109]	[115]	[61.9]	[63.8]	:	:
Côte d'Ivoire	90.4	124	119	359	[359]	[349]	[111]	[365]	[332]	:
Ethiopia	187	304	364	[88.0]	[111]	[109]	[353]	[112]	[126]	:
Gabon	45.2	[69.8]	(64.0)	[121]	90.3	72.2	[112]	(70.8)	[74.0]	:
Ghana	204	151	(99.5)	288	279	282	[41.5]	[190]	[207]	[218]
Kenya	251	325	354	:	:	:	236	:	:	:
Liberia	11.4	12.2	10.7	16.8	34.8	57.7	23.3	19.1	22.1	:
Libya	[2 311]	[2 924]	[3 799]	[3 276]	[3 439]	[3 518]	[2 269]	[1 840]	:	:

Madagascar	73.4	75.1	97.5	(91.4)	(85.2)	[75.1]	[68.2]	(66.6)	[66.4]	..
Malawi	21.7	35.1	51.6	53.1	38.5	(29.1)	(30.3)	(33.0)	[31.4]	[37.6]
Mali	94.2	78.1	88.7	77.1	72.6	79.6	76.3	(88.0)	[38.9]	[36.5]
Mauritania	123	94.9	104	80.6	64.8	52.6	42.4	[40.0]	[40.1]	[39.8]
Mauritius	2.2	2.3	2.9	5.5	5.4	3.1	3.3	3.2	[3.1]	[3.7]
Morocco	1 088	969	971	1 118	1 140	1 187	899	800	(833)	[978]
Mozambique[h]	38.8	74.6	76.3	97.2	114	126	[170]	(209)	(211)	[229]
Niger	13.2	16.0	18.3	19.4	16.5	14.6	[15.5]	[15.6]	..	..
Nigeria	3 461	2 701	2 257	2 613	2 077	1 636	1 326	[810]	[693]	[503]
Rwanda	23.3	17.2	19.7	21.8	25.3	23.6	22.7	[20.0]	[20.8]	..
Senegal	96.9	106	104	94.0	96.4	89.6	85.7	(82.5)	(75.9)	[72.5]
Sierra Leone	10.5	10.7	10.5	13.4	13.5	10.6	6.5	[4.7]	[3.4]	..
Somalia	69.0	161	139	95.5	92.7	75.9	87.2	(62.2)	[47.2]	..
South Africa[i]	(2 819)	(2 733)	(2 948)	(3 106)	(2 915)	[2 884]	[3 127]	[3 222]	[2 939]	[2 996]
Sudan	270	233	212	217	211	207	[242]	[294]	[234]	..
Tanzania	300	558	440	206	[277]	[248]	[173]	[158]	[122]	..
Togo	24.5	26.4	24.8	24.4	24.5	21.8	20.6	23.2	[26.3]	..
Tunisia	161	181	178	194	256	(566)	(666)	(500)	(558)	[600]
Uganda[k]	147	158	209	399	730	554	783	[1 021]	[759]	..
Zaire	154	[85.7]	[96.9]	[102]	[102]	[116]	78.2	[90.1]	[87.3]	..
Zambia	[97.7]	[96.3]	[181]	[134]	[156]	[98.9]	[99.2]	[84.7]	[100]	..
Zimbabwe	277	302	305	467	368	404	385	(339)	(337)	[408]
Central America										
Costa Rica	33.7	31.2	33.3	32.1	27.1	31.8	30.5	33.6	32.5	33.9
Cuba	957	1 028	1 068	986	1 080	1 221	1 196	1 406	1 313	1 239
Dominican Republic	100	111	127	99.4	117	[111]	106	106	..	..
El Salvador	87.1	85.5	82.0	102	112	123	122	142	[94.4]	[156]
Guatemala	111	127	131	143	145	[186]	(198)	(224)	(182)	..
Haiti	15.8	19.6	22.2	20.1	18.9	17.4	15.6	15.7	(17.1)	..
Honduras	43.9	56.0	58.5	79.0	(90.5)	(90.6)	93.0	93.0	118	137
Jamaica	95.2	99.2	89.7	76.7	83.2	[81.8]	[83.8]	(74.7)	[72.5]	(89.1)
Mexico	803	794	979	1 046	1 291	1 119	[1 360]	[1 194]	[1 136]	[1 228]
Nicaragua	75.7	91.5	(61.5)	(95.7)	(104)	(113)	(168)	(201)	[202]	..
Panama	[41.0]	[44.2]	[46.6]	[42.2]	[43.3]	[49.2]	[52.5]	75.9	(78.5)	[80.1]
Trinidad and Tobago	66.6	110	102	123	135	184	(153)	(121)	[107]	[98.4]

	1977	1978	1979	1980	1981	1982	1983	1984	1985	1986
South America										
Argentina	3 952	4 019	3 975	3 936	4 178	[8 784]	(6 536)	5 633	6 647	6 315
Bolivia	166	187	191	192	242	(257)	(209)	[210]	[229]	[230]
Brazil^f	2 009	1 858	1 656	1 296	1 347	1 526	(1 892)	[1 855]	[1 988]	..
Chile	1 286	1 446	1 726	1 744	1 918	2 160	1 913	1 950	(1 711)	[1 824]
Colombia	..	501	549	614	594	591	776	[966]	[879]	..
Ecuador	285	204	210	222	228	203	(190)	[211]	..	..
Guyana	40.7	35.3	30.0	38.4	30.2	28.2	(32.8)	(29.0)	(32.0)	[31.8]
Paraguay	57.9	60.9	56.3	60.7	73.7	76.2	[86.3]	[45.3]	60.3	59.1
Peru	1 120	850	667	(979)	(1 210)	(1 216)	(1 292)	[1 289]	[1 252]	[1 057]
Uruguay	201	209	244	296	391	356	..	..	(389)	..
Venezuela	1 158	1 114	1 413	1 607	1 798	1 813	1 461	(1 504)	1 543	1 593

Table 6A.3. World military expenditure as a percentage of gross domestic product

	1977	1978	1979	1980	1981	1982	1983	1984	1985	1986
NATO										
North America										
Canada	2.0	1.9	1.8	1.8	1.9	2.0	2.1	2.2	2.2	2.3
USA	6.1	5.9	5.9	6.3	6.6	7.0	7.1	7.0	7.0	6.7
Europe										
Belgium	3.2	3.3	3.3	3.3	3.5	3.3	3.3	3.1	3.0	(2.9)
Denmark	2.3	2.3	2.3	2.4	2.5	2.5	2.5	2.3	2.2	2.1
France	3.9	4.0	3.9	4.0	4.2	4.1	4.2	4.1	4.1	4.0
FR Germany	3.4	3.3	3.3	3.3	3.4	3.4	3.4	3.3	3.2	3.1
Greece	7.0	6.7	6.3	5.7	7.0	6.9	6.3	7.2	7.1	6.6
Italy	2.4	2.4	2.4	2.4	2.5	2.6	2.7	2.7	2.7	2.7
Luxembourg	0.9	0.9	0.9	1.0	1.1	1.0	1.1	1.1	1.1	1.1
Netherlands	3.3	3.1	3.2	3.1	3.2	3.2	3.2	3.2	3.1	3.1
Norway	3.1	3.2	3.1	2.9	2.9	3.0	3.1	2.8	3.1	3.1
Portugal	3.5	3.5	3.5	3.5	3.5	3.4	3.4	3.3	3.1	3.2
Spain[a]	2.8	2.7	2.8	3.1	3.2	3.3	3.3	3.3	3.3	..
Turkey	5.8	5.2	4.3	4.7	4.9	5.2	4.9	4.4	4.5	4.7
UK	4.6	4.4	4.5	4.8	5.0	5.2	5.2	5.4	5.2	5.2
WTO										
Bulgaria[l]	(3.0)	[3.1]	[3.1]	[3.1]	[3.1]	[3.0]	[3.1]	[3.1]	..	..
Czechoslovakia[l]	3.4	3.3	3.3	3.3	3.4	3.5	3.5	3.5	(3.6)	..
German DR[l]	4.0	4.1	4.1	4.2	4.4	4.5	4.5	4.7	4.6	(4.8)
Hungary	2.2	2.4	2.4	2.5	2.4	2.4	2.4	2.3	2.2	..
Poland[l]	2.7	2.6	2.7	2.8	2.9	3.0	2.6	..	..	..
Romania[l]	2.1	2.1	2.0	1.7	1.6	1.5	1.5	1.4	1.4	[1.3]
Other Europe										
Austria	1.2	1.3	1.3	1.2	1.2	1.2	1.2	1.1	1.2	1.3
Finland[b]	1.8	1.9	1.9	1.9	1.9	2.2	2.1	2.0	2.0	2.1

	1977	1978	1979	1980	1981	1982	1983	1984	1985	1986
Ireland	1.7	1.7	1.8	1.9	1.8	1.8	1.7	1.6	1.7	1.6
Sweden[c]	3.1	3.2	3.1	3.0	3.1	3.0	2.8	2.7	2.6	2.5
Switzerland[d]	1.8	1.8	1.9	1.9	1.8	1.8	1.8	1.8	1.9	1.9
Yugoslavia[m]	5.3	4.8	4.8	4.9	4.5	4.0	3.7	[5.2]	[6.1]	..
Middle East										
Bahrain	1.7	4.2	5.1	4.0	4.8	6.2	(3.6)	[3.1]	..	..
Cyprus	2.5	1.7	2.0	1.4	1.7	[1.7]	[1.6]	[1.5]	..	..
Egypt	[20.5]	[10.3]	[8.5]	[7.0]	[6.8]	[7.1]	[7.1]	[7.3]	..	..
Iran	10.6	10.6	6.3	5.4	[6.1]	[6.3]	[5.1]	..	..	..
Iraq	9.8	8.1	(6.9)	[6.3]	[13.1]	[23.2]	[33.7]	[51.2]	[57.1]	..
Israel	(27.1)	(22.8)	(25.8)	(26.0)	21.8	21.5	23.0	24.7	(17.9)	..
Jordan	18.8	16.2	17.7	13.9	13.7	13.5	13.7	13.2	(13.9)	..
Kuwait	5.1	5.8	4.2	4.0	(5.4)	(6.7)	[7.2]	..	..	..
Lebanon	3.1	5.6	6.6	..	..	..	18.1	11.7	..	..
Oman	26.9	28.0	20.9	19.7	20.8	22.3	24.5	24.2	..	..
Saudi Arabia	[15.5]	[17.3]	(21.1)	(16.6)	(14.5)	(16.7)	(20.3)	[20.4]	[21.9]	..
Syria	15.3	14.5	21.1	16.2	14.5	15.2	15.5	[16.8]	..	..
United Arab Emirates	3.0	5.0	5.5	5.8	6.3	6.5	6.9	[6.9]	..	..
Yemen Arab Republic	7.1	16.6	20.8	[19.2]	19.3	25.3	19.3	14.8	[7.8]	..
Yemen, People's Democratic Rep. of	12.5	17.5	17.5	17.8	19.7	[18.7]	[19.1]	[17.5]	14.8	..
South Asia										
Afghanistan	1.8	1.9	..	..	..	..	..	..	..	..
Bangladesh	1.2	1.1	1.1	1.2	1.3	1.4	1.3	(1.3)	(1.4)	..
India	3.6	3.4	3.5	3.6	3.8	3.9	3.9	4.0	..	..
Nepal	0.8	0.8	0.9	0.8	0.8	1.0	1.1	..	..	..
Pakistan	4.8	4.8	4.7	4.7	5.1	5.5	5.4	..	..	..
Sri Lanka	1.3	1.3	1.5	1.5	1.2	1.5	1.5	1.7	(2.7)	..
Far East										
Brunei	4.1	4.6	6.1	3.9	4.5	(5.3)	(6.5)	[6.5]	[6.4]	[6.6]
Burma	4.3	4.0	3.8	(3.7)	(3.8)	(3.5)	[3.3]	..	..	..

Hong Kong	0.5	0.7	0.6	1.0	0.9	0.8	0.7	0.6	..	..
Indonesia	(5.1)	(5.0)	(4.1)	(3.8)	(4.0)	[4.4]	[3.9]	(3.6)	[3.3]	..
Japan	0.9	0.9	0.9	0.9	0.9	0.9	1.0	..	..	..
Korea, North	9.6	10.1	10.4	10.7	11.5	11.8	12.3	..	..	..
Korea, South	5.6	6.0	5.1	6.0	6.0	6.0	5.7	5.1	5.3	5.3
Malaysia	6.1	5.8	5.5	6.3	8.1	7.8	6.9	(5.5)	(5.5)	(5.5)
Philippines	3.2	2.7	2.4	2.2	2.2	2.3	(2.2)	..	..	..
Singapore	6.3	5.6	5.1	5.4	5.4	5.2	4.5	5.9	6.5	5.9
Taiwan	7.9	7.8	6.8	6.6	(6.7)	7.3	6.8	..	..	..
Thailand	(4.4)	(4.9)	4.3	4.0	4.1	4.2	5.3	5.3	5.0	5.0
Oceania										
Australia	2.7	2.6	2.6	2.7	2.7	2.9	3.0	3.0	3.2	..
Fiji	0.5	0.5	0.5	0.4	0.3	0.4	0.4	0.3	0.3	..
New Zealand	1.6	1.7	1.7	1.8	2.0	2.0	2.0	1.9	1.9	..
Africa										
Algeria	2.4	2.4	2.1	2.1	1.8	1.9	1.9	1.9	..	..
Angola	..	..	(14.0)	(12.8)	(13.8)	(11.9)	(16.5)	(20.4)	..	..
Benin	1.4	1.2	1.9	2.0	1.9	2.0	[2.4]	..	..	..
Botswana	2.0	4.0	4.0	3.8	3.7	2.7	2.7	(2.5)	[2.4]	..
Burkina Faso	3.0	3.3	2.6	2.6	2.9	3.1	2.6	[3.3]	[3.2]	..
Burundi	2.5	(2.8)	(2.6)	(2.9)	[3.0]	[3.6]	[3.2]	[1.2]	..	..
Cameroon	1.5	1.3	1.2	1.2	1.2	1.1	1.1	..	..	..
Central African Rep.	1.5	(1.7)	(2.0)	[1.7]	[2.1]	[2.3]	[2.8]	[2.3]	..	..
Congo	..	5.0	3.7	2.8	[2.1]	[2.3]	[2.3]	(1.1)	..	..
Côte d'Ivoire	0.8	1.1	1.1	1.2	1.1	1.1	[1.2]	..	[2.9]	..
Ethiopia	4.0	6.8	8.8	8.5	[8.7]	[8.4]	[8.1]	[9.2]	..	..
Gabon	1.0	[2.3]	(1.9)	[2.1]	[2.4]	[2.4]	[2.5]	[2.4]	..	..
Ghana	1.3	0.9	(0.6)	[0.8]	0.7	0.6	(0.4)	(0.6)	..	..
Kenya	3.2	4.5	4.7	3.8	3.6	3.9	3.2	[2.6]	[3.0]	..
Liberia	1.2	1.2	1.1	1.8	4.3	7.9	3.3	2.8	[3.2]	..
Libya	[8.6]	[14.2]	[12.7]	[9.2]	[12.1]	[14.4]	[11.8]	[11.4]	..	[3.1]
Madagascar	2.4	2.5	3.0	(2.9)	(3.1)	[2.6]	[2.4]	(2.3)	[2.1]	..
Malawi	1.7	2.7	4.2	4.6	3.3	(2.5)	(2.5)	(2.5)	[2.4]	..
Mali	..	..	..	5.9	5.2	5.4	5.2	(5.6)	..	..
Mauritania	17.9	14.5	15.5	11.7	8.9	8.3	6.4	[6.6]	[6.6]	[6.6]

	1977	1978	1979	1980	1981	1982	1983	1984	1985	1986
Mauritius	0.2	0.2	0.2	0.5	0.5	0.3	0.3	0.3	[0.2]	..
Morocco	6.6	5.8	5.6	6.3	6.6	6.5	4.8	4.4	(4.3)	..
Mozambique	..	..	..	6.0	6.9	7.2	[10.7]	(11.9)	(11.7)	[10.4]
Niger	0.9	0.9	0.9	0.8	0.7	0.7	0.7	0.8	..	..
Nigeria	4.1	3.5	2.7	3.0	2.9	2.2	2.1	[1.8]	..	..
Rwanda	2.2	1.6	1.8	1.9	2.0	2.0	1.9	[1.6]	..	..
Senegal	3.4	3.8	3.5	3.2	3.2	2.8	2.7	(2.7)	..	..
Sierra Leone	0.9	0.9	0.9	1.1	1.2	1.0	0.8	[0.6]	..	..
South Africa	(4.5)	(4.2)	(4.3)	(3.9)	(3.7)	[3.7]	[4.1]	[3.9]	[3.7]	..
Sudan	2.6	2.3	2.3	2.4	2.4	2.3	[2.8]	..	..	..
Tanzania	5.0	9.3	7.6	3.9	[5.6]	[5.4]	[4.4]	[4.8]	..	..
Togo	2.5	2.4	2.2	2.2	2.4	2.3	2.2	2.4	[2.5]	..
Tunisia	2.4	2.5	2.2	2.2	2.7	(5.9)	(6.6)	(4.7)	(5.1)	[5.7]
Uganda	2.2	1.8	..	2.1	3.8	2.7	3.0	[4.0]	..	..
Zaire	2.5	[1.5]	[1.7]	[1.7]	[1.6]	[1.9]	1.2	[1.3]	[1.1]	..
Zambia	[2.8]	[2.8]	[4.8]	[3.5]	[4.0]	[2.8]	[2.9]	[2.6]	..	..
Zimbabwe	6.2	6.8	6.6	8.7	6.0	6.3	6.4	(5.9)	(5.5)	..
Central America										
Costa Rica	0.8	0.7	0.7	0.7	0.6	0.7	0.7	0.7	0.7	..
Cuba[m]	..	8.3	8.5	7.8	8.0	9.2	8.6	9.7	..	..
Dominican Republic	1.7	1.8	2.0	1.5	[1.7]	[1.6]	1.5	1.5	[1.4]	..
El Salvador	2.0	2.1	2.0	2.8	3.7	4.4	4.4	5.0	[6.4]	[5.5]
Guatemala	1.5	1.7	1.7	1.8	1.9	[2.4]	(2.6)	(2.9)	[3.6]	..
Haiti	1.2	1.3	1.4	1.4	1.4	1.3	1.2	1.1	..	..
Honduras	1.9	2.3	2.3	3.2	[3.7]	(3.9)	4.1	5.1	(4.7)	..
Jamaica	2.6	2.9	2.9	2.9	3.2	[3.0]	[2.9]	(2.4)	[2.3]	..
Mexico	0.6	0.5	0.6	0.6	0.6	0.6	[0.7]	[0.6]	[0.6]	[0.7]
Nicaragua	2.5	3.2	(3.1)	(4.4)	[5.0]	(5.9)	(9.6)	[11.7]	[12.0]	..
Panama	[1.5]	[1.5]	[1.5]	[1.2]	[1.2]	[1.3]	[1.4]	1.9	[1.9]	[1.9]
Trinidad and Tobago	1.4	2.3	1.9	1.9	2.2	3.2	(2.8)	(2.5)	[2.3]	[2.2]

South America

Argentina	2.4	2.7	2.5	2.6	2.9	[5.9]	(3.9)	3.3	3.9	3.7
Bolivia	3.3	3.5	3.5	3.7	4.9	4.8	4.4	4.2	:	:
Brazil[f]	1.1	0.9	0.8	0.5	0.6	0.6	(0.8)	[0.7]	[0.8]	:
Chile	6.9	6.4	6.5	6.3	7.0	8.9	8.0	8.1	(6.8)	[6.9]
Colombia	:	:	1.7	1.8	1.8	1.8	2.3	2.6	[2.3]	:
Ecuador	3.1	2.1	2.0	1.9	1.9	1.7	(1.7)	[1.7]	:	:
Guyana	6.0	5.3	5.1	6.5	6.0	7.5	(9.7)	(9.2)	(9.8)	:
Paraguay	1.6	1.5	1.3	1.4	1.5	1.6	(1.8)	[0.9]	1.1	:
Peru	7.3	5.5	3.9	(5.7)	(7.2)	(7.1)	(8.6)	[8.0]	[7.7]	[6.2]
Uruguay	2.3	2.3	2.4	2.9	3.9	4.0	:	:	4.4	:
Venezuela	2.2	2.1	2.4	2.7	3.1	3.4	2.9	(2.8)	[3.0]	3.0

Conventions

. . Information not available or not applicable

( ) Uncertain data

[ ] Estimates with a high degree of uncertainty

— Negligible or nil

t. Thousand

m. Million

b. Billion

Notes, definitions and sources for the tables of world military expenditure

[a] Spain became a NATO member on 30 May 1982. Military expenditure has been estimated on the basis of the NATO definition for the period 1980–86 and extrapolated to give estimates for 1977–79. For convenience, the whole series is presented here in the NATO section. See table 6.4.

[b] Finland's figures have been changed according to SIPRI's military expenditure definition. The new series includes: expenses for pensions, border guards, UN peace-keeping troops and military-related expenditures from the Ministry of Labour and the Ministry of Justice.

[c] In this edition of the *SIPRI Yearbook* Sweden's military expenditure series has been changed by excluding civil defence expenditures.

[d] In this edition of the *SIPRI Yearbook* Switzerland's military expenditure is lower than previously since costs for running the military university have not been included.

[e] The SIPRI estimate in square brackets is based on planned military expenditure in real terms.

[f] Recent evidence suggests that Brazilian military expenditure is considerably higher than the amount given here. The series is currently being revised.

[g] The SIPRI practice of using official consumer price indices, which tend to understate actual price changes in WTO countries, especially for recent years, results in overstated volume expenditure increases for the WTO countries.

[h] At current prices and 1980 exchange-rates.

[i] At current prices and an exchange-rate of 29.99 kwanzas per US dollar.

[j] At current prices and 1980 exchange-rates. Figures for 1980–83 are in constant prices.

[k] At current prices and 1980 exchange-rates for 1977–81. Figures for 1982–85 are in constant prices.

[l] Per cent of gross national product.

[m] Per cent of gross material product.

Table 6A.1: Military expenditure figures are given in local currency at current prices. Figures for recent years are budget estimates.
Table 6A.2: This series is based on the data given in the local currency series, deflated to 1980 price levels and converted into dollars at 1980 period-average exchange-rates. Local consumer-price indices (CPI) are taken as far as possible from *International Financial Statistics* (IFS) (International Monetary Fund: Washington, DC). For the most recent year, the CPI is an estimate based on the first 6–10 months of the year. Period-average exchange-rates are taken as far as possible from the IFS.
Table 6A.3: The share of gross domestic product (GDP) is calculated in local currency. GDP data are taken as far as possible from IFS. For WTO countries (except Hungary), military expenditure is given as a percentage of gross national product (GNP) up to and including 1978, and after 1978 as a percentage of net material product (NMP). For Romania, military expenditure is given as a percentage of GNP for the years 1977–86.

Definitions and sources

For more detailed information, readers are referred to previous editions of the *SIPRI Yearbook*.

The NATO definition of military expenditure is used as a guideline throughout. Where possible, the following items are *included*: all current and capital expenditure on the armed forces and on the running of defence departments and other government agencies engaged in defence projects; the cost of paramilitary forces and police when judged to be trained and equipped for military operations; military R&D, tests and evaluation costs; costs of retirement pensions of service personnel, including pensions of civilian employees. Military aid is included in the budget of the donor country. *Excluded*: civil defence, interest on war debts and some types of veterans' payments.

Problems encountered when applying this definition include: the absence of disaggregated expenditure series; the non-disclosure of certain expenditure categories, especially procurement and R&D; uncertainty as to the amount of military aid included in recipients' budgets; and the degree to which police forces, border and coastguards and the like play a military role.

The data cover 128 countries for the calendar years 1977–86. *Calendar year* figures are calculated from fiscal year data where necessary, on the assumption that expenditure takes place evenly throughout the year. All series are *revised* annually.

General remarks on the data and data presentation

Changes in data published in successive Yearbooks may be due to the revision of any component of the data base, i.e., military expenditure, consumer price indices, exchange-rates and GDP/GNP/NMP data.

Primary sources are official publications.

Secondary sources are press information, specialist literature and other background information.

Uncertain data (with round brackets in the tables) are figures from secondary sources or figures from primary sources, adjusted for known inconsistencies with the time-series in use. Estimates with a high degree of uncertainty (with square brackets in the tables) are data with components of primary and secondary sources and SIPRI estimates based on other country background material.

Main sources of military expenditure data

NATO
Official NATO data published in *Financial and Economic Data Relating to NATO Defence*, annual press release (NATO: Brussels).

Other WTO
1975–79: Alton, T. P., Lazaricik, G., Bass, E. M. and Znayenko, W., 'East European defense expenditures, 1965–1978', in *East European Assessment, Part 2*, a compendium of papers submitted to the Joint Economic Committee, US Congress (US Government Printing Office: Washington, DC, 1981); Alton, T. P., Lazaricik, G., Bass, E. M. and Znayenko, W., *Military expenditure in Eastern Europe, Post World War II to 1979* (L.W. International Financial Research, Inc: New York, 1980). After 1979: domestic sources.

Others
Domestic budgets, defence appropriations and final accounts. Official publications such as *Government Finance Statistics* (International Monetary Fund: Washington, DC); *Statistical Yearbook* (United Nations: New York); *Statistical Yearbook for Asia and the Pacific* (United Nations: Bangkok); *Statistik des Auslandes* (Federal Statistical Office: Wiesbaden); *Europa Yearbook* (Europa Publications: London). Journals and newspapers are consulted for the most recent figures.

7. The trade in major conventional weapons*

THOMAS OHLSON and ELISABETH SKÖNS

Superscript numbers refer to the list of notes and references at the end of the chapter.

I. Introduction

1986 was a dramatic year in the international arms trade—not because of drastic changes in the volume or direction of the flow of weapons, since these remain largely the same as they have been since the late 1970s, but rather because of the behaviour of actors on the market and the structural changes this market is undergoing. (Major weapons include aircraft, armour and artillery, guidance and radar systems, missiles and warships. For definitions of these five weapon categories, see appendix 7E).

The following are only a few examples of the controversial behaviour displayed by supplier countries, illustrating the clash between arms export legislation and short-term political or economic incentives. During 1986 the United States covertly supplied weapons to Iran with the active involvement of at least parts of the Reagan Administration. In FR Germany it was revealed that two companies in the naval industry had sold submarine blueprints to South Africa, thus violating the UN embargo and West German arms export restrictions. In Sweden it was revealed that an arms manufacturer, with the help of private middlemen and false end-use certificates, had supplied weapons and explosives to several countries in the Middle East in an open breach of Swedish guidelines for arms exports. According to SIPRI calculations, based on open sources, no fewer than 27 countries have supplied both belligerents in the Iraq-Iran War with weapons or other support since the war began in September 1980.

The arms market has for some time been characterized by the simultaneous presence of two factors: fierce competition among a growing number of producers and exporters; and a global reduction in the demand for major weapon systems, largely owing to the world-wide economic recession of the early 1980s. This shift towards a buyer's market has led to important structural changes. Arms deals today are concluded with complex financing arrangements, technology transfers and offset agreements involved. There is also an increasing demand among cost-conscious recipients for modernization of existing stocks of weaponry as an alternative to buying new systems. The suppliers have responded to this: there is an increasing flow of enhanced components and upgrading- and modernization kits on the market. Such items account for a rapidly growing share of the international arms trade.

Many arms-producing countries place fewer weapon orders with their

* Evamaria Loose-Weintraub participated in the collection of data for appendices 7A, B and C; appendix 7D was written by Michael Brzoska.

domestic arms industries as a result of shortage of funds and accelerating weapon costs. At the same time, governments are anxious, for political, security and economic reasons, to protect their arms industries. Thus, exports are promoted more intensely, competition increases, and the arms market becomes more and more commercialized. It also becomes more privatized, since the private, civilian sectors of the economies in both supplying and receiving countries are increasingly getting drawn into arms transfers through civil and dual-use technology transfers, offsets and so on. Commercial ambitions, in companies and in governments, often get the upper hand of sound political judgement. Still, it has been a widespread belief—at least among academic observers—that the bulk of the arms trade occurs as a result of politically controlled government-to-government negotiations.

This may still be true, but it is becoming increasingly clear that commercial aspirations and political considerations do not always pull in the same direction. The use of private arms dealers, obscure shipping lines, middlemen and false end-use certificates is not confined only to that part of the arms market which responds to the specific type of demand currently illustrated by Iran and Iraq. These phenomena occur throughout the arms market. They are a result of the competitiveness and commercialization of the arms trade. Arms industries have two roles: they are tools for government searches for national military capabilities and higher degrees of political independence and freedom of manoeuvre; they also represent big business and high profits. While the first role can be considered 'legitimate', it is doubtful—given the specific character of weapons as an industrial good and as a universal coin of power—whether the second one is. Given the lack of political grip on the arms trade today, this issue merits discussion.

There is a need for two major changes: first, the creation and reaffirmation among supplier nations of the political will and ability to control arms transfers. Second, recipients as well as suppliers should—more than now—take into account that security (national, regional or global) not only is a matter of military security but also includes minimum levels of economic and social well-being. Starting from such approaches, the search for restrictive measures that also offer advantages to all concerned parties can begin. For example, compensation schemes for arms industries converting parts of their capabilities towards civilian production are an important part of efforts to reduce the economic pressures to export arms. No agreement to restrict the flow of arms will be reached for its own sake.

II. The flow of arms: general trends

These are some of the major points that can be derived from the statistics on major-weapon exports during 1982–86. (The tables and figures on the arms trade in this chapter are based on the SIPRI values of major weapons *actually delivered* in the given year or years. In this *SIPRI Yearbook* a revised valuation system—including a new base year—for measuring the trade in major weapons is introduced; there are also minor changes in coverage. For a description of these methodological revisions, see appendices 7D and 7E.)

Table 7.1. The leading major-weapon exporting countries: the values and respective shares for 1982–86

Figures are SIPRI trend indicator values, as expressed in US $m., at constant (1985) prices; shares in percentages. Figures may not add up to totals due to rounding.

Country	1982	1983	1984	1985	1986	1982–86	Per cent of total exports to Third World, 1982–86
USA	12 707	12 011	10 276	9 104	10 462	54 562	51.6
	37.8	37.3	31.3	30.1	33.3	34.0	
USSR	9 552	8 850	9 433	11 134	9 881	48 850	76.1
	28.4	27.5	28.7	36.8	31.4	30.5	
France	3 472	3 380	4 170	4 170	4 196	19 387	86.1
	10.3	10.5	12.7	13.8	13.3	12.1	
UK	2 065	1 077	1 925	1 777	1 947	8 791	66.5
	6.1	3.3	5.9	5.9	6.2	5.5	
FR Germany	861	1 822	2 432	942	870	6 928	62.9
	2.6	5.7	7.4	3.1	2.8	4.4	
Third World	1 165	1 462	1 081	740	772	5 220	95.3
	3.5	4.5	3.3	2.4	2.4	3.3	
China	748	890	1 194	863	1 208	4 902	97.1
	2.2	2.8	3.6	2.9	3.8	3.1	
Italy	1 357	973	865	551	327	4 073	98.0
	4.0	3.0	2.6	1.8	1.0	2.5	
Others	1 673	1 720	1 456	938	1 797	7 586	61.0
	5.0	5.3	4.4	3.1	5.7	4.7	
Total	**33 600**	**32 185**	**32 833**	**30 219**	**31 460**	**160 298**	69.0

Source: SIPRI data base.

1. World-wide exports of major weapons remained at a steady level. Exports are still dominated by the superpowers. During 1982–86 the USA accounted for 34 per cent, while the Soviet share was around 31 per cent.

2. The Soviet Union was the leading supplier to the Third World with a share of close to 34 per cent; the US share was in the area of 26 per cent.

3. Annual values for the past 10 years show that the US and Soviet supply levels are out of pace. If one superpower increases its export share a certain year, then the share of the other superpower normally decreases.

4. The combined share of the USA and the USSR in exports of major weapons to the Third World has decreased markedly compared to the preceding five-year period: 59 per cent in 1982–86 as compared to 69 per cent in 1977–81.

5. The combined US–Soviet share in deliveries to industrialized countries has, however, increased slightly from the previous five-year period: from 75 to 77 per cent.

6. The major West European suppliers—France, the UK, FR Germany and Italy—have increased their share in exports to the Third World. Comparing 1977–81 with 1982–86, their share increased from 23 to 28 per cent. France alone accounted for 15 per cent during 1982–86.

7. Other countries that have increased their shares in sales to the Third World compared to 1977–81 are China (from 1.7 to 4.3 per cent), Spain (from

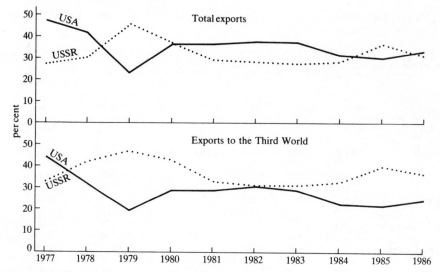

Figure 7.1. The Soviet and US shares of world exports of major weapons: total exports and exports to the Third World, 1977–86

Shares are based on annual values, as expressed in US $m., at constant (1985) prices.

Source: SIPRI data base.

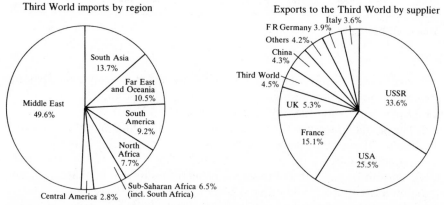

Figure 7.2. Percentage shares of the trade in major weapons with the Third World, 1982–86

Percentages are based on SIPRI trend indicator values, as expressed in US $m., at constant (1985) prices. The values are listed in appendix 7A.

0.2 to 1.6 per cent) and the group of Third World suppliers (from 3.3 to 4.5 per cent).

The statistics on imports of major weapons show that:

1. The Third World share of total imports of major weapons has remained largely constant, at 65–70 per cent, throughout the past 10 years.

2. The volume of Third World arms imports has stagnated—the five-year moving averages even indicate a slight decline from 1982.

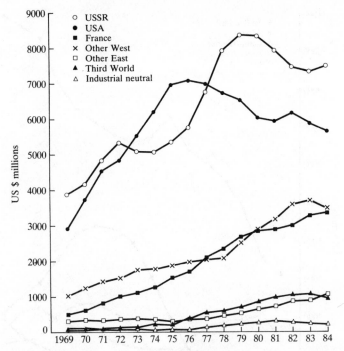

Figure 7.3. Exports of major weapons to Third World regions, by supplier, 1967–86
Based on SIPRI trend indicator values, as expressed in US $m., at constant (1985)
prices, 5-year moving averages.

Other West = Other NATO, Australia and Japan
Other East = Other WTO and China
Industrial neutral = Austria, New Zealand, Sweden, Switzerland and Yugoslavia

Source: Table 7A.2.

3. Regional trends differ. Middle Eastern arms imports have stagnated at the
level of 50 per cent of Third World arms imports. South Asian imports are
rising dramatically, while arms imports to the Far East are largely unchanged.
In other regions of the Third World, the trend is one of decline.[1]

4. The bulk of Third World major-weapon imports is concentrated among a
handful of countries. The five leading importers during 1982–86—Iraq, Egypt,
India, Syria and Saudi Arabia—accounted for 47 per cent of total Third World
arms imports. This degree of concentration is rising: during 1977–81 the share
of the five largest importers was considerably lower, 34 per cent.

5. The level trend in Third World imports of major weapons is in a way
illusory. Were it not for the rise in arms imports by a few major recipients, most
often involved in conflict or arms races for regional hegemony, the trend for the
Third World as a whole would be the same as that for the overwhelming
majority of individual Third World countries—one of decline. For example, if
the five leading Third World importers in 1982–86 are excluded, the combined
arms imports by all other Third World countries have declined by over 25 per
cent between the periods 1977–81 and 1982–86.

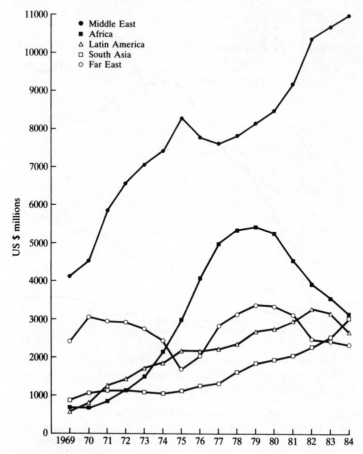

Figure 7.4. Third World imports of major weapons, by region, 1967–86
Based on SIPRI trend indicator values, as expressed in US $m., at constant (1985) prices; 5-year moving averages.

Source: Table 7A.1.

III. The suppliers

The Soviet Union

There are some commonplace statements to be made about Soviet arms production and Soviet arms exports. The USSR has the largest arms industry in the world in terms of output and number of employees; on the average, some 25 per cent of annual output was exported during the early 1980s; arms exports are the main tool for expanding Soviet influence in the Third World; arms exports make up for a considerable part—10–15 per cent—of total Soviet exports.[2] There is less clarity on two important points: Soviet arms export policy and the future of Soviet arms exports.

Soviet arms export policy is difficult to analyse, particularly because internal Soviet discussions on the subject only rarely reach the West. Arms transfer patterns suggest a complex picture: the importance of different determinants seems to vary from time to time depending on the relative power of particular interest groups within the Soviet bureaucracy and on external variables. The following assessment of present Soviet arms export policy is inferred from the arms trade statistics for the past decade.

First, there is the geographical factor. Soviet security needs are traditionally defined in terms of countries' proximity to the Soviet border. Second, high priority is assigned to arms clients that have concluded treaties of friendship and co-operation with the USSR. These two factors interact: close to 25 per cent of total Soviet arms exports were directed to its East European allies; two-thirds of Soviet deliveries to the Third World during 1982–86 were to three neighbouring treaty partners: Syria, India and Iraq (see table 7.2). Third, certain countries—often strong regional powers located far from the USSR—are supplied to create what the USSR sees as an appropriate regional balance. Another Soviet aim with deliveries to such countries is often to acquire access to base facilities for the Soviet Navy. Cuba and Viet Nam are cases in point: force modernization programmes were completed in both countries by the mid-1980s. In the Cuban case, the programme was mainly prompted by East–West tension in Central America. Libya is another example: the US attack on Tripoli in April 1986 resulted in transfers of replacement weapon systems, including transport aircraft and Nanuchka Class missile corvettes. New equipment, such as a Koni Class frigate and SA-5 surface-to-air missiles (SAMs), were also delivered. Fourth, the Soviet Union is supplying weapons to governments it supports and which face internal and/or

Table 7.2. Recipient shares in Soviet exports of major weapons to the Third World, 1977–81 and 1982–86

Percentage shares are based on SIPRI trend indicator values, as expressed in US $m., at constant (1985) prices.

Recipient	1977–81	Recipient	1982–86
Libya	18.7	Syria	24.7
Viet Nam	12.8	India	20.3
Top 2	**31.5**		**45.0**
India	12.3	Iraq	19.3
Iraq	11.3	Libya	8.2
Syria	10.6	Cuba	4.8
Top 5	**65.7**		**77.3**
Algeria	7.9	Angola	4.8
Ethiopia	5.8	North Korea	3.4
Cuba	3.0	Viet Nam	2.6
South Yemen	2.9	Afghanistan	2.6
Peru	2.6	Algeria	2.2
Top 10	**87.9**		**92.9**
Total value	$41 814 m.		$37 166 m.
Total no. of Third World recipients	41		36

Source: SIPRI data base.

external armed opposition, such as Angola, Ethiopia and Nicaragua. Soviet weapon deliveries to these countries were stepped up when the Reagan Administration declared them battlegrounds for challenging Soviet influence in the Third World. For example, among the Soviet deliveries to Nicaragua in 1986 were Mi-24 helicopters. Finally, the Soviet Union has—since the early 1970s—supplied arms as a way of obtaining hard currency to balance its financial and trade deficits with the West. This policy has applied to countries with high oil incomes, such as Algeria, Iraq and Libya, or with financial support from these countries, such as Syria.[3]

Table 7.2 illustrates other significant features of Soviet arms transfers to the Third World. They are declining in volume and numbers of recipients, and the trend towards concentrating on a few key clients continues. The three largest recipients accounted for 60 per cent of total Soviet deliveries to the Third World in 1982; by 1986 this share had risen to 77 per cent. These developments are not necessarily voluntary on the part of the Soviet Union: the explanations are instead largely to be found in the dynamics of the international environment.

The major reason why it can be assumed that Soviet arms transfers to the Third World are facing problems and need high-level policy decisions are to be found in the current structure of and trends in the global arms market. The comparative advantages of buying arms from the USSR—speedy delivery of large quantities of sturdy weapons on favourable credit terms—are diminishing. For countries that lack political choice or economic resources, such arguments are of course still persuasive. Many of these countries, however, can now also opt for affordable low- and middle-level technology weaponry from Third World exporters and from China (see below). This also holds for the more well-endowed Third World countries; the Iraqi 1986 repeat order for Brazilian armoured vehicles is a typical example. Furthermore, these richer countries in the Third World can currently exert considerable leverage on the arms-supplying countries, and this presents the Soviet Union with serious challenges.

First, the aim of earning hard currency from arms transfers has a longer-term backfire effect. The Soviet demand for hard currency forces the arms recipients to sell attractive goods and raw materials to the West, rather than to the Soviet Union. Soviet leverages in the civilian economic field are weakened and the overall dependence of recipients on the Soviet Union decreases. The increasing solitude of arms transfers as a foreign policy tool appears to be self-defeating, particularly at a time when offsets—such as counter-trade and civilian investments in the recipient country—are major bargaining-chips in the competition for arms contracts among the suppliers. Second, customers are looking for more sophisticated weapons than the Soviet Union has traditionally been prepared to offer. Third, the restrictive Soviet policy with respect to transfers of military technology and the supply of support equipment, spares and infrastructure is contrary to market trends.

Pressures are mounting on the Soviet Union to substitute weapons previously exported—on the average 15–20 years old in design and technology—with more state-of-the-art weaponry. Recent examples of Soviet compliance with market pressures include the sale to India of an initial batch of some 48 MiG-29 fighters, possibly including licence-production rights. Syria is also receiving the MiG-29, as well as more modern air-to-air missiles (AAMs) and SAM systems. A $3 billion arms-for-oil deal for more modern fighters, tanks and armoured vehicles was signed with Iraq in early 1986.[4] On a case-by-case basis, the Soviet restrictions are thus being relaxed in order to maintain especially favoured clients.

A second explanation for current Soviet problems *vis-à-vis* much of the Third World can be found in the interplay between US and Soviet Third World policies. When US Third World policy has emphasized the importance of arms transfers as a way of thwarting Soviet advances in the Third World—like today and in the early 1970s—Soviet policy has tended to be less assertive. When US exports have been restrained—for example, during the late 1970s—Soviet arms exports to the Third World have grown significantly. There is thus on the one hand an element of seizing the opportunity when it presents itself and, on the other hand, a reluctance to confront the United States—or US clients and allies—at times when US policy is assertive. In the early 1980s this latter approach was particularly visible in situations and areas of geographical disadvantage to the USSR; the muted support given to Southern Africa's front-line states (except to Angola) and the reluctance to provide the Sandinista Government in Nicaragua with MiG-21 fighters are symptomatic.

A third explanation for current Soviet caution is that the USSR is taking a more pessimistic view of the opportunity to promote socialism in the Third World.[5] Related to this, the Soviet leadership may feel that, under current market rules, arms production for exports diverts resources from domestic economic and technological reconstruction.[6]

In sum, just as in the US case, uncertain political benefits have to be weighed against economic and technological risk-taking at a higher level than before. Domestic military and consumer needs compete with the need to remain influential in the Third World. For the Soviet Union, arms transfers appear to be—by the mid-1980s—an increasingly unreliable, yet indispensible, instrument of foreign policy.

The United States

On 4 November 1986, White House spokesman Larry Speakes said: 'As long as Iran advocates the use of terrorism, the US arms embargo will continue'.[7] This embargo was imposed in 1979; since then over 40 cases of attempts to smuggle arms to Iran have been brought before the US courts (see chapter 8). A few days after the above statement was made, it became known that the United States, with the help of Israel, had supplied large quantities of arms to Iran and that the profits had partially been used to fund armed opposition in Nicaragua.

The number and types of major weapons supplied to Iran were not clarified by early 1987, but they included at least 500–600 TOW anti-tank missiles (ATMs) from Israeli stocks, over 2000 TOWs directly from the USA and about 235 Hawk SAMs (or a similar number of modernization kits for older Iranian missiles).[8] As the circuitous supply routes were becoming unravelled, a complex network emerged, involving companies, private middlemen and government officials in the United States and in other countries. Falsified end-use certificates were frequently used, especially in supplying arms to the contras.[9]

The Reagan Administration lost much credibility and public trust at home as well as among its European allies and in such pro-Western Arab countries as Egypt and Jordan.[10]

As a consequence, pressures to restore congressional powers over arms transfers—lost in 1983 when the US Supreme Court declared the legislative veto procedure to be unconstitutional (the so-called Chadha decision)—will mount. A bill, jointly sponsored by—among others—Senator Biden and Representative Levine, was introduced in September 1986—before the revelations of covert arms sales to Iran. Congress might further strengthen its proposed provisions as a result of the Iran–contras affair.[11]

Such changes in policy and legislation may in the future exacerbate the slightly downward trend in US arms exports to the Third World. On the other hand, in the aftermath of the Iran-contras affair, pressures will mount on the USA from countries such as Egypt, Jordan, Saudi Arabia and the smaller, moderate Gulf states to supply them with sophisticated weaponry. Despite President Reagan's relaxations of President Carter's measures of restraint of 1977,[12] significantly higher arms export levels have so far not been reached. There are three main explanations: first, even if different administrations try to implement their policies through changes in the legislative framework and the departmental processing routines, a combination of congressional action and bureaucratic inertia tends to some extent to level out the often drastic differences emerging from the rhetoric of policy formulations on the executive level. Second, US arms manufacturers are increasingly unwilling to plan arms production on the basis of hopes of selling on a volatile international market, especially since domestic demand is currently high and stable. Third, and most importantly, the USA (and the USSR) are at some disadvantage on the arms market of the 1980s. The changing climate—with decreased overall demand and increasing commercialization—tends in general to benefit suppliers that are less concerned with political factors and fear of unauthorized high-technology transfers than are the superpowers.

The arms trade statistics for 1982–86 show that US arms exports to the Third World are heavily concentrated to the Middle East and the Far East: it is only in these two regions that the USA accounts for a larger share of the region's total arms imports than the Soviet Union (table 7.3). A number of similarities between US and Soviet arms supply patterns to the Third World are visible in table 7.4. The USA tends—as does the USSR—to favour a handful of key allies; and the total value and number of recipients have decreased as compared to the previous five-year period.

Apart from the Iran affair, two other sensitive issues concerning US arms exports were particularly discussed during 1986. One was the perennial balancing act of arms sales to Taiwan and rapprochement with China; the other was the new US arms package to Pakistan and, in particular, the possibility that

Table 7.3. US and Soviet supply of major weapons to Third World regions, 1982–86: share of region's total imports and region's share of supplier's total exports

Percentage shares are based on SIPRI trend indicator values, as expressed in US $m., at constant (1985) prices.

Importing region	Supplier's share of region's total imports		Region's share of supplier's total exports to Third World	
	USA	USSR	USA	USSR
Middle East	32	31	62	46
South Asia	12	56	6	23
Far East	46	21	19	7
South America	12	0	5	0
North Africa	13	46	4	10
Sub-Saharan Africa	10	44	2	8
Central America	17	66	2	6

Source: SIPRI data base.

Table 7.4. Recipient shares in US exports of major weapons to the Third World, 1977–81 and 1982–86

Percentage shares are based on SIPRI trend indicator values, as expressed in US $m., at constant (1985) prices.

Recipient	1977–81	Recipient	1982–86
Iran	19.0	Egypt	25.5
Israel	16.3	Saudi Arabia	17.0
Top 2	**35.3**		**42.5**
Saudi Arabia	13.0	Israel	9.3
South Korea	9.0	Taiwan	7.4
Taiwan	5.5	Pakistan	5.8
Top 5	**62.8**		**65.0**
Jordan	5.2	South Korea	4.6
Egypt	5.1	Jordan	2.7
Morocco	3.4	Thailand	2.1
Thailand	3.1	Kuwait	1.9
Singapore	2.0	Venezuela	1.8
Top 10	**81.6**		**78.1**
Total value	$32 584 m.		$28 157 m.
Total no. of Third World recipients	69		61

Source: SIPRI data base.

the USA may supply airborne early-warning (AEW) capabilities to Pakistan while at the same time seeking military co-operation with India.

China views US arms sales to Taiwan as a symbol of US intentions concerning the future of Taiwan. So far, the United States has not endorsed the reunification concept of 'one country, two systems' as proposed by China. From the Chinese point of view, a more rapid reduction of US arms sales to Taiwan—in accordance with the joint Sino-US communiqué of 1982[13]—would signify a neutral US attitude towards the issue of reunification. China argues that present US policy suggests that the USA would rather like to perpetuate an independent Taiwan as long as possible. This possible intent was underlined in 1986 by the US decision to grant General Dynamics a licence to help design a new Taiwanese fighter aircraft, using a US engine and off-the-shelf US components, including avionics. The United States has refused Taiwanese requests for F-16 and F-20 fighters. The 1982 communiqué does not explicitly mention technology transfers; however, the Chinese view is that technology transfers and direct transfers of weapon systems are the same thing. Chinese protests have nevertheless been mild, presumably because China is unwilling to risk the benefits it is deriving from US technology transfers in connection with its economic-industrial modernization programme (see also below).[14]

US arms sales to Pakistan should primarily be interpreted in the context of overall US strategy in the region, rather than as a response to specific threats to Pakistani military security. Pakistan plays a critical role in US security planning in the region. Given the historical opposition of pro-Western Arab countries to US military bases on their soil, Pakistan has a key role to play in helping to establish regional military co-ordination—especially in connection with the regional air defence system now being established among the members of the Gulf Cooperation Council (GCC). Pakistan is a major exporter of military manpower; it has some 40 000–50 000 military personnel stationed in 22 countries in the Middle East and Africa.[15] However, whether the United States will risk its recently improved military relations with India by supplying Pakistan with sophisticated airborne surveillance capabilities remains to be seen (see also section IV).

Other Western industrialized suppliers

The Third World share in the combined sales of major weapons by other Western industrialized countries grew from 73 to 78 per cent between the five-year periods 1977–81 and 1982–86. For some of the major suppliers this share has increased substantially: from 71 to 86 per cent for France and from 42 to 63 per cent for FR Germany. Italy and Spain have in both these periods relied almost exclusively on Third World arms sales (see table 7.5). In France and Italy, where the share of exports in conventional arms production is substantial,[16] the dependence on arms sales to the Third World is thus significant.

For the United Kingdom the trend is reversed: the Third World share has declined from 85 to 67 per cent from the first period to the second. This is, however, not because their sales to the Third World have declined, but rather because of a rapid rise in arms sales to industrialized countries.

The stagnation during the early 1980s in the Third World arms market—from the previous long-term growth—has resulted in fierce competition among suppliers. Sales techniques include government and company representation in customer countries, co-operation in arms production and offers to transfer advanced military technology. In 1986 the Defence Export Services Organization (formerly called DSO) of the British Ministry of Defence opened an office in Malaysia; it is the fourth of its kind, the other three being located in India,

Table 7.5. Patterns of major-weapon exports of five West European arms suppliers, 1977–81 and 1982–86

Percentage shares are based on SIPRI trend indicator values, as expressed in US $m., at constant (1985) prices.

Supplier	Share in total arms exports to Third World		Third World share in supplier's arms exports		Top 5 Third World recipients, 1982–86	Combined share[a]
	1982–86	1977–81	1982–86	1977–81		
France	15.1	12.4	86	71	Iraq, Saudi Arabia, India, Argentina, Egypt	55
UK	5.3	5.1	67	85	India, Chile, Oman, Nigeria, Egypt	58
FR Germany	3.9	1.7	63	42	Argentina, Colombia, Malaysia, Bahrain, Kuwait	81
Italy	3.6	3.3	98	94	Libya, Venezuela, Ecuador, Peru, Malaysia	70
Spain	1.6	0.2	100	100	Egypt, Mexico, Morocco, Argentina, Iraq	84

[a] Share in supplier's total exports to the Third World.

Source: SIPRI data base.

Saudi Arabia and the USA. Two Italian arms producers, Agusta and OTO-Melara, were negotiating coproduction of military equipment with Singapore. In a policy reversal, the French aircraft company Dassault-Breguet offered Indonesia extensive co-operation in design and production of a new indigenous fighter aircraft, the philosophy being that it is 'better to co-operate with Indonesia and win over 30 per cent of the work load than [to] lose everything in the area [South East Asia]'.[17] While France already has arms production co-operation agreements with Egypt and India,[18] the offer to Indonesia represents a departure from previous policy in that design and engineering support was also offered, and in that the technology offered was the most advanced: on the level of the Rafale fighter, which has not yet entered service even in France itself. The West European suppliers have recently shown an increased interest in pushing arms sales to other industrialized countries, realizing that the growth potential in Third World demand for major weapons is limited.

British major weapons have for a long time had problems in competing on the Third World arms market. One major explanation is the relative sophistication and therefore high price of British weapons. In the campaign to promote arms exports, which started shortly after the Conservative Government took office in 1979, one of the ingredients has therefore been to encourage the development of weapons that are more tailored to Third World requirements.[19] Other measures include increased government support for arms exports: in channelling requests, in advertising and with financial arrangements. While the impact of this policy is not borne out in delivery rates of British major weapons (as measured by SIPRI), it can be seen in the national statistics for exports of all types of military equipment.[20] It is also evident from the pattern of newly received orders that British arms sales to the Third World are going to rise: with the exception of West German orders for Lynx helicopters and Sea Skua missiles, all confirmed orders in 1986 came from Third World countries. From the list of customers in appendices 7B and 7C (including Chile, India, Indonesia, Iran, Jordan, Oman, Pakistan, and Saudi Arabia), it can also be inferred that British arms export policy is highly permissive. One example is the approval of an export licence for the sale of a sophisticated air defence radar system to Iran. However, although a British embargo on arms sales to Iran and Iraq has been in force since 1979, it bans only the sale of 'lethal equipment' which could 'prolong or exacerbate the war'.

Although *French* deliveries of major weapons have continued to rise steadily, a temporary peak has been reached: arms export orders have decreased since 1984. In 1984 the order value for all types of military equipment was FRF 62 billion. declining to FRF 45 billion in 1985. Furthermore, in both 1984 and 1985 the total order value overstates the general competitiveness of the French arms industry, since in each of these years one single deal accounted for over half of this value.[21] No order of that magnitude was won in 1986, so it can be expected that the order value will be considerably lower than in 1985.

The stagnation in French arms exports is not due to a policy change: it rather reflects French dependence on the Third World market, in combination with increased supplier competition. The highly export-dependent aerospace sector is feeling this competition; expected orders for Mirage-2000 fighters from Morocco, Jordan and Indonesia were not concluded in 1986. The export sales of ground forces equipment have declined, a trend further aggravated in 1986 when GIAT, one of three major French producers of armoured vehicles, lost a sizeable Indian order for artillery to Sweden. GIAT has not received a major foreign contract since 1982, and is now pushing sales of its AMX-40 main battle tank in Saudi Arabia, and of the AMX-10RC reconnaissance vehicle in Qatar and the United Arab Emirates.

Although there has been some relaxation in recent years, the arms export policy of *FR Germany* is restrictive. Arms export policy is a hotly debated issue: economic and political pressures for liberalization clash with political pressures—mainly from the opposition—for tighter rules. In 1986 several cases of violation of West German arms export policy were under investigation. In a 1986 court case, top executives of an arms production company were sentenced for complicity in the illegal re-export of military equipment to Argentina, Saudi Arabia and South Africa.[22] In another court case—not completed during the year—the legality was examined of transfers to Libya—by West German companies without government approval—of missile and electronic parts and engineering support for the construction of rockets.[23] It was also revealed that the state-owned shipyard HDW and the engineering bureau IKL had delivered blueprints for the construction of submarines to South Africa[24]—in direct violation of West German adherence to the United Nations arms embargo on South Africa.[25] A parliamentary commission was formed to investigate the circumstances of this deal, including allegations that the Chancellor had been aware of, and even consented to, the sale.[26]

Two other examples demonstrate the boundaries of current arms export rules. Both concern sales to Iran, to which arms exports are banned in FR Germany. One is the delivery of floating bridges to Iran. This transfer did not require an export permit, since the bridges are not classified as military equipment, but Iran is reportedly using them for troop movements.[27] The other example is the export licence sought—after 18 months of negotiations—for 12 C-160 Transall transport aircraft to Iran. This request was rejected.

There has been a dramatic decline in *Italian* arms exports during the period 1982–86, and only a few minor orders have been reported for 1986. The surge in Italian arms exports during the late 1970s and early 1980s was mainly due to large naval orders from countries in South America, Africa and the Middle East. Apart from 10 frigates and corvettes awaiting delivery to Iraq, by late 1986 Italian shipyards had no major foreign military orders. While the reduction in ship exports may reflect a temporary saturation of the market, Italy's middle-level technology exports of other categories of weapons have suffered from their squeezed position on the world arms market: between competition from new suppliers producing unsophisticated and cheap weapons, and, on the other hand, efforts by established high-technology producers to scale down their weapons to meet Third World demands.

Italy is attempting to remedy this situation in several ways: through joint ventures with Third World arms producers; by raising the technological level of arms production through, for example, participation in co-production projects with major Western arms producers; and through restructuring of the Italian arms industry.[28]

Despite Italy's permissive attitude with respect to arms exports, reports in 1986 that an Italian port had been used for US shipments of arms to Iran—possibly from US bases in Italy—evoked a strong Italian reaction. An inquiry into the matter was immediately ordered, and arms exports were temporarily frozen to all areas of tension.[29] Italy was also one of the countries to join the USA in January 1986 in implementing an arms embargo on Libya.[30]

In a first break with its traditional policy of banning military exports in general, the *Japanese* Government in 1986 authorized two military technology export deals. These were for a shipbuilding technique and for a seeker technology for a shoulder-fired surface-to-air missile, both to the USA. The decision was an expected consequence of a 1983 decision to exempt the transfer of military technology to the USA from Japanese restrictions on military exports. The ban on export of finished military products remains, however. Arms production accounts for a small share of total industrial output in Japan: less than 1 per cent. For the leading arms producer, Mitsubishi Heavy Industries, accounting for about one-fifth of total Japanese defence contracts, the share of military sales in total revenues is significant, having increased to about 17 per cent.[31]

Spain has rapidly increased its exports of major weapons to the Third World. Low costs and lack of restrictions are the main reasons. Among exporters of major weapons to the Third World, Spain has moved to 8th place in the 1982–86 period, from 18th position in the previous five-year period. Most sales are to countries in Latin America and the Middle East. Exports of major weapons to industrialized countries are virtually non-existent. However, the

Spanish company Defex, S. A., responsible for the marketing of Spanish military equipment, has permanent representation in the USA.

Swedish arms exports were boosted in early 1986 when Sweden won an order from India for direct delivery and licensed production of field howitzers and associated services. The order, valued at more than US $1 billion, exceeded by a factor of four the annual average for total Swedish arms exports during the 1981–85 period.

Arms exports were intensively discussed in Sweden in 1986. Two types of deal were criticized. The first were deals in which arms manufacturers—without the prior knowledge or consent of the government—may have violated the Swedish guidelines for arms exports. By late 1986 the investigations of police and customs officials into the alleged smuggling of weapons and explosives to Middle Eastern countries by the private Swedish arms manufacturer Bofors were nearing completion. Second, there was discussion of sales approved by the government—with reference to the eligibility of the recipient countries, according to the arms export guidelines. Examples of such sales include howitzers to India, naval guns to Indonesia and RBS-70 SAMs to Pakistan.[32]

China

Chinese arms export policy—which during the 1960s and early 1970s centred on supporting friendly nations in East and South Asia, and revolutionary movements in the Third World free of charge—has in recent years become increasingly steered by commercial motives and the search for hard currency. The Chinese arms industry was reorganized along Western lines in the early 1980s,[33] and marketing campaigns were carried out through advertising and participation in international military exhibitions. The structural changes in the military–industrial sector and changes in arms export policy are part of the general reorientation of industrial policy towards commercialization of production units, modernization and a general opening towards the West.

The reliability of reports on Chinese arms exports is often low, as is the validity of numbers of weapons delivered in some cases. Keeping this need for caution in mind, the People's Republic of China ranked—according to SIPRI statistics for 1982–86—as the fifth largest exporter of major weapons to Third World countries, approximately on a par with FR Germany, Italy and the UK.

On a selective basis, Western military technology is being acquired with two interlinked aims in mind. One is to enhance the attraction of Chinese weapons on the world market. Arms exports will help generate the foreign currency needed to fulfil the other aim—the upgrading of China's obsolete military technologies. China is trying to substitute quality for quantity in its armed forces—a consequence of cutbacks in military spending and an announced demobilization of one million soldiers. If completed, this will cut by 25 per cent the total manpower of the Chinese armed forces.

In support of this modernization process, in 1986 China hosted two international arms shows in Peking: the International Defence Industries Expo in January and the Asian Defence Technologies Expo (ASIANDEX) in

November (see table 7.9). At the latter show, about 150 foreign arms manufacturers displayed their products in search of sales to the untapped Chinese market, while the six Chinese arms trade companies (listed in note 33) exhibited a wide range of new equipment—aimed mainly at Third World markets.[34]

Many of these weapons incorporate Western technology. The Chinese F-7 (MiG-21) fighter, for example, incorporates British GEC avionics, and during 1986 Aeritalia agreed to supply avionics for the A-5 (Mig-19) ground attack fighter. Both these aircraft are being supplied to Pakistan. In October, just before the ASIANDEX show, it was announced that the USA will supply 55 avionics kits for China's newest fighter, the F-8II, under a $550 million contract (this initial order is intended for the Chinese Air Force only). Similar developments are taking place in the production of equipment for ground forces. Tanks, APCs and artillery are being designed and produced with foreign assistance, and they incorporate foreign subsystems, for example from Austria, FR Germany, Israel, the UK and the USA. On the world market, these weapon systems will be comparatively cheap owing to the low Chinese labour costs.[35]

China is thus becoming increasingly competitive in what was previously largely a Soviet niche: the capability to quickly supply simple, yet functional weapon systems at low prices. Furthermore, the Chinese policy with respect to after-sales support, spare parts and so on is reportedly more forthcoming than that of the USSR.[36] Chinese arms supply patterns indicate that demand factors, rather than foreign policy priorities, guide sales decisions. Like other new, low-cost suppliers, China exports most of its weapons to crisis areas where foreign currency can be obtained, such as Iraq and Iran.[37] Egypt and Pakistan are two other large importers of Chinese weapons. China's arms export policy has come a long way since the 1960s. Little is known about possible internal debate or criticism about the predominance of pragmatic, commercial incentives over political considerations.

Third World suppliers

A few suppliers dominate in Third World exports of major weapons: 10 countries account for 96 per cent of total Third World arms exports in the period 1982–86; the top 5 countries account for three-quarters of the total (table 7.6). Third World arms suppliers mainly export to other countries in the Third World: 95 per cent of their exports in 1982–86. The Third World has slowly increased its share in total exports of major weapons to the Third World from 3.3 per cent in 1977–81 to 4.5 per cent in 1982–86. Recipients are to a large extent countries to which many industrialized countries are hesitant to sell arms, such as Taiwan, Iraq and Iran. Since 1983, however, the volume of Third World sales of major weapons has, on provisional figures, declined somewhat. In spite of the few restrictions these countries place on arms exports and their marketing of weapons well adapted for Third World conditions, they now seem to find it difficult to continue to expand their market share. The most likely reason, given the current structure of the market, is the difficulty of competing

Table 7.6. The top 10 Third World suppliers of major weapons, 1982–86

Percentage shares are based on SIPRI trend indicator values, as expressed in US $m., at constant (1985) prices.

Supplier	Share in total TW exports of major weapons 1982–86	Production of major weapons 1980–84 Share in total TW	Rank	Number of recipients TW	IC	Major recipient Region	Share	Country	Share
Israel	23.9	24.4	1	15	2	F. East	38.8	Taiwan	38.0
Brazil	23.3	10.3	3	24	4	M. East	48.3	Iraq	36.7
Egypt	14.1	2.9	9	9	0	M. East	89.2	Iraq	89.2
Jordan	7.3	0	–	2	1	M. East	91.4	Iraq	88.0
Libya	7.3	0	–	8	0	M. East	80.8	Syria	47.4
S. Korea	7.2	6.3	7	6	0	F. East	43.4	Malaysia	31.6
N. Korea	5.5	4.8	8	5	0	M. East	95.8	Iran	95.8
Syria	3.3	0	–	2	1	M. East	98.9	Iran	88.5
Singapore	2.1	1.0	10	6	0	F. East	50.9	Taiwan	40.7
Indonesia	1.6	0.5	12	3	0	M. East	64.3	Saudi Arabia	64.3
Others	4.4	49.8							

TW = Third World; IC = industrialized countries; F. East = Far East; M. East = Middle East.

Sources: SIPRI data base. For production estimates, see Brzoska, M. and Ohlson, T. (eds), *Arms Production in the Third World* (Taylor & Francis: London, 1986), appendix 1.

with the sales terms (credits and offsets) offered by richer countries. An associated reason is that, with few exceptions, they can seldom compete technologically, especially not in the crucial field of electronics. The types of weapon they can best produce—unsophisticated items such as small arms and ammunition—represent a small market compared to the market for more advanced major weapon systems. The competition at this lower end of the market has become more intense. The dilemma, then, is that what can be efficiently produced is in low demand, while products in high demand cannot be produced.

Brazil and Israel are the leading arms exporters in the Third World, accounting for almost half of Third World exports of major weapons. They are also among the top six Third World arms producers.[38] If re-exports[39] are excluded from the Third World arms export total, the dominance of Brazil and Israel is further accentuated: they account for approximately 80 per cent of Third World exports of domestically produced major weapons. None of the other four major arms producers in the Third World—India, Taiwan, Argentina and South Africa—were among the top 10 Third World arms exporters in the past five-year period.

Although the *Israeli* arms industry was built up in order to supply the Israeli armed forces, the economy has for many years been dependent on arms exports for both employment and foreign exchange earnings. In addition to selling major weapons, Israel is also a major supplier of small arms, ammunition and modernization and upgrading services. In recent years, export pressures have increased. Substantial reductions in the defence budget have since 1983 caused deep cuts in domestic arms sales,[40] although this effect was alleviated by the large US military and economic aid programme.

Until recently, 700–800 Israeli firms and individuals (mostly former military officers) were accredited as legitimate *carte blanche* arms dealers. In response to both international and domestic criticism, restrictions were introduced in late 1986.[41] The immediate cause was the major operation by the US Customs Service, in which four Israelis and 13 other international arms dealers were arrested in 1986. They were charged with conspiracy to smuggle military equipment to Iran, worth the astonishing sum of US $2 billion.[42] Possible links between this would-be deal and later revelations of the Israeli role as intermediary in covert US arms supplies to Iran during 1985–86 were not clear by early 1987. The major argument of the defendants has been that they believed that the deal would eventually be authorized by the US Government.[43] Other complications include Israeli arms sales to South Africa, estimated in a United Nations report[44] at about US $300 million a year, and recent reports of supplies to the South African-supported UNITA movement in Angola.[45]

In *Brazil*, as in Israel, reliable arms export data are hard to come by. However, while arms sales are played down in Israel, Brazilian arms exports are often exaggerated for the purpose of promoting sales, since the arms industry has from the outset been geared towards exports. In 1986 Argentina and Peru ordered Tucano fighter aircraft, and Brazil's major customer, Iraq, ordered Cascavel armoured cars. Throughout the year there were persistent reports, especially in the Brazilian press, of large arms deals with Saudi Arabia and Libya.[46]

In contrast to Israel, Brazil has tried to avoid US leverage over its arms exports. Brazil considers its non-restrictive arms export policy to be essential for its arms industry, and even uses it as a sales argument.[47] However, the argument is also put forward, not least by the Brazilian armed forces, that both the quality of Brazilian arsenals and Brazil's future competitiveness on the world market are dependent on access to US high technology. To achieve this, national control of the arms industry and exports would have to be sacrificed. Several of the major US defence contractors are interested in joint arms production ventures with Brazil, but only under the condition that Brazil signs an agreement which would prevent Brazil from transferring sensitive technology to countries hostile to the United States. It has, however, not been possible to reach any agreement on this issue.

The *South African* arms export drive in the early 1980s has not resulted in any significant major-weapon transfers.[48] Exports are mostly in the field of infantry weapons, often for South African-supported insurgent movements in neighbouring countries. During 1986 there were also reports about substantial munitions shipments to Iran. They claim that over the past three years South Africa has sold 300 000–400 000 155-mm artillery shells to Iran, probably in exchange for oil. According to unconfirmed sources, South Africa also manufactures spare parts for Iranian F-4 Phantom fighter aircraft.[49]

The main Third World re-exporters are *Egypt, Jordan, Libya, North Korea* and *Syria*. Re-export patterns differ markedly from the export pattern of the original supplier. Syria, Libya and North Korea ranked first, fourth and seventh, respectively, among Third World buyers of Soviet weapons in the period 1982–86. While all three countries delivered ex-Soviet weapons to Iran, the USSR is the main supplier of arms to Iraq. The increasing level of re-exports raises a number of important issues, especially with respect to the resupplier's relationship with the original producer. Re-exports may be the result of instructions or tacit approval from the original supplier, where the re-exporter functions as a proxy. They may also be an expression of a more independent foreign and economic policy, even in the absence of a domestic arms industry.

IV. The recipients

Latin America

There is a downward trend in the flow of major weapons to Latin America. While in South America this reflects a degree of declining militarization, in Central America it does not. The fall in the overall arms import trend for Central America is mainly due to declining arms imports in Cuba and Mexico. Especially Cuba received large amounts of major weapons from the Soviet Union in the early 1980s. Since then, arms imports of both countries have been increasingly constrained by sharply reduced export earnings (for sugar and oil).

Major weapon imports to the Central American isthmus countries—Costa Rica, El Salvador, Guatemala, Honduras and Nicaragua—are, however, increasing. Small arms and ammunition (not covered in the SIPRI statistics) have also been pouring in at high rates to both sides in the Nicaraguan conflict. Nicaragua's main supplier of weapons is the Soviet Union. According to the US Department of Defense, the USSR provided 43 ship-loads—or 18 000 metric tons—of 'military and military-associated' equipment during the first 10 months of 1986.[50] The content of these deliveries has not been revealed, apart from six Mi-24 Hind attack helicopters supplied in October. The Nicaraguan counter-revolutionary forces, the contras, have also received large supplies of military equipment,[51] mainly through private organizations operating from the United States.

During 1986 US policy towards the Nicaraguan conflict underwent two major changes. The first was the policy reversal of the US Congress with the approval in mid-1986 of US $100 million worth of military and humanitarian aid to the contras,[52] and the simultaneous permission to let the CIA be responsible for the transfer of part of the military aid. Since 1984 Congress had denied similar requests from the Reagan Administration.[53] In October, immediately upon presidential authorization, the first shipments started.[54] Military training of contra soldiers was also begun in the USA—after Costa Rica, El Salvador and Honduras had declared their opposition to training on their territories. Second, the Reagan Administration agreed in October to offer Honduras F-5E/F fighter aircraft, subject to congressional approval. If filled, this offer would represent a break with previous US policy of not being the first to supply advanced fighter aircraft to the isthmus area.[55] Subsequent developments during the year may, however, alter this picture. First, in US investigations late in the year of US arms sales to Iran, it was revealed that 'profits' from these sales had been diverted to the contras—during the period when US military support to the contras was forbidden.[56] Immediately upon this revelation a panel was appointed by President Reagan to conduct a review of the operations of the US National Security Council, and the US Justice Department began a criminal inquiry into the transfer of funds to the contras.[57] Second, a vote in the United Nations General Assembly showed that US NATO allies were critical of resumed US assistance to the contras. In reaction to 'the continued financing by the United States of America of military and other activities in and against Nicaragua', a resolution was approved which called for 'full and immediate compliance with the judgement of the International Court of Justice of 27 June 1986'.[58] Third, there was the reported accusation of the former US ambassador to Honduras (dismissed in June 1986) that US officials had put pressure on Honduras to request emergency military aid from the USA, upon Nicaraguan violation in March 1986 of Honduran borders, with the purpose to 'bolster the appearance of a threat from Nicaragua'.[59]

Major-weapon deliveries to South America have fallen substantially in 1985—and again in 1986, based on provisional figures. More importantly, few new orders have been made in recent years. Since 1984, arms imports by all but one of the region's six major arms importers—Peru—show a reduction: Argentina, Venezuela, Chile, Colombia and Ecuador.[60] One explanation for the decline is the economic situation prevailing in the region. With 35 per cent of Latin American export earnings required for interest payment on the foreign

Table 7.7. Rank order of the 20 largest Third World major-weapon importing countries, 1982–86

Percentage shares are based on SIPRI trend indicator values, as expressed in US $m., at constant (1985) prices. Rank order for the period 1981–85 is given in brackets.

Importing country	Percentage of total Third World imports	Importing country	Percentage of total Third World imports
1. Iraq (1)	12.1	11. Jordan (9)	2.0
2. Egypt (2)	9.8	12. Iran (20)	2.0
3. India (4)	9.5	13. Algeria (14)	1.8
4. Syria (3)	8.5	14. Angola (17)	1.7
5. Saudi Arabia (6)	7.2	15. Cuba (12)	1.6
6. Libya (5)	4.5	16. Nigeria (13)	1.5
7. Argentina (8)	3.3	17. Kuwait (19)	1.5
8. Pakistan (11)	2.9	18. Venezuela (15)	1.3
9. Israel (7)	2.4	19. North Korea (−)	1.3
10. Taiwan (10)	2.4	20. Thailand (−)	1.2
		Others	21.5
		Total	100.0
		Total value	**$110 571m.**

Source: SIPRI data base.

debt of US $382 billion, and with only a small amount of new loans received since 1983, the availability of foreign currency for arms imports is of course scarce. The attention given by the International Monetary Fund in 1983 to Peru's high defence burden may also be viewed as a precedent, warranting restraint.[61] Another factor is the change to civilian governments in many South American countries during the past five years. Attempts have been made by, for example, the Argentinian, Brazilian and Peruvian governments to substantially reduce military spending—in particular with respect to arms procurement from abroad. This is a difficult policy: the governments need to strike a balance with the interests of the military, which remain powerful actors. Reduced arms imports may, however, contribute to regional stabilization: directly by reducing the risk of armed conflict, and indirectly through the potentially benefical economic impact.

Africa

Two factors are currently shaping the flow of arms to Africa: the scarcity of economic resources, and the number and intensity of conflicts. The lack of funds exerts a downward pressure on military budgets. The acquisition by African countries of expensive prestige weapons, such as supersonic fighters, has—with few exceptions—ceased. On the other hand, social and economic problems and the weakness of civilian institutions fuel militarization processes. The inability of many African governments to fulfil the needs of the people increasingly translates into domestic or inter-state conflicts. The end-result of these contradicting pressures is a slow overall decrease in African arms imports, but with high levels and upward trends in some countries involved in conflict.

The Soviet Union is the main supplier of arms to Africa. During 1982–86 the USSR exported to the continent a volume of major weapons four times as great as that from the USA (excluding Egypt, which in the SIPRI statistics is included in the Middle East). The United States promotes its interests in Africa, as in South America, via economic rather than military means. France, the UK, FR Germany and Italy are also major suppliers to Africa—France has the largest share.[62]

In North Africa, Libyan arms purchases decreased during 1983–85 as a result of saturation effects, hard currency problems and political disagreements with the USSR.[63] However, Libyan arms imports from the USSR were boosted after the 1986 US bombing attack on Tripoli. Another major Soviet client, Algeria, is diversifying its sources of supply: the USA has recently delivered Hercules transport aircraft; patrol craft of British design are being assembled under licence; and French armoured vehicles were delivered during 1986.

In Sub-Saharan Africa the impact of the conflict determinant is clearly visible. The major recipients are Angola, Ethiopia, Somalia and Sudan. In Southern Africa, the struggle between South Africa and the front-line states is becoming increasingly militarized. Despite South Africa's use of military destabilization tactics against Mozambique, Soviet military support to the Frelimo Government remains limited and Mozambique is trying to diversify its sources of military support.[64] South Africa, subjected to a mandatory UN arms embargo since 1977, continues its 'sanctions-busting' efforts in both the military and civilian fields.[65] The embargo is circumvented in several ways. One is the purchase of equipment for South African police forces and for the defence forces of the homelands of Bophuthatswana, Ciskei, Transkei and Venda, which is not prohibited by the embargo.[66] Another is the import of dual-use high-technology equipment or components, mainly from the UK, the USA, Israel and Taiwan. These latter deliveries are vital since the arms embargo is most efficiently upheld in the field of major weapons. Components incorporating modern technology can then be used to upgrade South Africa's existing weapon inventories: the most recent example of such upgrading is the Cheetah (a modernized version of the Mirage-3 fighters acquired from France in the 1960s).[67]

In addition, there are also violations of the embargo. During 1986 it was revealed that two West German companies had illegally sold submarine blueprints to South Africa (see section II). Second, circuitous deliveries of machine-guns and rocket-launch equipment from unspecified sources, possibly intended for South African proxy forces in the neighbouring front-line states, reportedly took place.[68] Third, the operational radius of South Africa's Mirage F-1 and Buccaneer fighters was greatly enhanced by the delivery from Israel of two B-707 tanker aircraft.[69]

The Middle East

The Middle East remained by far the largest arms-importing region in the Third World during 1982–86. However, the region is also experiencing a severe economic recession, caused by the drastic decline in oil prices,[70] rising foreign debts and the oil-saving measures taken by consumer countries.

The drop in oil prices is the most important factor: a $10 drop in the per barrel price of oil implies a decrease of over $90 billion in the combined annual export income of Third World oil-exporting countries.[71] The total regional debt by late 1986 was estimated at approximately $225 billion: the most heavily indebted countries are Iraq, Israel and Egypt.[72]

The oil glut had an impact on some arms acquisitions during 1986. Saudi Arabia renegotiated the terms of its huge Tornado/Hawk/PC-9 aircraft package from the UK.[73] Saudi Arabia and some other members of the Gulf Cooperation Council have also, wholly or partly, for many years been financing arms imports by other countries in the region. That such philanthropy is becoming less common is illustrated by Oman's decision to postpone for financial reasons the receipt of the eight Tornado fighters ordered in 1985.

However, the recession coincides with the incurring of higher military costs in many countries. The Iraq-Iran War is enormously costly to the belligerents—the annual war cost for each of the two countries was, by 1986, roughly equal to the annual income from oil exports. Neighbouring countries—fearing that the war might spread throughout the region—are also strengthening their military capabilities. Syria is involved in a major arms buildup against Israel; it also has a costly military presence in Lebanon, and it supplies Iran in the war with Iraq. Egypt and Saudi Arabia are involved in major military modernization programmes. In 1986 Egypt took delivery of Mirage-2000 and F-16 fighters, E-2C Hawkeye AEW aircraft, M-60 tanks and various air defence systems. Saudi Arabia received its first AWACS aircraft, ordered in 1981, and the first of 72 Tornado fighters; it also received equipment and weapons related to its two major air defence programmes, the French *Al-Thakeb* contract and the US *Peace Shield* programme.

The Iraq–Iran War (more extensively treated in chapter 8) intensified during 1986. Three years ago, SIPRI conducted a study of the arms flows to Iraq and Iran.[74] Table 7.8 presents an update on these arms flows as of late 1986. A comparison with the 1984 data shows the following results. First, the 1984 table identified a total of 40 suppliers; by 1986 this number had risen to 53. Second, the number of countries supporting both parties has almost tripled (from 10 to 28). Third, the number of countries supporting only Iraq has declined (from 19 to 9), while the corresponding figure for Iran has risen (from 11 to 16). There are various explanations for these changes.

First, there has been a real increase in the number of suppliers. The huge profits to be made have particularly attracted private and semi-illegal brokers, middlemen and entrepreneurs in the sphere of export-import trading, shipping and so on. Second, there is a gradual relaxation of embargo policies in many supplying countries—a tendency given further impetus by the revelations of covert US Government support for Iran. Third, since the Iranian arms imports are more shrouded in secrecy than those of Iraq, more Iranian supply routes are identified as the war drags on. Another possible explanation is that, since Iran now appears to be the country most likely not to lose the war, suppliers are increasing their deliveries to Iran with a view to enhancing their future relations with Iran. In sum, the two main conclusions on the arms trade in the Iraq–Iran War made in the *SIPRI Yearbook 1984* are still valid:[75]

1. The weapon flows are in many ways different from those before the war. There is a dramatic increase in the number of suppliers, the patterns of supply are different from those before the war, and there are supplier groupings and interests which are not easily explained along standard political lines.
2. The procurement methods of wartime supply are different. Secret trade routes and arms merchants play a more significant role than in peace-time. The private, international arms market is booming. Many governments also profit markedly from the war.

Table 7.8. Arms supply and other support to Iran and Iraq, 1980–86

	Iran		Iraq	
Country[a]	Weapons[b]	Other support[c]	Weapons[b]	Other support[c]
Supporting both parties				
Austria	x		x	
Belgium	x		x	
Brazil	x	x	x	x
Bulgaria	x	x	x	x
Chile	x		x	
China	x	x	x	x
Czechoslovakia	x	x	x	x

Table 7.8 *cont*

Country[a]	Iran Weapons[b]	Iran Other support[c]	Iraq Weapons[b]	Iraq Other support[c]
Ethiopia		x	x	
FR Germany	x	x	x	x
France	x		x	x
German DR	x	x	x	x
Greece	x	x	x	x
Hungary	x	x	x	x
Italy	x	x	x	x
Korea, North	x		x	
Netherlands	x		x	
Pakistan	x	x	x	x
Poland	x	x	x	x
Portugal	x		x	
Saudi Arabia		x		x
South Africa	x		x	
Spain	x		x	x
Sweden	x	x	x	
Switzerland	x		x	
UK	x	x	x	x
USA	x	x	x	x
USSR	x	x	x	x
Yugoslavia	x	x	x	x
Supporting Iran only				
Algeria	x	x		
Argentina	x	x	(x)	
Canada	x	x		
Denmark		x		
Finland	x	x		
Israel	x	x	(x)	
Kenya		x		
Korea, South	x	x		
Libya	x	x		
Mexico	x	x		
Singapore		x		
Syria	x	x		
Taiwan	x	x		
Turkey	x	x		
Viet Nam	x			
Yemen, South		x		
Supporting Iraq only				
Egypt			x	x
Jordan			x	x
Kuwait				x
Morocco				x
Philippines			x	x
Sudan				x
Tunisia				x
United Arab Emirates				x
Yemen, North				x

[a] The purpose of this table is to identify the countries in order to underline the need for political control; it is not to identify governments that have acted in breach of, for example, an embargo. Many of these transactions take place without the knowledge and support of governments.

[b] The term 'weapons' includes major weapons, small arms, ammunition or explosives.

[c] 'Other support' includes military transport vehicles (jeeps, trucks, lorries), spare parts, training, military advisers, logistic support or financial support.

Source: SIPRI data base.

South Asia

South Asia shows a rising trend in the imports of major weapons: deliveries nearly doubled in 1985–86, and in 1986 accounted for over 20 per cent of Third World arms imports. India and Pakistan dominate the total: 70 and 21 per cent respectively in the period 1982–86. The conflicts of the region are many. In addition to internal conflicts between different ethnic groups in India, Pakistan and Sri Lanka, and the perennial conflict between India and Pakistan, external involvement has further fuelled the regional arms race: the Soviet invasion of Afghanistan in 1979, and the US response in terms of a large military aid programme to Pakistan. The importance attached to the region by both the United States and the Soviet Union appears to be increasing rather than diminishing (see also section III).[76] This was highlighted by the high-level delegations which visited South Asia in 1986: US Defense Secretary Caspar Weinberger visited India and Pakistan in October; and Soviet General Secretary Mikhail Gorbachev and the Soviet armed forces Chief of Staff Marshal Sergei Akhromeyev visited India in December.

Both India and Pakistan are moving ahead with major arms procurement and import plans. Although belonging to the world's poorest countries, both also can afford further arms purchases, owing to their financial arrangements with the USSR and the USA, respectively.[77] While the USSR is the major arms supplier to India, the USA has overtaken this role from China for Pakistan, starting with the US 1982–87 military aid programme. Several Western arms suppliers, including Sweden and the United Kingdom, continue to deliver arms to both countries.

As a result of India's high-technology ambitions and US interest in lessening India's reliance on the USSR for arms supplies, in late 1986 India ordered 11 US F-404 engines,[78] the engine used in such modern fighter aircraft as the US F/A-18 Hornet. The failure to agree on technology safeguards was the major obstacle to earlier attempts at US-Indian co-operation. India is also objecting to the US policy of reserving the right to unconditionally and at any time revoke an approved arms agreement. More substantive US-Indian co-operation in the field of military technology could, however, hardly be envisioned in the near future in view of the US position on technology transfer. Apart from strong economic ties between India and the Soviet Union, the Indian armed forces are also adjusted to Soviet weaponry, and there is close Soviet-Indian co-operation in the sphere of arms production.

Apart from the sale of MiG-29 fighters, the USSR also initiated deliveries of a number of new warships and about 10 Mi-26 Halo helicopters in 1986. Contracts with Western suppliers in 1986 include those for Swedish 155-mm howitzers, the British aircraft-carrier *Hermes*, British fighters and helicopters, and Dutch Flycatcher radar systems. Pakistan received 60 F-7 fighter aircraft (the Chinese version of the MiG-21) in 1986. There are also plans to establish a manufacturing facility (probably only an assembly plant) for F-7 fighters in Pakistan. US-made equipment, including engines and avionics, are reportedly to be fitted to the aircraft, and Pakistan has already budgeted for design studies and the construction of three prototypes. Pakistani arms deals in 1986 with

European suppliers include Swedish RBS-70 portable surface-to-air missiles, and British L7 105-mm tank guns for Pakistan's Chinese-built T-59 main battle tanks. A purchase of at least 200 Austrian GHN-45 155-mm howitzers was imminent in late 1986.

Future developments in South Asian arms imports largely depend on the content of the new US military aid programme for Pakistan, covering October 1987–September 1993. In 1986 the Reagan Administration promised a package of US $1.74 billion in Foreign Military Sales credits and US $2.28 billion in economic aid, subject to congressional approval. In addition to ships, missiles and upgrading of their older tanks and APCs, Pakistan has requested latest-generation equipment, including M-1 Abrams main battle tanks—which would be the first export sale of these tanks—a second batch of 40–60 F-16 fighter aircraft, and AEW aircraft. Under the current military aid programme, the USA refused to supply both the predecessor of the Abrams tank—the M-60—and AEW aircraft. US approval of the sale of AEW aircraft to Pakistan, which in late 1986 seemed likely,[79] is a highly sensitive issue. The official Pakistani justification for the request is to counter airspace violations at the Afghan border. However, this explanation has low credibility in India, since it is claimed that AEW aircraft would be ineffective for this mission owing to the topography of the mountain range of the border and the long reaction time for interceptor aircraft flying from the current location of Pakistani airfields. They would, on the other hand, be effective for monitoring both Indian and parts of Soviet air space.[80] Therefore, the unconfirmed reports that the Gorbachev visit to India resulted in a Soviet commitment to help India counter any Pakistani AEW capability[81] seem credible.

The Far East

A large and steady flow of arms characterizes most countries in the Far East. The national security policies of the region are—more than in any other part of the Third World—enmeshed in the global East-West conflict. The region's straits are important for the traffic from Soviet naval bases in Cam Ranh Bay, Viet Nam, and Vladivostok, USSR, and from US base facilities in the Philippines, and, more generally, for the traffic of naval forces and merchant fleets between the Indian and Pacific Oceans. The area is also gaining in economic importance. Whether or how future procurement patterns will be affected by the Soviet initiatives in 1986 towards the Asia-Pacific region is difficult to say. With Gorbachev's Vladivostok speech and the Soviet call for a Helsinki-type conference for the area, the situation in Indo-China was drawn into focus.[82] It is probably unrealistic to expect that the new Soviet foreign policy moves imply any significant decline in Soviet arms supplies to Viet Nam in the near future. It is also unlikely that arms imports by neighbouring countries will be reduced.

Procurement programmes currently focus on interceptor aircraft and various types of equipment for air defence. There is also an interest in the acquisition of submarines and maritime patrol aircraft. Viet Nam's imports of major weapons continue at a high level: arms are imported exclusively from the Soviet Union.[83]

The Soviet Union has also, since 1985, resumed arms supplies to North Korea, including MiG-23 fighters, following South Korea's order of US F-16s. In 1986 Indonesia decided to purchase F-16s (Thailand and Singapore placed orders for F-16s in 1985). Indonesia signed a third contract for Rapier SAM systems, while South Korea continued the product improvement programme for its Improved Hawk SAM systems.

Table 7.9. Major international exhibitions of military equipment held in the Asian-Pacific region in the 1980s

Date	Site	Name	Size[a]	Type[b]		Comments
Mar. 1980	Malaysia	Asian Defence Expo	n.a./234	V	E	First major arms expo in the ASEAN region
July 1983	China	NATSEDES (Naval Technology Shipboard Electronics Defence Equipment Exhibition)	9/81	N	E/S	First arms expo in China
Jan. 1984	Singapore	Asian Aerospace	19/400+	A	E	Second of its kind; the first, in 1981, was for civilian aircraft only
May 1984	Australia	AUSDES (Australian Exhibition of Defence and Security Equipment)	n.a.	V	E	Low participation; not supported by MOD; first Chinese participation in arms expo
Nov. 1984	China	Electronics Trade	n.a.	EC	E	Incl. defence electronics; the first, held in 1982, was for US companies only
Dec. 1984	China	Aviation Expo	14/208	A	E	
Jan. 1985	Singapore	ENSA (Electronics for National Security Asia)	16/60	EC	E	First of its kind in the region
Sep. 1985	S. Korea	AFCEA (Armed Forces Communications and Electronics Association)	n.a.	EC	E	
Jan. 1986	Singapore	Asian Aerospace	21/500	A	E	
Jan. 1986	China	International Defence Industries Expo	15/140	V	E	
Feb. 1986	Malaysia	Defence 86	25/384	V	E	Supported by the government
May 1986	Australia	PADEX (Pacific Area Defence Equipment Exhibition)	n.a.	V	E	First major international arms expo in Australia
June 1986	Indonesia	Indonesian Air Show	23/260	A	S	First major arms expo in Indonesia. USSR participated
Nov. 1986	China	ASIANDEX (Asian Defence Technologies Expo)	n.a./150	A	E/S	First time China displayed its weapons
Jan. 1987	Singapore	ENSA	n.a.	EC	E	
Mar. 1987	Thailand	Defence Asia 87	(21/200)	V	E	First arms expo in Thailand; supported by MOD

[a] Number of exhibitors: countries/companies.

[b] Type includes equipment exhibited (A=aircraft; EC=electronics/communications equipment; N=naval equipment; V=various types of equipment) and organizer (S=state/national organization; E=exhibition company).

Source: SIPRI.

It is clear that the arms suppliers expect the Asia–Pacific region, and the Far East in particular, to continue as a major arms market. This can, for example, be seen from the number of major international arms exhibitions which have been held in the area (table 7.9). While in the 1970s arms shows were held only in Western Europe and the USA, Western arms exhibitors have in 1986 crowded the Asia-Pacific area.[84]

During 1985–86 the economic burden of arms imports has, however, increased in most countries in the Far East. Their previously prosperous economic situation has deteriorated with the fall in prices for many of the region's raw material export commodities, especially oil and tin. Thus, oil export-dependent Indonesia decided in late 1986 to review all arms imports for which there were no firm commitments, including both the F-16 fighters and four Dutch frigates decided upon earlier in the year. On the other hand, arms imports are often seen as a vehicle for industrial modernization, owing in particular to the advantageous terms offered by arms suppliers in the race for market shares. Offset agreements involving local assembly or production of weapons and transfers of advanced technology are attractive to countries which aim for a role in high technology markets. Thus, in spite of increased economic constraints, prospects for lower arms import levels are bleak, at least in the short term.

Notes and references

[1] The list of countries in the Third World regions of Central America, South America and Sub-Saharan Africa follows general practice. For other regions, the countries included are as follows: *North Africa* (Algeria, Libya, Morocco, Tunisia); *Middle East* (Bahrain, Egypt, Iran, Iraq, Israel, Jordan, Kuwait, Lebanon, North Yemen, Oman, Qatar, Saudi Arabia, South Yemen, Syria, United Arab Emirates); *South Asia* (Afghanistan, Bangladesh, India, Nepal, Pakistan, Sri Lanka); *Far East* (Brunei, Burma, Indonesia, Kampuchea, Laos, Malaysia, Mongolia, North Korea, Philippines, Singapore, South Korea, Taiwan, Thailand, Viet Nam and the Oceanian states of Fiji, Papua New Guinea, Samoa, Solomon Islands, Tahiti, Tonga and Vanuatu).

[2] See Brzoska, M. and Ohlson, T., SIPRI, *Arms Transfers to the Third World 1971–85* (Oxford University Press: Oxford, 1987). A 1986 report concluded that the Soviet surplus in its trade balance with the Third World during the 1970s and 1980s is wholly accounted for by arms exports. Without these, a considerable deficit would have been incurred. See Machowski, H. and Schulz, S., 'Wirtschaftsbeziehungen der UdSSR zur Dritten Welt: Handel und Hilfe', *DIW Wochenberichte*, no. 22 (1986), pp. 276–81.

[3] Some observers claim that the massive flow of Soviet arms to Syria after 1982—valued at $12 billion—is increasingly driving Syria into debt, in part owing to greater reluctance in Saudi Arabia and other well-off oil states to finance such purchases (given the drop in oil prices in recent years). See Bruce, J., 'Huge weapons race with Israel driving Syria deeper into debt', *Jane's Defence Weekly*, 6 Dec. 1986.

[4] See, for example, *Defence and Armament*, no. 49 (Mar. 1986); and *International Defense Intelligence*, vol. 8, no. 1 (6 Jan. 1986).

[5] The discussion of the Soviet Third World debate in Hough, J., *The Struggle for the Third World: Soviet Debate and American Options* (Brookings: Washington, DC, 1986) suggests that Soviet leaders have lost much of their faith and some of their interest in radical Third World governments. The explanation for this is partly to be found in increasing political disagreements—illustrated by Libyan–Soviet relations during much of the early 1980s—but it also results from the view increasingly being put forward by Soviet theoreticians that, even if there are different political systems in the world, there is a single world economy which is dominated by the capitalist system. For an early discussion, see Tarabrin, Y., *USSR and Countries of Africa* (Progress: Moscow, 1977). A well-informed overview of the recent debate is found in Menon, R., *Soviet Power and the Third World* (Yale University Press: New Haven and London, 1986).

⁶ The argument here would be that since the prospects of earning hard currency from arms exports is decreasing due to the structure of the arms market, at least some of the resources now devoted to production for arms exports should be re-directed towards domestic military and civilian needs. Such conclusions can be derived from Becker, A., *The Soviet Union and the Third World: The Economic Dimension*, Rand Occasional Paper OPS-005 (Rand/UCLA: Santa Monica, Mar. 1986). See also Jacobs, G., 'Soviet arms exports', *Jane's Defence Weekly*, 1 Nov. 1986, pp. 1039–41.

⁷ *Washington Post*, 12 Nov. 1986.

⁸ See, for example, Pressman, S., 'Trade of arms and money took a long and often shadowy path', *Congressional Quarterly*, 29 Nov. 1986, pp. 2972–73.

⁹ Portugal was an important link in the supplies both to Iran and to the contras. Portuguese, Polish and Romanian arms and munitions were supplied to the contras with end-use certificates claiming the recipient to be Guatemala. The contras prefer ammunition from Eastern Europe, since such deliveries conceal the origin of the Western money that pays for the equipment; see *International Herald Tribune*, 19 Jan. 1987.

¹⁰ Zbigniew Brzezinski, former National Security Council (NSC) member and national security adviser to President Carter, describes the Iran-contras deal as 'a would-be Machiavellian policy in a manner more reminiscent of Inspector Clouseau'; see *The Times*, 16 Dec. 1986. Former CIA Director William Colby claims that President Reagan's hopes of bringing the Iranian moderates to the succession to Ayatollah Khomeini are naive and 'ignorant of the geopolitical and ideological realities of the Gulf'; see *Washington Post*, 9 Nov. 1986. For some critical reactions from the Arab world, see *The Times*, 24 Nov. 1986 and 28 Nov. 1986.

¹¹ Dubbed the Arms Export Reform Act of 1986, the Biden-Levine proposal defines arms sales subject to congressional review in qualitative terms rather than by monetary value. The term 'sensitive weapons' is introduced, and in cases of proposed sales of such weapons a majority in both Houses must consent in order for the sale to go forward. For details of the proposal, see *Congressional Record*, 18 Sep. 1986, pp. S12909–13. For a description of the AECA and other arms export regulations, see chapter 3 in Brzoska and Ohlson (note 2).

¹² For a survey of the Carter efforts at restraint, see SIPRI, *World Armaments and Disarmament: SIPRI Yearbook 1982* (Taylor & Francis: London, 1982), p. 177; and the section on the USA in Brzoska and Ohlson (note 2), chapter 3.

¹³ This communiqué requires the USA to reduce the quantity and quality of weapons sold to Taiwan. See SIPRI, *World Armaments and Disarmament: SIPRI Yearbook 1983* (Taylor & Francis: London, 1983), p. 274.

¹⁴ The USA-China-Taiwan arms triangle is thoroughly discussed in e.g. *Far Eastern Economic Review*, 24 Jul. 1986, pp. 26–30 and 25 Aug. 1986, pp. 26–27.

¹⁵ See Lifschultz, L., 'The strategic connection', *Far Eastern Economic Review*, 18 Dec. 1986; and Singh, J., 'US arms for Pakistan', *Strategic Analysis*, vol. 11, no. 9 (Dec. 1986).

¹⁶ Estimated at 50 per cent for France and 70 per cent for Italy. See SIPRI, *World Armaments and Disarmament: SIPRI Yearbook 1986* (Oxford University Press: Oxford, 1986), table 17.3, p. 336.

¹⁷ *Flight International*, 5 July 1986, p. 11. quoting 'a Dassault-Breguet international affairs executive'.

¹⁸ Egypt assembles Mirage fighters and produces Alpha Jet trainer aircraft and Gazelle helicopters under licence. India has licensed production of Alouette and Lama helicopters, and Milan and SS-11 anti-tank missiles.

¹⁹ An example of a Third World-adapted product is a new family of armoured vehicles, the RO-2000 series, which according to the designer, the Royal Ordnance Factories, is designed to be made and overhauled in Third World countries where the engineering skills and equipment available are limited. See *Defense News*, 16 June 1986.

²⁰ See the section on the UK in Brzoska and Ohlson (note 2), chapter 3.

²¹ A FRF 35 billion order from the US Army in 1985 for the French communications system RITA, and an order of the same size in 1984 from Saudi Arabia for Shahine air defence missile systems.

²² See 'Rüstungskonzern Rheinmetall hält Mitarbeiter für unschuldig', *Frankfurter Rundschau*, 13 Jan. 1986; and 'Rheinmetall-Manager kamen mit Bewährungsstrafen davon', *Frankfurter Rundschau*, 28 May 1986.

²³ See 'Ermittlung wegen Waffenexports: Staatsanwaltschaft untersucht Lieferung von Raketenteilen', *Frankfurter Rundschau*, 24 Dec. 1986.

²⁴ Deliveries were confirmed by HDW on 27 Nov. 1986 (see 'HDW-Vorstands-Vorsitzender gibt Verkauf der U-Boot-Pläne zu', *Frankfurter Allgemeiner Zeitung*, 28 Nov. 1986). The government confirmed on 28 Nov. 1986 that it had been informed on 18 June 1985 that deliveries of

blueprints to South Africa had already started (see 'Lieferung von U-Booten und Plänen nach Südafrika nicht genehmigt', *Frankfurter Allgemeiner Zeitung*, 29 Nov. 1986; and 'Bonn bestätigt Lieferung von Plänen für U-Boote', *Frankfurter Rundschau*, 29 Nov. 1986).

[25] FR Germany reported in 1978 to the United Nations that it would fully comply with the 1977 decision of the UN Security Council, and that it would not approve exports of weapons, weapon parts and associated licences to South Africa. See, Dolzer, R., 'Der Sicherheitsrat und das Waffenembargo', *Frankfurter Allgemeiner Zeitung*, 23 Dec. 1986.

[26] See, 'Untersuchungsausschuss zur "U-Boot-Affäre"', *Frankfurter Allgemeiner Zeitung*, 11 Dec. 1986.

[27] See, 'Deutsche Schwimmbrücken für Iran', *Frankfurter Allgemeiner Zeitung*, 25 Nov. 1986; and 'Pontonbrücken', *Frankfurter Rundschau*, 12 June 1986.

[28] In September 1986 the Italian Parliament approved the merger of the two major aerospace companies, Aeritalia and Agusta, both state-controlled, within one holding company.

[29] According to one source, however, the Italian Government has approved a wide range of arms sales to both Iran and Iraq after June 1984. See *Jane's Defence Weekly*, 29 Nov. 1986.

[30] Libya was the leading recipient of Italian major weapons in 1982–86, accounting for 23 per cent of total Italian arms exports. No new orders have been received from Libya since 1982.

[31] 'Survey: Japan', *Financial Times*, 16 Dec. 1986.

[32] The (very strict) guidelines for Swedish arms exports are described in the section on Sweden in Brzoska and Ohlson (note 2), chapter 3.

[33] In 1980 the Chinese Government founded six companies to be the export and import arms of the key Chinese military-related ministries and industries. The six firms are CATIC (China National Aero Technology Import and Export Corp.), NORINCO (China North Industries Corp.), CPMIEC (China Precision Machinery Import and Export Corp.), CSSC (China State Shipbuilding Corp.), CEIEC (China National Electronics Import and Export Corp.) and CNEIC (China Nuclear Energy Industry Group). These firms are grouped under the corporate management of the China Xinshidai (New Era) Co. See *Defense News*, 17 Nov. 1986, pp. 21–22.

[34] See 'China's arms bazaar', *Far Eastern Economic Review*, 18 Dec. 1986, pp. 23–24.

[35] Unofficial sources in the Chinese arms industry claim that the industry is sometimes in competition with the armed forces over export revenues. Equipment supplied to the Chinese armed forces at prices fixed by the General Staff at levels far below market prices is sometimes re-sold on the world market at full market prices by the General Staff's own commercial company, Poly Technologies. The profits can be used to finance equipment purchases from abroad; see *International Defense Review*, Jan. 1987, p. 25.

[36] See Namboodiri, P., 'China's arms exports: new initiatives', *Strategic Analysis*, Feb. 1985, p. 1097.

[37] China is supplying Iraq via Egypt and Iran via North Korea and directly. Although this has been frequently reported in the international military press since 1982, Chinese officials either routinely deny the existence of such sales or maintain silence. For recent assessments of Chinese arms exports to the Middle East, see Brigantini, G., 'Chinese long have maintained a leadership in military supply to Iran', *Defense News*, 15 Sep. 1986, p. 20; and *Milavnews*, vol. 26, no. 303 (Jan. 1987), p. 8.

[38] Brzoska, M. and Ohlson, T. (eds), SIPRI, *Arms Production in the Third World* (Taylor & Francis: London, 1986), table 2.2, p. 10.

[39] For an estimate see SIPRI (note 16), table 17.4, p. 338.

[40] According to professor Aaron Klieman, an Israeli expert on the Israeli arms industry, existing domestic contracts are now expiring and there is little work to replace them. The export share of production has since 1983 increased from 50 to 80 per cent for the Israeli Military Industries, and the share for the Israeli Aircraft Industries (IAI, the leading Israeli arms producer) was 60 per cent in 1985. See 'How Israel's economy got hooked on selling arms abroad', *New York Times*, 7 Dec. 1986, section 3. IAI plans to raise exports from US $435 million in 1984–85 to US $626 million in 1986–87. One-tenth of the Israeli labour force is engaged in arms production.

[41] The new system requires permits from the Ministry of Defence for each individual arms deal, instead of a general letter of accreditation. See 'Scandals prompt change in permits to sell weaponry', *Jerusalem Post*, 29 Oct. 1986.

[42] Most of it was to have been supplied from Israeli surplus stocks of US weapons and allegedly included at least 36 F-4 Phantom and F-5 Tiger aircraft, 46 A-4 Skyhawk fighter-bombers, 5 C-130 Hercules transport aircraft, 8750 TOW anti-tank missiles, 100 000 artillery shells and thousands of spare parts and engines. (See for example, '17 charged with illegal weapons sales', *Flight International*, 5 May 1986, p. 29; and 'Israel linked to arms deal', *Chicago Tribune*, 3 Aug. 1986, p. 1). Both the Israeli and the Iranian governments have denied any involvement in these plans. (See

'Israel denies approving plan for sale of arms to Iranians', *International Herald Tribune*, 24 Apr. 1986; and 'Israel not involved in Iran arms plot', *Jerusalem Post*, 3 May 1986).

43 'Disclosures muddy an arms-sale case', *International Herald Tribune*, 3 Dec. 1986; 'US employed a sting setup for arms to Iran', *New York Times*, 29 Nov. 1986; and 'Walsh may take over more Iran arms cases', *New York Times*, 31 Dec. 1986.

44 *Recent Developments Concerning Relations Between Israel and South Africa*, report by the United Nations Special Committee against Apartheid, quoted in *Jane's Defence Weekly*, 15 Nov. 1986, p. 1144. Termination of US military aid to any country supplying weapons to South Africa is one of the further sanctions that could be imposed within a year, according to the US Bill on South Africa sanctions, which was enacted on 2 Oct. 1986. See 'The next step: sanctions take effect', *Congressional Quarterly Weekly Report*, 4 Oct. 1986, p. 2338.

45 'US investigates Israel arms link with S. Africa', *Financial Times*, 11 Dec. 1986.

46 The agreement with Saudi Arabia, the major part of which was reportedly for 500–1000 Osorio main battle tanks with an assembly plant in Jiddah, was denied in early 1986 by both the Brazilian and the Saudi governments. A Libyan delegation was to have visited Brazil in March to resume negotiations for a major arms purchase which were interrupted in 1983, following the Brazilian seizure of a Libyan aircraft that reportedly carried weapons destined for Nicaragua. However, the visit was cancelled by Brazil, and the official position of the Brazilian Government at the time was that it had not decided whether to comply with US pressures to join the boycott of Libya. See Council on Hemispheric Affairs, *COHA's Washington Report on the Hemisphere*, 23 May 1986, p. 5.

47 In the 1986 volume of the annual Brazilian catalogue of military equipment, the publishers of which include the Foreign Ministry, it is declared that 'Brazil abides by the principle that sales of defence material is not a part of Brazilian foreign policy', and that 'no restrictions regarding the re-export of military equipment are imposed by Brazil because it believes that any possible decisions in this area pertain to the sovereignty of the purchasing country'. See, 'Brazil arms industry competes worldwide', *Washington Post*, 2 Nov. 1986. There are some exceptions, however: a ban on arms exports to South Africa, and an instruction not to sell war material to Iran. See 'Libya buys Brazilian spare parts to sell to Iran', *Veja* (São Paulo), 22 Oct. 1986, p. 59.

48 Although not invited to the 1986 Farnborough arms exposition in the UK, the South African arms industry gave parallel briefings of their new weapons in a nearby hotel (see *Defence News*, 8 Sep. 1986, p. 24). The United Nations Security Council has adopted a resolution (in December 1984), requesting all states 'to refrain from importing arms, ammunition of all types and military vehicles produced in South Africa'.

49 'Who keeps the Gulf war going?', *Business Week*, 29 Dec. 1986; and 'S. Africa barters arms for oil: Iran, Iraq get same weapons', *Washington Times*, 23 Dec. 1986.

50 See, for example, 'Soviets ship more arms to Nicaragua', *Washington Post*, 29 Oct. 1986. A sum of US $700 million for Soviet military aid to Nicaragua in 1986 has also been reported by the US DOD. See 'Increased shipments of arms to Nicaragua', *San Fransisco Chronicle*, 12 Nov. 1986.

51 Hundreds of thousands of kilograms since April 1986, according to an interview with six former crew members of the flights supplying the contras with arms, a project which ended with the downing of one aircraft over Nicaragua on 5 October 1986. See 'Arming contras: high-risk venture', *International Herald Tribune*, 6–7 Dec. 1986.

52 The total sum was divided as follows: US $70 million in military equipment and training, US $27 million in non-lethal aid, and US $3 million for human rights monitoring.

53 US military aid to the contras was prohibited by the so-called Boland amendment passed by the Congress in June 1984 in response to the revelations that the CIA had mined Nicaraguan harbours. For a full account of security assistance to Central America, see Tullberg, R. and Millán, V., 'Security assistance: the case of Central America', SIPRI, *World Armaments and Disarmament: SIPRI Yearbook 1986* (note 16), 309–22.

54 The content of these shipments was classified, but it is believed that the first transfers would include small arms, surface-to-air missiles (probably Stingers to which the contras have given first priority) and transportation equipment, while the second part (US $40 million) released from February 1987 onwards could be used for heavy weapons such as artillery. The FIM-92A Stinger is the most modern among US man-portable, shoulder-fired surface-to-air missiles.

55 The USA now argues that deliveries of F-5 fighters would not change the military balance in the isthmus area, since they would only represent a replacement of the existing 12 Mystère B-2 fighters in Honduras. However, these aircraft, delivered from Israel in 1977, are of 1950 vintage, although modernized in the early 1970s by Israel. Nicaragua has no fighters, but has previously threatened to order Soviet MiG-21s, should the USA supply more modern fighters to Honduras. See, for example, 'US set to offer newer jet fighter to the Hondurans', *New York Times*, 31 Oct. 1986, p. 1.

56 According to a statement on 25 November 1986 by US Attorney General Edwin Meese III, money received from Iran was transferred to the CIA which, after having repaid the US Department of Defense for arms, deposited the remaining sum in bank accounts which were under the control of representatives of the contras. According to the same source, all these transactions took place from January 1986 onwards under an executive order signed by President Reagan on 17 January 1986. See, 'Reagan, Meese on Iran-Nicaragua arms deals', *Congressional Quarterly Weekly Report*, 29 Nov. 1986, p. 3001.

57 'Iran arms and contras: a Reagan bombshell', *Congressional Quarterly Weekly Report*, 29 Nov. 1986, pp. 2971–76. On 25 November 1985 National Security Council (NSC) aide Lt. Col. Oliver L. North was fired and the head of the NSC staff, Vice Admiral John Pointdexter, had resigned. There had been indications earlier of official US involvement in military support for the contras. One example is the testimony by Mr Hasenfus, the only survivor of the C-123 transport aircraft shot down over Nicaragua on October 1986, that he participated in a contra supply operation directed by two persons working for the CIA.

58 *Judgment of the International Court of Justice of 27 June 1986 Concerning Military and Paramilitary Activities in and against Nicaragua: Need for Immediate Compliance*, UN Resolution 41/31, 3 Nov. 1986. Only El Salvador and Israel joined the US vote against the UN resolution. Six NATO countries voted for the resolution, and eight (including France, FR Germany, Italy and the UK) abstained from voting. See also 'UN tells Reagan to end rebel aid', *Times*, 5 Nov. 1986.

59 'GAO probing origin of Honduran bid for aid', *Washington Post*, 8 Jan. 1987. The US General Accounting Office (GAO) subsequently started an investigation of this issue.

60 Major weapons delivered to Peru since 1984 include Mirage fighters and one Lupo Class frigate.

61 Two IMF reports of November 1983 pointed to military outlays as a major factor in the sharp deterioration in Peru's public finances since the signing of an extended IMF facility agreement in June 1982. See 'IMF team slams economic management', *Latin America Weekly Report*, 2 Dec. 1983, pp. 1–2; and 'IMF leaves without a deal', *Latin America Weekly Report*, 23 Dec. 1983, pp. 6–7.

62 Apart from arms sales, France had by 1986 military assistance agreements with 23 African countries (including some 5000 military advisers, mainly in the Central African Republic, Chad and Senegal).

63 These disagreements include the Lebanon War, the Iraq–Iran War and Libya's policy towards some other African countries. However, Libya will remain an important, albeit unpredictable, client of the USSR. Libya's attempts at diversifying its sources of arms were thwarted in 1986 after many West European countries declared—following US demands—an arms embargo on Libya due to alleged Libyan support for Arab terrorists operating in Western Europe. Brazil is the most likely alternative source of arms in the near future.

64 The presence of General Evgeny Ivanovsky—Commander-in-Chief of the Soviet ground forces—at the funeral of President Samora Machel may signal a stronger Soviet commitment to Mozambican security. However, British rifles are being delivered to the Mozambican Army along with a training programme, and Zimbabwean and Tanzanian troops are helping to fight the South African-supported MNR-insurgents in Mozambique. It is also believed that US relations with Mozambique will improve; see *Africa Confidential*, vol. 27, no. 22 (29 Oct. 1986); and *CAAT Newsletter*, no. 81 (11 Dec. 1986).

65 During 1986 South Africa concluded new trade agreements with Israel and Taiwan and reaffirmed their trade links with South Korea and Switzerland. See *Financial Times*, 19 Aug. 1986; and *Dagens Nyheter* (Stockholm), 6 Sep. 1986.

66 For example, during 1985–86 FR Germany supplied helicopters from MBB to the South African police and to the homelands of Bophuthatswana, Ciskei and Venda, while Spain supplied a CASA Aviocar transport aircraft to Bophuthatswana in 1985.

67 The modernization programme includes airframe reconstruction and new navigation and attack systems, including forward-looking sensors and laser rangefingers. The avionics were almost certainly supplied by Israel or manufactured with Israeli assistance. Much of this equipment is similar to the Israeli Kfir 'upgrade kit' originally developed with US technical assistance. Its supply to South Africa would break the spirit, if not the letter, of US adherence to the UN embargo. See *Milavnews*, Aug. 1986.

68 See *International Defense Intelligence*, vol. 8, no. 51 (22 Dec. 1986); and *International Herald Tribune*, 10 Dec. 1986.

69 See *Milavnews*, vol. 25, no. 302 (Dec. 1986), p. 22.

70 The price of a barrel of oil by the end of the oil boom in 1984 was $32. By April 1986 it had plummeted to $12, and later in 1986 it stabilized at around $15–18.

71 See World Bank, *World Development Report 1986* (Oxford University Press: New York, 1986), pp. 50–51.

72 The Iraqi debt is estimated at $65–85 b., of which some 60 per cent military; the Israeli at $30 b., of which some 20 per cent military; and the Egyptian at $38 b., of which about 22 per cent military. The Egyptian Government initially tried to turn to private, commercial banks in Europe and in the USA for low-interest (about 7 per cent) loans to finance its $4.6 b. military debt to the USA. Instead, the US Administration proposed measures to relieve the military debt burden of Egypt and Israel by introducing lower interest rates and possibly also permission to use Economic Support Fund aid from the USA for the servicing of military debts. See *Defense Week*, 1 Dec. 1986, p. 12; *Flight International*, 3 Jan. 1987, p. 9; and *Milavnews*, vol. 26, no. 303 (Jan. 1987), p. 9.

73 In the Saudi case three options were available: halving the order, extending the delivery schedule or adjusting the amount of crude oil delivered as payment. The last option was chosen, complemented with a £1.5 billion bank guarantee to cover short-term financing problems. Saudi Arabia has increased the number of barrels of oil per day paid for the aircraft package from 300 000 to 400 000. See *Flight International*, 20 Sep. 1986. Further increases could interfere with British oil production or with agreed OPEC quotas.

74 Brzoska, M. and Ohlson, T., 'The trade in major conventional weapons', in SIPRI, *World Armaments and Disarmament: SIPRI Yearbook 1984* (Taylor & Francis: London, 1984), pp. 195–201.

75 Note 74, p. 200.

76 A reputed US expert on South Asian security matters has even hinted at the possibility of using Pakistani territory for facilities associated with the US Strategic Defense Initiative: 'Some regional states, especially Pakistan, might also make useful sites for radar and other facilities in connection with an SDI system that ringed the Soviet Union.' See, Cohen, S. P., *The Security of South Asia: Regional Conflicts and External Induction*, paper presented to the Wilson Center Core Seminar Series on the Third World and International Security, Washington, DC, 30 Apr. 1985, p. 30.

77 According to World Bank statistics, India ranked 15th and Pakistan 28th in poverty level in 1984 (as measured by GNP/capita) among the world's 128 countries with a population exceeding one million. In its trade with the USSR, India has a large surplus (estimated at about US $2 billion for the period 1981–85), which India can use—and is using—for arms imports from the USSR. (See 'Thrust on trade', *Far Eastern Economic Review*, 11 Dec. 1986, pp. 18–19.) Pakistan receives economic and military aid from the USA.

78 India will fit these engines in the prototypes of its indigenously designed fighter, the Light Combat Aircraft, planned for service entry in the mid-1990s.

79 See, for example, Weinberger's statement that Pakistan needs an AEW system 'as quickly as possible'. ('US AWACS plan offends both India and Pakistan', *New York Times*, 9 Nov. 1986, p. 24). Although Pakistan has given first priority to the most powerful (and expensive) of available models, the E-3A Sentry, a more realistic alternative is the E-2C Hawkeye or either P-3 Orion or C-130 Hercules aircraft converted to an AEW configuration.

80 Singh (note 15), pp. 1003–19.

81 'With guns and goodwill', *Far Eastern Economic Review*, 11 Dec. 1986, p. 19. The status of Soviet capability in AEW aircraft production is unclear. An AEW version (Il-76 Mainstay) of the Il-76 Candid aircraft has been under development since the 1970s, and the first examples are operational. According to the US DOD, they have the capability to detect aircraft and cruise missiles flying at low altitude over land and water, to help direct fighter operations and to enhance air surveillance. See *Jane's All the World's Aircraft 1986–87* (Jane's: London, 1986), p. 236. India ordered some 20 Il-76 Candid transport aircraft in 1984.

82 In his July 1986 Vladivostok speech, Gorbachev addressed two of China's three obstacles to improved Sino-Soviet relations: the Soviet military presence in Afghanistan and the Soviet troops on the Chinese border, expressing a willingness to compromise. China responded that their condition for improved Sino-Soviet relations was that the USSR urge Viet Nam to withdraw its troops from Kampuchea. Subsequently Viet Nam made some moves to improve relations with China; the USSR started in October to withdraw 8000 troops from Afghanistan; and in December the Mongolian President Jambyn Batmonk announced an accord with the USSR on the withdrawal of a part of the Soviet troops from Mongolia. For the agenda of an Asia-Pacific conference, the Soviet Union proposes the reduction of naval forces, the decrease of military activities along the main sea lanes of communication and general confidence-building measures. (See, for example, 'Moscow's new tack' and an interview with Mikhail Kapitsa in *Far Eastern Economic Review*, 14 Aug. 1986, pp. 30–35; 'Diplomacy on the air', *Far Eastern Economic Review*, 18 Sep. 1986, p. 26; and the series of articles on the Vladivostok initiative in *Far Eastern Economic Review*, 13 Nov. 1986, pp. 32–41.)

[83] The unprecedented visit in 1986 by a Vietnamese delegation to a Western arms exhibition (in Indonesia) sparked off some speculations that Viet Nam would start to diversify its arms imports.

[84] Arms industry marketing directors even complain that there are too many arms exhibitions in this region, considering the costs involved in participation. This has resulted in a proposal to regulate the shows by having one major biannual arms exhibition for all three armed services, rotated to five countries in the Far East. (See, 'Beating the defence exhibition boom', *International Defense Review*, Dec. 1986, p. 1729.)

Appendix 7A. Aggregate tables of the value of the trade in major weapons with the Third World, 1967–86

Table 7A.1. Values of imports of major weapons by the Third World: by region, 1967–8

Figures are SIPRI trend indicator values, as expressed in US $m., at constant (1985) prices.
A = yearly figures, B = five-year moving averages.[b]

Region[c]		1967	1968	1969	1970	1971	1972	19
Middle East	A	3 228	3 634	3 240	4 893	5 601	5 339	10 2
	B	2 514	3 278	4 119	4 541	5 868	6 572	7 0
South Asia	A	758	817	865	798	1 208	1 734	1 0
	B	789	869	889	1 085	1 131	1 145	1 1
Far East	A	2 328	2 392	1 935	2 249	3 166	5 601	1 8
	B	1 887	2 133	2 414	3 069	2 955	2 925	2 7
South America	A	305	330	601	285	922	1 156	2 2
	B	355	357	488	659	1 044	1 170	1 4
North Africa	A	354	167	343	185	224	373	3
	B	316	287	255	258	293	342	6
Sub-Saharan Africa	A	198	161	126	357	393	266	4
	B	178	213	247	260	322	465	5
Central America	A	28	51	60	181	135	261	3
	B	101	105	91	138	189	237	2
South Africa	A	310	169	67	275	104	292	4
	B	197	209	185	181	240	333	3
Total[d]	**A**	**7 509**	**7 721**	**7 238**	**9 223**	**11 752**	**15 023**	**16 9**
	B	**6 338**	**7 451**	**8 688**	**10 191**	**12 042**	**13 191**	**14 0**

[a] The values include licensed production of major weapons in Third World countries (see appendix 7E). For the values for the period 1951–66, see Brzoska, M. and Ohlson, T., *Arms Transfers to the Third World 1971–85* (Oxford University Press: Oxford, 1987).

[b] Five-year moving averages are calculated as a more stable measure of the trend in arms imports than the often erratic year-to-year figures.

[c] The regions are listed in rank order according to their five-year average values in the column for 1984.

[d] Items may not add up to totals due to rounding.

.. Not applicable.

Source: SIPRI data base.

1975	1976	1977	1978	1979	1980	1981	1982	1983	1984	1985	1986
7 248	7 398	9 833	7 605	6 003	8 319	8 966	11 522	11 182	11 877	9 751	10 526
8 302	7 769	7 617	7 831	8 145	8 483	9 199	10 373	10 660	10 972	. .	. .
573	1 044	1 958	1 789	1 181	2 088	2 202	2 449	2 313	2 297	3 315	4 768
1 112	1 260	1 309	1 612	1 844	1 942	2 047	2 270	2 515	3 028	. .	. .
1 451	1 468	1 970	3 520	5 644	2 934	2 832	1 711	2 412	2 507	2 608	2 375
1 700	2 039	2 811	3 107	3 380	3 328	3 106	2 479	2 414	2 323	. .	. .
1 473	1 809	2 547	2 238	1 599	2 090	3 160	2 288	2 638	2 930	1 325	937
1 864	1 861	1 933	2 057	2 327	2 275	2 355	2 621	2 468	2 023	. .	. .
1 747	2 629	2 595	3 702	5 435	3 016	2 492	2 888	1 677	1 558	1 027	1 351
1 580	2 253	3 222	3 476	3 448	3 507	3 102	2 326	1 929	1 700	. .	. .
645	968	2 449	2 532	929	1 394	1 876	1 514	1 143	1 688	1 690	892
1 074	1 487	1 505	1 654	1 836	1 649	1 371	1 523	1 582	1 386	. .	. .
201	234	557	202	238	185	644	1 067	864	538	311	312
320	299	286	283	365	467	600	660	685	618	. .	. .
232	371	171	343	102	109	4	4	158	5	4	147
353	330	244	219	146	112	75	56	35	64	. .	. .
13 571	**15 921**	**22 082**	**21 932**	**21 130**	**20 135**	**22 176**	**23 444**	**22 387**	**23 401**	**20 031**	**21 308**
16 306	**17 297**	**18 927**	**20 240**	**21 491**	**21 763**	**21 854**	**22 308**	**22 288**	**22 114**	. .	. .

Table 7A.2. Values of exports of major weapons to regions listed in table 7A.1: by supplier, 1967–86[a]

Figures are SIPRI trend indicator values, as expressed in US $m., at constant (1985) prices. A = yearly figures, B = five-year moving averages.[b]

Supplier[c]		1967	1968	1969	1970	1971	1972	1973
USSR	A	4 317	3 787	2 164	4 121	4 967	5 874	7 025
	B	2 845	3 398	3 871	4 183	4 830	5 344	5 094
USA	A	1 816	2 215	3 118	3 551	3 830	5 924	6 264
	B	2 017	2 442	2 906	3 728	4 538	4 810	5 515
France	A	274	580	274	693	677	786	1 643
	B	333	433	500	602	815	1 012	1 102
UK	A	478	518	1 038	472	1 212	1 195	1 307
	B	537	564	744	887	1 045	1 052	1 196
China	A	214	162	86	101	321	417	232
	B	154	159	177	218	232	291	335
FR Germany	A	66	36	56	3	86	108	—
	B	52	44	50	58	51	121	173
Italy	A	96	121	85	37	95	137	148
	B	73	75	87	95	100	137	157
Spain	A	6	12	6	—	—	10	—
	B	12	8	5	5	3	2	3
Israel	A	*	1	9	5	1	34	4
	B	2	3	3	10	10	22	45
Brazil	A	—	—	1	—	—	—	—
	B	*	*	*	*	*	2	7
Other Third World	A	44	13	15	26	48	134	30
	B	77	81	29	47	51	84	108
Other Industrialized, West[d]	A	67	105	241	68	223	327	254
	B	117	102	141	193	223	191	221
Other Industrialized, neutral[e]	A	4	7	6	3	232	5	10
	B	12	4	50	51	51	52	57
Other Industrialized, East[f]	A	126	163	139	143	60	72	56
	B	107	135	126	115	94	70	46
Total[g]	A	7 509	7 721	7 238	9 223	11 752	15 023	16 974
	B	6 338	7 451	8 688	10 191	12 042	13 191	14 060

[a] The values include licences sold to Third World countries for production of major weapons (see appendix 7E). For the values for the period 1951–66, see Brzoska, M. and Ohlson, T., *Arms Transfers to the Third World 1971–85* (Oxford University Press: Oxford, 1987).

[b] Five-year moving averages are calculated as a more stable measure of the trend in arms exports than the often erratic year-to-year figures.

[c] The countries are listed in rank order according to their five-year average values in the column for 1984.

[d] Other NATO, Australia and Japan.

[e] Austria, New Zealand, Sweden, Switzerland and Yugoslavia.

[f] Other WTO.

[g] Items may not add up to totals due to rounding.

* < $0.5 million.

— Nil.

.. Not applicable.

Source: SIPRI data base.

	1975	1976	1977	1978	1979	1980	1981	1982	1983	1984	1985	1986
	2 874	4 875	7 233	9 065	9 786	8 590	7 141	7 112	6 904	7 521	7 948	7 681
	5 348	5 756	6 766	7 910	8 363	8 339	7 906	7 454	7 325	7 433	. .	. .
	7 074	7 257	9 722	6 852	4 020	5 712	6 277	7 192	6 336	5 230	4 291	5 108
	6 960	7 077	6 985	6 713	6 517	6 011	5 907	6 150	5 865	5 631	. .	. .
	1 144	1 398	2 157	2 409	3 264	2 356	3 134	2 892	2 778	3 654	3 796	3 566
	1 521	1 674	2 074	2 317	2 664	2 811	2 885	2 963	3 251	3 337	. .	. .
	1 196	834	1 641	1 200	773	703	1 161	1 670	579	1 135	942	1 516
	1 210	1 189	1 129	1 030	1 096	1 102	977	1 050	1 098	1 169	. .	. .
	320	211	114	459	412	548	328	736	877	1 146	792	1 208
	252	297	303	349	372	497	580	727	776	952	. .	. .
	261	166	204	258	162	283	931	321	1 172	1 820	505	541
	208	259	210	215	368	391	574	905	950	872	. .	. .
	139	163	294	323	975	653	1 332	1 346	970	811	539	324
	202	237	379	481	715	926	1 055	1 022	999	798	. .	. .
	5	7	13	30	21	9	97	371	542	525	247	107
	5	11	15	16	34	106	208	309	356	358	. .	. .
	121	59	55	470	228	209	277	375	310	174	184	144
	61	155	187	204	248	312	280	269	264	237	. .	. .
	25	154	130	120	112	268	273	202	298	269	185	121
	64	88	108	157	181	195	231	262	245	215	. .	. .
	146	157	187	95	507	177	385	542	789	573	310	498
	141	154	218	225	270	341	480	493	520	542	. .	. .
	218	514	184	464	301	226	287	437	438	152	129	261
	251	293	336	338	292	343	338	308	289	284	. .	. .
	24	63	71	41	445	272	320	181	282	251	107	182
	36	42	129	178	230	252	300	261	228	201	. .	. .
	23	63	76	144	124	129	232	68	111	137	57	50
	48	65	86	107	141	139	133	135	121	85	. .	. .
82	**13 571**	**15 921**	**22 082**	**21 932**	**21 130**	**20 135**	**22 176**	**23 444**	**22 387**	**23 401**	**20 031**	**21 308**
94	**16 306**	**17 297**	**18 927**	**20 240**	**21 491**	**21 763**	**21 854**	**22 308**	**22 288**	**22 114**	**. .**	**. .**

Appendix 7B. Register of the trade in major conventional weapons with industrialized and Third World countries, 1986

This appendix lists major weapons on order or under delivery during 1986. Certain deals close to finalization by early 1987 are included with order year (1987). Deliveries made before 1982 for the same sales agreement have been excluded for space reasons. The sources and methods for the data collection, and the conventions, abbreviations and acronyms used, are explained in appendix 7E. The entries are made alphabetically, by recipient, supplier and weapon designation.

Region code/ Recipient	Supplier	No. ordered	Weapon designation	Weapon description	Year of order	Year of delivery	No. delivered	Comments
I. Industrialized countries								
7 Australia	Italy	..	HSS-1	Surveillance radar	1986			Unspecified number of air surveillance radars ordered; total value: $20 m
	Sweden	60	RBS-70	Port SAM	1985	(1986)	(30)	Follow-on order expected; Sweden agreed not to apply embargo on military sales to Australia
						(1987)	(30)	
	UK	..	Rapier	Landmob SAM	1975	1982	(50)	Final assembly in Australia from 1983
						1983	(50)	
						1984	(50)	
						1985	(50)	
						(1986)	(50)	
	USA	10	P-3C Orion	Mar patrol/ASW	1982	1984	(1)	Update-2 version; in addition to 20 P-3B/Cs in service; will probably replace 10 P-3Bs
						1985	(4)	
						(1986)	(5)	
		8	SH-60B Seahawk	Hel	1985			Total requirement: 32; first batch of 8 for delivery from 1987; for use on FFG-7 frigates; also designated S-70B
		8	SH-60B Seahawk	Hel	1986			In addition to 8 ordered 1985; for Navy
		14	UH-60 Blackhawk	Hel	1986			For Army; for delivery from 1988; total requirement: approx 50
		7	AN/TPQ-36	Tracking radar	1982	(1986)	(7)	
		(30)	AGM-84A Harpoon	AShM	1982	1984	(10)	To arm P-3C Orions, F-111s and F/A-18s
						1985	(10)	
						1986	(10)	
		..	AIM-7M Sparrow	AAM/SAM	1984	1986	(50)	Arming F/A-18 Hornets
		..	AIM-9M	AAM	1984	1986	(72)	Arming F/A-18 Hornets

No.	Supplier/Recipient	Weapon designation	Weapon description	Year of order	Year(s) of deliveries	No. delivered	Comments
28		RGM-84A Harpoon	ShShM		1986		Probably additional missiles for FFG-7 Class frigates; total cost: $47 m
6	Austria						
300	Netherlands	Centurion	MBT	1984	(1985)	(120)	For use as L-7A2 SPHs
24	Sweden	J-35 Draken	Fighter/strike	1985	(1986)	(180)	Total cost incl refurbishment: $127 m; 130% offsets; first delivery due 1987
4	Belgium						
(1 000)	France	SATCP Mistral	Port SAM	1985			Order incl 150 launchers; total cost: approx $66 m; for delivery from 1988
5	Bulgaria						
..	USSR	SA-13 TELAR	AAV(M)	(1984)	(1985)	(4)	
					(1986)	(4)	
..		SA-13 Gopher	Landmob SAM	(1984)	(1985)	(288)	
					(1986)	(288)	In service
4	Canada						
36	Switzerland	M-113 ADATS	AAV(M)/TD(M)	1986			Part of ADATS contract; number also reported as 32
10		Skyguard SAMS	Mobile SAM system	1986			Part of ADATS contract
(864)		ADATS	SAM/ATM	1986			36 ADATS systems on M-113 vehicles; order incl 10 Oerlikon 35mm AA-guns and 10 Skyguard fire control systems; total cost: $145 m; possibly for licensed production
41	UK	SSR	Surveillance radar	1984	(1985)	(20)	
					(1986)	(21)	
2	USA	C-130H Hercules	Transport	1986	1986	2	
138		F/A-18 Hornet	Fighter/strike	1980	1982	2	Order incl 113 single-seat fighters and 25 two-seat operational trainers; delivery schedule: 1982-89
					1983	19	
					1984	17	
					1985	24	
					1986	24	
6		Seasparrow VLS	ShAM/PDM launcher	1984			To arm 6 Halifax Class destroyers
4		Seasparrow VLS	ShAM/PDM launcher	1986			Arming Tribal Class frigates; for delivery 1988-90
408		AIM-7M Sparrow	AAM/SAM	1984	1985	(124)	Arming F/A-18 Hornets; total cost incl spares and training: $113 m
					1986	(124)	
184		AIM-7M Sparrow	AAM/SAM	1985			To arm CF-18 Hornet aircraft
416		AIM-9M	AAM	1984			Arming F/A-18 Hornets; total cost incl 40 training missiles: $41 m
2 160		BGM-71D TOW-2	ATM	1985			For delivery 1987-88
(168)		Seasparrow	ShAM/ShShM/PDM	1984	1985	(124)	To arm 6 Halifax Class destroyers; total value: $92 m
					1986	(124)	

Region code/Recipient	Supplier	No. ordered	Weapon designation	Weapon description	Year of order	Year of delivery	No. delivered	Comments
		(80)	Seasparrow	ShAM/ShShM/PDM	1986			To arm 4 Tribal Class frigates; for delivery 1988-90
3 China	Canada	3	Challenger-601	Transport	(1985)	1986	3	For Army
	France	6	AS-332	Hel	(1984)	(1985)	(3)	Unconfirmed
	USA	..	Rasit-3190B	Surveillance radar	1986	(1986)	(3)	
		4	AN/TPQ-37	Tracking radar	(1987)			Total cost: $62 m
		..	BGM-71A TOW	ATM	(1987)			Agreed in principle Jun 1984
		..	MIM-23B Hawk	Landmob SAM	(1987)			Agreed in principle Jun 1984
6 Cyprus	France	84	VAB	APC	1984	1985	(28)	66 of the VII version and 18 of the VCI-type
						1986	(28)	
						(1987)	(28)	
5 Czechoslovakia	USSR	..	Mi-17 Hip-H	Hel	(1985)	1985	(12)	To replace Mi-4
						1986	(12)	
		..	Su-25 Frogfoot	Fighter/grd attack	(1984)	(1985)	(25)	
						(1986)	(25)	
		..	BMP-1	MICV	(1979)	(1982)	(100)	
						(1983)	(100)	
						(1984)	(100)	
						(1985)	(100)	
						(1986)	(100)	
		..	BMP-1 Spigot	TD(M)	1979	1982	(24)	
						1983	(24)	
						1984	(24)	
						(1985)	(24)	
						(1986)	(24)	
		..	BRDM-2 Gaskin	AAV(M)	1979	(1982)	(10)	
						(1983)	(10)	
						(1984)	(10)	
						(1985)	(10)	
						(1986)	(10)	
		..	SA-13 TELAR	AAV(M)	(1984)	(1984)	(5)	In service; 72 SA-13 SAMs per vehicle
						(1985)	(5)	
		(5)	SS-21 L	Mobile SSM system	(1985)	(1985)	(5)	Replacing Frog-7s
						(1986)	(2)	
							(3)	

Recipient	Supplier	No. ordered	Weapon designation	Weapon description	Year of order	Year(s) of deliveries	No. delivered	Comments
		..	AT-4 Spigot	ATM	1979	(1982)	(240)	In service; 72 SA-13 SAMs per vehicle
						(1983)	(240)	
						(1984)	(240)	
						(1985)	(240)	
						(1986)	(240)	
		..	SA-13 Gopher	Landmob SAM	(1984)	1984	(360)	
						1985	(360)	
						1986	(360)	
		..	SA-9 Gaskin	Landmob SAM	1979	(1982)	(200)	
						(1983)	(200)	
						(1984)	(200)	
						(1985)	(200)	
						(1986)	(200)	
		(40)	SS-21	SSM	(1985)	(1985)	(10)	Replacing Frog-7s
						(1986)	(30)	
4 Denmark	Germany, FR							
	Norway	:	RAM	ShAM/PDM	(1985)			To arm 3 Niels Juel Class frigates
		3	Type 207	Submarine	1985			Agreement to first borrow and then buy 3 Kobben Class submarines
	UK	2	S-723 Martello	3-D radar	(1984)	(1985)	(1)	
						(1986)	(1)	
	USA	8	F-16A	Fighter/strike	1985			For delivery 1987-89; in addition to 58 in service; total cost incl spares and technical support: $210 m
		4	F-16B	Fighter/trainer	1985			For delivery 1987-89
		840	FIM-92A Stinger	Port SAM	(1987)			Final decision postponed until 1987
6 Finland	Italy	3	AB-412 Griffon	Hel	(1984)	1985	(1)	In addition to 1 delivered 1984; replacing Mi-8s; for border patrol
						1986	(2)	
	Sweden	18	J-35 Draken	Fighter/strike	1984	1984	(2)	
						1985	(6)	
						1986	(6)	
						1987	(4)	
		..	RBS-15	ShAM/ShShM	1983	1986	(16)	Ordered Mar 1983; first export order; arming Helsinki Class FACs
						1987	(16)	
	USA	(26)	BGM-71C I-TOW	ATM	(1985)	1986	(18)	Undisclosed number ordered
	USSR	..	MiG-21bis	Fighter	(1984)	1985	(8)	
		(60)	MT-LB	APC	1984	1984	(20)	
						1985	(20)	
						1986	(20)	
		(100)	MT-LB	APC	(1986)	1986	(10)	
		(60)	T-72	MBT	(1986)	1986	(12)	For delivery 1986-90

Region code/Recipient	Supplier	No. ordered	Weapon designation	Weapon description	Year of order	Year of delivery	No. delivered	Comments
		..	AT-4 Spigot	ATM	(1986)	(1986)	(60)	Part of $400 m 5-year agreement also incl T-72 tanks and MT-LB APCs
4 France	Netherlands USA	6 (3)	Atlantic-4 E-3A Sentry	Mar patrol/ASW AEW	1985 (1987)	1986	6	
5 German DR	Bulgaria	..	MT-LB	APC	(1982)	(1984) (1985) (1986)	(10) (10) (10)	Unconfirmed
	USSR	..	BRDM-2 Spigot	TD(M)	1978	(1982) (1983) (1984) (1985) (1986)	(12) (12) (12) (12) (12)	
		..	BTR-70	APC	(1982)	(1983) (1984) (1985) (1986)	(50) (100) (100) (100)	Replacing BTR-60; also designated SPW-70
		..	SA-13 TELAR	AAV(M)	(1984)	(1985) (1986)	(10) (10)	Unconfirmed
		..	T-72	MBT	(1978)	1982 1983 1984 1985 1986	(100) (100) (100) (100) (100)	
		..	T-74	MBT	(1981)	1982 1983 (1984) (1985) (1986)	(15) (15) (15) (15) (15)	
		1	SA-N-4 L	ShAM launcher	(1984)	1986	1	Arming third Koni Class frigate
		..	SA-N-5 L	ShAM launcher	1981	1982 1983 1984 1985	6 10 2 4	Arming Parchim Class
		..	SA-N-5 L	ShAM launcher	(1982)	1984 1985	1 2	Arming Tarantul Class FACs
		..	SSN-2 Styx L	ShShM launcher	(1982)	1986 1984	(1) (1)	Arming Tarantul Class FACs

	Weapon designation	Description	Year of order	Year of delivery	No. delivered	Comments
..	AT-4 Spigot	ATM	1978	1985	(2)	
				1986	(1)	
				(1982)	(240)	
				(1983)	(240)	
				(1984)	(240)	
				(1985)	(240)	
				(1986)	(240)	
..	SA-13 Gopher	Landmob SAM	(1984)	(1985)	(10)	Unconfirmed
				(1986)	(10)	
(20)	SA-N-4	ShAM	(1984)	1986	(20)	Arming third Koni Class frigate
..	SA-N-5	ShAM	1981	1982	(72)	Arming Parchim Class corvettes
				1983	(120)	
				1984	(24)	
				1985	(48)	
..	SA-N-5	ShAM	(1982)	1984	(24)	Arming Tarantul Class FACs
				1985	(48)	
				1986	(24)	
..	SSN-2 Styx	ShShM	(1982)	1984	(24)	Arming Tarantul Class FACs
				1985	(24)	
				1986	(12)	
1	Koni Class	Frigate	(1984)	1986	1	
..	Tarantul Class	Corvette	(1982)	1984	1	More expected; to replace 15 Osa-1s
				1985	2	
				1986	1	
Canada						
7	Challenger-601	Transport	1984	(1985)	(3)	
UK						
2	Lynx	Hel	1984	(1986)	(4)	For delivery 1986; in addition to 12 in service
5	Lynx	Hel	1986	(1986)	(2)	For new F-122 Class frigates; for delivery 1988–89; offset value: 30%
USA						
(100)	Sea Skua	AShM	1986			To arm Sea King helicopters
(80)	M-109-A2 155mm	SPH	(1987)	(1985)	(22)	
44	AN/TPS-24	PAR	(1983)	(1986)	(22)	
28	Patriot Unit	Mobile SAM system	(1983)			Order number refers to fire units; each unit has 8 launchers with 4 missiles per launcher and 32 reload missiles
(4)	RGM-84A L	ShShM launcher	(1986)			To arm 2 Bremen Class frigates
(2)	Seasparrow L	ShAM/PDM launcher	1986			To arm 2 Bremen Class frigates
120	AGM-65B	ASM	1985	(1986)	120	
310	AGM-65B	ASM	1986	(1987)	(310)	In addition to 450 ordered 1981 and 120 ordered 1985; total value: $40 m

4 Germany, FR

Region code/ Recipient	Supplier	No. ordered	Weapon designation	Weapon description	Year of order	Year of delivery	No. delivered	Comments
		368	AGM-88 Harm	ARM	1986			To arm Tornado fighters; option on 576 more
		(1 792)	MIM-104 Patriot	Landmob SAM	1984			28 fire units with 64 missiles each; FRG will pay for 14 units and get the rest in exchange for Roland-2 air defence of West German and US air bases in FRG; total cost: $1000 m
		(150)	RAM	ShAM/PDM	(1985)			Prior to licensed production; probably for 10 S-143A Class FACs
		(48)	RGM-84A Harpoon	ShShM	(1986)			To arm 2 Bremen Class frigates
		110	RIM-66A/SM-1	ShAM/ShShM	1985			Total cost incl 70 containers and spares: $44 m
		(48)	Seasparrow	ShAM/ShShM/PDM	(1986)			To arm 2 Bremen Class frigates
4 Greece	France	40	Mirage-2000	Fighter/strike	1985			36 fighters and 4 trainers; for delivery 1988-89
	Italy	(240)	Magic-2	AAM	(1986)			To arm Mirage-2000
		25	A-109 Hirundo	Hel	(1987)			Negotiating
		5	C-47	Transport	(1986)	(1987)	(5)	
		(30)	G-222	Transport	(1987)			Negotiating
		20	Model 300C	Hel	(1985)	1985 1986	(2) 18	For Army training and observation; in addition to 6 for civilian duties
	Norway	4	F-5A	Fighter	1984	1986	4	
	Switzerland	(10)	Skyguard SAMS	Mobile SAM system	1982	(1985)	(5)	For AIM-7M Sparrow SAMs
	USA	40	F-16C	Fighter/strike	1985	(1986)	(5)	Some version D trainers; part of Mirage/ F-16 purchase; option on 20 more; bought directly from General Dynamics
		8	Model 209 AH-1S	Hel	1980	(1986) (1987)	(4) (4)	Armed with TOW ATMs; total cost: $66 m
		48	M-109-A2 155mm	SPH	1985	(1985) (1986)	(36) (12)	
		58	M-198 155mm	TH	1982	(1984) (1985) (1986)	(20) (20) (18)	
		200	M-48 Patton	MBT	1986			M-48-A1; total cost incl 300 M-48-A5: $138 m
		300	M-48-A5	MBT	1986			US LoO Aug 1983; total cost: $186 m; competing with Leopard-1
		(110)	M-60-A3	MBT	(1987)			

Recipient	Supplier	No.	Weapon designation	Weapon description	Year of order	Year(s) of deliveries	No. delivered	Comments
		(54)	M-901 TOW	TD(M)	1984	1985, 1986, (1987)	(14), (20), (20)	
		2	HADR	Air defence radar				Part of NADGE system; US LoO July 1986; total cost: $28 m
		2	Phalanx	CIWS				
		4	Phalanx	CIWS				
		280	AIM-7M Sparrow	AAM/SAM	1982	1985, (1986)	(140), (140)	Incl in sale of Skyguard SAM system; test firings on Crete Dec 1984
		300	AIM-9L	AAM	1984	(1986)	(300)	Arming A-7H Corsairs
		(160)	BGM-71A TOW	ATM	(1983)	(1986), (1987)	(80), (80)	Arming 8 Model 209 AH-1S helicopters
		1 097	BGM-71C I-TOW	ATM	1984	1985, 1986, (1987)	(280), (400), (417)	
		32	RGM-84A Harpoon	ShShM	1986			Total cost incl spares and containers: $43 m; arming Elli (Kortenaer) Class frigates
6 Ireland	France	5	AS-365F	Hel	1982	1985, 1986	2, 3	For Air Corps
	Italy	5	SF-260 Warrior	Trainer/COIN	(1987)			
4 Italy	France	2	Falcon-50	Transport	1984	1985, 1986	1, 1	
	Germany, FR	..	Kormoran-2	AShM	(1986)			To arm Tornado fighters
	Switzerland	..	Fledermaus II	Mobile AA system	(1970)	(1982), (1983), (1984), (1985), (1986)	(4), (4), (4), (4), (4)	Details unconfirmed
	USA	1	Gulfstream-3	Transport	1985	1986	1	For VIP use
		2	HADR	Air defence radar	1985			Part of NADGE system
		6 629	BGM-71C I-TOW	ATM	1984	(1986)	(2 000)	Total cost incl 1239 practice missiles: $67 m
		450	FIM-92A Stinger	Port SAM	1984	(1986)	(200)	Total cost incl 150 launchers: $51 m
7 Japan	France	3	SA-330L Puma	Hel	(1985)	1986	3	For VIP use; total cost: $22 m
	UK	(400)	FH-70 155mm	TH	1984	(1985), (1986)	(43), (43)	Ordered Jul 1984; 375 to be locally assembled
	USA	2	C-130H Hercules	Transport	1984	1986	2	In addition to 4 in service; total cost: $54 m
	USA	2	C-130H Hercules	Transport	1985			Third order; total cost: $51 m

Region code/Recipient	Supplier	No. ordered	Weapon designation	Weapon description	Year of order	Year of delivery	No. delivered	Comments
		2	C-130H Hercules	Transport	1986	1986	4	First 2 delivered directly; 5 assembled from kits; licensed production of at least 47 to follow
		7	CH-47D Chinook	Hel	1984	(1987)	(3)	
		16	King Air C-90	Trainer	(1979)	1982	3	
						1983	2	
						1984	1	
		4	MH-53E	Hel	(1985)	1986	4	Replacing SH-3Bs; for ASW
		2	SH-60B Seahawk	Hel	1983	1985	1	
						1986	1	
		130	Patriot SAMS	Mobile SAM system	1984	(1985)	(10)	For delivery 1985-91; 130 launchers (10 training) in 24 Patriot launch units; to be produced under licence after delivery of initial batch from USA
						(1986)	(20)	
		4	Phalanx	CIWS	(1984)	(1985)	(2)	Refitted on Haruna Class
						(1986)	(2)	
		(2)	Phalanx	CIWS	(1985)	(1986)	(1)	On Hatakaze Class
		6	Phalanx	CIWS	1986			US LoO July 1986; for Hatsuyuki Class
		..	RGM-84A L	ShShM launcher	(1979)	(1982)	(2)	Arming various Japanese destroyers and frigates
						(1983)	(5)	
						(1984)	(5)	
						(1985)	(5)	
						(1986)	(3)	
		..	AGM-84A Harpoon	AShM	(1980)	(1982)	(10)	Arming P-3C Orions
						(1983)	(20)	
						(1984)	(20)	
						(1985)	(20)	
						(1986)	(20)	
		..	FIM-92A Stinger	Port SAM	1982	(1984)	(50)	51 launchers approved in FY 1985
						(1985)	(100)	
						(1986)	(150)	
		..	RGM-84A Harpoon	ShShM	(1979)	(1982)	(24)	Arming various Japanese destroyers and frigates
						(1983)	(72)	
						(1984)	(72)	
						(1985)	(72)	
						(1986)	(72)	
		38	RGM-84A Harpoon	ShShM	1986			Incl some AGM/UGM-84 versions

Recipient	Supplier	No.	Weapon designation	Weapon description	Year of order	Year of delivery	No. delivered	Comments
4 Netherlands	Germany, FR	445	Leopard-2	MBT	1979	1982 / 1983 / 1984 / 1985 / 1986	(88) / (88) / (88) / (88) / (89)	
	USA	22	MLRS 227mm	MRS	1986			Total cost incl 2700 rocket pods: $192 m
	USA	4	AN/TPQ-37	Tracking radar	1986			
	USA	20	Patriot SAMS	Mobile SAM system	1984			Final decision Dec 1983; total cost: $300 m incl 160 missiles and 4 AN/MPQ-53 radar sets
	USA	2	RGM-84A L	ShShM launcher	(1983)	(1985) / (1986)	(1) / (1)	Arming 2 Heemskerck Class frigates
	USA	8	RGM-84A L	ShShM launcher	1986	(1986)	(1)	To arm 8 M Class frigates
	USA	(2)	RIM-67A L	ShAM launcher	(1983)	(1986)	(1)	For Tartar missiles on 2 Heemskerck Class frigates
	USA	(2)	Seasparrow L	ShAM/PDM launcher	(1983)	(1986)	(1)	Arming 2 Heemskerck Class frigates
	USA	900	AIM-9L	AAM	1983	1985 / 1986	(200) / (200)	Total cost: $78 m
	USA	1 878	BGM-71D TOW-2	ATM	1986	(1985) / (1986)	(200) / (200)	Total cost: $22 m
	USA	646	FIM-92A Stinger	Port SAM	1982			
	USA	160	MIM-104 Patriot	Landmob SAM	1983			Contract signed Dec 1983; total cost: $300 m incl 20 launchers and 4 AN/MPQ-53 radar sets in 4 units
	USA	(48)	RGM-84A Harpoon	ShShM	(1983)	(1985) / (1986)	(24) / (24)	Arming 2 Heemskerck Class frigates
	USA	25	RGM-84A Harpoon	ShShM	1986			To arm 8 M Class frigates; cost: $37 m
	USA	(48)	RIM-24 Tartar	ShAM	(1983)	(1985) / (1986)	(24) / (24)	Arming 2 Heemskerck Class frigates
	USA	78	RIM-67A/SM-1	ShAM/ShShM	1985	(1986)	78	Replacing older missiles
	USA	(48)	Seasparrow	ShAM/ShShM/PDM	(1983)	(1986)	(24)	Arming 2 Heemskerck Class frigates
7 New Zealand	Australia	24	Hamel 105mm	TG	1986	1986	(6)	For delivery 1986-89
	UK	..	Seacat	ShAM/ShShM	1985	1986	(24)	Replacement order; for Leander Class
4 Norway	Germany, FR	6	Type 210	Submarine	1982			Contract signed Sep 1983; for delivery 1989-92; offsets incl delivery of 12 fire control systems for West German submarines; designated Ula Class
	Sweden	4	MFI-15 Safari	Lightplane	1986	(1987)	(4)	
	Sweden	..	Ersta 120mm	CG	1986	1986	(4)	Unspecified number; for coastal defence

Region code/ Recipient	Supplier	No. ordered	Weapon designation	Weapon description	Year of order	Year of delivery	No. delivered	Comments
		..	Giraffe	Fire control radar	1985	(1986)	(10)	Unspecified number; for RBS-70 SAMs
		..	RBS-70	Port SAM	1983	(1984), (1985), (1986)	(100), (100), (100)	Fourth order
		..	RBS-70	Port SAM	1985			Fifth order; cost: $90 m; some Norwegian production; for delivery 1987-90
	USA	(24)	F-16A	Fighter/strike	1983			Ordered as attrition aircraft; for delivery early 1990s; F-16 A/Bs
		2	F-16A	Fighter/strike	1986	1986	(1)	For attrition; total cost: $30 m
		18	Model 412	Hel	1986	(1987)	(5)	For AF; for delivery 1986-89; last 17 for local assembly
		4	P-3C Orion	Mar patrol/ASW	1986			For delivery 1989
		16	M-113-A2	APC	(1986)			
		36	M-48-A5	MBT	1986	(1986)	(20)	In addition to 44 M-901 TOW TDs
		44	M-901 TOW	TD(M)	(1986)			Refurbished; total cost: $26 m
		..	AN/PPS-15	Surveillance radar	(1984)	(1985)	(2)	
		3	HADR	Air defence radar	1981	(1986)	(1)	
		6	I-Hawk SAMS	Mobile SAM system	1983	(1987)	(6)	
		432	AIM-9L	AAM	1977	(1982), (1983), (1984), (1985), (1986)	(60), (100), (100), (100), (100)	NATO co-production programme
		7 612	BGM-71D TOW-2	ATM	1985	(1987)	(162)	Total cost incl 300 launchers and spares: $126 m
		(162)	MIM-23B Hawk	Landmob SAM	1983			Purchase of 2 more btys (54 missiles) planned
5 Poland	USSR	(24)	Mi-24 Hind-D	Hel	(1984)	1985, 1986	(12), (12)	
		5	SA-N-5 L	ShAM launcher	(1985)			To arm 5 Tarantul Class corvettes
		5	SSN-2 Styx L	ShShM launcher	(1985)			To arm 5 Tarantul Class corvettes
		(480)	AT-2 Swatter	ATM	(1984)	(1985), (1986)	(240), (240)	Arming Hind-D helicopters
		(60)	SA-N-5	ShAM	(1985)			To arm 5 Tarantul Class corvettes
		(60)	SSN-2 Styx	ShShM	(1985)			To arm 5 Tarantul Class corvettes
		(3)	Kilo Class	Submarine	(1984)	1986	1	Replacing Whiskey Class
		5	Tarantul Class	Corvette	(1985)			In addition to 3 in service

Recipient	Supplier	No.	Weapon designation	Weapon description	Year of order	Year(s) of deliveries	No. delivered	Comments
4 Portugal	France	24	TB-30 Epsilon	Trainer	(1986)	(1986)	(14)	Ex-Luftwaffe
	Germany, FR	(14)	SE-313B	Hel	(1986)	(1986)		Total cost: $700 m
		3	Meko-200 Type	Frigate	1986			
	Italy	4	A-109 Hirundo	Hel	1986			
	USA	6	P-3B Orion	Mar patrol/ASW	1985			Ex-Australian; one to be refurbished in USA, five in Portugal
		5	M-730 Chaparral	AAV(M)	1986			Total cost incl 66 missiles and 2 AN/MPQ-54 radars: $45 m
		2	AN/MPQ-54	Guidance radar	1986			Part of low-level air defence system
		1	HADR	Air defence radar	1985			Part of NADGE system
		3	Phalanx	CIWS	1986			
		3	RGM-84A L	ShShM launcher	1986			To arm 3 Meko-200 frigates
		3	Seasparrow VLS	ShAM/PDM launcher	1986			To arm 3 Meko-200 frigates
		66	MIM-72F	SAM/ShAM	1986			To arm 3 Meko-200 frigates
		24	RGM-84A Harpoon	ShShM	1986			To arm 3 Meko-200 frigates
		24	Seasparrow	ShAM/ShShM/PDM	1986			To arm 3 Meko-200 frigates
5 Romania	France	(2)	AS-365N	Hel	1985	(1986)	(2)	
4 Spain	Chile	40	T-35 Pillan	Trainer	1984	1985 1986 (1987)	(10) (15) (15)	Offsetting Chilean purchase of C-101s; Spanish designation: E-26 Tamiz
	France	18	AS-332	Hel	1986	(1986)	(500)	For Army; local assembly of last 12
		(2 000)	HOT	ATM	1984	(1986)	(1 000)	Ordered Dec 1984; incl 150 launchers
		(3 500)	Milan	ATM	1984	1986	(138)	Ordered Dec 1984; incl 250 launchers
		414	Roland-2	Landmob SAM	1984	(1987)	(138)	Total cost incl 18 AMX-30 Roland launch units: $124 m; 50% of work to be done by Spanish industry; offsets at 65% of order value
	Italy	28	Skyguard Unit	Mobile SAM system	1985	(1987)	(5)	For delivery over 5 years; 28 launch units in 6 btys
		(200)	Aspide	AAM/SAM/ShAM	1985	(1987)	(36)	Total cost incl 13 Aspide/Spada launch systems: $129 m; 40% of value assigned to Spanish industry as offset
	USA	12	AV-8B Harrier	Fighter	1983			For delivery 1987-88; cost: $378 m; off-set value: $130 m; to equip AC carrier
		6	CH-47D Chinook	Hel	1985	1986 (1987)	4 (2)	For Army; in addition to 12 in service; total cost: $80 m; Model 414
		72	F/A-18 Hornet	Fighter/strike	1983	1986 (1987)	11 (26)	60 fighters and 12 trainers; future delivery schedule: 1988-15, 1989-2, 1990-8
		2	KC-135	Tanker/transport	(1985)	(1987)	(2)	

Region code/Recipient	Supplier	No. ordered	Weapon designation	Weapon description	Year of order	Year of delivery	No. delivered	Comments
		6	SH-60B Seahawk	Hel	1984			For delivery 1988-89
		96	M54 Chaparral	Mobile SAM system	1981	(1986)	(6)	
		(5)	RGM-84A L	ShShM launcher	(1977)	(1987)	(12)	Arming 5 FFG-7 Class frigates
		(6)	RGM-84A L	ShShM launcher	1983	(1986)	(1)	To arm Lazaga Class FACs
		(5)	RIM-67A L	ShAM launcher	(1977)	(1986)	(1)	Arming 5 FFG-7 Class frigates
		20	AGM-84A Harpoon	AShM	(1987)			
		(80)	AGM-88 Harm	ARM	(1987)			
		1 760	MIM-72C	Landmob SAM	1981	(1986) (1987)	(108) (216)	
		80	RGM-84A Harpoon	ShShM	1977	(1986)	(16)	Arming 5 FFG-7 Class frigates; partial batch of 25 Harpoons ordered 1985
		55	RGM-84A Harpoon	ShShM	1983			To arm Lazaga Class FACs
		(120)	RIM-67C/SM-2	ShAM/ShShM	(1977)	(1986)	(24)	Arming 5 FFG-7 Class destroyers
6 Sweden	Germany, FR	20	Bo-105CB	Hel	1984	1986 (1987)	(4) (16)	For Army; to carry 4 TOW ATMs
		4	Bo-105CB	Hel	1985	1985 (1986)	2 2	For AF search and rescue duties; in addition to 20 ordered 1984 for anti-tank use; option on 7 more
	Spain	3	C-212-200	Transport	1985	1986	3	For maritime patrol
	UK	..	Sky Flash	AAM	1981	1983 (1984) (1985)	(50) (100) (100)	Additional quantity for JA-37 Viggen; total cost: approx $26.5 m
	USA	1	Metro-2	Transport	(1985)	1986	1	To evaluate new Ericsson AEW system
		16	Model 300C	Hel	1985			For training; total value: SEK 28 m
		24	GPS-100	Surveillance radar	(1984)			
		(1 000)	AGM-114A	ASM/ATM	1984	(1985) (1986)	(12) (12)	Adapted for shore defence; Sweden to develop new warhead, container and one-rail launcher; for delivery 1987-88
		(864)	AIM-9M	AAM	1984	(1986) (1987)	(432) (432)	US DoD agreed to sell May 1982; delay due to funding problems; to arm JA-37 Viggen; total cost: approx $75 m
		1 000	BGM-71D TOW-2	ATM	1984			
6 Switzerland	France	3	AS-332	Hel	1986	(1987)	(3)	
	Germany, FR	35	Leopard-2	MBT	1983			345 more to be built under licence; for delivery from 1987

Supplier	No.	Weapon designation	Weapon description	Year of order	Year of delivery	No. delivered	Comments
UK	60	DN-181 Rapier	Mobile SAM system	(1980)	1983 1984 1985 1986	(10) (20) (20) (10)	60 Rapier systems with Blindfire radar
	(720)	Rapier	Landmob SAM	1980	1983 1984 1985 1986	(120) (240) (240) (120)	
USA	30	Model 300C	Hel	(1985)			
	12 000	BGM-71D TOW-2	ATM	(1985)			12 000 missiles and 3000 inert practice rounds; total cost incl 400 night vision sights, 400 components for launcher assembly and support equipment: $209 m
4 Turkey							
Canada	(20)	CF-104	Fighter/strike	(1984)	(1986)	(20)	20 for active duty, 30 for spares
	50	CF-104	Fighter/strike	1985	1986	44	
Egypt	33	F-4E Phantom	Fighter	(1987)	(1987)	(6)	USA approved of resale Mar 1983; Saudi financing expected; negotiating
Germany, FR	40	Tornado IDS	Fighter/MRCA	(1987)			Negotiations deadlocked due to funding problems
	(200)	Leopard-1	MBT	1986			Negotiations on Leopard-2 resulted in contract for Ex-West German Leopard-1s
	2	Meko-200 Type	Frigate	1983			Followed by licensed production of 2; armed with 2x4 Harpoon ShShMs and Aspide ShAMs using Seasparrow launcher; for delivery 1987
Indonesia	52	CN-235	Transport	(1986)			For delivery from 1988; co-production expected; supplier unconfirmed--possibly Spain
Italy	4	Seaguard	CIWS	(1985)			For 4 Meko-200 Type frigates
	(96)	Aspide	AAM/SAM/ShAM	(1986)			Negotiating; to arm Meko-200 frigates; credit arrangement not finalized
UK	5	T-67M	Trainer	1985	1986	(5) (12) (12) (12)	
	(36)	Rapier SAMS	Mobile SAM system	1983	1984 1985 1986		
USA	(432)	Improved Rapier	Landmob SAM	1983	1984 1985 1986	(144) (144) (144)	Total value incl 36 launch units and 18 Blindfire radars: $225 m; deal incl technology transfers and assembly rights
	2	Citation-2	Transport	1985	1986	2	For VIP use
	128	F-16C	Fighter/strike	1984			32 to be assembled in Turkey; licensed production of 24 trainers and 96 fighters to start 1988

Region code/Recipient	Supplier	No. ordered	Weapon designation	Weapon description	Year of order	Year of delivery	No. delivered	Comments
		32	F-16D	Fighter/trainer	1984	(1986)	(8)	8 trainers delivered directly
		15	F-4E Phantom	Fighter	(1986)	(1987)	(15)	Total cost: $70 m; from US surplus stocks; to be refurbished before delivery; attrition replacements
		(6)	F-5B	Fighter/trainer	(1985)	1986	(6)	MAP
		15	Model 205 UH-1H	Hel	1985	(1986)	(9)	Local assembly; total cost: $33 m
		18	S-2E Tracker	Fighter/ASW	(1985)	(1987)	(9)	MAP; in addition to 18 in service
		36	M-198 155mm	TH	(1986)			US LoO Sep 1986
		6	AN/TPQ-36	Tracking radar	(1986)			US LoO Sep 1986
		3	HADR	Air defence radar	1985			Part of NADGE system
		4	RGM-84A L	ShShM launcher	1983			To arm 4 Meko-200 frigates
		(4)	Seasparrow L	ShAM/PDM launcher	(1986)			To arm 4 Meko-200 frigates
		(320)	AIM-7M Sparrow	AAM/SAM	(1983)	(1986)	(50)	
						(1987)	(50)	
		(32)	RGM-84A Harpoon	ShShM	1983	1983		To arm 4 Meko-200 frigates
4 UK	France	(5)	Falcon-20G	Mar patrol	1985	1984	2	Ordered number reportedly 5-10
		(6)	MM-38 L	ShShM launcher	(1981)	1986	1	Arming Type-22 destroyers
						(1987)	(2)	
		(72)	MM-38 Exocet	ShShM	(1981)	1984	(24)	Arming second batch of 6 Type-22 destroyers
						1986	(12)	
						(1987)	(24)	
	Netherlands	15	Goalkeeper	CIWS	1985			6 systems for Type-22 destroyers; 9 for Invincible Class AC carriers
	Switzerland	11	AS-202 Bravo	Trainer	1986	(1987)	(6)	
		30	PC-9	Trainer	1985			
	USA	8	CH-47D Chinook	Hel	1982	1984	3	For delivery to Saudi Arabia
						1985	4	
						1986	1	
		6	E-3A Sentry	AEW	1986	(1987)	(10)	Option on two more
		19	PA-28 Warrior	Lightplane	1986	(1987)	(3)	
		6	PA-34 Seneca-2	Lightplane	1986			
		4	Phalanx	CIWS	(1985)			For Type-23 frigates
		(12)	RGM-84A L	ShShM launcher	1984			Arming 4 Type-22 destroyers and 8 Type-23 frigates
		(192)	RGM-84A Harpoon	ShShM	1984			Arming 4 Type-22 destroyers and 8 Type-23 frigates; offsets worth 130% of

Recipient	Supplier	No.	Weapon designation	Weapon description	Year of order	Year(s) of deliveries	No. delivered	Comments
		(210)	COMPUTA Harpoon	...		1983 / 1984 / 1985 / 1986 / (1987)	(30) / (30) / (30) / (30) / (30)	submarines
1 USA	Canada	386	LAV-25	APC	1982	1983 / 1984 / 1985 / 1986 / (1987)	(30) / (120) / (120) / (116) / (10)	For US Marine Corps; developed from Swiss Piranha APC; reduced from 758
	France	10	Milan-2	ATM	1985	1986 / (1986)	(10)	For evaluation as replacement for Dragon ATM
	Israel	13	Kfir-C1	Fighter/MRCA	1986			Lease; in addition to 12 leased 1985
	Norway	193	Penguin-3	AShM	1984	(1987)	(60)	In part offsetting Norwegian purchase of Hawk SAMs; to arm LAMPS helicopter
	Sweden	(100)	RBS-56 Bill	ATM	1986	(1987)	(100)	For trials
	UK	(4)	Rapier SAMS	Mobile SAM system	1985	(1987)	(4)	
		(100)	Rapier	Landmob SAM	1985	(1987)	(100)	To protect 2 USAF bases in Turkey
2 USSR	Czechoslovakia	..	L-39 Albatross	Jet trainer	1972	1982 / 1983 / 1984 / 1985 / 1986	(20) / (20) / (20) / (20) / (20)	Replacing L-29 Delfin
6 Yugoslavia	Canada	1	CL-215	Amphibian	1986	1984 / 1985 / (1986)	(2) / (2) / (2)	Replacing 1 lost 1984
	USSR	..	SSC-3 L	SShM launcher	1983			
		..	AT-3 Sagger	ATM	(1978)	1982 / 1983 / 1984 / 1985 / 1986	(60) / (60) / (60) / (60) / (60)	Arming Gazelle helicopters
		..	SA-7 Grail	Port SAM	(1978)	1982 / 1983 / 1984 / 1985 / 1986	(60) / (60) / (60) / (60) / (60)	Arming Gazelle helicopters
		..	SSC-3	SShM	1983	1984 / 1985 / 1986	(10) / (10) / (10)	Coastal defence missile derived from Styx ShShM; replacing Samlet SShMs

II. Third World countries

Region code/ Recipient	Supplier	No. ordered	Weapon designation	Weapon description	Year of order	Year of delivery	No. delivered	Comments
9 Afghanistan	Egypt	..	SA-7 Grail	Port SAM	(1984)	(1985)	(50)	For Mujahideen forces
	Egypt	..	Sakr Eye	Port SAM	(1984)	(1986)	(50)	For Mujahideen forces
	UK	(30)	Blowpipe	Port SAM	(1986)	(1985) (1986)	(50) (30)	For Mujahideen; paid for by the USA and supplied via Nigeria
	USA	(200)	FIM-92A Stinger	Port SAM	(1986)	1986 (1987)	(150) (50)	For Mujahideen forces
12 Algeria	Brazil	..	EE-9 Cascavel	AC	(1987)			Negotiating package incl Urutu APCs, trucks and technology transfers; total value: approx $400 m
	France	(4 000)	VP-2000	APC	1983	(1984) (1985) (1986)	(500) (1 000) (1 000)	
	Yugoslavia	..	G-4 Super Galeb	Jet trainer	(1987)			Negotiating
13 Angola	France	4	AS-365N	Hel	1985	1986	4	Part of Mar 1985 order incl 4 AS-365Ns; total cost: $47 m
	France	6	SA-342K Gazelle	Hel	1985	1986	(2)	
	Spain	(100)	HOT	ATM	1985	(1986)	(36)	Arming SA-365 and Gazelle helicopters
	Spain	8	C-212-200	Transport	(1984)	1985	(4)	
	Switzerland	4	PC-9	Trainer	(1985)	1986 (1987)	(2) (2)	
	USA	1	Gulfstream-3	Transport	(1986)	1986	1	For VIP use
	USA	(200)	FIM-92A Stinger	Port SAM	(1986)	(1986)	(200)	Unconfirmed; reportedly delivered via Zaire; for UNITA
	USSR	(30)	An-26 Curl	Lightplane	(1982)	(1983) (1984) (1985) (1986)	(1) (10) (10) (9)	Unconfirmed; acc to South African reports
		..	Mi-17 Hip-H	Hel	(1985)	(1985) (1986)	(10) (10)	Unconfirmed
		..	Mi-24 Hind-C	Hel	(1983)	(1984) (1985)	(5) (5)	

No.	Weapon designation	Weapon description	Year of order	Year(s) of delivery	No. delivered	Comments
..	Mi-8 Hip	Hel	(1982)	(1983)	(10)	
				(1984)	(10)	
				(1985)	(10)	
				(1986)	(10)	
(70)	MiG-21bis	Fighter	(1982)	(1983)	(7)	
				(1984)	(5)	
				(1985)	(6)	
				(1986)	(6)	
(20)	BRDM-2 Gaskin	AAV(M)	(1983)	(1983)	(6)	
				(1984)	(6)	
				(1985)	(5)	
				(1986)	(2)	
(4)	SA-13 TELAR	AAV(M)	(1984)	(1985)	(2)	
				(1986)	(5)	
(33)	SA-3 SAMS	Mobile SAM system	(1980)	(1982)	(5)	
				(1983)	(5)	
				(1984)	(5)	
				(1985)	(5)	
				(1986)	(5)	
				(1987)	(3)	
(288)	SA-13 Gopher	Landmob SAM	(1984)	(1985)	(144)	Unconfirmed; for 4 SA-13 TELAR vehicles
				(1986)	(144)	
(165)	SA-3 Goa	Landmob SAM	(1980)	(1982)	(45)	Unconfirmed
				(1983)	(45)	
				(1984)	(45)	
				(1985)	(45)	
				(1986)	(45)	
				(1987)	(45)	
(240)	SA-9 Gaskin	Landmob SAM	(1983)	(1983)	(30)	
				(1984)	(72)	
				(1985)	(72)	
				(1986)	(60)	
				(1986)	(36)	

15 Argentina

Supplier	No.	Weapon designation	Weapon description	Year of order	Year(s) of delivery	No. delivered	Comments
Brazil	30	EMB-312 Tucano	Trainer	1986			Contract signed Sep 1986; partly to be offset by Brazilian technology purchase
France	(6)	MM-40 L	ShShM launcher	1980	1985	(2)	Arming 6 Meko-140 frigates
	(144)	MM-40 Exocet	ShShM/SShM	1980	1985	(48)	Arming 6 Meko-140 frigates
Germany, FR	2	Type TR-1700	Submarine	1977	1984	1	Prior to licensed production of 4
					1986	1	
Israel	1	B-707-320C	Transport	(1985)	(1987)	(1)	For electronic intelligence duties
Italy	6	SH-3D Sea King	Hel	1982	1984	2	
	(15)	Palmaria 155mm	SPH	(1983)	(1987)	(4)	Possibly order for turret only; (for adaption on TAM chassis)

Region code/Recipient	Supplier	No. ordered	Weapon designation	Weapon description	Year of order	Year of delivery	No. delivered	Comments
	Korea, South	2	SHORAR	Tracking radar	(1986)	1986	1	
		2	Hyundai Type	LS	(1982)			
14 Bahamas	UK	3	Protector Class	PC	1985	1986	3	
8 Bahrain	France	2	MM-38 L	ShShM launcher	1985	1986	1	Arming 2 TNC-45 FACs
		(24)	MM-38 Exocet	ShShM	1985	1986	(12)	Arming 2 TNC-45 FACs
	Germany, FR	2	TNC-45	FAC	1985	1986	1	In addition to 2 ordered 1979
		2	Type 62-001	Corvette	1984	1986	2	Ordered Feb 1984
	USA	12	F-5E Tiger-2	Fighter	1985	1985	(2)	Three separate orders during 1985
						1986	(2)	
						(1987)	(7)	
		7	M-198 155mm	TH	(1985)	(1987)	(3)	US LoO; total cost: $90 m
		(54)	M-60-A3	MBT	1986	(1987)	(18)	To arm 2 Type 62-001 corvettes
		2	RGM-84A L	ShShM launcher	1984	1985	(2)	Arming F-5E/F fighters; further order expected
		60	AIM-9P	AAM	1985	1985	(30)	
						1986	(30)	Arming 2 Type 62-001 corvettes
		(24)	RGM-84A Harpoon	ShShM	1984	(1987)	(24)	
13 Benin	France	2	ATR-42	Transport	(1987)	(1985)	(80)	Negotiating
		(111)	VLRA	Recce AC	(1984)	(1986)	(31)	Unconfirmed
15 Bolivia	Argentina	(12)	IA-63 Pampa	Jet trainer/strike	(1987)			Negotiating
	Brazil	3	HB-315B Gavaio	Hel	1985			Total cost: $3.8 m
	France	18	T-33A	Jet trainer	1984	1985	12	Total cost incl spares: $6.2 m; ex-Canadian AF; refurbished in France
	USA	6	Model 205 UH-1H	Hel	(1986)	1986	6	
13 Botswana	USA	6	Model 206B	Hel	(1986)			Unconfirmed
		(12)	V-150 Commando	APC	(1986)			Unconfirmed
15 Brazil	Argentina	..	IA-63 Pampa	Jet trainer/strike	(1987)			Negotiating
	France	6	AS-332	Hel	1985			For Navy; reduced from 10; possibly from Brazilian production line
		20	AS-332	Hel	1986	1986		For AF: 6 used Brazilian Pumas will be part of payment
		11	AS-350 Ecureuil	Hel	1985			For Navy: reduced from 15

Recipient	Supplier	No.	Weapon designation	Weapon description	Year of order	Year of deliveries	No. delivered	Comments
(continued)	Germany, FR	(8)	MM-40 L	ShShM launcher	1984	(1986)	(6)	To arm 2 frigates under construction
		(24)	AM-39 Exocet	AShM	1985	(1987)	(14)	To arm 6 AS-332 helicopters on order
		(24)	MM-40 Exocet	ShShM/SShM	1984	(1986)	(16)	To arm 2 frigates under construction
		1	Type 209/3	Submarine	1982	(1987)	(16)	Order incl 1 submarine for licensed production; also designated Type 1400
	Korea, South	25	F-5E Tiger-2	Fighter	(1986)	1985		Incl some F-5F trainers
	Sweden	24	BOFI 40mm	Mobile AA system	1985	(1987)		For delivery 1986-87; total value: SEK 200 m
	UK	32	Sea Skua	AShM	1985	(1986)	(3)	Arming Lynx helicopters
	USA	4	B-707-320C	Transport	1985	(1987)		In tanker/transport configuration
		(12)	Model 205 UH-1H	Hel	1984	(1985)	(10)	
		16	Model 206B	Hel	1985	1986	16	US Army surplus; total cost: $14 m
		1	Model 412	Hel	(1985)	1986	1	For Navy
10 Brunei	USA	2	S-70C	Hel	1986	(1987)	(2)	
13 Burkina Faso	Italy	2	S-211	Trainer	(1986)			Unconfirmed
		4	SF-260S	Trainer	(1986)	1986	4	
	Philippines	6	SF-260 Warrior	Trainer/COIN	(1986)	1986	6	
10 Burma	Switzerland	(11)	PC-9	Trainer	1985	1986	(4)	
13 Cameroon	Germany, FR	4	Do-228-200	Transport	(1985)	(1985)	(4)	
	Israel	4	IAI-202 Arava	Transport	(1985)	(1985)		
		(10)	Kfir-C7	Fighter/MRCA	(1985)	(1985)		
	USA	(6)	UH-60 Blackhawk	Hel	(1986)	(1986)		
13 Chad	France	(20)	M-3	APC	1985	1986	(20)	Military assistance
	Libya	(4)	SF-260 Warrior	Trainer/COIN	(1986)	(1986)	(4)	Ex-Libyan AF; delivered to GUNT forces
	USA	2	C-130B Hercules	Transport	1986	1986	2	Gift
		6	V-150 Commando	APC	1985	1986	6	
		(1)	Hawk SAMS	Mobile SAM system	(1986)	(1986)	(1)	Unconfirmed
		(100)	FIM-43A Redeye	Port SAM	(1986)	(1986)	(100)	Emergency MAP
		(27)	MIM-23B Hawk	Landmob SAM	(1986)	(1986)	(27)	Unconfirmed
15 Chile	France	(3)	Mirage-50	Fighter/MRCA	(1987)			Negotiating
	Germany, FR	(30)	Bo-105CB	Hel	1985	1986	1	1 delivered complete; assembly of up to 30 planned
	Spain	(6)	C-212-200	Transport	(1986)			Unconfirmed

Region code/Recipient	Supplier	No. ordered	Weapon designation	Weapon description	Year of order	Year of delivery	No. delivered	Comments
	UK	1	MM-38 L	ShShM launcher	(1986)	1986	1	Arming third County Class destroyer
		1	Seacat L	ShAM launcher	1986	1986	1	Arming third County Class destroyer
		(12)	MM-38 Exocet	ShShM	1986	1986	(12)	Arming third County Class destroyer
		(2)	Sea Eagle	AShM	(1985)	1986	(2)	At least 2 delivered; evaluated for T-36 Halcons
		(8)	Seacat	ShAM/ShShM	1986	1986	(8)	Arming third County Class destroyer
		1	County Class	Destroyer	1986	1986	1	Arming third County Class destroyer
15 Colombia	Spain	5	C-212-200	Transport	1984	1986	5	Total cost: $14.5 m; for AF airline SATENA
		3	C-212-200	Transport	1986	1986	1	For AF airline SATENA
						(1987)	(2)	
	USA	2	Model 500E	Hel	(1984)	1985	(1)	
						1986	(1)	
		6	Model 530MG	Hel	(1984)	1985	(2)	
						1986	(4)	
14 Costa Rica	USA	3	Model 321	Lightplane	1986	1986	3	For border surveillance
		(3)	M-113-A2	APC	(1984)	(1986)	(3)	
13 Côte d'Ivoire	USA	1	Metro-2	Transport	(1985)	(1987)	(1)	
14 Cuba	USSR	..	BMP-1	MICV	(1980)	(1982)	(10)	Unconfirmed
						(1983)	(10)	
						(1984)	(10)	
						(1985)	(10)	
						(1986)	(10)	
		(100)	BTR-152	APC	(1984)	(1985)	(50)	Replacements
						(1986)	(50)	
		(100)	BTR-60P	APC	(1984)	(1985)	(50)	Replacements
						(1986)	(50)	
		(40)	PT-76	LT	(1984)	(1985)	(20)	Replacements
						(1986)	(20)	
		(120)	T-62	MBT	(1984)	(1984)	(40)	Replacements
						(1985)	(40)	
						(1986)	(40)	
		(500)	SA-14 Gremlin	Port SAM	1985	(1986)	(250)	Unconfirmed
						(1987)	(250)	

Recipient	Supplier	No.	Weapon designation	Weapon description	Year of order	Year(s) of deliveries	No. delivered	Comments
						(1984)	(50)	
						(1985)	(50)	
						(1986)	(50)	
13 Djibouti	Spain	2	C-212-200	Transport	1985	1986	2	French military aid
15 Ecuador	Canada	1	DHC-5D Buffalo	Transport	1985	1986	1	
		3	DHC-6	Transport	1985	(1987)	(1)	
	France	4	AS-350 Ecureuil	Hel	(1985)	1986	4	For Army; more expected
	Netherlands	1	F-28 Mk-4000	Transport	1985	1986	1	
	Spain	(10)	BLR	APC	(1986)	1986	(10)	
	USA	25	T-33A	Jet trainer	1985	(1987)	(10)	Ex-US reserves; refurbished to AT-33 standard before transfer
8 Egypt	China	(80)	F-7	Fighter	1982	1982	(20)	Locally assembled in Egypt; following delivery of 30 in 1980
						1983	(15)	
						1984	(15)	
						1985	(15)	
						1986	(15)	
	France	2	Romeo Class	Submarine	(1984)	1986	2	3rd pair of ex-Chinese Navy submarines
		20	Mirage-2000	Fighter/strike	1981	1986	4	Ordered Dec 1981; total cost: $1000 m
		(20)	Mirage-2000	Fighter/strike	(1986)	(1987)	(16)	Option on 16-20 more taken up 1984 but still under discussion; assembly in Egypt possible
		(60)	ARMAT	ARM	1984	(1986)	(30)	Arming Mirage-2000s
						(1987)	(30)	
		(60)	AS-30L	ASM	1983	(1986)	(30)	Arming Mirage-2000s
						(1987)	(30)	
		(120)	R-550 Magic	AAM	1983	(1986)	(90)	Arming Mirage-2000s
						(1987)	(30)	
		(80)	Super-530	AAM	1983	(1986)	(60)	Arming Mirage-2000s
						(1987)	(20)	
	Italy	(18)	Skyguard Unit	Mobile SAM system	1982	1985	(2)	18 btys comprising 2 twin 35mm AAGs and 2 quadruple Sparrow launchers
	USA	6	Commuter-1900	Transport	1985	1986	6	For delivery from 1988; for electronic surveillance
		4	E-2C Hawkeye	AEW	1983	(1987)	(4)	Total cost for 4 aircraft: $689 m
		1	E-2C Hawkeye	AEW	1985	(1987)	(1)	Total cost: $50 m
		34	F-16C	Fighter/strike	1982	(1986)	(8)	Agreement in principle for a total of 150 aircraft; total cost incl 6 F-16D trainers: $1.2 b

Region code/Recipient	Supplier	No. ordered	Weapon designation	Weapon description	Year of order	Year of delivery	No. delivered	Comments
		6	F-16D	Fighter/trainer	1982	1986 / (1987)	(3) / (3)	
		..	Commando Scout	Recce AC	(1986)	(1986) / (1987)	(50) / (150)	Unspecified number for delivery 1986-87; total cost: $22.8 m
		48	M-109-A2 155mm	SPH	1985	1986 / (1987)	(24) / (24)	In addition to 100 supplied in 1984
		472	M-113-A2	APC	(1984)	(1985) / (1986) / (1987)	(150) / (150) / (172)	US LoO Mar 1984; total cost incl M-125s, M-577s and M-548s: $157 m
		90	M-113-A2	APC	(1987)	(1986)	(19)	Total cost: $27 m
		19	M-125-A2	APC	1984	(1986)	(18)	US LoO Mar 1984
		42	M-198 155mm	TH	1983	(1986)	(16)	US LoO Oct 1983
		33	M-548	APC	1984	(1987)	(17)	US LoO Mar 1984
		13	M-577-A2	CPC	1984	(1986)	(13)	US LoO Mar 1984
		94	M-60-A3	MBT	1985	1986	94	Exempted from temporary US ban on arms sales to Middle East imposed Jan 1985
		56	M-88-A1	ARV	1984	(1985) / (1986) / (1987)	(20) / (20) / (16)	Total cost: $63 m
		2	AN/TPQ-37	Tracking radar	1986			Ordered Jan 1986
		1	AN/TPS-59	3-D radar	1986			Total value: $190 m; assembly in Egypt planned
		..	AN/TPS-63	Surveillance radar	1986			
		24	I-Hawk SAMS	Mobile SAM system	1982	(1985) / (1986)	(12) / (12)	
		(10)	I-Hawk SAMS	Mobile SAM system	(1985)			Third order
		26	M54 Chaparral	Mobile SAM system	1983	1986 / (1987)	(13) / (13)	
		424	AIM-7M Sparrow	AAM/SAM	(1984)	1985 / 1986	(48) / (144)	Arming Skyguard air defence system
		560	AIM-9L	AAM	(1986)			To arm F-16 fighters; total cost: $42 m
		72	MIM-23B Hawk	Landmob SAM	1982	(1985) / (1986)	(36) / (36)	Order incl 24 launch units in 4 btys; in addition to 12 btys ordered 1979
		(120)	MIM-23B Hawk	Landmob SAM	(1985)			Third order
		483	MIM-72F	SAM/ShAM	1983	1986 / (1987)	(240) / (243)	Total cost incl 26 towed launchers: $160 m

	Recipient	Supplier	No. ordered	Weapon designation	Weapon description	Year of order	Year of delivery	No. delivered	Comments
14	El Salvador	USA	10	Model 205 UH-1H	Hel	1985	1985	(4)	6 UH-1H and 4 UH-1M with night vision equipment
			(6)	Model 300C	Hel	(1986)	(1986)	(6)	
							1986	(6)	
13	Ethiopia	Italy	(20)	SF-260TP	Trainer	(1984)	(1986)	(20)	Unconfirmed
		USSR	(12)	MiG-23	Fighter/interceptor	(1985)	(1985)	(6)	
							1986	(6)	
			(40)	BRDM-1	SC	(1985)	(1985)	(20)	Replacements
							(1986)	(20)	
			(40)	T-55	MBT	(1985)	(1985)	(20)	Replacements
10	Fiji	Israel	(3)	IAI-202 Arava	Transport	(1986)	(1986)		
13	Gabon	France	3	AS-350 Ecureuil	Hel	(1984)	1984	1	
							(1986)	(2)	
			5	SA-342L Gazelle	Hel	(1985)	(1986)	(2)	3 armed with HOT ATMs; part of package incl aircraft, missiles and ships
							(1987)	(3)	
			(24)	AML-90	AC	(1985)	(1986)	(12)	Unconfirmed
							(1987)	(12)	
			4	ERC-20 Kriss	Recce/AAV	1985	(1986)	(3)	
			6	ERC-90 Sagaie	AC	1985	(1987)	(3)	
			(72)	HOT	ATM	1985	(1986)	(24)	Arming 3 Gazelle helicopters
							(1987)	(48)	
			(100)	Milan	ATM	(1985)	(1986)	(50)	
							(1987)	(50)	
		Italy	2	P-400 Class	PC/FAC	1985	(1987)	(1)	
			1	ATR-42	Transport	(1985)	(1987)		For Presidential Guard
		USA	(15)	V-150 Commando	APC	(1985)	(1987)	(15)	
13	Ghana	India	1	HTT-34	Trainer	(1985)	(1986)	1	
13	Guinea	USSR	8	MiG-21MF	Fighter	(1985)	1986	8	
14	Honduras	Brazil	12	EMB-312 Tucano	Trainer	(1984)	1985	8	
		UK	2	Jetstream-31	Transport	(1986)	1986		
		USA	(18)	F-5E Tiger-2	Fighter	(1987)		4	
			5	Model 412	Hel	1985	1986	5	Option on 6 more
			5	Model 412	Hel	1986	(1986)	(5)	In addition to 5 ordered Nov 1985

Region code/Recipient	Supplier	No. ordered	Weapon designation	Weapon description	Year of order	Year of delivery	No. delivered	Comments
9 India	France	40	Mirage-2000	Fighter/strike	1982	1985	(20)	36 fighters and 4 trainers
						(1986)	(20)	
		9	Mirage-2000	Fighter/strike	1986			In addition to 40 ordered 1982
		..	MM-38 L	ShShM launcher	(1983)			To arm new Indian missile corvettes; unconfirmed
		..	MM-38 Exocet	ShShM	(1983)			To arm new missile corvettes; unconfirmed
		(240)	Magic-2	AAM	(1984)	(1986)	(120)	Arming 40 Mirage-2000s
						(1987)	(120)	
		(558)	R-550 Magic	AAM	(1979)	1982	(204)	Arming 93 Jaguar fighters
						1983	(24)	
						1984	(30)	
						1985	(60)	
						1986	(108)	
						(1987)	(42)	
		(186)	R-550 Magic	AAM	(1984)	(1986)	(120)	To arm 31 Jaguar fighters
		(240)	Super-530	AAM	1984	(1987)	(120)	Arming 40 Mirage-2000s
	Germany, FR	2	Type 1500	Submarine	1981	1986	1	Licensed production to follow
						(1987)	(1)	
	Netherlands	..	Flycatcher	Mobile AA system	1985	1985	1	Assembly planned
	Poland	2	Polnocny Class	LS	(1984)	1986	1	In addition to 6 in service
		4	Polnocny Class	LS	(1985)			Unconfirmed; possibly for licensed production; in addition to 8 in service
	Sweden	(400)	FH-77 155mm	TH	1986	1986	(60)	Total cost incl ammunition, vehicles and other support: $1.2 b; for delivery over 5 years; licensed production to follow
	UK	10	Sea Harrier	Fighter/strike	1985			Total cost incl 1 trainer: $230 m
		7	Sea Harrier	Fighter/strike	1986			In addition to 19 ordered earlier
		1	Sea Harrier T-4	Fighter/trainer	1985			
		1	Sea Harrier T-4	Fighter/trainer	1986			
		12	Sea King HAS-5	Hel	1983	1984	2	Option on 8 more; to be armed with Sea Eagle AShMs; total cost: approx $125 m
						1985	(4)	
						(1986)	(6)	
		20	Sea King HAS-5	Hel	1984	(1986)	(6)	In addition to 12 ordered 1983; to carry Sea Eagle AShMs; total cost: $80 m
		6	Sea King HAS-5	Hel	1986			For delivery 1987-88; in addition to 35 ordered earlier

USSR

No.	Weapon designation	Weapon description	Year of order	Year(s) of delivery	No. delivered	Comments
(84)	Sea Eagle	AShM	1983			Arming 12 Sea King helicopters; follow-on orders expected; for delivery 1987
(48)	Sea Eagle	AShM	1985	1986	1	To arm Sea Harriers
1	Hermes Class	AC carrier	1986			Total cost approx $74 m
95	An-32 Cline	Transport	1980	1984 / 1985 / 1986 / (1987)	(9) / (24) / (36) / (26)	Delivery rate: 2/month; some Western avionics integrated
20	Il-20	Transport	(1985)			Unconfirmed
(20)	Il-76 Candid	Transport	1984	1985 / 1986	5 / (5)	Some may be Il-76 Mainstay AEW version
(8)	Ka-27 Helix	Hel	(1985)	(1985) / (1986) / (1987)	(1) / (2) / (2)	8-18 ordered; on Kashin Class destroyers
(100)	Mi-17 Hip-H	Hel	(1984)	1984 / 1985 / 1986	(10) / (20) / (20)	Replacing Mi-8s
(10)	Mi-26 Halo	Hel	(1985)	1986	2	First two for evaluation
(48)	MiG-29	Fighter	1986	(1987)	(8)	Locally assembled; licensed production may follow
3	Tu-142 Bear	Recce/ASW	(1987)			For Navy
..	SA-8 SAMS	Mobile SAM system	(1982)	1986 / (1987)	12 / (36)	Reportedly operational early 1984
6	SA-N-1 L	ShAM launcher	1982	1986	2	Arming 3 Kashin Class destroyers
3	SA-N-4 L	ShAM launcher	(1978)	(1987)	(2)	Arming 3 Godavari Class frigates
(5)	SA-N-4 L	ShAM launcher	1982	1983	1	For Nanuchka Class corvettes
(6)	SSN-2 Styx L	ShShM launcher	(1978)	1986	(1)	For Godavari Class frigates
3	SSN-2 Styx L	ShShM launcher	1982	1986	2	Arming 3 Kashin Class destroyers
(5)	SSN-2 Styx L	ShShM launcher	1982	(1987)	(2)	Arming 5 Nanuchka Class corvettes
80	AA-7 Apex	AAM	(1984)	(1984)	(50)	To arm MiG-29s
160	AA-8 Aphid	AAM	(1984)	(1985)	(100)	To arm MiG-29s
(250)	SA-8 Gecko	Landmob SAM	(1982)	(1986)	(100)	Reportedly operational early 1984
(72)	SA-N-1	ShAM	1982	1986 / (1987)	(24) / (24)	Arming 3 Kashin Class destroyers

Region code/ Recipient	Supplier	No. ordered	Weapon designation	Weapon description	Year of order	Year of delivery	No. delivered	Comments
		(60)	SA-N-4	ShAM	(1978)	1983 / 1986 / (1987)	(20) (20) (20)	Arming Godavari Class frigates
		(100)	SA-N-4	ShAM	1982	(1986)	(20)	Arming 5 Nanuchka Class corvettes
		(36)	SSN-2 Styx	ShShM	(1978)	1983 / 1986 / (1987)	(12) (12) (12)	Arming Godavari Class frigates
		(36)	SSN-2 Styx	ShShM	1982	1986 / (1987)	(12) (12)	Arming 3 Kashin Class destroyers
		(60)	SSN-2 Styx	ShShM	1982	1986 / (1987)	(12) (12)	Arming 5 Nanuchka Class corvettes
		3	Kashin Class	Destroyer	1982	1986	1	In addition to 3 previously delivered
		6	Kilo Class	Submarine	(1984)	(1987)	(1)	Replacing Foxtrot Class
		(3)	Kresta-2 Class	Cruiser	(1983)	1986	1	For delivery from 1988
		5	Nanuchka Class	Corvette	1982	1986	(1)	In addition to 3 in service; for delivery 1986-89
		6	Natya Class	MSO	1982	(1986) / (1987)	(2) (2)	In addition to 6 delivered earlier; for delivery 1986-88
		(5)	Tarantul Class	Corvette	(1985)	(1986)	(3)	Unconfirmed
		6	Yevgenia Class	MSC	(1985)	(1987)	(3)	In addition to 6 in service
10 Indonesia	Australia	..	Attack Class	PC	(1984)	1985 / 1986	2 / 1	In addition 5 in service
	France	(10)	AM-39 Exocet	AShM	(1985)	1986	(10)	Initial batch for trials on CN-235s and Super Pumas
	Netherlands	4	RGM-84A L	ShShM launcher	1986	(1986) / (1987)	(2) (1)	Arming 4 Van Speijk Class frigates
		(8)	Seacat L	ShAM launcher	1986	(1986) / (1987)	(4) (2)	Arming 4 Van Speijk Class frigates
		(32)	RGM-84A Harpoon	ShShM	1986	(1986) / (1987)	(16) (8)	Arming 4 Van Speijk Class frigates
		(96)	Seacat	ShAM/ShShM	1986	(1986) / (1987)	(48) (24)	Arming 4 Van Speijk Class frigates
		2	Alkmaar Class	Minehunter	1985			First export order of Tripartite design; for delivery 1987-88
		4	V. Speijk Class	Frigate	1986	(1986) / (1987)	(2) (1)	Contract possibly being reconsidered

Supplier	No.	Weapon designation	Weapon description	Year of order	Year(s) of deliveries	No. produced/delivered	Comments
UK	(600)	FV-101 Scorpion	LT	(1987)			Negotiating
	(25)	Rapier SAMS	Mobile SAM system	1984	(1986)	(5)	Total value: $128 m; offsets for Indonesian electronics industry
	(20)	Rapier SAMS	Mobile SAM system	1985			Repeat order; total value incl missiles: approx $100 m
	(10)	Rapier SAMS	Mobile SAM system	1986			Third order
	(6)	Seacat L	ShAM launcher	1984	1985, 1986	(4), (2)	Arming 3 Tribal Class frigates
	(300)	Improved Rapier	Landmob SAM	1984	1986	(60)	
	(240)	Improved Rapier	Landmob SAM	1985			Repeat order; total value incl missiles: $100 m
	(120)	Improved Rapier	Landmob SAM	1986			Third order; total value: $60 m
	(72)	Seacat	ShAM/ShShM	1984	1985, 1986	(38), (24)	Arming 3 Tribal Class frigates
	1	Hecla Class	OPV	(1985)	(1985)	1	Ex-British 'HMS Hydra'
	3	Tribal Class	Frigate	1984	1985, 1986	2, 1	Ex-UK Navy; refurbished before delivery
USA	8	F-16A	Fighter/strike	(1986)			Decision delayed due to devaluation; for delivery from 1988; total cost incl 4 F-16Bs: $432 m
	4	F-16B	Fighter/trainer	(1986)			To arm F-16s
	(72)	AIM-9P	AAM	(1986)			In addition to 1 in service; total cost: $150 m; option on 6 more and licensed production of 36
	4	Jetfoil	Hydrofoil FAC	1983	1984, 1985, 1986	2, 1, 1	

8 Iran

Supplier	No.	Weapon designation	Weapon description	Year of order	Year(s) of deliveries	No. produced/delivered	Comments
China	12	F-6	Fighter	(1985)	(1985), (1986)	(3), (9)	Unconfirmed; reportedly part of $1.6 b deal allegedly signed Mar 1985
	(60)	F-7	Fighter	(1985)	(1986)	(20)	Unconfirmed
	200	T-59	MBT	(1985)	(1985), (1986)	(100), (100)	Incl in $1.6 b deal; unconfirmed
	(100)	Type 59/1 130mm	TG	(1985)	(1985), (1986)	(50), (50)	Incl in $1.6 b deal; unconfirmed
	(100)	Type 60 122mm	TG	(1985)	(1985), (1986)	(50), (50)	Incl in $1.6 b deal; unconfirmed
	(6)	CSA-1 SAMS	Mobile SAM system	(1985)	(1985), (1986)	(3), (3)	Unconfirmed
	(130)	CSA-1	SAM	(1985)	(1985), (1986)	(65), (65)	Incl in $1.6 b deal; unconfirmed
	(300)	Hong Ying-5	Port SAM	(1985)	(1985), (1986)	(150), (150)	Incl in $1.6 b deal; unconfirmed
Germany, FR	6	Type 209/3	Submarine	1985			Originally ordered in 1979; cancelled same year; order reopened for delivery after end of Iraq-Iran War

Region code/ Recipient	Supplier	No. ordered	Weapon designation	Weapon description	Year of order	Year of delivery	No. delivered	Comments
	Korea, North	(60)	F-6	Fighter	(1985)	(1986)	(30)	Unconfirmed
	Korea, South	3	Hyundai Type	LS	(1984)	1986	3	Designation probably wrong; may have been built at Inchon SY
	Libya	(12)	SCUD-B	Landmob SSM	(1986)	(1986)	(12)	Unconfirmed
	Switzerland	(15)	PC-9	Trainer	(1985)			Unconfirmed
	Syria	..	Scud-B L	Mobile SSM system	(1984)	(1984)	(8)	
						(1985)	(8)	
						(1986)	(8)	
		..	SCUD-B	Landmob SSM	(1984)	(1984)	(40)	
						(1985)	(40)	
						(1986)	(40)	
	UK	6	AR-3D	3-D radar	1986			Negotiating
		(5)	Watchman	Surveillance radar	1987			
	USA	..	AIM-9L	AAM	(1985)	(1985)	(150)	Unconfirmed; allegedly via Israel or from Israeli stocks
						(1986)	(150)	
		(2 008)	BGM-71A TOW	ATM	(1986)	1986	(2 008)	Number unconfirmed; possibly only spares
		(235)	MIM-23B Hawk	Landmob SAM	(1986)	1986	(235)	Unconfirmed; reportedly part of $400 m arms package for old US equipment
		(12)	F-5E Tiger-2	Fighter	(1986)			Unconfirmed
	Viet Nam	(12)	Model 205 UH-1H	Hel	(1986)			Unconfirmed
		(200)	M-107 175mm	SPG	(1986)			Unconfirmed
			M-113-A1	APC	(1986)			Unconfirmed
		(80)	M-48 Patton	MBT	(1986)			Unconfirmed
		..	AIM-9E	AAM	(1986)			Unconfirmed
8 Iraq	Argentina	20	IA-58A Pucara	COIN	(1986)	(1986)	(19)	Unconfirmed
	Brazil	(38)	Astros-II SS-30	MRS	(1985)	(1987)	(19)	
		200	EE-3 Jararaca	SC	(1987)			Negotiating; in addition to 300 supplied 1984-85
		250	EE-9 Cascavel	AC	1986	(1987)	(100)	25mm AA cannon
	China	..	T-59	MBT	(1981)	(1982)	(100)	
						(1983)	(100)	
						(1984)	(100)	
						(1985)	(100)	
						(1986)	(100)	
		..	T-69	MBT	(1982)	(1983)	(100)	
						(1984)	(100)	
						(1985)	(100)	
							(100)	

	No.	Weapon designation	Weapon description	Year of order	Year(s) of delivery	No. delivered	Comments
Egypt	(80)	EMB-312 Tucano	Trainer	1983	1985	(10)	From Brazil and from Egyptian licensed production
					1986	(20)	
	(70)	F-7	Fighter	1983	1983	(14)	Chinese version of MiG-21 assembled in Egypt
					1984	(14)	
					1985	(14)	
					1986	(14)	
France	24	Mirage F-1C	Fighter/interceptor	1985	(1987)	(24)	In addition to 89 acquired earlier
	(150)	AMX-30 Roland	AAV(M)	1981	(1982)	(15)	At least 30 delivered by 1983
					(1983)	(15)	
					(1984)	(15)	
					(1985)	(15)	
					(1986)	(15)	
	..	AM-39 Exocet	AShM	1983	1983	(70)	Arming (now returned) Super Etendards and Mirages
					1984	(280)	
					1985	(96)	
					1986	(96)	
	(200)	AS-30L	ASM	(1984)	(1985)	(20)	Unconfirmed; to arm Mirage F-1s
					(1986)	(180)	
	..	Roland-2	Landmob SAM	1981	(1982)	(150)	
					(1983)	(150)	
					(1984)	(150)	
					(1985)	(150)	
					(1986)	(150)	
Italy	2	A-109 Hirundo	Hel	1984			On 2 Wadi Class corvettes; total cost incl 5 AB-212ASW helicopters: $164 m; delivery halted due to war with Iran
	5	AB-212ASW	Hel	1984			On 4 Lupo Class frigates; delivery halted due to war with Iran
	(10)	Aspide/Albatros	ShAM/ShShM launcher	(1981)			Arming Lupo and Wadi Class; delivery halted due to war with Iran
	(14)	Otomat-2 L	ShShM launcher	(1981)			Arming Lupo and Wadi Class; delivery halted due to war with Iran
	(224)	Aspide	AAM/SAM/ShAM	(1981)			Arming 4 Lupo Class frigates and 6 Wadi Class corvettes; delivery halted due to war with Iran
	(60)	Otomat-2	ShShM	(1981)			Arming 4 Lupo Class frigates and 6 Wadi Class corvettes; delivery halted due to war with Iran
	4	Lupo Class	Frigate	1981			Order incl 6 Wadi Class corvettes and 1 Stromboli Class support ship; delivery halted due to war with Iran

Region code/Recipient	Supplier	No. ordered	Weapon designation	Weapon description	Year of order	Year of delivery	No. delivered	Comments
		6	Wadi Class	Corvette	1981			Iraqi designation: Assad Class; delivery halted due to war with Iran
	Jordan	(200)	GHN-45 155mm	TH/TG	(1984)	(1985)	(100)	Unconfirmed
	Poland	(200)	SA-6 Gainful	Landmob SAM	(1985)	(1986)	(100)	Unconfirmed
	Saudi Arabia	(12)	FH-70 155mm	TH	(1986)	(1986)	(12)	Unconfirmed
	USA	45	Model 214ST	Hel	1985	(1985)	(10)	Commercial deal; may be for civil use
	USSR	..	Mi-24 Hind-D	Hel	(1986)	(1986)	(15)	Designation unconfirmed; reportedly part of $3 b deal
		..	MiG-23BN	Fighter/grd attack	(1986)			Designation unconfirmed; reportedly part of $3 b deal
		..	MiG-29	Fighter	(1986)	(1987)	(4)	Unconfirmed
		..	BM-21 122mm	MRS	(1986)			Designation unconfirmed; reportedly part of $3 b deal
		..	BRDM-2 Gaskin	AAV(M)	1982	(1982) (1983) (1984) (1985) (1986)	(5) (5) (5) (5) (5)	
		..	BTR-80	APC	(1986)			Designation unconfirmed; reportedly part of $3 b deal
		..	M-1974 122mm	SPH	(1986)			Designation unconfirmed; reportedly part of $3 b deal
		(600)	T-72	MBT	1984	1984 1985 1986	(200) (200) (200)	
		..	T-74	MBT	(1986)			Designation unconfirmed; reportedly part of $3 b deal
		..	SA-6 SAMS	Mobile SAM system	1979	1982 1983 1984 1985 1986	(6) (6) (6) (6) (6)	
		..	SA-8 SAMS	Mobile SAM system	(1982)	1982 1983 1984 1985 1986	(6) (6) (6) (6) (6)	Designation unconfirmed; reportedly part of $3 b deal

Recipient / Supplier	No.	Weapon designation	Weapon description	Year of order	Year(s) of delivery	No. delivered	Comments
	..	SA-6 Gainful	Landmob SAM	1979	(1982)(1983)(1984)(1985)(1986)	(60)(60)(60)(60)(60)	
	..	SA-8 Gecko	Landmob SAM	(1982)	1982 1983 1984 (1985)(1986)	(72)(72)(72)(72)(72)	
	..	SA-9 Gaskin	Landmob SAM	1982	(1982)(1983)(1984)(1985)(1986)	(40)(40)(40)(40)(40)	On BRDM-2 Gaskin vehicles
8 Israel							
USA	(12)	AS-365N	Hel	1986	1986	11	12-20 ordered
	11	F-15A Eagle	Fighter	1982	1986	(15)	Total cost: $2200 m of which half grant and half credit; for delivery 1986-88
	75	F-16C	Fighter/strike	1983	(1986)	(75)	
	25	Model 209 AH-1S	Hel	1986	(1986)	(75)	
	150	AIM-7M Sparrow	AAM/SAM	1983	(1987)	(75)	Arming F-15s; total cost: $52 m
	200	AIM-9L	AAM	1983	(1985)(1986)	(100)(100)	US LoO Mar 1983
8 Jordan							
Argentina	60	TAM	MT	(1986)			Turrets to be made in Israel; unconfirmed
Austria	(200)	GHN-45 155mm	TH/TG	(1984)			Unconfirmed
Brazil	..	EE-11 Urutu	APC	(1986)			Unconfirmed
France	(6)	AS-332	Hel	(1986)			
Spain	14	C-101 Aviojet	Jet trainer	1986	(1987)	(8)	
	1	C-212-200	Transport	1985			
UK	2	CN-235	Transport	1985			Option taken Jun 1985
	(248)	Khalid	MBT	(1987)			Negotiating
	..	S-723 Martello	3-D radar	1985			Deal signed during Thatcher visit 1985; designation unconfirmed
	(1 500)	Blowpipe	Port SAM	(1987)			May order as result of US withdrawal of offer to sell Stinger SAMs
USA	(1 500)	Javelin	Port SAM	(1987)			Reportedly negotiating
	2	Gulfstream-3	Transport	(1984)	1986	2	For AF Royal Flight
	24	Model 209 AH-1S	Hel	1982	(1985)(1986)	(12)(12)	Armed with TOW ATMs

Region code/ Recipient	Supplier	No. ordered	Weapon designation	Weapon description	Year of order	Year of delivery	No. delivered	Comments
	USSR	(192)	BGM-71A TOW	ATM	1981	(1985)	(96)	Arming 24 Model 209 Cobras
						(1986)	(96)	
	USSR	..	BRDM-2 Gaskin	AAV(M)	(1984)			Unconfirmed
		..	ZSU-23-4 Shilka	AAV	(1984)	(1986)		Unconfirmed
		(18)	SA-8 SAMS	Mobile SAM system	1984	(1986)	(8)	Unspecified number ordered
		..	SA-7 Grail	Port SAM	1984	(1986)	(18)	Unconfirmed
		(216)	SA-8 Gecko	Landmob SAM	1984	(1986)	(100)	Unconfirmed
		..	SA-9 Gaskin	Landmob SAM	(1984)		(216)	Unconfirmed
13 Kenya	Canada	4	DHC-5D Buffalo	Transport	1986	(1986)	(2)	
						(1987)	(2)	
	France	2	Otomat-2 L	ShShM launcher	1984	(1987)	(2)	On 2 FACs ordered from UK
	UK	(24)	Otomat-2	ShShM	1984	(1987)	(24)	Arming 2 Type 56M FACs on order from UK
		2	Type 56M	PC/FAC	1984	(1987)	(2)	Similar to Omani Province Class
10 Korea, North	USSR	(8)	Mi-14 Haze	Hel	(1985)	(1986)	(8)	For ASW
		(24)	Mi-17 Hip-H	Hel	(1985)	(1986)	(24)	Unconfirmed
		(45)	Mi-24 Hind-D	Hel	(1985)	(1985)	(15)	
						(1986)	(15)	
						(1987)	(15)	
		(24)	Mi-8 Hip	Hel	(1985)	(1986)	(24)	
		(50)	MiG-23	Fighter/interceptor	1984	1985	(26)	
						1986	(24)	
		(300)	AA-7 Apex	AAM	(1984)	(1985)	(90)	Reportedly arming MiG-23s
						(1986)	(90)	
10 Korea, South	France	..	MM-38 L	ShShM launcher	(1982)	1983	(1)	Arming HDC-1150 Class corvettes
						1985	(1)	
		..	MM-38 Exocet	ShShM	(1982)	1983	(6)	Arming HDC-1150 Class corvettes
						1985	(6)	
	Indonesia	10	CN-235	Transport	1986			For delivery from 1988
	USA	30	F-16C	Fighter/strike	1981	1986	4	Cost incl 6 F-16Ds: $931 m; future delivery schedule: 1988-12, 1989-2
						1987	(12)	
		6	F-16D	Fighter/trainer	1981	1986	(2)	
						(1987)	(2)	
		50	Model 205 UH-1H	Hel	1986			US LoO (incl 60 engines) worth $115 m
		21	Model 209 AH-1S	Hel	1986			Cost incl spares and training: $178 m; to be armed with TOW ATMs

Recipient/supplier	No.	Weapon designation	Weapon description	Year of order	Year(s) of deliveries	No. delivered	Comments
	12	AN/TPQ-36	Tracking radar	(1985)	(1985) (1986)	(6) (6)	
	(3)	RGM-84A L	ShShM launcher	(1985)	(1985)	(1)	Arming Ulsan Class frigates
	(680)	AIM-9L	AAM	(1979)	(1982) (1983) (1984) (1985) (1986)	(30) (120) (180) (180) (170)	For licence-produced F-5E/F fighters; unconfirmed
	(504)	BGM-71C I-TOW	ATM	(1985)	(1985)	(24)	To arm 21 Model 209 Cobra helicopters
	(732)	FIM-92A Stinger	Port SAM	1986	(1986)		Total cost incl 133 launch units: $57 m
	..	RGM-84A Harpoon	ShShM	(1985)	(1985)		Arming Ulsan Class frigates
8 Kuwait							
Argentina	20	IA-58A Pucara	COIN	1983	(1985)	(12)	Total cost: $120 m; option on 40 more
France	24	AM-39 Exocet	AShM	1983	(1985) (1986)	(12) (12)	To arm 6 AS-332 Super Pumas
	..	ARMAT	ARM	1983	1986		To arm 6 AS-332 Super Pumas
	(78)	Super-530	AAM	1983	1986 (1987)	(48) (30)	Arming 13 Mirage F-1Cs
UK	12	Hawk	Jet trainer/strike	1982	(1985) (1986)	(2) (10)	Mk-64 trainer/ground attack version; total cost: $105 m
USA	(188)	M-113-A2	APC	1982	1984 (1985) (1986)	(50) (50) (50)	
	62	V-300 Commando	APC	1984	(1985) (1986)	(30) (32)	
	4 840	BGM-71C I-TOW	ATM	1982	(1984) (1985) (1986)	(1 000) (1 000) (1 000)	Cost incl M-901s and M-113s: $97 m
12 Libya							
Brazil	(8)	EMB-111	Mar patrol	(1987)			Negotiating
	25	EMB-121 Xingu	Transport	(1987)			Negotiating
	(100)	EMB-312 Tucano	Trainer	(1987)			Negotiating for 100-150 aircraft
	(15)	Astros-II SS-40	MRS	(1987)			Negotiating
	(15)	Astros-II SS-60	MRS	(1987)			Negotiating
	:	EE-11 Urutu	APC	(1987)			Negotiating
	:	EE-3 Jararaca	SC	(1987)			Negotiating
	:	EE-9 Cascavel	AC	(1987)			Negotiating
Czechoslovakia	6	Let L-410	Transport	1985	1986	6	Ordered Jun 1985
Greece	..	Steyr-4K 7FA	APC	(1987)			Negotiating
USA	2	L-100-30	Transport	1984	1986	2	Covertly acquired via Benin
USSR	3	Il-76 Candid	Transport	1986	1986	3	Replacing aircraft destroyed during US Apr attack

Region code/Recipient	Supplier	No. ordered	Weapon designation	Weapon description	Year of order	Year of delivery	No. delivered	Comments
		(24)	SA-5 SAMS	Mobile SAM system	(1985)	(1985)	(12)	
		(1)	SA-N-4 L	ShAM launcher	(1984)	1986	1	Arming first Koni Class frigate
		2	SA-N-4 L	ShAM launcher	1986	1986	2	Arming 2 Nanuchka Class corvettes
		..	SSN-2 Styx L	ShShM launcher	(1982)	1983	4	Land-based version
						1984	4	
						1985	4	
						(1986)	4	
		1	SSN-2 Styx L	ShShM launcher	(1984)	1986	1	Arming first Koni Class frigate
		2	SSN-2 Styx L	ShShM launcher	1986	1986	2	Arming 2 Nanuchka Class corvettes
		(72)	SA-5 Gammon	SAM	(1985)	(1985)	(36)	
						(1986)	(36)	
		(20)	SA-N-4	ShAM	(1984)	1986	(20)	Arming first Koni Class frigate
		(40)	SA-N-4	ShAM	1986	1986	(40)	Arming 2 Nanuchka Class corvettes
		..	SSN-2 Styx	ShShM	(1982)	1983	(36)	Land-based version for protection of Gulf of Sirte
						1984	(36)	
						1985	(36)	
						(1986)	(36)	
		(12)	SSN-2 Styx	ShShM	(1984)	1986	(12)	Arming first Koni Class frigate
		(24)	SSN-2 Styx	ShShM	1986	1986	(24)	Arming 2 Nanuchka Class corvettes
		..	Koni Class	Frigate	(1984)	1986	1	Arming first Koni Class frigate
		2	Nanuchka Class	Corvette	1986	1986	2	Arming 2 Nanuchka Class corvettes
	Yugoslavia	4	Koncar Class	FAC	1985			Replacing 1 destroyed and 1 damaged in Mar 1986 US attack. Based on Swedish Spica design; contract signed Jun 1985
13 Malawi	France	1	AS-365	Hel	(1985)	1986	1	For VIP use
	Germany, FR	3	Do-228-200	Transport	1985	1986	2	Third for delivery 1988
	UK	1	HS-125/700	Transport	(1984)	1986	1	For Army Air Wing; probably 800-version
10 Malaysia	Belgium	186	Sibmas	APC	1982	1983	(50)	162 APCs (AFSV-90) and 24 ARVs
						1984	(50)	
						(1985)	(50)	
						(1986)	(36)	
	Indonesia	4	CN-235	Transport	(1987)			Negotiating
	Italy	4	Lerici Class	Minehunter	1981	1986	4	Different engines and armament than version produced for Italian Navy
	UK	6	Wasp	Hel	1986	(1987)	(6)	

Recipient	Supplier	No.	Weapon designation	Weapon description	Year of order	Year(s) of deliveries	No. delivered	Comments
	USA	40	A-4E Skyhawk	Fighter/bomber	1981	1984 / 1985 / 1986	(10) / (20) / (10)	63 A-4Ls and 25 A-4Cs; 40 A-4Ls to be refurbished by Grumman; remaining 23 A-4Ls to be stored in USA; the A-4Cs to be used for spares
	USA	2	HU-16B Albatros	Mar patrol/ASW	1985	1986	2	
	USA	(1)	HADR	Air defence radar	(1982)	(1986)	(1)	Refurbished by Grumman; unit cost: $4 m
14 Mexico	France	40	ERC-90 Lynx	AC	1986			Also designated Ultrav; some reportedly armed with Milan ATMs
	France	(40)	VBL-M11	AC	1984	(1985) / (1986)	(20) / (20)	
	France	(120)	Milan	ATM	1984	(1985) / (1986)	(60) / (60)	Unspecified number ordered; arming M-11 VBL vehicles
	Germany, FR	6	Bo-105	Hel	(1985)	1986	6	
	Spain	10	C-212-200	Transport	1985	1986	6	For Navy
	Switzerland	20	PC-7	Trainer	1985	1986	(6)	
	USA	21	F-33C Bonanza	Trainer	1985	(1987)	(4)	
12 Morocco	Argentina	(20)	IA-58A Pucara	COIN	(1985)	(1985)		17 on loan from Libya for training prior to delivery from Brazil
	Brazil	60	EE-11 Urutu	APC	(1985)	(1986)	(20)	
	France	24	Mirage-2000	Fighter/strike	(1987)			Negotiating
	France	108	AMX-10RC	Recce AC	1978	1982 / 1983 / (1984) / (1985) / (1986)	(10) / (20) / (10) / (10) / (20)	
	Spain	6	Vigilance Class	PC	1985			Development of Lazaga Class; for fishery protection
	USA	1	KC-130H	Tanker/transport	(1985)	(1987)	(1)	In addition to 4 in service
	USA	..	BGM-71C I-TOW	ATM	(1985)			Undisclosed number ordered
13 Mozambique	USSR	..	BTR-60P	APC	1979	(1982) / (1983) / (1984) / (1985) / (1986)	(10) / (10) / (10) / (10) / (10)	
14 Nicaragua	USA	1	Model 204 UH-1B	Hel	1986	1986	1	For contras; delivered by private US organization after official approval
	USA	(50)	SA-7 Grail	Port SAM	1986	1986	(50)	For contras

Region code/ Recipient	Supplier	No. ordered	Weapon designation	Weapon description	Year of order	Year of delivery	No. delivered	Comments
	USSR	(15)	Mi-17 Hip-H	Hel	(1985)	1986	(15)	Unconfirmed; in addition to approx 6 in service
		(6)	Mi-24 Hind-D	Hel	(1985)	1986	(6)	
		..	T-55	MBT	(1986)	(1986)	(20)	Unconfirmed
		..	ZSU-57-2	AAV	(1986)	(1986)	(10)	Unconfirmed
		(100)	SA-14 Gremlin	Port SAM	(1986)	(1986)	(50)	Unconfirmed
						(1987)	(50)	Unconfirmed
13 Niger	France	3	VBL-M11	AC	1986	1986	3	French MAP
	Germany, FR	1	Do-228-200	Transport	1985	1986	1	
13 Nigeria	Brazil	5	EMB-110	Transport	(1985)	1986	5	Possibly for civil use
	Czechoslovakia	(24)	L-39 Albatross	Jet trainer	(1984)	(1986)	(1)	Unconfirmed
	France	12	SA-330L Puma	Hel	1985	(1986)	(6)	Deal incl trade-in of 9 old Pumas
						(1987)	(6)	
	Germany, FR	40	ERC-90 Sagaie	AC	(1986)	(1986)	(10)	In addition to 12 in service
		12	Alpha Jet	Jet trainer/strike	1983	1985	(6)	In addition to 3 delivered 1984
						1986	(6)	
		3	Do-228-200	Transport	(1985)	1985	(1)	
						1986	(2)	
	Italy	25	Palmaria 155mm	SPH	1982	1983	2	
						1985	8	
						(1986)	(15)	
		2	Lerici Class	Minehunter	1983			Ordered Jun 1983; for delivery 1987; option for second ship taken up 1984
	UK	(18)	Lightning F-53	Fighter/interceptor	(1987)			Negotiating; re-purchased by UK as part of Tornado package
		(4)	Lightning T-55	Fighter/trainer	(1987)			Negotiating; re-purchased by UK as part of Tornado package
	USA	(36)	MBT Mk-3	MBT	1984	(1985)	(12)	In addition to 36 ordered 1981
						(1986)	(24)	
		5	CH-47C Chinook	Hel	(1987)			Ordered Feb 1983; delivery halted due to funding problems; being re-negotiated
	USSR	12	MiG-21MF	Fighter	1984			Agreed late 1984
		6	MiG-21UTI	Jet trainer	1984			Agreed late 1984
8 Oman	France	(1)	MM-40 L	ShShM launcher	1986			To arm fourth Province Class FAC
		(24)	MM-40 Exocet	ShShM/SShM	1986			To arm fourth Province Class FAC
	UK	8	Tornado ADV	Fighter/MRCA	1985			Deliveries postponed until 1991 for lack

Recipient / Supplier	No. ordered	Weapon designation	Weapon description	Year of order	Year(s) of deliveries	No. delivered	Comments
	4	S-723 Martello	3-D radar	(1984)	(1985)	(2)	
	1	Watchman	Surveillance radar	1986	(1986)	(2)	
	48	Sky Flash	AAM	1985	1986	1	Arming 8 Tornado ADV fighters
	1	Province Class	FAC	1986			In addition to 3 in service; for delivery 1988
USA	1	C-130H Hercules	Transport	(1985)	(1986)	(1)	In addition to 3 in service
	300	AIM-9P	AAM	1985	(1986)	(300)	Arming Jaguar and Hunter fighters
9 Pakistan							
Austria	(200)	GHN-45 155mm	TH/TG	(1987)	(1986)	(60)	Negotiating
China	60	F-7	Fighter	(1983)	1986	35	Licensed production to follow
	(100)	Q-5 Fantan-A	Fighter/grd attack	1984	(1987)	(35)	For delivery 1986-88
	..	T-59	MBT	(1975)	(1982)	(75)	
					(1983)	(75)	
					(1984)	(75)	
					(1985)	(75)	
					(1986)	(75)	
Sweden	..	Giraffe	Fire control radar	(1986)			Ordered with RBS-70 SAMs
	(800)	RBS-70	Port SAM	(1985)	(1985)	(400)	Version RBS-70+; total value incl Giraffe radars: SEK 700 m
					(1986)	(400)	
USA	34	F-16A	Fighter/strike	1981	1984	(15)	Total cost incl 6 trainers: $1.1 b; may be 28 fighters and 12 trainers
					1985	(15)	
					1986	(4)	
	12	Model 209 AH-1S	Hel	1982	(1986)	(12)	In addition to 12 ordered 1981
	88	M-109-A2 155mm	SPH	(1985)	(1986)	(22)	US LoO Sep 1985; total value: $78 m
	110	M-113-A2	APC	(1985)	(1986)	(30)	US LoO Sep 1985; total value: $25 m
	75	M-198 155mm	TH	1981	(1984)	(20)	
					(1985)	(25)	
					(1986)	(30)	
	4	AN/TPQ-37	Tracking radar	(1985)	(1986)	(2)	
	(2)	RGM-84A L	ShShM launcher	(1985)			Arming 1 Gearing Class destroyer
	500	AIM-9M	AAM	1985	1986	100	Arming F-16 fighters; total cost: $50 m; quick delivery of 100
	1 005	BGM-71A TOW	ATM	1981	1983	(200)	Arming Model-209 helicopters and M-901 AVs
					1984	(100)	
					1985	(240)	
					1986	(300)	
						(365)	
	2 030	BGM-71C I-TOW	ATM	1986			Total cost: $20 m
	16	RGM-84A Harpoon	ShShM	(1985)	(1986)	(16)	To arm 1 Gearing Class destroyer; also planned for other 5 ships of same type

Region code/ Recipient	Supplier	No. ordered	Weapon designation	Weapon description	Year of order	Year of delivery	No. delivered	Comments
14 Panama	Spain	7	C-212-200	Transport	(1987)			Negotiating
10 Papua New Guinea	Australia	4	ASI-315	PC	1985	(1987)	(4)	
15 Paraguay	Brazil	(10)	EMB-110	Transport	(1985)			
	Israel	..	IAI-201 Arava	Transport	(1985)			
15 Peru	Brazil	3	EMB-111	Mar patrol	(1986)			Unconfirmed
		20	EMB-312 Tucano	Trainer	(1986)			Unconfirmed
	Canada	8	DHC-6	Transport	1985	(1986)	(2)	Total cost: $21.1 m
	France	12	Mirage-2000	Fighter/strike	1982	1986	4	Order reduced from 26 for financial reasons; option on 2 more; armed with AM-39 Exocets
						(1987)	(8)	
		(24)	AM-39 Exocet	AShM	1982	(1985)	(2)	Ordered Dec 1982; arming Mirage-2000s
						(1986)	(12)	
						(1987)	(10)	
	Spain	(24)	BMR-600	ICV	(1986)			Unconfirmed
	USA	3	L-100-30	Transport	(1985)			Delivery delayed for financial reasons
		12	Model 214ST	Hel	1983	1985	6	
						1986	6	
		5	UH-60 Blackhawk	Hel	(1984)	(1983)	(25)	Status of deal uncertain
		(75)	M-113	APC	1980	(1985)	(25)	
						(1986)	(25)	
10 Philippines	Korea, South	3	PSMM-5 Type	FAC	1986			Old order possibly re-opened; arms: 2 MM-38 Exocet ShShMs and Bofors 57mm gun
	USA	2	S-70C	Hel	(1985)	(1986)	(2)	Unconfirmed
8 Qatar	France	4	Mirage F-1C	Fighter/interceptor	(1986)	1985	(50)	Total cost incl Roland SAMs: $243 m
	UK	..	Blowpipe	Port SAM	(1984)	1986	(50)	
13 Rwanda	France	1	Noratlas 2501	Transport	(1984)	1986	1	MAP
10 Samoa	Australia	1	ASI-315	PC	1985	(1987)	(1)	
8 Saudi Arabia	Brazil		Astros II SS-40	MRS	(1986)			Unconfirmed

Supplier	No.	Weapon designation	Weapon description	Year of order	Year(s) of deliveries	No. delivered	Comments
	24	AS-365F	Hel	1980	1983 1984 1985 (1986)	(6)(6)(6)(6)	20 armed with AS-15TT; some arming 4 F-2000 Class frigates
	(80)	AMX-30 Shahine	AAV(M)	1984	1986	(8)	Improved version developed with Saudi financial assistance
	600	ERC-90 Sagaie	AC	(1987)			Negotiating; deal incl modernization of French vehicles in Saudi arsenal
	4	Crotale Naval L	ShAM launcher	1980	1985 1986	(2)(2)	1x4 launchers on 4 F-2000 Class frigates
	8	Otomat-2 L	ShShM launcher	1980	1985	(4)	On F-2000 frigates
	..	Otomat-2 L	ShShM launcher	1984	(1986)	(4)	Coastal defence btys; 'Al Thakeb' deal
	(54)	Shahine-2 L	Mobile SAM system	1984	(1986)	(6)	'Al Thakeb' deal; launch canisters for defence of fixed installations; 134 launch systems of which rest are AMX-30s
	221	AS-15TT	AShM	1980	1983 1984 1985 1986	(55)(55)(55)(56)	Arming SA-365F helicopters
	104	Crotale Naval	ShAM	1980	1985 1986	(52)(52)	First export order of naval version; arming F-2000 Class frigates
	(96)	Otomat-2	ShShM	1980	1985 1986	(48)(48)	Arming 4 F-2000 Class frigates
	..	Otomat-2/Teseo	SShM	1984	(1986)	(24)	'Al Thakeb' deal; for coastal defence
	(1 000)	Shahine-2	Landmob SAM	1984	1986	(100)	Total value of 'Al Thakeb' deal: $4.1 b
	4	F-2000 Class	Frigate	1980	1985 1986	2 2	Part of 'Sawari' naval deal
Germany, FR	(60)	Wildcat	AAV	(1986)			Unconfirmed
Indonesia	40	CN-212	Transport	1979	(1983)(1984)(1985)(1986)	(2)(5)(8)(12)	
Japan	10	KV-107/2A	Hel	1982	1984 1985 (1986)	(4)(4)(2)	
Spain	4	CN-235	Transport	(1985)	(1986)	(4)	Order may be increased to 10
	140	BMR-600	ICV	1984	(1986)	(20)	Total cost: $62 m
Switzerland	30	PC-9	Trainer	1986	1986	(1)	UK workshare: 10%
UK	30	Hawk	Jet trainer/strike	1986	(1987)	(24)	
	2	Jetstream-31	Transport	1986	(1987)	(2)	

Region code/Recipient	Supplier	No. ordered	Weapon designation	Weapon description	Year of order	Year of delivery	No. delivered	Comments
		24	Tornado ADV	Fighter/MRCA	1986	1986	(2)	Remainder for delivery 1989-91
		48	Tornado IDS	Fighter/MRCA	1986	(1987)	(6)	Total value incl 72 Tornados, 30 Hawks, 30 PC-9s and missiles: approx $5.5 b
		..	SSR	Surveillance radar	(1984)	1986	(4)	
		..	ALARM	ARM	(1986)	(1987)	(8)	To arm Tornado fighters
		..	Sea Eagle	AShM	(1986)	(1985)	(10)	To arm Tornado fighters
		..	Sky Flash	AAM	(1986)	(1986)	(10)	To arm Tornado fighters
	USA	5	E-3A Sentry	AEW	1981			
		8	KC-135	Tanker/transport	1981	1986	(2)	Order increased from 6 to 8 in 1984; total cost: $2.4 b; for delivery 1986-88
						(1987)	(3)	
		12	UH-60 Blackhawk	Hel	(1986)	1986	(2)	
						(1987)	(3)	
		(505)	M-113-A2	APC	1983	(1984)	(100)	Also incl M-578s, M-992s, M-106s, M-577s and M-88/125s; total cost: $271 m
						(1985)	(200)	
						(1986)	(205)	
		(214)	M-88-A1	ARV	(1985)			Unconfirmed
		579	V-150 Commando	APC	(1980)	1982	(100)	For modernization of National Guard
						1983	(100)	
						1984	(100)	
						1985	(100)	
						1986	(79)	
		..	AN/TPS-32	3-D radar	(1985)			
		..	AN/TPS-43	3-D radar	1985			
		1 600	AGM-65D	ASM	(1984)	(1986)	(400)	Arming F-15s
		100	AGM-84A Harpoon	AShM	1986			To arm F-15s
		1 177	AIM-9L	AAM	1981	1982	(200)	Arming F-15s
						1983	(150)	
						1984	(200)	
						1985	(200)	
						1986	(200)	
		995	AIM-9L	AAM	1986			Number ordered also reported to be 495
		671	AIM-9P	AAM	1986			For delivery 1989-91
		2 538	BGM-71C I-TOW	ATM	1983			Total cost: $26 m
13 Senegal	France	1	EDIC/EDA Type	LC	1985	1986	1	EDIC-3 version
10 Singapore	France	22	AS-332	Hel	1984	1985	5	
						1986	(8)	

Recipient	Supplier	No.	Weapon designation	Weapon description	Year of order	Year of deliveries	No. produced/delivered	Comments
	Germany, FR	1	Type 62-001	Corvette	(1985)	1984	2	Prior to licensed production of 5
	Italy	30	S-211	Trainer	1983	1985	8	First 6 to be delivered directly; last 24 to be assembled in Singapore; total cost: approx $60 m
						1986	(12)	
						(1987)	(8)	
	USA	4	E-2C Hawkeye	AEW	1983	(1987)	(2)	Total cost: $601 m
		8	F-16A	Fighter/strike	1985			For delivery 1988; Singapore requested F-18s instead 1986
		24	M-167 Vulcan	Mobile AA system	(1984)	(1985)	(12)	Total cost: $30 m
		6	Phalanx	CIWS	(1986)	(1986)	(12)	For 6 Type 62-001 corvettes
		6	RGM-84A L	ShShM launcher	(1986)			For 6 Type 62-001 corvettes
		31	AGM-84A Harpoon	AShM	1985			To arm AS-332s; chosen over AM-39 Exocets
		(72)	RGM-84A Harpoon	ShShM	(1986)			For 6 Type 62-001 corvettes
10 Solomon Islands	Australia	1	ASI-315	PC	1985	(1987)	(1)	
13 Somalia	Italy	(6)	S-211	Trainer	(1985)			Unconfirmed
		(50)	M-47 Patton	MBT	(1985)	(1986)	(50)	In addition to 100 delivered earlier
	Spain	6	C-212-200	Transport	1984	(1985)	(3)	
						(1986)	(3)	
16 South Africa	Germany, FR	(2)	Bo-105CB	Hel	(1985)	1986	(2)	For Bophuthatswana AF
	Israel	2	B-707-320C	Transport	(1985)	1986	2	For use as tanker aircraft
		..	Gabriel L	ShShM launcher	1974	1983	2	Arming Reshef Class FACs
						1986	1	
		(162)	Gabriel-2	ShShM	1974	1983	(36)	Arming Reshef Class FACs
	Spain	(3)	C-212-200	Transport	(1986)	1986	(18)	For Bophuthatswana AF
9 Sri Lanka	China	(6)	Y-12	Transport	1986	1986	2	
						(1987)	(4)	
	Israel	8	Dvora Class	FAC	1986	(1987)	(8)	In addition to 6 delivered earlier
	Italy	(6)	SF-260TP	Trainer	1985	(1986)	(6)	Replacing losses
		2	SF-260TP	Trainer	(1986)	(1987)	(2)	
	Singapore	2	Type 33M	LC	1985	1986	2	200t mechanized-infantry landing craft; ordered from Vosper Aug 1985
	UK	..	HS-748-2	Transport	(1985)	(1985)	(1)	
						(1986)	(1)	
	USA	4	Model 212	Hel	1985	(1985)	(2)	For COIN duties; via Singapore
						(1986)	(2)	

Region code/ Recipient	Supplier	No. ordered	Weapon designation	Weapon description	Year of order	Year of delivery	No. delivered	Comments
	China	3	Model 212	Hel	(1986)	1986	3	
		4	Model 412	Hel	(1986)	1986	4	
		1	Super King Air	Transport	(1985)	1986	1	
13 Sudan	China	(4)	F-7	Fighter	(1986)			Unconfirmed
	Egypt	(44)	Walid	APC	(1986)	1986	(44)	MAP
		250	Swingfire	ATM	(1982)	(1985)	(100)	Part of $50 m aid package
	France	2	Alouette-3	Hel	(1985)	1986	2	
	Italy	6	AB-212	Hel	1984			Designation unconfirmed
	Oman	1	DHC-5D Buffalo	Transport	(1985)	1986	1	
	Spain	6	C-212-200	Transport	1984	(1985)	(2)	
						(1986)	(4)	
	UK	10	BAC-167	Trainer/COIN	(1983)	(1984)	3	Delivery halted for financial reasons
	USA	24	V-150 Commando	APC	(1986)			
	Yemen, North	1	F-27 Mk-400	Transport	(1985)	1986	1	
15 Suriname	Switzerland	2	PC-7	Trainer	(1985)	1986	2	Delivered Oct 1986
8 Syria	USSR	..	MiG-23M	Fighter/interceptor	1981	1982	(15)	Incl some MiG-23BNs (grd attack version)
						1983	(20)	
						1984	(20)	
						(1985)	(20)	
						(1986)	(20)	
		..	MiG-25 Foxhound	Fighter	(1984)	(1985)	(10)	Unconfirmed
						(1986)	(10)	
		..	MiG-27	Fighter/strike	(1980)	1982	(6)	
						1983	(6)	
						1984	(6)	
						1985	(6)	
						1986	(6)	
		(80)	MiG-29	Fighter	(1986)	(1987)	(15)	
		..	BMP-1	MICV	1981	1982	(200)	
						1983	(200)	
						1984	(200)	
						1985	(200)	
						1986	(200)	
		..	BTR-80	APC	(1984)	(1985)	(100)	Unconfirmed
						(1986)	(100)	

No.	Weapon designation	Weapon description	1981	1982	1983	1984	1985	1986	Comments
(500)	M-1974 122mm	SPH		(100)	(100)	(100)	(100)	(100)	Designation unconfirmed
(6)	SA-13 TELAR	AAV(M)	(1984)				(3)	(3)	
..	T-72	MBT	1980	(150)	(150)	(150)	(150)	(150)	
(250)	T-74	MBT	(1985)					(250)	Up to 250; unconfirmed
..	ZSU-23-4 Shilka	AAV	1981	(25)	(25)	(25)	(25)	(25)	
(10)	SA-11 SAMS	Mobile SAM system	(1985)					(10)	Unconfirmed
..	SA-8 SAMS	Mobile SAM system	(1982)	(8)	(8)	(8)	(8)	(8)	
..	SS-23 L	Mobile SSM system	(1986)						Unconfirmed
..	AA-6 Acrid	AAM	(1984)			(50)	(50)	(50)	Unconfirmed; arming MiG-25s
..	AA-7 Apex	AAM	(1984)			(50)	(50)	(50)	Unconfirmed; arming MiG-21s and MiG-23s
..	AA-8 Aphid	AAM	(1984)			(20)	(20)	(20)	Unconfirmed; arming MiG-21s andMiG-23s
..	AT-4 Spigot	ATM	(1980)	(50)	(100)	(100)	(100)	(100)	Captured by Israeli forces in Lebanon
..	AT-5 Spandrel	ATM	(1984)			(100)	(100)	(100)	Unconfirmed

Region code/ Recipient	Supplier	No. ordered	Weapon designation	Weapon description	Year of order	Year of delivery	No. delivered	Comments
		(30)	SA-11	Landmob SAM	(1985)	(1986)	(30)	Unconfirmed
		(432)	SA-13 Gopher	Landmob SAM	(1984)	(1985)	(216)	
						(1986)	(216)	
		..	SA-7 Grail	Port SAM	1978	(1982)	(25)	
						(1983)	(50)	
						(1984)	(50)	
						(1985)	(50)	
						(1986)	(50)	
		..	SA-8 Gecko	Landmob SAM	1982	(1982)	(64)	
						(1983)	(64)	
						(1984)	(64)	
						(1985)	(64)	
						(1986)	(64)	
		..	SA-9 Gaskin	Landmob SAM	1978	(1982)	(48)	
						(1983)	(48)	
						(1984)	(48)	
						(1985)	(48)	
						(1986)	(48)	
		(500)	SS-23	Landmob SSM	(1986)			Unconfirmed
		4	Nanuchka Class	Corvette	(1984)			Reportedly on order
		2	Romeo Class	Submarine	(1984)	1986	2	
		1	Sonya Class	MSC	(1985)	1986	1	
10 Taiwan	Indonesia	(15)	AS-332	Hel	(1986)			Negotiating
	Netherlands	2	Zwaardvis Class	Submarine	1981			
	USA	12	C-130H Hercules	Transport	1984	(1986)	(12)	Total cost: $325 m
		14	S-70C	Hel	1984	(1986)	(14)	Option on 10 more
		42	T-34C-1	Trainer	1984	(1985)	(21)	
						(1986)	(21)	
		357	M-113-A2	APC	1982	(1984)	(100)	140 APCs, 90 M-106-A2 and 72 M-125-A2 mortar carriers, 31 CPCs and 24 of the ambulance version
						(1985)	(100)	
						(1986)	(157)	
		(75)	M-60-A3	MBT	1984			For local assembly; hulls to be fitted with locally produced engines and equipment; some sources report 215 on order and 140 more on option
		33	M-88-A1	ARV	1983	(1985)	(16)	
						(1986)	(17)	

No.	Supplier	Quantity / Weapon designation	Weapon description	Year of order	Year(s) of deliveries	No. delivered	Comments
		(1) AN/TPQ-37	Tracking radar	1986	1986		
		(12) M54 Chaparral	Mobile SAM system	1983	(1985) (1986)	(5) (5)	For Army
		(8) M54 Chaparral	Mobile SAM system	(1985)	(1985) (1986)	(5) (5)	
		(10) RIM-66A L	ShAM launcher	(1983)	(1986) (1987)	(50) (50)	
		(100) AIM-7M Sparrow	AAM/SAM	1983	(1985) (1986)	(150) (150)	
		384 MIM-72F	SAM/ShAM	1983	(1985) (1986)		
		262 MIM-72F	SAM/ShAM	(1985)	(1985)	(85)	For Army; cost incl launchers: $94 m
		170 RIM-66A/SM-1	ShAM/ShShM	1983	(1986)	(85)	
10 Thailand	Germany, FR	(2) M-40 Type	MSC/PC	1984	(1986)	(1)	Option on 4-6 more; unit cost: $18 m; for delivery 1986-87
	Indonesia	1 M-40 Type	MSC/PC	1986	(1985)		In addition to 2 ordered 1984
		3 CN-212	Transport	1985	(1986)	(2) (1)	In addition to 5 in service (4 from Spain and 1 from Indonesia)
		(25) NBo-105	Hel	(1979)	(1983) (1984) (1985) (1986)	(2) (3) (5) (5)	
	Italy	(2) Aspide/Albatros	ShAM/ShShM launcher	1984	(1986)	(1)	Arming 2 Tattankesin Class corvettes ordered from USA
	Netherlands	(48) Aspide	AAM/SAM/ShAM	1984	(1986)	(24)	Arming 2 Tattankesin Class corvettes
		1 F-27 Maritime	Mar patrol	1985	1986	1	In addition to 3 in service
		2 F-27 Mk-400M	Transport	1986	(1986) (1987)	(1) (1)	In addition to 4 supplied earlier
	Singapore	20 T-33A	Jet trainer	(1985)	1986	20	
	USA	8 F-16A	Fighter/strike	1985			Number reduced from 16 for cost reasons; for delivery 1988-89; total cost incl 4 F-16Bs: $378 m
		4 F-16B	Fighter/trainer	1985	(1987)		
		10 Model 208	Lightplane	1985	(1987)	(5)	For Army
		4 Model 209 AH-1S	Hel	1986	1986	(5)	Armed with TOW ATMs; US LoO Jul 1986
		(5) Model 214ST	Hel	(1986)	1986	(5)	For Navy
		(24) Model 300C	Hel	(1986)	(1986)	24	
		148 M-113-A2	APC	1982	(1984) (1985) (1986)	(40) (40) (68)	Total cost incl 40 trucks: $33 m

Region code/Recipient	Supplier	No. ordered	Weapon designation	Weapon description	Year of order	Year of delivery	No. delivered	Comments
		..	AN/MPQ-4	Tracking radar	(1986)			
		2	AN/TPQ-37	Tracking radar	1985	(1986)	(1)	
		..	AN/TPS-70	Air defence radar	1985	(1987)	(2)	
		(1)	Phalanx	CIWS	(1984)			For refit of one Yarrow Type frigate; order unconfirmed
		(2)	RGM-84A L	ShShM launcher	1983	(1986)	(1)	Arming 2 Tattankesin Class corvettes on order from USA
		(24)	RGM-84A Harpoon	ShShM	1983	(1986)	(12)	Arming 2 Tattankesin Class corvettes
		2	Tattankesin Cl	Corvette	1983	(1986)	(1)	Ordered May 1983; for delivery 1986-87
13 Togo	France	1	Alouette-2	Hel	(1986)	1986	1	Refurbished
	USA	3	TB-30 Epsilon	Trainer	1984	1986	3	First export order
		2	Baron	Lightplane	(1985)	1986	2	
12 Tunisia	USA	57	M-198 155mm	TH	1986			Total cost incl 70 trucks, ammunition, spares and support equipment: $60 m
13 Uganda	Italy	6	AB-412 Griffon	Hel	1982	1985	(2)	Held in storage due to funding problems; at least 2 delivered late 1985
8 United Arab Emirates	France	18	Mirage-2000	Fighter/strike	1983	1985	1	For Abu Dhabi
						(1987)	(17)	
		(18)	Mirage-2000	Fighter/strike	1985			For delivery 1988-89
		(108)	Magic-2	AAM	(1985)	1985	(6)	To arm second batch of 18 Mirage-2000s
		(108)	R-550 Magic	AAM	1983	1986	(48)	Arming Mirage-2000s
						(1987)	(54)	
		(72)	Super-530	AAM	(1983)	1985	(4)	Arming Mirage-2000s
						1986	(32)	
						(1987)	(36)	
	Italy	(72)	Super-530	AAM	(1985)	1984	2	To arm second batch of 18 Mirage-2000s
		4	MB-339A	Jet trainer	(1984)	(1985)	(2)	For Dubai
	Switzerland	10	PC-7	Trainer	1984	(1986)	(8)	In addition to 14 delivered 1982
	UK	24	Hawk	Jet trainer/strike	1983	1984	(2)	Ordered Jan 1983; Mk 61
						1985	(12)	
						(1986)	(10)	
		2	Model 206B	Hel	(1985)	1986	2	For Sharjah

Recipient / Supplier	No.	Weapon designation	Weapon description	Year of order	Year(s) of delivery	No. delivered	Comments
10 Vanuatu							
Australia	1	Shorts 330-UTT	Transport	1985	1986	1	For Sharyah
	1	Skyvan-3M	Transport	(1985)	1986	1	For Sharyah
	(44)	FV-101 Scorpion	LT	(1983)	(1984)(1985)(1986)	(15)(15)(14)	Unconfirmed
15 Venezuela							
Australia	1	ASI-315	PC	1985	(1987)	(1)	
Brazil	30	EMB-312 Tucano	Trainer	(1985)	1986 (1987)	(12)(18)	Total cost: $50 m; option on 14 more
Korea, South	4	Tacoma Type	LS	1982	1984 1985	2 2	
Spain	4	C-212-200	Transport	(1984)	1985 1986	(1)(3)	For Navy
10 Viet Nam							
USSR	..	MiG-23	Fighter/interceptor	(1986)	(1986)	(12)	Unconfirmed; possibly confused with Soviet MiG-23s
	5	Turya Class	Hydrofoil FAC	(1983)	1984 1986	3 2	
8 Yemen, South							
USSR	(4)	An-26 Curl	Lightplane	(1984)	1984 1985 1986	(1)(2)(1)	
13 Zaire							
Italy	..	S-211	Trainer	(1985)			Unconfirmed
13 Zimbabwe							
China	(12)	F-6	Fighter	(1983)		(12)	Unconfirmed offer for 1 squadron; may be cancelled due to absorption problems
	(12)	F-7	Fighter	(1983)	(1987)	(12)	
	(35)	T-59	MBT	(1984)	(1985)(1986)	(20)(15)	Unconfirmed
Italy	10	AB-412 Griffon	Hel	1985	1986 (1987)	(5)(5)	

Appendix 7C. Register of licensed production of major conventional weapons in industrialized and Third World countries, 1986

This appendix lists licensed production of major weapons for which either the licence was bought, production was under way, or production was completed during 1986. Certain deals close to finalization by early 1987 are included with licence year (1987). Deliveries made before 1982 for the same sales agreement have been excluded for space reasons. The sources and methods for the data collection, and the conventions, abbreviations and acronyms used, are explained in appendix 7E. The entries are made alphabetically, by recipient, licenser and weapon designation.

Region code/ Country	Licenser	No. ordered	Weapon designation	Weapon description	Year of licence	Year of delivery	No. produced	Comments
I. Industrialized countries								
7 Australia	France	1	Durance Class	Support ship	1977	1986	1	Modified Durance design
	Switzerland	67	PC-9	Trainer	1985	(1987)	(2)	Selected as new basic trainer for RAAF; first 2 delivered directly; for delivery 1987-91
	UK	59	Hamel 105mm	TG	(1982)	1985	(2)	To be produced 1985-89
						1986	(20)	
	USA	73	F/A-18 Hornet	Fighter	1981	1985	3	In addition to 2 delivered directly; total cost: A $3396 m; incl 17 TF/A-18 trainers
						(1986)	(15)	
		2	FFG-7 Class	Frigate	1983			For completion 1991-93
4 Belgium	USA	44	F-16A	Fighter/strike	1983	1982	(50)	In addition to 116 F-16A/Bs in service; offset share: 80%; for delivery 1988-89
						1983	(80)	
						1984	(80)	
						1985	(80)	
						1986	(80)	
		514	AIFV	MICV	1979	1982	(50)	Total number ordered: 1189 incl 525 M-113s; unit cost: $100 000; for production 1982-88
						1983	(80)	
						1984	(80)	
						1985	(80)	
						1986	(80)	
		525	M-113-A2	APC	1979	1982	(50)	For production 1982-88
						1983	(80)	
						1984	(80)	
						1985	(80)	
						1986	(80)	

Recipient	Supplier	No. ordered	Weapon designation	Weapon description	Year of order	Year(s) of deliveries	No. delivered	Comments
5 Bulgaria	USSR	..	MT-LB	APC	(1980)	(1982) (1983) (1984) (1985) (1986)	(10) (20) (20) (20) (20)	Also produced with BMP-2 turret
3 China	France	(25)	AS-365N	Hel	1980	1984 1985 1986 (1987)	10 (4) (4) (4)	Ordered Jul 1980; initial batch of 50, of which about half for military use; may carry HOT ATMs
		..	Super Frelon	Hel	(1981)	(1985)	(2)	Prototypes flying Dec 1985; possibly reverse-engineered Super Frelons
5 Czechoslovakia	USSR	(1 900)	T-72	MBT	1978	(1982) (1983) (1984) (1985) (1986)	(50) (100) (100) (100) (100)	
4 France	USA	..	FTB-337	Trainer	1969	1982 1983 (1984) (1985)	(5) (5) (5) (5)	Designation: FTB-337 Milirole; exported to Africa
4 Germany, FR	USA	..	AIM-9L	AAM	1977	1982 1983 1984 1985 1986 (1987)	(1 600) (2 500) (2 400) (2 386) (2 405) (1 865)	For delivery 1981-89; NATO co-production programme; 7277 produced by end-1984
		10 000	NATO Stinger	Port SAM	1983			Dornier/Diehl (FRG) main contractor for FRG, Belgium, Greece, Italy, Netherlands, Turkey; production to begin 1987
		(10 000)	RAM	ShAM/PDM	1985			MoU signed between USA, FRG and Denmark; 4 West German companies to provide second-source production
4 Italy	France	23 000	Milan	ATM	1980	1985 1986	920 1 270	Actual contract signed 1984
		..	Roland-2	Landmob SAM	(1986)			OTO-Melara negotiating with Euromissile for licensed production

Region code/ Country	No. ordered	Weapon designation	Weapon description	Year of licence	Year of delivery	No. produced	Comments
USA	..	AB-205	Hel	(1963)	1982	(60)	
					1983	(60)	
					1984	(30)	
					1985	(30)	
					1986	(30)	
	..	AB-206B	Hel	1972	1982	(50)	Jetranger-3 version available from 1984
					1983	(50)	
					1984	(50)	
					1985	(50)	
					1986	(50)	
	..	AB-212	Hel	1970	1982	(10)	In production since 1971
					1983	(10)	
					1984	(10)	
					1985	(10)	
					1986	(10)	
	..	AB-212ASW	Hel	1975	1982	(20)	
					1983	(25)	
					1984	(25)	
					1985	(20)	
					1986	(20)	
	..	AB-412 Griffon	Hel	1980	1983	(3)	Military version of Bell Model 412; Italy holds marketing rights
					1984	(5)	
					1985	(10)	
					1986	(10)	
	(170)	CH-47C Chinook	Hel	1968	1982	(12)	Licensed production began 1970
					1983	(12)	
					1984	(12)	
					1985	(12)	
					1986	(12)	
	..	S-61R	Hel	1972	1982	(3)	In production since 1974
					1983	(3)	
					1984	(3)	
					1985	(3)	
					1986	(3)	
	..	SH-3D Sea King	Hel	1965	1982	(2)	In production since 1969
					1983	(2)	
					1984	(2)	
					1985	(3)	
					1986	(3)	

Unshaded whether joint NATO-European or only Italian production for NATO Europe

(15 000) AGM-65D   ASM   (1985)

	No.	Weapon designation	Weapon description	Year	Year(s) of deliveries	No.	Comments
7 Japan							
USA	47	CH-47D Chinook	Hel	(1984)	(1987)	(4)	For Army and AF
	88	F-15J Eagle	Fighter/interceptor	1978	1982 1983 1984 1985 1986	(10) (13) (17) (14) (12)	In addition to 12 delivered directly from USA; total order of 100 incl 12 trainers
	55	F-15J Eagle	Fighter/interceptor	1985	(1986)	(2)	MoU signed Dec 1984; in addition to 100 on order; for delivery 1986-90
	..	KV-107/2A	Hel	(1982)	1984 1985	(3) (5)	In addition to 61 produced earlier; improved version
	..	Model 205 UH-1H	Hel	1972	1982 1983 1984 1985 1986	(4) (6) (6) (4) 4	
	54	Model 209 AH-1S	Hel	1982	1984 1985 1986	(6) (8) 8	
	..	OH-6D	Hel	1977	1982 1983 1984 1985 1986	(8) (4) (9) (7) 12	Identical to Hughes Model 500D
	42	P-3C Orion	Mar patrol/ASW	1978	1982 1983 1984 1985 1986	(5) (7) (8) (10) 10	
	30	P-3C Orion	Mar patrol/ASW	1985	(1987) (1986)	(2) (2)	MoU signed Oct 1985; in addition to 45 previously ordered
	90	S-61B	Hel	1965	1982 1983 1984 1985 1986	(4) (4) (1) (1) (1)	
	51	SH-3B	Hel	1979	1982 1983 1984 1985 1986	(8) (5) (7) (10) 13	

Region code/Country	Licenser	No. ordered	Weapon designation	Weapon description	Year of licence	Year of delivery	No. produced	Comments
		(72)	M-110-A2 203mm	SPH	(1981)	1983	(6)	
						1984	(12)	
						1985	(12)	
						1986	(12)	
		1 350	AIM-7F Sparrow	AAM	(1979)	1982	(200)	Arming F-15s
						1983	(250)	
						1984	(250)	
						1985	(150)	
						1986	(150)	
		..	AIM-9L	AAM	(1982)	1983	(146)	
						1984	(500)	
						1985	690	
						1986	740	
		..	BGM-71C I-TOW	ATM	(1983)	1985	40	Total requirement: up to 10 000
						1986	(236)	
		..	MIM-104 Patriot	Landmob SAM	1984	(1987)	(440)	For delivery 1985-91; 130 launchers (10 for training); 24 Patriot launch units; to be produced under licence after delivery of initial batch from USA; total cost: $2800 m
						(1985)	(40)	
						(1986)	(80)	
		..	MIM-23B Hawk	Landmob SAM	1978	1982	(280)	
						1983	(260)	
						1984	(260)	
						1985	(260)	
						1986	260	
		..	Seasparrow	ShAM	1980	(1982)	(18)	Arming various Japanese-built frigates and destroyers
						(1983)	(18)	
						(1984)	(36)	
						(1985)	(10)	
						(1986)	(18)	
4 Netherlands	USA	18	F-16A	Fighter/strike	1982	(1985)	(6)	For delivery 1985-87
						(1986)	(6)	
		57	F-16A	Fighter/strike	1983			For delivery 1987-92
		840	AIFV	MICV	1981	(1983)	(200)	In addition to 880 in service; 173 will be M-901 TOW version; Dutch designation: YPR-765
						(1984)	(200)	
						(1985)	(200)	
						(1986)	(200)	

						Year(s)	No.	
4 Norway	USA	18	LASR	Tracking radar	1984			Selected for Norwegian Adapted Hawk System
5 Poland	USSR	..	An-28	Transport	1978	1984 (1985) (1986)	4 (10) (10)	Series production transferred from the USSR to Poland in 1978; first flight of Polish-built aircraft in 1984
		..	Mi-2 Hoplite	Hel	(1956)	1982 1983 1984 1985 1986	(200) (200) (200) (200) (200)	In production since 1957; 3000 built by end-1979
		(1 900)	T-72	MBT	(1978)	(1982) (1983) (1984) (1985) (1986)	(50) (100) (100) (100) (100)	
5 Romania	France	..	SA-316B	Hel	1971	1982 1983 1984 1985 1986	(20) (20) (20) (20) (20)	Initial order of 180; more than 185 produced by Spring 1985
		..	SA-330 Puma	Hel	1977	1982 1983 1984 1985 1986	(15) (15) (15) (15) (15)	Initial order of 100; 112 delivered by Spring 1985
	UK	20	BAC-111	Transport	1979	1982 1983 1984 1985 (1986)	(3) (3) (3) (3) (2)	Total cost: $410 m plus $205 m for licensed production of Rolls-Royce Spey engine; 20 aircraft for Romanian AF
	USSR	..	Yak-52	Trainer	(1979)	1982 1983 (1984) (1985) (1986)	(150) (150) (150) (150) (150)	Two-seat piston-engined primary trainer; 500th delivered in 1983; production started in 1979
		..	T-72	MBT	(1984)			Reportedly to be built with French engine; unconfirmed

Region code/ Country	Licenser	No. ordered	Weapon designation	Weapon description	Year of licence	Year of delivery	No. produced	Comments
4 Spain	France	18	AMX-30R	AAV(M)	1984	1986 (1987)	(6) (6)	
		4	S-70 Class	Submarine	1975	1983 1985 1986	2 1 1	
	USA	3	FFG-7 Class	Frigate	1977	1986 (1987)	1 (2)	
		1	FFG-7 Class	Frigate	1985			In addition to 3 now under construction
6 Switzerland	Germany, FR	345	Leopard-2	MBT	1983	(1987)	(2)	Total cost incl 35 delivered directly: $1400 m; final deliveries due 1993
4 Turkey	Germany, FR	2	Meko-200 Type	Frigate	1983		(2)	In addition to 2 built in FR Germany; will probably be armed with 2x4 Harpoon ShShMs and Aspide ShAMs using 1x8 Seasparrow launcher
		13	SAR-33	PC	1976	1982 1983 1984 1985 (1986)	(2) (2) (2) (2) (2)	Prototype delivered from FR Germany 1977 for trials; 13 built in Turkey; for Coast Guard; can carry ShShMs
		(9)	Type 209/1	Submarine	1974	1985	1	Built under licence in addition to 3 delivered from FR Germany; planned production rate: 1 ship/year
	Italy	(50)	G-222	Transport	(1984)			To commence as assembly from kits and then progress to complete indigenous production; partly financed by US MAP; may be cancelled in favour of Spanish CN-235s
4 UK	Brazil	130	EMB-312 Tucano	Trainer	1985	1986 (1987)	(4) (22)	Total cost: $145-150 m; powered by Garrett TPE-12B turboprop engine; for delivery 1986-91; option on further 17
	France	..	Milan	ATM	1976	1982 1983 1984 1985 1986 (1987)	(6 000) (10 000) (10 000) (7 500) (7 105) (2 865)	UK requirement: 50 000; also produced for export as Euromissile production is phased out

	No.	Weapon designation	Weapon description	Year of order	Year(s) of deliveries	No.	Comments
1 USA							
USA	..	BGM-71A TOW	ATM	1980	1982 / 1983 / 1984 / 1985 / 1986 / (1987)	(400) / (1 500) / (3 500) / (3 600) / (3 705) / (3 900)	
Israel	..	EL/2106	Point defence radar	(1983)			
UK	302	T-45 Hawk	Jet trainer/strike	1981			First deliveries expected 1989; total cost incl simulators and training: $3200 m
6 Yugoslavia							
France	..	SA-342 Gazelle	Hel	1971	1982 / 1983 / 1984 / 1985 / 1986	(10) / (10) / (10) / (10) / (10)	SA-341/342 Gazelles produced since 1973
USSR	..	T-72	MBT	(1977)	(1984) / (1985) / (1986)	(30) / (30) / (30)	Upgraded T-72 with Yugoslavian-designed laser aiming device

II. Third World countries

	No.	Weapon designation	Weapon description	Year of order	Year(s) of deliveries	No.	Comments
12 Algeria							
Bulgaria	..	Kebir Type	Corvette	1983			Unconfirmed whether licensed production, assembly or sale
UK	4	Kebir Class	PC	1981	1985	(3)	In addition to 2 delivered from UK; 3 more on order
	3	Kebir Class	PC	1985	1986	1	For delivery by 1987
15 Argentina							
Germany, FR	(300)	TAM	MT	1976	(1982) / (1983) / (1984) / (1985) / (1986)	(55) / (55) / (40) / (40) / (40)	220 for Argentina plus for export; developed by Thyssen (FRG); orders from Panama and Peru cancelled; Jordan order of 60 in 1986
	6	Meko-140 Type	Frigate	1980	1985	2	Armed with MM-40 Exocet ShShMs; last 2 possibly for export
USA	4	Type TR-1700	Submarine	1977	(1982)	(10)	In addition to 2 delivered directly
	120	Model 500D	Hel	1972	(1984) / (1985) / (1986)	(5) / (5) / (5)	Assembly of knocked-down components

Region code/Country	Licenser	No. ordered	Weapon designation	Weapon description	Year of licence	Year of delivery	No. produced	Comments
15 Brazil	Austria	..	GHN-45 155mm	TH/TG	(1985)			Unconfirmed
	France	6	HB-350M Esquilo	Hel	(1985)			Requirement for 40 more
	Germany, FR	1	Type 209/3	Submarine	1982			Hull and some components to be built in Brazil; in addition to 1 delivered directly; production of 3 more planned
	UK	1	Niteroi Class	Frigate	1981	1986	1	Ordered Jun 1981; training ship; completion delayed
15 Chile	Spain	(20)	T-36 Halcon	Jet trainer	1984	1986	2	In addition to 16 delivered 1982-83; at least 1 armed with Sea Eagle AShMs
						(1987)	(6)	
	Switzerland	(150)	Piranha	APC	1980	1982	(20)	
						1983	(20)	
						1984	(20)	
						1985	(20)	
						(1986)	(20)	
	USA	(120)	T-35 Pillan	Trainer	1980	(1985)	(10)	Developed from Piper PA-28 by US and Chilean engineers; 80 for Chile, 40 for Spain
						(1986)	(20)	
8 Egypt	Brazil	110	EMB-312 Tucano	Trainer	1983	1985	(12)	30 for Egypt, 80 for Iraq
						(1986)	(48)	
	France	..	AS-332	Hel	1983			Ordered Dec 1983; mainly assembly
		15	Alpha Jet	Jet trainer/strike	1985			
		36	SA-342L Gazelle	Hel	1981	1983	(1)	
						1984	(15)	
						1985	(15)	
						(1986)	(5)	
	UK	..	SA-342L Gazelle	Hel	(1986)			Negotiating continued production
		(5 000)	Swingfire	ATM	1977	1982	(500)	3320 produced by end-1985
						1983	(500)	
						1984	(500)	
						1985	(500)	
						1986	1 127	
						(1987)	(1 136)	
9 India	France	..	SA-316B Chetak	Hel	(1962)	1982	(20)	Also for civilian use; some production of parts for French AS-316s
						1983	(20)	
						1984	(20)	

Supplier	No. Weapon designation	Weapon type	Year of order	Year(s) of deliveries	No. delivered	Comments
Germany, FR	(10 000) Milan	ATM	1982	1985 1986 (1987)	(1 272) (4 060) (3)	First missile completed early 1985
	(150) Do-228	Transport	1982			For civil and military use; production for AF, Navy and Coast Guard began 1986; deliveries from 1987
	2 Type 1500	Submarine	1981			In addition to 2 directly delivered; first delivery due 1988
UK	2 Type 1500	Submarine	(1987)			Option from 1981
	45 Jaguar	Fighter	1978	1982 1983 1984 1985 (1986) (1987)	(1) (4) (5) (10) (18) (7)	Local production of components; in addition to 40 purchased directly
	31 Jaguar	Fighter	1982			Local production of components; plans for complete local manufacture abandoned
USSR	(220) MiG-21bis	Fighter	1976	(1982) (1983) (1984) (1985) (1986) (1987)	(30) (30) (30) (30) (20) (10)	
	(185) MiG-27	Fighter/grd attack	1983	1984 1985 1986	(2) (10) (20)	Agreement signed July 1983; first flight Nov 1984
	.. BMP-1	APC/ICV	1983			
	(1 000) T-72	MBT	(1980)			Prototype ready Mar 1984; for entry into service 1987; production initially 10% indigenous; Indian designation: T-72M; possibly similar to Soviet T-74
	(2 200) AA-2 Atoll	AAM	(1963)	1982 1983 1984 1985 1986 (1987)	(140) (140) (140) (140) (60) (35)	Arming MiG fighters
	.. AA-8 Aphid	AAM	(1986)			Unconfirmed
10 Indonesia France	(56) AS-332	Hel	(1982)	1985 1986	2 2	Production switched from Puma to Super Puma 1983; total orders by end-1984: 69; military orders: 56

Region code/ Country	Licenser	No. ordered	Weapon designation	Weapon description	Year of licence	Year of delivery	No. produced	Comments
	Germany, FR	(100)	BK-117	Hel	1982	1984	2	Total production schedule: 100; 2 pre-production aircraft delivered 1984
		(50)	NBo-105	Hel	1976	1982 1983 1984 1985 1986	(5) (5) (5) (5) (5)	Military order for approx 50 helicopters
	Spain	6	PB-57 Type	PC	1982	(1985)	(1)	Probably 4 for Coast Guard
		(80)	CN-212	Transport	1976	1982 1983 1984 1985 1986	(3) (2) (2) (2) (2)	For civil and military use; 18 delivered to armed forces by early 1986
	USA	(28)	Model 412	Hel	1982	1986	1	More than 100 to be assembled from 1985; military orders by 1986: 28
8 Israel	USA	..	Westwind 1124	Transport	1968	1982 1983 1984 1985 1986	(2) (2) (2) (2) (2)	Production transferred to Israel 1968
10 Korea, South	USA	(68)	F-5E Tiger-2	Fighter	1979	1982 1983 1984 1985 1986	(3) (12) (18) (18) (17)	Incl 36 F-5Es and 32 F-5Fs; local assembly of aircraft, incl engines
		..	Model 205 UH-1H	Hel	(1987)			Negotiating
		(139)	Model 500MD	Hel	1976	1982 1983 1984 1985 1986	(15) (15) (15) (15) (15)	
		..	M-101-A1 105mm	TH	(1971)	(1982) (1983) (1984) (1985) (1986)	(10) (10) (10) (10) (10)	Possibly without US consent

No.	Recipient	Supplier	Number	Weapon designation	Weapon description	Year of order	Year(s) of deliveries (Nos.)	Comments
			.. ..	M-109-A2 155mm M-114-A1	SPH TH	1983 (1971)	(1982) (10) (1983) (10) (1984) (10) (1985) (10) (1986) (10)	Possibly without US consent
			..	PSMM-5 Type	FAC	(1974)		4 for S. Korea; rest for Indonesia and the Philippines
10	Malaysia	Korea, South	1	Mash Class	OPV	(1983)	1986 (1)	In addition to 1 delivered directly
14	Mexico	UK	5	Azteca Class	PC	1983		In addition to 31 in service
13	Nigeria	Austria	(200)	Steyr-4K 7FA	APC	(1981)		Various versions to be built; possibly also Cuirassier LT/TD; status uncertain due to financial problems
9	Pakistan	Sweden	(180)	Supporter	Trainer	1974	1982 (5) 1983 (5) 1984 (10) 1985 (15) (1986) (15)	Assembly of 90 from imported kits began 1976; from 1982 with local raw materials; production transferred to Kamra 1981
10	Philippines	Germany, FR	..	Bo-105C	Hel	1974	1982 (1) 1983 (1) 1984 (1) 1985 (1) (1986) (1)	Approx 15 in service incl 5 from FRG
		UK	(100)	BN-2A Islander	Lightplane	1974	1982 (10) (1983) (10) (1984) (10) (1985) (10) (1986) (10)	
10	Singapore	Germany, FR	3 5	PB-57 Type Type 62-001	PC/FAC Corvette	1980 (1985)		Luerssen design; status unclear Mini-corvettes of Luerssen design
16	South Africa	Israel	..	Reshef Class	FAC	1974	1983 (2) 1986 (1)	In addition to 3 previously acquired; armed with 6 Scorpioen ShShMs derived from Israeli Gabriel ShShM

Region code/ Country	Licenser	No. ordered	Weapon designation	Weapon description	Year of licence	Year of delivery	No. produced	Comments
10 Taiwan	Israel	..	Gabriel L	ShShM/SShM launcher	(1978)	1982 1983 (1984) (1985)	(8) (8) (8) (8)	Taiwanese designation: Hsiung Feng; no deliveries in 1986 but production line reportedly still open
	Israel	..	Gabriel-2	ShShM/SShM	(1978)	1982 1983 1984 1985	(75) (75) (50) (50)	
	Singapore	(8)	Suikiang Class	FAC	(1983)			To be armed with 2 Hsiung Feng ShShMs; up to 22 considered
	USA	30	F-5E Tiger-2	Fighter	1982	1983 1984 1985 1986	(6) (6) (6) (6)	Total cost incl 30 F-5Fs: $620 m; for delivery 1983-87
	USA	30	F-5F Tiger-2	Jet trainer	1982	1983 1984 1985 1986	(6) (6) (6) (6)	
10 Thailand	France	1	PS-700 Class	LS	1984	(1987)	(1)	To be built by Ital Thai Ltd; due for delivery 1987
	Germany, FR	1	PS-700 Class	LS	(1985)	1985	(1)	In addition to 1 ordered in 1984
		45	Fantrainer	Trainer	1983	1986	(3)	After 2 from FRG; local assembly and some component manufacture; first delivery mid-1985

Appendix 7D. The SIPRI price system

I. Introduction

The aggregation of disparate data requires a common unit of measurement. Only one such unit is available for weapon systems—monetary value. Despite many efforts there is no measure of military-use value as such.[1]

The purpose of SIPRI's valuation method for the arms trade is to measure changes in the total flow of weapons and its geographical pattern. In order to do this, the prices used by SIPRI cannot always be equal to the prices actually paid, since these vary considerably from case to case (see also appendix 7E, section III). The price of an F-16 fighter aircraft, for example, varied in the mid-1980s from zero (when supplied as military aid to Egypt), to $9.7 million (US Navy fly-away cost for a simplified version), to $15 million (US Air Force fly-away cost), to $21 million (US Air Force average unit programme acquisition cost) to $35 million (average unit cost for the Singaporean Air Force, including spares and support).[2]

Matters are further complicated by inflation, currency conversion problems, training costs and the wide range of weapon types available. How, for example, can a reasonable price relation be established between a US nuclear-powered aircraft-carrier and a Chilean armoured personnel carrier?

SIPRI has designed its own price system for the valuation of the flow of major conventional weapons. This price system was first introduced in 1968 and has since undergone a major revision. The purpose of this appendix is to describe this revision.

II. SIPRI rules

One assumption and one convention constitute the core of the SIPRI price system. The assumption is that there is a competitive global market for armaments and that—over a wide range of arms deals—actual prices paid approximate to the military-use value of the weapons. The convention is that among the various prices of a weapon system—including or excluding R&D outlays, support, spares and so on—the unit production cost is chosen. To the cost of producing one unit as part of a long production run is then added a percentage to represent the average cost of armaments (unless separately priced), spares, support and so on.

There are problems both with the assumption and the convention. There is in many areas and sectors no competitive arms market. Often the distinction between unit production cost and other cost levels is impossible to make. These two basic rules are only guidelines.

III. The former system

The 1968 prices

The original price system was constructed from a long list of comparable prices in 1968 US dollars.[3] These prices were then grouped into four weapon categories and 27 sub-categories. Within each sub-category, the prices obtained were compared with such performance criteria as weight, speed and role of the weapon. A price reflecting these criteria was set, both for weapons for which prices were available and for those weapons for which no price data existed. A percentage was added to reflect costs for spare parts, and so on. This percentage varied from one weapon category to another. Ships were valued differently: for each sub-category a 1968 US dollar price per ton was estimated. In addition, a technical improvement factor of 3.5 per cent per year was assumed. Each new ship traded thus received an individual price depending on sub-category, displacement and year of transfer. Second-hand and refurbished ships were treated separately. An exponential depreciation was assumed, with different time lengths for different sub-categories. For the other weapon categories, blanket percentage assumptions were used in determining prices for second-hand and refurbished weapons.

Later additions

Prices for weapon systems introduced into SIPRI's arms trade data collection after 1968 were estimated in the same way as for the original price systems. Existing prices were continuously updated as new data became known. In order to get more recent base years, the total price system was updated by applying a weighted average of British, French and US wholesale price indexes, first to 1973 and then to 1975.

With the computerization of the data base, the special valuation of ships was changed. Ships were grouped into individual ship classes and these classes received new, second-hand and refurbished prices. These prices were calculated using the 1968 prices per ton, multiplied by the appropriate technical improvement factor.

IV. Price system revision

The main reason why a revision was necessary was the constantly changing relations between prices, often caused by changes in the mix of inputs of labour, capital and pre-products. New production technologies also affect input mixes and prices. Another very important factor is the embodiment of new technologies and materials, particularly for weapon systems.

Additional reasons for the price system revision were the introduction of a new weapon category (see appendix 7E) and a wish to use the same valuation for all weapon categories.

Some early decisions had to be made concerning the collection and systematization of the data. A first decision concerned currency conversion and deflation; another concerned the choice of estimation method.

Currency conversion

The prices for weapon systems quoted in government papers, journals and so on, are normally expressed in current prices and national currencies. They have to be converted into a common currency and deflated to an appropriate base year.

The rule used for currency conversion follows from the basic assumption mentioned above. The conversion is made for the year to which the quoted price refers. The US dollar was chosen as the standard currency—it is the most frequently used currency in arms sales. The ordinary exchange-rate (average market rate) is used.

The choice of the US dollar has another advantage. It allows for the use of special military price deflators for the different SIPRI weapon categories. Such deflators are only available for a few countries, but they are to be preferred to other price deflators such as consumer price index or GNP deflators.[4]

Deflation

The variation in price over time of a unit such as one ton of a weapon system (or a succession of weapon systems performing similar tasks) can be attributed to three components of change: (a) changes in the input mix, (b) changes in the production process and (c) changes in the military-use value of the product.

The first component concerns changes in the prices of raw materials, pre-products and labour as well as changing profit margins and interest rates. To the extent that the input mix in the production of weapon systems is different from the inputs used to calculate other available deflators, military price deflators will vary. This difference varies from one weapon category to another—and within weapon categories—with the use of specialized labour, special materials and costly pre-products, such as advanced electronics.

The second component that changes over time—the production process—tends in most cases to lower prices. The introduction of better tools and machinery and the growing experience of workers all make production progressively more efficient and thus less expensive. Another element influencing the production cost is the number of items produced in a given time period. Differences in the price of a weapon system owing to varying lengths of production runs can be quite substantial.[5] Since the number of items produced varies from year to year, the influence of this factor on a deflator is erratic and not representative of changes in production costs. Its effects should therefore be eliminated to the largest possible extent in the construction of a deflator.

The US military price deflators are designed to capture these two types of effect, thus eliminating them from the measurement of real price changes of weapon systems.

The third influence on prices remains outside the deflator, since it reflects real changes in the product. The extent to which the US authorities are able to distinguish between the various components of price change is a matter of debate. However, the military price deflators are not very different from the broader ones mentioned, and they are much lower than the increases of prices quoted for individual weapon systems.[6] This third factor was called the technical improvement factor in the 1968 SIPRI price system. Deflating quoted prices with the US military price deflator implies the assumption that price increases to a considerable extent result from qualitative improvements.

Parametric costing

A second decision referred to the extent to which the revision of the price system should be based on the use of statistical estimation techniques. In the 1960s, the use of mathematical equations for estimating the cost of weapon systems became widespread in the US Department of Defense. There were two main reasons: the availability of computers and the general trend to introduce more systematic judgement in procurement decisions. The main use of the various models, developed by the RAND Corporation and other 'braintrust' contractors, was in the projection of costs of future weapons. With the help of these models, unknown future costs could be estimated and, for example, used to judge tenders by prospective contractors.[7] Such models are probably also in wide use in order to estimate prices of weapon systems in the Soviet Union and in other countries.

In most models, physical parameters of weapon systems—such as weight, speed and thrust of engines or the extent of high-cost materials embodied—are used as independent variables in a regression analysis, with the known price as a dependent variable. The resulting coefficients for the various parameters can then be multiplied by the physical parameters of a weapon system for which the price is unknown.

Regression equations using only the two parameters weight and speed have been found to give a good fit for weapon systems such as fighter aircraft. The introduction of more complex equations has not added to the confidence in the price estimates.

Parametric costing is a very mechanistic pricing method. The more that is known about a weapon system—its characteristics, uses and the prices involved—the less relevant parametric costing becomes. It can therefore only be used as a guideline: it cannot substitute for examination of the specific weapon system. For the purpose of SIPRI's price system revision, it was decided to estimate equations, but to use them prudently, that is, only as a basis for further judgement of individual weapon prices.

Intra- and inter-generational price changes

It is widely believed that there is a distinct difference between the technical improvement during the life-cycle of a weapon system and the embodiment of technological improvements in new generations of weapon systems. While in the second case there is ample evidence of large improvement and thus real price increases, in the first case opinions are divided as to the level of improvement that takes place.[8]

With the SIPRI price system there is no problem in identifying improvements in successive generations since each weapon system becomes a separate entry in the register and, thus, gets its own price. Questions arise with respect to incorporations of new technology during the life-cycle of a weapon system. The SIPRI rule is a compromise: on the one hand, no technical improvement is automatically assumed for a weapon system within its life-cycle: on the other hand, whenever actual improvements do take place, a new version—or model—of the weapon system is introduced into the register. Each version has a different price. Substantial improvements can result from design changes, incorporation of different sub-systems or improved component performance. Often, such improvements are reflected in slightly different weapon designations given by the producer of the weapon system. There are, however, many borderline cases. Sometimes, differing designations do not reflect different capabilities and substantial improvements are sometimes made without any change in the weapon designation.

Procedures

As a first step, prices were collected from a large number of open sources over a period of more than two years. These were converted into dollars and deflated as described above. After examination and elimination of several prices for the same weapon system, newly-collected prices were available for approximately 550 weapon systems. These were then compared to the prices for the same weapons from the upated 1968 price system. After further detailed examination a final price for these weapons was determined.

Next, a regression analysis was performed. The weapon categories were divided into two groups of sub-categories (with a total of 16 and 90 weapon types, respectively) reflecting physical capabilities. Average prices were estimated for these weapon types on the basis of weight and first production year. Separate estimates were made for the 5 weapon categories and the two groups of sub-categories. In the end, average prices per unit of weight were taken from the sample with 90 weapon types. The technical improvement factor was taken from the most detailed categorization yielding significant results (see table 7D.1).

Table 7D.1. Percentage product improvement rates calculated from the SIPRI arms production data base (rounded to nearest 0.5 per cent)

5 weapon categories		16 weapon types		90 weapon types[a]	
Aircraft	3.0	Fighter aircraft	3.5	Fighters	4.5
		Helicopters	5.5	Fighters/	
		Patrol aircraft	3.0	interceptors	6.5
		Utility aircraft	4.5	Jet trainers	5.5
				Helicopters	5.5
				Trainers	2.5
				Transports	5.0
Armour and artillery	3.5	Light vehicles	1.5	APCs	0.5
		Artillery	5.0	MBTs	3.5
		Special vehicles	6.5		
		Tanks	4.0		
Guidance and radar systems	4.0	Ground radar, etc.	4.0		
Missiles	5.5	Anti-air	4.5	AAMs	5.5
		Anti-surface	3.5	Landmob SAMs	6.0
		Anti-ship	7.0		
		Anti-tank	10.0		
Ships	3.0	Major ships	3.5	Destroyers	2.0
		Small combatants	2.0	Fast attack craft	3.0
		Support ships	0.0		

[a] Only statistically significant results are given.

Source: SIPRI data base.

Prices were then estimated for those weapons that had not been included in the regression analysis. These estimates were compared with the price in the updated 1968 system. The final price was settled, after case by case examination considering technical characteristics, military use value, market response and so on. A complete set of new prices was sent to reviewers at the Swedish Defence Material Administration (FMV). Their comments are fully integrated in the new price system.

Mark-up for weapons, spares and initial support

Information was gathered on the cost of actual arms deals including goods and services in addition to the weapon system. The range of these additional costs is a wide one, ranging from less than 1 per cent and up to more than 100 per cent. An average mark-up of 25 per cent was decided upon.

Second-hand and refurbished weapons

The SIPRI data base has separate prices for second-hand and refurbished weapons. Again, the data collected showed a wide range of prices. It is doubtful whether the introduction of a depreciation procedure would improve the estimate of second-hand prices; in the case of refurbished weapons this is highly unlikely. Depreciation is highly dependent on the assumption made about depreciation rates and the form of depreciation (see table 7D.2). Not enough information on second-hand prices could be collected to make an empirically-based choice of depreciation form or rates. For reasons of simplicity in the calculation of second-hand values, it was decided to set all second-hand values at 40 per cent of the value of a new weapon system. With respect to refurbished weapons—where it is even more difficult to establish an empirical basis because of varying degrees of refurbishment—a blanket assumption of a value of 66 per cent of the new price was made.

Table 7D.2. Average time span between introduction of major weapon systems and trade as second-hand or refurbished weapons and examples of implied rest values with different depreciation formulae

Weapon category	Refurbished (years)	Second-hand (years)	Implied rest values (%)					
			a	b	c	d	e	f
Aircraft	11.4	14.7	44	62	65	4	13	39
Armour and artillery	16.3	17.9	19	46	51	1	5	26
Missiles	Not applicable							
Guidance and radar systems	Not available							
Ships	14.4	18.0	29	52	57	1	7	30

Implied rest values:
   a) Life span 20 years, scrap value 1%, linear depreciation
   b) Life span 30 years, scrap value 1%, linear depreciation
   c) Life span 30 years, scrap value 10%, linear depreciation
   d) Life span 20 years, scrap value 1%, exponential depreciation
   e) Life span 30 years, scrap value 1%, exponential depreciation
   f) Life span 30 years, scrap value 10%, exponential depreciation

Source: SIPRI data base.

V. Effects of the new price system

The new price system re-establishes a comprehensive set of prices. Prices are now in 1985 US dollars. Some earlier estimating errors have been corrected. All prices are now based on the same deflators and currency conversion methods. As with all base year revisions, the change of base year from 1968 to 1985 created new price relations between years. In comparison with the old price system, the new system makes weapons produced in the 1970s and 1980s appear 'cheaper' than those produced earlier. This is not surprising since the 1985 prices better reflect the input mixes used for the production of weapons in the 1970s and 1980s. As a result, growth rates in the arms trade are reduced.

The relations between the prices of different weapon categories or of weapons from different producer/supplier countries have not changed much. The ratios between prices of weapons produced in NATO countries and WTO countries are approximately the same. Some types of ship have been given higher prices since the technical improvement factor used earlier was too low. Other types have received lower prices.

Notes and references

[1] See Sköns, E., 'Military prices', in SIPRI, *World Armaments and Disarmament: SIPRI Yearbook 1983* (Taylor & Francis: London, 1983), pp. 195–211; and GAO, *Measures of Military Capability: a Discussion of their Merits, Limitations and Interrelationships*, GAO/NSIAD-85-75, 13 June 1985 (US General Accounting Office: Washington, DC, 1985).

[2] Fly-away costs are quoted from: *Department of Defense Appropriations for 1986*, Hearings before a Subcommittee of the Committee on Appropriations, House of Representatives, 99th Congress (US Government Printing Office: Washington, DC, 1985), Part 2, p. 336; programme acquisition costs from: *Programme Acquisition Costs by Weapon System*, Department of Defense Budget for Fiscal Year 1986 (US Department of Defense: Washington, DC, 1985), p. 39; the price for the Singaporean Air Force from: Chanda, N., 'For you, US $280 million', *Far Eastern Economic Review*, 1 Aug. 1985, p. 31.

[3] The procedures involved in the production of the original price system are described in: SIPRI, *The Arms Trade with the Third World* (Almqvist & Wiksell: Stockholm, 1971), pp. 789–92; the procedures used to update the information thereafter is described in the appendices to the arms trade chapters in all *SIPRI Yearbooks*.

[4] A detailed analysis of military prices used in various countries is given in Sköns (note 1); the various aspects involved in constructing a military price deflator are described in: US Department of Commerce, Bureau of Economic Analysis, *Measuring Price Changes of Military Expenditures*, Prepared for the US Arms Control and Disarmament Agency (US Government Printing Office: Washington, DC, 1975). See also: US Congress, Congressional Budget Office, *Budgeting for Defense Inflation* (CBO: Washington, DC, 1986) and the various published deliberations of the UN expert group on the measurement and limitation of military expenditures, e.g., United Nations, Department of Disarmament Affairs, Report of the Secretary General, *Reduction of Military Budgets: Construction of Military Price Indexes and Purchasing-Power Parities for Comparison of Military Expenditures* (United Nations: New York, 1986), UN document A/40/421.

[5] Such differences were at the bottom of much political debate in the USA in the early 1980s. US procurement agencies had paid outrageous prices for single items, such as a $9609 wrench. The same wrench was quoted to cost only 12 cents when supplied from mass production, see Comeau, L., *Nuts and Bolts at the Pentagon: A Spare Parts Catalogue* (Defense Budget Project, Center on Budget and Policy Priorities: Washington, DC, 1974).

[6] See Sköns (note 1); also Maisonneuve, P., 'Prix des materiels d'armament', *Défense Nationale*, July 1980, pp. 65–80.

[7] A short overview can be found in: Large, J. P., *Development of Parametric Cost Models for Weapon Systems*, Rand Corporation, P-6604, Santa Monica, CA, Apr. 1981.

[8] See Sköns (note 1); Maisonneuve (note 6); Albrecht, U., 'Rüstung und Inflation' in Sonntag, P. (ed.), *Rüstung und Ökonomie* (Haag & Herchen: Frankfurt, 1982), pp. 209–36.

Appendix 7E. Sources and methods

I. Introduction

When compared to earlier SIPRI assessments of the volume changes in the global flow of major conventional weapons, the methods employed as of the *SIPRI Yearbook 1987* incorporate two important changes. First, SIPRI has adopted a new price system. The reasons for this revision and the nature and methodology of the current system are described in appendix 7D. Second, SIPRI has introduced a fifth weapon category—guidance and radar systems—in addition to those used earlier. This marks an attempt to adapt to the changing nature of the arms market so as to be able to cover as much as possible of the arms transfers that occur—especially in the field of electronics (see below).

II. Selection criteria

The SIPRI arms trade data cover five categories of 'major' weapons: aircraft, armour and artillery, guidance and radar systems, missiles and warships. The statistics presented refer to the value of the trade in these five categories only.

There are two criteria for the selection of major weapon items. The first is that of military application. The *aircraft* category exludes aerobatic aeroplanes, remotely piloted vehicles, drones and gliders. The *armour and artillery* category includes all types of tank, tank destroyer, armoured car, armoured personnel carrier, infantry combat vehicle as well as multiple rocket launchers and self-propelled and towed guns and howitzers with a calibre equal to or above 100 millimetres. Military trucks, lorries and jeeps are not included. The category *guidance and radar systems* is a residual category for electronic acquisition, launch and guidance systems that are either (*a*) deployed independently of a weapon system listed under another weapon category (e.g., certain ground-based SAM launch systems) or (*b*) shipborne missile launch or point defence (CIWS) systems. The values of acquisition, launch and guidance systems on aircraft and armoured vehicles are included in the value of the respective aircraft or armoured vehicle. The reason for treating shipborne systems separately is that a given type of ship is often equipped with numerous combinations of different acquisition, launch and guidance systems. The *missile* category includes only guided missiles; unguided rockets are excluded. The *ship* category excludes some types of ship, such as small patrol craft (with a displacement of less than 100t, unless they carry missiles or torpedoes), research vessels, tugs and ice-breakers.

The second criterion for selection of major weapon items is the identity of the buyer—that is, items either destined for or purchased by the armed forces of the buyer country are included. Arms supplies to guerrilla forces pose a problem. For example, if weapons are delivered to the Afghani resistance they are listed as imports to Afghanistan with a comment in the arms trade register indicating the local recipient. Weapons for police and para-military forces are as a rule not included.

The entry of any arms transfer is made according to the five categories listed above. This means that when, for example, a missile-armed ship is purchased, the missiles and the launch and guidance equipment are entered separately under their respective category in the arms trade register.

Both the order dates and the delivery dates for arms transactions are continuously revised in the light of new information. The *order date* should ideally be the date on which the sales contract was signed. The exact number of weapons ordered as well as the number of weapons delivered may not always be known and is sometimes estimated.

III. The value of the arms trade

The SIPRI system for evaluating the arms trade (described more fully in appendix 7D) was designed as a *trend-measuring device*, to enable the measurement of changes in the total flow of major weapons and its geographic pattern. Expressing the evaluation in monetary terms reflects both the quantity and the quality of the weapons transferred. Aggregate values and shares are based only on *actual deliveries* during the year or years covered in the relevant tables and figures.

The SIPRI valuation system is not comparable to official economic statistics such as gross domestic product, public expenditure and export/import figures. The monetary values chosen do not correspond to the actual prices paid, which vary considerably depending on different pricing methods, the length of production runs and the terms involved in individual transactions. For instance, a deal may or may not cover spare parts, training, support equipment, compensation and offset arrangements for the local industries in the buying country, and so on. Furthermore, to use only actual sales prices—even assuming that the information were available for all deals, which it is not—military aid and grants would be excluded, and the total flow of arms would therefore not be measured.

Production under licence is included in the arms trade statistics in such a way that it should reflect the import share embodied in the weapon. In reality, this share is normally high in the beginning and then it gradually decreases over time. SIPRI has attempted to estimate an average import share for each weapon produced under licence.

IV. The SIPRI sources

The sources of the data presented in the registers are of five general types: official national documents; journals and periodicals; newspapers; books, monographs and annual reference works; and documents issued by international and intergovernmental organizations. These are all open sources, available to the general public. The total number of sources regularly perused for data is at present about 200. The sources listed below represent a selection of the first-priority sources of the arms trade and arms production data.

Journals and periodicals

Afrique Défense (Paris)
Air et Cosmos (Paris)
Air Force Magazine (Washington)
Antimilitarismus Information (Frankfurt/M)
Armed Forces Journal (Washington)
Asia Monitor (Hong Kong)
Asian Defence Journal (Kuala Lumpur)
Aviation Week & Space Technology (New York)
Beiträge zur Konfliktforschung (Cologne)
Campaign against Arms Trade (London)
Current News (Washington)

Defence Journal (Karachi)
Defence Today (Rome)
Defensa (Madrid)
Defense & Economy World Report and Survey (Washington)
Defense & Foreign Affairs Daily (Washington)
Defense & Foreign Affairs Digest (Washington)
Defense Daily (Washington)
Defense Electronics (Palo Alto)
Defense & Armament (Paris)
DMS Intelligence (Greenwich)
Far Eastern Economic Review (Hong Kong)
Flight International (Sutton, UK)
IDF Journal (Jerusalem)
Interavia (Geneva)
Interavia Airletter (Geneva)
International Defense Review (Geneva)
Jane's Defence Weekly (London)
Keesing's Contemporary Archives (Bristol)
Latin America Weekly Report (London)
Marine-Rundschau (Stuttgart)
Martime Defence International (London)
Middle East Review (New York)
Milavnews (Stapleford)
Military Electronics & Countermeasures (Santa Clara, CA)
Military Technology (Cologne)
NACLA Report on the Americas (New York)
NATO's Sixteen Nations (Brussels)
Naval Forces (Aldershot, UK)
Navy International (Dorking, UK)
News Review (Institute for Defence Studies & Analyses, New Delhi)
Pacific Defence Reporter (Victoria)
Soldat und Technik (Frankfurt/M)
Der Spiegel (Hamburg)
Technología Militar (Bonn)
Wehrtechnik (Bonn)
World Missile Forecast (Ridgefield)

Newspapers

Dagens Nyheter (Stockholm)
Daily Telegraph (London)
Financial Times (London)
Frankfurter Rundschau (Frankfurt/M)
Hsin Hua News (London)
International Herald Tribune (Paris)
Izvestia (Moscow)
Jerusalem Post (Jerusalem)
Le Monde (Paris)
Le Monde Diplomatique (Paris)
Neue Zürcher Zeitung (Zürich)
New York Times (New York)

Pravda (Moscow)
Svenska Dagbladet (Stockholm)
The Guardian (London)
The Times (London)
Washington Post (Washington)

Annual reference publications

Aerospace Forecast and Inventory, annually in *Aviation Week & Space Technology* (McGraw-Hill: New York)
Combat Fleets of the World (Naval Institute Press: Annapolis, MD)
Defense and Foreign Affairs Handbook (Copley & Associates: Washington, DC)
Interavia Data: Air Forces of the World (Interavia: Geneva)
Interavia Data: Aircraft Armament (Interavia: Geneva)
Interavia Data: World Aircraft Production (Interavia: Geneva)
Interavia Data: World Helicopter Systems (Interavia: Geneva)
International Air Forces and Military Aircraft Directory (Aviation Advisory Services: Stapleford, UK)
Jane's All the World's Aircraft (Macdonald: London)
Jane's Fighting Ships (Macdonald: London)
Jane's Weapon Systems (Macdonald: London)
Jane's Armour and Artillery (Macdonald: London)
Labayle Couhat, J. (ed.), *Flottes de Combat* (Editions Maritimes et d'Outre Mer: Paris)
'Military Aircraft of the World' and 'Missile Forces of the World', annually in *Flight International* (IPC Transport Press: Sutton, UK)
The Military Balance (International Institute for Strategic Studies: London)

Other reference books

Conway's All the World's Fighting Ships 1922–1946 (Conway Maritime Press: London, 1980)
Conway's All the World's Fighting Ships 1947–1982 (Conway Maritime Press: London, 1983)
Hewish, M. et al., *Air Forces of the World* (Salamander Books: London, 1979)
Keegan, J. (ed.), *World Armies*, second edition (Macmillan: London, 1983).

V. Conventions

The following conventions are used in the appendices to the arms trade chapter:

..	Data not available or not applicable
—	Negligible figure (<0.5)
()	Uncertain data or SIPRI estimate

Abbreviations and acronyms

AA	Anti-aircraft
AAG	Anti-aircraft gun
AAM	Air-to-air missile
AAV	Anti-aircraft vehicle (gun-armed)
AAV(M)	Anti-aircraft vehicle (missile-armed)

AC	Aircraft/armoured car
AC carrier	Aircraft carrier
Acc to	According to
ADV	Air defence version
Adv	Advanced
AEV	Armoured engineering vehicle
AEW	Airborne early-warning system
AF	Air Force
AFSV	Armoured fire support vehicle
Amph	Amphibious/amphibian
APC	Armoured personnel carrier
Approx	Approximately
ARM	Anti-radar missile
ARV	Armoured recovery vehicle
AShM	Air-to-ship missile
ASM	Air-to-surface missile
ASW	Anti-submarine warfare
ATM	Anti-tank missile
AV	Armoured vehicle
AWACS	Airborne early warning and control system
BL	Bridge-layer
Bty	Battery
CIWS	Close-in weapon system
CG	Coastal gun
COIN	Counter-insurgency
CPC	Command post carrier
DoD	Department of Defense (USA)
ECM	Electronic countermeasures
EW	Early warning
Excl	Excluding/excludes
FAC	Fast attack craft (missile/torpedo-armed)
FMS	Foreign Military Sales (USA)
FY	Fiscal year
Grd	Ground
Hel	Helicopter
ICV	Infantry combat vehicle
IDS	Interdictor/strike version
Incl	Including/includes
Landmob	Land-mobile (missile)
LC	Landing craft (<600t displacement)
LS	Landing ship (>600t displacement)
LT	Light tank
LOA	Letter of Offer and Acceptance (USA)
LoO	Letter of Offer (USA)
MAP	Military Assistance Program
Mar patrol	Maritime patrol aircraft
MBT	Main battle tank
MCM	Mine countermeasures (ship)
MICV	Mechanized infantry combat vehicle
Mk	Mark
MoU	Memorandum of Understanding

MRCA	Multi-role combat aircraft
MRL	Multiple rocket launcher
MRS	Multiple rocket system
MSC	Minesweeper, coastal
MSO	Minesweeper, ocean
MT	Medium tank
OPV	Offshore patrol vessel
PAR	Precision approach radar
PC	Patrol craft (gun-armed/unarmed)
PDM	Point defence missile
Port	Portable
RAAF	Royal Australian Air Force
Recce	Reconnaissance (aircraft/vehicle)
RN	Royal Navy (UK)
SAM	Surface-to-air missile
SC	Scout car
SEK	Swedish crowns
ShAM	Ship-to-air missile
ShShM	Ship-to-ship missile
ShSuM	Ship-to-submarine missile
SPG	Self-propelled gun
SPH	Self-propelled howitzer
SShM	Surface-to-ship missile
SSM	Surface-to-surface missile
SuShM	Submarine-to-ship missile
SY	Shipyard
TD	Tank destroyer (gun-armed)
TD(M)	Tank destroyer (missile-armed)
TG	Towed gun
TH	Towed howitzer
Trpt	Transport
UNITA	National Union for the Total Independence of Angola
VIP	Very important person

Region codes
 1 USA
 2 USSR
 3 China
 4 NATO, excluding USA
 5 WTO, excluding USSR
 6 Other Europe, neutral
 7 Industrialized, Pacific
 8 Middle East
 9 South Asia
10 Far East & Oceania
12 North Africa
13 Sub-Saharan Africa (excluding South Africa)
14 Central America
15 South America
16 South Africa

8. Armed conflicts in 1986, and the Iraq– Iran War

STEPHEN D. GOOSE, Center for Defense Information, Washington, DC

Superscript numbers refer to the list of notes and references at the end of the chapter.

I. Summary

At the end of 1986, there were 36 armed conflicts around the world. An armed conflict is defined as: prolonged combat involving the use of weapons between two or more governments or between the military forces of a government and an organized, armed opposition force.[1] Table 8.1 identifies the location, combatants, starting date, number of troops and number of deaths in each of the conflicts.

Approximately five and one-half million soldiers from 41 countries—one-quarter of the world's 165 nations—are directly involved in the fighting. Many additional countries are involved through provision of weapons, military equipment, military advisers, military training, base facilities and/or sanctuary for rebels. Three to five million people have died as a result of these wars, with perhaps three times that many wounded.

All of the conflicts take place in the Third World, with the exception of that in Northern Ireland: 4 in South Asia, 8 in the Far East, 6 in the Middle East, 11 in Africa and 6 in Latin America. Almost all of the conflicts are guerrilla struggles within nations. Iraq–Iran is the only major conventional war. Other conflicts between two nations include the Viet Nam–China and Ethiopia–Somalia border conflicts.

Most of these conflicts have been in existence for many years. Of the 36 conflicts in progress at the end of 1986, 4 started in the 1940s, 7 in the 1960s, 17 in the 1970s and 8 in the 1980s. One outstanding feature of post-World War II armed conflict appears to be that conflicts rarely come to a definitive conclusion; fighting may wane for months or even a year or two, only to resume at even higher levels.

The level of violence and fighting in these conflicts varies greatly, from the Iraq–Iran War where tens of thousands die in a single week-long battle between hundreds of thousands of troops, to hit-and-run insurgencies in places such as Malaysia. In about half of the conflicts the death toll for 1986 exceeded 1000 (a common criteria used for full-scale war). The other half were lower-level conflicts which nevertheless required the use of military force by a government. The most violent conflicts in the 1980s, in terms of number of deaths, are Iraq–Iran, Afghanistan, Uganda, El Salvador, Lebanon, Kampuchea, Guatemala, Ethiopia (Eritrea), the Philippines and India (see table 8.1).

Conflict and tension seem to be on the rise in nearly every region of the world. Since 1980, eight new conflicts have erupted, most recently in Ecuador, Sri Lanka and Sudan. Meanwhile, only three conflicts have come to an end: the mismatches in Grenada and the Falkland/Malvinas Islands (a conflict which technically is not over since no peace treaty has been signed), and a low-level guerrilla war in Honduras. However, Honduras is on more of a war-footing today because of the contra camps inside that nation than it was in 1983 when the government defeated insurgent forces.

The escalation of violence within individual conflicts in the 1980s is even more striking than the increased number of conflicts. Over 100 000 Soviet troops entered Afghanistan in 1979 and at least that many are still there; over 100 000 Israeli troops invaded Lebanon to oust Palestinian fighters and Syrian forces (most of the Israelis have left Lebanon, but the Palestinians and Syrians have returned); the Iraq–Iran War has emerged as one of the bloodiest since World War II, including the use of chemical weapons; El Salvador and Nicaragua expanded from low-level struggles into full-scale civil wars; the Philippines and South Africa threaten to do the same; the war in Kampuchea has increasingly involved clashes between Vietnamese and Thai forces; the United States has instituted a global programme of aid to non-communist rebels fighting against communist governments; and so on.

Several nations are engaged in both internal and external conflicts, most notably Iraq, Iran and Ethiopia. Viet Nam, in addition to its border conflict with China, is fighting in two foreign nations (Kampuchea and Laos). South Africa has carried out attacks inside Angola, Botswana, Lesotho, Mozambique, Swaziland, Zambia and Zimbabwe, supposedly to quell rebels fighting against white minority rule in South Africa and Namibia.

The reasons for these conflicts are nearly as numerous as the conflicts themselves. There are border wars, wars for independence or autonomy, wars against foreign invaders, religious wars, wars for territorial or economic gain, wars for political power, and wars which combine many of these factors.

Common perceptions to the contrary, there is no dominant theme of communism versus democracy or East versus West. In Kampuchea, a communist government is fighting communist rebels. The Sino–Vietnamese border dispute pits two communist governments against each other. In many conflicts non-communist governments are fighting non-communist rebels. Although political factors are important in the origins of most conflicts, religious, economic and ethnic factors are usually more important than ideological factors. Nationalism remains the most powerful motive around the globe.

Regardless of the indigenous nature of the origins of conflicts, foreign countries—especially the USA and the USSR—are involved in virtually every conflict. Nearly one-half million foreign combat troops are involved in at least seven different conflicts. At least nine nations have a significant number of combat troops involved in foreign wars (see table 8.1). Soviet, Vietnamese and Libyan troops have taken over the main burden of fighting in Afghanistan, Kampuchea and Chad, respectively. Those totals do not include the many countries which may have smaller numbers of volunteers fighting in foreign wars, or the countries which have troops committed to multi-national peacekeeping forces in, for example, the Sinai (10 nations), Cyprus (7 nations) and Lebanon (9 nations). Foreign weapons, and other forms of foreign military involvement, have tended to escalate and prolong conflicts. The superpowers see many of these conflicts as proxy wars. The United States is a major supplier to 16 governments engaged in conflict, and the Soviet Union to 14.

There is no absolutely 'correct' number for conflicts around the world. A very strict definition of conflict, with specifiic parameters for number of casualties, number of troops involved, duration and intensity of conflict, could result in a much lower number than 36. On the other hand, a much higher figure could also be reasonably cited. Not included in this tally are: other conflicts which still are technically unresolved (North Korea–South Korea, Cyprus, the Falklands/Malvinas, Israel and various Arab nations); lower-level conflicts which might better be described as terrorist wars (e.g., the Basques in Spain, Armenians and others in Turkey, and renegade army forces in Suriname); extensive civil unrest in nations such as Chile and Bolivia; and sporadic border conflicts (North Yemen–South Yemen, Burkina Faso–Mali, India–Pakistan and others).

There are also many instances in which a government faces more than one armed opposition group and, in effect, is fighting more than one conflict. The Philippine armed forces, for example, are fighting two distinct conflicts against the New People's Army and the Moro National Liberation Front. In this study, however, guerrilla conflict inside a nation is counted as a single war, regardless of the number of independent armed factions operating against the government.

Widespread armed conflict is, of course, not new. There have been more than 200 wars in the 20th century, and more than 120 since 1945, by one estimate.[2] Still, several salient points emerge regarding global armed conflict in 1986: (a) There probably have never been as many wars as there are today, nor so many combatants armed with such highly destructive weapons. (b) Because of the nature of most of these wars, civilians are at greater risk and are dying in greater numbers than ever before. (c) Numerous local conflicts have the potential for escalating into regional wars or superpower confrontations.

II. The Iraq–Iran War

Of the 36 conflicts in progress around the globe at the end of 1986, the Iraq–Iran War is by far the most bloody and costly. It has become in many respects one of the most significant conventional wars of the century. Not since the Korean War (1950–53) has the world witnessed battles of such size and intensity, or losses of such magnitude. The Iraq–Iran War, which started in September 1980, has already lasted longer than the Korean War or either world war, and no end is in sight. It has resulted in more deaths and destruction than all the Arab–Israeli wars combined. Many more deaths will certainly occur as nearly two million troops remain poised for further combat along the 1200-km front.

The Iraq–Iran War is potentially the most dangerous conflict in the world today. The strategic importance of Iran and Iraq—mainly because of their location and oil reserves—makes this conflict central not only to the Middle East and the Persian Gulf countries, but also to the superpowers and the rest of the world. There have been widespread fears of the war expanding to embroil the entire Gulf region, with severe repercussions around the globe. The war could have devastating spill-over effects on stability throughout the region and on Western and Japanese economies. The high level of interest on the part of the USA and the USSR holds out the possibility of a superpower confrontation.

The effects of the war on oil availability and prices have thus far proven to be minimal, but it remains an issue of primary concern because of uncertainties about the future course of the war. An oil crisis could be triggered by an attempt by one of the belligerents to halt the flow of oil traffic out of the Persian Gulf, by expansion of the conflict to involve other oil exporters in the region, or by an Iranian victory, which could also lead to the spread of Islamic fundamentalism and the overthrow of moderate Arab governments.

The war has brought about new political and military alignments in the region and created doubts about future relations between Arab nations, their neighbours, the superpowers and other countries. Regardless of the outcome of the war, one can anticipate new tensions and new arms buildups in the Middle East and Persian Gulf as nations react to new realities.

Origins

A multitude of factors contributed to the outbreak of hostilities, ranging from personal animosity between Iraq's President Saddam Hussein and Iran's Ayatollah Khomeini to centuries-old religious (Sunni versus Shi'ite Muslims) and ethnic (Arab versus Persian) disputes between the two peoples. Above all, the war has been fought to determine which nation will become the more dominant political, economic, cultural and religious force in the region. Like most international conflicts, the origins of this war had little, if anything, to do with superpower politics or East–West competition.

Iraq and Iran had engaged in border clashes for many years, and the immediate spark that started the war was their dispute over the Shatt al 'Arab waterway. Iraq's stated war aims for its 22 September 1980 attack on Iran were to 'recover' rights of exclusive navigation of the Shatt al 'Arab, to regain several islands held by Iran since 1971, and to end Iranian interference in Iraqi internal affairs.

President Hussein may have seen war as inevitable because of the incompatibility of Iran's Islamic fundamentalism and Iraq's state and pan-Arab nationalism, and because of Khomeini's personal hatred for him. Iraq, at the Shah's request, had expelled Khomeini in 1978 following 15 years in exile. Khomeini later identified Hussein as one of three 'mortal enemies', along with the Shah and the United States. After overthrowing the Shah, Khomeini declared that the government of Iraq 'belongs in the dustbin of history' and called for the Shi'ite Muslims in Iraq to overthrow Hussein's secular, 'unholy' Ba'athist regime.[3]

President Hussein may also have seen it as a propitious time for Iraq to attack. Iran appeared to be weak, vulnerable and in chaos. The Iranian military, in particular, was assumed to be in disarray after extensive purges and the cut-off of military supplies and training by its former major supplier, the USA. Hussein probably expected victory in a matter of days, with little international criticism and considerable regional support.

In addition to pre-empting a possible Iranian attack, Hussein could make political, economic and territorial gains. By recovering territorial rights ceded to the Shah, he could simultaneously bolster the security of Iraq's border and the security of the Ba'athist regime. Potential bonuses included the overthrow of Khomeini and control of Iran's oil-rich Khuzestan province through 'liberation' of the Arabs there.

Hussein had badly miscalculated the situation. Iran, with the initiative since 1981, now views the war as a *jihad* (holy war) to crush the 'blasphemous' Iraqi regime and gain control of the Shi'ite holy sites in Iraq. Khomeini's demands for an end to the war include the ouster of Hussein, an end to the Ba'athist rule, and $300 billion in war reparations.

The course of the war

A brief chronology of the war follows.

Iraq launched its invasion of Iran on 22 September 1980, quickly driving up to 8 km inland and occupying 1000 km^2 of Iranian territory. But by mid-October Iran was slowing Iraqi advances. The last Iraqi successes came in early November with the capture of Khorramshahr and Abadan.

Iran began a series of counter-offensives in January 1981, unveiling its 'human wave assaults' which use huge numbers of troops from the regular Army, the Revolutionary Guards and the 'Baseeji' (including thousands of young teenagers). Iran's first major victory—the recapture of Abadan—came in September 1981.

Iran's Operation Undeniable Victory in March 1982 marked a major turning-point as Iran penetrated Iraqi lines, split Iraq's forces and put them into retreat. In late June, Iraq stated its willingness to negotiate a settlement to the war and withdrew its forces from Iran. Iran refused to negotiate and demanded $150 billion in reparations and the removal of Hussein.

In July 1982 Iran launched its first assault into Iraqi territory, near Basra, and was repulsed. In August 1982 Iraq declared a maritime exclusion zone in the northern Gulf and began attacking both Iranian ports and oil complexes and neutral tankers and ships sailing to or from Iran. The ground war of attrition set in as Iranian ground offensives throughout the fall and winter were repulsed, with heavy casualties.

In 1983 three major Iranian human wave assault offensives, and several smaller operations, in all three war sectors (north, central and south) were unsuccessful, resulting in massive casualties. Iran's 'final offensive' in February 1984, involving 250 000 troops, failed.

In March 1984 Iraq, newly armed with French Super-Etendard combat aircraft and Exocet missiles, greatly expanded the so-called 'tanker war'.

Attacks on neutral merchant shipping became much more frequent—72 in 1984 compared to 28 in the first three years of the war—and were no longer limited to the northern Persian Gulf.[4]

The major development in 1985 was the increased attacks by both combatants on strategic targets such as population centres and industrial complexes. In May Iraq began launching aircraft, artillery and surface-to-surface missile (SAM) attacks on Tehran and other Iranian cities. In August Iraq began a campaign of air attacks on Kharg Island—a total of 44 raids from August through November. Iran responded with air raids and missile attacks on Baghdad and other Iraqi towns and by stopping and searching neutral ships in the Strait of Hormuz.[5]

Iran's only major ground offensive in 1985, involving 60 000 troops, came in March near Basra. It was repelled, again with heavy Iranian losses. In February 1986 Iran launched an amphibious assault across the Shatt al 'Arab waterway and captured the disused Iraqi oil port of Faw, marking the first time Iran has held territory that was indisputably Iraqi. Unable or unwilling to dislodge the Iranians, Iraq in May made its first attack into Iranian territory since 1982 and captured Mehran. In July, Iran recaptured Mehran. Throughout the rest of the year Iran carried out only small hit-and-run attacks in Iraq, while massing about 500 000 troops for another promised 'final offensive'. Increased co-operation between Iran and Kurds in Iraq caused Baghdad to divert 100 000 Iraqi troops to the northern region.

In July 1986 the Iraqi Air Force began a campaign of vastly expanded air strikes, using higher-risk but much more effective tactics, primarily against oil refineries and oil shipping installations. Heavy attacks on Kharg Island in August and September forced Iran to rely on new installations farther south in the Gulf at Sirri Island and Larak Island. Iraqi jets then hit Sirri and Larak, reportedly refuelling in the air and using a Saudi military base. Ninety neutral ships were attacked in the Gulf in 1986.[6]

On 24 December 1986, Iran began an assault in the Basra region that some believed could be the 'final offensive'. By mid-January 1987 very heavy fighting had resulted in over 40 000 dead, according to some estimates.[7]

Costs of the war

The Iraq-Iran War is without question the most destructive and costly conflict in the world today, whether measured in terms of lives lost or of damage to property and the economic well-being of the belligerents. Since the end of World War II, only the wars in Korea and Viet Nam have resulted in more battle casualties than the Iraq–Iran War had by the end of 1986.

As is the case with most wars, reliable estimates of casualty figures are very hard to acquire. Observers are rarely allowed to visit combat areas, so impartial first-hand information is almost non-existent. At the end of 1986, the most frequently cited estimate of casualties since September 1980 was about one million—350 000 dead and 650 000 wounded. Iran accounted for 250 000 dead and 500 000 wounded; Iraq for 100 000 dead and 150 000 wounded.[8] Other reliable sources have put the combined death toll at much higher figures of 600 000–880 000.[9] The Iraqi Defence Minister has claimed that up to one million Iranians have been killed and three million wounded.[10] Reports indicate 10 000–40 000 casualties in a single week's fighting during the largest offensives.

The extremely high casualty rates are attributable primarily to Iran's human wave assaults—using tens and sometimes hundreds of thousands of troops—and its willingness to sustain huge losses in order to offset Iraq's numerical and technological superiority in weaponry. The human wave assaults—and shocking death tolls—are perhaps cynically motivated by Iran's population advantage and made possible by the religious zeal of its citizens.

The financial and economic costs of the Iraq–Iran War have been similarly staggering. Economic development in Iraq and Iran has come to a virtual halt. Even with a quick resolution to the conflict, it could take Iraq 10 years and Iran 20 years to complete reconstruction.[11]

Iran's Planning and Budget Minister put the country's losses due to the war, during 1980–85, at $309 billion, with damage to the oil sector accounting for one-half thereof.[12] Losses in 1986 have been substantial, as Iraq's air war has slashed Iran's oil production from 1.3 million to 500 000–600 000 barrels per day. Iran's oil income is expected to fall to $6 billion in 1986 from $16 billion in 1985, which was considered a lean year.[13] Iranian Government officials have said that one-third of the nation's budget is devoted to the war.[14]

Iraq's war bill is estimated at $600 million to $1 billion per month.[15] Iraqi oil revenues have plunged from over $20 billion per year before the war to $5–8 billion per year in 1986.[16] Iraq has exhausted the $35 billion in foreign exchange reserves that it had when the war began, and has gone into debt for another $40–85 billion. Most of the money ($30–60 billion) has come from members of the Gulf Cooperation Council (GCC), especially Saudi Arabia and Kuwait, and probably will not have to be repaid.[17] Hussein adopted a strategy of 'guns and butter', trying to sustain the war effort along with a civilian service economy, in an attempt to isolate the population from the hardships of war. In doing so he has mortgaged the nation's future. As the war drags on, the strategy will be difficult, if not impossible, to sustain.

Force comparisons

Recent assessments indicate that, after a major Iraqi military expansion in 1986, Iraq and Iran have roughly equal numbers of regular and reserve troops—slightly more than one million for each nation.[18] Iran, however, retains a significant manpower advantage because of its huge para-military forces—particularly the 'Baseeji' army—and because of Iran's willingness to commit larger numbers of troops to battle and sustain much higher casualties than Iraq has done.

In addition to 305 000 regular army troops, Iran has the 350 000-strong 'Pasdaran' or Revolutionary Guard. It has grown greatly in size and effectiveness over the course of the war, evolving from a local vigilante force into one comparable to the professional army. These 'Shi'ite shock troops' have been the principle fighting force in most ground assaults. The Baseeji,

Khomeini's so-called 'Army of 20 Million', are mostly unskilled street recruits. Iran claims to have trained about three million Baseeji and sent one million to the front.[19] Prepared for martyrdom, they lead the human wave assaults, walking through minefields and other obstacles, wearing death shrouds and carrying their own coffins to the front lines. It has been widely reported that Iran has sent thousands of teenagers and school children to the front to die as part of the human wave assaults.[20]

Iraq's Army grew in 1986 from 550 000 to about 800 000.[21] Much of the increase resulted from forced recruiting, including 16-year-olds. Iraq has a clear-cut advantage in both the quantity and the quality of modern weapons, particularly combat aircraft, armour and artillery. Iraq has an advantage of: 4.5-to-1 in tanks (4500 vs. 1000; 3-to-1 in armoured fighting vehicles (4000 vs. 1360); and 9-to-1 in artillery pieces (5500 vs. more than 600). It has over 170 Soviet Hind, French Gazelle, Super-Frelon and Alouette, and other army attack helicopters, while Iran has only a handful of US Cobra helicopters.[22] Iraq's overall air-power superiority is most striking. It has about 500 combat aircraft, including high-performance Soviet MiGs and French Mirages armed with Exocet missiles. Iran is thought to have fewer than 70 serviceable combat aircraft, and perhaps only a dozen of its most advanced aircraft, the US-made F-14.[23] Iraq's edge in ground weaponry and air power, combined with Iraq's in-place defensive structure, make a successful Iranian 'final offensive' very unlikely.

Chemical warfare

In March 1986 United Nations Secretary-General Perez de Cuellar for the first time directly accused Iraq of using chemical weapons against Iran, citing the report of four chemical warfare experts sent to Iran at the UN's request in February and March 1986. The report concluded, 'On many occasions Iraqi forces have used chemical warfare against Iranian forces', noting that mustard gas was most common and that nerve gas was also used.[24] The experts also said that 'the use of chemical weapons appears to be more extensive than in 1984'.[25] It was the third UN-sponsored investigation. The two previous investigations confirmed chemical weapons usage, but did not specifically name Iraq (see also *SIPRI Yearbook 1985*, page 181).

Iran has accused Iraq of using chemical weapons from the early stages of the war. From May 1981 to March 1984 Iran charged Iraq with 49 uses of chemical weapons.[26] The first international team of specialists, sent in March 1984, concluded that mustard gas and the nerve agent Tabun had been used during heavy fighting in February. In September 1985, US Assistant Secretary of State Richard Murphy told the Congress that the Iraq–Iran War involved 'the largest use of chemical warfare since World War I'.[27] A British representative at the Conference on Disarmament in Geneva said in July 1986 that Iraqi chemical warfare was responsible for about 10 000 casualties.[28]

The use of chemical weapons is a violation of the Geneva Protocol of 1925, which both Iraq and Iran have signed. Iraq has officially denied that it has used chemical weapons, and has levelled counter-charges at Iran. Iran has acknowledged that it has the ability to make chemical weapons and has warned that it may use chemical weapons as a last resort. While UN and US officials say there is no evidence of Iranian use of chemical weapons, the US State Department has expressed its concern that Iran already has a chemical weapon arsenal.[29]

Strategy and tactics

The conduct of the war has been curious in many ways. In some respects, it has been an all-out unlimited war of great intensity, including Iraq's use of chemical weapons and Iran's use of human wave tactics. Both nations have bombarded population centres. Yet, the war has also been strangely limited. Battles have not been fought to decisive conclusions. Fighting has often been sporadic, with long periods of relative inactivity. There has been little movement of front lines. Drastic escalatory steps such as attempts to close the Strait of Hormuz or attacks on neighbouring countries have been avoided.

Since 1982 Iraq has been content with an essentially defensive strategy, and has not fully used its overwhelming superiority in aircraft, armour and artillery. The defensive strategy is aimed at keeping casualties and equipment losses low, while inflicting heavy damage on Iran's economic and military infrastructure. This minimizes costs to Iraq—and internal opposition to Hussein—while attempting to force Iran to accept a negotiated end to the fighting. Iraqis speak of a 'red line' for casualties, which if crossed could result in widespread domestic opposition to Hussein and the Ba'athists.

To carry out the defensive strategy Iraq has built very impressive fortifications along much of the length of the 1200-km war front. In particular, the area in the south near Basra and Abadan has line after line of concrete-roofed bunkers, tank- and artillery-firing positions, minefields and stretches of barbed wire, all shielded by an artificially flooded lake 30 km long and 1800 metres wide.[30] Iraq has been widely acknowledged for its effective use of combat engineering to create barriers.

In 1984, Iraq combined its defensive ground war with an offensive air war. By escalating the 'tanker war' against oil ships, Iraq hoped to deny Iran oil revenues and internationalize the war to bring pressures on Iran to negotiate a settlement. However, until mid-1986 Iraqi air tactics were characterized by under-sized attack forces flying too few missions and dropping bombs ineffectively from great heights. Since the summer of 1986 the Air Force has engaged in the first truly sustained bombing campaign of the war. It is flying many more sorties, striking at greater distances, and using more aggressive, higher-risk tactics to accomplish more destructive air strikes on economic targets.

Since 1981 Iran has seemed to follow a dual-track strategy: (a) fight a war of attrition, counting on Iran's larger population and willingness to sacrifice to bring eventual victory; and (b) mount massive human wave assaults in the hope of accomplishing an immediate breakthrough which could lead to the downfall of Hussein. For the past several years Iran has mounted a major offensive early in the year, then fallen into a retaliatory pattern of air raids and artillery bombardments, resulting in mounting civilian casualties for both sides.

The arms trade and foreign involvement

In a period of general decline in the global arms trade, the Iraq-Iran War has been a boon to arms merchants, particularly those who operate outside, or just within, the boundaries of official channels. The murky business of private arms dealers and black-marketeers has gained the most from this conflict. (The arms flow is also discussed in chapter 7; see also *SIPRI Yearbook 1984*, chapter 7.)

Initially, the USA and the USSR—the traditional major arms suppliers for Iran and Iraq, respectively—declared neutrality and refused to ship new weapons. Neither Iran nor Iraq was significantly hampered by this fact, as many alternative suppliers became available. The rush to take advantage of the arms market has created some very strange bedfellows. Iran has been supplied by both sides in other conflicts: China and Viet Nam, North Korea and South Korea, Israel and Syria. In 1982 the Soviet Union resumed major arms shipments to Iraq, yet most of Iran's ardent supporters are Soviet allies (e.g., Syria, Libya and North Korea).

The war has demonstrated that national boundaries or political ideology mean little in the arms trade business. Governments, arms manufacturers, private dealers and criminals wanting profits or political benefits have made arms readily available. The availability—given enough money—of weapons, whether US, Soviet or of other manufacture, has been a key factor in Iran's ability to continue to prosecute the war. Deliveries of highly sophisticated aircraft and missiles to Iraq have enabled it to expand the war through its escalation of the tanker war and attacks on Iranian oil facilities anywhere in the Persian Gulf.

A major advantage to Iraq in the war has been its steady and reliable supply of all types of weapons. Iraq had since 1973 been diversifying its arms suppliers and decreasing its reliance on the Soviet Union, so that when the Soviet Union withheld direct arms shipments to Iraq for the first year and a half of the war, other nations, especially France, picked up the slack. In addition, Iraq was able to get Soviet weapons from China, North Korea, Egypt and other nations.

French weapon deliveries to Iraq since September 1980 have been estimated at values as high as $5–9 billion, which would make it the largest supplier to either side.[31] However, in late 1986 US officials claimed that China's $3 billion worth of arms to Iraq, plus $1 billion to Iran, made it the number one arms supplier in the war.[32] Most of China's deliveries to Iraq were made in 1981 and 1982. Other major suppliers to Iraq include the Soviet Union, with over $2 billion in arms deliveries since the spring of 1982 (perhaps as much as $7 billion), and Egypt, which has also shipped over $2 billion in weapons.[33]

Iran has not had the reliable sources of weaponry, especially modern weaponry, that Iraq has, but has nonetheless found many willing supliers. It is estimated that Iran has imported about $9 billion in weapons since 1980.[34] Iran has purchased arms from all the available sources—as seen by its secret deals with its acknowledged enemies, the USA and Israel. Iran has also received

US-made weapons from South Korea, several European nations and Viet Nam, but has often had to settle for less capable, usually Soviet-made, weaponry. It has had to rely more on private and illegal arms deals. The US Government has brought 44 prosecutions for illegal shipments, or attempted shipments, of arms to Iran.[35] Some reports indicate that private dealers have purchased Iranian weapons captured by Iraq, and then re-sold them to Iran.[36]

US officials stated in August 1986 that China had surpassed North Korea as Iran's major supplier. Chinese sales are thought to be in excess of $1.6 billon.[37] North Korea's military deliveries are estimated at over $1 billion.[38] Other major arms suppliers are Israel (over $500 million) and Viet Nam (over $400 million).[39]

The US-led arms embargo against Iran—Operation Staunch, implemented in 1983—was reported to have had a significant impact on Iran's weapon purchases, although the revelations about the US 'arms for hostages' deal indicate otherwise.[40] So far as is known, the weapons that the United States sold to Iran will not make any significant difference in Iran's military capabilities, but could open the floodgates for renewed shipments by other nations.

Foreign military support has not been limited to major arms supply. Many nations have provided small arms, ammunition, spare parts, training and advisers. The United Kingdom, for example, has acknowledged that British companies have provided technical training in the UK for Iraqi pilots and Iranian artillery officers.[41] There have been reports of 'volunteer' soldiers assisting Iraq from Egypt (15 000–17 000), Jordan (5000), North Yemen, Morocco, Tunisia and Sudan.[42] In late 1986 Saudi Arabia reportedly permitted Iraq to use Saudi bases to refuel aircraft attacking Iranian oil facilities in the mouth of the Persian Gulf.[43] Syrian pilots have reportedly flown MiG-23 escorts for Iranian F-4 strikes into Iran.[44]

The war has induced other nations of the region to seek additional weapons to protect against possible expansion of the conflict. Perhaps the most notable example is the Saudi purchase of 400 Stinger missiles from the USA in 1984 to protect its shipping, and of Harpoon and Sidewinder missiles in 1986.

Lessons

The Iraq–Iran War has not generated the huge professional literature on 'military lessons' that other recent conflicts, such as the Falklands/Malvinas, Lebanon or Grenada conflicts, have. In large part that reflects the lack of confirmed information, particularly about the performance of individual weapon systems. It also reflects the unusual tactics of the war, and the nearly complete absence of air-to-air or naval combat.

Two US officers have written that 'The Iraq–Iran war has shattered illusions about the nature of modern conflict in many quarters. Virtually none of the early expectations of this war have been realized'.[45] Some contend that this is because there are 'amateur armies on both sides', noting the consistent failures to use combined arms, the use of tanks without infantry support, poor use of artillery and counter-battery fire, and failure to shift and mass firepower to support manoeuvre, among other things.[46]

The key military lessons that analysts have drawn are the advantage of defensive positions, the importance of combat engineering, and the important role that can be played by reserve, volunteer and local forces. One central observation about the war is that the most advanced weapons money can buy have not had the impact of tens of thousands of troops armed with rifles and machine-guns, willing to die for the cause. 'Super weapons' such as F-14s and MiG-25s have been used sparingly. Highly sophisticated or large numbers of forces are of little value if armies are inadequately trained to use and repair them, and if there is poor command and control and faulty tactical and strategic planning.

The war has shown how easy it is to start a war, with the expectation of easy and quick gains, and how difficult it is to stop a war or contain it. The history of the dispute over the Shatt al 'Arab waterway imparts the lesson that if settlements are to last, they must not be imposed or based on shifting power equations, but must reflect the mutual interests of both sides.

The Iraq–Iran conflict clearly demonstrates that the superpowers do not control wars and that the origins of all wars are not linked to superpower concerns. It also provides a reminder that a nation which exports arms has no control over how or against whom they will eventually be used. The war is evidence of the destabilizing nature of huge arms-buying sprees such as those by Iraq and Iran in the 1970s.

The future

Predictions about the Iraq–Iran War have usually proved wrong. It has been a war of surprises and is likely to stay that way. Of the many paths the war could take, the only one that can be readily ruled out is a quick end to the fighting. Neither side has the military power to achieve victory, and neither is yet close enough to economic collapse to give in. Iran refuses to negotiate, but cannot dictate peace. Iraq will negotiate, but cannot accept Iran's terms. Khomeini and Hussein may see the risks of peace as greater than the costs of the war. Khomeini needs turmoil and an external enemy to keep revolutionary fervour alive and perpetuate his rule. Hussein wants peace, but not at any cost; if he is perceived to have 'lost' the war, his political support could crumble.

The most likely future is a continuing war of attrition, with an intensification of air strikes on both sides, perhaps additional loss of territory by Iraq, and the economic and political weakening of both regimes. An escalation and widening of economic warfare are distinct possibilities as both sides seek to break the deadlock. The question is not so much who will win but who will collapse first. Some feel that eventually a war of attrition will favour Iran because of its larger population and gross national product and the Messianic determination of Iran's leaders and people. However, Iraq has advantages that could permit it to drag out the war for an indefinite period: reliable sources of military re-supply, Arab financial underpinning, and the military benefits of defensive posture and superiority in air power and firepower.

In late 1986 it appeared likely that Iran would mount one major ground offensive in the first three months of the year to probe for a possible breakthrough, to attempt to gain more territory, to feed Iranian revolutionary fervour while weakening Iraqi morale, and to try to inflict unacceptable casualties on Iraqi forces; the rest of the year would be devoted to smaller-scale attacks all along the frontier, keeping pressure on Iraq. Iran will probably also increase assistance to Kurds in order to divert Iraqi resources, as well as increasing harassment of shipping and bombardment of Iraqi cities.

A military breakthrough by Iran is very unlikely, given Iraq's defensive fortifications, superior firepower and air power, and willingness to use chemical weapons, and Iran's inability to sustain high levels of combat for an extended period of time. If a breakthrough attempt is made, it will probably be aimed at Basra, Iraq's second largest city, which is literally on the front line. The capture of Basra could lead to the downfall of Hussein.

A drastic escalation of the war by Iran, such as an attempt to block the Strait of Hormuz, would be too risky, given its limited military capability to do so and the potential for devastating military retaliation by other nations. A large-scale attack on other Gulf states is also unlikely, but Iran may well increase terrorist activities and political and subversive pressures against the states that support Iraq.

Iraq will search for ways to better implement its strategy of pressuring Iran economically and trying to bring international pressure to bear on Iran to seek a negotiated solution. That probably means continued increased use of air power, with an escalation of the tanker war and attacks on key oil facilities, and intensified strikes against population centres. An attempt to dislodge Iranian forces from Faw is a possibility, but one that is almost certainly seen as too costly in terms of casualties.

The best hope for a negotiated settlement is through multinational peace initiatives. Yet, the international community does not seem very interested. As the dangers of regional escalation seem to have faded, many nations, such as Israel, probably see the prolonged weakening of both nations as a positive development; they are so uncertain about the results of a victory by either side that they prefer to see the war continue. The feeling may be shared by the superpowers, since the war limits the ability of both nations to create mischief. If there is to be a negotiated solution, the multitude of foreign countries involved in the war must limit their war-making support and make a concerted effort to pressure belligerents to exercise restraint.

As bleak as the picture appears, indefinite large-scale conflict is not inevitable. Different factors could undermine the political will or the economic and military capability for either side to fight. Psychological attrition could induce Iran to reduce its demands, or Iraq to make greater concessions. As decreasing oil income and dwindling resources lead to shortages of food and military hardware for both sides, economic and military exhaustion could produce a slow-down in the fighting. The war could subside to the level of occasional border clashes and mutual subversion, as has happened to China and Viet Nam following their 1979 war. War-weariness could result in a *de facto* ceasefire or an armistice, but the high costs the war has already engendered make a long period of hostility probable. A ceasefire, armistice or even a peace treaty are likely to be only a prelude to rearmament or revenge. Future conflicts between the two nations are a near certainty.

Many unpredictable factors could affect the course of the war: the death of Khomeini, an assassination of Hussein or a *coup d'etat*, a new Arab–Israeli war, interaction with other regional wars, sudden influx of weapons (especially for Iran), changes in Soviet–Iranian or US–Iraqi relations, and many others. One safe prediction is that the war will take many more lives. While neither side has the strength to deliver a definitive blow or even to carry out sustained offensive action, they both still have the weaponry and willpower to inflict heavy losses.

Table 8.1. Armed conflicts in the world, 1986

Conflicts	Year began	Warring parties	No. of troops (thousands)[a]	No. killed (thousands)[b]
Europe				
Northern Ireland	1969	British Government and Protestant Irish paramilitary *vs.* IRA	9 10? 0.5	>2.5

Comments: British troops and Protestant paramilitary forces in Northern Ireland battle against Catholic Irish nationalists—primarily Irish Republican Army (IRA), which seeks reunification of Northern Ireland with the Republic of Ireland. Protestant majority wants to remain part of United Kingdom. Nov. 1985 Anglo–Irish agreement granting increased rights to Ulster Catholics has not diminished violence. Sixty-two deaths in year after agreement was signed. Armed rebels of the Provisional Wing of the IRA continue bombings, assassinations and other terrorist activities.

Middle East				
Iran	1979	Government *vs.* Kurds (pesh mergas), People's Mujahideen, other separatist and anti-government rebels	100? 10–15? ? ?	?

Comments: Kurds, who make up 3% of Iran's population and want greater autonomy or independence in mountainous north–west, became very active militarily following overthrow of Shah. Largest of several armed Kurdish groups, the Kurdistan Democratic Party, claims to have killed more than 20 000 Iranian soldiers. Rebel establishment of 'liberated zones' led to partially successful 1983–84 campaign by Iranian forces to regain control. Iranian Kurds have received support from Iraq. Other ethnic minorities—nearly 40% of Iran's population is non-Persian—are in armed revolt against Khomeini as well, including Baluchis, Azerbaijanis and Khuzistani Arabs. Besides Kurds, the most powerful armed opposition comes from the People's Mujahideen, which wants to topple the Khomeini Government. It also receives aid from—and its leader is based in—Iraq. Iran is accused of executing from 6000 to more than 20 000 political opponents since 1979.

Iraq	1980	Government *vs.* Kurds (pesh mergas), ICP	100 12 1	?

Comments: Most serious armed internal opposition comes from three main Kurdish groups. Kurds make up 15–20% of Iraq's population. Kurdish armed rebels, known as pesh mergas, have used government's war with Iran to expand operations, after being mostly dormant 1975–80.

Conflicts	Year began	Warring parties	No. of troops (thousands)[a]	No. killed (thousands)[b]

Rebels conduct attacks on oil installations and military facilities, kidnappings and bombings. Government troops have destroyed entire villages, launched air strikes. Kurds have received aid from Iran and fought alongside Iranian troops. Iraqi Army controls only the major towns and roads in mountainous northern region of Kurdistan. Iraq reportedly forced to deploy 100 000 troops to Kurdistan in 1986. Armed opposition from Iraqi Communist Party (ICP) also.

| Iraq–Iran | 1980 | Iraqi Government vs. Iranian Government | 845 700 | 350–880 |

Comments: See section II.

| Israeli–Palestinians/ Syria | 1948 | Israeli Government vs. PLO rebels and Syrian troops | 149* 8 25 | >10 |

Comments: Israel and Palestinian rebels (mainly the Palestine Liberation Organization) backed primarily by Syria fight their war in Lebanon. Israel's invasion of Lebanon in 1982 to expel 7000–10 000 Palestinian guerrillas did not bring peace, or even slow pace of warfare much. An estimated 3500 armed Palestinians have returned to Lebanon. Some 25 000 Syrian troops remain entrenched in Lebanon. About 1000 Israeli troops are in southern Lebanon. Conflict has resumed pre–1982 pattern: PLO launches rocket attacks, bombings, other attacks on Israeli citizens and property in Lebanon and Israel; Israel carries out raids, usually air strikes against rebel bases, in Lebanon.

| Lebanon | 1975 | Government troops, Christian militia, Muslim militia | 15 40? 40? | >125 |

Comments: General civil war between and among Lebanese Christians and Muslims. Muslims form majority of population, but Christians have dominated political and economic life. Lebanese armed forces—divided into Christian units (loyal to President Gemayel) and Muslim units— exercise little control on national scale. Numerous Christian and Muslim militia fight each other, among themselves and with government troops. Most intense fighting since May 1985 is between Amal Shi'ite Muslim militiamen and Palestinian rebels—more than 1400 dead. Syria sent several hundred 'peacekeeping' troops into Beirut in July 1986 for first time since 1982. Violence between Christian groups (Army and militias) also heavy in 1986.

| Syria | 1976 | Government vs. Sunni rebels, anti-government rebels | 392.5* 42 ? | >6–26 |

Comments: Main armed opposition to government has come from Islamic fundamentalist groups, most notably Sunni Muslim rebels known as Muslim Brotherhood. Sunnis make up 74% of population, but Alawite Muslims control politics and economy. Disaffection with Assad regime erupted into warfare in 1976; fighting climaxed with destruction of town of Hamah—a suspected Muslim Brotherhood stronghold—in Feb. 1982, resulting in 5000–25 000 deaths. Support for President Assad after Israel's invasion of Lebanon in June 1982 halted most fighting until spring 1986, when new wave of bombings and assassinations occurred. Assad also faces armed opposition from pro-Iraqi Ba'athists and Palestinian extremists.

South Asia

| Afghanistan | 1978 | Afghan Government and USSR vs. Mujahideen | 40–45 115 50 | >200 |

Conflicts	Year began	Warring parties	No. of troops (thousands)^a	No. killed (thousands)^b

Comments: Conflict began as insurrection mainly by religious groups against new Marxist government. Soviet invasion in support of government in Dec. 1979. Soviet troops do most fighting, as Afghan Army has disintegrated to half its former size. Military situation remains a stand-off with neither side able make significant or lasting gains. USSR effectively controls only Kabul and smaller urban areas. War may cost USSR $3–4 billion per year. Soviet deaths estimated at 10 000–15 000. USSR claims to withdraw 6000–8000 troops in Oct. 1986; USA says is only troop rotation, not real reduction. USA reported to have provided more than $1 billion in aid to rebels, including Stinger missiles. War increasingly spills into Pakistan; Pakistan claims over 650 airspace violations in 1986, lodged 20 formal protests.

India	1947	Government *vs.* separatist, ethnic, religious rebels	1 260* 9	1983–86: 10

Comments: Since 1983, ethnic and religious violence has been at highest level since independence in 1947. Sharpest conflict is with Sikhs in Punjab (13 million total), who desire greater autonomy or independence. Escalating attacks by Sikh rebels (Khalitan Liberation Army and Khalistan Commando Force) led to government's military assault on Golden Temple (holiest Sikh shrine) in June 1984, resulting in 1000 deaths. About 5000 died from Sikh violence 1984–86, including more than 650 in 1986. Rebels in state of Assam have quieted after massive violence in 1983. Government must also deal with militant Hindu groups (Hindu–Moslem and Hindu–Christian violence) and separatist struggles in the north-eastern region (Manipur, Tripura).

Pakistan	1972	Government *vs.* separatist and anti-government rebels	480.6* 5? ?	>9?

Comments: Low-level separatist guerrilla campaigns since early 1970s in the three provinces dominated by an ethnic minority. Baluchi, Pushtan (Pathan) and Sindhi constitute about 40% of population (majority are Punjabi). Army–rebel clashes in Baluchistan left thousands dead in 1970s and continue today, as do terrorist bombings by Pathans in the North–West Frontier Province. Currently, Sind province is main trouble spot for government. Heavily armed gangs roam countryside robbing, kidnapping, attacking police and sabotaging transportation. Army patrols back up police. Sindhis resent domination of central government by Punjab. Additionally, fighting between ethnic groups in Sind in Nov. and Dec. left about 200 dead; Army troops were sent to restore order four times in latter half of 1986. Widespread unpopularity of Zia's regime has led to massive rioting. Opposition headed by Movement for the Restoration of Democracy, an alliance of banned political parties. Violence in Aug. 1986 (clashes with police and attacks on banks, government buildings, railroad lines) left more than 37 dead.

Sri Lanka	1983	Government *vs.* Tamils	38 5–7	>3–4.5

Comments: Long simmering ethnic- and religious-based conflict between Buddhist Sinhalese (74% of population) and Hindu Tamilese (18% of population) erupted into sustained civil war in 1983. Tamils want separate nation. Liberation Tigers of Tamil Eelam are biggest of six Tamil rebel groups. Rebels carry out bombings, minings, hit-and-run assaults on government forces and facilities; rebels control countryside in the north. Extensive attacks on civilians by both sides. Rebels use southern India as sanctuary, base of operations.

Far East

Burma	1948	Government *vs.* BCP, KNLA and other rebels	186* 10–15 4–10 12–20	2–3/year

Conflicts	Year began	Warring parties	No. of troops (thousands)[a]	No. killed (thousands)[b]

Comments: At least 14 different separatist and revolutionary armed groups have been fighting against the government since Burma gained independence in 1948. None currently poses a serious threat, but government control in many areas is weak. The largest is the Burma Communist Party (BCP), although its activities have lessened in recent years as China's support has decreased. Heaviest fighting is now with the Karen National Liberation Army (KNLA), which seeks an autonomous state for 2–3 million ethnic Karen. Other significant rebellions in Kachin and Shan states, plus many smaller ethnic minority armed opposition groups.

China–Viet Nam	1979	Chinese Government *vs.*	250	1979: 47
		Vietnamese Government	250	1980–86: >1

Comments: Low-level border conflict has continued since China's 'lesson-teaching' invasion in 1979. Mostly artillery exchanges, cross-border raids and limited ground attacks. Casualties are not high, but a very tense border with large number of forces deployed in the region. China claims 10 000 incursions and over half a million artillery shells fired by Viet Nam since 1980. Viet Nam claims 20 000 shells a day during Chinese offensives. Chinese attacks are usually tied to Vietnamese actions in Kampuchea.

Indonesia	1975	Government *vs.* Fretilin,	281*	>0.1
(East Timor)		other separatists	0.2–8	

Comments: Government is plagued by several low-level separatist insurgencies. Invasion of East Timor, a former Portuguese colony seeking independence, in 1975 resulted in over 100 000 deaths by 1979. Indonesian troops still occupying East Timor (since 'annexed' by Indonesia), conduct 'final offensives' against remaining Fretilin rebels every year or two. Other armed separatist movements include those in West Irian (Free Papua Movement) and northern Sumatra (Free Aceh Movement).

Kampuchea	1970	Government and Viet Nam	30	1970–78:
		vs. Khmer Rouge,	40	2000–3000
		KPNLF and ANS	30	1979–86: 24
			11	
			5	

Comments: Civil war, invasion and war-related famine have resulted in 2–3 million deaths since 1970—the most of any current conflict. Most deaths occurred during brutal reign of Pol Pot's Khmer Rouge (1975–78). Viet Nam invasion toppled Pol Pot in Jan. 1979. 140 000 Vietnamese troops remain in Kampuchea and conduct most of the fighting against a fragile coalition of communist Khmer Rouge rebels and two non-communist rebel groups (Khmer People's National Liberation Front, KPNLF, and Armée Nationale Sihanoukiste, ANS). The rebel alliance (Coalition Government of Democratic Kampuchea) is recognized by UN as legitimate government of Kampuchea. The war has increasingly spilled into Thailand, which houses rebel camps. Soviet Union supports Heng Samrin Government, China supports Khmer Rouge, USA and ASEAN support non-communist guerrillas. US Government has accused Samrin, Government and Viet Nam with use of chemical warfare ('yellow rain').

Laos	1975	Government and	54*	10–50
		Viet Nam *vs.* National	40–45*	
		Liberation Front	2–3	

Comments: Widespread warfare in 1975–79 following communist Pathet Lao's assumption of power has dwindled to low-level insurgency. Four rebel groups formed coalition (National Liberation Front) in 1981 aimed at ouster of Pathet Lao government and Vietnamese troops, but co-operation is sporadic. Largest rebel group is Hmong tribesmen led by Gen. Vang Pao (remnants of CIA's 'secret army'). Rebels are largely based in Thailand. US Government has charged Pathet Lao and Viet Nam with use of chemical warfare ('yellow rain').

Conflicts	Year began	Warring parties	No. of troops (thousands)[a]	No. killed (thousands)[b]
Malaysia	1945	Government vs. CPM	110* 1–2	. . (0.1/year)

Comments: Government has been fighting low-level insurgency against the Communist Party of Malaysia (CPM) since World War II. CPM guerrillas are mostly based in Thailand; Thai and Malaysian armed forces conduct joint operations against the CPM.

| Philippines | 1970 | Government vs. NPA and MNLF | 113*
16–22
10 | 50–100
1983–86: 10–15 |

Comments: Communist New People's Army (NPA) doubled in size in 1983–85. Major increase in number and scale of clashes as NPA became active in every province in the country. Aquino government's 60-day cease-fire with NPA, starting 10 Dec. 1986, did not result in permanent end to warfare. Extensive fighting in the 1970s against the Muslim Moro National Liberation Front (MNLF) resulted in more than 50 000 dead. MNLF, which desires independence, has declined from armed strength of 30 000 to about 10 000. Little co-ordination with NPA.

| Thailand | 1965 | Government vs. CPT, separatist rebels | 256*
0.8–1
2 | . . (0.1/year) |

Comments: Since late 1970s, once-powerful communist and separatist rebel movements have been reduced to low levels. Number of Communist Party of Thailand (CPT) armed rebels has decreased from 12 000–14 000 in 1978 to less than 1000. Thai forces also combat Muslim separatists in the south (Patani United Liberation Organization and others). Diminished internal threat accompanied by increased external threat from Vietnamese troops in Kampuchea. Viet Nam and Thailand each have roughly 20 000 troops in the border region. Vietnamese forces have frequently crossed into Thailand in search of Kampuchean rebels and clashed with Thai troops.

Africa

| Angola | 1975 | Government vs. anti-communist rebels (UNITA) | 50
40 | Thousands
(1985: 2) |

Comments: UNITA (Union for the Total Independence of Angola) controls one-third of the country. Main supporter is South Africa. South African troops regularly attack inside Angola. The USA has an open 'covert' aid programme for UNITA. The Angolan Government is supported by Cuba (25 000–30 000 troops) and the USSR (arms and advisers). Deep intensification of fighting in recent years.

| Chad | 1965 | Habre government and Oueddai forces vs. Libya and rebels | 14.2
3
5
0.3 | >21 |

Comments: Decades of war with North vs. South, Arab vs. Black, Muslims vs. Christians and animists. Frequent Libyan military intervention; several thousand Libyan troops have occupied Aozou strip in north since 1973. Conflict in 1980s has mainly pitted President Hissan Habre vs. Libyan-backed forces of Goukouni Oueddai. Multinational OAU peacekeeping force deployed in Nov. 1981. French troops intervened on behalf of Habre July 1983–Nov. 1984 and Feb. 1986, troops from Zaire in 1983. Major development in Oct. 1986—Oueddai switched sides and joined Habre in fighting Libyan troops in Chad.

Conflicts	Year began	Warring parties	No. of troops (thousands)[a]	No. killed (thousands)[b]
Ethiopia	1962	Government vs. EPLF, TPLF, other separatist guerrillas	227* 50–60	>45

Comments: Largest rebel group is Eritrean People's Liberation Front (EPLF), about 30 000 strong, fighting for independence since annexation of Eritrea in 1962. Conflict pits Marxist government vs. Marxist rebels. Other major threat is Tigre People's Liberation Front (TPLF), about 10 000 strong. Smaller opposition groups in the Oromo, Wollo and Gondar regions. Annual government offensives are largely ineffective. Rebels attack towns, roads, military facilities and control 85% of countryside in northern Ethiopia. Cuban troops supporting government number less than 5000, down from peak of 20 000 in 1977.

Conflicts	Year began	Warring parties	No. of troops (thousands)[a]	No. killed (thousands)[b]
Ethiopia–Somalia	1964	Ethiopian Government and anti-Somalia rebels vs. Somalian Government and anti-Ethiopian rebels	227* 3.5 42.7* 1	38 1980–86: 2

Comments: This conflict combines a border war and several guerrilla conflicts. Ethiopia and Somalia dispute their border in the Ogaden region. Rebels in Ogaden desiring independence have been fighting Ethiopian Government since 1964. Most deaths occurred during Somalian invasion of Ogaden in 1977. The Ethiopian Government now supports the Democratic Front for the Salvation of Somalia (DFSS) and the Somali National Movement (SNM)—which are based in Ethiopia—while the Somalian Government supports the Western Somalian Liberation Front (WSLF) and the Somali Abu Liberation Front (SALF)—which are based in Somalia. Ethiopia conducts occasional air strikes, ground attacks and artillery bombardments in the border region.

Conflicts	Year began	Warring parties	No. of troops (thousands)[a]	No. killed (thousands)[b]
Mozambique	1978	Mozambican Government vs. MNR	25 15	1985: 2–3

Comments: The National Resistance Movement (MNR, or RENAMO) has grown rapidly from 3000–5000 rebels in 1983 to 15 000 in 1986. MNR receives weapons, training, logistic and other support from South Africa. Apparent MNR goal is to disrupt and destroy government infrastructure. Mozambican Government has received military aid from the Soviet Union, and combat support from Zimbabwean and Tanzanian troops. Some 10 000 Zimbabwean troops are deployed in Mozambique.

Conflicts	Year began	Warring parties	No. of troops (thousands)[a]	No. killed (thousands)[b]
Namibia	1966	South African Government vs. SWAPO	21 SWATF 6–9	10

Comments: In 1966 the UN renunciated South Africa's mandate over South West Africa (and renamed it Namibia), but South Africa has ignored the UN. SWAPO (South West African People's Organization), the national anti-colonial movement leading the war for independence, has widespread support among Namibia's population, which is 97% black. SWAPO's military arm, the People's Liberation Army of Namibia (PLAN), is based in Angola. South Africa keeps the 21 000-strong South West African Territory Force (SWATF) based in Namibia, and deploys additional troops for some operations. South African troops regularly attack the rebels inside Angola. It is estimated that South Africa spends $2–3 million per day on the war in Namibia, but profits greatly from the gem mines it controls and taxes it collects.

Conflicts	Year began	Warring parties	No. of troops (thousands)[a]	No. killed (thousands)[b]
South Africa	1970s	Government vs. ANC	106.4* 10	1984–86: 3

Comments: Years of predictions of inevitable civil war between 90% non-white population and white minority government appear to be coming true. New phase of increased violence since 1984. Increasing use of South African military in townships where police forces cannot quell unrest. The African National Congress (ANC) has emerged as the main armed anti-apartheid

Conflicts	Year began	Warring parties	No. of troops (thousands)[a]	No. killed (thousands)[b]

organization; its military wing, the Spear of the Nation, has grown to perhaps 10 000 armed and trained rebels but remains weak. Main warfare is economic sabotage and hit-and-run attacks on police and military facilities.

Sudan	1983	Government vs.	56.75	3
		SPLA	20	

Comments: Resumption of bloody 17-year civil war which killed hundreds of thousands in 1955–72. Moslem, Arab north vs. Christian and animist, Black south. South desires greater autonomy and better distribution of national income. Sudan People's Liberation Army (SPLA) is main rebel group; it receives arms and sanctuary from Ethiopia. A second rebel group, Anyana II, broke from the SPLA and is now fighting with the government forces against the SPLA.

Uganda	1981	Government (NRA) vs.	6?	>250
		anti-government rebels	6?	
		(Obote, Okello, Amin)		

Comments: Uganda has been plagued for decades with fighting among various ethnic, tribal and private armies. The guerrilla National Resistance Army (NRA), which took up arms in 1981, seized power in Jan. 1986. The NRA is now battling forces led by three previous leaders of Uganda—Okello, Obote and Amin. Widespread massacres and attacks on the civilian population resulted in 250 000 deaths in 1983–85.

Western Sahara	1975	Moroccan Government	100–120	7–10
		vs. Polisario	4–15	

Comments: Former Spanish colony of Western Sahara was divided between Morocco and Mauritania in 1975; Morocco annexed Mauritania's half in 1979. Polisario Liberation Front is fighting for independence. It is based mainly in Algeria. Morocco has built a 2500-km wall, enclosing 75% of Western Sahara, to force rebels out.

Zimbabwe	1980	Government vs.	42*	>1.5
		'dissidents'	?	

Comments: Dec. 1979 defeat of white minority government of then-Rhodesia did not bring peace. Subsequent fighting between forces loyal to leaders of two main black guerrilla groups (Robert Mugabe, elected Prime Minister in March 1980, and Joshua Nkomo) effectively ended in 1986 with attempted unity of the two groups, but warfare continues against so-called 'dissidents'. Dissidents are collection of disaffected guerrilla fighters (mostly former Nkomo-loyalists), South African proxies and criminals conducting campaign of terrorism and economic sabotage in Matabeleland Province, with aim of destabilizing government.

Latin America

Colombia	1978	Government vs. M-19,	66.2*	1/year
		FARC, other rebels	0.1–1.5	
			10–12	
			1–1.5	

Comments: At least half a dozen armed leftist revolutionary groups engage in bombings, kidnappings and attacks on police stations, Army patrols and small towns. Government armed forces mount offensives and counter-offensives with some success, but are unable to defeat rebels. May 1984 peace accord with four main groups has not ended violence, although biggest group—Colombian Revolutionary Armed Forces (FARC)—has largely abided by it. Most active group is M-19 (April 19 Movement). When M-19 seized Palace of Justice in Nov. 1985, government military assault resulted in more than 100 deaths, including 12 Supreme Court justices.

Conflicts	Year began	Warring parties	No. of troops (thousands)[a]	No. killed (thousands)[b]
Ecuador	1985	Government vs. Alfaro Vive	42* 1–1.5	2?

Comments: Alfaro Vive has grown from a very small terrorist group into an insurgent organization capable of threatening the government. Reportedly closely aligned with Colombia's M-19, Alfaro Vive engages in kidnappings, bank robberies and attacks on radio stations and newspapers.

El Salvador	1977	Government vs. FMLN	43 4.5–6	>60

Comments: Farabundo Marti Front for National Liberation (FMLN) is coalition of leftist rebel groups fighting to defeat Salvadorean armed forces, which have traditionally ruled El Salvador along with small wealthy élite. War is rooted in political, economic and social disparities. Full-scale civil war since 1979 with widespread rebel assaults on military and economic targets. Rebels control portions of countryside. Extensive arms deliveries, military training, other combat support for government forces by USA. Since 1984, government has regained military initiative and mounted extensive air war campaign, forcing rebels to abandon major engagements and turning conflict into war of attrition. Vast majority of casualties are non-combatant civilians.

Guatemala	1967	Government vs. URNG	32* 2–2.5	1967–74: 20 1979–86: >21

Comments: Civil war 1967–74, rooted largely in poor socio-economic conditions and government repression, rekindled in 1979. Four guerrilla groups formed Guatemalan National Revolutionary Unity (URNG) in 1982. Massive counter-insurgency campaign 1982–83 cut rebel strength by more than half; extensive civilian casualties with entire villages destroyed. Civil defence patrols (rural militia) and 'model villages' established. Rebels still conduct hit-and-run attacks, occasionally striking military installations.

Nicaragua	1981	Government vs. contras	72 12–17	5–10

Comments: Contras (counter-revolutionaries) are attempting to overthrow the leftist Sandinista Government. They are based in Honduras and, to a lesser extent, Costa Rica and inside Nicaragua. Largest contra group is Democratic Forces of Nicaragua (FDN); others include two Indian groups (Misura and Misurasata) and the Southern Opposition Bloc (BOS). Eden Pastora's ARDE collapsed in 1986. Contras have received arms, training, other combat support from USA; CIA mining of harbours condemned by the International Court of Justice. US Congress cut off military aid in mid-1984, slowing pace of war, but resumed aid in Oct. 1986. Major border clash between Nicaraguan and Honduran forces in Dec. 1986. Extensive Soviet military deliveries to Sandinistas; several thousand Cuban military advisers, according to US sources.

Peru	1980	Government vs. Sendero Luminoso	127* 2–3	6–8

Comments: Sendero Luminoso (Shining Path) describes itself as 'Maoist', with goal of putting workers and peasants in power, though observers say it is more closely linked to Inca warriors than international communism. Sendero carries out assassinations and attacks on Army patrols, police posts, power stations and other economic targets, haciendas of the wealthy, government buildings and embassies. Tremendous expansion of conflict since late 1982, as Sendero has moved from main base in Ayacucho region to become active in more provinces, launched many more and much larger assaults and increasingly attacked in urban areas, including Lima. Government forced to deploy ever-larger numbers of Army troops. Widespread abuse of civilians by both Army and Sendero.

*a*Figures in this column refer to the warring parties in the previous column, and correspond to the order in which they are named in that column.

*b*Figures for number killed refer to total casualties.

Conventions: * Not all troops are engaged in combat
  . . Not known

Notes on sources for table 8.1:

Data in this table were collected by the World at War Project of the CDI from a multitude of sources. Information was gathered from the US Government, the governments of nations at war and from guerrilla organizations when possible; but, because of the scarcity and unreliability of 'official' information from combatants, extensive use has been made of secondary sources. Most government armed forces totals were taken from the International Institute for Strategic Studies, *The Military Balance 1986–87*. Ruth Sivard's annual *World Military and Social Expenditures* was the single best source for casualty figures.

Interviews were conducted with US State Department and/or Defense Department specialists for nearly every conflict. Also interviewed were Embassy officials and regional and country experts in Washington, DC. The US Government's Foreign Broadcast Information Service provided extensive coverage of non-US media and government statements. The US State Department's *Country Reports on Human Rights Practices* (annual) had relevant material for numerous conflicts. Many other publications from the State Department, Defense Department, Arms Control and Disarmament Agency, Congressional Research Service, and other US Government agencies were utilized. Congressional hearings and prints were extensively used; of particular interest were foreign assistance hearings.

The newspapers most heavily used were the *New York Times* and *Washington Post*. Others include (not exclusively) the *Christian Science Monitor*, *Los Angeles Times*, *Miami Herald*, *Wall Street Journal* and *Washington Times*. The US Defense Department's newspaper clipping service *Current News* provided coverage of dozens of US papers. Non-US newspapers, from nations such as France, the United Kingdom, Israel, Lebanon, Algeria, South Africa, Thailand, El Salvador and Nicaragua, were also used.

Publications useful for all regions included *Defense and Foreign Affairs*, *Defense and Foreign Affairs Weekly*, *Jane's Defence Weekly*, *Journal of Defense and Diplomacy*, *Proceedings*, *Armed Forces Journal International*, *Army Times*, *International Defense Review*, *World Press Review*, *South*, *Le Monde*, *Nation*, *Newsweek*, *Time* and *US News and World Report*. Also helpful were *Strategic Survey*, *Survival*, *Adelphi Papers*, *Foreign Affairs*, *Foreign Policy*, *Third World Quarterly*, *World Policy Journal* and *Problems of Communism*. A variety of Amnesty International publications were valuable.

Particularly useful for Asian conflicts were the *Asian Defense Journal*, *Far Eastern Economic Review* and *Pacific Defense Reporter*, plus information from Asia Watch and the Indochina Project. For Middle Eastern conflicts, most useful were *American-Arab Affairs*, *MERIP Middle East Report* and *Middle East Journal*. For African conflicts, most useful were the *Africa Contemporary Record*, *Africa News* and *AfricAsia*. For Latin American conflicts, most useful were *Central America Bulletin*, *Central American Historical Institute Update*, *Central America Report*, *Latin American Monitor*, *Latinamerica Press*, *Latin America Update*, *Report on the Americas* and *Washington Report on the Hemisphere*, plus material from Americas Watch and the American Friends Service Committee.

Notes and references

[1] This definition intentionally avoids citing as criteria specific numbers for casualties incurred, duration of fighting or size of opposition forces. The selection of arbitrary numbers as 'cut-off points' tends to distort and understate the degree to which armed violence exists throughout the world. As a practical matter, however, only those conflicts which have resulted in more than 1000 deaths have been included.

[2] Sivard, R. L., *World Military and Social Expenditures 1986* (World Priorities: Washington, DC, 1986), pp. 26–27.

[3] Khomeini quotations are from *Time*, 26 July 1978, p. 45; and Foreign Broadcast Information Service (US Department of Commerce), 10 Apr. 1980, cited in Evans, D. and Campany, R., 'Iran–Iraq: bloody tomorrows', *Proceedings*, Jan. 1985, p. 33.

⁴ Preece, R. M., *The Iran–Iraq War: Implications for US Policy*, Congressional Research Service (CRS) Issue Brief IB 84016, 24 Sep. 1986, p. 7 gives the 1984 figure. 'The course of the Iran–Iraq war', *Strategic Survey 1985–86* (IISS: London, 1986), p. 126 gives the 1980–83 figure.

⁵ IISS, *Strategic Survey 1985–86* (note 4), p. 127.

⁶ *Washington Post*, 26 Nov. 1986.

⁷ *New York Times*, 28 Dec. 1986.

⁸ See, for example, *New York Times*, 19 Oct. 1986; *Washington Post*, 11 Nov. 1986; *Army Times*, 24 Nov. 1986, p. 47.

⁹ Sivard (note 2) cites 627 000 dead. *New York Times*, 23 Sep. 1985, cites 'intelligence estimates' of 720 000–880 000 dead (300 000 Iraqi and 420 000–580 000 Iranian).

¹⁰ Chubin, S., 'Reflections on the Gulf War', *Survival*, July-Aug. 1986, p. 312, citing *Al-Siyasah*, 14 Oct. 1985.

¹¹ Preece (note 4), p. 9, citing *Economist* Intelligence Unit Study.

¹² *Washington Post*, 23 Sep. 1986.

¹³ *Army Times*, 24 Nov. 1986, p. 47.

¹⁴ *Washington Post*, 5 Oct. 1986; *New York Times*, 26 Oct. 1986.

¹⁵ Preece (note 4), p. 6.

¹⁶ Preece (note 4), p. 6.

¹⁷ Most sources put the Iraqi debt at the lower end of the range given. See, for example, Preece (note 4), p. 13; and Chubin (note 10), p. 311. IISS, *Military Balance 1986–87*, p. 92 gives $85 billion in total debt, with $60 billion from the GCC.

¹⁸ IISS, *Military Balance 1986–87*, pp. 96–98. See also *Army Times*, 24 Nov. 1986; *New York Times*, 1 Oct. 1986.

¹⁹ Chubin (note 10), p. 320.

²⁰ See for example, *Washington Post*, 5 Oct. 1986; Preece (note 4), p. 4; Daly, M., 'The enduring Gulf War', *Proceedings*, May 1985, pp. 153–54; Senate Foreign Relations Committee Print, *War in the Gulf*, Aug. 1984, p. 7.

²¹ *New York Times*, 26 Sep. 1986; IISS, *Military Balance 1985–86*, p. 76; and IISS, *Military Balance 1986–87*, p. 97.

²² IISS, *Military Balance 1986–87*, pp. 96–98.

²³ See note 22. See also *Jane's Defence Weekly*, 29 Nov. 1986, p. 1257; *Army Times*, 25 Nov. 1986, p. 47, 50; *Defense and Foreign Affairs*, Nov. 1986, p. 1; *Washington Post*, 23 Sep. 1986; *Washington Times*, 25 Nov. 1986.

²⁴ *Washington Post*, 15 Mar. 1986.

²⁵ *New York Times*, 15 Mar. 1986.

²⁶ Preece (note 4), p. 8.

²⁷ *Washington Post*, 27 Sep. 1985.

²⁸ Preece (note 4), p. 9.

²⁹ *New York Times*, 15 Mar. 1986; Preece (note 4), pp. 8–9.

³⁰ Good descriptions of Basra defences are to be found in *Washington Post*, 2 Nov. 1986; and *New York Times*, 12 Oct. 1986.

³¹ The figure of $9 billion is cited in Evans and Campany (note 3), p. 1; $5 billion is cited in Stork, J., 'Arms merchants in the Gulf War', *MERIP Reports*, July-Sep. 1984, p. 39.

³² *Defense Week*, 29 Sep. 1986, p. 2.

³³ In its annual volumes on *Soviet Military Power* (*1986* and *1987*), the Pentagon reports that the USSR delivered $6 billion worth of arms and equipment to Iraq during 1984–86; the Senate Foreign Relations Committee cites 'several billion dollars worth' through mid–1984 (see note 20, p. 10). Egypt has also shipped over $2 billion in weapons to Iraq (see Evans and Campany, note 3, p. 37, and Hiro, D., 'Chronicle of the Gulf War', *MERIP Reports*, July–Sep. 1984, p. 8).

³⁴ *New York Times*, 5 Dec. 1986 and 25 Nov. 1986, citing a high-ranking Administration official.

³⁵ *Washington Post*, 3 Dec. 1986.

³⁶ *Jane's Defence Weekly*, 29 Nov. 1986, p. 1257.

³⁷ *New York Times*, 25 Nov. 1986, citing a high-ranking Administration official. Many sources cite an unconfirmed $1.6 billion deal in March 1985, including *SIPRI Yearbook 1986*, p. 371. Also widely reported was a $1.3 billion deal in spring 1983 (*Washington Post*, 3 Apr. 1984, and *Jane's Defence Weekly*, 21 Apr. 1984, p. 606) confirmed by the US State Department.

³⁸ *New York Times*, 25 Nov. 1986, citing an Administration official.

³⁹ *Jane's Defence Weekly*, 29 Nov. 1986, p. 1256 and 1 Nov. 1986, p. 1023; *International Defense Review*, Mar. 1985, pp. 303–304.

⁴⁰ *Washington Post*, 10 Dec. 1986, discusses the failure of Operation Staunch to stop sales from Israel, the United Kingdom, FR Germany, Switzerland, China and other nations.

⁴¹ *Washington Post*, 3 Apr. 1984.

[42] Hiro (note 33), p 8, citing the Iraqi Deputy Prime Minister.
[43] *Washington Post* and *New York Times*, 30 Nov. 1986.
[44] *Defense Electronics*, Sep. 1984, p. 138.
[45] Evans and Campany (note 3), p. 43.
[46] See Cordesman, A., 'Lessons of the Iran–Iraq War', *Armed Forces Journal International*, June 1982, pp. 68–85.

Part III. Developments in arms control

Chapter 9. US–Soviet nuclear arms control

The Reykjavik summit meeting / Narrowing the gap / Critique from NATO allies / The basic flaws / The outlook

Chapter 10. The future of conventional arms control in Europe, A tale of two cities: Stockholm, Vienna

Introduction / An assessment of Stockholm from NATO's perspective / What does Stockholm's outcome imply for the future of operational arms control?

Chapter 11. Multilateral arms control efforts

Introduction / Chemical disarmament / Nuclear test ban / Arms control in outer space / The South Pacific nuclear-free zone / Arms control in Central America / Zone of peace in the South Atlantic

Chapter 12. The review of the Biological Weapons Convention

Scope of the prohibitions / Compliance with the obligations / Strengthening the effectiveness of the Convention / Peaceful uses of biological agents / Evaluation

9. US-Soviet nuclear arms control

CHRISTOPH BERTRAM, diplomatic correspondent, *Die Zeit*,
FR Germany

Superscript numbers refer to the list of notes and references at the end of the chapter.

1986 was an extraordinary year for East–West arms control. Never before have the positions of the USSR and the USA seemed so close. Much of the year witnessed the often encouraging diplomatic efforts towards compromise between the world's major powers. Yet, at the end of the year, the barriers blocking major agreement still seemed dauntingly high although there was some positive movement in early 1987 on a separate accord over intermediate-range nuclear forces in Europe and Asia.

I. The Reykjavik summit meeting

No other event during the year symbolized the failure to agree more than the meeting between President Reagan and General Secretary Gorbachev held on 11–12 October 1986 in Reykjavik, Iceland. Mr Gorbachev had called for the conference because, in his own words, 'the situation is such that we should leave our daily business for one or two days and get together without delay'.[1] Gorbachev, who had announced major arms control initiatives earlier in the year, felt impatient with the lack of progress in the Geneva negotiations; he did not want to commit himself to the long-awaited summit meeting (which, although originally expected to be held before 1987, did not occur) without some visible achievements in arms control.

When the Soviet team arrived in Reykjavik, it was not just for an exploratory exchange—it was to negotiate. The Soviet offer that knowledgeable observers had expected for a long time to be tabled was finally presented. The Soviet Union proposed to the United States a package deal of two stages: within the first five years, the halving of strategic delivery systems, to be followed in the second five-year period by their total elimination; the reduction of inter-mediate-range nuclear forces (INF) to 100 systems each in the Asian part of the Soviet Union and in the United States, and to zero in Europe; an agreed slow-down in nuclear tests; and finally, a firm undertaking by both sides to adhere to the Anti-Ballistic Missile (ABM) Treaty for a period of 10 years while restricting tests for space-based defences to the laboratory.[2]

President Reagan, in contrast, went to the Reykjavik summit meeting without much of a plan. He had been intrigued by Gorbachev's request. His advisers had counselled acceptance since a summit meeting would be helpful both to push the awkward Daniloff issue (the arrest in Moscow of a US reporter) into the background and to enhance Republican changes in the mid-term elections a few weeks later; and the President counted, as he had done so successfully at the November 1985 Geneva summit meeting, on his well-known ability to engage his counterpart in a friendly exchange of views.

As to specific issues, the United States hoped to achieve a compromise on INF and expected strong Soviet pressure to agree on a joint moratorium on nuclear tests. The US side was prepared to advance talks on strategic forces but not for a 'Grand Compromise'—deep cuts in offensive systems in exchange for some limitations on space-based defences—which had been rumoured before-hand in the US press. In contrast to the Soviet delegation, which included Marshall Akromeyev, the Chief of the Soviet General Staff, the US delegation had no senior representative from the Joint Chiefs of Staff.

However, the President's team, to their surprise, soon discovered that the Soviet Union wanted real negotiations, pressing for a compromise across the board. After his first session with Gorbachev, the President remarked to his advisers: 'He's brought a whole lot of proposals, but I'm afraid he is going after SDI'[3]—Reagan's Strategic Defense Initiative, designed to explore the possibilities of space-based missile defences. It was this issue which, a day later, not unexpectedly became the decisive stumbling-block. While the Soviet side proposed a series of concessions to facilitate agreement on INF and strategic forces, it did not budge on its demand for a drastic curtailment of SDI. And the President, while prepared to contemplate the removal of all ballistic missiles within the 10-year period (and even, according to Soviet if not US accounts, the removal of all nuclear weapons) remained adamant that there should be no restrictions, during the 10 years of ABM Treaty compliance agreed by both sides, on SDI research, testing and development.

At the end of the nearly 10 hours of top-level dialogue, it was the inability to bridge this gap which turned the Reykjavik meeting into failure. Perhaps Mr Gorbachev lacked authority to loosen the strings around the package deal he had brought from Moscow, and certainly Mr Reagan saw no basis for compromise on SDI. 'It became more and more clear that the Soviet Union's objective was effectively to kill off the SDI', Secretary of State Shultz stated at his press conference in Reykjavik. 'We are deeply disappointed at this outcome'.[4]

As a result of the inconclusive Reykjavik meeting, strategic arms control was effectively adjourned to an uncertain and distant future. Despite assurances from both sides that dialogue and negotiations would continue, there were no signs, in early 1987, that the breakthrough that was missed in Reykjavik would again come within reach of the world's most powerful statesmen for a long time to come.

II. Narrowing the gap

The failure in October could not entirely hide the progress that had been made earlier in the year on a number of issues, largely owing to a new and—for many—unexpected flexibility on the part of the Soviet Union. At the beginning of the year, both sides had not yet moved significantly from the positions taken prior to and during the November 1985 Geneva summit meeting: both pledged to seek cuts in their strategic nuclear forces of 50 per cent, to try to negotiate an

On 12 October 1986, the second day of the negotiation, the US and Soviet delegations each presented their proposals on strategic arms control. The USA revised its proposals after hearing the Soviet proposal.

First US proposal

Both sides would agree to confine itself to research, development and testing which is permitted by the ABM treaty for a period of five years, through 1991, during which time a 50 per cent reduction of strategic nuclear arsenals would be achieved. This being done, both sides will continue the pace of reductions with respect to the remaining ballistic missiles with the goal of the total elimination of all offensive ballistic missiles by the end of a second five-year period. As long as these reductions continue at the appropriate pace, the same restrictions will continue to apply. At the end of the 10-year period, with all offensive ballistic missiles eliminated, either side would be free to deploy defenses.

Soviet proposal

The Soviet Union and the United States will oblige themselves not to use their right to withdraw from the ABM Treaty, which has no time-limit, for a period of ten years and during this period to ensure strict observance of all of its provisions. All testing on the space elements of the ABM defence in outer space will be prohibited excluding research and testing conducted in laboratories.

In the first five years of this decade (until 1991 inclusive) the strategic offensive arms of both sides will be reduced by 50 per cent.

In the next five years of this period the remaining 50 per cent of the strategic offensive arms of both sides will be eliminated.

Thus, the strategic offensive arms of the USSR and the USA will be completely eliminated by the end of the year 1996.

Second US proposal

The USSR and the United States undertake for 10 years not to exercise their existing right of withdrawal from the ABM Treaty, which is of unlimited duration, and during that period strictly to observe all its provisions while continuing research, development and testing, which are permitted by the ABM treaty. Within the first five years of the 10-year period (and thus through 1991), the strategic offensive arms of the two sides shall be reduced by 50 per cent. During the following five years of that period, all remaining offensive ballistic missiles of the two sides shall be reduced. Thus, by the end of 1996, all offensive ballistic missiles of the USSR and the United States will have been totally eliminated. At the end of the 10-year period, either side could deploy defenses if it so chose unless the parties agree otherwise.

Figure 9.1. US and Soviet proposals made at the 1986 Reykjavik summit meeting

Sources: Official US texts provided by the State Department, reprinted in *New York Times*, 18 Oct. 1986. Official English translation of Soviet text, from speech by General Secretary Gorbachev on Soviet television, 14 Oct. 1986, in Gorbachev, M., *The Results and Lessons of Reykjavik: Summit Meeting in the Icelandic Capital, October 11–12, 1986* (Novosti Press Agency Publishing House: Moscow, 1986), p. 37.

interim agreement on INF and, in addition, to 'prevent an arms race in space and end it on earth'. But—even leaving aside the fundamental issue of strategic defences—they remained far apart on specific issues.

1. The Soviet definition of strategic forces still included not only those so defined in the SALT II Treaty of 1979 but also all the forward-based systems (INF, nuclear-capable aircraft on land and on US aircraft-carriers) which, because of their range, could reach targets in the Soviet Union. Thus the Soviet proposals inflated US arsenals while excluding all similar systems in their own arsenals.

2. The Soviet definition of 'nuclear charges' differed considerably from the US definition of 'nuclear warheads': it included nuclear explosives not only on strategic delivery vehicles but also on theatre-range missiles and also free-fall bombs on aircraft.

3. The United States insisted on halving not only strategic missile forces and warheads but also the related throw-weight (claiming a figure of 5.7 million kg for the USSR to 2 million kg for the US side).

4. The United States, pursuing its priority aim of deep cuts in Soviet heavy missiles, called for cuts in the intercontinental ballistic missile (ICBM) forces of both sides that, while limiting nuclear warheads to 3000 (the Soviet figure was 3500) would have an asymmetric effect on the arsenals of both sides.

5. Both sides favoured modernization restraints but with a different bias: the Soviet Union, having completed a major missile modernization programme, wanted to prohibit all new, untested strategic weapons; the United States, which was just beginning its own force modernization, insisted that only new heavy and mobile ICBMs should be so prohibited.

6. As to INF, the Soviet Union, while prepared to accept a force of up to 120 cruise missiles in Western Europe, insisted that it needed a similar SS-20 force plus sufficient INF to compensate for the British and French strategic forces.

This was scarcely a basis on which agreements could be built. But as the year progressed there were growing signs that at least some of the barriers to compromise were being removed.

On 15 January 1986, the Soviet General Secretary launched a major, ambitious proposal, suggesting a detailed schedule to achieve the total abolition of nuclear weapons by the year 2000.[5] This Utopian perspective—to which Gorbachev returned in Reykjavik—seemed designed more to compete with the Reagan vision of an SDI world in which nuclear missiles were to become 'impotent and obsolete'. And the main initial step of halving the strategic arsenals of both superpowers was still tied to restrictions on SDI: 'It goes without saying that such a reduction is only possible if both the USSR and the United States renounce the development, testing and deployment of space strike weapons' (the Soviet term for active missile defences in space).[6] Yet the proposal also contained important new moves which, though still far from meeting Western demands, indicated a Soviet readiness to get negotiations moving.

In particular, this applied to an area which the General Secretary had singled out on previous occasions for treatment separate from the SDI impasse: intermediate-range nuclear forces. What many among NATO's military experts had feared, what many among West European politicians had advocated and what President Reagan had made his official position in the INF negotiations since 1981, was now being proposed from Moscow—a zero solution for all INF in Europe.

The initiatives still did not quite bridge the gap between the former Soviet and US positions: Gorbachev showed no readiness to reduce Soviet INF forces in Asia (where they amounted to about 170 systems) and continued to insist on the Soviet right to build up their own INF forces to compensate for British and French strategic forces, which should be frozen at their present level. At the same time, however, this was the first Soviet proposal suggesting the total disappearance of the Soviet SS-20 missile in the 'European zone'—a decisive departure from all previous Soviet statements.

The other important element in the 15 January statement concerned one of the hitherto most controversial issues of East–West arms control: verification. While Soviet leaders before Mr Gorbachev had shown some readiness in individual cases to accept a degree of on-site inspection, he was the first to formulate Soviet readiness for comprehensive verification. All the steps in his disarmament plan were to be subject to verification by national means (such as satellite surveillance) as well as through on-site inspection. And he added: 'The Soviet Union is prepared to agree to any additional means of verification'.[7]

Yet the January speech was still a halfway-house, not yet a consistently argued and negotiable proposal. It contained a strong element of popular appeal, clearly directed at a West European audience. Not only were the most concrete suggestions made on INF, the area of primary European concern, but Mr Gorbachev also emphasized that the Europeans were the obvious addressees: 'It is by no means a coincidence, that a major part of the new Soviet initiatives are addressed directly to Europe. In case of a fundamental shift towards a policy of peace Europe could be charged with a special mission. This mission would be to erect anew a building of détente'.[8]

As a result, there were many in the West who dismissed the text as an exercise in propaganda. Yet that was inaccurate, not only in the light of subsequent events. Significantly, the January speech contained a large number of fairly specific undertakings, indicating that its author wished the West to put his words to the test. Perhaps it was as much an exercise intended for the world outside as for the bureaucracy within; by staking out future positions, the Soviet leader sought to commit the Soviet foreign policy machine to his objectives. Western diplomats soon pointed out that the new policy on verification was still not visible in Soviet position papers presented to the chemical weapon negotiations in the Conference on Disarmament in Geneva or the Mutual and Balanced Force Reduction (MBFR) talks in Vienna. Indeed, it took another six months before the principles announced from above percolated through to the diplomatic frontline—when, for the first time in history, the Soviet Union agreed, in the Stockholm negotiations on confidence- and security-building measures in Europe, to compulsory inspections on its territory conducted by foreign inspection teams.

So movement was clearly intended in Moscow, even if it did not occur swiftly, and the stalemate in Soviet–US nuclear arms control continued. It was not until early summer that Mr Gorbachev took new steps towards agreement. Suddenly there were reports from the strategic nuclear weapon talks in Geneva that the negotiations had begun in earnest. To underline this new seriousness, the Soviet delegation dropped its attempts to redefine US strategic forces by the inclusion of forward-based systems (FBS), although it ceded ground only gradually, still claiming initially that all FBS should at least be frozen at their present level or otherwise constrained. Sea-launched cruise missiles with over 600-km range which earlier Soviet proposals had sought to ban should now be permitted, at least on submarines.

SDI and the ABM Treaty

The most important indication that the talks were moving into a decisive phase was provided by a new Soviet approach to the problem of how to combine reductions in offensive strategic forces with constraints on strategic defences. Since late 1985, the Soviet Union had proposed what it termed a 50 per cent cut in the strategic forces of both sides to 6000 'nuclear charges' (in fact, this would represent a reduction of between 30 and 40 per cent) with 3600 of these charges on ICBMs. But that had been proposed on the basis of a permanent ban on SDI efforts. Now, in a letter to the US President, General Secretary Gorbachev declared the Soviet willingness to end the SDI restrictions imposed by the ABM Treaty after a 15- to 20-year period if the United States so desired, provided that during that period all SDI activities beyond the laboratory would cease. In other words, the USSR was willing to trade away the unlimited duration of the treaty (and the unilateral right to give six months' notice to withdraw from the treaty if a party 'decides that extra-ordinary events related to the subject matter of this Treaty have jeopardized its supreme interests') in exchange for a more strictly interpreted commitment for a finite period. The corollary to this less ambitious approach to restraints on SDI was that the Soviet Union now also offered less in limitations of offensive forces: the proposed ceiling for warheads on strategic delivery systems (excluding sea-launched cruise missiles) was increased to 8000 (instead of 6000) with 4800 (instead of 3600) on ICBMs.

At the end of July, President Reagan responded to these proposals in a letter to General Secretary Gorbachev which raised hopes that, at last, the United States was willing to negotiate in some fashion about its strategic defence programme. Yet the US flexibility was more apparent than real. While Mr Reagan made astonishing proposals on strategic offensive forces, suggesting even a total ban on ballistic missiles (an idea he was to return to in Reykjavik), he remained adamant on SDI. The deployment of strategic defences in space, so the President proposed, should be delayed for seven years, and only then would the six-month period of notice apply. In the meantime, all other restrictions on the SDI programme imposed by the ABM Treaty would be waived. The USA would be entitled to do what the Department of Defense had been claiming with increasing force for some time—namely, to research, develop and test SDI as it saw fit. The apparent US concession turned out to be none at all. At the end of the seven and a half-year period, the Administration suggested that a new treaty which would allow both sides to deploy active defences in space should replace the ABM Treaty.

Movement on INF

The major stumbling-block remained as solid as ever, and little progress was registered on strategic nuclear forces, with the Soviet Union in particular rejecting US ideas of sublimits on Soviet ICBM forces, which were clearly designed to diminish drastically the number of Soviet multi-warhead, highly accurate heavy missiles. Instead, attention refocused on the INF issues. Two special meetings of Soviet and US officials which included not only the chief negotiators but also the top officials from the two capitals as well, held near Moscow and Washington in August and September, were able to move the matter forward. The Soviet Union dropped its traditional insistence that the French and British nuclear forces should somehow be included, albeit indirectly, in any INF agreement, at least for a transitory period; how long this would last remained uncertain in the run-up to the Reykjavik meeting. There was also still the open question of reductions in the Soviet INF forces stationed in Asia, outside the 'European zone', and both sides continued to disagree on how to treat shorter-range INF (below a range of 1000 km)—whether to freeze them at their present level (which would give a clear advantage to the Soviet Union) or to decide on a common ceiling (to which the United States could then build up).

Yet despite this movement and the repeated Soviet declaration that an INF interim deal would not be held up by the deadlock over strategic defences, there were doubts even before the Reykjavik summit meeting whether a separate INF agreement would be a realistic outcome—for the simple reason that a zero-rule for INF in Europe and major reductions in Asia would put much the larger burden of concessions on the Soviet Union without it obtaining much in return. But such speculation had become, at least for the time being, academic. All Soviet proposals, even that of the General Secretary in Reykjavik, were now tied into one package. And the Politbureau of the Communist Party of the Soviet Union confirmed that this was no isolated decision but one endorsed (and enforced) by the collective leadership of the Soviet Union as a whole.[9]

III. Critique from NATO allies

The post-Reykjavik period confirmed the old rule that an opportunity lost once may be lost forever. It would have been difficult enough for the two world leaders to push an agreement through their respective bureaucracies; the fact that they left Reykjavik without a result meant that whatever compromise they envisaged would now be infinitely harder to resurrect. Only a few days after the Reykjavik meeting, the superpowers voiced public disagreement on what had and what had not been agreed. While the opponents in Moscow of an arms control deal with the Reagan Administration reacted by tying the knots around the Gorbachev package even tighter, Western opponents to some of the aspects of the reported Reagan concessions also made their views heard. This criticism came above all from Europe (although some of it was shared in the United States) and centred on two issues: the zero-solution for INF, and the total ban on ballistic missiles within a 10-year period.

For most military experts in NATO the total removal of Pershing II and cruise missiles had never been an attractive outcome for arms control, and not without reason: after all, the Soviet SS-20 threat had not been the only military concern behind Western INF deployments; and other concerns—over the feared vulnerability of NATO nuclear-capable aircraft to Warsaw Pact air defence, and over the assumed importance for NATO to reach targets on Soviet territories with INF delivery systems from Western Europe—came to the surface once the total removal of the SS-20 systems within range of West European targets became a distinct possibility. No less an authority than General Bernard Rogers, the Supreme Allied Commander in Europe, warned that zero INF would handicap NATO's strategy of flexible response and weaken deterrence against the Warsaw Pact's conventional forces.[10]

While political leaders in Western Europe shared at least some of these misgivings, having for years offered the zero-option on INF to the USSR, they realized the political impossibility of refusing their own proposal now that the Soviet Union was offering it. Yet some governments insisted that, in addition to the removal of long-range INF (over 1000 km), shorter-range systems (for which a common definition betwen East and West apparently does not yet exist; they cover ranges of 300–1000 km) should be subjected to some immediate constraints (the West: a ceiling; the East: a freeze) and should be urgently dealt with in direct negotiations. Whatever misgivings about a zero-solution on INF existed in NATO, these were unlikely to block a Soviet–US INF deal if it should, once again, materialize. Indeed, this was later confirmed when General Secretary Gorbachev on 28 February 1987 removed the linkage between an INF deal and restrictions on strategic defences.

The second issue of Western and particularly European criticism of the US negotiating proposals in Reykjavik concerned not the medium- but the long-term perspective, as outlined by the US President: the removal of all ballistic nuclear missiles within 10 years (and, perhaps, of all nuclear weapons in the more distant future).

The idea, although aired earlier in Mr Reagan's July letter to Mr Gorbachev, had all the ingredients of worrying the USA's allies as well as most US strategists. For one, it demonstrated the cavalier way in which the Reagan Administration approached strategic matters: never discussed with its allies, incompletely consulted with the Joint Chiefs of Staff, the suggestion indicated the worrying absence of a long-term concept of strategic stability and deterrence apart from the visionary notion of a comprehensive and leak-proof strategic defence. Moreover, it awakened long-held, if dormant, fears in Western Europe that the United States, even under a President for whom 'making America strong again' had been the most consistent objective, was losing the will to extend nuclear deterrence to its overseas allies in such a way that US survival would continue to be directly at stake. To remove all ballistic missiles would limit the nuclear systems of the future to the manned and the unmanned (cruise missiles) aircraft, thus giving a bonus to the Soviet Union with its traditionally strong emphasis on air defence. At the same time, it would reduce the US deterrent capability against nuclear attacks on Western Europe.

European governments were thus reminded that their security policies continued to be based on nuclear deterrence and on the threat of nuclear escalation. As a result of the Reykjavik meeting, they sought to couple the President's willingness to reduce strategic forces beyond a 50 per cent cut to a series of conditions, the most important of which was the undertaking that any further reductions in nuclear arsenals would have to be accompanied by major reductions in the conventional forces of the East and the West. In a statement issued by British Prime Minister Thatcher following discussions with President Reagan on 15 November (and published with his agreement), the most important sentence read: 'We confirmed that NATO's strategy of forward defence and flexible response would continue to require effective nuclear deterrents based on a mix of systems. At the same time, reductions in nuclear weapons would increase the importance of eliminating conventional disparities. Nuclear weapons cannot be dealt with in isolation, given the need for stable overall balance at all times'.[11]

IV. The basic flaws

Such declarations would become relevant only if, indeed, as the USSR and the USA continued to assert, most of the Reykjavik compromises were still on the table. But as the year moved towards its end, it became increasingly doubtful if this was still the case. The brief post-Reykjavik euphoria, aroused by a successful publicity campaign on the part of the White House, had little substance in fact, just as earlier statements and hopes about arms control had reflected more a general sense of unreality than any reliable guide to future agreements. Despite the fact that, on the surface, the positions of both sides on a number of specific issues had moved rather closer together during 1986, the very basis for Soviet–US arms control simply did not exist, neither before, during nor after the Reykjavik summit meeting.

SDI: the divisive issue

The most obvious barrier, whose importance was again confirmed at Reykjavik, was the different perspectives of the Soviet and the US sides on strategic defences. But behind it other, no less fundamental, obstacles became visible. Many of these were more apparent in the United States than in the Soviet Union, owing to the openness of the US political system. In the end, however, that may be irrelevant. What counts for arms control is the ability of *both sides* to come to an agreement, and that ability was fundamentally lacking.

The first example of the absence of a sound basis for agreement was that of strategic defences, particularly space-based systems. In contrast to the predominant mood in the Soviet Union several years ago, the main Soviet concern no longer seemed to be caused by any belief that, in the future, the United States would be able to deploy an effective operational missile defence system to protect its territory against attack. The Soviet Union, which had itself for many years invested heavily in research and development for active defences, probably realized the technical difficulties involved the closer it studied the US effort. Studies emerging from the Soviet Union emphasized Soviet confidence that, instead of competing with the United States, it would be possible, through highly accurate strikes against the command and control elements, to blind a US strategic defence system.[12] But neither this nor the growing resistance in the US Congress to providing the President with the SDI funds he had requested seemed to alter the adamancy of Soviet opposition to the testing of strategic defences in space. While after the Reykjavik meeting Soviet officials hinted repeatedly that the insistence on allowing only laboratory testing did not have to be the last word, the limits of Soviet flexibility nevertheless were clear. What motivated the Soviet Union may have been the concern that the environment of space should be denied to the kinds of test envisaged under the US SDI programme—not in order to prevent an effective system of defences but to delay, for as long as possible, the development of military technology predominantly considered within SDI but increasingly relevant for the whole spectrum of future weaponry; sensor technology, optics and kinetic-energy weapons chief among them. For the Soviet Union, so its approach suggested, SDI was a problem not because it might alter the nuclear doctrine of the United States but because it might push the military-technical competition between East and West into a new environment in which the technologically underdeveloped Soviet Union was bound to lag dangerously behind.

If this explained the limits of Soviet flexibility on SDI, the US case was very different. Here SDI was seen by some—above all by the President himself—as the major Reagan legacy, and hence, whatever the current difficulties in proving that it could satisfy the exalted expectations formulated by the President in March 1983, as a programme that under no condition must be jeopardized, least of all through an arms control agreement. Others in the Administration who were philosophically opposed to arms control made use of this presidential determination both for trying to undermine the ABM Treaty (see below) and for preventing any concessions on SDI which might have broken the deadlock in the negotiations.

Competing visions

The second and perhaps more significant obstacle to agreement was the maximalist or deliberately Utopian approach to arms control which not only the US but also the Soviet side displayed. Rather than exploring the possible, both superpowers, perhaps motivated by the outburst of anti-nuclear public sentiments in Western societies during the early 1980s, demanded the unattainable: Mr Reagan, a shield against missile attack which would render nuclear missiles 'impotent and obsolete'; and Mr Gorbachev, the total elimination of all nuclear weapons by the year 2000.

Both notions contained an element of *realpolitik* in their instrumental effect—the US President felt he had devised a good method both to strengthen the United States and to extract concessions from the Soviet Union. The Soviet leader may have wanted to profit from anti-nuclear feelings in Western Europe by promoting, in the guise of a universal plan, the old Soviet objective of a nuclear-free Europe. But as contributions to arms control, these initiatives, if they were intended as such, were counter-productive. This was not only because the vision of the East was incompatible with the vision of the West; even if both sides had agreed on the same objective, this would at best have regulated a very distant future, but not the present competition and the problems that it now created.

For behind this competition of visions lay a fundamental misunderstanding of what arms control, as opposed to disarmament, can be expected to accomplish. The understanding that arms control and disarmament are two very different matters and that only the former stands some chance of being realized between rival powers dates back to the late 1950s. Without it, neither the limited test ban treaties nor the SALT agreements and the ABM Treaty would ever have been successfully negotiated. The same basic fact remains true today: arms control is a modest means for regulating military competition, but no more than that. Any more ambitious approach, from deep cuts to the complete elimination of weapons that are central to the military force relationship between the superpowers, runs contrary to so many more and much larger obstacles—differences of doctrine, technology, the specific interests of the services, bureaucracy, industry, and so on—so as to become highly unlikely. Disarmament denies what arms control recognizes, namely, that deep asymmetries (which are represented by weaponry) exist and that with good will they might be curtailed but never entirely removed. Those who make the latter the aim of arms control are likely to fail—and they risk, in the process, producing disillusion and apathy in a public in which exaggerated expectations have been nurtured.

The compliance issue

The third fundamental obstacle to agreement, finally, was the divisions within the US Government and the unwillingness or inability of the President to overcome them. Perhaps some similar divisions existed within the Soviet leadership and government, and they might have emerged if there had been serious negotiations; as it was, the Soviet Union was able to display an increasingly coherent position *vis-à-vis* the US Administration which, by tolerating its internal divisions, had sent a highly ambiguous message to the outside world, with both the few—supporters of arms control—and the many—opponents in Washington—claiming to do no more than implement the President's wishes. In the end, the opponents usually carried the day.

This was particularly pronounced in two instances, both raising the question of how seriously an Administration, which professed to be seeking new agreements with the Soviet Union, was treating agreements that its predecessors had entered into.

The first instance concerned the 1979 SALT II Treaty, signed by Leonid Brezhnev and Jimmy Carter but not ratified by either the Soviet Union or the United States. The Reagan Administration had wavered in its early days on whether to observe the unratified accord which the President had in his election campaigns labelled 'fatally flawed'. But the Administration soon found out that the only constraints imposed by the treaty were, in practice, on Soviet forces, while the United States was still well below the permitted ceilings of nuclear forces and could continue its programmes. Even when the United States had to dismantle older Poseidon submarines to accommodate the new Trident I systems, the President decided to remain within the treaty limits. When he announced in May 1986 that the United States would henceforth not base its procurement decisions on the SALT II Treaty but on its military requirements, there were some who hoped that this was still not the end of the accord; but on 28 November the United States deliberately exceeded the treaty limits when a B-52 bomber, modified to carry cruise missiles, entered service.

There was no pressing military reason for the USA to break away from SALT II. None of the major US strategic programmes was prohibited under the treaty, while the constraints on Soviet programmes remained in the US strategic interest. Yet the President had allowed the SALT II agreement to become hostage to a campaign against treaty violations that he had been waging for a number of years. Although the evidence of such violations was imperfect, the pressure within the Administration, coupled with the President's own instincts in the matter, determined the outcome—over protestations from the Congress and the USA's European allies.

Of course, the need for compliance in arms control cannot be denied, and the most serious sanction against treaty violations must be the abrogation of the treaty itself. The Reagan Administration, however, while credibly suggesting that the Soviet Union had gone to the limits of the activities permitted under SALT II, was unable to produce hard evidence that violations had actually taken place. After presenting on repeated occasions a long list of supposed treaty infringements, in 1986 the Administration claimed only two kinds of Soviet violation of the SALT II Treaty.

The first allegation followed from the stipulation in the treaty that limits both sides to developing and deploying only one new type of ICBM. The Soviet Union had brought into its arsenal two 'new' missiles: the SS-24 (with over six warheads) and the mobile SS-25 (with one warhead only). The USA regarded the SS-25 missile as a new and therefore prohibited system. The Soviet Union, on the other hand, claimed that the missile was merely a permitted modernization of the SS-13. Modifications of no more than 5 per cent in volume, length, launch-weight and throw-weight are allowed under the treaty; moreover, in order to discourage the clandestine introduction of multiple-warhead weapons, tests of an existing or modernized missile with a single warhead are permissible only if the weight of the warhead exceeds 50 per cent of the total throw-weight of the missile. Yet despite repeated claims, the United States did not succeed in proving the Soviet contention wrong, perhaps because of the imperfection of means of detection and a comparable data base. The Soviet Union, possibly in order to strengthen its argument that the SS-25 was no more than a permitted updating of the SS-13 missile, tested a few of these old missiles in late 1985, but US intelligence remained divided on the data.

The second US claim of a Soviet SALT II Treaty violation related to a provision that telemetry during missile tests by either side should not be unduly encoded. However, the treaty itself does not prohibit the encoding of telemetry as such but only to the degree that this inhibits verification of the treaty provisions. The treaty does not define this distinction with any precision. Hence the US claim rested on uncertain grounds—enough to raise questions about the Soviet practice of encoding, but not enough to prove a violation. If the evidence provided did not match the magnitude of the accusation, it was difficult not to conclude that it was less the commitment to arms control than the desire to throw off whatever restrictions remained on US military programmes which prompted the Administration's actions.

This was even more strongly suggested by moves within the Reagan Administration to reinterpret those provisions of the ABM Treaty that might stand in the way of SDI. Until October 1985, the Administration, as former US administrations, had maintained that article V of the treaty prohibits the development, testing and deployment of space-based ABM systems and components—and hence, by definition, of systems and components of SDI. During the summer of 1985, the Pentagon authorized an examination of the treaty's negotiation record and, jointly with the Legal Counsel of the State Department, arrived at the conclusion that 'esoteric' technology (i.e., that which did not exist or was not seriously considered when the treaty was negotiated, signed and ratified in 1972) was not covered by article V but by an Agreed Statement in the annex of the treaty which merely required consultations. In other words, the definition in article V which pertains to the environment of ballistic missile defences (air, space, sea and so on) was reinterpreted to refer to specific techniques. The argument advanced by the Pentagon study amounted to no less than the claim that the restrictions on space-based defences in article V related to 1972 technology only—which plainly was not capable of such performance. At any rate, the new interpretation was declared to be legally correct by the President, although he emphasized that, for the time being, the old, restrictive interpretation would continue to apply.

As the year progressed, it was the new and broader rather than the old and restrictive interpretation which was increasingly presented as the only viable one. The ability of the United States 'to research, test and develop' strategic defences in space became the corner-stone of any agreement with the Soviet Union—precisely what the Administration sought with its new inter-pretation.

Had the President, at the Reykjavik meeting, agreed to maintain, for a 10-year period, the traditional, restrictive interpretation of article V, the SDI compromise which the Soviet Union had been trying to obtain might have been within reach. Yet no less important than the substantive issue was the attitude of powerful forces within the Administration which the incident revealed. The post-Reykjavik period saw a renewed effort within the Administration to move to a reading of the ABM Treaty which would lift all limitations on SDI testing and development. Clearly, there was pressure within the Administration to dismantle past accords, if need be unilaterally. This was not a record which suggested any coherent positive approach to the task of controlling military competition through agreement between East and West.

V. The outlook

If the present deadlock in East–West arms control is to be overcome, the mere narrowing of specific positions will not produce a breakthrough. This can only come about as a result of a deliberate departure from the flawed concepts and practices that governed the issue in 1986: the confusion of strategic defences with strategic stability, the confusion of disarmament and arms control, and the confusion of will within the US Administration. There was, as the year drew to a close, little prospect that such advice would soon be heeded. In particular, the Reagan Administration, following the adverse impact on its authority of the Iran–Nicaragua (contras) affair, seemed even less capable than before of producing a coherent position on arms control. For the remaining two years of President Reagan's tenure, little more than an agreement on INF—however welcome—seemed probable; however, a major breakthrough on the main arms control issues in terms of negotiated agreements between the super-powers still seemed remote.

However, a new if more modest alternative of practised but not negotiated arms control might have a chance to evolve. In the United States, the Congress—particularly after the November 1986 mid-term elections, which confirmed the Democratic majority in the House and established it in the Senate—promised to play a much more active role in putting budget constraints on US military programmes and in maintaining treaty limitations which the Administration itself seemed eager to undermine. On the SALT II Treaty, the Congress was contemplating tying the Administration to the treaty's ceiling by refusing to fund exceeding programmes. And on the ABM Treaty, the Senate had obtained the secret negotiating record to examine for itself the case for a wider as opposed to the stricter interpretation of article V. There were signs that the Senate would seek to obstruct Administration plans to forgo the ABM Treaty limits on SDI testing as long as the Soviet Union, too, stayed within the 'strict interpretation' of the treaty.[13]

Indeed, there was a distinct possibility of arms control resulting from reciprocal restraint. Significantly, the Soviet Union reacted to the US breakout of SALT II by declaring that, for the time being, the Soviet side would continue to abide by the treaty limitations.[14] If the Senate were successful in forcing on the Administration the 'strict' interpretation of the ABM Treaty, much of the Soviet demand formulated at the Reykjavik summit meeting would be met. In the field of anti-satellite (ASAT) weapons, both the US Congress and the Soviet leadership had previously demonstrated the possibility of arms control by unilateral example: Congress had denied the Air Force the right to test its ASAT system against targets in space, and in return the Soviet Union had refrained from any new tests of its own ASAT system.

Of course, unilateral example, dependent on reciprocation, cannot replace the binding quality of negotiated agreements. For arms control, however, the choice probably did not present itself at the end of 1986. Unilateral restraint may be an even more modest instrument of arms control, but it may be the only instrument for some time to come.

Notes and references

[1] Gorbachev's Press Conference in Iceland, 12 Oct. 1986, Novosti Press Agency (APN).

[2] For the best account, see Oberdorfer, D., *International Herald Tribune*, 18 Feb. 1987.

[3] Quoted in Mandelbaum, M. and Talbot, S., 'Reykjavik and beyond', *Foreign Affairs*, Winter 1986/87, p. 228.

[4] Press briefing on 12 Oct. 1986, in *Document on Foreign Policy*, US Information Service, US Embassy, Stockholm, Sweden, 13 Oct. 1986.

[5] Reprinted in *Neues Deutschland*, 16 Jan. 1986.

[6] See note 5.

[7] See note 5.

[8] See note 5.

[9] Published 15 Oct. 1986, Novosti Press Agency (APN).

[10] *Süddeutsche Zeitung*, 20 Nov. 1986.

[11] Distributed in English and German by the British Embassy, Bonn, 18 Nov. 1986.

[12] *The Large-Scale Anti-Missile System and International Security*, Report of the Committee of Soviet Scientists against the Nuclear Threat, Moscow, Feb. 1986; also *International Herald Tribune*, 18 Dec. 1986.

[13] See Mawby, M., 'Arms control prospects in the 100th Congress', *Arms Control Today*, Jan./Feb. 1987.

[14] Taubman, P., 'Soviet to abide by arms treaty "for time being"', *New York Times*, 6 Dec. 1986, p. 1.

10. The future of conventional arms control in Europe, A tale of two cities: Stockholm, Vienna*

RICHARD E. DARILEK, Rand Corporation, Santa Monica, California

Superscript numbers refer to the list of notes and references at the end of the chapter.

I. Introduction

Since the early 1970s, two competing approaches to arms control involving conventional military forces in Europe have vied for public attention, governmental support and negotiated results. One approach centres around Vienna, where NATO and the Warsaw Pact have been engaged since 1973 in the 'Mutual and Balanced Force Reduction' (MBFR) talks, as NATO calls them. As their title implies, these talks focus on reducing the numbers of military forces currently encamped in central Europe—i.e., on scaling down military structures (e.g., manpower, units, equipment); hence, they represent a characteristically 'structural' approach to arms control.

The second approach to conventional arms control in Europe culminated in September 1986, after almost three years of negotiations, in the 'Document of the Stockholm Conference' on confidence- and security-building measures (CSBMs). That Document, which is reprinted in appendix 10A, focuses on regulating the 'activities' of military forces: forecasting far in advance or otherwise notifying exercises or concentrations of troops in excess of various thresholds, inviting observers to such activities and permitting on-site inspections of questionable activities. 'Not a single soldier will return to civilian life and not a single weapon will be beaten into a plowshare as a result of it', however, for the Stockholm Document and its CSBMs represent a distinctively 'operational' approach to arms control.[1] Although they share many of the same participants and some of the same measures (there are CSBM-like 'associated measures' in MBFR for regulating the 'activities' of forces subject to reductions), the operational approach sets Stockholm's CSBMs clearly apart from the structural alternative to conventional arms control in Europe represented by MBFR in Vienna.[2]

Historically, the two approaches to arms control are intimately linked, both to each other and to the East–West competition. MBFR negotiations were the US and Western price in the early 1970s for agreeing to convene the Conference on Security and Co-operation in Europe (CSCE), a long-standing objective of Soviet foreign policy. CSCE and its hallmark, the Helsinki Final Act of 1975, constitute the broader framework in which the Stockholm

* This chapter is an expanded version of an article which appeared in *Survival*, Jan./Feb. 1987, for which the International Institute for Strategic Studies, London, holds the copyright. The views expressed are those of the author and do not necessarily represent the views of the RAND Corporation or its research sponsors.

Document of 1986 was eventually negotiated. It was the CSCE forum that originally commissioned Stockholm's CSBM negotiations—in 1983 at the second CSCE Review Meeting in Madrid—and it was to the CSCE that the satellite conference in Stockholm had ultimately to report. (Ironically, that report was made in Vienna, the traditional negotiating venue of MBFR, because the third CSCE Review Meeting happened to convene there shortly after the Stockholm Conference ended.)

There are other differences as well. MBFR is a bloc-to-bloc negotiation. As such it embodies the well-founded perception that military forces concentrated by the rival alliances in central Europe are of a size and disposition more likely to wreak uncontrollable havoc, should a conflict between them occur, than the forces of neutral or non-aligned states (NNAs). The CSBM agreement, on the other hand, covers a broader area—'all of Europe'—and thus a greater number as well as variety of forces. While recognizing the right of its signatories to form alliances, it also counts NNAs as well as NATO and Warsaw Pact members among its signatories. Moreover, throughout the process of negotiating the agreement, participants time and again eschewed possibilities for bloc-oriented solutions to problems (e.g., a proposal, considered but rejected in Stockholm, that aircraft from neutral countries be used to ferry inspectors about during the investigation of a questionable activity).[3]

MBFR, therefore, and the structural approach to arms control that it represents, constitutes a distinctly Western—perhaps even a distinctly US—approach. From the US perspective, MBFR has always been the 'real' military negotiation in the sense that it was dealing directly with the possibility of removing the physical accoutrements of military force (Soviet and US personnel in the first instance; other components later) from their area of greatest concentration, central Europe. CSCE, on the other hand, was primarily a political negotiation about the fate of post-war Europe. It had originally been proposed by the USSR as a way of settling that fate, but had since been confined largely to dealing with such outstanding non-military problems as human rights and contacts, economic interchanges and information flows. For its part, the USSR 'showed the low priority it assigned to MBFR when it pushed its proposal for a follow-on conference of Helsinki Accord signatories on European security despite its knowledge that this rival conference, which ultimately took the form of the Stockholm Conference on Disarmament in Europe (CDE), would undermine the authority of the MBFR forum'.[4]

It does not follow, however, that the operational alternative to MBFR embodied in Stockholm's CSBMs is necessarily an Eastern or a Soviet phenomenon. From their inception in the early 1970s, the MBFR negotiations excluded the NNAs. The latter responded to this exclusion, in part by pushing for inclusion of a stronger security component within the CSCE framework. As a result, despite misgivings initially by both the USA and the USSR, the Helsinki Final Act signed at the summit in 1975 contained several rudimentary 'confidence-building measures' (CBMs).[5] These called for prior notification of military manoeuvres and movements, as well as the occasional presence of observers, on a voluntary basis. They were forerunners and embryonic examples of operational arms control. Their shortcomings, combined with the desire to do more, ultimately led the NNAs to support attempts to improve them via the Stockholm Conference and its CSBMs. (The addition of the 's' for 'security', in fact, was proposed by non-aligned Yugoslavia at Madrid as a way of distinguishing the new, more militarily significant measures to be negotiated at Stockholm from their less militarily significant predecessors.)

Meanwhile, the NNAs were not the only ones looking for alternatives to both Vienna and Helsinki. MBFR had also failed to include the French, who had themselves refused to participate in the negotiations on the Western side because they disagreed with MBFR's narrow geographic scope (central Europe only), as well as its emphasis on structural versus operational arms control. The French argued that regulating activities should, logically and otherwise, precede reducing forces, and in the late 1970s they cast these beliefs in the form of a proposal for a new conference on disarmament in Europe. This conference would first negotiate operational arms-control measures, namely, CSBMs for all of Europe, 'from the Atlantic to the Urals'. Once these had been obtained, the conference would proceed to negotiate conventional force reductions throughout the same geographic area in a second phase.

The French proposal attracted considerable support, not only from NNAs but also from European NATO allies like the Federal Republic of Germany. A unique phenomenon in recent arms control history with potentially important implications for the future, European pressures for an agreement played a key role in helping the French proposal reach fruition in Stockholm. Despite initial opposition by both the USA and the USSR to various aspects of the proposal, it ultimately made its way into the CSCE process where, at the Review Meeting in Madrid, it was accepted by all 35 participants. Shortly thereafter, the 35 began negotiating what eventually became the Stockholm Document. That Document consists of six main elements:

1. A 19-paragraph statement on the principle of refraining from the threat or use of force which says, among other things, that 'no consideration may be invoked . . . in contravention of this principle' (paragraph 10).

2. A section on 'prior notification of certain military activities', which requires notification 42 days or more in advance of (a) an 'exercise' or 'concentration' in the field or a 'transfer' in the CSBM zone of at least 13 000 troops or 300 battle tanks 'if organized into a divisional structure or at least two brigades/regiments, not necessarily subordinate to the same division' (paragraph 31.1.1), and (b) an amphibious landing or parachute drop of at least 3000 troops. Such activities, when carried out without advance notice to the troops involved (i.e., as alerts), are notifiable at commencement of the activity (versus 42 days in advance).

3. A provision for 'observation of certain military activities', which requires the invitation of observers from all other participating states to all activities notifiable under (a) and (b) above if they exceed 17 000 troops in the first case and 5000 in the second, or if they are conducted as alerts lasting longer than 72 hours.

4. An annual calendar to be provided by 15 November of each year that forecasts activities notifiable in the following year.

5. Constraining provisions that call for placing on the calendar, two years in advance, any notifiable activity in excess of 75 000 troops and of 40 000 troops, with exceptions implied for the latter, but not the former.

6. A compliance and verification measure providing that: three on-site inspections per year of any participating state by air, ground or both, with the state being inspected in effect supplying any transports and communications required; the 'number and extent of restricted areas should be as limited as possible . . . and consequently those areas will not be used to prevent inspection of notifiable military activities' (paragraph 74).

Having thus reviewed the origins of Stockholm's CSBMs, as well as the background of both the operational and the structural approaches to conventional arms control in Europe, this chapter will now turn its attention to two tasks. The first is to evaluate the outcome of the Stockholm negotiations in terms of its contribution to operational arms control and, by extrapolation, the contribution of the latter to European arms control in general. This evaluation will be conducted by assessing the CSBM package agreed upon in Stockholm primarily from the perspective of the USA and NATO. The second task will be to array and evaluate likely options for the future of conventional arms control in Europe. For this task, several options will be considered. These range from combining the operational and structural approaches to arms control in Europe together into a single negotiating framework, on the one hand, to maintaining their individuality, as conceptually and practically different enterprises, on the other.

Before moving to address these tasks, however, a few comments are in order here on the outcome of Stockholm when considered from the perspectives of NNAs and of Warsaw Pact members. As noted above, operational arms control negotiations originated largely as a result of NNAs. Their continuing interest in confidence-building helped sustain CBMs during the dramatic downturn in East–West détente that followed the Soviet invasion of Afghanistan. NNAs can even lay claim to the change in emphasis that added 'security' to the name of such measures and, thus, to the full name of the Stockholm Conference.

En route to Stockholm from Helsinki and Madrid, various NNAs stressed the need for an evolutionary or gradualistic approach to confidence- and security-building, incorporating what was new (CSBMs) without abandoning what had gone before (CBMs) and improving political as well as military relationships in the process.[6] Judged by prior NNA expectations, therefore, the Stockholm Document represents a highly successful accomplishment, both politically and militarily. Politically, Stockholm builds upon Helsinki's CBMs and, in doing so, suggests the possibility of recapturing a lost 'spirit' of Helsinki (i.e., of détente); militarily, it improves upon the original CBMs considerably, especially by including constraining and verification provisions but also by providing notification and observation measures that are both more specific and less discretionary that those in the Final Act.

To most NNAs, maintaining an acceptable balance between East–West political and military interests was probably Stockholm's most significant goal and achievement. In fact, when certain military issues—e.g., a proposal that mobilizations be notified in advance—appeared to threaten their own national interests, certain NNAs clearly objected. Such objections tend to suggest that structural arms control, as currently practised by the two alliances in Vienna, would be hard for some NNAs to accept for themselves because of its strong emphasis on militarily (versus politically) significant outcomes. Operational arms control as practised at Stockholm, in other words, may continue to be some NNAs' preferred alternative.

Soviet and East European preferences seem to be moving in the opposite direction, however. Warsaw Pact proposals for a new or expanded forum to negotiate structural arms control agreements emerged early in 1986, even before the Stockholm Conference had concluded its work. These proposals are addressed in more detail below. The interesting question to raise here is what their announcement tends to suggest about Eastern assessments of the outcome at Stockholm.

If one accepts that Soviet and Warsaw Pact objectives in Stockholm were primarily political (not military) objectives, as evidenced by their concerted efforts to include a fundamentally political prohibition against the use of force (as well as other such declaratory pledges) in the concluding document, then Stockholm went further than the East initially intended to go. While incorporating a non-use-of-force provision in the document, the conference produced, for example, a compliance and verification measure that permits three on-site inspections per year on Soviet (as well as any other participating CSCE European) territory—a provision that, in principle, the USSR had previously opposed in Vienna as well as in Stockholm. Furthermore, the conference solidified agreement on an 'Atlantic to the Urals' geographic definition—specifically, on inclusion of all the European territory of the USSR—as the area of application for CSBMs, without providing additional compensation in the West as the Soviet Union had requested.

From a variety of perspectives, therefore, including its own, the USSR might appear to have given more away militarily than it received politically at Stockholm. If accurate, such an assessment might suggest that Moscow's shift in emphasis towards the new negotiating focus on structural arms control (where the problems have been intractible, hence more likely to remain unresolved) is a kind of escape from the less predictable, less manageable environs of operational arms control. On the other hand, the Soviets may believe that they gained politically as much as or more than they supposedly sacrificed militarily at Stockholm. Perhaps they calculate that the military results are manageable, particularly because—to give one example—they still control any transports or communications required for an inspection. If so, the Soviets may not be escaping from Stockholm at all by changing their focus to structural arms control. Instead, they might simply be trying to extend a pan-European framework and process that they have learned to deal with in the operational context to the structural dimension of conventional arms control.

II. An assessment of Stockholm from NATO's perspective

NATO entered the negotiations at Stockholm seeking CSBMs that would be more militarily significant, politically binding, verifiable and geographically extensive (from the Atlantic to the Urals) than the Helsinki CBMs. Each of these criteria had both a political and a military dimension. For example, the applicability of CSBMs from the Atlantic to the Urals was intended to establish, as a political principle, that the European part of the USSR was subject to European security negotiations, but it was also intended to encompass, militarily, more Soviet forces as a result. Verifiability was aimed at the political need to have new measures, so that compliance (or the lack thereof) could be established more effectively than in the case of Helsinki's CBMs, as well as a military need to ensure reciprocity of implementation—not simply reciprocity of commitment. Even the politically binding and militarily significant criteria had their respective counterparts. The more binding an agreement the more seriously it could be taken, from a military point of view, as a potential indicator of national political will or intent; the more militarily significant an agreement, the greater its potential contribution to political confidence and security building.

The Western Alliance had worked hard to have these four politico-military criteria included in the mandate for Stockholm that was ultimately produced by the CSCE Review Meeting in Madrid. When the Stockholm Conference began in January 1984, NATO quickly tabled a package of six measures designed to meet the various criteria. These measures are briefly summarized below:

1. Exchange of military information, on a yearly basis, covering the structure of ground and air forces in all of Europe, giving unit designations, normal headquarters locations and the composition of the forces.

2. Exchange of forecasts of activities notifiable in advance, on a yearly basis; the annual forecast would include the name and the purpose of notifiable activities, the countries participating, the size and type of forces involved, and the places and times of occurrence.

3. Notification of military activities, 45 days in advance, that involve field training of units at division level or above and certain mobilization and amphibious exercises.

4. Observation of certain military activities, a requirement that states invite observers from all other states to all prenotified activities and to certain alert activities.

5. Compliance and verification provisions, by which states would agree (*a*) not to interfere with other states' 'National Technical Means' (e.g., photoreconnaissance satellites) for monitoring compliance with the provisions of an agreement and (*b*) to allow each other to send observers, on a limited basis, to observe activities that seem not to be in compliance with negotiated agreements.

6. Development of means of communication, to enhance capabilities and procedures for urgent communication.[7]

All of the foregoing measures were intended to apply throughout the whole of Europe, 'from the Atlantic to the Urals', thus satisfying the geographic criterion laid down in Stockholm's mandate. Notwithstanding its military dimension, noted above, this criterion had been pushed by NATO primarily for its political significance. It clearly moved away from the idea, implicit both in the Helsinki CBMs and in MBFR, that the USSR's European territory was, and of necessity must remain, largely exempt from conventional arms control, whether operational or structural. The criterion that all the above measures should be binding was also driven largely by political considerations. In particular, NATO sought to curtail the highly discretionary authority permitted and practised under the Helsinki Final Act over whether and to what extent compliance with the original CSBM was actually required.

Verification, likewise a political requirement, was to be ensured primarily through the strong on-site inspection measure envisaged in the original NATO package, which was also supposed to help meet the criterion of military significance. Elsewhere, that criterion was to be pursued via the promise of thresholds and other requirements for notification of various military activities that were based on more militarily relevant yardsticks—e.g., units, especially main combat units at the level of divisions, whenever they are in the field—than the simpler, less inclusive definitions and thresholds provided in the Final Act (e.g., 'major maneuvers in excess of 25 000 troops').[8] Additional military significance was to be achieved in NATO's package through annual exchanges of military information covering the structure, composition, location, unit designation and headquarters of ground and air forces throughout all of Europe.

In the process of NATO's gaining acceptance of its criteria for the new conference and developing its package of CSBMs for Stockholm, two things were happening. First, both the USA and NATO were positively embracing the framework and advancing the frontiers of operational arms control. Both were acknowledging that operational arms control could be militarily, not simply politically (as in the Helsinki CBMs), significant, and they were embarking on an exploration of what the militarily significant possibilities might actually be. For the USA, this was something of a departure from past preferences for structural arms control, but it was a part of a trend that had already been developing, even in the Western MBFR position in Vienna. Over the years in those negotiations, the number of structural (manpower and unit) reductions being asked of the East and offered by the West had steadily diminished, while the operational component of the Western position had been enhanced with, among other things, introduction of a new package of associated measures in 1979. Many of the CSBMs in NATO's original package for Stockholm were, in fact, modelled on these MBFR measures.[9] Thus, the positive US/NATO approach to Stockholm was neither a reversal of past practice nor an outright switch from one form of arms control to the other, but rather an expansive move to broaden the field of possibilities—to take operational arms control as seriously as structural arms control.

In the second place, NATO was developing a theory of CSBMs, or hierarchy of CSBM criteria and objectives, that said, in effect: militarily significant, verifiable, politically binding, geographically extensive CSBMs can lead to greater openness and predictability, which in turn can help realize certain other objectives. The first four items—military significance, verifiability, etc.—might be considered specific design criteria for CSBMs, while the last two (openness, predictability) might qualify either as more general criteria or as intermediate objectives to be sought once the measures have been properly designed. Beyond these, NATO specified three more pointed objectives for CSBMs:

– reduce the risk of surprise attack;

- diminish the threat of armed conflict in Europe resulting from misunderstanding and miscalculation;
- inhibit the use of force for the purpose of political intimidation.

These might be considered NATO's core objectives for any CSBMs coming out
of Stockholm. If they could be achieved, NATO held out the hope that CSBMs
would ultimately 'enhance stability, contribute to the preservation of peace
and could open up prospects for new progress in disarmament'. This hierarchy,
or theory of relatively specific criteria leading to more wide-ranging objectives
over time, was embodied in the opening paragraphs of the Document that
introduced the original NATO package of CSBMs in Stockholm.[10]

How did the results of Stockholm compare with NATO's original
objectives? In particular, to what degree were the four basic criteria for CSBMs
upheld in the final package? To the extent that these criteria were not met in
full, what does this imply for the 'theory' of CSBMs as posited above? To what
extent were other criteria or objectives achieved in the outcome, and what does
this imply for the future of operational arms control, of which the Stockholm
experience was undoubtedly a significant test? Each of these questions will be
addressed here in turn.

How did the NATO package fare in Stockholm?

NATO lost its bid for an information measure and a communication measure,
the first and last proposals in the original NATO package outlined above. It
gained the right to inspect suspicious activities; the Stockholm Document
provided for that. It did not provide, however, for inspections to be conducted
solely at the discretion of the inspecting state, with that state supplying its own
transports (air and ground) and communications as NATO's proposal
envisaged. Instead, the Document invests the state being inspected with rights
to furnish any transport and communications equipment required. The
language in the Document says that both the inspecting and the inspected states
must agree on these modalities of inspection; in practice, this gives the state to
be inspected a veto, hence the right to dictate that its own equipment be used or
else the inspection may not take place as requested—not because of the refusal
of the inspection, which neither the Document nor the original NATO measure
allow, but because of a disagreement over whose equipment to use. As a result,
the Stockholm Document's ability to meet the criteria of verifiability may
suffer substantially.

Elsewhere in the Document, it looks as if NATO gained much of what it had
originally proposed in the way of relying on significant units (i.e., divisions) as
well as personnel and equipment thresholds to trigger obligations to notify and
rights to inspect under the Document. In contrast to the outcome on
inspections the outcome on thresholds for notification may help recoup some of
the ground lost with respect to verifiability. Stockholm's new, more militarily
specific thresholds should prove somewhat easier to monitor and verify than
the Helsinki CBM's simple aggregates of personnel. On the political front, the
West seems to have fully satisfied the criterion of having the new CSBMs apply

to all of Europe, including all Soviet territory west of the Urals. It also seems to have satisfied the criterion of making any agreement that came out of Stockholm more politically binding than the politically voluntary Helsinki CBMs.

To what extent were all four basic criteria achieved at Stockholm?

Although it obtained some of its criteria for CSBMs without question, the Alliance did not meet equally well each of the four criteria it had set itself at Madrid for any CSBM to be negotiated at Stockholm. As indicated above, the four criteria must be understood in two dimensions, i.e., the political and the military. In other words, as the table below illustrates, there are eight cases to be taken into account in answering this question, not simply four.

Table 10.1. Madrid criteria versus Stockholm accomplishments

	Accomplishments	
Criteria	Political	Military
Atlantic to Urals	yes	yes?
Binding	yes	no
Verifiable	yes	no
Militarily significant	yes	no

The Stockholm package upheld the Atlantic-to-Urals criterion in both dimensions. Politically, all Soviet European territory is included; militarily, more Soviet force activities are subject to the provisions of the CSBMs, although serious questions can be raised about whether this will detract from the area where the focus of attention really ought to be, that is, on Soviet forces in central Europe. In terms of its language, if nothing else, obligations in the Stockholm Document are much more clearly put as 'politically binding' obligations than in the Helsinki Final Act's Document on CBMs and Certain Aspects of Disarmament. The latter is replete with numerous 'voluntary' obligations couched in terms of what participating states 'may' or 'are encouraged' to do. Stockholm's obligations are phrased in much less discretionary terms. Politically, this is important and a definite advance; issues of compliance, while no easier to resolve under the Stockholm Document than under the Helsinki Final Act, can now be argued, at least, on the basis of clearer terminology. Militarily, however, the Document is not binding enough to permit a letting down of one's guard or a lessening of necessary defence efforts. It is not, after all, an international treaty. Furthermore, the Document is replete with significant exceptions—e.g., no-notice alert activities are not subject to prior notification and the constraining provisions provided for exercises in excess of 40 000 and 75 000 troops also permit both explicit (less than two-year forecasting for exercises below 75 000) and implicit (any exercise can be called as an alert) exceptions.

An important political inroad, making the USSR's European territory subject to on-site inspections, was reached at Stockholm. Militarily, this development is still questionable because the number of such inspections is small (three per year) and the state being inspected is permitted a *droit de regard* over any communications and transports involved. Finally, the criterion of military significance itself has a political dimension that the Stockholm Document reaffirms by incorporating various unit and equipment thresholds into its requirements for notification. In other words, the Document implicitly and explicitly endorses the need to have militarily significant measures. In its purely military dimension, however, this criterion is not as well served as it might have been at Stockholm, in part because of the permissible exceptions for most, if not all, of the military obligations finally agreed upon. Moreover, certain significant military activities are not included in the Stockholm Document. Mobilization activities, for example, are not subject to notification, as they were in the original NATO package.

The CSBM package negotiated in Stockholm, therefore, neither fully meets NATO's criterion of military significance nor the military dimension of at least two other criteria. Moreover, the package does not move very far into the area of applying constraints upon, as opposed to providing notification of, certain military activities. There are too few 'thou shalt nots' provided in the Stockholm Document to make it an example of really serious arms 'control'. As with the Helsinki CBMs, Stockholm's CSBMs are primarily 'thou shalt' commitments designed not to interfere very much with intended military activities, but to encourage positive actions having to do with how (versus whether) those activities take place. For operational arms control even to become as potentially militarily significant as structural arms control, it will ultimately have to explore the realm of constraining provisions more thoroughly than it has thus far. Such explorations will undoubtedly raise questions about whether it is preferable to constrain forces, rather than reduce them. The latter is hard enough; the former may or may not be harder (and may ultimately raise insurmountable obstacles to further progress in operational arms control). Nevertheless, additional constraining provisions have yet to be widely discussed on their own merits, much less as potential alternatives to structural arms control proposals that could actually prove more onerous.

What does the outcome at Stockholm imply for the 'theory' of CSBMs?

How does the failure to meet more completely both the military criterion itself and the military dimension of the other criteria affect the NATO 'theory of CSBMs' discussed above? One thing it may mean is that NATO is unlikely to see its core objectives—inhibiting the use of force for political intimidation, lessening the risk of war by misunderstanding and miscalculation, and making surprise attacks less likely—realized fully or even in significant part as a result of Stockholm. Since most of the CSBMs are invitations to positive action, not barriers to undesirable activities, they may be more likely to be used in the long run as 'legitimate' vehicles for political intimidation, rather than inhibitions against it. Because the CSBMs are defined in an internationally agreed Document, one implication is that any military activity properly notified in accordance with the Document's provisions, even an obviously intimidating one, is a legitimate activity. In view of the possibilities for such 'letter-of-the-law' employment of the CSBMs, Stockholm's 19-paragraph non-use-of-force provision seems unlikely to impose a significant enough block to shows of force that have the effect of intimidating. A state set on manipulating the measures for purposes of intimidation will be able to find sufficient refuge in other provisions of the Document to justify its objectives.

There is, however, one significant exception to this judgement. Stockholm's 'constraining provisions' stipulate that states 'will not carry out military activities subject to prior notification involving more than 75 000 troops' (paragraph 60), unless they have been forecast on an annual calendar well over a year in advance. Although a state can still, legitimately, notify such an activity at the last minute as an alert, such a procedure clearly contravenes not only the spirit of the Document but also some of its language. This constraining provision, therefore, could add to the calculation of political costs that a state undertakes in deciding whether to use a show of force in the first place; it may not add decisively to that calculation, but it does none the less add a cost—that of greater potential for reaction by other participants.

Table 10.2. Comparison of Helsinki CBMs of 1975 and Stockholm CSBMs of 1986

	Helsinki CBMs	Stockholm CSBMs
Zone of application	European territory, extending 250 km into the USSR and Turkey	The whole of Europe, extending 250 km into Turkey, and the adjoining sea and air space
Degree of commitment	On a voluntary basis[a]	All provisions are politically binding
Activities covered	Confined to manoeuvres (incl. movements at parties' discretion)	Agreed military activities, incl. exercises, movements and transfers of troops from outside the zone
Notification thresholds	25 000 troops	Ground forces: 13 000 troops or 300 battle tanks Amphibious landings: 3000 troops Parachute assaults: 3000 troops Air forces: 200 sorties
Prior notification period	At least 21 days, no annual calendar	At least 42 days, with annual calendar and 2-year forecast
Observation threshold	None specified	Ground forces: 17 000 troops Amphibious landings: 5000 troops Parachute assaults: 5000 troops
Observation regime	Rudimentary	Detailed specification of host country obligations and observer rights
Constraining provisions	None	Time constraints: activities with 40 000 and >70 000 troops not permitted unless they are notified 1 and 2 years in advance, respectively
Verification provisions	None	Each state must accept up to 3 obligatory on-site inspections per year (from different states), from the ground, air or both

[a] However, in practice it was understood that the provision for notification of troops above 25 000 amounted to an obligation.

Another core objective—lessening the risks of war resulting from misunderstanding of the true intent of military activities, which could lead to miscalculation, in a crisis and conflict—could conceivably be served by Stockholm's CSBMs in a case where intent on both sides was benign, but the tools available for communicating that intent are limited. In such circumstances, faithful implementation of the CSBMs, even going beyond the letter of their requirements in some cases, might provide a useful auxiliary vehicle for communicating the intent and help prevent the escalation of an incipient crisis. On the other hand, in an already developing crisis, where suspicions (for example, of intimidation or surprise attack) already abound, it is difficult to see how any message conveyed by CSBMs would not be suspect. Military activities undertaken in such circumstances are inherently ambiguous, even if undertaken for strictly defensive motives. Nor can CSBMs change the external circumstances in which they are being invoked. For the same reason— the inevitable ambiguity, calculated or inherent, that is part of crisis escalation—it seems unlikely that Stockholm's CSBMs will contribute very positively, much less decisively, to NATO's third core objective, namely, reducing the risk of surprise attack. Perhaps the best that can be said for them in this context is that at some point during the escalation of a crisis, they will probably cease being looked upon as significant indicators of intent.

Nevertheless, short of a crisis, these measures might contribute positively to those middle-range objectives, or more general criteria, identified earlier as part of the NATO hierarchy. The Stockholm CSBMs might actually promote greater openness and predictability with regard to military activities, even if that does not lead immediately, as in the NATO theory, to achievement of the core objectives. Much depends on how the measures are implemented, of course, and the outcome in Stockholm on the inspection measure provides a case in point. On the one hand, the fact of agreement on this measure gives rise to the hope that openness and predictability regarding military activities will be better served; on the other hand, if continually discouraging experiences over implementation of the measure occur, the intermediate goals of openness and predictability will not be well served.

III. What does Stockholm's outcome imply for the future of operational arms control?

The foregoing judgement, that Stockholm may have benefited middle-range but not longer-term objectives for CSBMs in Europe, holds several implications for the future of operational arms control. One implication is that more ground needs to be ploughed in the relatively narrow fields cultivated thus far at Stockholm before venturing beyond those fields to more expansive operational, much less structural, arms control domains. Stockholm affords hope that the cultivation of CSBMs will yield productive harvests, but better seeds can and should be sown on the same ground, and those crops harvested, before moving on to supposedly greener pastures.

More work needs to be done, in other words, to ensure that the measures adopted at Stockholm actually result in the mid-term benefits of predictability and greater openness attributed to them above. More work is also required to develop other measures, or other types of measures (e.g., additional constraining provisions), that could move operational arms control closer to achieving the core objectives identified earlier. In practical terms, this probably means that there should be a Phase II or follow-on to the Stockholm Conference, but that its mandate should be essentially the same as it was before (following Madrid): more of the same, only better. For operational arms control, this means continuing to focus on improving the military significance of what it is trying to accomplish on its own terms. For the near future, this also means exercising restraint by declining to move CSBM negotiations into other areas, such as structural arms control, before operational arms control itself has become more fully developed.

Soviet leader Mikhail Gorbachev made a proposal in April 1986 that, depending on how it evolves, could provide a tempting diversion from further operational arms control efforts. Gorbachev called for 'substantial reductions in all the components of the land forces and tactical air forces of the European states and the relevant forces of the USA and Canada deployed in Europe'. In a departure from MBFR's geographical focus on central Europe as the preferred area for such reductions, he proposed that force reductions should now 'cover the entire European territory from the Atlantic to the Urals'. Gorbachev also suggested that 'operational-tactical nuclear weapons could be reduced simultaneously with conventional weapons', and that both 'National Technical Means and international forms of verification, including, if need be, on-site inspection are possible'.[11]

At first glance, it appeared that Gorbachev's proposal had breathed new life into the long search for structural arms control, making it possible, as he said, 'to cut the knot which has been growing tighter at the Vienna talks over so many years now'.[12] Over time, and on reflection, however, it began to appear as if this proposal were aimed as much at striking a blow to the existing MBFR negotiations in Vienna as at producing any structural breakthroughs. The new Western MBFR proposals of December 1985, which emphasized on-site inspections in exchange for de-emphasizing the need for agreement on data for each side's forces prior to any reductions, had seemed to promise a breakthrough in the negotiations. Disagreement over the data provided by the East for its forces and over the need to resolve that issue before any reductions could be taken were literally the 'knot' that had tied up progress in the negotiations for over 10 years. Coming in the wake of this Western proposal, which already had offered to cut that knot, Gorbachev's initiative and its subsequent elaboration by the Warsaw Pact's Political Consultative Committee in June 1986 seemed more like an escape from, than support for, structural arms control.

In a sense, these Eastern proposals represented an 'escape forward' from MBFR into a broader negotiating arena where solutions to previously difficult problems, impossible to find before, were now held out as incentives for making the change. Indeed, the Warsaw Pact's gloss on Gorbachev's proposal even said that 'the sides would exchange, at an agreed-upon moment, data on the total numerical strength of the land forces and tactical strike aviation in the

cutback area and, separately, data on that part of them that is to be reduced'.[13]
In other words, as a *quid* for altering the MBFR negotiations because they were
'all knotted up', the Pact offered to loosen its hold on the knot, which owed
much to Eastern refusal to provide data in the first place. As its bottom line,
therefore, the Pact statement suggested that reduction proposals could be
negotiated either in a second phase of the CDE or in MBFR talks expanded to
include other European states.

If these proposals were accepted, the MBFR talks in Vienna could no longer
survive in their current format and structural arms control negotiations, as we
have known them for the past 15 years, could be subject to considerable
change. That change is also likely to affect operational arms control since, as
just noted, one Warsaw Pact option endorses the original French idea of adding
a structural arms control component to CDE in its second phase. (It is
important to note, however, that Gorbachev and the Pact envisage the
possibility of shorter-range nuclear weapons being included in such talks, while
the French confined their original proposal exclusively to conventional forces.)
In practical terms, therefore, three distinct options for the future relationship
of operational and structural arms control seem possible.

- Maintain CDE (for operational arms control) and MBFR (for structural
  arms control) in their current forms;
- Maintain CDE and expand MBFR to 'all of Europe';
- Establish a combined (operational and structural), expanded (to 'all of
  Europe') arms control negotiation—in CDE Phase II or elsewhere.

Variations on each of these options are, of course, possible. NATO's
'Brussels Declaration on Conventional Force Reductions', for example,
constitutes a recent variant of the second option. Issued in December 1986 as a
response to the Warsaw Pact proposals noted above, the Brussels Declaration
appears to envisage distinct negotiations that would, on the one hand, build
upon the Stockholm experience and, on the other, create new talks on
conventional arms reductions covering all of Europe but including only the 16
NATO and the seven Warsaw Pact states as participants.[14] Nevertheless, if one
assumes as here that, in some form, the options listed above represent the main
choice, what can one then say about each of these options?

The third option seems potentially to be the least productive, in the sense of
actually producing an agreement, as opposed to interminable negotiations.
The history of their relationships to date does not suggest that operational and
structural arms control, when combined in the same negotiating forums, result
in productive choices and trade-offs. In theory, one might expect that decisions
about whether to accept operational constraints upon the use of forces might be
weighed against the possibility of deep cuts in their size to come up with optimal
solutions for all parties concerned. In practice, the parties have differing
interests that make it more difficult to address the alternatives simultaneously
than it does to address them separately.

The history of the potential trade-offs between (operational) associated
measures and (structural) reductions in MBFR noted above—a classic example
of which is embodied in the most recent Western proposal—is instructive in this

regard. Rather than deal with this proposal directly, the East proposed changing the negotiating form. There were undoubtedly other, possibly more decisive, reasons for the proposed switch, but the intended mix of operational and structural components that the West had in mind for an initial MBFR agreement cannot be discounted entirely as a reason for the continued failure to produce negotiated results in Vienna. Stockholm (even Helsinki), it can be argued, succeeded in producing an agreement on operational arms control because it focused exclusively on that particular type of arms control.

This is not to say that the structural and operational approaches to conventional arms control in Europe should never be mixed. On the contrary, trade-offs between the two ultimately will have to be made. In the end, states will have to decide both individually and collectively which types of arms control best suit their interests. In the meantime, however, they would probably be best served by having a much fuller menu of possibilities before them. Thus, it is still an open question whether Western interests in arms control for conventional forces in Europe are best served, in the extreme, by: (a) agreements that severely constrain forces operationally, which may lead to their reduction as a by-product of such constraints; (b) agreements that drastically reduce force structure, which necessarily constrain how forces can operate; or (c) some mix of both that lies short of either extreme.

Europe is very far from such extremes when it comes to considering current arms control alternatives. The only two agreements that exist are those reached at Helsinki and Stockholm. Both of those leave much to be desired militarily, and much more work needs to be done simply to improve upon the operational arms control path that they have only just begun to carve out. At this early stage in the evolutionary process, attempts to direct these fledgling efforts towards structural arms control possibilities as well (for example, in a Phase II CDE) will probably harm more than help the effort. At a minimum, they will delay it by further complicating already complicated matters. The potential addition of NNAs to the reductions process via a Phase II CDE, moreover, injects yet another complicating factor that promises additional confusion and delay.

Hence, either of the first two options listed above might be preferable to the third. Separate negotiations for structural and operational arms control are envisaged in each. The second option, which comes closest to matching the thrust of NATO's Brussels Declaration, would expand the structural approach to the broader geographic area already encompassed in the Stockholm Agreement. This ostensibly improves the potential effectiveness of a structural agreement by covering more forces. It is unclear, however, if the additional forces to be covered represent the same kind of threat as that posed by the forces already encompassed within MBFR's central European focus. After all, the largest peacetime concentration of military force in history is located in central Europe. Perhaps there is something to be gained for the central region by including the forces in Hungary and the Western military districts of the USSR, for example, or perhaps security concerns on NATO's flanks can be addressed more directly than heretofore. At this point, however, it remains unclear what an expansion of the focus of structural arms control to additional territory achieves militarily: the useful inclusion of additional forces in negotiations or simply a dilution of the negotiations' focus upon specific forces. If territorial expansion serves more as a distraction from, than a contribution to, the central European problem, then much would have been squandered and little gained by altering the current framework of MBFR.

Structural arms control, in other words, marches to a different drummer than operational arms control. What works for the latter may not work as well for both. That is yet another reason why care must be taken either in trying to combine the two approaches in one negotiation or in assuming that specific features of Stockholm (for example, 'all of Europe') can be applied successfully in other contexts. The lesson of Stockholm for Vienna, therefore, is not necessarily to cover more of Europe or to include more operational arms control but, rather, to focus as directly as possible at this stage on the unique and thus far intractable problems of structural arms control in Europe. The lesson for future Stockholms, meanwhile, is to maintain and develop their own unique focus on additional possibilities for operational arms control.

Notes and references

[1] 'A small cheer for Stockholm', *The Economist*, 27 Sep. 1986, p. 50.

[2] The distinctions between the 'structural' and 'operational' arms control employed in this article are discussed further in Lawrence, M. F., *A Game Worth the Candle: The Confidence and Security Building Process in Europe—An Analysis of US and Soviet Negotiating Strategies* (Rand Corporation: Santa Monica, CA, 1987), R. 7264–RGS, p. 3. This study also draws together in one convenient place copies of numerous confidence-building proposals made and documents issued prior to the Stockholm Document.

[3] *The Economist* (note 1), p. 50.

[4] Dean, J., *Watershed in Europe: Dismantling the East–West Military Confrontation* (D. C. Heath and Co.: Lexington, MA and Toronto, 1986), p. 169. For more on the historic interest of the USA in the Vienna MBFR negotiations versus the Stockholm Conference, see Blaker, J. R., 'Stockholm carves out a new path', *Wall Street Journal*, 9 Oct. 1986, p. 32.

[5] 'Document on Confidence-Building Measures and Certain Aspects of Disarmament', in the 'Final Act' of the Conference on Security and Co-operation in Europe, Helsinki, Finland, 1975, which may be found in Lawrence (note 2), pp. 213–16.

[6] The discussion of non-US and non-NATO perspectives in this and the following four paragraphs in the text draws on a previous analysis of NNA and Soviet/Warsaw Pact perspectives on the Stockholm Conference to be found in Darilek, R. E., 'Building confidence and security in Europe: the road to and from Stockholm', *Washington Quarterly*, Winter 1985, pp. 131–40.

[7] This description of the NATO measures is excerpted from Goodby, J., 'Security for Europe', *NATO Review*, June–July 1984, p. 12.

[8] Lawrence (note 2), p. 213.

[9] For further discussion of MBFR, its associated measures and the relationships of both to confidence-building efforts prior to but in the general context of Stockholm, see Darilek, R. E., 'Separate processes, converging interest: MBFR and CBMS', in H. G. Brauch and D. L. Clark, *Decisionmaking for Arms Limitation: Assessment and Prospects* (Ballinger: Cambridge, MA, 1983), pp. 237–57; and Darilek, R. E., 'Reducing the risks of miscalculation: the promise of the Helsinki CBMS', in F. S. Larrabee and D. Stobbe (eds), *Confidence-building Measures in Europe* (East–West Security Studies: New York, 1983), pp. 59–90.

[10] The quotations are from CSCE/S.C.I., which may be found in Ben-Horin, Y., Darilek, R., Jas, H., Lawrence, M. and Platt, A., *Building Confidence and Security in Europe: The Potential Role of Confidence and Security-building Measures*, R-3431-USDP (Rand Corporation: Santa Monica, CA, 1986), pp. 45–48.

[11] 'Reportage on Gorbachev visit to GDR: Addresses SED Congress', *Foreign Broadcast Information Service/Soviet Union*, vol. 3, no. 075 (18 Apr. 1986), p. F8.

[12] See note 11, p. F8.

[13] 'Address to NATO, European states', *FBIS/Soviet Union*, vol. 3, no. 114 (13 June 1986), p. BB-10; this is from Moscow *Pravda* in Russian, 12 June 1986, first edn, pp. 1, 2.

[14] 'NATO seeking wider talks on cuts in forces', *Los Angeles Times*, 12 Dec. 1986, pp. 1, 16.

Appendix 10A. Stockholm Document

Document of the Stockholm Conference on Confidence- and Security-Building Measures and Disarmament in Europe Convened in Accordance with the Relevant Provisions of the Concluding Document of the Madrid Meeting of the Conference on Security and Co-operation in Europe

(1)   The representatives of the participating States of the Conference on Security and Co-operation in Europe (CSCE), Austria, Belgium, Bulgaria, Canada, Cyprus, Czechoslovakia, Denmark, Finland, France, the German Democratic Republic, the Federal Republic of Germany, Greece, the Holy See, Hungary, Iceland, Ireland, Italy, Liechtenstein, Luxembourg, Malta, Monaco, the Netherlands, Norway, Poland, Portugal, Romania, San Marino, Spain, Sweden, Switzerland, Turkey, the Union of Soviet Socialist Republics, the United Kingdom, the United States of America and Yugoslavia, met in Stockholm from 17 January 1984 to 19 September 1986, in accordance with the provisions relating to the Conference on Confidence- and Security-Building Measures and Disarmament in Europe contained in the Concluding Document of the Madrid Follow-up Meeting of the CSCE.

(2)   The participants were addressed by the Prime Minister of Sweden, the late Olof Palme, on 17 January 1984.

(3)   Opening statements were made by the Ministers of Foreign Affairs and other Heads of Delegation. The Prime Minister of Spain as well as Ministers and senior officials of several other participating States addressed the Conference later. The Minister for Foreign Affairs of Sweden addressed the Conference on 19 September 1986.

(4)   The Secretary-General of the United Nations addressed the Conference on 6 July 1984.

(5)   Contributions were made by the following non-participating Mediterranean States: Algeria, Egypt, Israel, Lebanon, Libya, Morocco, Syria and Tunisia.

(6)   The participating States recalled that the aim of the Conference on Confidence- and Security-Building Measures and Disarmament in Europe is, as a substantial and integral part of the multilateral process initiated by the Conference on Security and Co-operation in Europe, to undertake, in stages, new, effective and concrete actions designed to make progress in strengthening confidence and security and in achieving disarmament, so as to give effect and expression to the duty of States to refrain from the threat or use of force in their mutual relations as well as in their international relations in general.

(7)   The participating States recognized that the set of mutually complementary confidence- and security-building measures which are adopted in the present document and which are in accordance with the Madrid mandate serve by their scope and nature and by their implementation to strengthen confidence and security in Europe and thus to give effect and expression to the duty of States to refrain from the threat or use of force.

(8)   Consequently the participating States have declared the following:

REFRAINING FROM THE THREAT OR USE OF FORCE

(9)   The participating States, recalling their obligation to refrain, in their mutual relations as well as in their international relations in general, from the threat or use of force against the territorial integrity or political independence of any State, or in any other manner inconsistent with the purposes of the United Nations, accordingly reaffirm their commitment to respect and put into practice the principle of refraining from the threat or use of force, as laid down in the Final Act.

(10)   No consideration may be invoked to serve to warrant resort to the threat or use of force in contravention of this principle.

(11)   They recall the inherent right of individual or collective self-defence if an armed attack occurs, as set forth in the Charter of the United Nations.

(12)   They will refrain from any manifestation of force for the purpose of inducing any other State to renounce the full exercise of its sovereign rights.

(13)   As set forth in the Final Act, no occupation or acquisition of territory resulting from the threat or use of force in contravention of international law, will be recognized as legal.

(14)   They recognize their commitment to peace and security. Accordingly they reaffirm that they will refrain from any use of armed forces inconsistent with the purposes and principles of the Charter of the United Nations and the provisions of the Declaration on Principles Guiding Relations between Participating States, against another Participating State, in particular from invasion of or attack on its territory.

(15)   They will abide by their commitment to refrain from the threat or use of force in their relations with any State, regardless of that State's political, social, economic or cultural system and irrespective of whether or not they maintain with that State relations of alliance.

(16)   They stress that non-compliance with the obligation of refraining from the threat or use of force, as recalled above, constitutes a violation of international law.

(17)   They stress their commitment to the principle of peaceful settlement of disputes as contained in the Final Act, convinced that it is an essential complement to the duty of States to refrain from the threat or use of force, both being essential factors for the maintenance and consolidation of peace and security. They recall their determination and the necessity to reinforce and to improve the methods at their disposal for the peaceful settlement of disputes. They reaffirm their resolve to make every effort to settle exclusively by peaceful means any dispute between them.

(18)   The participating States stress their commitment to the Final Act and the need for full implementation of all its provisions, which will further the process of improving security and developing co-operation in Europe, thereby contributing to international peace and security in the world as a whole.

(19)   They emphasize their commitment to all the principles of the Declaration on Principles Guiding Relations between Participating States and declare their determination to respect and put them into practice irrespective of their political, economic or social systems as well as of their size, geographical location or level of economic development.

(20)   All these ten principles are of primary significance and, accordingly, they will be equally and unreservedly applied, each of them being interpreted taking into account the others.

(21)   Respect for the application of these principles will enhance the development of friendly relations and co-operation among the participating States in all fields covered by the provisions of the Final Act.

(22)   They reconfirm their commitment to the basic principle of the sovereign equality of States and stress that all States have equal rights and duties within the framework of international law.

(23)   They reaffirm the universal significance of human rights and fundamental freedoms. Respect for and the effective exercise of these rights and freedoms are essential factors for international peace, justice and security, as well as for the development of friendly relations and co-operation among themselves as among all States, as set forth in the Declaration on Principles Guiding Relations between Participating States.

(24)   They reaffirm that, in the broader context of world security, security in Europe is closely linked with security in the Mediterranean area as a whole; in this context, they confirm their intention to develop good neighbourly relations with all States in the region, with due regard to reciprocity, and in the spirit of the principles contained in the Declaration on Principles Guiding Relations between Participating States, so as to promote confidence and security and make peace prevail in the region in accordance with the provisions contained in the Mediterranean chapter of the Final Act.

(25)   They emphasize the necessity to take resolute measures to prevent and to combat terrorism, including terrorism in international relations. They express their determination to take effective measures, both at the national level and through international co-operation, for the prevention and suppression of all acts of terrorism. They will take all appropriate measures in preventing their respective territories from being used for the preparation, organization or commission of terrorist activities. This also includes measures to prohibit on their territories illegal activities, including subversive activities, of persons, groups and organizations that instigate, organize or engage in the perpetration of acts of terrorism, including those directed against other States and their citizens.

(26)   They will fulfil in good faith their obligations under international law; they also stress that strict compliance with their commitments within the framework of the CSCE is essential for building confidence and security.

(27)   The participating States confirm that in the event of a conflict between the obligations of the members of the United Nations under the Charter of the United Nations and their obligations under any treaty or other international agreement, their obligations under the Charter will prevail, in accordance with Article 103 of the Charter of the United Nations.

(28)   The participating States have adopted the following measures:

PRIOR NOTIFICATION OF CERTAIN MILITARY ACTIVITIES

(29)   The participating States will give notification in writing through diplomatic channels in an agreed form of content, to all other participating States 42 days or more in

advance of the start of notifiable* military activities in the zone of application for confidence- and security-building measures (CSBMs).**

(30)   Notification will be given by the participating State on whose territory the activity in question is planned to take place even if the forces of that State are not engaged in the activity or their strength is below the notifiable level. This will not relieve other participating States of their obligation to give notification, if their involvement in the planned military activity reaches the notifiable level.

(31)   Each of the following military activities in the field conducted as a single activity in the zone of application for CSBMs at or above the levels defined below, will be notified:

(31.1)   The engagement of formations of land forces*** of the participating States in the same exercise activity conducted under a single operational command independently or in combination with any possible air or naval components.

(31.1.1)   This military activity will be subject to notification whenever it involves at any time during the activity:
– at least 13 000 troops, including support troops, or
– at least 300 battle tanks
if organized into a divisional structure or at least two brigades/regiments, not necessarily subordinate to the same division.

(31.1.2)   The participation of air forces of the participating States will be included in the notification if it is foreseen that in the course of the activity 200 or more sorties by aircraft, excluding helicopters, will be flown.

(31.2)   The engagement of military forces either in an amphibious landing or in a parachute assault by airborne forces in the zone of application for CSBMs.

(31.2.1)   These military activities will be subject to notification whenever the amphibious landing involves at least 3000 troops or whenever the parachute drop involves at least 3000 troops.

(31.3)   The engagement of formations of land forces of the participating States in a transfer from outside the zone of application for CSBMs to arrival points in the zone, or from inside the zone of application for CSBMs to points of concentration in the zone, to participate in a notifiable exercise activity or to be concentrated.

(31.3.1)   The arrival or concentration of these forces will be subject to notification whenever it involves, at any time during the activity:
– at least 13 000 troops, including support troops, or
– at least 300 battle tanks
if organized into a divisional structure or at least two brigades/regiments, not necessarily subordinate to the same division.

(31.3.2)   Forces which have been transferred into the zone will be subject to all provisions of agreed CSBMs when they depart their arrival points to participate in a notifiable exercise activity or to be concentrated within the zone of application for CSBMs.

(32)   Notifiable military activities carried out without advance notice to the troops

---

* In this document, the term notifiable means subject to notification.
** See Annex I.
*** In this context, the term land forces includes amphibious, airmobile and airborne forces.

involved, are exceptions to the requirements for prior notification to be made 42 days in advance.

(32.1)   Notification of such activities, above the agreed thresholds, will be given at the time the troops involved commence such activities.

(33)   Notification will be given in writing of each notifiable military activity in the following agreed form:

(34)   **A—General Information**

(34.1)   The designation of the military activity;

(34.2)   The general purpose of the military activity;

(34.3)   The names of the States involved in the military activity;

(34.4)   The level of command, organizing and commanding the military activity;

(34.5)   The start and end dates of the military activity.

(35)   **B—Information on different types of notifiable military activities**

(35.1)   The engagement of formations of land forces of the participating States in the same exercise activity conducted under a single operational command independently or in combination with any possible air or naval components:

(35.1.1)   The total number of troops taking part in the military activity (i.e., ground troops, amphibious troops, airmobile and airborne troops) and the number of troops participating for each State involved, if applicable;

(35.1.2)   Number and type of divisions participating for each State;

(35.1.3)   The total number of battle tanks for each State and the total number of anti-tank guided missile launchers mounted on armoured vehicles;

(35.1.4)   The total number of artillery pieces and multiple rocket launchers (100 mm calibre or above);

(35.1.5)   The total numbers of helicopters, by category;

(35.1.6)   Envisaged number of sorties by aircraft, excluding helicopters;

(35.1.7)   Purpose of air missions;

(35.1.8)   Categories of aircraft involved;

(35.1.9)   The level of command, organizing and commanding the air force participation;

(35.1.10)   Naval ship-to-shore gunfire;

(35.1.11)   Indication of other naval ship-to-shore support;

(35.1.12)   The level of command, organizing and commanding the naval force participation.

(35.2)   The engagement of military forces either in an amphibious landing or in a parachute assault by airborne forces in the zone of application for CSBMs:

(35.2.1)   The total number of amphibious troops involved in notifiable amphibious landings, and/or the total number of airborne troops involved in notifiable parachute assaults;

(35.2.2)   In the case of a notifiable amphibious landing, the point or points of embarkation, if in the zone of application for CSBMs.

(35.3)   The engagement of formations of land forces of the participating States in a transfer from outside the zone of application for CSBMs to arrival points in the zone, or from inside the zone of application for CSBMs to points of concentration in the zone, to participate in a notifiable exercise activity or to be concentrated:

(35.3.1)   The total number of troops transferred;

(35.3.2)   Number and type of divisions participating in the transfer;

(35.3.3)   The total number of battle tanks participating in a notifiable arrival or concentration;

(35.3.4)   Geographical co-ordinates for the points of arrival and for the points of concentration.

(36)   **C—The envisaged area and timeframe of the activity**

(36.1)   The area of the military activity delimited by geographic features together with geographic co-ordinates, as appropriate;

(36.2)   The start and end dates of each phase (transfers, deployment, concentration of forces, active exercise phase, recovery phase) of activities in the zone of application for CSBMs of participating formations, the tactical purpose and corresponding geographical areas (delimited by geographical co-ordinates) for each phase;

(36.3)   Brief description of each phase.

(37)   **D—Other information**

(37.1)   Changes, if any, in relation to information provided in the annual calendar regarding the activity;

(37.2)   Relationship of the activity to other notifiable activities.

OBSERVATION OF CERTAIN MILITARY ACTIVITIES

(38)   The participating States will invite observers from all other participating States to the following notifiable military activities:

(38.1)   – The engagement of formations of land forces* of the participating States in the same exercise activity conducted under a single operational command independently or in combination with any possible air or naval components.

(38.2)   – The engagement of military forces either in an amphibious landing or in a parachute assault by airborne forces in the zone of application for CSBMs.

(38.3)   – In the case of the engagement of formations of land forces of the participating States in a transfer from outside the zone of application for CSBMs to arrival points in the zone, or from inside the zone of application for CSBMs to points of concentration in the zone, to participate in a notifiable exercise activity or to be concentrated, the concentration of these forces. Forces which have been transferred into the zone will be subject to all provisions of agreed confidence- and security-building measures when they depart their arrival points to participate in a notifiable exercise activity or to be concentrated within the zone of application for CSBMs.

* In this context, the term land forces includes amphibious, airmobile and airborne forces.

(38.4) The above-mentioned activities will be subject to observation whenever the number of troops engaged meets or exceeds 17 000 troops, except in the case of either an amphibious landing or a parachute assault by airborne forces, which will be subject to observation whenever the number of troops engaged meets or exceeds 5000 troops.

(39) The host State will extend the invitations in writing through diplomatic channels to all other participating States at the time of notification. The host State will be the participating State on whose territory the notified activity will take place.

(40) The host State may delegate some of its responsibilities as host to another participating State engaged in the military activity on the territory of the host State. In such cases, the host State will specify the allocation of responsibilities in its invitation to observe the activity.

(41) Each participating State may send up to two observers to the military activity to be observed.

(42) The invited State may decide whether to send military and/or civilian observers, including members of its personnel accredited to the host State. Military observers will, normally, wear their uniforms and insignia while performing their tasks.

(43) Replies to the invitation will be given in writing not later than 21 days after the issue of the invitation.

(44) The participating States accepting an invitation will provide the names and ranks of their observers in their reply to the invitation. If the invitation is not accepted in time, it will be assumed that no observers will be sent.

(45) Together with the invitation the host State will provide a general observation programme, including the following information:

(45.1) – the date, time and place of assembly of observers;

(45.2) – planned duration of the observation programme;

(45.3) – languages to be used in interpretation and/or translation;

(45.4) – arrangements for board, lodging and transportation of the observers;

(45.5) – arrangements for observation equipment which will be issued to the observers by the host State;

(45.6) – possible authorization by the host State of the use of special equipment that the observers may bring with them;

(45.7) – arrangements for special clothing to be issued to the observers because of weather or environmental factors.

(46) The observers may make requests with regard to the observation programme. The host State will, if possible, accede to them.

(47) The host State will determine a duration of observation which permits the observers to observe a notifiable military activity from the time that agreed thresholds for observation are met or exceeded until, for the last time during the activity, the thresholds for observation are no longer met.

(48) The host State will provide the observers with transportation to the area of the notified activity and back. This transportation will be provided from either the capital or another suitable location to be announced in the invitation, so that the observers are in position before the start of the observation programme.

(49)   The invited State will cover the travel expenses for its observers to the capital, or another suitable location specified in the invitation, of the host State, and back.

(50)   The observers will be provided equal treatment and offered equal opportunities to carry out their functions.

(51)   The observers will be granted, during their mission, the privileges and immunities accorded to diplomatic agents in the Vienna Convention on Diplomatic Relations.

(52)   The host State will not be required to permit observation of restricted locations, installations or defence sites.

(53)   In order to allow the observers to confirm that the notified activity is non-threatening in character and that it is carried out in conformity with the appropriate provisions of the notification, the host State will:

(53.1)   – at the commencement of the observation programme give a briefing on the purpose, the basic situation, the phases of the activity and possible changes as compared with the notification and provide the observers with a map of the area of the military activity with a scale of 1 to not more than 500 000 and an observation programme with a daily schedule as well as a sketch indicating the basic situation;

(53.2)   – provide the observers with appropriate observation equipment; however, the observers will be allowed to use their personal binoculars, which will be subject to examination and approval by the host State;

(53.3)   – in the course of the observation programme give the observers daily briefings with the help of maps on the various phases of the military activity and their development and inform the observers about their positions geographically; in the case of a land force activity conducted in combination with air or naval components, briefings will be given by representatives of these forces;

(53.4)   – provide opportunities to observe directly forces of the State/States engaged in the military activity so that the observers get an impression of the flow of the activity; to this end, the observers will be given the opportunity to observe major combat units of the participating formations of a divisional or equivalent level and, whenever possible, to visit some units and communicate with commanders and troops; commanders or other senior personnel of participating formations as well as of the visited units will inform the observers of the mission of their respective units;

(53.5)   – guide the observers in the area of the military activity; the observers will follow the instructions issued by the host State in accordance with the provisions set out in this document;

(53.6)   – provide the observers with appropriate means of transportation in the area of the military activity;

(53.7)   – provide the observers with opportunities for timely communication with their embassies or other official missions and consular posts; the host State is not obligated to cover the communication expense of the observers;

(53.8)   – provide the observers with appropriate board and lodging in a location suitable for carrying out the observation programme and, when necessary, medical care.

(54)   The participating States need not invite observers to notifiable military activities

which are carried out without advance notice to the troops involved unless these notifiable activities have a duration of more than 72 hours. The continuation of these activities beyond this time will be subject to observation while the agreed thresholds for observation are met or exceeded. The observation programme will follow as closely as practically possible all the provisions for observation set out in this document.

ANNUAL CALENDARS

(55)   Each participating State will exchange, with all other participating States, an annual calendar of its military activities subject to prior notification*, within the zone of application for CSBMs, forecast for the subsequent calendar year. It will be transmitted every year, in writing, through diplomatic channels, not later than 15 November for the following year.

(56)   Each participating State will list the above-mentioned activities chronologically and will provide information on each activity in accordance with the following model:

(56.1)   – type of military activity and its designation;

(56.2)   – general characteristics and purpose of the military activity;

(56.3)   – States involved in the military activity;

(56.4)   – area of the military activity, indicated by appropriate geographic features and/or defined by geographic co-ordinates;

* as defined in the provisions on Prior Notification of Certain Military Activities.

(56.5)   – planned duration of the military activity and the 14-day period, indicated by dates, within which it is envisaged to start;

(56.6)   – the envisaged total number of troops* engaged in the military activity;

(56.7)   – the types of armed forces involved in the military activity;

(56.8)   – the envisaged level of command, under which the military activity will take place;

(56.9)   – the number and type of divisions whose participation in the military activity is envisaged;

(56.10) – any additional information concerning, *inter alia*, components of armed forces, which the participating State planning the military activity considers relevant.

(57)   Should changes regarding the military activities in the annual calendar prove necessary, they will be communicated to all other participating States no later than in the appropriate notification.

(58)   Information on military activities subject to prior notification not included in an annual calendar will be communicated to all participating States as soon as possible, in accordance with the model provided in the annual calendar.

* as defined in the provisions on Prior Notification of Certain Military Activities.

CONSTRAINING PROVISIONS

(59) Each participating State will communicate, in writing, to all other participating States, by 15 November each year, information concerning military activities subject to prior notification* involving more than 40 000 troops*, which it plans to carry out in the second subsequent calendar year. Such communication will include preliminary information on each activity, as to its general purpose, timeframe and duration, area, size and States involved.

(60) Participating States will not carry out military activities subject to prior notification involving more than 75 000 troops, unless they have been the object of communication as defined above.

(61) Participating States will not carry out military activities subject to prior notification involving more than 40 000 troops unless they have been included in the annual calendar, not later than 15 November each year.

(62) If military activities subject to prior notification are carried out in addition to those contained in the annual calendar, they should be as few as possible.

(63) According to the Madrid Mandate, the confidence- and security-building measures to be agreed upon 'will be provided with adequate forms of verification which correspond to their content.'

(64) The participating States recognize that national technical means can play a role in monitoring compliance with agreed confidence- and security-building measures.

(65) In accordance with the provisions contained in this document each participating State has the right to conduct inspections on the territory of any other participating State within the zone of application for CSBMs.

(66) Any participating State will be allowed to address a request for inspection to another participating State on whose territory, within the zone of application for CSBMs, compliance with the agreed confidence- and security-building measures is in doubt.

(67) No participating State will be obliged to accept on its territory within the zone of application for CSBMs, more than three inspections per calendar year.

(68) No participating State will be obliged to accept more than one inspection per calendar year from the same participating State.

(69) An inspection will not be counted if, due to *force majeure*, it cannot be carried out.

(70) The participating State which requests an inspection will state the reasons for such a request.

(71) The participating State which has received such a request will reply in the affirmative to the request within the agreed period of time, subject to the provisions contained in paragraphs (67) and (68).

(72) Any possible dispute as to the validity of the reasons for a request will not prevent or delay the conduct of an inspection.

---

* as defined in the provisions on Prior Notification of Certain Military Activities.

(73)   The participating State which requests an inspection will be permitted to designate for inspection on the territory of another State within the zone of application for CSBMs, a specific area. Such an area will be referred to as the 'specified area'. The specified area will comprise terrain where notifiable military activities are conducted or where another participating State believes a notifiable military activity is taking place. The specified area will be defined and limited by the scope and scale of notifiable military activities but will not exceed that required for an army level military activity.

(74)   In the specified area the representatives of the inspecting State accompanied by the representatives of the receiving State will be permitted access, entry and unobstructed survey, except for areas or sensitive points to which access is normally denied or restricted, military and other defence installations, as well as naval vessels, military vehicles and aircraft. The number and extent of the restricted areas should be as limited as possible. Areas where notifiable military activities can take place will not be declared restricted areas, except for certain permanent or temporary military installations which, in territorial terms, should be as small as possible, and consequently those areas will not be used to prevent inspection of notifiable military activities. Restricted areas will not be employed in a way inconsistent with the agreed provisions on inspection.

(75)   Within the specified area, the forces of participating States other than the receiving State will also be subject to the inspection conducted by the inspecting State.

(76)   Inspection will be permitted on the ground, from the air, or both.

(77.)   The representatives of the receiving State will accompany the inspection team, including when it is in land vehicles and an aircraft from the time of their first employment until the time they are no longer in use for the purposes of inspection.

(78)   In its request, the inspecting State will notify the receiving State of:

(78.1)   – the reasons for the request;

(78.2)   – the location of the specified area defined by geographical co-ordinates;

(78.3)   – the preferred point(s) of entry for the inspection team;

(78.4)   – mode of transport to and from the point(s) of entry and, if applicable, to and from the specified area;

(78.5)   – where in the specified area the inspection will begin;

(78.6)   – whether the inspection will be conducted from the ground, from the air, or both simultaneously;

(78.7)   – whether aerial inspection will be conducted using an airplane, a helicopter, or both;

(78.8)   – whether the inspection team will use land vehicles provided by the receiving State or, if mutually agreed, its own vehicles;

(78.9)   – information for the issuance of diplomatic visas to inspectors entering the receiving State.

(79)   The reply to the request will be given in the shortest possible period of time, but within not more than twenty-four hours. Within thirty-six hours after the issuance of the request, the inspection team will be permitted to enter the territory of the receiving State.

(80)   Any request for inspection as well as the reply thereto will be communicated to all participating States without delay.

(81)   The receiving State should designate the point(s) of entry as close as possible to the specified area. The receiving State will ensure that the inspection team will be able to reach the specified area without delay from the point(s) of entry.

(82)   All participating States will facilitate the passage of the inspection teams through their territory.

(83)   Within 48 hours after the arrival of the inspection team at the specified area, the inspection will be terminated.

(84)   There will be no more than four inspectors in an inspection team. While conducting the inspection the inspection team may divide into two parts.

(85)   The inspectors and, if applicable, auxiliary personnel, will be granted during their mission the privileges and immunities in accordance with the Vienna Convention on Diplomatic Relations.

(86)   The receiving State will provide the inspection team with appropriate board and lodging in a location suitable for carrying out the inspection, and, when necessary, medical care; however this does not exclude the use by the inspection team of its own tents and rations.

(87)   The inspection team will have use of its own maps, own photo cameras, own binoculars and own dictaphones, as well as own aeronautical charts.

(88)   The inspection team will have access to appropriate telecommunications equipment of the receiving State, including the opportunity for continuous communication between the members of an inspection team in an aircraft and those in a land vehicle employed in the inspection.

(89)   The inspecting State will specify whether aerial inspection will be conducted using an airplane, a helicopter or both. Aircraft for inspection will be chosen by mutual agreement between the inspecting and receiving States. Aircraft will be chosen which provide the inspection team a continuous view of the ground during the inspection.

(90)   After the flight plan, specifying, *inter alia*, the inspection team's choice of flight path, speed and altitude in the specified area, has been filed with the competent air traffic control authority the inspection aircraft will be permitted to enter the specified area without delay. Within the specified area, the inspection team will, at its request, be permitted to deviate from the approved flight plan to make specific observations provided such deviation is consistent with paragraph (74) as well as flight safety and air traffic requirements. Directions to the crew will be given through a representative of the receiving State on board the aircraft involved in the inspection.

(91)   One member of the inspection team will be permitted, if such a request is made, at any time to observe data on navigational equipment of the aircraft and to have access to maps and charts used by the flight crew for the purpose of determining the exact location of the aircraft during the inspection flight.

(92)   Aerial and ground inspectors may return to the specified area as often as desired within the 48-hour inspection period.

(93)   The receiving State will provide for inspection purposes land vehicles with cross country capability. Whenever mutually agreed taking into account the specific

geography relating to the area to be inspected, the inspecting State will be permitted to use its own vehicles.

(94)   If land vehicles or aircraft are provided by the inspecting State, there will be one accompanying driver for each land vehicle, or accompanying aircraft crew.

(95)   The inspecting State will prepare a report of its inspection and will provide a copy of that report to all participating States without delay.

(96)   The inspection expenses will be incurred by the receiving State except when the inspecting State uses its own aircraft and/or land vehicles. The travel expenses to and from the point(s) of entry will be borne by the inspecting State.

(97)   Diplomatic channels will be used for communications concerning compliance and verification.

(98)   Each participating State will be entitled to obtain timely clarification from any other participating State concerning the application of agreed confidence- and security-building measures. Communications in this context will, if appropriate, be transmitted to all other participating States.

★   ★   ★

(99)   The participating States stress that these confidence- and security-building measures are designed to reduce the dangers of armed conflict and of misunderstanding or miscalculation of military activities and emphasize that their implementation will ·contribute to these objectives.

(100)   Reaffirming the relevant objectives of the Final Act, the participating States are determined to continue building confidence, to lessen military confrontation and to enhance security for all. They are also determined to achieve progress in disarmament.

(101)   The measures adopted in this document are politically binding and will come into force on 1 January 1987.

(102)   The Government of Sweden is requested to transmit the present document to the follow-up meeting of the CSCE in Vienna and to the Secretary-General of the United Nations. The Government of Sweden is also requested to transmit the present document to the Governments of the non-participating Mediterranean States.

(103)   The text of this document will be published in each participating State, which will disseminate it and make it known as widely as possibly.

(104)   The representatives of the participating States express their profound gratitude to the Government and people of Sweden for the excellent arrangements made for the Stockholm Conference and the warm hospitality extended to the delegations which participated in the Conference.

Stockholm, 19 September 1986

ANNEX I

Under the terms of the Madrid mandate, the zone of application for CSBMs is defined as follows:

"On the basis of equality of rights, balance and reciprocity, equal respect for the security interests of all CSCE participating States, and of their respective obligations concerning confidence- and security-building measures and disarmament in Europe, these confidence- and security-building measures will cover the whole of Europe as well as the adjoining sea area* and air space. They will be of military significance and politically binding and will be provided with adequate forms of verification which correspond to their content.

As far as the adjoining sea area* and air space is concerned, the measures will be applicable to the military activities of all the participating States taking place there whenever these activities affect security in Europe as well as constitute a part of activities taking place within the whole of Europe as referred to above, which they will agree to notify. Necessary specifications will be made through the negotiations on the confidence- and security-building measures at the Conference.

Nothing in the definition of the zone given above will diminish obligations already undertaken under the Final Act. The confidence- and security-building measures to be agreed upon at the Conference will also be applicable in all areas covered by any of the provisions in the Final Act relating to confidence-building measures and certain aspects of security and disarmament.

* In this context, the notion of adjoining sea area is understood to refer also to ocean areas adjoining Europe.

Wherever the term 'the zone of application for CSBMs' is used in this document, the above definition will apply.

ANNEX II

CHAIRMAN'S STATEMENT

It is understood that, taking into account the agreed date of entry into force of the agreed confidence- and security-building measures and the provisions contained in them concerning the timeframes of certain advance notifications, and expressing their interest in an early transition to the full implementation of the provisions of this document, the participating States agree to the following:

The annual calendars concerning military activities subject to prior notification and forecast for 1987 will be exchanged not later than 15 December 1986.

Communications, in accordance with agreed provisions, concerning military activities involving more than 40 000 troops planned for the calendar year 1988 will be exchanged by 15 December 1986. Participating States may undertake activities involving more than 75 000 troops during the calendar year 1987 provided that they are included in the annual calendar exchanged by 15 December 1986.

Activities to begin during the first 42 days after 1 January 1987 will be subject to the relevant provisions of the Final Act of the CSCE. However, the participating States will make every effort to apply to them the provisions of this document to the maximum extent possible.

This statement will be an annex to the Document of the Stockholm Conference and will be published with it.

Stockholm, 19 September 1986

ANNEX III

CHAIRMAN'S STATEMENT

It is understood that each participating State can raise any question consistent with the mandate of the Conference on Confidence- and Security-Building Measures and

Disarmament in Europe at any stage subsequent to the Vienna CSCE Follow-up Meeting.

This statement will be an annex to the Document of the Stockholm Conference and will be published with it.

Stockholm, 19 September 1986

CHAIRMAN'S STATEMENT

It is understood that the participating States recall that they have the right to belong or not to belong to international organizations, to be or not to be a party to bilateral or multilateral treaties including the right to be or not to be a party to treaties of alliance; they also have the right of neutrality. In this context, they will not take advantage of these rights to circumvent the purposes of the system of inspection, and in particular the provision that no participating State will be obliged to accept on its territory within the zone of application for CSBMs, more than three inspections per calendar year.

Appropriate understandings between participating States on this subject will be expressed in interpretative statements to be included in the journal of the day.

This statement will be an annex to the Document of the Stockholm Conference and will be published with it.

Stockholm, 19 September 1986

Appendix 10B. Calendar of planned notifiable military activities in 1987 and forecast for 1988, as required by the Stockholm Document

Prepared by RICHARD W. FIELDHOUSE

One of the requirements of the Document of the Stockholm Conference is that each of the participating states must prepare and exchange with all the other CSCE states, by 15 November each year, an annual calendar of notifiable military activities planned for the following year (paragraph 55). Each state is also required to provide information on activities involving more than 40 000 troops that are planned for the second subsequent year (paragraph 59). The first results of these requirements, the annual calendar for 1987 and the advance forecast for 1988, are presented in the table.

Since the Stockholm Conference concluded less than two months before the deadline for the exchange of calendars, the states agreed to extend the deadline by one month for the first calendars, to 15 December 1986. The Stockholm Document specifies the information to be included in each calendar (paragraph 56). Participating states are also required by the Stockholm Document to make a formal notification of each military activity at least 42 days before it begins (paragraph 29). The information in the notifications is more detailed than in the calendars. Consequently, the first 10 activities of 1987 were notified shortly after being placed on the calendar, and the more detailed information from the subsequent notifications is included in SIPRI's calendar table in the 'Equipment' column, although these are not strictly calendar items.

It is useful to keep in mind the following points when using the table. The table is a compilation (based on the limited official information available to SIPRI) of the information from 35 states' calendars, and thus gives the overall picture of all their notifiable military activities. States are required to report all notifiable military activities occurring on their territory or in which their participation reaches the notifiable level. Twenty states have not reported any activities for 1987 (see notes to the table), although some are participating in notifiable activities. The table presents activities in chronological order rather than by participating state. Each activity is listed as one event, regardless of the number of states notifying or participating, or the number of exercises occuring simultaneously. States agreed to include in the calendars the duration of each activity and the 14-day period during which it will start—the so-called 'start window' (paragraph 56.5). In the table some of the dates are more precise and some less so than prescribed. In the column for the number and type of divisions, the table has maintained the names of units given by notifying states. Abbreviations are provided at the end of the table.

For all activities at or above the threshold for observation, observers must be invited from all other participating states (paragraph 38). The details of each activity listed in the calendars may change as plans are revised. States are required to make such changes known in the formal notification for each activity.

Calendar of planned notifiable military activities in 1987 and forecast for 1988, as required by the Stockholm Document

State(s)/ Location	Dates/ Start window	Type/Name of activity	Area	Level of command	No. of troops	Equipment or type of forces[a]	No. and type of divisions[a,b]	Comments
1. Czechoslovakia	2–6 Feb.	Ground forces exercise	Cheb–Jachymov–Decin–Liberec–Melnik–Plana–Marienbad	Western Military District	17 500	285 tanks 180 aircraft	1 mot. inf. div. 1 arm. div.	Notified and observers invited 19 Dec. 1986
2. USSR and Czechoslovakia in Czechoslovakia	14–21 Feb.	Allied ground forces exercise DRUZBA 87	Jachymov–Karlovy–Melnik–Liberec–Decin	Commander, Central Group of Forces	15 000 (11 000 USSR) (4 000 CSSR)	330 tanks . . aircraft 36 cmbt. hels. 32 trans. hels.	2 mot. rifle divs. (−)	Notified 23 Dec. 1986
3. Austria	16–20 Feb.	Ground forces exercise WINTER-STURM 87	Lower Austria (North of Alps)	Armoured Infantry Division	13 000	Ground forces	2 arm. inf. brigs.	Notified
4. USSR	24 Feb.–1 Mar.	Ground forces exercise to improve training	Kostopol–Rovno–Dovbych–Yemil'chino	Commander, Armies of the Carpathian Military District	14 000	400 tanks 350 AT sys. 180 arty. pieces 35 MRLs 25 combt. hels. 5 trans. hels.	2 tanks divs. (−)	Notified 9 Jan. 1987
5. USSR	1–7 Mar.	Ground forces exercise	Radun–Grodno–Iratsevichi–Bara Novichi	Commander, Armies of the Belorussian Military District	>14 000	430 tanks 180 AT sys. 90 arty. pieces 12 MRLs 16 cmbt. hels. 3 trans. hels.	2 tank divs.	Notified 14 Jan. 1987
6. Poland	9–14 Mar.	Ground forces exercise OPAL 87	Lobez–Recz–Wiebork–Chojnice	Pommeranian Military District	18 000	150 tanks 130 AT sys. 100 arty. pieces 12 hels.	1 mot. inf. div. 1 arm. div.	Notified 23 Jan. 1987; observers to be invited

	Dates	Type	Location	Level	Troops	Equipment	Formations	Notes
7. USSR	10–16 Mar.	Ground forces exercise	Komarin–Oster–Kozelets–Chernigov	Deputy Commander, Kiev Military District	16 000	360 tanks 260 AT sys. 200 arty. pieces 34 MRLs 50 cmbt. hels. 70 trans. hels.	1 tank div. 1 mot. rifle div.	Notified 26 Jan. 1987
8. USSR	12–19 Mar.	Ground forces exercise	Gardabani–Akstafa–Gettebe–Sagaredzho	Deputy Commander, Transcaucasus Military District	16 000	240 tanks 250 AT sys. 100 arty. pieces 16 MRLs 54 combt. hels. 30 trans. hels.	2 mot. inf. divs.	Notified 28 Jan. 1987
9. Norway, Netherlands, UK and USA in Norway	13–30 Mar.	Annual field training exercise COLD WINTER 87 (combined arms)	Narvik–Offersøe–Sortland–Kinn–Tovik–Bardujord–Tjeldøya–Hinnøya	6th Division (Nor.)	14 600 (6 000 Nor.) (4 000 USA) (3 800 UK) (800 Neth.)	20 tanks 50 arty. pieces 48 hels. 250 aircraft sorties	Elements of 1 div. (Nor.) 1 commando brig. (UK) 1 marine amph. brig. (USA)	Notified 30 Jan. 1987; amphibious troops in land exercise; observers to be invited
10. USSR and GDR in GDR	23–30 Mar.	Ground forces exercise	Gardelegen–Magdeburg–Wittenberg–Lübben–Brandenburg	Commander, Group of Soviet Forces in Germany	25 000 (23 500 USSR) (1 500 GDR)	500 tanks 190 AT sys. 270 arty. pieces 30 MRLs 50 combt. hels. 70 trans. hels.	1 mot. rifle div. 1 tank div.	Notified 9 Feb. 1987; observers to be invited
11. USSR	1–14 Apr.	Airborne forces exercise	Kirzan–Kirovobad–Mingechaur–Taxtapa–Kazach–Telavi	Deputy Commander, Air Assault Forces	3 000	Air assault and air forces	Air assault regt. with reinforcement units	
12. GDR	1–16 Apr.	Ground forces exercise	Cottbus–Wittenberg–Torgau–Görlitz	Deputy Defence Minister	17 000	Ground and air forces	2 inf. divs. (−)	Observers to be invited

State(s)/Location	Dates/Start window	Type/Name of activity	Area	Level of command	No. of troops	Equipment or type of forces[a]	No. and type of divisions[a,b] Comments	
13. Bulgaria, USSR and Romania in Bulgaria	14–27 May	WTO ground forces exercise BALKAN 87	Velingrad–Dimitrovgrad–Burgas–Varna	Division	13 000	Ground and air forces	..	Plan of the United Command of WTO Armed Forces
14. USSR	15–28 May	Ground forces exercise	Lyady–Strugi–Xrasnye–Tesovskiy–Druzhnaya Gorka	Deputy Commander, Leningrad Military District	14 000	Ground and air forces	2 mot. rifle divs. (–)	
15. France	3–15 June	Amphibious exercise KORRIGAN 87	Quiberon–Auray–Vannes–Port Navalo	Rapid Action Force, i.e., Corps	3 500	Ground, naval and air forces (1 air wing and 1 hel. regt.)	1 marine inf. div.	Exercise may be replaced by a smaller one, which would cancel observation
16. USSR and GDR in GDR	15–28 June	Ground forces exercise	Brandenburg–Magdeburg–Wittenberg–Jüterbog	Commander, Group of Soviet Forces in Germany	15 000	Ground and air forces	1 tank div. (+)	
17. USSR	15–28 June	Ground forces exercise	Yuzha–Vyazniki–Dzerzinsk–Balakhna	Commander, Moscow Military District	13 000	Ground and air forces	1 tank div. (–) with reinforcement units	
18. USA and FRG in FRG	6–19 July	Field training exercise COMPASS POINT 2–87	Kassel–Bad Kissingen–Aschaffenburg–Marburg	Division	19 500	Ground forces	1 mech. inf. div. 1 arm. cavalry regt. 1 tank brig. (FRG)	Observers to be invited; exercise in agreement with FRG
19. USSR and GDR in GDR	15–28 July	Ground forces exercise	Gardelegen–Magdeburg–	Commander, Group of Soviet	25 000	Ground and air forces	1 inf. div. 1 tank div.	Observers to be invited

	Dates	Exercise	Location	Command	Number	Forces	Units	Observers
20. USSR and Czechoslovakia in Czechoslovakia	15–28 July	Ground forces exercise	Jachymov–Karlovy–Vary–Melnik–Liberec–Decin	Soviet Central Group of Forces	17 000	350 tanks, air forces	1 tank div. (+) 1 mot. inf. div. 1 pontoon bn.	Observers to be invited
21. USSR, GDR and Poland in Poland	7–9 days, end of July	Ground forces exercise FRIENDSHIP 87	Lobez–Recz–Walcz–Barwice	General Director of Combat Training of Polish Army	18 000	300 tanks, 1000 aircraft sorties	2 arm. divs. (–) 1 mech. inf. div. (–)	Observers to be invited; no dates for start window
22. Bulgaria	8–21 Aug.	Ground forces exercise	Kaskovo–Topolovgrad–Yambol–Zagora	Division	13 700	Ground and air forces	2 mot. inf. divs. (–)	Plan of the United Command of the WTO Armed Forces
23. USSR	10–24 Aug.	Ground forces exercise	Rava–Russkaya–Yavarov–Gorodok–Nesterov	Commander, Carpathian Military District	18 000	Ground and air forces	2 mot. rifle divs. (–) with reinforcement units	Observers to be invited
24. USSR	15–28 Aug.	Airborne forces exercise	Gvardeysk–Bagrationovsk–Vilkavishkis–Krasnoznamensk	Commander, Air Assault Forces	3 500	Air assault and air forces	1 airborne assault regt. (+)	
25. USSR	25 Aug.–7 Sep.	Ground forces exercise	Serezh–Minsk–Berezino–Obol	Commander, Belorussian Military District	16 000	Ground and air forces	1 tank div. (–) 1 mot. rifle div. (–)	
26. USA in FRG	31 Aug.–13 Sep.	REFORGER deployment VIKING LANDING	Espelkamp–Lippstadt–Marl–Lingen	Theatre Army (US 3d Corps)	35 000	Ground forces	2 mech. inf. divs. 1 arm. div.	Observers to be invited; in agreement with FRG Government

State(s)/Location	Dates/Start window	Type/Name of activity	Area	Level of command	No. of troops	Equipment or type of forces[a]	No. and type of divisions[a,b]	Comments
27. USSR and Hungary in Hungary	1–14 Sep.	Ground forces exercise	Celldömölk–Keszthely–Szekesfeherrar–Unay–Varos–Ercsi	Commander, Southern Army Group	15 000 (8 000 Hun.)	Ground and air forces	1 mech. inf. div. (+)	
28. USSR and GDR in GDR	1–14 Sep.	Ground forces exercise	Jüterbog–Wittenberg–Cottbus–Guben	Group of Soviet Forces in Germany	14 000	Ground and air forces	1 arm. div. (+)	
29. UK and FRG in FRG	4–17 Sep.	Logistic exercise PLAIN SAILING	Northern FRG	Division	13 500 (UK)	Logistic and movement control units, and non-mechanized infantry forces	1 inf. div.	Activity expected to be below notification threshold
30. USA, UK, FRG, Netherlands, Belgium and France in FRG	7–20 Sep.	Field training exercises CERTAIN STRIKE, REFORGER, SACHSEN-ROSS, BELLENDE MEUTE	Lüneberg–Braunschweig–Lippstadt–Espelkamp	Northern Army Group, Central Europe (NORTHAG)	78 000 (35 000 USA) (8 000 UK)	Ground and air forces	2 mech. inf. divs. 3 arm. divs. from 3d Corps(US) Elements of FRG 1st Corps	Participation planned from Netherlands, Belgium and France; observers to be invited; connected to activity No. 26
31. USA and FRG in FRG	7–30 Sep.	Field training exercise GOLDENER LÖWE PARTNER	Waldkappel–Fulda–Limburg–Friedberg–Siegen	Commander, 5th Armoured Division	18 000 (15 500 FRG) (2 500 USA)	Ground and air forces	1 arm. div. (FRG)	Observers to be invited
32. France	7–19 Sep.	Ground forces exercise EXTEL 3	Peronne–Compiègne–Rouen–Abbeville	3d Army Corps	35 000	Ground and air forces 450 tanks	2 arm. divs. (2d + 10th) 1 inf. div. (8th)	Observers to be invited

33. France and FRG in FRG	13–27 Sep.	Ground forces exercises MOINEAU HARDI and KECKER SPATZ	Schwandorf-Deggendorf-Bad Waldsee-Horb-Pforzheim Markt Erlbach-Hilpostein	2d Corps	80 000 (55 000 FRG) (25 000 Fr.)	Ground and air forces (Fr: FAR, FRG: 2d Corps) 150 tanks (Fr.)	Fr: 1 arm. div. 1 marine div. 1 air-mobile div. FRG: 1 mountain div 1 arm. inf. div.	Bilateral training for French Rapid Action Force (FAR): observers to be invited
34. USSR	15–28 Sep.	Ground forces exercise	Gardabani-Akstafa-Gettebe-Sagaredzho	Commander, Transcaucasus Military District	18 000	Ground and air forces	2 mot. rifle divs. (−)	Observers to be invited
35. USA in FRG	17–30 Sep.	REFORGER REDEPLOYMENT to exercise redeployment of US forces to FRG	Northern FRG (Wunstorf-Wieren-Lippstadt-Wulfen-Lehrte)	Theatre Army	35 000	Ground and air forces	2 mech. inf. divs. 1 arm. div.	Observers to be invited; activity connected to Nos. 26 and 29
36. France	19 Sep.–2 Oct.	Ground forces exercise EXTEL 1	Thionville-Metz-Chateau-Salins-Forbach	1st Army Corps	16 000	Mech. ground forces, 200 tanks	7th div.	Will include elements of corps troops and logistic brigade
37. Turkey	21–27 Sep.	Ground forces exercise MEHMETCIK 87	Askale-Erzurum-Sarikanis-Eleskirt	Army	38 000	Infantry, arty. and tank units	3 inf. divs. 2 arm. brigs. 2 mech. brigs.	Observers to be invited; reservists will participate
38. Switzerland	(5 days, 4–19 Oct.)	Exercise CORMOESA (deployment of mountain div.)	South of Alps	Mountain Division	20 000	Ground and air forces plus aircraft defence	1 mountain div. (+)	Observers to be invited

State(s)/ Location	Dates/ Start window	Type/Name of activity	Area	Level of command	No. of troops	Equipment or type of forces[a]	No. and type of divisions[a,b]	Comments
39. Hungary	6–20 Oct.	Ground forces exercise BASALT 87	Celldömölk–Keszthely–Dunaújvaros–Ercsi	Army	8 000	Ground forces and army aviation	1 mech. inf. div. (−)	Below notification threshold
40. UK and FRG in FRG	7–27 Oct.	Field training exercise KEYSTONE	Braunschweig–Bad Sachsa–Minden–Hannover	Commander, Infantry Division (UK)	26 000 (24 000 UK) (2 000 FRG)	Non-mechanized infantry forces	1 inf. div. (UK)	Observers to be invited
41. USA in FRG	19 Oct.–1 Nov.	Field training exercise IRON FORGE 87	Herzogenaurath–Nabburg–Coburg–Schweinfurt	Division	13 400	Ground forces	1 armoured div. (−) 1 mech. inf. div (−)	Exercise of divisional command and control
42. Yugoslavia	23–25 Oct.	Tactical war games JESEN 87	Southern Slovenia in Krka river valley, direction of Novo Mesto–Brezice	Division	15 000	Ground, air, and air defence and territorial defence forces	1 mech. inf. div.	
43. Switzerland	26–29 Oct.	Exercise DIANA (deployment of mountain division)	East of Alps	Mountain Division	13 000	Ground and air forces plus aircraft defence	1 mountain div. (+)	
44. FRG, UK and Denmark in FRG	30 Oct.–6 Nov.	Exercise BRISK FRAY	Fehmarn–Lübeck–Hamburg–Kiel–Putgarden–Lauenburg–Neumünster	Division	c. 14 000 (13 000 FRG) (500 UK) (500 Den.)	Ground and air forces	1 arm. inf. div.	

45. Switzerland	2–5 Nov.	Exercise EIGER (deployment of mountain division)	West of Alps	Mountain Division	18 000	Ground and air forces plus aircraft defence	1 mountain div. (+)	Observers to be invited
46. UK	4–21 Nov.	Amphibious exercise PURPLE WARRIOR	Scotland (Galloway, Arran, Kintyre)	Division	10 000	Amphibious and airborne forces	1 div. (−) of 2 brigs.	7000 troops in amphibious operations; will include an airborne assault by up to 1000 troops; observers to be invited
47. FRG	5–13 Nov.	Alternate types of combat operations (name not designated)	Beverungen–Eschwege–Bad Hersfeld–Marburg	Commander, Armoured Infantry Division	c. 13 500	Ground forces	1 mot. inf. div.	

Advance forecast for 1988

1. Belgium in FRG	..	..		..	<22 000	..	..	Observers to be invited
2. USA in FRG	Jan.–Feb. (11 days)	Field training exercise CARAVAN GUARD	Central FRG	Corps	45 000	..	..	Observers to be invited
3. USA and FRG in FRG	Aug.–Sep. (15 days)	Field training exercise REFORGER	Southern FRG	Corps	60 000–75 000	Ground forces	..	Observers to be invited; exercise will likely include other states

State(s)/Location	Dates/Start window	Type/Name of activity	Area	Level of command	No. of troops	Equipment or type of forces[a]	No. and type of divisions[a,b]	Comments
4. UK and others in Denmark	1 Sep. (26 days)	Ground forces exercise	Denmark	Division	12 500 (UK element)	..	1 inf. brig. 1 amph. brig.	Observers possible; other states will participate
5. UK	7 Sep.–2 Nov.	UK District Home Defence Exercise	Throughout UK	..	poss. >40 000 at certain times	..	Non-mech. army dist. units; troops will exercise as series of mil. dist. exercise, and not in divisions or equivalent formations	Observers to be invited
6. Netherlands, FRG and USA in FRG	19 Sep.–1 Oct.	Field training exercise FREE LION	Osnabrück–Hannover–Braunschweig–Göttingen–Dortmund–Münster	Corps	50 000	Ground forces	2 mech. inf. divs., incl. 3 Neth. brigs. 1 FRG brig. 1 US brig.	Observers to be invited
7. UK, Belgium and FRG in FRG	20 Sep.–16 Oct.	Ground forces exercise IRON HAMMER	North-west Niedersachsen	Corps	> 40 000 (20 000 UK)	..	3 arm. divs.	Belgium and FRG will also participate; observers to be invited
8. USSR	Sep. (10 days)	Ground forces exercise	Verkhedvinsk–Brest–L'vov–Brichany–Krasnodar–Orhl (point in Black Sea c. 43°00'N, 32°00'E)	..	> 40 000	..	..	

a See the list of abbreviations below.

b (−) means that the division is below full strength or not comprised of all its component units; (+) means that the division is at full strength or with reinforcement units assigned to it.

Abbreviations used in the table:

amph.	amphibious
arm.	armoured
arty.	artillery
AT	anti-tank
bn.	batallion
brig(s).	brigade(s)
cmbt.	combat
dist.	district
div(s).	division(s)
hel(s).	helicopter(s)
inf.	infantry
mech.	mechanized
mot.	motorized
MRL	multiple rocket launcher
regt.	regiment
sys.	system
trans.	transport

States participating in notifiable military activities in 1987, by activity number:

Austria: 3
Belgium: 30
Bulgaria: 13, 22
Czechoslovakia: 1, 2, 20
Denmark: 44
France: 15, 30, 32, 33, 36
GDR: 10, 12, 16, 19, 21, 28
FRG: 18, 29, 30, 31, 33, 40, 44, 47
Hungary: 27, 39
Netherlands: 9, 30
Norway: 9
Poland: 6, 21
Romania: 13
Switzerland: 38, 43, 45
Turkey: 37
UK: 29, 30, 40, 44, 46
USSR: 2, 4, 5, 7, 8, 10, 11, 13, 14, 16, 17, 19, 20, 21, 23, 24, 25, 27, 28, 34
USA: 9, 18, 26, 30, 31, 35, 41
Yugoslavia: 42

States not notifying military activities in 1987: Belgium,* Canada, Cyprus, Denmark,* Finland, Greece, Holy See, Iceland, Ireland, Italy, Liechtenstein, Luxembourg, Malta, Monaco, Netherlands,* Portugal, Romania,* San Marino, Spain and Sweden.

(* States participating in activities but not responsible for notification.)

11. Multilateral arms control efforts

JOZEF GOLDBLAT

Superscript numbers refer to the list of notes and references at the end of the chapter.

I. Introduction

In 1986, for the ninth consecutive year, the Geneva-based arms control and disarmament negotiating body, now called the Conference on Disarmament (CD), failed to reach agreement on any of the items on its agenda. This failure was not due to a lack of efforts on the part of the international community. On the contrary, the discussions of arms control issues in multilateral forums, within and outside the United Nations, and at both the political and technical levels, have rarely been as lively as they were in the past few years. It was rather the continuous impasse in the bilateral talks between the USA and the USSR and the generally tense international political climate that hindered the CD from moving ahead.

Some progress was made in the negotiations for a ban on chemical weapons, but the draft treaty which was intended to incorporate the ban remained in a rudimentary form. Moreover, the threat of chemical weapon proliferation is growing, both vertical proliferation—through the continued or resumed manufacture of these weapons by the major powers—as well as horizontal proliferation—through their wider spread among nations—as exemplified by the uses of poison gas in the Iraq–Iran War.

The talks on the cessation of nuclear weapon tests were conducted at cross-purposes: the Soviet Union insisted on an immediate halt to testing, whereas the United States saw a test ban as only a distant goal, to be sought in the context of far-reaching nuclear arms reduction measures. Since these antagonistic positions are unlikely to change in the foreseeable future, a multilateral comprehensive test ban treaty will certainly not be among the next arms control agreements to be concluded. Nevertheless, a few interesting proposals recently made with regard to verification of compliance may facilitate meaningful limitations to US and Soviet nuclear testing.

The discussions at the CD of measures to prevent an arms race in outer space were of a very general nature. The issues to be negotiated were not fully identified, and the weapons to be dealt with were not properly defined. However, the need to reinforce the legal regime of outer space is widely recognized, mainly with a view to protecting satellites against possible attack. In this connection, suggestions for confidence-building undertakings have been put forward.

On the regional level, the 1986 Contadora Act on Peace and Co-operation in Central America, a comprehensive arms control proposal, remained unsigned. It will probably remain in abeyance as long as the conflict between the United States and Nicaragua continues.

These reversals in the process of arms control were to some extent compensated by two regional achievements. The Treaty of Rarotonga entered into force in 1986: it set up the South Pacific nuclear-free zone, preventing further nuclearization of the South Pacific region and strengthening thereby the global nuclear non-proliferation regime. The Stockholm Conference adopted a Document on confidence- and security-building measures in Europe, which has considerably amplified the obligations of the parties contained in the relevant part of the 1975 Helsinki Declaration. (The Stockholm Document is not dealt with in this chapter.)

II. Chemical disarmament

In 1986, negotiations on a convention prohibiting the development, production and stockpiling of chemical weapons, and providing for their destruction, continued in the CD as a priority item on its agenda. These multilateral talks were stimulated by several rounds of complementary bilateral US-Soviet discussions. As a result, there is now agreement on the general scope of the envisaged treaty, and a step forward has been made with regard to verification of compliance, as well as in establishing distinct categories of agents and other chemicals of importance that are subject to prohibitions or restrictions.

However, there are considerable gaps in the draft under consideration, with 'details to be elaborated later'. Annexes describing the arrangements for the implementation of the provisions of the convention also remain to be completed.[1] The major issues that are still unresolved, or only partially resolved, concern: (a) the declaration and monitoring of chemical weapon stockpiles; (b) the order of elimination of these stockpiles; (c) the elimination of chemical weapon production facilities; (d) the prevention of misuse of the chemical industry for chemical weapon production; and (e) the nature of on-site inspection. The threat of further chemical weapon proliferation among nations, which may complicate the efforts to reach a universal ban on these weapons, must also be dealt with, even before the convention is concluded.

Declaration of stockpiles

It is agreed that after a chemical weapon convention entered into force each party would submit declarations stating whether it possessed or did not possess chemical weapons on its territory or elsewhere, and whether it had on its territory chemical weapons under the jurisdiction or control of any other state. The parties possessing chemical weapons would also have to state the aggregate quantity and detailed composition of their stocks, and a format was developed for the submission of this type of information.

The United States proposed that the location of stockpiles should also be stated in order to make it possible to confirm through on-site inspection the accuracy of the declarations and to have the stockpiles monitored continuously until they are completely eliminated. For a long time, the Soviet Union had been opposed to revealing what it considered to be a military secret, arguing that locations of stockpiles need not be disclosed before the beginning of the elimination process, but in February 1987 it agreed to do so and to subject the declared stocks to international inspection.[2] The modalities remain to be worked out.

Elimination of stockpiles

Elimination of stockpiles of chemical weapons would take place through destruction not later than 10 years after the entry into force of the convention (a period considered too long by some countries, e.g., Morocco[3]). In the process of destruction, chemicals would be converted to a form unsuitable for production of chemical weapons, and chemical munitions would be rendered unusable.

The negotiators agreed that elimination of stocks must start simultaneously by all states possessing chemical weapons. The order of elimination should take account of the degree of harmfulness of the agents in question and should ensure undiminished security of the parties during the entire elimination process. Belgium proposed that the destruction should be spread over a number of periods, with minimal established quantities of the stocks to be destroyed within each period, and that the order of elimination for lethal substances and that for harmful substances should be considered independently.[4]

Elimination of production facilities

It is understood that chemical weapon production facilities should be promptly declared and their elimination over a 10-year period be carried out under international controls. But no agreement was reached on what exactly must be declared and subsequently eliminated, inasmuch as the definition of the term 'chemical weapons production facility' has not as yet been definitively determined.

Nevertheless, a move was made to ensure verification of the destruction of facilities. In particular, the Soviet Union agreed that the correctness of the declarations of the production facilities, made by the parties, should be open to verification; that the facilities closed should be sealed by inspectors; and that those seals should be periodically checked until each facility has been destroyed or dismantled. Systematic, international on-site inspections would be conducted until the industrial base for chemical weapon production has been completely abolished. The conversion of facilities for the purpose of destruction of stocks of chemical weapons as well as their subsequent elimination would also be carried out under international supervision.[5]

Prevention of misuse of chemical industry

The need to monitor the civilian chemical industry to ensure that it is not illicitly manufacturing lethal chemical agents is generally acknowledged, but the difficulties of instituting reliable verification are also recognized. To test the relevant procedures, the Netherlands organized in 1986 an experimental inspection in a modern multi-purpose Dutch plant. The conclusions drawn from this exercise are as follows. For the chemical industry, which is already accustomed to a rather intrusive system of inspection (for purposes of public health, safety and environmental protection), additional inspections in connection with a chemical weapons convention would not be unusually burdensome. It would be important, however, to protect sensitive information, in particular information on production and on the destination of sales. The experience obtained from the Netherlands' test has strengthened the view that an adequate system of verification can be elaborated and obtained at reasonable cost. Moreover, it is believed that a well-developed system of routine on-site inspection would diminish the need for recourse to inspections upon special request.[6]

A report was also presented to the CD on a 'trial inspection' of an Australian chemical facility. According to this report, a system of material accountancy and routine, random inspections of chemical plants would provide a strong deterrent to both the production of super-toxic lethal chemicals or their key precursors and to the diversion of 'other lethal' chemicals for use in chemical weapons.[7]

The view shared by the Western participants in the negotiations was that an effective verification system to prevent the misuse of the civilian chemical industry for weapon production could be developed, taking into account the legitimate interests of this industry.[8] The Soviet Union concurred with the proposition that the use of the commercial industry for the development and production of chemical weapons should be prevented.

Inspection 'on challenge'

Routine inspections as envisaged in the draft convention are meant to ensure confidence in the initial declarations as well as in the actual elimination of the chemical weapon stockpiles and production facilities. They are also intended to guard against diversion of chemicals from the civil industry to weapon production. Certain concerns, however, may not be resolved by routine measures. There is an avowed need for bilateral and multilateral consultation and co-operation on any matter which may be raised relating to the objectives or the implementation of the provisions of the convention. It is also accepted that there must be a fact-finding procedure, but opinions differ as regards the nature of inspections that may be required by such a procedure.

In its 1984 draft convention the United States provided for special international inspections, permitting unimpeded access to any relevant location or facility owned or controlled by the government of a party, including military facilities.[9] This proposal was found by the Soviet Union to be discriminatory against parties with state-owned or partly nationalized industries in that it put them in an unfavourable position compared to states with predominantly private enterprise. Responding positively to this objection, the United States amended the draft, making it clear that on-site inspections would encompass all relevant locations and facilities regardless of the economic or political systems of parties, but it still insisted that they must be mandatory. This would mean that a country which was concerned that another country was not complying with the ban on chemical weapons would have the right to request that an inspection be conducted on very short notice, and that such inspection could not be refused.[10] The Soviet Union and its allies, however, contended that acceptance of these so-called on-challenge inspections should be voluntary and thus that there should be a right of refusal.[11]

Two compromise proposals were put forward in the CD to reconcile these diametrically opposed positions. Pakistan suggested that in special cases a party may be expected to refuse a fact-finding mission the right to visit the facilities or sites to be inspected. However, the refusal would have to be accompanied by a detailed explanation of the reason. If the explanation was found unsatisfactory, the request for sending a fact-finding team could be renewed. In case of repeated refusals, an extraordinary session of the consultative committee, the principal organ of the convention, could be convened to consider the situation.[12] The United Kingdom also recognized that a state may have legitimate security interests in refusing inspection, and that in very limited circumstances it should have the right to do so. The challenged party would then have to propose alternative measures to resolve the matter. Were alternative measures to fail to provide a satisfactory answer, the state under challenge would still be obliged to find ways to demonstrate its compliance. The time-limit for this process would be a maximum of seven days. If the requesting state were not satisfied that the challenged state was fulfilling its obligations, the matter would be transmitted for consideration to the executive council, established by the convention, where measures to be taken against the suspected party could be collectively decided, including the withdrawal of that party's rights and privileges under the convention. These measures would be without prejudice to the right of other parties to take unilateral action up to and including withdrawal from the convention, if they decided that 'extraordinary' events related to the subject-matter of the convention had jeopardized their supreme interests.[13]

So far, a convergence of views has emerged on the following points: (a) that confidence in the convention should be built up and maintained by routine inspection; (b) that any party must have the right to voice its suspicions that another party is not complying with its obligations and have confidence that these suspicions would be promptly allayed by agreed procedures; (c) that such procedures should be regarded as a fundamental source of confidence in the convention and recourse to them should be a rare event; and (d) that once these procedures have been invoked a very short time scale for resolution of the issue is essential both for reasons inherent in the nature of chemical weapons as well as for wider political reasons.[14]

Proliferation of chemical weapons

In the absence of a universal ban on the possession of chemical weapons, the international taboo against their use is being eroded. In 1986, Iran submitted new complaints of use of chemical weapons by Iraqi forces (previous complaints having been made and investigated in 1984 and 1985), and a UN team of specialists found the allegations to be well-founded.[15] These patent violations of the 1925 Geneva Protocol were criticized or condemned by a number of states but, on the whole, the reaction of the international community was weak. No collective action was recommended by the UN Security Council against the transgressor of this important international agreement. The verbal exhortations did not deter the Iraqi Government from continuing to employ gas in combat. Moreover, recent statements made by Iran implied the possibility of retaliation in kind.[16]

According to the United Kingdom, as many as 10 000 people may already have been casualties of chemical warfare in recent years. Iraq has full-scale production facilities capable of producing many hundreds of tons of mustard gas and of nerve agents, and new production complexes are under construction. The United Kingdom claims to be in possession of evidence that in the Middle East alone, apart from Iraq, there are countries developing an offensive chemical weapon capacity. 'World-wide, there may be more than 20 nations which now either possess chemical weapons or are looking at the option of acquiring them.'[17]

Some measures to deal with the problem of chemical weapon proliferation have been taken parallel to US–Soviet consultations on this subject. Thus, the United States now requires export licences on chemicals related to the manufacture of chemical weapons and has prohibited exports of certain dangerous chemicals to Iran, Iraq and Syria. Many Western countries have enacted analogous or even wider controls. The Soviet Union proceeded in a similar way by deciding on 23 January 1986 on a 'Statute on the export of chemicals which have a peaceful purpose but can be used to produce chemical weapons'. This document, adopted by the Soviet Council of Ministers, stipulates that the chemicals in question may be exported from the USSR only if guarantees have been given by the importing countries that they will not be used to produce chemical weapons, and will not be re-exported or transferred from the jurisdiction of the recipient country without the written consent of the corresponding Soviet foreign-trade organization.[18] All such measures, although clearly desirable, are not sufficient, since any country with a modern chemical industry can convert intermediate chemicals (for example, for the production of pesticides or fertilizers) into chemical weapons with relative ease.

Whereas the possibility of concluding a chemical 'non-proliferation treaty', patterned after the 1968 Treaty on the Non-Proliferation of Nuclear Weapons, has been categorically ruled out by most CD members, there is some measure of support for interim regional chemical disarmament undertakings, which might reduce the proliferation risks pending the conclusion of a global ban.[19]

Conclusion

A host of problems still remains to be dealt with before a chemical weapons convention could be finalized. Most of the obstacles are of a technical nature and could be resolved by technical experts. The crucial obstacles are of a political nature. Among the latter the central issue is inspection on challenge. However, here also, the compromise proposals made in 1986 could facilitate progress.

Time is pressing. Allegations continue to be made of massive production and storage of chemical weapons by the Soviet Union. The USA may soon begin manufacture of modern, binary chemical weapons after a unilateral 18-year moratorium on production. For the first time, France has openly stated (in its programme for arms procurement for 1987–91) that it could not renounce chemical weapons and would have to possess an 'appropriate' deterrent capacity as long as others possessed one.[20] A chemical disarmament convention is ripe for conclusion, and it would be a pity to make it dependent on other arms control measures.

III. Nuclear test ban

Much of the time devoted in 1986 to multilateral discussions of a nuclear test ban was absorbed by the continued dispute (lasting almost three years) over the mandate of a working committee to deal with this measure within the framework of the CD. The dispute is clearly a cover-up for the fundamental difference between the main partners as to whether cessation of nuclear weapon explosions—a central arms control issue for decades—is still a desirable and urgent measure.

The United States is of the view that nuclear testing plays a role in ensuring the security of the Western Alliance and that, therefore, a test ban is an objective to be sought only in the context of significant reductions in the existing arsenals of nuclear weapons and the development of substantially improved verification measures. The Soviet Union, on the other hand, considers an immediate halt to nuclear testing as an indispensable practical step towards diminishing the nuclear threat, and maintains that reductions in nuclear arsenals alone, without a prohibition on tests, would not help in reaching this objective, because continued testing may serve to modernize the remaining weapons and to develop ever more sophisticated ones.[21] Nevertheless, a series of important proposals have been made regarding verification of compliance, both within and outside the usual arms control and disarmament forums. They may facilitate the resumption of test ban or test limitation negotiations.

Initiatives at the CD

In recent years proposals have been made at the CD for the creation of a world-wide seismic network on the basis of existing seismic facilities and communications systems, and for progressively expanding and refining it in order to maximize confidence in its ability to detect and identify underground nuclear explosions.[22] Pending the conclusion of a comprehensive test ban treaty, the network would be used to monitor nuclear tests and would also benefit international co-operation in seismology. In 1986, Australia referred to these proposals and suggested that the CD should 'call the global network into being' by deciding to establish it 'forthwith', pledge to make available to it appropriate national facilities and equipment, and invite non-member countries to do the same.[23] The USSR 'warned' that premature establishment of an international system of seismic data exchange could give a misleading impression that something was being done to prevent nuclear testing. It said that a verification system was to serve as a means to ensure compliance with a ban and not to monitor continued testing, and that it should therefore start operating only upon the entry into force of a treaty.[24] However, the USSR still voted for a UN General Assembly resolution urging the CD to take immediate steps for the establishment of an international seismic monitoring network with a view to the further development of the potential to monitor and verify compliance with a comprehensive test ban.[25] (The United Kingdom and the United States abstained.)

Sweden claimed that the verification limits depended primarily on the number of stations used in the seismic system, their location and their technical performance. To obtain a homogeneous global network producing identical data, Sweden suggested using modern standardized stations, the technical specifications of which could be worked out by the CD *Ad Hoc* Group of Scientific Experts (GSE) which considers international co-operative measures to detect and identify seismic events.[26]

Norway proposed that the global seismological network should incorporate, to the extent possible, small-aperture seismic arrays (an array being a station consisting of several seismometers placed in a certain pattern). The usefulness of such mini-arrays was demonstrated during the first year of operation (from May 1985) of the Norwegian Regional Seismic Array System (NORESS), which had been designed to detect seismic events at regional distances (less than 3000 km), and which had been added to the Norwegian Seismic Array (NORSAR), designed to detect seismic events at longer, so-called teleseismic distances. (Both installations are part of a joint Norwegian-US undertaking.)[27]

The GSE envisages that the operators of each seismic station would derive basic parameters, called 'Level I' data, from the recordings of all the detected events. These parameters would be transmitted to the international data centres to enable them to locate and assign magnitudes to seismic events and to characterize the observed signals, so as to form a preliminary idea about the nature of the event. Should a participant in the seismic system want to pursue the examination of the event, he could request waveform data, i.e., the original recordings, called 'Level II' data, from one or more of the participating stations.

The issue of waveform exchange has been the subject of considerable debate during the past few years. With the advances in digital seismometry, computer technology and data transmission, it was felt that much greater use could be made of the raw waveform data in the global system, but for a long time the USSR was opposed to any modification of the parameter-based system. In 1986, however, its position changed: in a statement in the CD, the USSR expressed the belief that timely transmission of Level II data would significantly increase the effectiveness of the envisaged international system of seismic data exchange.[28]

Consequently, the Soviet Union formally proposed that the *Ad Hoc* Group should devise a system for prompt transmission of Level II seismic data to underpin international seismic verification. Such data would be transmitted from the seismic stations belonging to the global network using satellite communication channels, and would be processed at the international data centres. Provision would be made for automatic data exchange among these centres using specially selected communication channels. The Soviet Union considered that it would be useful to carry out an international experiment in Level II data exchange.[29] Realization of the Soviet proposal would have a considerable impact on the work of the GSE.

Six-Nation Initiative

In a document adopted on 7 August 1986 at Ixtapa, Mexico, the heads of state or government of Argentina, Greece, India, Mexico and Sweden and the first President of Tanzania stated that they were prepared to assist in the monitoring of a moratorium on nuclear weapon tests or of a test ban.

In case of a halt in nuclear testing by the USA and the USSR, the six nations would establish, in co-operation with both powers, temporary monitoring stations at existing test sites and operate them for an initial period of one year. All data would be available to these nations, as well as to the USA and the USSR. Data analysis could be a joint undertaking, and preliminary analysis would be done at the sites. To reduce the risk of falsely identifying shallow earthquakes as nuclear explosions, a scheme of on-site inspections at the test sites could be contemplated and the six nations were prepared to participate in such inspections in co-operation with the host country. They were also willing to co-operate with the two powers in the establishment of specific verification arrangements outside the test sites, in some of those areas where the availability of large cavities or unconsolidated rock might reduce the strength of the seismic signals, as well as in regions of shallow seismicity. The six nations further suggested 'internationalizing' a number of selected stations (tentatively 20-30) in each of the two nuclear weapon powers by placing observers at these stations. The task of the observers would be to verify that the instruments were properly operated and that all information obtained was reported without omission.

To replace these temporary measures, experts from the six nations were ready to co-operate with experts from the USA and the USSR in the development of permanent verification facilities at test sites, and in the development of an optimal network of internal stations in the territory of both powers. Moreover, to ensure that large chemical explosions were not mistaken for nuclear tests, the six nations were willing to establish, together with the USA and the USSR, procedures for on-site inspections of large chemical explosions and to take part in such inspections. And, finally, they pledged to strengthen co-operation among themselves with a view to monitoring and announcing ongoing test activities, and to support the establishment of an international verification system by actively participating in its elaboration by the GSE at the CD.[30] In separate letters to President Reagan and General Secretary Gorbachev the six leaders proposed that a meeting of their experts with those from the USA and the USSR be held to discuss the verification issue.[31]

It is remarkable that of the participants in this so-called Six-Nation Initiative only Sweden and India had previously been active in the work of the GSE, which is open to all states. It is also noteworthy that of the six nations Argentina is not party either to the 1967 Treaty of Tlatelolco prohibiting nuclear weapons in Latin America or the 1968 Non-Proliferation Treaty. Argentina, moreover, claims for itself the right to conduct nuclear explosions for peaceful purposes, including explosions which involve devices similar to those used in nuclear weapons, even though it is impossible to develop nuclear explosives which would be capable only of peaceful applications. Tanzania and India have refused to join the NPT. The latter country has even conducted a nuclear explosion; it declines to submit its nuclear activities to comprehensive international safeguards and consistently rejects the proposals for the setting-up of a nuclear weapon-free zone in South Asia. It is possible that the Six-Nation Initiative signifies a change in the attitudes of these countries to nuclear weapon proliferation. Indeed, ratification by Argentina of the Partial Test Ban Treaty (PTBT) in November 1986, more than 23 years after its signature, may be considered a step in that direction.

Reacting to the six-nation proposal the Soviet Union said that it would follow it up 'if, of course, it was accepted by the other side'.[32]

Installations of US seismometers in the USSR

The two US–Soviet test-limitation treaties—the Threshold Test Ban Treaty (TTBT) and the Peaceful Nuclear Explosions Treaty (PNET), signed in 1974 and 1976 respectively—have still not been ratified. The Soviet Union has often stated its readiness to do so, although after its unilateral suspension of underground testing it emphasized preference for the conclusion of a comprehensive ban, bypassing the TTBT. On the other hand, the United States, which in signing the Treaty expressed full confidence that it would be able to recognize violations owing to the data-exchange provision, now claims that the verification clauses are insufficient. It alleges that the Soviet Union has on a number of occasions exceeded the 150-kt explosion yield limit which both signatories had committed themselves to observe during the pre-ratification period. (The extent of the suspected breaches is a controversial issue within the US Administration.)

To tighten the relevant TTBT clauses so as to ensure that the agreed threshold was actually being observed, the US Government proposed in 1985 mutual visits of Soviet and US experts to the respective test sites to measure directly the yield of explosions. The USA claimed that such visits would help to establish the basis for the verification of 'effective limits' on underground nuclear testing.[33] It is clear that measurements taken on the spot could validate the data supplied by the other side and add confidence in the yields of explosions conducted for calibration purposes in accordance with the provisions of the TTBT. (Because seismic signals produced by a given underground explosion vary, yield determination requires knowledge of the environment in which the test has been carried out as well as of previous explosions conducted at the same site.)

The Soviet Union rejected the US Government's proposal, but in the summer of 1986 the Soviet Academy of Sciences and the Natural Resources Defense Council (NRDC), a private US environmental group, concluded an agreement on the basis of which scientists from both countries installed US-manufactured seismometric equipment on Soviet territory near the testing site in the area of Semipalatinsk (Kazakhstan).[34] While the equipment could not be used for calibration purposes as long as the Soviet test moratorium was in force, it could have been helpful in monitoring compliance with the moratorium. Identical stations, jointly manned and operated, were to be (but had not been) set up to monitor US tests at the Nevada Test Site.[35]

Prospects

The 1985 and 1986 UN General Assemblies recommended the parties to the PTBT to convert the PTBT through an amendment into a comprehensive treaty.[36] Indeed, upon request from one-third or more of the parties, a conference of all the parties must be convened by the depositary governments to consider any proposed amendments. The supporters of this recommendation seem to think that a conference of this nature would put irresistible pressure on the nuclear weapon powers to reach a comprehensive ban. However, considering the present firm opposition of the UK and the USA to stopping their nuclear weapon tests, such an undertaking is unlikely to succeed.

The 1985 Review Conference of the parties to the Non-Proliferation Treaty urged the conclusion of a comprehensive nuclear test ban treaty 'as a matter of the highest priority'.[37] However, judging by the developments at the CD, such a treaty is not achievable in the foreseeable future. Bilateral US–Soviet talks on issues related to nuclear testing, held in several rounds since the summer of 1986, have reinforced this impression. It would seem, nevertheless, that there exist prospects for bringing about at least some further limitations on testing. They opened up at the end of 1986.

In the course of the US–Soviet summit meeting at Reykjavik, the United States said that it was prepared—upon achieving 'adequate verification' of the TTBT and the PNET and upon ratification of these treaties—to embark on negotiations for further testing limitations 'in association with nuclear-weapon reductions'.[38] The Soviet Union expressed its willingness to initiate a negotiating process in order to consider 'the questions of thresholds, the yield of nuclear explosions, the number of nuclear explosions a year, and the fate of the 1974 and the 1976 treaties'.[39] The Soviet Government reiterated this offer in December 1986 in a statement regarding possible termination of its unilateral nuclear test moratorium.[40] Another positive development was that China became the second nuclear weapon state, after France, to renounce testing in the atmosphere without formally joining the PTBT. All the atmospheric nuclear tests have thus ceased.

Short of a total ban, meaningful restraints on tests are no doubt better for the cause of arms control than unrestrained nuclear testing.

IV. Arms control in outer space

An *Ad Hoc* Committee of the CD was re-established in 1986 to deal with the issue of the prevention of an arms race in outer space. The mandate of the Committee was not to negotiate an agreement, but only to examine and 'identify' the relevant issues. Consequently, the discussion was of a general nature; various opinions were stated and proposals put forward without an attempt to reconcile the differences.

The debate[41]

Many delegations, mainly from non-aligned and socialist countries, asserted that outer space is the common heritage of mankind and should be used 'exclusively' for peaceful purposes to promote the development of all nations. This point of view was disputed by certain Western delegations on the grounds that the 'common heritage' status of outer space had not been unambiguously established by the international treaties in force. Those who held the latter view also argued that outer space was analogous to other environments beyond national jurisdiction, such as the high seas, where non-aggressive military activities are permitted under the existing legal regime. It was further pointed out that certain activities of a military nature which have been conducted in outer space had contributed to strategic stability and arms control.

Several delegations said that an arms race in outer space would undermine the international agreements in force relating to outer space, as well as jeopardize the arms limitation and disarmament process as a whole. The danger of the 'weaponization' of outer space was particularly stressed,[42] and it was contended by some that even Article 51 of the UN Charter, providing for self-defence in case of armed attack, would not justify the use of space weapons or the possession of defensive systems based on space weapons.

Attention was also drawn to the present military uses of space, as having negative consequences for international peace and security, because the majority of objects in orbit constitute integral parts of weapon systems and are associated with a possible use of nuclear weapons on earth. The group of socialist countries in the CD insisted that to prevent an arms race in outer space it was essential to prevent the emergence of 'space strike weapons', including anti-satellite (ASAT) weapons, space-based anti-ballistic missile (ABM) systems and space-to-earth weapons.

Definitions

To facilitate the discussion, it was considered useful to define the characteristics and principal elements of the weapons to be dealt with. Venezuela put forward the following definition of 'space strike weapons':

'Space strike weapons' means any offensive or defensive device, including its operational components, whatever the scientific principle on which its functioning is based:
(a) capable of destroying or damaging from its place of deployment in outer space an object situated in outer space, in the air, in water or on land,
(b) capable of destroying or damaging from its place of deployment in the air, in water or in land an object situated in outer space.
The following are also space strike weapons: any offensive or defensive device including its operational components, and any system of such devices, whatever the scientific principle on which its functioning is based, that is capable of intercepting, from outer space or from land, water or the atmosphere, ballistic projectiles during their flight.[43]

China defined space weapons as devices or installations, either space-, land-, sea-, or atmosphere-based, which are designed to attack or damage vehicles in outer space, or disrupt their normal functioning, or change their orbits, and all devices or installations based in space (including those based on the moon and other celestial bodies) which are designed to attack or damage objects in the atmosphere, or on land, or at sea, or disrupt their normal functioning.[44]

In the view of Sri Lanka, any device, whether ground-based or space-based, in earth orbit or in any trajectory beyond earth orbit, designed physically to damage or interfere with a space object or to attack ground or airborne targets from space, is a space weapon which should be banned.[45]

A paper discussing the terminology relevant to arms control and outer space was submitted by Canada.[46] It has not proved possible so far to agree on a definition of 'outer space', or on a demarcation between airspace, which is subject to national sovereignty, and outer space, which is open for utilization by all states. There are also conflicting interpretations of the terms 'peaceful purposes', 'militarization' and 'weaponization', used in connection with space activities.

Proposals

Some delegations saw as the main objective of their endeavours the attainment of a prohibition on the development, testing, production and deployment of space weapons. However, before such a comprehensive goal was attained, they considered it important that partial measures should be adopted—in the first place, a multilateral ban on ASAT weapons or their components, as well as on systems adaptable for use in an ASAT mode. They also suggested that, pending a formal agreement on these measures, a moratorium be declared on the development, testing and deployment of ASAT weapons. Reference was made to the 1983 Soviet draft treaty for the prohibition of the use of force in outer space.[47] Pakistan proposed, as an interim measure, the adoption of an international instrument to supplement the US–Soviet ABM Treaty with a view to ensuring that the self-restraint accepted by the two powers under the Treaty was not negated by acts of omission or commission by either of these powers or by other technologically advanced states. Such an instrument could: (a) recognize and re-confirm the importance of the ABM Treaty in preventing the escalation of an arms race, especially in outer space; (b) note the commitment of the USA and the USSR to continue to abide strictly by the provisions of this Treaty, in particular its Article V under which they have undertaken not to develop, test or deploy ABM systems or components of such systems that are sea-based, air-based, space-based or mobile land-based; (c) provide a clear interpretation of the research activities permissible under the ABM Treaty; (d) include a commitment by other technologically advanced states not to take their own research beyond the limits accepted by the USA and the USSR; and (e) include a mechanism to provide for the redress of such activities that are contrary to the limitations contained in the ABM Treaty.[48]

A great amount of attention was devoted to the need for confidence-building measures, including an increased exchange of information related to outer space. In this context, elaboration of 'rules-of-the-road' for space, similar to those valid for the seas, was found worthy of consideration in order to limit the risks arising from misunderstandings (for example, from unintended collisions of satellites with space debris or other space objects). And, finally, various delegations expressed their support for the idea of establishing a world space organization to promote the exploration and use of outer space for peaceful purposes.

Verification

The difficulty of verifying compliance with measures related to the prevention of an arms race in outer space was one of the dominant features in the CD debate. The particular complexity of the issue is due, among other reasons, to the vastness of space and the possibility of concealment of certain systems on earth. However, many delegations felt that the subject of verification should not be dealt with in abstract, but must be examined in the context of specific agreements to be concluded. The feasibility of using both national and international technical means of verification was mentioned. Some thought that verification functions could be entrusted to a world space organization (see above); reference was also made to the 1978 French proposal for the establishment of an international satellite monitoring agency.[49]

Possible confidence-building measures

While the importance of the bilateral US–Soviet negotiations is generally acknowledged, the need for a multilateral approach to issues which relate to the prevention of an arms race in outer space and which affect the vital interests of all nations is also recognized. In particular, it is believed that the CD has a role to play in the negotiation of multilateral measures which may be necessary to complement the existing legal regime of outer space. But the CD has so far been unable to identify and agree upon any such measure.

One option for a multilateral undertaking would be to bring about a general ban on actions intended to destroy or damage satellites, or to interfere in any other way with their functioning. Reaching such a no-use (or no-first-use)-of-force agreement reinforcing pertinent international law would, however, require dealing with complications caused by the overlap between civilian and military as well as between stabilizing and destabilizing uses of satellites. These complications may prove difficult to overcome, as selective protection is nearly impossible. A blanket prohibition, implying immunity for *all* satellites, would therefore seem to be the only rational solution. It might not be fully credible, considering the importance of satellites for modern warfare, but it would not be less dependable than other laws of armed conflict according protection to objects which may have military significance.

A legal 'immunization' regime for satellites, as suggested above, would benefit from confidence-building measures. A first, relatively modest step in this area could be the improvement and amplification of the existing international requirement for the registration of space objects.

The 1972 Convention on registration of objects launched into outer space provides for an obligation of the parties to furnish, as soon as practicable, to the UN Secretary-General information on the designator of the space object or its registration number, the date and territory or location of launch, basic orbital parameters and general function of the object. 'This mandatory registration provision seems to be more honoured in the breach than in compliance, since space powers do not describe any military functions.'[50] Moreover, there are inordinate delays in the announcement of launches—on the average several months; many delays are of up to one year and in a few cases even years. As corroborated by information from non-governmental sources, certain launches have never been announced.

To strengthen the Registration Convention for the purposes of building confidence some supplementary information should be required, such as a precise description of the space object or the changes in the stated orbit. The term 'as soon as practicable' used for the provision of notification should be understood as meaning no more than, for example, 24 hours. A constraint measure limiting the rate of launch, and perhaps a prohibition on multiple launches as well as on threatening actions (such as aiming a weapon at a space object or using another country's satellite for target practice) would also be advisable in terms of confidence building. An agency for overseeing the Convention and checking compliance might be needed.

Any state party to the Registration Convention has the right to propose amendments, which would enter into force for each accepting party upon their acceptance by the majority. It would seem useful, nonetheless, that before any amendments were to be formally submitted, a review conference should be convened (as envisaged in the Convention) to discuss the possibility and the desirability of a revision of the Convention.

V. The South Pacific nuclear-free zone

As a result of negotiations among Australia, the Cook Islands, Fiji, Kiribati, Nauru, New Zealand, Niue, Papua New Guinea, the Solomon Islands, Tonga, Tuvalu, Vanuatu and Western Samoa—all member states of the South Pacific Forum—a treaty was concluded on 6 August 1985 in Rarotonga (in the Cook Islands) establishing the South Pacific nuclear-free zone. In its basic provisions the Treaty of Rarotonga forbids its adherents to manufacture or otherwise acquire or have control over nuclear weapons and prohibits other countries from stationing such weapons in the territories of the parties as well as from conducting nuclear tests in the zone. In addition, there is a ban on the dumping of radioactive wastes and other radioactive material at sea within the zone.[51] (For the text and an analysis of the Treaty of Rarotonga, see *SIPRI Yearbook 1986*.)

Status of implementation of the Treaty of Rarotonga

The Treaty of Rarotonga entered into force on 11 December 1986, upon deposit of the eighth instrument of ratification with the Director of the South Pacific Bureau for Economic Co-operation who is the depositary.

Three protocols annexed to the Treaty were opened for signature on 1 December 1986. Under Protocol 1, meant to be signed by France, the United Kingdom and the United States, the signatories would undertake to apply the prohibitions contained in the Treaty in respect of the territories in the zone for which they are internationally responsible. Under Protocol 2, open for signature by China, France, the United Kingdom, the Soviet Union and the United States, the signatories would undertake not to contribute to a violation of the Treaty or its protocols, and not to use or threaten to use a nuclear explosive against the parties to the Treaty or against any territory within the nuclear-free zone for which a state that had become a party to Protocol 1 was internationally responsible. Also Protocol 3, prohibiting tests of any nuclear explosive device anywhere within the zone, is to be signed by all the nuclear weapon powers, but it is clearly addressed to France, the only state which is still engaged in such tests in the region. This circumstance makes France's acceptance of this protocol and, for that matter, of the other two protocols as well highly improbable—at least for the foreseeable future.

Another difficulty which arises in connection with the protocols is the problem of transit. The Treaty of Rarotonga does not require an absolute absence of nuclear weapons in the zone under any circumstance: in Article 5 it allows each party to make an exception for nuclear weapons that may be aboard nuclear states' ships visiting its ports or navigating its territorial seas or archipelagic waters, and for weapons that may be aboard aircraft visiting its airfields or transiting its airspace. The frequency and duration of such visits and transits have not been limited. This provision, which is intended to suit the interests of the Western nuclear weapon powers, has proved to be unacceptable to the USSR. Indeed, in signing Protocols 2 and 3 on 15

December 1986, the Soviet Union stated the view that 'admission' of transit of nuclear weapons or other nuclear explosive devices by any means, as well as of visits by foreign military ships and aircraft with nuclear explosive devices on board to the ports and airfields within the nuclear-free zone, would contradict the aims of the Treaty of Rarotonga and would be inconsistent with the status of the zone. This statement amounts to a rejection of Article 5 of the Treaty.

The Soviet Union also warned that in case of action taken by a party or parties violating their major commitments connected with the nuclear-free status of the zone, as well as in case of aggression committed by one or several parties to the Treaty, supported by a nuclear weapon state, or together with it, with the use by such a state of the territory, airspace, territorial sea or archipelagic waters of the parties for visits by nuclear weapon-carrying ships and aircraft or for transit of nuclear weapons, the USSR will have the right to consider itself free of its no-use commitments assumed under Protocol 2. A similar warning was given by the Soviet Union several years before, when it joined an additional protocol of the 1967 Treaty of Tlatelolco, which prohibits nuclear weapons in Latin America. Since then, however, under a unilateral declaration made in 1982, the USSR is formally and unconditionally committed not to be the first to use nuclear weapons against any country. Its reservation to the Treaty of Rarotonga, as formulated above, seems to contradict this declaration.

On 10 February 1987, China signed Protocols 2 and 3 to the Treaty of Rarotonga, but reserved the right to reconsider the assumed obligations, if other nuclear weapon states or the contracting parties to the Treaty took action in 'gross violation' of the Treaty and its Protocols, thus changing the status of the nuclear-free zone and endangering the security interests of China.

The United States decided in early 1987 that it would not sign the protocols 'at this time'.[52]

It should be noted that no prior consultation is known to have been conducted by the drafters of the Treaty with the powers eligible to become parties to its protocols. Such consultation was held only after the signing of the Treaty by a team of officials from the South Pacific Forum countries, resulting in some amendments in the text of the three protocols.[53] In particular, a withdrawal clause was added reading as follows:

This Protocol is of a permanent nature and shall remain in force indefinitely, provided that each Party shall, in exercising its national sovereignty, have the right to withdraw from this Protocol if it decides that extraordinary events, related to the subject matter of this Protocol, have jeopardized its supreme interests. It shall give notice of such withdrawal to the depositary three months in advance. Such notice shall include a statement of the extraordinary events it regards as having jeopardized its supreme interests.

This clause appears in most arms control treaties, but the parties to the Treaty of Rarotonga itself may withdraw from it only in the event of a violation of its essential provisions.

The Treaty of Rarotonga and the ANZUS alliance

The conclusion of the Treaty of Rarotonga coincided with the *de facto* collapse of the ANZUS alliance, the 1951 defence pact linking Australia, New Zealand and the United States. The collapse was brought about by the New Zealand Government's refusal to allow nuclear-armed or nuclear-powered naval units into its ports. This anti-nuclear posture (planned to be embodied in a special law underpinning the South Pacific nuclear-free zone) has proved unacceptable to the United States, which follows a policy of neither confirming nor denying the presence of nuclear weapons aboard its ships and submarines. In response then, the United States cancelled its naval exercises with New Zealand, stopped its long-established intelligence relationship with that country, and suspended its security obligations to it. At one point, even sanctions in the field of trade were contemplated. (In December 1986, the US Navy Secretary recommended that the United States block imports of New Zealand agricultural products, including lamb and beef.[54]) The formal argument, put forward by the United States, was that by barring US warships New Zealand had placed in jeopardy the collective capacity of the alliance to resist armed attack,[55] for 'we only have one navy; we do not have a nuclear navy and a nonnuclear navy'.[56]

On the other hand, the New Zealand Government insists that its policy does not damage US strategic interests, and that it only confirms that the South Pacific is not a zone of nuclear confrontation. New Zealand further emphasizes that ANZUS is essentially a conventional defence alliance, no nuclear arms having been deployed in conjunction with, or because of, this agreement.[57] Consequently, the New Zealand Government declared that although ANZUS had become inoperative, New Zealand did not intend to withdraw from it, and was prepared to fulfil its alliance obligations in non-nuclear terms. This attitude reflects public opinion in New Zealand. It is estimated that 72 per cent of the public desire to be in alliance with larger countries, but 73 per cent—many of them the same people—desire that their defence be arranged in a way which ensures that their country is nuclear free. Thus, the most preferred defence option would seem to be membership of ANZUS but separated from all nuclear aspects. Among those who prefer to withdraw from ANZUS rather than accept the visits of nuclear ships, there is no consensus on a preferred defence policy. From the poll carried out by New Zealand's National Research Bureau, it is clear, however, that most citizens do not wish their country to be neutral or non-aligned. In its report issued in July 1986, the New Zealand Defence Committee of Enquiry has formulated the view that an 'enhancement of the bilateral ANZUS relationship with Australia is the most promising option left open to New Zealand'.[58]

Significance of the Treaty of Rarotonga

The Treaty of Rarotonga was the first nuclear arms control agreement signed since the 1979 US–Soviet SALT II Treaty. Its actual geographical scope is rather limited: it bans the presence of nuclear weapons only within the territories of South Pacific states, and does not seek to have nuclear weapon prohibitions applied outside the 12-mile territorial limits of the parties. Nevertheless, the Treaty serves the purpose of preventing the wider spread of nuclear weapons.

In setting up a second nuclear weapon-free zone in a populated part of the world, after the Latin American zone, the Treaty of Rarotonga has confirmed the right of states under the 1968 Non-Proliferation Treaty (Article VII) to conclude agreements in order to ensure the denuclearized status of their respective territories. It may thus have set yet another example for other regions.

VI. Arms control in Central America*

Since 1983 the so-called Contadora group of countries—Colombia, Mexico, Panama and Venezuela—has been engaged in a mediation process aimed at bringing about peace in Central America. The countries directly involved are those situated on the Central American isthmus: Costa Rica, El Salvador, Guatemala, Honduras and Nicaragua. All these countries want to avoid a generalized conflict, which may break out as a result of the growing militarization of the area. In 1985, Argentina, Brazil, Peru and Uruguay formed a support group for the Contadora efforts. The latest proposals contained in the Contadora Act on Peace and Co-operation in Central America were delivered by the four Contadora Foreign Ministers to their five Central American counterparts in Panama on 6 June 1986.[59] (The previous version of the Act was described and analysed in the SIPRI Yearbook 1986.)

The Contadora proposals

Commitments regarding security matters form the most elaborate part of the Contadora Act and are the most controversial. The emphasis is on the removal of foreign military presence and of outside military pressure.

The parties are required to provide detailed notification, at least 30 days in advance, of national military manoeuvres held in areas less than 30 km from the territory of another state. International military manoeuvres, involving armed forces of states situated outside the Central American region, are to be suspended within 90 days of the entry into force of the Act. This suspension could be subsequently extended until the agreed maximum limits for armaments and troop strength had been introduced. If no agreement can be reached on the extension, the parties will have to ensure that the manoeuvres would not involve any form of intimidation against a Central American state or any other state; prior detailed notification would also be required.

Additional constraints on international manoeuvres involving non-Central American forces include: a ban on holding them within a zone less than 50 km

* Section VI was written in collaboration with Victor Millán.

from the territory of a state that is not participating, without that state's express consent; limitation of such manoeuvres to only one a year, with a duration not longer than 15 days; and limitation of the total number of participating troops to 3000, with a proviso that 'under no circumstances' shall the number of troops of other states exceed the number of participating nationals. Once the maximum limits for armaments and troop strength had been reached, the conduct of military manoeuvres involving the participation of states not located in the Central American region would be prohibited.

Control and reduction of the inventory of weapons and of the number of troops would take place in two stages. In the first stage, after the entry into force of the Act and pending the establishment of the maximum limits for 'military development', the parties would undertake to suspend the acquisition of any military material with the exception of supplies needed to keep existing matériel in operation, and not to increase their military forces. Within 15 days of the entry into force of the Act, they would submit simultaneously to the Verification and Control Commission (VCC), a body established by the Act, their current inventories of weapons, military installations and troops, in accordance with the guidelines specified in the Annexe to the Act. Within 60 days, the VCC would suggest to the parties (without prejudice to any negotiations that they might initiate themselves) maximum limits for their military development, as well as timetables for appropriate reductions and dismantling. The actual establishment of these limits and timetables would have to be agreed in the second stage. If the parties failed to reach such agreement within a specified period, the levels suggested by the VCC would apply provisionally. The parties would then set a new period for the establishment of these levels.

A separate clause describes the basic criteria to be taken into account in fixing limits for military development in Central America. These criteria, of potential application also in other regions, are: security needs and defence capabilities; area and population; extent and characteristics of the boundaries; military expenditure in relation to gross domestic product; military budget in relation to public expenditure and other social indicators; military technology, combat preparedness, military manpower, quantity and quality of the military installations and of military resources; armaments subject to control and armaments subject to reduction; and military presence as well as presence of foreign advisers. The intention seems to be to assign a value to each of these criteria, according to their military importance. The limits for military development would thus probably be expressed first in an aggregate number of points allowed for each country.

The parties would undertake not to allow the use of their territories by foreign armed forces whose actions could signify a 'threat to the independence, sovereignty and territorial integrity of any Central American state'.

All foreign military schools, bases or installations would have to be closed down within 180 days of the signing of the Act, and the parties would undertake not to authorize their establishment in the respective territories. Within a period of no more than 180 days after the signing of the Act, foreign advisers and foreign elements 'likely' to participate in military, paramilitary and security activities would have to be withdrawn. As regards advisers performing technical functions related to the installation and maintainence of military equipment, a control register would have to be maintained, and 'reasonable' limits on their numbers would be proposed by the VCC.

The parties would undertake to stop all illegal flow of arms, meaning transfer by governments, individuals or regional or extra-regional groups, of weapons intended for irregular forces or armed bands that are seeking to destabilize governments in the region; an elaborate control mechanism has been provided for. With a view to preventing incidents, a regional communications system would be established to guarantee timely liaison between the competent government, civilian and military authorities, and with the VCC. Joint security commissions would help settle disputes between neighbouring states.

Verification of compliance would be carried out by the VCC, composed of four commissioners representing four states generally recognized to be impartial and genuinely interested in helping to resolve the Central American crisis, and of a Latin American executive secretary responsible for the operation of the VCC.

The Act would remain in force for five years, but its duration could be extended for additional periods of five years, unless a notification to the contrary had been given by any party six months before the expiration of any such period.

To ensure the widest possible support for the Act, and to reinforce it thereby, four additional protocols, containing pledges of co-operation in achieving its objectives, have been drawn up for signature by states other than the parties: Protocol I, by the Contadora Group of states; Protocol II, by states of the 'American continent'; Protocol IV, by states participating in the implementation and follow-up machinery; and Protocol III, by any other state.

Reaction of the parties

As distinct from some previous Contadora proposals, the latest one does not seem to be objectionable to Nicaragua. In expressing its readiness to sign it, the Nicaraguan Government specified 14 categories of weapons and other military items, as well as military activities, which it qualified as 'offensive' and therefore subject to reduction, limitation, regulation or elimination.

Honduras has rejected the draft Act as failing to establish sufficient obligations to guarantee its security. It stated that a distinction between offensive and defensive weapons, as proposed by Nicaragua, was unacceptable. It furthermore pointed out that almost all the items on the Nicaraguan list were in the possession of Honduras and El Salvador, while Nicaragua possessed only some of them. El Salvador shares these views and considers the latest text of the Act to be a sign of complacency towards Nicaragua. Costa Rica insists that all relevant matters, especially those concerning the levels of armaments and military manpower, should be settled before the signing of the Act. It is also dissatisfied with the verification provisions, which, in its opinion, do not provide an assurance of compliance.[60] Guatemala has not clearly expressed its position regarding the Act; it seems to have adopted a policy of neutrality by declaring that it would not form any bloc with any country or countries designed to lead to the 'isolation' of a neighbour.[61]

The future of the Contadora process

The criticism of the Act put forward by Honduras, El Salvador and Costa Rica carries weight, but the fundamental conflict is that between the United States and Nicaragua. The United States is opposed to the Contadora Act, formally on the grounds that the document leaves open the issues of democratization, demilitarization and verification, and is therefore flawed. The actual problem, however, is the refusal by the US Government to recognize under any circumstance the legitimacy of the Sandinist regime; hence its material support for the contras, aiming at the overthrow of that regime. Hence also the reluctance of Nicaragua to reduce significantly its armed forces, threatened as it is by the contras as well as by the United States.

In 1986, the International Court of Justice (ICJ) found that US actions against Nicaragua constituted a breach of the obligation under international law not to intervene in the affairs of another state. The actions referred to included training, arming and financing the contra forces, attacks on Nicaraguan territory, and laying mines in the internal or territorial waters of Nicaragua. The ICJ decided that the USA was under a duty immediately to cease and to refrain from such actions and to make reparation for all injury caused.[62] Nevertheless, US authorities continued their support for the contras, including supplies of arms.

On the isthmus itself, inter-state relations deteriorated when in July 1986 new complaints were brought by Nicaragua to the ICJ. Costa Rica and Honduras were accused of allowing armed attacks by the contras to be launched from their territories against Nicaragua. In the case of Honduras it was also alleged that the armed forces of this country participated in such attacks.[63] Subsequently, in December 1986, Nicaraguan troops crossing the border in pursuit of the contras clashed with Honduran forces transported to the border area with US helicopters. For the first time Honduran military planes bombed targets in Nicaragua.[64] Costa Rica suspended its participation in the Contadora process.[65] Under these conditions, the Contadora group finds it difficult to bring its activities to a successful conclusion.

In an attempt to revitalize the peace-making process, the Secretaries-General of the United Nations and of the Organization of American States, together with the foreign ministers of the Contadora group and their counterparts from the states constituting the support group, visited the five Central American isthmus countries in January 1987. However, the key differences preventing a constructive dialogue have not been removed.

VII. Zone of peace in the South Atlantic

The repertory of proposals for the establishment of zones of peace in various parts of the world has been enriched by an initiative put forward at the 1986 UN

General Assembly to set up such a zone in the South Atlantic.[66] (Similar proposals were made in previous years with regard to the Indian Ocean, the Mediterranean and South-East Asia.)

Declaration of the zone

The proposal for a declaration proclaiming the Atlantic Ocean between Africa and South America to be a 'zone of peace and co-operation' was submitted by Brazil together with several other states situated on both sides of the Atlantic Ocean—Angola, Argentina, Cape Verde, Congo, Côte d'Ivoire, Equatorial Guinea, Gabon, Guinea-Bissau, Liberia, Nigeria, Sao Tome and Principe, and Uruguay. The resolution containing the declaration (subsequently co-sponsored by Bangladesh, Ghana, Nepal and Saint Lucia) was adopted on 27 October 1986 with 124 votes.[67] It calls upon states of other regions, in particular the militarily significant states, to respect the status of the zone, especially through the reduction and eventual elimination of their military presence there, the non-introduction of nuclear weapons or other weapons of mass destruction and the non-extension into the region of rivalries and conflicts that are foreign to it.

All states are requested to co-operate in the elimination of the sources of tension in the zone,[68] to refrain from the threat or use of force, to observe the principle that no territory should be the object of military occupation resulting from the use of force, as well as the principle that the acquisition of territories by force is inadmissible. The declaration also makes an appeal that all acts of aggression and subversion against the states in the zone should cease.

The sponsors of the declaration stressed that co-operation within the South Atlantic zone must be carried out with full respect for the principles and norms of the law of the sea, in particular those relating to the freedom of navigation on the high seas and the right of innocent passage through territorial waters. Nigeria and Uruguay underlined that one of the special aims was to convert the South Atlantic region into a nuclear weapon-free zone, while the Soviet Union stressed its interest in the elimination of all foreign military bases in the zone.

Objections to the declaration

The only country which voted against the resolution was the United States. The most important reasons for this opposition, as given in the debate, were the following. The declaration inadequately defines the waters to be covered by its provisions, and specifically excludes the littoral and hinterland states of the South Atlantic region from the zone. It attempts to create an internationally recognized zone of peace through the adoption of a UN resolution rather than through multilateral negotiations. It moreover implies that restrictions should be placed on naval access to and activity in the South Atlantic Ocean, such restrictions being inconsistent with the generally recognized principles of international law.[69]

Of the other great powers, China, the UK and the USSR voted in favour of the resolution, while France abstained.

Assessment

The UN declaration of the South Atlantic as a zone of peace is an abstruse document. Not only are the geographical limits of the zone ill-described; even the proposed state obligations, other than those already embodied in the UN Charter, appear unclear. Furthermore, the stated requirement to keep the area nuclear weapon-free, if not demilitarized,[70] seems incompatible with the use of the high seas for all military purposes, which the authors of the declaration seem to tolerate in the name of 'international law applicable to ocean space'. The only unequivocal requirements are those regarding the elimination of *apartheid* and the granting of independence to Namibia, but these have already been dealt with in numerous other UN resolutions.

To acquire political importance as well as arms control significance, the declaration would need to be transformed into a treaty containing concrete, legally binding commitments. A first step towards such a treaty could be for Argentina and Brazil—the two largest and most developed countries on the Latin American continent and the main proponents of the zone of peace—to join the 1968 Non-Proliferation Treaty, or at least to become fully-fledged parties to the 1967 Treaty of Tlatelolco, and for Nigeria—one of the most important countries on the African continent and co-sponsor of the South Atlantic zone declaration—to accept international nuclear safeguards. Such measures would demonstrate seriousness of intent to 'shield' the South Atlantic from the arms race and especially from the presence of nuclear arms, as was postulated by the President of Brazil in 1985.[71]

Note: The UN General Assembly resolutions and decisions on arms control and disarmament in 1985–86 may be obtained from SIPRI.

Notes and references

[1] Conference on Disarmament document CD/727.
[2] Soviet statement at the CD on 17 Feb. 1987.
[3] Conference on Disarmament document CD/PV.367.
[4] Conference on Disarmament documents CD/697 and CD/CW/WP.135.
[5] Conference on Disarmament document CD/PV.358 and *Pravda*, 23 Apr. 1986.
[6] Conference on Disarmament document CD/706.
[7] Conference on Disarmament documents CD/698 and CD/CW/WP.140.
[8] Conference on Disarmament documents CD/CW/WP.L33; CD/575.
[9] Conference on Disarmament document CD/500.
[10] Conference on Disarmament documents CD/685, CD/CW/WP.132 and CD/PV.353.
[11] Conference on Disarmament document CD/CW/WP.136.
[12] Conference on Disarmament document CD/664.
[13] Conference on Disarmament document CD/715.
[14] Conference on Disarmament document CD/734.
[15] UN document S/17911.
[16] Conference on Disarmament document CD/PV.379.
[17] Statement by the UK Minister of State at the Foreign and Commonwealth Office, Conference on Disarmament document CD/PV.370.
[18] *International Affairs*, Moscow, 4 Apr. 1986.
[19] SIPRI, *World Armaments and Disarmament: SIPRI Yearbook 1986* (Oxford University

Press: Oxford, 1986), pp. 460–62; Conference on Disarmament documents CD/PV.373, CD/648 and CD/CW/WP.128.

20 *Le Monde*, 7 Nov. 1986.

21 Conference on Disarmament document CD/732.

22 Conference on Disarmament documents CD/612, CD/624, CD/626.

23 Conference on Disarmament document CD/717.

24 Conference on Disarmament document CD/701.

25 UN General Assembly Resolution 41/47.

26 Conference on Disarmament documents CD/712, CD/PV.343 and CD/PV.371.

27 Conference on Disarmament document CD/714.

28 Conference on Disarmament document CD/PV.372.

29 Conference on Disarmament document CD/724.

30 Conference on Disarmament document CD/723.

31 Conference on Disarmament document CD/725.

32 Conference on Disarmament document CD/730.

33 Conference on Disarmament document CD/PV.290.

34 Conference on Disarmament document CD/PV.372.

35 *New York Times*, 6 July 1986; and *New Scientist*, 24 July 1986.

36 UN General Assembly Resolutions 40/80 B and 41/46 B.

37 NPT Review Conference document NPT/CONF.III/64/I, Annex I.

38 Statement by the Director of the US Arms Control and Disarmament Agency in the First Committee of the UN General Assembly, 20 Oct. 1986.

39 Statement by the Soviet Deputy Foreign Minister in the First Committee of the UN General Assembly, 14 Oct. 1986.

40 *Pravda*, 19 Dec. 1986.

41 Conference on Disarmament document CD/732.

42 The imprecise neologism 'weaponization' was repeatedly used throughout the debate.

43 Conference on Disarmament documents CD/709/Rev.1 and CD/OS/WP.13/Rev.1.

44 Conference on Disarmament document CD/PV.372.

45 Conference on Disarmament document CD/PV.354.

46 Conference on Disarmament documents CD/716 and CD/OS/WP.15.

47 Conference on Disarmament document CD/476.

48 Conference on Disarmament documents CD/708, CD/OS/WP.12 and CD/PV.358.

49 UN document A/S-10/AC 1/7.

50 Statement by Jonathan Alford, former deputy director of the International Institute for Strategic Studies, at the 13–15 June 1985 Colloquium on the prevention of an arms race in space, at Les Avants, Switzerland.

51 It will be noted that on 25 November 1986 the countries of the South Pacific Region, the United States and France reached agreement on a convention which, among other things, prohibits the dumping of radioactive waste in the South Pacific region.

52 *International Herald Tribune*, 6 Feb. 1987.

53 *New Zealand Foreign Affairs Review*, Jan.-Mar. 1986.

54 Washington Post, 18 Dec. 1986.

55 *New York City Tribune*, 7 May 1986.

56 Samuel, P. and Serong, F. P., 'The troubled waters of ANZUS', *Strategic Review*, Winter 1986.

57 Rowling, Sir W., New Zealand Ambassador to the United States, 'New Zealand and ANZUS', *Armed Forces and Society*, Winter 1986, vol. 12, no. 2.

58 *Defence and Security: What New Zealanders Want*, Report of the Defence Committee of Enquiry and *Public Opinion Poll on Defence and Security*, annexed to the Report, Wellington, July 1986.

59 *Contadora Act on Peace and Co-operation in Central America*, Boletín Informativo, Secretaría de Relaciones Exteriores de México, México, D. F. (7 June 1986); UN document A/40/1136 of 2 July 1986.

60 *La Republica*, Lima, 16 July 1986.

61 *Christian Science Monitor*, 26 July 1986.

62 International Court of Justice, Communiqué No. 86/8 (27 June 1986).

63 International Court of Justice, Communiqué No. 86/10 (29 July 1986).

64 *New York Times*, 8, 9 and 10 Dec. 1986.

65 *El País*, 10 Nov. 1986.

66 UN document A/41/PV.50.

67 UN document A/RES/41/11.

[68] One such source of tension identified in the course of the discussion was the British–Argentine dispute over the Falkland/Malvinas Islands.

[69] See note 66.

[70] The term 'demilitarization' with regard to the South Atlantic was used by the Argentine Foreign Minister, in UN document A/41/PV.5, p. 96.

[71] UN document A/40/PV.4, pp. 14-15.

12. The review of the Biological Weapons Convention

JOZEF GOLDBLAT

Superscript numbers refer to the list of notes and references at the end of the chapter.

The Convention on the prohibition of the development, production and stockpiling of bacteriological (biological) and toxin weapons and on their destruction (BW Convention), signed in 1972 and in force since 1975, is so far the only international agreement (of unlimited duration) outlawing the possession of an entire category of weapons.[1] The first Review Conference of the parties, mandated by Article XII of the Convention, was held in 1980 to ensure that the contracted obligations were being realized. The second Review Conference took place on 8–26 September 1986, with 63 of more than 100 states parties (including China, France, the UK, the USA and the USSR) and 4 signatory states (Egypt, Iraq, Morocco and Sri Lanka) participating. It was expected that in reviewing the operation of the Convention the Conference would clarify uncertainties regarding the scope of the prohibitions, which had arisen as a result of recent advances in the biological field, and restore confidence in this important international instrument, which had been seriously shaken by allegations of non-compliance. The salient features of the review are discussed here. (For the full text of the Final Declaration of the Conference[2] see appendix 12A.)

I. Scope of the prohibitions

In response to a request by the preparatory committee of the Conference, the depositaries of the BW Convention—the USA, the USSR and the UK—submitted information on new scientific and technological developments relevant to the Convention.

The United States stated that advances in biotechnology have increased man's ability to design new or modify known substances. It is now also possible to manufacture biological or toxin agents in much smaller, less easily identifiable facilities than in the past. These capabilities, if misused, could pose a significant threat; in addition they have further complicated verification of compliance with the BW Convention.[3] Nevertheless, the United States believes that Article 1, which defines the scope of the Convention, has proved sufficiently comprehensive to have covered recent scientific and technological developments.[4]

The Soviet Union stated that the emergence of new pathogens, and the application of the methods of genetic engineering to modify or create micro-organisms with enhanced virulence and considerable resistance to therapeutic preparations and external environmental factors, may cause apprehension as regards their suitability as biological weapons. However, in the Soviet view, all new natural or artificially created pathogenic micro-organisms fall, without reservation, under the terms of the BW Convention, and there are no grounds for placing them in any special category of weapons of mass destruction. Similarly, the dual classification of synthesized toxins as chemical and toxin weapons does not remove the ban on their development, production and stockpiling (still less on their military use). In other words, all micro-organisms and toxins of both natural and synthetic origin, which could be regarded as agents for military use, are covered by the prohibitions.[5]

The United Kingdom also supported the view that the BW Convention covered all agents which could result from the application of genetic engineering or any other new technology.[6]

Following these statements, the Conference reaffirmed that the undertaking given by the parties to the Convention applies to all relevant scientific developments. It also emphasized that the Convention 'unequivocally' applies to all natural or artificially created microbial or other biological agents or toxins, whatever their origin or method of production. Consequently, toxins of a microbial, animal or vegetable origin and their synthetically produced analogues are covered. In the light of this clarification, elaboration of a precise definition of toxins, as suggested by some delegations, was considered unnecessary.

Related to the scope of the prohibition is the problem of transfer. The Conference pointed out that Article III, forbidding transfers of biological and toxin weapons, is comprehensive enough to cover any recipient, whether at the international, national or subnational level. The latter remark was clearly addressed to terrorist or rebel groups fighting governments in power.

II. Compliance with the obligations

The United States expressed its conviction that the Soviet Union maintained an offensive biological warfare programme and capability. In particular, the USA claimed to have 'determined' that a biological warfare facility was in active use at Sverdlovsk, USSR. It furthermore contended that the Soviet Union was involved in the development, production, transfer and use of toxins for hostile purposes in Laos, Kampuchea and Afghanistan, and failed to co-operate to resolve the compliance concerns. The Soviet Union was thus accused of having violated both the BW Convention (Articles I and III), and the 1925 Geneva Protocol prohibiting the use of chemical and biological weapons.[7] However, the United States had not made recourse to Article VI of the Convention, which gives the accusing state the right to lodge its complaints with the UN Security Council.

Responding to the above allegations, the Soviet Union stated that it did not possess any biological or toxin weapons, was not engaged in research and development with the aim of creating or upgrading them, had not transferred such weapons or information on their development or manufacture to any recipient, nor assisted, encouraged or induced other states to acquire them, and did not keep stockpiles outside its territory. In a demonstration of its concern for the integrity of the BW Convention, the Soviet Union formally proposed that an additional protocol to the Convention be adopted to strengthen the system of verification of compliance with the prohibitions. To bring this about, a conference would be convened.[8]

This Soviet proposal marked a retreat from the position which the Soviet Union had maintained for years in opposing any modification or addition to the BW Convention. Indeed, in 1982 the USSR voted against a UN resolution recommending that a special conference be held to establish a 'flexible, objective and non-discriminatory' procedure to deal with the issues of compliance with the BW Convention.[9] It was precisely because of the Soviet opposition that the recommended conference was never convened. The Soviet reversal announced at the Review Conference was welcomed by some, but the parties nevertheless decided that not until the next Review Conference would they consider whether legally binding improvements should be introduced to the Convention. The postponement of action was justified by the argument that it would be appropriate to await the conclusion of a chemical weapons convention and only then—in the light of what had been agreed to with regard to the verification of chemical weapon prohibitions—consider whether the BW Convention needed supplementary formal obligations. In the meantime, it was believed, the strengthening of the procedures for verification of compliance could be achieved within the framework of the original text of the BW Convention through informal, voluntary undertakings.

As regards the machinery for verification, considered unsatisfactory by a number of states, Nigeria proposed that the UN Secretary-General should be explicitly empowered to initiate investigations of allegations of breaches of the BW Convention using a consultative committee of experts—to be appointed by him—before consideration had been given and a decision taken by the UN Security Council, the only body which under the Convention has a clearly expressed right to carry out such investigations. The idea, supported by several other countries, was to separate the fact-finding stage from the political stage of the complaints procedure and thereby to remove the possibility of misuse of the veto power by the permanent members of the Security Council. For a veto would hinder the Council from carrying out inquiries concerning the nature of suspected activities and from meeting its responsibilities under the Convention.[10]

Several Western countries insisted on giving the UN Secretary-General clear authority to carry out investigations of alleged use of biological and toxin weapons, arguing that a confirmed use of these weapons would not only be a violation of the 1925 Geneva Protocol, but would also violate the BW Convention in that it would contradict its basic objective (as stated in the preamble) to 'exclude completely' the possibility of biological warfare. In fact, the Secretary-General is already authorized by the UN General Assembly to set in motion such investigations (procedures have been established, based on lists of qualified experts and laboratories), but the relevant Assembly resolutions, adopted by a majority vote, are controversial.[11] The Soviet Union, its allies and several other countries voted against these resolutions, objecting to the role accorded the United Nations in the implementation of international treaties concluded outside the Organization. Practice has shown, however, that even without invoking the established procedures, the UN Secretary-General is able to undertake a fact-finding mission in case of suspected violations of the Geneva Protocol and, in so doing, refer to the moral responsibilities vested in his office. This was the case with the UN mission to Iran to investigate the use of gas by Iraq. Another proposal, submitted by Colombia, was to entrust the World Health Organization (WHO) with full powers of verification, but the Conference considered that only advice may be sought from the WHO.

The Conference agreed that, to strengthen the relevant Convention provisions, a consultative meeting of experts, open to all parties, must be promptly convened when requested by any party. The meeting may consider any problems which could arise in relation to the objective of, or in the application of, the Convention, initiate 'appropriate' international procedures within the framework of the United Nations and in accordance with its Charter, and request specialized assistance.

III. Strengthening the effectiveness of the Convention

The Conference noted the importance of legislative, administrative and other measures designed to guarantee compliance with the provisions of the Convention, as well as of legislation regarding the physical protection of laboratories and facilities to prevent unauthorized access to and removal of pathogenic or toxic material. It was also recommended that information dealing with the prohibition of biological and toxin weapons and the provisions of the 1925 Geneva Protocol be included in textbooks and in medical, scientific and military educational programmes.

Moreover, in order to prevent or reduce ambiguities, it was found advisable to recommend increased transparency of the activities pertaining to the use of biological agents and toxins for permitted purposes. Indeed, the prohibitions under the BW Convention are not absolute. They do not apply to types and to (albeit unspecified) quantities of biological agents and toxins that have justification for prophylactic, protective or other peaceful purposes. Consequently, research on and production of certain agents may continue, giving rise to suspicions; hence the need to generate trust among the parties. In recognition of this need, the Conference proposed the following confidence-building undertakings: exchange of data on relevant research centres and laboratories; exchange of information on outbreaks of infectious diseases and similar occurrences caused by toxins that seem to deviate from the normal pattern; encouragement of publication of results of biological research directly related to the Convention; and promotion of contacts between scientists engaged in biological research. It was decided to hold in 1987 an *ad hoc* meeting of scientific and technical experts from states parties to work out standardized procedures for the envisaged exchange of information and data.

An interesting proposal was made by Finland and France to the effect that states should provide information on vaccinations undergone by their armed forces. In explaining the reasons for this proposal, Finland drew attention to the fact that continued vaccination of military personnel against smallpox could give rise to suspicion that a state was immunizing its forces while making preparations for the use of the smallpox microbe as a warfare agent, because in most countries vaccination discontinued after the WHO certification that the microbe had been eradicated.[12]

IV. Peaceful uses of biological agents

The BW Convention provides for co-operation among the parties in the peaceful uses of biological agents and toxins (Article X). It is agreed that such co-operation can include exchange of information, training of personnel, and transfer of materials and equipment. It is uncertain, however, whether the Convention is the best instrument for organizing this type of activity. There exist more competent bodies for this purpose—inter-governmental agencies and specialized international non-governmental scientific associations which function irrespective of the BW Convention. Since the Convention is primarily a disarmament measure, one should not expect too much from it (as some developing countries seem to do) as regards redressing the existing inequalities among states in the field of science and technology or the promotion of economic development. Moreover, since research activities in the area of biotechnology are often classified as industrial secrets, there are obvious limits to what kind of information can be expected to be shared.

V. Evaluation

It is technically possible to produce biological agents for use against enemy forces and at the same time devise vaccines and antidotes to such agents to protect one's own forces. New biological or toxin weapons can also be produced that are less costly, easier to handle and store, more potent, faster acting and less sensitive to weather conditions than those already known. One could have imagined that such 'improvements' have decidedly increased the attractiveness of biological agents and toxins for the military by making them more useful as means of warfare than hitherto. There is, however, no evidence that this is actually the case. The potentials for misuse of biotechnology, including genetic engineering, 'appear to be no greater than standard microbiological techniques which have existed since the inception of the 1972 Convention'.[13] In other words, the Convention does not seem to have been overtaken by technology, and the military appeal of the still hypothetical, exotic weapons is apparently not strong enough to endanger its survival. It is doubtful whether biological and toxin weapons could do anything particularly devastating in war that chemical weapons (especially nerve gas), the possession of which is not yet forbidden, could not do. In fact, since at least the early 1920s, biological weapons have been associated in the public mind in one single taboo with chemical weapons, and the parties to the BW Convention have recognized that the Convention was to be only a step towards an agreement effectively prohibiting chemical weapons as well. Without a formal commitment included in the Convention that such an agreement should be reached at an 'early' date (Article IX), many countries would probably have refrained from joining it.

The polemics regarding compliance have, in spite of their harshness, produced some constructive ideas for additional procedures to clarify controversial issues, adding to the effectiveness of the Convention. It was generally acknowledged that verification was needed not only to provide confidence that the terms of the Convention were adhered to, but also to provide those whose compliance might be called into question with the means of proving their innocence. The agreed confidence-building measures introduced to create greater openness in the field of biological research may be useful in removing suspicions of breaches if, in fact, the governments honour the commitments expressed in the Final Declaration.

However, the significance of the second BW Review Conference lies mainly in the reaffirmation by the parties of their dedication to the objectives of the BW Convention and of their commitment to implement effectively its provisions, as well as in that it unreservedly upheld the comprehensive scope of the Convention, which excludes loopholes for the use of biological science for other than peaceful purposes. The authority of the Convention has been strengthened and the Conference can rightly be called a success.

The parties agreed to convene a third review of the BW Convention not later than 1991.

Notes and references

[1] For the full text of the BW Convention, see Goldblat, J., SIPRI, *Agreements for Arms Control: A Critical Survey* (Taylor & Francis: London, 1982).

[2] BW Review Conference document BWC/CONF.II/13.

[3] US statement at the BW Review Conference on 9 Sep. 1986 and Conference document BWC/CONF.II/4/Add. 2

[4] US statement at the BW Review Conference on 16 Sep. 1986.

[5] Soviet statement at the BW Review Conference on 9 Sep. 1986 and Conference document BWC/CONF.II/4/Add. 1.

[6] BW Review Conference document BWC/CONF.II/4.

[7] US statement at the BW Review Conference of 16 Sep. 1986 and Conference document BWC/CONF.II/SR.3.

[8] Soviet statement at the BW Review Conference on 15 Sep. 1986.

[9] UN General Assembly resolution 37/98 C.

[10] BW Review Conference document BWC/CONF. II/SR.7.

[11] UN General Assembly resolutions 37/98 D and 39/65 E.

[12] BW Review Conference documents BWC/CONF. II/SR.5 and BWC/CONF.II/9.

[13] Statement of the Pugwash Executive Committee in *Pugwash Newsletter*, vol. 23, no. 4 (Apr. 1986).

Appendix 12A. Final Declaration

Final Declaration of the Second Review Conference of the Parties to the Convention on the Prohibition of the Development, Production and Stockpiling of Bacteriological (Biological) and Toxin Weapons and on their Destruction

Preamble

The States Parties to the Convention on the Prohibition of the Development, Production and Stockpiling of Bacteriological (Biological) and Toxin Weapons and on their Destruction, having met in Geneva 8–26 September 1986 in accordance with a decision by the First Review Conference 1980 and at the request of a majority of States Parties to the Convention, to review the operation of the Convention with a view to assuring that the purposes of the preamble and the provisions of the Convention are being realized:

Reaffirming their determination to act with a view to achieving effective progress towards general and complete disarmament, including the prohibition and elimination of all types of weapons of mass destruction, and convinced that the prohibition of the development, production and stockpiling of chemical and bacteriological (biological) weapons and their elimination, through effective measures, will facilitate the achievement of general and complete disarmament under strict and effective international control,

Recognizing the continuing importance of the Convention and its objectives and the common interest of mankind in the elimination of bacteriological (biological) and toxin weapons,

Affirming their belief that universal adherence to the Convention would enhance international peace and security, would not hamper economic or technological development and, further, would facilitate the wider exchange of information for the use of bacteriological (biological) agents for peaceful purposes,

Confirming the common interest in strengthening the authority and the effectiveness of the Convention, to promote confidence and co-operation among States Parties,

Affirming the importance of strengthening international co-operation in the field of biotechnology, genetic engineering, microbiology and other related areas,

Reaffirming their adherence to the principles and objectives of the Geneva Protocol of 17 June 1925 and calling upon all States to comply strictly with them,

Recalling that the General Assembly of the United Nations has repeatedly condemned all actions contrary to the said principles and objectives,

Recognizing the importance of achieving as a matter of high priority an international convention on the complete and effective prohibition of the development, production and stockpiling of chemical weapons and on their destruction,

Noting the relevant provisions of the Final Document of the first special session of the General Assembly devoted to disarmament,

Appealing to all States to refrain from any action which might place the Convention or any of its provisions in jeopardy,

Declare their strong determination, for the sake of all mankind, to exclude completely the possibility of microbial, or other biological agents, or toxins being used as weapons and reaffirm their strong support for the Convention, their continued dedication to its principles and objectives and their legal obligation under international law to implement and strictly comply with its provisions.

Article I

The Conference notes the importance of Article I as the Article which defines the scope of the Convention and reaffirms its support for the provisions of this Article.

The Conference concludes that the scope of Article I covers scientific and technological developments relevant to the Convention.

The Conference notes statements by some States Parties that compliance with Articles I, II and III was, in their view, subject to grave doubt in some cases and that efforts to resolve those concerns had not been successful. The Conference notes the statements by other States Parties that such a doubt was unfounded and, in their view, not in accordance with the Convention. The Conference agrees that the application by States Parties of a positive approach in questions of compliance in accordance with the provisions of the Convention was in the interest of all States Parties and that this would serve to promote confidence among States Parties.

The Conference, conscious of apprehensions arising from relevant scientific and technological developments, *inter alia*, in the fields of microbiology, genetic engineering and biotechnology, and the possibilities of their use for purposes inconsistent with the objectives and the provisions of the Convention, reaffirms that the undertaking given by the States Parties in Article I applies to all such developments.

The Conference reaffirms that the Convention unequivocally applies to all natural or artificially created microbial or other biological agents or toxins whatever their origin or method of production. Consequently, toxins (both proteinaceous and non-proteinaceous) of a microbial, animal or vegetable nature and their synthetically produced analogues are covered.

Article II

The Conference notes the importance of Article II and welcomes the statements made by States which have become Parties to the Convention since the First Review Conference that they do not possess agents, toxins, weapons, equipment or means of delivery referred to in Article I of the Convention. The Conference believes that such statements enhance confidence in the Convention.

The Conference stresses that States which become Parties to the Convention, in implementing the provisions of this Article, shall observe all necessary safety precautions to protect populations and the environment.

Article III

The Conference notes the importance of Article III and welcomes the statements which States that have acceded to the Convention have made to the effect that they have not transferred agents, toxins, weapons, equipment of means of delivery, specified in Article I of the Convention, to any recipient whatsoever and have not furnished assistance, encouragement or inducement to any State, group of States or international organizations to manufacture or otherwise acquire them. The Conference affirms that Article III is sufficiently comprehensive so as to cover any recipient whatsoever at international, national or sub-national levels.

The Conference notes that the provisions of this Article should not be used to impose restrictions and/or limitations on the transfer for purposes consistent with the objectives and the provisions of the Convention of scientific knowledge, technology, equipment and materials to States Parties.

Article IV

The Conference notes the importance of Article IV, under which each State Party shall, in accordance with its constitutional processes, take any necessary measures to prohibit or prevent any acts or actions which would contravene the Convention.

The Conference calls upon all States Parties which have not yet taken any necessary measures in accordance with their constitutional processes, as required by the Article, to do so immediately.

The Conference notes that States Parties, as requested by the First Review Conference, have provided to the United Nations Department of Disarmament Affairs information on and the texts of specific legislation enacted or other regulatory measures taken by them, relevant to this Article. The Conference invites States Parties to continue to provide such information and texts to the United Nations Department for Disarmament Affairs for purposes of consultation.

The Conference notes the importance of
— legislative, administrative and other measures designed effectively to guarantee compliance with the provisions of the Convention within the territory under the jurisdiction or control of a State Party;
— legislation regarding the physical protection of laboratories and facilities to prevent unauthorized access to and removal of pathogenic or toxic material; and
— inclusion in textbooks and in medical, scientific and military educational programmes of information dealing with the prohibition of bacteriological (biological) and toxin weapons and the provisions of the Geneva Protocol

and believes that such measures which States might undertake in accordance with their constitutional process would strengthen the effectiveness of the Convention.

Article V

The Conference notes the importance of Article V and reaffirms the obligation assumed by States Parties to consult and co-operate with one another in solving any problems which may arise in relation to the objective of, or in the application of the provisions of, the Convention.

The Conference reaffirms that consultation and co-operation pursuant to this Article may also be undertaken through appropriate international procedures within the framework of the United Nations and in accordance with its Charter.

The Conference confirms the conclusion in the Final Declaration of the First Review Conference that these procedures include, *inter alia*, the right of any State Party to request that a consultative meeting open to all States Parties be convened at expert level.

The Conference stresses the need for all States to deal seriously with compliance issues and emphasizes that the failure to do so undermines the Convention and the arms control process in general.

The Conference appeals to States Parties to make all possible efforts to solve any problems which may arise in relation to the objective of, or in the application of the provisions of, the Convention with a view towards encouraging strict observance of the provisions subscribed to. The Conference further requests that information on such efforts be provided to the Third Review Conference.

The Conference, taking into account views expressed concerning the need to strengthen the implementation of the provisions of Article V, has agreed:

— that a consultative meeting shall be promptly convened when requested by a State Party,
— that a consultative meeting may consider any problems which may arise in relation to the objective of, or in the application of the provisions of the Convention, suggest ways and means for further clarifying, *inter alia*, with assistance of technical experts, any matter considered ambiguous or unresolved, as well as initiate appropriate international procedures within the framework of the United Nations and in accordance with its Charter,
— that the consultative meeting, or any State Party, may request specialized assistance in solving any problems which may arise in relation to the objective of, or in the application of the provisions of, the Convention, through, *inter alia*, appropriate international procedures within the framework of the United Nations and in accordance with its Charter,
— the Conference considers that States Parties shall co-operate with the consultative meeting in its consideration of any problems which may arise in relation to the objective of, or in the application of the provisions of the Convention, and in clarifying ambiguous and unresolved matters, as well as co-operate in appropriate international procedures within the framework of the United Nations and in accordance with its Charter.

The Conference, mindful of the provisions of Article V and Article X, and determined to strengthen the authority of the Convention and to enhance confidence in the implementation of its provisions, agrees that the States Parties are to implement, on the basis of mutual co-operation, the following measures, in order to prevent or reduce the occurrence of ambiguities, doubts and suspicions, and in order to improve international co-operation in the field of peaceful bacteriological (biological) activities:

1. Exchange of data, including name, location, scope and general description of activities, on research centres and laboratories that meet very high national or international safety standards established for handling, for permitted purposes, biological materials that pose a high individual and community risk or specialize in permitted biological activities directly related to the Convention.
2. Exchange of information on all outbreaks of infectious diseases and similar occurrences caused by toxins that seem to deviate from the normal pattern as regards type, development, place, or time of occurrence. If possible, the information provided would include, as soon as it is available, data on the type of disease, approximate area affected, and number of cases.
3. Encouragement of publication of results of biological research directly related to the Convention, in scientific journals generally available to States Parties, as well as promotion of use for permitted purposes of knowledge gained in this research.
4. Active promotion of contacts between scientists engaged in biological research directly related to the Convention, including exchanges for joint research on a mutually agreed basis.

The Conference decides to hold an *ad hoc* meeting of scientific and technical experts from States Parties to finalize the modalities for the exchange of information and data by working out, *inter alia*, appropriate forms to be used by States Parties for the exchange of information agreed to in this Final Declaration, thus enabling States Parties to follow a standardized procedure. The group shall meet in Geneva for the period 31 March–15 April 1987 and shall communicate the results of the work to the States Parties immediately thereafter.

Pending the results of this meeting, the Conference urges States Parties to promptly apply these measures and report the data agreed upon to the United Nations Department for Disarmament Affairs.

The Conference requests the United Nations Department for Disarmament Affairs to make available the information received to all States Parties.

Article VI

The Conference also notes the importance of Article VI, which in addition to the procedures contained in Article V, provides for any State Party, which finds that any other State Party is acting in breach of its obligations under the Convention, to lodge a complaint with the United Nations Security Council and under which each State Party undertakes to co-operate in carrying out any investigation which the Security Council may initiate.

The Conference notes the need to further improve and strengthen this and other procedures to enhance greater confidence in the Convention. The Conference considers that the Security Council may, if it deems it necessary, request the advice of the World Health Organization in carrying out any investigation of complaints lodged with the Council.

Article VII

The Conference notes that these provisions have not been invoked.

Article VIII

The Conference reaffirms the importance of Article VIII and stresses the importance of the Protocol for the Prohibition of the Use in War of Asphyxiating, Poisonous or other Gases and of Bacteriological Methods of Warfare.

The Conference reaffirms that nothing contained in the Convention shall be interpreted as in any way limiting or detracting from the obligations assumed by any State under the Protocol for the Prohibition of the Use in War of Asphyxiating, Poisonous or other Gases and of Bacteriological Methods of Warfare, signed at Geneva on 17 June 1925. Noting the report of the Security Council (S/17911), the Conference appeals to all States Parties to the Geneva Protocol of 1925 to fulfil their obligations assumed under that Protocol and urges all States not yet Parties to the said Protocol to adhere to it at the earliest possible date.

Article IX

The Conference reaffirms the obligation assumed by States Parties to continue negotiations in good faith towards an early agreement on effective measures for the prohibition of the development, production and stockpiling of chemical weapons and for their destruction.

All States Parties participating in the Conference reiterate their strong commitment to this important goal.

The Conference notes with satisfaction the substantial progress made in the negotiations on a convention on the prohibition of chemical weapons in the Conference on Disarmament during the period under review. The Conference also takes note of the bilateral talks between the Union of Soviet Socialist Republics and the United States of America on all aspects of the prohibition of chemical weapons.

The Conference nevertheless deeply regrets that an agreement on a convention on chemical weapons has not yet been reached.

The Conference urges the Conference on Disarmament to exert all possible efforts to conclude an agreement on a total ban of chemical weapons with effective verification provisions by the earliest possible date.

Article X

The Conference emphasizes the increasing importance of the provisions of Article X, especially in the light of recent scientific and technological developments in the field of biotechnology, bacteriological (biological) agents and toxins with peaceful applications, which have vastly increased the potential for co-operation between States to help promote economic and social development, and scientific and technological progress, particularly in the developing countries, in conformity with their interests, needs and priorities.

The Conference, while acknowledging what has already been done towards this end, notes with concern the increasing gap between the developed and the developing countries in the field of biotechnology, genetic engineering, microbiology and other related areas. The Conference accordingly urges States Parties to provide wider access to and share their scientific and technological knowledge in this field, on an equal and non-discriminatory basis, in particular with the developing countries, for the benefit of all mankind.

The Conference urges that States Parties take specific measures within their competence for the promotion of the fullest possible international co-operation in this field through their active intervention. Such measures could include, *inter alia*:

— transfer and exchange of information concerning research programmes in bio-sciences,
— wider transfer and exchange of information, materials and equipment among States on a systematic and long-term basis,
— active promotion of contacts between scientists and technical personnel on a reciprocal basis, in relevant fields,
— increased technical co-operation, including training opportunities to developing countries in the use of bio-sciences and genetic engineering for peaceful purposes,
— facilitating the conclusion of bilateral, regional and multiregional agreements providing on a mutually advantageous, equal and non-discriminatory basis, for their participation in the development and application of biotechnology,
— encouraging the co-ordination of national and regional programmes and working out in an appropriate manner the ways and means of co-operation in this field.

The Conference calls for greater co-operation in international public health and disease control.

The Conference urges that co-operation under Article X should be actively pursued both within the bilateral and the multilateral framework and further urges the use of existing institutional means within the United Nations system and the full utilization of the possibilities provided by the specialized agencies and other international organizations.

The Conference, noting that co-operation would be best initiated by improved institutionalized direction and co-ordination, recommends that measures to ensure co-operation on such a basis be pursued within the existing means of the United Nations system. Accordingly, the Conference requests the Secretary-General of the United Nations to propose for inclusion on the agenda of a relevant United Nations body a discussion and examination of the means for improving institutional mechanisms in order to facilitate the fullest possible exchange of equipment, materials and scientific and technological information for the use of bacteriological (biological) agents and toxins for peaceful purposes. The Conference recommends that invitations to participate in this discussion and examination should be extended to all States Parties, whether or not they are members of the United Nations and concerned specialized agencies.

The Conference requests the States Parties and the United Nations Secretariat to include in the document materials prepared for the above-mentioned discussion of States Parties, information and suggestions on the implementation of Article X, taking into account the preceding paragraphs. Furthermore, it urges the specialized agencies, *inter alia*, FAO, WHO, UNESCO, WIPO and UNIDO, to participate in this discussion and fully co-operate with the Secretary-General of the United Nations and requests the Secretary-General to send all relevant information of this Conference to these agencies.

The Conference, referring to paragraph 35 of the Final Document of the first special session of the General Assembly devoted to disarmament, stresses the importance of the obligations under Article X in promoting economic and social development of developing countries, particularly in the light of the United Nations Conference on the Relationship between Disarmament and Development, for the States participating therein, scheduled for 1987.

The Conference, to ensure compliance with Article X, also requests States Parties and the United Nations Secretariat to provide information relevant to the implementation of the Article for examination by the next conference of States Parties.

The Conference upholds that the above-mentioned measures would positively strengthen the Convention.

Article XI
The Conference notes the importance of Article XI and that since the entry into force of the Convention the provisions of the Article have not been invoked.

Article XII
The Conference decides that a Third Review Conference shall be held in Geneva at the request of a majority of States Parties not later than 1991.

The Conference, noting the differing views with regard to verification, decides that the Third Review Conference shall consider, *inter alia*:

— the impact of scientific and technological developments relevant to the Convention,
— the relevance for effective implementation of the Convention of the results achieved in the negotiations on prohibition of chemical weapons,
— the effectiveness of the provisions in Article V for consultation and co-operation and of the co-operative measures agreed in this Final Declaration, and
— in the light of these considerations and of the provisions of Article XI, whether or not further actions are called for to create further co-operative measures in the context of Article V, or legally binding improvements to the Convention, or a combination of both.

Article XIII
The Conference notes the provisions of Article XIII and expresses its satisfaction that no State Party to the Convention has exercised its right to withdraw from the Convention.

Article XIV

The Conference notes with satisfaction that a significant number of States have ratified or acceded to the Convention since the First Review Conference and that there are now more than 100 States Parties to the Convention, including all the permanent Members of the Security Council of the United Nations.

The Conference calls upon states which have not yet ratified or acceded to the Convention to do so without delay and upon those States which have not signed the Convention to join the States Parties thereto thus contributing to the achievement of universal adherence to the Convention.

The Conference makes an urgent appeal to all States Parties to the Convention on the Prohibition of the Development, Production and Stockpiling of Bacteriological (Biological) and Toxin Weapons and on their Destruction, which did not participate in its work, to give their effective co-operation and take part more actively in the common endeavour of all the Contracting Parties to strengthen the objectives and purposes of the Convention. In this connection, the Conference urges all States Parties that were absent to take part in the future work envisaged in this Final Declaration.

Article XV

The Conference notes the provisions of Article XV.

Part IV. Special features

Chapter 13. The Chernobyl reactor accident: the international significance and results

Introduction / The role of the IAEA / Conclusion

Chapter 14. Recent developments in arms control verification technology

Introduction / Seismology / Adaptive optics / Ground-based radar imaging / Conclusion

13. The Chernobyl reactor accident: the international significance and results

HANS BLIX, Director General, International Atomic Energy Agency

Superscript numbers refer to the list of notes and references at the end of the chapter.

I. Introduction

At 1:23 a.m. on 26 April 1986, a steam explosion at the fourth unit of the Chernobyl nuclear power station resulted in the destruction of this light water-cooled, graphite-moderated (LWGR) reactor, the subsequent death of 31 persons and the radioactive contamination of a region surrounding the plant. The causes of the accident were complex. Just before the scheduled normal shut-down of the unit for maintenance, it was to be tested whether the kinetic energy in the turbogenerators could support reactor cooling for a short period of 40 seconds—which could be of value during a major station blackout. While preparing for and performing the test, the plant staff committed a series of violations of operating rules and procedures, thereby neutralizing reactor safety features and resulting in the reactor being brought to an inherently unsafe state.

When the test was started, a power excursion (that is, an accidental increase in the power level) occurred, pulverizing the fuel and causing a steam explosion. This blew open the reactor vault, and a second explosion destroyed the reactor building. The graphite moderator caught fire. Thus, immediately after the fuel destruction, the core was bare to the atmosphere, and the explosions and fire created a mechanism which transported radioactivity to a height of about 1000 metres, just above an existing inversion layer (inversion is a reversal in the normal temperature lapse rate, the temperature rising with increased elevation instead of falling). A south-easterly wind (atypical of the region) then carried it initially toward Poland and Scandinavia, where the first elevated radiation levels were reported on 29 April; the radiation plume later swung over central and south-eastern Europe.

The impact of the airborne radioactivity was fundamentally different from that of atmospheric nuclear weapon tests, where the radioactivity is carried to a higher altitude and fall-out is relatively evenly dispersed over large areas. In the case of the Chernobyl accident, fall-out distribution was to a very great extent determined by local rainfall, which caused higher levels of activity in small areas both in Scandinavia and in central Europe.

Initial reports in some Western media predicted a disaster of major proportions with estimates of deaths running into the thousands. To be sure, the impact of the Chernobyl accident was manifold, involving health, psychological, technical, economic and political problems. In retrospect, however, the radiological consequences outside the USSR have been small. It has been authoritatively estimated that even within the Soviet Union the collective radiation dose and possible resulting cancers attributable to the Chernobyl accident would represent only a fraction of the cancers that will occur in the same population over the same period (70 years) as a result of other causes. This is not at all to minimize the accident which occurred or the urgency of taking substantial and vigorous measures to prevent recurrences and to meet such emergency situations as may occur on a timely basis and in a comprehensive manner, but only to put Chernobyl and its aftermath in perspective.

II. The role of the IAEA

The Chernobyl accident can be examined from many perspectives. The purpose here is to focus on the international implications with emphasis on the role that international organizations, in particular the International Atomic Energy Agency (IAEA),[1] played and can play in radiological situations involving public health and safety.

Nuclear energy has brought with it new opportunities, new problems and new institutions. The opportunities relate to the numerous ways in which nuclear technology can contribute to the achievement of national social and economic goals. The problems are of the kind often associated with the management of complex high technologies, but go beyond that in two respects: one is the magnitude of damage that potentially could be caused by a nuclear accident; the other is the fact that some of the technologies connected with the peaceful use of nuclear energy can also serve military ends. International society has taken important steps to try to foreclose the diversion of peaceful nuclear activities to military ends, but the enormous tasks of overcoming the risk of nuclear weapon proliferation and of ridding the planet of the nuclear weapon threat remain.

The main responsibility for nuclear safety rests with national authorities. They have the necessary legislative and executive means at their disposal to develop and implement a nuclear safety programme, and it may be assumed that they are attentive to the welfare and safety of their citizens and will take appropriate protective measures when authorizing industrial or other activities. The primacy of national responsibility has not meant the absence of international involvement in civilian nuclear safety. Indeed, a considerable degree of bilateral, multilateral and international co-operation has existed for some time. The Statute of the IAEA, for example, authorizes the Agency to establish safety standards and to provide for their implementation in its own operations or in operations carried out under bilateral and multilateral arrangements, when requested to do so by the parties to those arrangements. The focus of Agency activities in the safety field has reflected the interests of its member states, commencing with the safe transportation of radioactive materials, the safe handling of radioactive sources and radiation protection.

With the coming of age of commercial nuclear power, the IAEA, beginning in 1974, initiated a programme on nuclear power plant safety standards (NUSS), which today consists of five internationally agreed Codes of Practice covering governmental organization, design, siting, operation and quality assurance, and sixty Safety Guides dealing with methods and procedures for implementing the Codes. Although the contents of the documents in the NUSS programme reflect state practices upon which they are often based, they are not binding or mandatory, except when an Agency activity such as a technical co-operation or project agreement is involved, in which case they are incorporated into the agreement. Nevertheless, a number of states have used NUSS standards, at least partially, in their national regulations.

After the Three Mile Island reactor accident in the United States in 1979, the IAEA's safety programme was reviewed, resulting in its expansion and the establishment in 1981 of a separate Division of Nuclear Safety. Several elements were added, including the Operational Safety Review Teams (OSARTs), the Incident Reporting System (IRS) and the establishment of an International Nuclear Safety Advisory Group (INSAG), composed of eminent safety experts from the industrial, research and regulatory sectors.

OSARTs, consisting of a dozen Agency staff and external experts, assist member states in the safe operation of nuclear facilities by reviewing the operating processes of specific facilities. They are sent only on invitation, and their reports are both advisory and confidential to the host government authorities. As such, they offer in-depth analysis and recommendations regarding operational safety. Under the IRS, states learn from each other's experience of events with safety significance. Reports help identify generic problems and are of use to improve safety in nuclear facilities. INSAG provides an international forum for examining safety issues and gives the Agency an added source of expertise and advice. All of these elements of the IAEA safety programme have drawn even greater interest and attention in the wake of the Chernobyl accident. OSART requests have substantially increased and include invitations from leading nuclear nations. The IRS is a focal point for increased use, and INSAG has been closely involved in the Agency's post-accident analysis of Chernobyl: it has prepared an international consensus report of the accident, based on the review held by the Agency.

The IAEA has also sought to promote adequate emergency planning and preparedness. An expanded programme, emphasizing technical guidance, training and emergency plan development, has been in place since January 1981. Guidelines were developed in 1984 for mutual emergency assistance management in the case of nuclear accidents or radiological emergencies, and in 1985 a Radiation Protection Advisory Team (RAPAT) programme, focused primarily on non-power applications of nuclear energy, was established.

III. Conclusion

It is clear from this review of some of the elements of the IAEA nuclear programme that safety-related issues were on the international agenda at the time of the Chernobyl accident. Does this mean that the international community was prepared for such an incident? The answer to that question is both yes and no: yes, in the sense that a number of elements that would be essential to an eventual international nuclear safety regime already had been identified and in place. It was not a case of *tabula rasa*. International institutions existed that were ready and able to respond to public calls for information and, to the extent possible, understanding about what was happening. The IAEA began receiving enquiries from its member states in Europe from the moment that increased levels of radioactivity began to be recorded. These same countries began sending the IAEA information on their radiological measurements of dose rates in the environment and in foodstuffs. The Agency offered itself as a channel of communication to member states, maintained close contact with the Soviet Mission to the Agency, and quickly disseminated information as it was received. On 6 May 1986 the World Health Organization (WHO) Regional Office for Europe convened a meeting of experts in Copenhagen, Denmark, to evaluate immediate problems related to radioactivity released from the accident. National authorities themselves were taking responsive action to reports which they received from domestic and international sources regarding levels of radioactivity, and bilateral assistance was offered to the Soviet Union by a number of countries in a position to do so once the nature and magnitude of the accident were known.

The answer to the question of whether the international community was prepared for an incident like Chernobyl is also no, in the sense that there was not a viable, functioning international nuclear safety regime in place. Important elements were missing. Despite their inclination to increase co-operation, member states had tended to take a minimalist approach, preserving as much independence of decision as possible. This is most vividly reflected in the critical areas of notification and assistance in the case of nuclear reactor accidents. Following the Three Mile Island accident in the United States, an effort had been made to reach agreement on binding rules on these issues. In both cases, the best that could be achieved was agreement for non-binding guidelines, leaving it up to individual states to decide whether to enter into bilateral or multilateral arrangements and how much, if any, of the guidelines to accept.

In striking contrast, after Chernobyl, political leaders from many quarters emphasized the need to broaden international co-operation in nuclear safety, including especially the drafting of international agreements committing their parties to early notification and comprehensive information about nuclear accidents, and co-ordination of emergency response and assistance in the event of nuclear accidents, which could in both cases involve trans-boundary radiological releases. What had shortly before been perceived as a virtue, binding co-operation, had now become a necessity in the eyes of the international community.

The IAEA Board of Governors[2] convened government expert groups in July 1986, and within a month's time the texts of two conventions on notification and assistance were adopted by consensus. They were unanimously adopted by a special session of the General Conference in September. The speed with which these conventions were negotiated, adopted and brought into force (27 October 1986 in the case of the notification convention, and 8 February 1987 in the case of the emergency assistance convention) demonstrates international co-operation at its best: governments determined to reach concrete results of mutual benefit, willing to make concessions to achieve them, and making full use of the competent international organization.

The two conventions make a substantial contribution towards the establishment of an international nuclear safety regime. The Early Notification Convention covers all uncontrolled releases of radioactive material from *any* source, irrespective of its nature and location, that may result in transboundary effects which could be of radiological safety significance to another state. In plain language, this means uncontrolled releases from civil *or* military nuclear facilities. In the case of accidents connected with nuclear weapons, the Convention provides that states parties may voluntarily notify such accidents, and at the Special Session of the IAEA's General Conference (noted above), all of the nuclear weapon states committed themselves to make such notifications. This step toward greater openness, even in the military field, must count as one of the most positive 'effects' of the Chernobyl accident. This Convention furthermore makes the IAEA the focal point for receiving notification of a nuclear accident and for providing states and concerned international organizations with relevant information received by it. This gives added assurance that information will be forthcoming and on a timely basis.

The Convention on Assistance in the Case of a Nuclear Accident or Radiological Emergency sets out an international framework aimed at facilitating the prompt provision of such assistance, directly among states parties or through the IAEA and from it, as well as from other international organizations. States parties are required to notify the IAEA of experts, equipment and materials that they could make available for the provision of emergency assistance. Overall direction and control of assistance are the responsibility of the requesting state, which also grants to personnel provided by the assisting party the necessary privileges and immunities for carrying out the assistance functions.

This Convention assigns a major role to the IAEA with a view to facilitating and supporting co-operation among states parties in emergency assistance. The IAEA would make available its good offices to states parties and member states for securing the assistance needed, maintain liaison with other international organizations for this purpose, and assist states parties and member states in various ways—in particular, in expert services and manpower training and development—with a view to strengthening their capabilities to cope with a nuclear accident or radiological emergency.

Ten days after the conventions had been adopted by the expert working groups, some 500 technical experts from 62 countries and 21 national and international organizations assembled at IAEA headquarters for a 'first' in international relations: the first international post-accident review to analyse available data and draw lessons from a severe industrial accident with trans-frontier consequences.

The meeting turned out to be a most interesting and rewarding dialogue between experts. All came away with a feeling of having jointly explored important scientific and technological problems. The causes of the accident were more clearly understood, the actions taken to contain the accident and alleviate the consequences drew considerable appreciation, and the experts agreed to a number of recommendations for international actions, many of which were subsequently endorsed by the Special Session of the IAEA's General Conference and incorporated in an expanded nuclear safety programme (at the cost of an additional $2 million in 1987). The willingness of states to expand their co-operation through an international agency in a time of zero-growth budgets was another encouraging implication of the Chernobyl experience. It confirmed the awareness that nuclear safety has an international dimension and that a severe accident *anywhere* is of concern *everywhere*.

The recommendations of the post-accident review meeting reflected areas in which the international community recognized a need for better preparedness and for international follow-up of the consequences of the Chernobyl accident. International support for research and exchange of information in a variety of areas was identified and approved, including: man-machine interface (given the fact that operator defeat of safety measures played the most important role in the accident); operator qualification and training methods and international accreditation of operator training programmes; fire protection procedures in the case of nuclear accidents; medical treatment and biological dosimetry studies; and harmonization of intervention levels following radioactive releases. This latter point deserves some further explanation. Radioactivity levels recorded following the Chernoby accident triggered widely differing responses on the part of governmental authorities. This was primarily the consequence of the absence of harmonization of levels at which public authorities would intervene to regulate use of foodstuffs or access to the environment. Discrepancies in intervention levels, particularly in densely populated regions of the world where national boundaries are close together as in Western Europe, can exacerbate public fears about radiation. In Sweden, the United Kingdom, France and Finland, milk and vegetables containing more than 2000 becquerels of iodine–131 per kilogram were considered unsuitable for consumption. In Poland, the limit was 1000 becquerels; in Hungary, 500; in Austria, 385; and in Land Hesse in the Federal Republic of Germany, the limit was 20 becquerels. These figures speak for themselves in terms of the need for international harmonization.

These are important developments and they offer promise for more effective international co-operation in nuclear safety in the future. But one must also frankly recognize that there are practical limits to what can be achieved. In the period immediately following the accident, there was much discussion about the need for binding international safety norms and the possibility of making the IAEA's international nuclear safety standards mandatory. The NUSS are going to be reviewed, but whether one can go further and envisage basic mandatory rules or criteria embracing the whole field of nuclear safety, or even further, to consider some kind of obligatory international control and inspection as some have called for, is very doubtful. No government is eager to turn the IAEA into a supranational authority, even if the interest in the safety of nuclear installations everywhere is now firmly entrenched. It is more likely that the interest in increasing international assurances regarding safety will be pursued through the expansion of the Operational Safety Review Team programme and the development of other kinds of review mechanisms that serve to enhance international confidence and assurance while respecting national responsibility for public health and safety.

One certain effect of the Chernobyl accident has been to weaken public confidence in nuclear power. This reverses a trend of growing confidence during the first half of the present decade as a result of improving performance and a good safety record in the nuclear industry. It will take a certain accident-free period of time and a new record of excellence to restore confidence. In the public mind, the nuclear industry is back to square one—if not minus one. Public opinion is very unforgiving when it comes to accidents in the nuclear industry, and the public's fear of radioactivity has to be taken into account by political decision-makers. The psychological impact of the Chernobyl accident far exceeds any health, technical or direct economic consequences. In some countries, such as Austria and Denmark, Chernobyl served to reconfirm earlier decisions to renounce nuclear power. In others, such as Finland, the Netherlands and Yugoslavia, decisions to order new nuclear plants have been postponed.

Nonetheless, nuclear power continues to play a very significant role in the energy economies of a large number of states, many of whose leaders show a strong commitment to continued reliance on nuclear power. Nuclear energy today accounts for 15 per cent of the world's electricity supply, providing 70 per cent of all electricity produced in France, 60 per cent in Belgium, 50 per cent in Sweden, 40 per cent each in Finland and Switzerland, 31 per cent in the Federal Republic of Germany and 23 per cent in Japan. The leaders of seven economically important countries, meeting in Tokyo, Japan, immediately after the Chernobyl accident, declared their view that 'properly managed' nuclear power will continue to produce an increasing share of the world's electricity. General Secretary Gorbachev has stated that it is unthinkable to envisage a world economy without nuclear power. Numerous statements to the effect that nuclear power will continue to be an important source of energy for social and economic development were heard at the Special Session of the IAEA's General Conference in September 1986.

The restoration of public confidence and the fulfilment of the expectations of a continued important role for nuclear energy require a consistent effort to make the technology as workable and as safe as possible. The major efforts are no doubt to be made at the national level, but the objective cannot be achieved in isolation or on an independent basis, for nuclear radioactivity will not stop at the national boundaries created by political man. Technological considerations compel co-operation by all in the interest of all.

We face a twofold challenge: one is to make the most of the window of opportunity that opened with the shock of the Chernobyl accident. While the political will to improve and reinforce international co-operation still remains strong, one can already sense some relenting, as public interest slackens. Co-operation requires not only political will to accomplish positive goals but also readiness to support the economic costs that such co-operation often entails. The expanded Agency nuclear safety programme for 1987 will cost $2 million, and it is clear that continued and new activities will also require additional financial support. In a time of zero-growth budgets, especially in international organizations, securing the financial commitment is a very difficult task. International secretariats can outline plans of action and implement agreed programmes, but they cannot themselves provide the needed resources. That must come from the member states. As the Chernobyl accident recedes in time, the sense of urgency in developing and implementing a comprehensive and reliable programme of international nuclear safety co-operation diminishes. But the problems and the risks associated with nuclear technology and radioactivity remain as real and as present as ever. It is in the nature of things that states act most resolutely when the danger is clear and present. Hence, the time for consolidating the international efforts to strengthen nuclear safety is now.

This evokes a second challenge: to make the most effective use of the international institutions that states have established for given purposes. The experience of co-operation in the IAEA in the post-Chernobyl period is very encouraging, particularly coming as it does during a time when international organizations have generally been facing much scepticism from important member states.

Notes and references

[1] The Statute of the IAEA entered into force in 1957. The seat of the Agency is in Vienna, Austria. As of 31 December 1986, the 113 member states of the General Conference are: Afghanistan, Albania, Algeria, Argentina, Australia, Austria, Bangladesh, Belgium, Bolivia, Brazil, Bulgaria, Burma, Byelorussia, Cameroon, Canada, Chile, China, Colombia, Costa Rica, Côte d'Ivoire, Cuba, Cyprus, Czechoslovakia, Denmark, Dominican Republic, Ecuador, Egypt, El Salvador, Ethiopia, Finland, France, Gabon, German Democratic Republic, Federal Republic of Germany, Ghana, Greece, Guatamala, Haiti, Holy See, Hungary, Iceland, India, Indonesia, Iran, Iraq, Ireland, Israel, Italy, Jamaica, Japan, Jordan, Kampuchea, Kenya, North Korea, South Korea, Kuwait, Lebanon, Liberia, Libya, Liechtenstein, Luxembourg, Madagascar, Malaysia, Mali, Mauritius, Mexico, Monaco, Mongolia, Morocco, Namibia, Netherlands, New Zealand, Nicaragua, Niger, Nigeria, Norway, Pakistan, Panama, Paraguay, Peru, Philippines, Poland, Portugal, Qatar, Romania, Saudi Arabia, Senagal, Sierra Leone, Singapore, South Africa, Spain, Sri Lanka, Sudan, Sweden, Switzerland, Syria, Tanzania, Thailand, Tunisia, Turkey, UK, Uganda, Ukraine, United Arab Emirates, Uruguay, USA, USSR, Venezuela, Viet Nam, Yugoslavia, Zaire, Zambia and Zimbabwe.

[2] The IAEA Board of Governors is composed of members from among the most advanced in the technology of atomic energy, including the production of source materials, so that it at all times includes representatives of specified geographical areas. See the IAEA Statute, Article VI, as amended in GC(XXX)/780, 17 Aug. 1986, Annex.

14. Recent developments in arms control verification technology

ALLAN KRASS, Professor of Physics and Science Policy, Hampshire College, Amherst, MA, and Senior Arms Analyst, Union of Concerned Scientists, Cambridge, MA

Superscript numbers refer to the list of notes and references at the end of the chapter.

I. Introduction

Despite the brief flurry of hope generated by the October Reykjavik summit meeting, 1986 came to an end with no discernible progress in US–Soviet arms control. In fact, the overall trend was clearly negative, with the USA officially renouncing its political commitment to abide by the terms of the unratified SALT II Treaty and then exceeding the Treaty's limit on strategic nuclear delivery vehicles. President Reagan's unshakeable commitment to the Strategic Defense Initiative (SDI) promises no better fate for the ABM Treaty, which could effectively be abrogated by the end of this decade if the SDI programme proceeds as planned.

In such a climate discussions of verification are somewhat academic. It is obvious from the record of the past seven years that the erosion of existing agreements, and the almost total failure to arrive at new ones, has had little or nothing to do with verification. While US officials have frequently criticized such potential agreements as a comprehensive test ban or an anti-satellite weapons ban as inadequately verifiable, the public record makes clear that these treaties and others have been opposed far more for their perceived negative impact on US security interests than for their verification weaknesses. Meanwhile, the negotiations that have taken place in Geneva on strategic and intermediate-range nuclear forces and space weapons do not appear to have progressed far enough to make detailed discussions of verification useful, and none of the accounts of the Reykjavik summit suggest that the issue was raised there at all.

Nevertheless, there are good reasons to follow the progress of monitoring technology. First, concerns about verifiability are often surrogates for political objections to arms control, and it is important to be able to distinguish those verification concerns which have a legitimate technical basis from those which do not. Second, it may be possible to identify areas of research which could lead to more effective monitoring techniques, thereby removing some of the technical obstacles to future agreements, if and when such agreements become politically feasible.

This chapter focuses on three important technologies which have shown recent progress and which promise to contribute significantly to future agreements if research and development are encouraged: seismology, for monitoring nuclear explosions; and adaptive optics and ground-based radar imaging, both for observing details of satellites.

II. Seismology

Possibly the most significant recent advances in monitoring technology have taken place in seismology, a field that has long been one of the most sophisticated and successful. Almost 30 years ago a conference of US and Soviet experts was able to agree that a comprehensive test ban could be adequately verified relying largely on seismic methods,[1] and scientific understanding and technical competence have continued to advance steadily since that time. The United States alone has spent over $500 million on such research, and more than $1 billion have been spent world-wide.[2]

It is important to keep clear the distinction between a threshold and a comprehensive test ban. Unless the threshold is set very low the verification requirements for the two are in principle quite different, but there has been a tendency in public and policy discussions to discuss the verification of a 'test ban' as if the problems were comparable in the two cases. Much of the confusion can be attributed to the widely different proposals currently advocated by the United States and the Soviet Union. While the USSR advocates a comprehensive test ban and has undertaken a unilateral moratorium to promote its case,[3] the USA is still worried about the verifiability of the Threshold Test Ban Treaty (TTBT) signed in 1974 and has gone no further than to suggest improving the monitoring of this treaty as a prerequisite for its ratification.

Under a comprehensive test ban the verification problem consists in detecting and identifying nuclear explosions which might be of small yield and conducted in remote and unexpected locations, and for which any of several measures may have been taken to muffle or conceal the seismic waves emanating from the explosion. On the other hand, the verification of a threshold test ban involves estimating the yields of explosions, most or all of which will take place at known and agreed test sites. Since the intelligence agencies of both the USA and the USSR want to obtain as much information as possible about the other's nuclear capabilities, considerable effort has gone into developing sophisticated techniques for accomplishing both of these tasks using only national technical means. These techniques, designed primarily for military intelligence purposes, would also permit the verification with high confidence of either a threshold or a comprehensive test ban treaty.

Verification of the Threshold Test Ban Treaty

Current US seismic monitoring capabilities can estimate the yields of underground nuclear explosions at known Soviet test sites with a precision of 30 per cent or better.[4] In addition there is an almost solid consensus among informed Western seismologists that the Soviet Union has not violated the TTBT limit of 150 kilotons as the Reagan Administration has repeatedly alleged.[5] After many years of intense bureaucratic dispute the US Government officially revised its yield-estimating procedures in April 1986.[6] A key element of the procedure is the assignment of a 'bias factor' to the Soviet Kazakh test site to account for differences between its geology and that of the US Nevada Test Site used to calibrate the yield estimates against explosions of known yield.[7] The new bias factor reduces the previously estimated yields of Soviet tests by 30 per cent, leaving, according to one account, only 'about a dozen' Soviet tests 'above the limit' and only three or four which 'exceed the limit enough to warrant special concern'.[8]

Once systematic biases have been accounted for, the remaining uncertainties in seismic yield measurements are purely statistical. It is to be expected that yields in excess of the permitted threshold will be observed if weapon tests are conducted close to the threshold. An elementary statistical analysis shows that one-sixth of all the measured yields from a series of identical 150-kt tests will appear to be greater than 195 kt if the uncertainty (i.e., standard deviation) is 30 per cent. One test in 40 can be expected to show a yield of 240 kt or more. Since the new procedure suggests that the largest Soviet test since 1974 showed a yield of 250 kt,[9] the data appear to be consistent with a finding of Soviet compliance with the TTBT.

Nevertheless, the Reagan Administration refused to submit the treaty for ratification until January 1987 and only under the condition that its verification provisions be renegotiated to include on-site yield measurements with the CORRTEX procedure. This technique was first developed to help monitor the Peaceful Nuclear Explosions Treaty signed in 1976 and since then has been employed at the Nevada Test Site to measure nuclear explosive yields.[10] President Reagan has invited Soviet scientists to the Nevada Test Site to make their own yield measurements, evidently hoping that the USSR will return the invitation. So far, the Soviet Union has refused such an arrangement, first arguing that the TTBT should be ratified as it stands and, more recently, showing a willingness to discuss improving its verification but only in the context of discussions on a comprehensive test ban.[11]

The CORRTEX technique employs a long coaxial cable inserted into the emplacement hole of the nuclear device being tested or a satellite shaft 10–30 m away. Repetitive electric pulses are sent down the cable at intervals of 10 to 90 microseconds, and the elapsed time is recorded for each pulse to return to the generator after reflection from the end of the cable several hundred or more metres underground. When the nuclear device explodes, the shock wave crushes the cable, creating a short-circuit which travels up the cable at the speed of the shock wave. The expanding shock front is tracked by observing the decreasing transit times of pulses reflected from the shock front. Only simple portable equipment is required, and the method's accuracy is given as 'within 30 percent or better of . . . "standard" radiochemical measurements',[12] similar to that quoted for seismic methods.[13] However, so far it seems useful only for tests with yields 'larger than several tens of kilotons'.[14] It has not been demonstrated that CORRTEX will be significantly more accurate than existing seismic methods when applied to the Soviet test site, and it is also inapplicable to many relatively low-yield, but militarily significant tests. Unless further research on the use of CORRTEX for low-yield tests shows otherwise, the method seems to offer few benefits that would warrant the difficulties of renegotiating the TTBT and arranging for a particularly intrusive form of on-site inspection.

Verification of a comprehensive test ban

All of this is irrelevant to the verification of a comprehensive test ban (CTB). Under a CTB violations would take the form of clandestine tests with at most 5-kt yield. Difficult, expensive and risky measures would have to be employed to hide even such small tests. To verify a CTB it is necessary to be able to identify all detected seismic events down to some low, militarily insignificant yield as either explosions or earthquakes. Such identification must rely primarily on seismic means, although these can and would be supplemented by other measures, both national (e.g., satellite observation and atmospheric radiation monitoring) and co-operative (e.g., exchanges of geological information and advance notice of large chemical explosions). Some provision for on-site inspection of suspicious events may also be negotiable and the achievement of such a provision could have a salutary political effect. But the usefulness of such inspections is often exaggerated and the high quality of modern monitoring technology makes on-site inspection virtually redundant and probably not worth the political, legal and technical difficulties inherent in its achievement and implementation.[15]

Two important advances, one scientific and the other technical, have added substantially to the capability to monitor a comprehensive test ban. Scientifically it can now be said that seismologists understand the theoretical basis for discriminating earthquakes from explosions down to very low yields.[16] The vast majority of events can be identified as earthquakes by their location (e.g., under the ocean more than 25 km offshore) or depth (e.g., more than 30 km below the surface of the earth). Only 1 per cent of earthquakes occur at locations or depths such that further discrimination is required to identify them.[17]

More seismic discrimination techniques rely on the very different frequency spectra produced by explosions and earthquakes.[18] Explosions are highly localized in both space and time and therefore put a large fraction of their energy into high-frequency compression waves (so-called 'body-waves'). Earthquakes are much slower events which involve highly asymmetric earth motions over large areas ('Effectively, the entire world relaxes a bit for each earthquake of any magnitude'[19]). Consequently, the seismic signal from most earthquakes will be dominated by low-frequency surface waves and look very different from a signal generated by an explosion. It is now possible to distinguish with high confidence the spectral content of explosion and earthquake signals, especially if seismographs are designed to respond at frequencies of 30 Hz or higher. At these frequencies not only are signals from earthquakes greatly attenuated, but background seismic noise is also suppressed, allowing the detection of much weaker seismic signals.[20] Therefore by monitoring at 30 Hz it is possible to identify very small explosions at distances up to at least 1000 km even if they have been 'decoupled'[21] or conducted under cover of an earthquake. Such high-frequency monitoring is already being conducted at the NORSAR array in northern Norway, a particularly advantageous spot from which to monitor the Soviet test sites. So far the NORSAR high-frequency observations have produced dramatic improvements in identification of very low yield explosions within the USSR (see figure 14.1).[22]

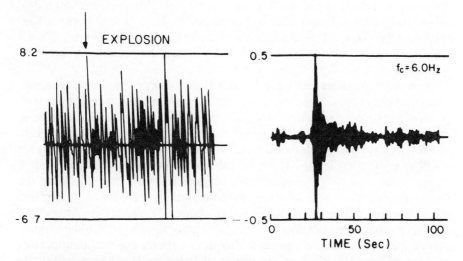

Figure 14.1. Comparison of seismic records of a small, distant explosion recorded at the NORSAR array in different frequency bands
On the left is the signal as observed in the normal seismic recording band centred at 1 Hz. In this band the seismic noise is comparable in amplitude to the signal from the explosion and it is unlikely that the explosion would have been detected. On the right is the signal as recorded in a narrow frequency band centred at 6 Hz. Here the noise is dramatically reduced and the explosion stands out clearly. At higher frequencies (e.g., 30 Hz) the signal-to-noise ratio would be even larger.

Source: Evernden, J. F. and Archambeau, C. B., 'Some seismological aspects of monitoring a CTBT', in Tsipis, K., Hafemeister, D. W. and Janeway, P. (eds), *Arms Control Verification: The Technologies that Make it Possible* (Pergamon-Brassey's: Washington, DC, 1986), p. 255. Based on NORSAR data and reproduced by permission of Pergamon-Brassey's International Defense Publishers, Inc., McLean, VA.

The technical advance in seismic monitoring involves the development and successful testing of simple, unmanned seismic stations which can operate for long periods in remote areas, and transmit continuous streams of secure seismic data via satellite links to data analysis centres.[23] A world-wide network of such stations separated by 1000 km or more and designed to detect both surface waves and high-frequency body waves would be capable of monitoring a CTB with high confidence down to yields of small fractions of a kiloton. Indeed even a few tonnes of explosives produce an easily detectable signal at 1000 km.[24] A less sophisticated type of remote station has been deployed at three locations around the Soviet Kazakh test site by the US Natural Resources Defense Council in collaboration with the Soviet Academy of

Sciences. Soviet officials announced that these stations would be allowed to operate when nuclear testing is resumed in 1987,[25] which should result in even better calibration of the Kazakh site.

At yields under 1 kt the problem arises of distinguishing small nuclear explosions from large chemical ones. Here seismic methods appear to be of little value. Chemical explosions occur on a time-scale roughly 1000 times slower than nuclear explosions (milliseconds as opposed to microseconds), and therefore produce a narrower frequency spectrum. However, the difference is not observable at frequencies as low as 30 Hz. Detection at roughly 1000 Hz would be required to separate chemical from nuclear explosions, but it appears unlikely that seismic observation will ever be feasible at such high frequencies.

Chemical explosions involving thousands of tonnes of explosives are rare events, so the chemical-nuclear ambiguity is relevant only to explosions with yields of 1 kt or less, far below the yields required to create new nuclear weapon designs. Surveys of the US testing programme have shown that only 5 per cent of US tests have had yields below 1 kt,[26] and such tests are useful primarily for studying nuclear radiation effects on other systems rather than for weapon design itself. If a criterion of military significance were used to define the necessary capabilities of a seismic monitoring system, and if it were recognized that other possibilities exist for learning about any clandestine attempt to ᴗ nduct a programme of very small nuclear explosions, then it could be argued that no special efforts would be needed to provide for the positive identification of large chemical explosions. However, if it were politically necessary to provide for positive identification even at such low levels, some form of co-operation involving prior notification of large chemical explosions and possibly the invitation of observers would have to be negotiated.

Further research is necessary to learn more about the propagation of high-frequency (10–100 Hz) seismic waves, to develop better high-frequency seismometers and to improve data analysis capabilities. However, all of the components for a highly effective CTB monitoring system are now in existence.

III. Adaptive optics

The most common method of observing a distant object involves collecting and focusing the electromagnetic radiation, such as light or radar, emitted or reflected by the object. Each illuminated point on the target serves as a source of spherical wave-fronts which move outward from the point at the speed of light. In empty space the waves can propagate long distances during which the spherical wave-fronts expand until their radius of curvature is very large. At distances of many kilometres these wave-fronts appear to be parallel planes, just as the surface of the large spherical earth appears flat to an observer on the ground.

Optical telescopes or radar antennas are generally designed on the assumption that they will collect and focus plane wave-fronts. But as electromagnetic radiation passes through a variable medium like the atmosphere, its wave-fronts are distorted. The distortion is observable to the naked eye as the twinkling of stars and is also responsible for the phenomenon of 'scintillation' of radar waves. If a telescope or antenna is to achieve its maximum resolution, these distortions must somehow be corrected for.

One method for removing distortions from incoming light waves is adaptive optics. It uses a reflecting telescope with a flexible mirror, whose face can be altered rapidly by small amounts to restore distorted wave-fronts to their proper shape. Without such corrections the resolution of a telescope cannot be improved indefinitely by increasing its diameter; all that is achieved is the collecting of more light. Such 'photon buckets' can detect, but not resolve, very faint objects. With adaptive optics, however, the resolution of a telescope can be made 'diffraction-limited', meaning that resolution is determined by the diameter of the telescope aperture.[27]

During the 1970s considerable progress was made in understanding the origins of atmospheric density variations and the effect they have on image quality.[28] Along with this theoretical understanding came technological developments in flexible optics, wave-front sensing and information processing, which permitted the design of telescopes able to measure the degree of distortion in the incoming light, convert these measurements into feedback signals and then use the signals to change the surface shape of the primary mirror. Wave-front distortions were largely eliminated, producing an image with a quality close to the theoretical capability of the telescope.[29] This is feasible because electronic instruments can analyse the wave-front distortion, perform the analysis and transmit the necessary correction signals in times considerably shorter than the 0.1 second which is the typical duration of atmospheric fluctuations (see figure 14.2).

In the 10 years since these developments were made public, research has continued on adaptive optics, but at a relatively low level. In particular, the technique was seen to have little application to satellite photography, since atmospheric fluctuations have a much smaller effect on images of targets on the earth photographed from space than they do on images of objects outside the atmosphere photographed from earth. The effect of density fluctuations increases when they are closer to the telescope, so it is much harder to get good resolution looking up through the atmosphere than looking down through it from above. In fact, the sharpness of a satellite photograph is almost completely independent of the altitude of the satellite as long as it is greater than about 30 km, a condition fulfilled by all photoreconnaissance satellites.[30]

Now that arms control discussions are showing some possibility of focusing on weapons in space, interest in the use of ground-based optical devices to identify space objects is growing.[31] The United States has had some capabilities in this area for several years in the form of the Ground-Based Electro-Optical Deep Space Surveillance (GEODSS) system.[32]

There are currently five GEODSS sites operating or nearing completion (in New Mexico, Hawaii, South Korea, Portugal and Diego Garcia), each using two 1-metre telescopes and a 38-cm auxiliary telescope.[33] Silicon sensors at each telescope's focal plane convert reflected light from the satellite to electrical signals which are used to produce an image of the target in the form of

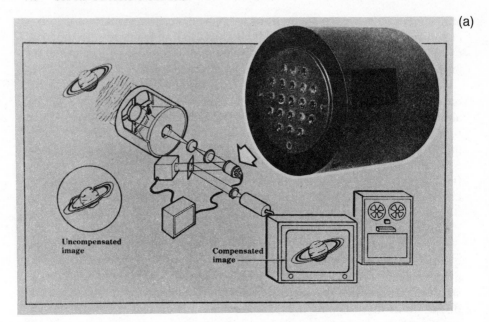

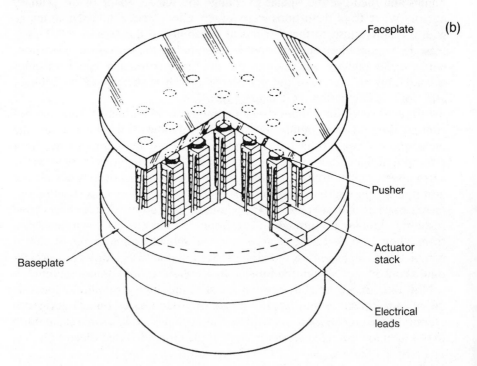

a bright streak against the black background of space. In an alternate mode of operation the sensors can record the fluctuations in intensity of light from the target and infer whether the target is tumbling in orbit, in which case it is most likely to be a piece of debris or an inoperative satellite. GEODSS is capable of observing and tracking an object the size of a soccer ball in geosynchronous orbit, 36 000 km above the earth's surface.[34] However, because of atmospheric distortions no details of the satellite's structure can be resolved, even in the case of low-orbit satellites.

If these distortions could be removed by adaptive optics, the 1-metre telescope could achieve its optimum diffraction-limited angular resolution, ideally as good as 0.6 microradians for visible light.[35] This would permit the resolution of details as small as 18 cm on a satellite passing over the telescope at an altitude of 300 km. Such resolutions are considered adequate by US intelligence agencies to allow the 'precise identification' of most military vehicles and structures and the even more detailed 'description' of others, such as radars, aircraft and submarines.[36] For satellites in higher orbits the target resolution is not as good, and the same telescope, even with adaptive optics, could resolve only to about 20 metres at geosynchronous orbit. With this resolution only the general features of very large satellites could be distinguished. If greater resolution were desired, larger-diameter telescopes would be needed or some different principle would have to be used (see section IV).

As an example of an application for such a system consider the verification of a treaty banning the deployment of so-called 'space-strike' weapons. Most designs currently under consideration for such weapons, such as chemical lasers, large orbiting mirrors, particle-beam weapons, or kinetic-energy kill vehicles, will have to be large objects with readily identifiable structures.[37] For example, one device currently under consideration for the US Strategic Defense Initiative is a neutral particle-beam accelerator which might ultimately be used to discriminate warheads from decoys in the mid-course phase of ballistic missile flight.[38] The current design concept for this system calls for an accelerator weighing about 20 000 kg and 30 metres in length to be deployed at an altitude of 300 km. If a ground-based telescope similar in size to GEODSS and using adaptive optics could resolve details on the accelerator down to 18 cm in size, this would be more than adequate to determine its structure and purpose. In particular, a particle accelerator would require more

---

Figure 14.2. Adaptive optics

a. Schematic diagram of an adaptive optics system with a deformable mirror. Light from the target (the planet Saturn in this illustration) enters a reflecting telescope and is directed by a system of lenses to the deformable mirror (shown by the arrow). The reflected light is divided by a beam splitter, with a portion of it entering a wave-front sensor and the rest going to form the image. The signals from the wave-front sensor are processed and transmitted back to the deformable mirror as a stream of correction signals. These drive the force actuators attached to the rear of the mirror face, and the mirror is deformed to produce an undistorted reflected wave.

b. Drawing of a deformable mirror assembly showing arrangement of force actuators.

Figures courtesy of Itek Corporation, Lexington, MA

power than could practically be supplied by solar panels. The absence of such panels could easily be discerned and the inference drawn that an on-board power source, possibly a nuclear reactor, was in use. An 18-cm resolution would also be sufficient to determine the number, size and shape of antennas deployed on the satellite, giving information about its target acquisition and command-control mechanisms.

There are some technical difficulties with this method. First, adaptive optics can be used to improve resolution only over a very narrow field of view, no greater than about 20 microradians.[39] At an altitude of 300 km, 20 microradians represents a length of only 6 metres, so only about 20 per cent of the particle-beam weapon could be resolved in any single image. Some method would have to be devised for scanning the target to provide a complete detailed image. Second, the assumption of diffraction-limited performance of the optics may be overly optimistic, and other factors may limit resolution to less favourable values. Finally, although reflected sunlight has been shown to provide sufficient intensity to allow operation of wave-front sensing devices,[40] this is true only when the target is viewed against the black background of the night sky. Therefore, satellites could be photographed with reflected sunlight only during the brief periods close to sunrise and sunset when the satellite is illuminated while the earth's surface remains in shadow.

One method for solving several of these problems at once is to employ an active illumination system, analogous to using a flash unit in photography rather than relying on ambient light. A large ground-based laser could direct a well-focused pulse of light at a satellite, and the pulse duration could be made short compared to the typical duration of atmospheric density fluctuations. For a satellite at an altitude of 300 km the pulse would take only two milliseconds for a round trip, about one-fiftieth of the fluctuation time. This would allow for the transmission of many pulses through an effectively static atmosphere, enabling the telescope to use adaptive optics or optical phase conjugation to produce a high-resolution image.[41]

The sunlight reaching an earth satellite has an intensity of roughly 0.1 watt/cm² spread out over the entire visible spectrum, while lasers can easily produce intensities 10 to 100 times this amount in a very narrow spectral band with high spatial coherence. This would permit photographs to be taken at any time of day or night, as well as the use of interference techniques to obtain even higher resolutions than are possible with individual telescopes. Atmospheric compensation of laser beams has already been tested, apparently successfully, by the USA as part of the SDI programme.[42]

Recently two facilities which appear to be large lasers under construction have been observed on mountain tops in the Soviet Union by US intelligence agencies.[43] One possible purpose for these lasers could be for anti-satellite (ASAT) weapons, but another, suggested recently by a Soviet expert,[44] could be for photographing US satellites. It should be possible to distinguish these two missions, since the power densities required for damaging satellites are at least 100 to 1000 times those needed for photographing objects in low earth orbit. It would seem a relatively simple matter to determine the potential brightness of the lasers by observing their sizes and power supplies, though observation of such features could be made more difficult by camouflage or concealment. The only conclusive way to determine their function would be to observe their energy output during tests.

Active laser imaging of objects in *geosynchronous* orbit is not promising as a verification measure because of the large-diameter mirrors required to obtain useful resolutions. In addition, the illumination of objects in geosynchronous orbit could be threatening to satellites in low orbits and would therefore be inconsistent with an ASAT treaty.

IV. Ground-based radar imaging

Laser imaging has the advantage of using short-wavelength visible light, enabling high resolution with relatively small telescope apertures. But, as noted above, laser imaging will probably be limited to low orbits by both technical and political constraints. It is also useless under cloud cover. On the other hand radar radiation will penetrate clouds, permitting continuous surveillance of orbiting objects. And with the proper antenna arrangements radar can obtain resolutions comparable to those just described for optical systems.

One such antenna arrangement involves a single ground-based transmitter/receiver which can track a moving object for a substantial period of time. As the target moves, a series of radar pulses is directed at it and the reflected signals collected by the receiver. The information carried by the reflected pulses is stored and analysed to produce an image of the target in much the same way as is done for synthetic aperture radar (SAR).[45]

In SAR the object to be observed is stationary and the radar antenna is moving. The distance moved during the relevant processing time (i.e., the time during which the receiver collects and stores reflected pulses from the target) determines the effective length of the 'synthetic aperture' and therefore the resolution of the image. The larger this aperture the better the resolution, up to a maximum of half the size of the radar antenna in the along-track direction. With a stationary radar and a moving target the situation is essentially the same, only here it is the motion of the target during the relevant processing time that determines the effective size of the aperture. In this configuration the process is called *inverse* synthetic aperture radar (ISAR).[46]

An important property of ISAR is that its resolution is determined only by the size of the antenna and does not decrease with distance.[47] Assuming that one can compensate for atmospheric scintillation effects, a 1-metre antenna would produce a theoretical 50-cm target resolution at all altitudes that the radar had sufficient power to reach. While a 50-cm resolution is not as good at low altitude as the 18-cm value obtained with the optical system described above, at altitudes greater than 1000 km the ISAR resolution is superior to that of the optical system. Since the provision of adequate power to ground-based systems is not a difficult problem, such systems ought in principle to be useful out to distances of many thousands of kilometres.

Of course an ISAR cannot be used to observe a target in geosynchronous orbit, since by definition such a target has no velocity relative to the earth's surface. In this case another form of radar observation, called very long baseline interferometry (VLBI), should be useful. In this technique radar pulses are reflected off a target and observed by two or more receivers located far apart on the earth's surface, or even by a combined earth-based and satellite-based array. Because the coherence of radar waves is preserved over long distances it is possible to combine the signals from several widely spaced receivers as if they were all part of a single large antenna. In this way angular resolutions of hundredths or, conceivably, thousandths of microradians can be obtained, leading to target resolutions of 1 metre or better, even in geosynchronous orbit. For example, 10-gigahertz radiation (3-cm wavelength) could be used with an array of receivers with a baseline of 1000 km to obtain a resolution of 0.03 microradians (about 1 metre in geosynchronous orbit), far better than could be obtained with any currently feasible optical system.

One interesting application of the VLBI principle has recently been demonstrated in radio astronomy.[48] The US Tracking and Data Relay Satellite (TDRS) was used in conjunction with ground-based radio telescopes to produce a baseline of 1.4 earth diameters (18 400 km), giving an angular resolution of 0.01 microradians. In order to establish coherence between the signals at the ground-based and space-based receivers, the location of the satellite had to be determined with great precision and its antenna precisely synchronized in time with the ground-based antennas. The latter was accomplished by compensating the synchronization signal for atmospheric scintillation, demonstrating that such compensation can be carried out with excellent precision. In another demonstration of the viability of VLBI techniques, the Soviet Union was able to monitor the descent of a balloon in the atmosphere of Venus with accuracies of a few kilometres, corresponding to a resolution of about 0.1 microradian.[49]

All of this suggests that negotiated limitations on many forms of space weapon would be highly verifiable by national technical means. Weight is such an important constraint in space-based systems that form tends to be closely related to function, especially on large satellites. It is possible to determine a great deal about a satellite's mission simply by observing its external configuration.[50] Therefore it is unlikely that satellites with significant military capabilities could be deployed in space clandestinely, even if all the research, development, production and preparations for their launching into orbit could be concealed, already an unlikely prospect.

V. Conclusion

This chapter has reviewed only a few of the ways in which scientific and technological innovation might contribute to the verification of arms control and disarmament agreements. No attempt has been made to be comprehensive and there are undoubtedly many other potentially useful ideas which could be developed and implemented if more support were available and the relevant agreements could be reached. Indeed, if effective verification by technical means were to become a high priority, there is no question that remarkable improvements could be made in current monitoring capabilities.

Yet it is necessary to end this discussion of monitoring technology by emphasizing the primarily political nature of the verification process. The intelligence agencies of the two great nuclear powers already possess elaborate and sophisticated means for monitoring the activities of other states. Each knows far more about the other than is revealed to the public and probably more than enough to verify adequately any but the most extreme disarmament agreements. Yet suspicion and the military competition it engenders persist. And, ironically, this military competition provides the primary motivation for the very improvements in monitoring technology which would make verification of disarmament possible. This paradox, and the inability so far of anyone to find a way out of it, must temper enthusiasm for even the most ingenious new monitoring devices.

Notes and references

[1] Gilpin, R., *American Scientists and Nuclear Weapons Policy* (Princeton University Press: Princeton, NJ, 1962), pp. 186–200.

[2] Sykes, L. R., 'Advancing United States national security interests through verifiable limitations on nuclear testing', preprint of testimony before Committee on Foreign Relations, US Senate, 26 June 1986, Lamont-Doherty Geological Observatory of Columbia University, Palisades, NY, p. 6.

[3] As this is written in December 1986 the Soviet Union has just announced its intention to resume testing after the first US test in 1987.

[4] See Sykes (note 2), pp. 16–18.

[5] *Soviet Noncompliance With Arms Control Agreements*, Special Report No. 136, United States Department of State, Bureau of Public Affairs, Washington, DC, Dec. 1985, pp. 7–8.

[6] Gordon, M. R., 'CIA changes way that it measures Soviet atom tests', *New York Times*, 2 Apr. 1986, pp. A1, 10.

[7] Krass, A. S., *Verification: How Much Is Enough?*, SIPRI (Taylor & Francis: London, 1985), p. 72.

[8] See Gordon (note 6), p. A10.

[9] See Gordon (note 6), p. A10.

[10] Virchow, C. F., Conrad, G. E., Holt, D. M. and Hodson, E. K., 'Microprocessor-controlled time domain reflectometer for dynamic shock position measurements', *Review of Scientific Instruments*, vol. 51, no. 5 (May 1980), pp. 642–46. 'CORRTEX' stands for Continuous Reflectometry for Radius versus Time Experiments.

[11] Gordon, M. R., 'U.S. group can study Soviet A-test', *New York Times*, 20 Dec. 1986, p. 8.

[12] 'CORRTEX', Fact Sheet published by US Department of Energy, Nevada Operations Office, Los Alamos National Laboratory, Los Alamos, NM, Apr. 1986.

[13] See note 2.

[14] See note 12.

[15] See Krass (note 7), pp. 212–23.

[16] Evernden, J. F. and Archambeau, C. B., 'Some seismological aspects of monitoring a CTBT', in Tsipis, K., Hafemeister, D. W. and Janeway, P. (eds), *Arms Control Verification: The Technologies That Make It Possible* (Pergamon-Brassey's: Washington, DC, 1986), pp. 223–63.

[17] See Evernden and Archambeau (note 16), p. 225.

[18] See Krass (note 7), pp. 66–70.

[19] See Evernden and Archambeau (note 16), p. 233.

[20] See Evernden and Archambeau (note 16), p. 257.

[21] A decoupled explosion is one which has been conducted inside a large cavity or in a very soft, inelastic medium. This causes a substantially smaller fraction of the energy to be 'coupled' to seismic waves and effectively muffles the explosion. However, the muffling effect is far less effective at high frequencies.

[22] See Evernden and Archambeau (note 16), p. 255.

[23] Stokes, P. A., 'Unattended in-country stations for seismic verification', in Tsipis, Hafemeister and Janeway (note 16), pp. 264–74.

[24] Dahlman, O., remarks at conference on 'Scientific Aspects of Verification of Arms Control Treaties', Hamburg, FRG, 13–14 Nov. 1986.

[25] See Gordon (note 11).

[26] Kidder, R. E., 'Militarily significant nuclear explosive yields', F.A.S. Public Interest Report, Sep. 1985, Federation of American Scientists, Washington, DC, pp. 1–3.

[27] See Krass (note 7), pp. 24–25.

[28] Fante, R. L., 'Electromagnetic beam propagation in turbulent media', Proceedings of the IEEE, vol. 63, no. 12 (Dec. 1975), pp. 1669–92.

[29] Hardy, J. W., 'Active optics: a new technology for control of light', Proceedings of the IEEE, vol. 66, no. 6 (June 1978), pp. 651–97.

[30] Evvard, J. C., 'Limits on observational capabilities of aerospacecraft', NASA TN D-2933, National Aeronautics and Space Administration, Washington, DC, 1965, p. 1.

[31] Vyce, R. J. and Hardy, J. W., 'Adaptive optics: potential for verification', in Tsipis, Hafemeister and Janeway (note 16), pp. 97–103.

[32] 'GEODSS photographs orbiting satellite', Aviation Week & Space Technology, 28 Nov. 1983, pp. 146–47.

[33] US Congress, Office of Technology Assessment, Anti-Satellite Weapons, Countermeasures and Arms Control, OTA-ISC-281, (US Government Printing Office: Washington, DC, Sep. 1985), pp. 55–57.

[34] See note 32.

[35] Angular resolution is defined as the smallest angular separation two point objects can have and still appear as two objects on the focal plane of the telescope. It is calculated by taking the ratio of the wavelength of the radiation to the diameter of the telescope and multiplying by 1.2. (This last factor is often omitted in approximate calculations.) The 'target resolution' is the actual distance between the two resolved points on the target. For a given angular resolution the target resolution increases linearly with the distance of the object from the telescope.

[36] See Krass (note 7), p. 26, table 2.

[37] US Congress, Office of Technology Assessment, Ballistic Missile Defense Technologies, OTA-ISC-254 (US Government Printing Office, Washington, DC, Sep. 1985), chapter 7.

[38] Klass, P. J., 'Neutral particle beams show potential for decoy discrimination', Aviation Week & Space Technology, 8 Dec. 1986, pp. 45–52.

[39] See Vyce and Hardy (note 31), p. 100.

[40] See Vyce and Hardy (note 31), pp. 101–102.

[41] Shkunov, V. V. and Zel'dovich, B. Ya, 'Optical phase conjugation', Scientific American, Dec. 1985, pp. 54–59.

[42] Jasani, B., 'The military use of outer space', in SIPRI, World Armaments and Disarmament: SIPRI Yearbook 1986 (Oxford University Press: Oxford, 1986), p. 135.

[43] 'White House assesses reports of Soviet Asat laser facilities', Aviation Week & Space Technology, 15 Sep. 1986, p. 21.

[44] Sagdeyev, R., remarks at Hamburg conference, see note 24.

[46] Brookner, E., 'Radar imaging for arms control', in Tsipis, Hafemeister and Janeway (note 16), pp. 142–44, 151–54.

[47] See Brookner (note 46), pp. 158–61.

[48] Dornheim, M. A., 'TDRS, ground antennas link for radio astronomy observations', Aviation Week & Space Technology, 1 Dec. 1986, pp. 32–33.

[49] See Sagdeyev (note 44).

[50] Osborne, F. J. F., 'The PAXSAT concept', Talk delivered at the Third Annual Symposium on Arms Control and Disarmament Verification, Carleton University, Ottawa, 19 Apr. 1986.

Annexe A. Chronology

RAGNHILD FERM

January–December 1986

10 January A declaration appeal by the presidents of Bulgaria and Romania concerning the creation of a chemical weapon-free zone in the Balkans is transmitted to the Ad Hoc Committee on Chemical Weapons of the Conference on Disarmament.

10 January The first US cruise missiles arrive in FR Germany.

15 January General Secretary Gorbachev proposes a step-by-step process to eliminate nuclear weapons. First stage: A 50 per cent reduction of those US and Soviet nuclear weapons which can reach the other's territory, a mutual renunciation of space-strike weapons and a ban on US and Soviet nuclear tests. The UK and France should pledge not to build up their nuclear forces. Second stage: All nuclear states should join the process by 1990. Third stage: All remaining nuclear weapons should be eliminated at the latest by 1999. All steps in the disarmament plan should be subject to comprehensive verification. As regards chemical weapons the Soviet Union will make timely announcement of the location of enterprises producing these weapons and ensure the cessation of their production. A multilateral agreement could be reached not to transfer or deploy chemical weapons in other states. The Soviet nuclear test moratorium is extended by three months.

28 January The US space shuttle Challenger explodes shortly after take-off, killing all seven astronauts on board. The accident postpones the US shuttle programme for at least two years.

31 January The French President, François Mitterrand, rejects the Soviet proposal of 15 January for a freeze on French nuclear forces.

18 February Australia and the UK agree on measures for a clean-up of former British test sites in Australia.

20 February At the MBFR talks in Vienna, the Warsaw Treaty Organization (WTO) presents a new draft treaty. The proposal includes an initial reduction of 11 000 Soviet and 6500 US troops followed by a three-year commitment not to increase troops. There is a plan for verification measures, such as permanent check-points.

24 February In response to the Soviet disarmament proposals of 15 January President Reagan supports the 50 per cent reduction of US and Soviet strategic forces but states that total elimination of nuclear weapons will require correction of the conventional and other force balance.

25 February–6 March In his report to the 27th CPSU Congress General Secretary Gorbachev states that tasks underlying the country's economic and social development also determine its strategy on the world scene. He suggests principles for creating an international security system: non-use of force, prevention of an arms race in outer space, a ban on nuclear weapons and weapons of mass destruction, a lowering of the levels of military capabilities, disbanding of military alliances and a reduction of military budgets.

28 February   In a message to President Reagan and General Secretary Gorbachev the leaders of Argentina, Greece, India, Mexico, Sweden and Tanzania (the Six-Nation Initiative, also called the Five-Continent Initiative) urge the two nations to refrain from nuclear tests in the period up to the next summit meeting.

2 March   US arms control adviser Paul Nitze rejects the Soviet proposal of 15 January for a freeze on British and French nuclear forces.

5–6 March   US-Soviet talks on the prevention of the spread of chemical weapons, as agreed in the summit meeting in November 1985, are held in Berne. Another round of these talks, with an expanded scope, is held in Berne on 4–6 September.

7 March   The US Arms Control and Disarmament Agency (ACDA) releases its report, alleging Soviet violations of arms control agreements. The report follows the US Administration's report to the Congress of 23 December 1985.

10 March   British Prime Minister Margaret Thatcher rejects the Soviet proposal of 15 January for a freeze on British nuclear forces.

12 March   In a referendum Spain's continued membership of NATO is supported by a 53 per cent majority. (Against: 40 per cent; remaining votes invalid; 60 per cent participation.)

12 March   The report of the mission dispatched by the UN Secretary-General to investigate allegations of the use of chemical weapons in the Iraq–Iran War is released. It confirms the use of chemical weapons by Iraqi forces against Iranian forces.

13 March   In reply to the Six-Nation Initiative proposal of 28 February General Secretary Gorbachev declares that the Soviet Union shall not conduct nuclear explosions even after 31 March 1986—until the USA carries out its next nuclear explosion.

14 March   President Reagan reiterates his proposal (29 July 1985) for monitoring of nuclear tests by a hydrodynamic yield measurement method called CORRTEX. This method could improve verification of compliance with the 150-kiloton threshold on underground tests established in the unratified Threshold Test Ban Treaty (TTBT) and Peaceful Nuclear Explosions Treaty (PNET). He also invites Soviet scientists to inspect the system at a US test site and to monitor a US nuclear weapon test.

20 March   The WTO Foreign Ministers, meeting in Warsaw, issue a communiqué stating that if the US intermediate-range missiles are eliminated from Europe there will no longer be a need for Soviet extended-range tactical missiles to remain in those countries where they have been deployed. The ministers support the creation of nuclear weapon-free zones in Northern Europe and in the Balkans as well as a nuclear weapon-free corridor in Central Europe and chemical weapon-free zones in the Balkans and Central Europe.

21 March   In a communiqué, issued at the NATO Nuclear Planning Group meeting in Würzburg, FR Germany, a US proposal, presented at the Nuclear and Space Talks (NST) in Geneva, for global elimination of US and Soviet intermediate-range nuclear missiles is supported.

21 March   In a speech in Beijing, Chinese Prime Minister Zhao Ziyang announces that China will no longer conduct atmospheric nuclear tests. He urges that a convention banning chemical weapons should be reached at an early date. Until then, all countries capable of manufacturing chemical weapons should pledge never to use them and to stop their testing, production, transfer and deployment.

21 March   After having considered the report of the mission of specialists dispatched by the UN Secretary-General (see *12 March*) the members of the UN Security Council strongly condemn Iraq's continued use of chemical weapons in clear violation of the 1925 Geneva Protocol.

26 March   General Secretary Gorbachev says that if the USA withdraws its fleet in the Mediterranean the USSR would simultaneously do the same. He is prepared to enter talks on the issue.

27 March   FR Germany signs an agreement with the USA on conditions for its participation in the SDI research programme.

29 March   General Secretary Gorbachev repeats his announcement (*13 March*) of the extension of the Soviet test moratorium until the USA conducts another test. He reiterates his invitation to the USA to join the moratorium and suggests a summit meeting to reach agreement on the testing issue.

29 March   In a reply to General Secretary Gorbachev's speech of the same day President Reagan again rejects the proposal for a test moratorium and states that at a possible summit meeting the nuclear testing issue will only be one of a number of items to be discussed by the two countries.

11 April   As a consequence of the US nuclear weapon test on 10 April, the Soviet Government declares itself free from its unilateral commitment to refrain from nuclear testing. However, it expresses readiness to return any time to the question of a mutual moratorium on nuclear explosions if the USA declares that it is prepared to abandon nuclear testing.

14 April   The USA conducts an air strike on Libya from the UK. 130 aircraft are involved in the attack. France and Spain forbid use of their airspace.

15 April–26 May   An expert meeting within the Conference on Security and Co-operation in Europe (CSCE) process on humanitarian issues is held in Berne, Switzerland. The meeting fails to reach an agreement.

18 April   In a speech before the East German Socialist Unity Party (SED) Congress in East Berlin, General Secretary Gorbachev proposes reductions in tactical nuclear weapons and conventional forces, aiming to reduce the troops on each side by 500 000 by the early 1990s from the Atlantic to the Urals.

23 April   The US Administration announces US rejection of General Secretary Gorbachev's proposal of 18 April.

26 April   The fourth unit of the Chernobyl nuclear power station 130 km north of Kiev blows up, resulting in radioactive releases beyond the Soviet Union.

30 April   The Soviet Union officially notifies the IAEA of the Chernobyl nuclear-reactor accident.

1 May   France deploys its first nuclear air-to-surface missile, the ASMP.

5–6 May   US and Soviet officials meet in Geneva to discuss establishing centres in Washington and Moscow to reduce the risk of an accidental nuclear war. One more such meeting is held during the year: 25 August.

6 May   Israel signs an agreement with the USA on conditions for its participation in the SDI research programme.

14 May   In a speech concerning the Chernobyl nuclear-reactor accident of 26 April General Secretary Gorbachev announces that the Soviet Union will extend its moratorium on nuclear tests until 6 August 1986, which will make the moratorium period one whole year.

15 May   The NATO Defence Planning Committee, in permanent session, approves the package of NATO force goals for 1987–92, including the US resumption of the production of chemical binary munitions.

15 May   The West German Bundestag is informed of an agreement between Chancellor Kohl and President Reagan on the future of US binary chemical weapons in FR Germany: existing US stocks of chemical weapons in FR Germany should be withdrawn by 1992 and there is to be no deployment of binaries to NATO Europe during peacetime; binary munitions are not to be deployed in Europe without prior consultation with NATO and may not be deployed in FR Germany without the consent of its government.

27 May   President Reagan announces that he has determined that, in the future, the USA must base decisions regarding its strategic force structure on the threat posed by Soviet strategic forces, and not on the standards of the SALT agreements which have been undermined by Soviet non-compliance. He intends to continue deployment of US B-52 heavy bombers with cruise missiles beyond the 131st aircraft, without dismantling additional systems, thus disregarding the terms of the SALT II Treaty.

28 May   An agreement is reached between US and Soviet scientists (the Natural Resources Defense Council—NRDC—and the Soviet Academy of Sciences) on setting up seismic monitoring stations adjacent to each of the principal test sites in the two countries. The findings of the project will be helpful in demonstrating verification procedures to be used during a test moratorium or under a nuclear test ban treaty.

29 May   The Soviet Union presents its position on space weapons at the Geneva Nuclear and Space Talks (NST). Basic research on ABM systems would be permitted within the ABM Treaty, but testing in space would be constrained. Both sides should agree not to invoke the six-month termination clause for a period of 15–20 years.

30 May   The North Atlantic Council, meeting in ministerial session at Halifax, Canada, decides to set up a high-level task force on conventional arms control. The ministers call for a treaty totally eliminating chemical weapons.

31 May   Reacting to President Reagan's announcement of 27 May the Soviet Government states that it will consider itself free from the relevant commitments under the SALT treaties and will take the necessary steps to prevent the military-strategic parity from being upset.

6 June   A new version of the Contadora Act on peace and co-operation in Central America is presented at a meeting of the Contadora group in Panama.

11 June   The Political Consultative Committee of the Warsaw Treaty Organization, meeting in Budapest, issues an appeal to the member states of NATO and all European countries. A substantial reduction of land and tactical air forces of European states and US and Canadian forces stationed in Europe is proposed. In a first step NATO and WTO troops should be cut by 100 000–150 000. By the early 1990s the opposing armed forces in Europe would be reduced by over one million troops. A special forum should be convened with the participation of the European states as well as the USA and Canada to explore the reduction proposals.

23 June   In a private letter to President Reagan General Secretary Gorbachev proposes that both parties should abide by the ABM Treaty for 15–20 years, which means abstaining during this period from deploying space defence systems.

26 June   In the 'Report to Congress on the Strategic Defense Initiative (SDI)', issued by the US Department of Defense, it is stated that the ABM Treaty allows the development and testing of systems based on physical principles other than those upon which the current ABM systems are based, regardless of basing mode.

26 June   The US House of Representatives, for the first time in three years, approves the Administration's request for military aid to the contras. (The Senate approves legislation providing $70 million on 13 August.)

27 June   The International Court of Justice (ICJ) states that US actions against Nicaragua constitute a breach of the obligations under international law not to intervene in the affairs of another state. The Court decides that the USA is under a duty immediately to cease and to refrain from such actions and to make reparation for all injury caused.

8 July   Nicaragua institutes proceedings in the International Court of Justice (ICJ) against Costa Rica and Honduras for allowing armed attacks by the contras to be launched from their territories against Nicaragua.

13 July   US scientists set up seismographs in the vicinity of the Semipalatinsk test site area in the Soviet Union, in accordance with the agreement of 28 May.

15 July   The UK and the Soviet Union sign an agreement designed to reduce the risk of dangerous incidents at sea by regulating the manoeuvres of ships and aircraft of their armed forces when operating close to each other. It also establishes channels of communication between the two navies in order to provide means of quickly resolving difficulties arising from incidents at sea.

15 July   At the Conference on Disarmament the UK presents a new proposal for verification of a ban on chemical weapons. Each party should have the right, in exceptional cases, directly to request a challenge inspection of another. In very limited circumstances there would be a right to refuse an inspection, in which case the challenged state would propose alternative measures.

25 July   President Reagan responds in a private letter to General Secretary Gorbachev's letter of 23 June. He proposes that both sides agree not to deploy space weapons for seven years. During this period research, including testing, is to be permitted. After the seven years both sides would be free to deploy space weapons.

25 July–1 August   US–Soviet talks covering 'the entire scope of issues relating to nuclear testing' take place in Geneva. Two more rounds of such talks are held during the year: 4–18 September and 13–25 November.

28 July   In a speech, given in Vladivostok, USSR, General Secretary Gorbachev proposes measures for the reduction of nuclear and conventional weapons in Asia and the Pacific. He also suggests that talks be held on the reduction of naval activity, especially that of nuclear-armed warships in the Pacific, as well as on confidence-building measures and non-use of force in the region. He announces that a withdrawal of a substantial part of the Soviet troops in Mongolia is being examined with the Mongolian leadership and that six regiments will return home from Afghanistan before the end of 1986.

5 August   At the Conference on Disarmament Indonesia reports that the six countries of ASEAN (Association of South East Asian Nations) have reached an agreement to undertake a study on the creation of a nuclear weapon-free zone in South-East Asia.

7 August   The US Senate calls on President Reagan to seek ratification of the 1974 Threshold Test Ban Treaty (TTBT) and the 1976 Peaceful Nuclear Explosions Treaty (PNET).

7 August   In a document adopted at Ixtapa, Mexico, the leaders of Argentina, Greece, India, Mexico, Sweden and Tanzania (the Six-Nation Initiative) state that they are prepared to assist in the monitoring of a moratorium on nuclear weapon tests or a test ban.

11–12 August   US and Soviet arms control expert groups (led by Paul Nitze and Richard Perle for the USA, and Victor Karpov and Nicolai Chervov for the USSR) meet in Moscow to discuss a broad range of arms control issues. Details of the talks are not announced. Two more rounds of these talks are held in Washington, 5–6 September, and in Vienna, 2–5 December.

15 August   The USA announces that it is suspending its security obligations to New Zealand under the ANZUS Treaty, owing to New Zealand's refusal to allow nuclear naval units into its ports.

18 August   General Secretary Gorbachev announces a further extension of the Soviet moratorium on nuclear tests, to remain in effect until 1 January 1987.

20 August   The Chinese Government announces that it will allow the IAEA to inspect a Chinese nuclear power plant to be built close to Hong Kong, in accordance with the Chinese statement to the IAEA General Conference, 24 September 1985.

25 August   US-Soviet talks on risk reduction centres. See *5–6 May*.

1–6 September   The Eighth Conference of heads of state or government of non-aligned countries is held in Harare, Zimbabwe. In the final document from the conference it is noted that collaboration with the South African regime violates many UN resolutions and the final documents of the first and second special sessions of the UN General Assembly devoted to disarmament. It is asserted that the militarization of South Africa, especially in the nuclear field, would not have occurred without the support of certain Western states and Israel and that some of these states have violated the UN Security Council embargo imposed on South Africa.

4–6 September   US–Soviet talks on the prevention of the spread of chemical weapons, Berne. See *5–6 March*.

4–18 September   US–Soviet talks on nuclear testing. See *25 July–1 August*.

5–6 September   US–Soviet talks on risk reduction centres. See *5–6 May*.

5–6 September   US and Soviet arms control experts meet in Washington. See *11–12 August*.

8–26 September   The Biological Weapons (BW) Convention Review Conference is held in Geneva. A final declaration which strengthens the authority of the Convention is adopted by consensus.

9 September The Japanese Cabinet approves in principle Japanese participation in SDI research. (Negotiations on formal agreement will follow.)

18 September The USA presents its proposal on the reduction of Intermediate-range Nuclear Forces (INF) at the Nuclear and Space Talks (NST) in Geneva. It would set a global limit of 200 warheads for each side; of these, 100 warheads could be on missiles within range of Europe; 100 Soviet warheads in Asia and 100 US warheads in the USA would be permitted.

19–20 September The US and Soviet Foreign Ministers meet in Washington. A letter from General Secretary Gorbachev is delivered to President Reagan (reply to President Reagan's letter of 25 July). He insists that both parties should abide by the ABM Treaty for a 15-year period. He also outlines arms control concessions pertaining to medium-range missiles in Europe.

19 September A Philippine Government commission unanimously accepts a draft constitutional provision opposing nuclear weapons on the soil of the country.

19 September Italy signs an agreement with the USA on the conditions for participating in the SDI research programme.

22 September The Conference on Confidence- and Security-Building Measures and Disarmament in Europe (the Stockholm Conference) adopts a final document (dated 19 September 1986) in which the confidence-building measures adopted in Helsinki in 1975 are improved and expanded.

22 September In addressing the UN General Assembly President Reagan says that the USA is prepared to sign an agreement with the Soviet Union on strategic defence. Under the agreement both sides would agree to confine themselves until the end of 1991 to research, development and testing which is permitted by the ABM Treaty. If, by the end of 1991, either side should have deployed such a system that side must offer a plan for sharing defence benefits and for eliminating offensive ballistic missiles. If the two sides cannot reach an agreement after two years, either side would be free to deploy an advanced strategic defence system after six months' notice.

23 September–6 October The preparatory meeting for the Conference on Security and Co-operation (CSCE) in Europe is held in Vienna.

26–27 September Western reporters visit a Soviet test site at the invitation of the Soviet Government.

26 September Two IAEA conventions on nuclear safety (the Convention on early notification of a nuclear accident and the Convention for the provision of assistance in the case of a nuclear accident or radiological emergency) are opened for signature.

2 October The British Labour Party decides at its annual conference to officially adopt a policy of unilateral nuclear disarmament.

3 October A Soviet Yankee-1 Class nuclear-powered ballistic missile submarine (SSBN)—on patrol in the Atlantic *circa* 970 km north-east of Bermuda—experiences a fire and explosion which kill three crew members and later cause the submarine to sink. On the following day the Soviet Union notifies the IAEA about the accident.

10 October President Reagan agrees to submit the 1974 Threshold Test Ban Treaty (TTBT) and the 1976 Peaceful Nuclear Explosions Treaty (PNET) to the Senate for consent to ratification if the Soviet Union will accept additional verification measures which could accompany the treaties as a protocol.

11–12 October   General Secretary Gorbachev and President Reagan meet in Reykjavik, Iceland, for talks on disarmament matters. No agreement is concluded.

12 October   At a press conference in Reykjavik General Secretary Gorbachev reports on the summit meeting. The USSR had presented the following proposals: a 50 per cent reduction of each component of the strategic offensive weapons within five years with a view to fully eliminate these weapons by the end of the century; total elimination of US and Soviet medium-range missiles in Europe (not including the French and British missiles); and a freeze on missiles of less than 1000-km range. If the US and Soviet missiles are eliminated the USSR would agree to keep only 100 warheads on medium-range missiles in Asia, while the USA has the same number on its territory. Verification must be comprehensive and include the right to on-site inspection. Both sides should pledge not to withdraw from the ABM Treaty within a 10-year period during which the nuclear arsenals are reduced. ABM research and testing should be allowed only in laboratories.

15 October   At the WTO Foreign Ministers' meeting in Bucharest, proposals by the GDR, Czechoslovakia, Romania and Bulgaria for chemical and nuclear weapon-free zones in the Balkans and Central and Northern Europe are supported. The ministers call for an international conference on the Middle East under UN aegis and propose that a preparatory committee for that purpose, including the five permanent members of the Security Council, be established in 1986.

15 October   The Soviet Defence Ministry announces the start of the withdrawal of 8000 Soviet troops from Afghanistan in accordance with the decision announced by General Secretary Gorbachev in his speech in Vladivostok on 28 July. The withdrawal is to be completed by 31 October.

15 October   The NATO Supreme Allied Commander, Europe, General Bernard Rogers, says that the 'zero level option' for the long-range intermediate nuclear force needs to be coupled with an attempt to strike a balance in conventional forces as well as on shorter-range intermediate nuclear forces.

17 October   The US State Department presents the final US proposals, offered at the Reykjavik meeting. The strategic offensive arms of the two sides should be reduced by 50 per cent over a period of five years. During the following five years all remaining offensive ballistic missiles should be eliminated. During this 10-year period both sides should undertake not to withdraw from the ABM Treaty. Research, development and testing—which is permitted by the Treaty—should proceed. At the end of the 10-year period either side could deploy defences.

21 October   The West German Social Democratic Party (SPD) and the East German Socialist Unity Party (SED) release an outline on basic principles for the establishment of a nuclear weapon-free zone in Europe, 150 km on either side of the border between the two states.

24–26 October   The Palme Commission on disarmament and security issues, meeting in Budapest, proposes that the ABM Treaty should not be amended, broadened or narrowed. Each party should specify its planned activities, if any, and identify which of these activities it considers to be permitted by the Treaty. The Commission also suggests that a first step towards a ban on nuclear tests could be to limit the yield of tests to one kiloton.

26 October   The UN General Assembly adopts a resolution, submitted by Brazil, proclaiming the Atlantic Ocean between Africa and South America to be a zone of peace and co-operation.

27 October The IAEA Convention on early notification of a nuclear accident (see *26 September*) enters into force.

3 November In a speech before the First Committee of the UN General Assembly the Soviet delegate announces that the USSR would agree to declare, together with the USA, a moratorium on the production and deployment of chemical weapons. He suggests that the proposal submitted to the Conference on Disarmament by the UK (see *15 July*) be used as a basis for procedures for on-site challenge inspections.

4 November The third follow-up meeting of the Conference on Security and Co-operation (CSCE) in Europe opens in Vienna.

6 November The French Cabinet approves the defence programme for 1987–91 which includes the manufacture of chemical weapons.

10 November The EEC Foreign Ministers agree on sanctions against Syria to show disapproval of alleged Syrian involvement in terrorism. The sanctions include a ban on arms sales.

13 November At a press conference in Helsinki, Yegor Ligachev, a member of the Soviet Politburo, announces that the USSR has dismantled the launchers for medium-range missiles in the Kola Peninsula as well as most of the launchers for such missiles in the Leningrad and Baltic military districts. He reports that several battalions of operational tactical missiles have been moved from the area for deployment elsewhere. Withdrawal of ballistic missile submarines from the Baltic is also envisaged, if there is an agreement on a Nordic nuclear weapon-free zone.

13 November President Reagan publicly acknowledges US shipment of weapons to Iran.

13–25 November US–Soviet talks on nuclear testing. See *25 July–1 August.*

14 November President Reagan signs into law the US 1987 Defence Authorization Act. It allows purchase of the M687 nerve-gas artillery projectile and the Bigeye nerve-gas bomb. However, the final assembly of complete Bigeyes may not take place before 1 October 1988. The Act also contains a decision on retaining the current ban on tests of anti-satellite (ASAT) missiles against targets in space.

15 November British Prime Minister Thatcher meets President Reagan at Camp David, USA. They confirm that NATO's strategy of forward defence and flexible response should continue to require effective deterrents based on a mix of systems. Reductions in nuclear weapons would increase the importance of eliminating conventional weapon disparities.

19 November The President of Mozambique, Samora Machel, is killed in an aeroplane crash in South Africa.

23 November In a referendum in Romania, voters approve a proposal by the President to reduce military spending by 5 per cent.

25 November The US Administration reports on the US role in arms shipment to Iran and the transfer of funds to anti-government rebels in Nicaragua. Money received from Iran has been deposited in bank accounts under the control of representatives of the contras in Central America.

27 November   Speaking to Indian parliamentarians (during an official visit to Delhi) General Secretary Gorbachev says that the Soviet Union is prepared to start negotiations with the USA on reducing naval forces in the Indian Ocean.

28 November   The USA exceeds the limits stated in the unratified SALT II Treaty, when a B-52 bomber, modified to carry cruise missiles, enters into service.

2–5 December   US and Soviet arms control experts meet in Vienna. See *11–12 August*.

3 December   The UN General Assembly decides to convene its third special session on disarmament in 1988.

5 December   In a communiqué, issued by the NATO Defence Planning Committee, meeting in Brussels, NATO's strategy of forward defence and flexible response is reaffirmed. Reductions in nuclear arms will increase the importance of eliminating the current imbalance in conventional forces.

5 December   The Soviet Government declares that it will for the time being abide by the unratified SALT II Treaty in spite of the USA abandoning it.

11 December   The South Pacific Nuclear Free Zone Treaty (Treaty of Rarotonga) enters into force.

11–12 December   The NATO Council, meeting in ministerial session in Brussels, welcomes the US proposal at the Reykjavik meeting on a 50 per cent reduction of strategic offensive forces. It also supports the envisaged elimination of INF in Europe and their limitation to 100 warheads in Asia and the USA. The ministers propose East–West discussions on the question of a new mandate for negotiating conventional arms control, covering the whole of Europe from the Atlantic to the Urals. The ministers stress that an INF agreement must not neglect the existing imbalances in shorter-range US and Soviet INF missiles and must provide for negotiations on these missiles.

15 December   The Soviet Union signs Protocols 2 and 3 of the South Pacific Nuclear Free Zone Treaty (Treaty of Rarotonga)—with significant reservations.

15 December   The first annual calendars concerning military activities, in accordance with the final document of the Stockholm Conference, are exchanged.

18 December   In a Soviet Government statement it is announced that the USSR is prepared to continue to abide by its nuclear test moratorium. However, it will resume nuclear testing after the first US nuclear explosion in 1987.

22 December   The US Air Force achieves initial operational capability for the first 10 MX missiles.

29 December   The Japanese Government decides to put forward a military budget for the coming fiscal year which would exceed the 10-year-old limit of 1 per cent for defence costs as a share of the GNP.

Annexe B. Major multilateral arms control agreements

JOZEF GOLDBLAT and RAGNHILD FERM

For the full texts of the arms control agreements, see Goldblat, J., SIPRI, *Agreements for Arms Control: A Critical Survey* (Taylor & Francis: London, 1982).

I. Summaries of the agreements

Protocol for the prohibition of the use in war of asphyxiating, poisonous or other gases, and of bacteriological methods of warfare (Geneva Protocol)

Signed at Geneva on 17 June 1925; entered into force on 8 February 1928.

Declares that the parties agree to be bound by the above prohibition, which should be universally accepted as part of international law, binding alike the conscience and the practice of nations. (Reservations made by a number of states have limited the applicability of the Protocol to nations party to it and to first use only.)

Antarctic Treaty

Signed at Washington on 1 December 1959; entered into force on 23 June 1961.

Declares the Antarctic an area to be used exclusively for peaceful purposes. Prohibits any measure of a military nature in the Antarctic, such as the establishment of military bases and fortifications, and the carrying out of military manoeuvres or the testing of any type of weapon. Bans any nuclear explosion as well as the disposal of radioactive waste material in Antarctica, subject to possible future international agreements on these subjects.

Representatives of the contracting parties hold at regular intervals so-called consultative meetings to exchange information and consult each other on matters of common interest pertaining to Antarctica, as well as to recommend to their governments measures in furtherance of the principles and objectives of the Treaty.

Treaty banning nuclear weapon tests in the atmosphere, in outer space and under water (Partial Test Ban Treaty—PTBT)

Signed at Moscow on 5 August 1963; entered into force on 10 October 1963.

Prohibits the carrying out of any nuclear weapon test explosion or any other nuclear explosion: (*a*) in the atmosphere, beyonds its limits, including outer space, or under water, including territorial waters or high seas; or (*b*) in any other environment if such explosion causes radioactive debris to be present outside the territorial limits of the state under whose jurisdiction or control the explosion is conducted.

Treaty on principles governing the activities of states in the exploration and use of outer space, including the moon and other celestial bodies (Outer Space Treaty)

Signed at London, Moscow and Washington on 27 January 1967; entered into force on 10 October 1967.

Prohibits the placing in orbit around the earth of any objects carrying nuclear weapons or any other kinds of weapons of mass destruction, the installation of such weapons on celestial bodies, or the stationing of them in outer space in any other manner. The establishment of military bases, installations and fortifications, the testing of any type of weapons and the conduct of military manoeuvres on celestial bodies are also forbidden.

Treaty for the prohibition of nuclear weapons in Latin America (Treaty of Tlatelolco)

Signed at Mexico City on 14 February 1967; entered into force on 22 April 1968.

Prohibits the testing, use, manufacture, production or acquisition by any means, as well as the receipt, storage, installation, deployment and any form of possession of any nuclear weapons by Latin American countries.

The parties should conclude agreements with the IAEA for the application of safeguards to their nuclear activities.

Under *Additional Protocol I* the extra-continental or continental states which, *de jure* or *de facto*, are internationally responsible for territories lying within the limits of the geographical zone established by the Treaty (France, the Netherlands, the UK and the USA), undertake to apply the statute of military denuclearization, as defined in the Treaty, to such territories.

Under *Additional Protocol II* the nuclear weapon states undertake to respect the statute of military denuclearization of Latin America, as defined and delimited in the Treaty, and not to contribute to acts involving a violation of the Treaty, nor to use or threaten to use nuclear weapons against the parties to the Treaty.

Treaty on the non-proliferation of nuclear weapons (NPT)

Signed at London, Moscow and Washington on 1 July 1968; entered into force on 5 March 1970.

Prohibits the transfer by nuclear weapon states, to any recipient whatsoever, of nuclear weapons or other nuclear explosive devices or of control over them, as well as the assistance, encouragement or inducement of any non-nuclear weapon state to manufacture or otherwise acquire such weapons or devices. Prohibits the receipt by non-nuclear weapon states from any transferor whatsoever, as well as the manufacture or other acquisition by those states of nuclear weapons or other nuclear explosive devices.

Non-nuclear weapon states undertake to conclude safeguard agreements with the International Atomic Energy Agency (IAEA) with a view to preventing diversion of nuclear energy from peaceful uses to nuclear weapons or other nuclear explosive devices.

The parties undertake to facilitate the exchange of equipment, materials and scientific and technological information for the peaceful uses of nuclear energy and to ensure that potential benefits from peaceful applications of nuclear explosions will be made available to non-nuclear weapon parties to the Treaty. They also undertake to pursue negotiations in good faith on effective measures relating to cessation of the nuclear arms race at an early date and to nuclear disarmament, and on a treaty on general and complete disarmament.

Treaty on the prohibition of the emplacement of nuclear weapons and other weapons of mass destruction on the sea-bed and the ocean floor and in the subsoil thereof (Sea-Bed Treaty)

Signed at London, Moscow and Washington on 11 February 1971; entered into force on 18 May 1972.

Prohibits emplanting or emplacing on the sea-bed and the ocean floor and in the subsoil thereof beyond the outer limit of a sea-bed zone (coterminous with the 12-mile outer limit of the zone referred to in the 1958 Geneva Convention on the Territorial Sea and the Contiguous Zone) any nuclear weapons or any other types of weapons of mass destruction as well as structures, launching installations or any other facilities specifically designed for storing, testing or using such weapons.

Convention on the prohibition of the development, production and stockpiling of bacteriological (biological) and toxin weapons and on their destruction (BW Convention)

Signed at London, Moscow and Washington on 10 April 1972; entered into force on 26 March 1975.

Prohibits the development, production, stockpiling or acquisition by other means or retention of microbial or other biological agents, or toxins whatever their origin or method of production, of types and in quantities that have no justification of prophylactic, protective or other peaceful purposes, as well as weapons, equipment or means of delivery designed to use such agents or toxins for hostile purposes or in armed conflict. The destruction of the agents, toxins, weapons, equipment and means of delivery in the possession of the parties, or their diversion to peaceful purposes, should be effected not later than nine months after the entry into force of the Convention.

Convention on the prohibition of military or any other hostile use of environmental modification techniques (Enmod Convention)

Signed at Geneva on 18 May 1977; entered into force on 5 October 1978.

Prohibits military or any other hostile use of environmental modification techniques having widespread, long-lasting or severe effects as the means of destruction, damage or injury to states party to the Convention. The term 'environmental modification techniques' refers to any technique for changing—through the deliberate manipulation of natural processes—the dynamics, composition or structure of the Earth, including its biota, lithosphere, hydrosphere and atmosphere, or of outer space.

The understandings reached during the negotiations, but not written into the Convention, define the terms 'widespread', 'long-lasting' and 'severe'.

Convention on the prohibitions or restrictions on the use of certain conventional weapons which may be deemed to be excessively injurious or to have indiscriminate effects ('Inhumane Weapons' Convention)

Signed at New York on 10 April 1981; entered into force on 2 December 1983.

The Convention is an 'umbrella treaty', under which specific agreements can be concluded in the form of protocols.

Protocol I prohibits the use of weapons intended to injure by fragments which are not detectable in the human body by X-rays.

Protocol II prohibits or restricts the use of mines, booby-traps and similar devices.

Protocol III prohibits or restricts the use of incendiary weapons.

South Pacific Nuclear Free Zone Treaty (Treaty of Rarotonga)

Signed at Rarotonga, Cook Islands, on 6 August 1985; entered into force on 11 December 1986.

Prohibits the manufacture or acquisition by other means of any nuclear explosive device, as well as possession or control over such device by the parties anywhere inside or outside the zone area described in an annex. The parties also undertake not to supply nuclear material or equipment unless subject to IAEA safeguards; and to prevent in their territories the stationing as well as the testing of any nuclear explosive device. Each party remains free to allow visits, as well as transit, by foreign ships and aircraft.

Under Protocol 1, France, the UK and the USA would undertake to apply the treaty prohibitions relating to the manufacture, stationing and testing of nuclear explosive devices in the territories situated within the zone, for which they are internationally responsible.

Under Protocol 2, China, France, the UK, the USA and the USSR would undertake not to use or threaten to use a nuclear explosive device against the parties to the Treaty or against any territory within the zone for which a party to Protocol 1 is internationally responsible.

Under Protocol 3, China, France, the UK, the USA and the USSR would undertake not to test any nuclear explosive device anywhere within the zone.

II. Status of the implementation of the major multilateral arms control agreements, as of 1 January 1987

Number of parties

1925 Geneva Protocol	111
Antarctic Treaty	33
Partial Test Ban Treaty	116
Outer Space Treaty	89
Treaty of Tlatelolco	23
Additional Protocol I	3
Additional Protocol II	5
Non-Proliferation Treaty	136 ·
NPT safeguards agreements	78
Sea-Bed Treaty	78
BW Convention	107
Enmod Convention	51
'Inhumane Weapons' Convention	25
Treaty of Rarotonga	9

Notes

1. The table records year of ratification, accession and succession.

2. The Partial Test Ban Treaty, the Outer Space Treaty, the Non-Proliferation Treaty, the Sea-Bed Treaty and the Biological Weapons Convention provide for three depositaries—the governments of the UK, the USA and the USSR. The dates given for these agreements are the earliest dates on which countries deposited their instruments of ratification, accession or succession—whether in London, Washington or Moscow. The dates given for the other agreements, for which there is only one depositary, are the dates of the deposit of the instruments of ratification, accession or succession with the depositary in question.

3. Key to abbreviations used in the table:

S: Signature without further action

PI, PII: Additional Protocols to the Treaty of Tlatelolco

P1, P2, P3: Additional Protocols to the Treaty of Rarotonga

CP: Party entitled to participate in the consultative meetings provided for in Article IX of the Antarctic Treaty

SA: Nuclear safeguards agreement in force with the International Atomic Energy Agency as required by the Non-Proliferation Treaty or the Treaty of Tlatelolco, or concluded by a nuclear weapon state on a voluntary basis.

4. The footnotes are listed at the end of the table and are grouped separately under the heading for each agreement. The texts of the statements contained in the footnotes have been abridged, but the wording is close to the original version.

5. A complete list of UN member states and year of membership appears on page 486.

State	Geneva Protocol	Antarctic Treaty	Partial Test Ban Treaty	Outer Space Treaty	Treaty of Tlatelolco	Non-Proliferation Treaty	Sea-Bed Treaty	BW Convention	Enmod Convention	'Inhumane Weapons' Convention	Treaty of Rarotonga
Afghanistan	1986		1964	S		1970 SA	1971	1975	1985	S	
Algeria			S								
Antigua and Barbuda	1969		1986		1983²	1985¹					
Argentina	1969	1961 CP	1963	1969	S¹		1983¹	1979		S	1986
Australia	1930¹	1961 CP	1964	1967		1973 SA	1973	1977	1984	1983	
Austria	1928			1968		1969 SA	1972	1973¹		1983	
Bahamas			1976¹	1976¹	1977²	1976¹		1986			
Bangladesh			1985	1986		1979 SA		1985	1979		
Barbados	1976²			1968	1969²	1980		1973			
Belgium	1928¹	1960 CP	1966	1973		1975 SA	1972	1979	1982	S	

Country										
Belize	1986					1985[1]		1986		
Benin	1986		1964	1986		1972	1986	1975	1986	
Bhutan	1978		1978			1985		1978		
Bolivia	1985		1965	S	1969[2]	1970	S	1975	S	
Botswana			1968[1]	S		1969	1972	S		
Brazil	1970	1975	1964	1969[2]	1968[3]		S[2]	1973	1984	
Brunei Darussalam					1985			1985		
Bulgaria	1934[1]	1978	1963	1967		1969 SA	1971	1972	1978	1982
Burkina Faso (formerly Upper Volta)	1971		S	1968		1970				
Burma			1963	1970			S	S		
Burundi			S	S		1971	S	S		
Byelorussia	1970[3]		1963[3]	1967[3]			1971	1975	1978	1982

State	Geneva Protocol	Antarctic Treaty	Partial Test Ban Treaty	Outer Space Treaty	Treaty of Tlatelolco	Non-Proliferation Treaty	Sea-Bed Treaty	BW Convention	Enmod Convention	'Inhumane Weapons' Convention	Treaty of Rarotonga
Cameroon			S[2]	S		1969	S				
Canada	1930[1]		1964	1967		1969 SA	1972[3]	1972	1981	S	
Cape Verde			1979			1979	1979	1977	1979		
Central African Republic	1970		1964	S		1970	1981	S			
Chad			1965			1971					
Chile	1935[1]	1961 CP	1965	1981	1974[4]			1980			
China	1929[4]	1983 CP		1983	PII: 1974[5]		S	1984[2]		1982[1]	[1]
Colombia			1985	S	1972[2] SA	1986	S	1983			
Congo						1978	1978	1978			
Cook Islands											1985

Costa Rica	1970		1967		1969[2] SA[16]	1970 SA	S	1973		
Côte d'Ivoire	1966		1965			1973 SA	1972	S		
Cuba	1966[2]	1984		1977[4]			1977[4]	1976	1978	S
Cyprus	1966		1965	1972		1970 SA	1971	1973	1978	
Czechoslovakia	1938[5]	1962	1963	1967		1969 SA	1972	1973	1978	1982
Denmark	1930	1965	1964	1967		1969 SA	1971	1973	1978	1982
Dominica						1984[1]				
Dominican Republic	1970		1964	1968	1968[2] SA[16]	1971 SA	1972	1973		
Ecuador	1970		1964	1969	1969[2] SA[16]	1969 SA		1975		1982
Egypt	1928		1964	1967		1981[2] SA		S	1982	S
El Salvador	S		1964	1969	1968[2] SA[16]	1972 SA		S		

State	Geneva Protocol	Antarctic Treaty	Partial Test Ban Treaty	Outer Space Treaty	Treaty of Tlatelolco	Non-Proliferation Treaty	Sea-Bed Treaty	BW Convention	Enmod Convention	'Inhumane Weapons' Convention	Treaty of Rarotonga
Equatorial Guinea						1984	S				
Ethiopia	1935		S	S		1970 SA	1977	1975	S		
Fiji	1973[1,2]		1972[1]	1972[1]		1972[1] SA		1973			1985
Finland	1929	1984	1964	1967		1969 SA	1971	1974	1978	1982	
France	1926[1]	1960 CP		1970	PI: S[6] PII: 1974[7]	SA[3]		1984		S[2]	
Gabon			1964			1974		S			
Gambia	1966[2]		1965[1]	S		1975 SA	S	S			
German Dem. Republic	1929	1974[1]	1963	1967		1969 SA	1971	1972	1978	1982	
FR Germany	1929	1979[2] CP	1964[4]	1971[5]		1975[4] SA	1975[5]	1983[3]	1983[1]	S	
Ghana	1967		1963	S		1970 SA	1972	1975	1978		

Country										
Greece	1931		1963	1971		1970 SA	1985	1975	1983	S
Grenada					1975[2]	1975[1]		1986		
Guatemala	1983		1964[2]		1970[2] SA[16]	1970 SA	S	1973		1983
Guinea						1985	S			
Guinea-Bissau			1976	1976		1976	1976	1976		
Guyana				S				S		
Haiti			S	S	1969[2]	1970		S		
Holy See (Vatican City)	1966			S		1971[5] SA			S	
Honduras			1964	S	1968[2] SA[16]	1973 SA	S	1979		
Hungary	1952	1984	1963	1967		1969 SA	1971	1972	1978	1982
Iceland	1967		1964	1968		1969 SA	1972	1973	S	S
India	1930[1]	1983 CP	1963	1982			1973[6]	1974[4]	1978	1984

State	Geneva Protocol	Antarctic Treaty	Partial Test Ban Treaty	Outer Space Treaty	Treaty of Tlatelolco	Non-Proliferation Treaty	Sea-Bed Treaty	BW Convention	Enmod Convention	'Inhumane Weapons' Convention	Treaty of Rarotonga
Indonesia	1971[2]		1964	S		1979[6] SA		S			
Iran	1929		1964	S		1970 SA	1971	1973	S		
Iraq	1931[1]		1964	1968		1969 SA	1972[4]	S	S		
Ireland	1930[6]		1963	1968		1968 SA	1971	1972[5]	1982	S	
Israel	1969[7]		1964	1977							
Italy	1928	1981	1964	1972		1975[7] SA	1974[7]	1975	1981	S[3]	
Jamaica	1970[2]		S	1970	1969[2] SA[16]	1970 SA	1986	1975			
Japan	1970	1960 CP	1964	1967		1976[8] SA	1971	1982	1982	1982	
Jordan	1977[8]		1964	S		1970 SA	1971	1975			

Kampuchea	1983[9]			1972	S	1983		
Kenya	1970	1965	1984	1970		1976		
Kiribati				1985[1]				S	1986
Korea, Democratic People's Republic	1986			1985			1984	
Korea, Republic of		1964[2]	1967[4]	1975[9,10] SA	S[4]	S[6]	1986[2]	
Kuwait	1971[10]	1965[5]	1972[6]	S	1971	1972[7]		1980[3]
Lao People's Dem. Republic		1965	1972	1970	1971	1973	1978	1983
Lebanon	1969	1965	1969	1970 SA	S	1975	S	S
Lesotho	1972[2]		S	1970 SA	1973	1977	S	
Liberia	1927	1964		1970	S		S	
Libya	1971[11]	1968	1968	1975 SA		1982	S	S
Liechtenstein				1978[11] SA				S

State	Geneva Protocol	Antarctic Treaty	Partial Test Ban Treaty	Outer Space Treaty	Treaty of Tlatelolco	Non-Proliferation Treaty	Sea-Bed Treaty	BW Convention	Enmod Convention	'Inhumane Weapons' Convention	Treaty of Rarotonga
Luxembourg	1936		1965	S		1975 SA	1982	1976	S	S	
Madagascar	1967		1965	1968[7]		1970 SA	S	S			
Malawi	1970		1964[1]			1986	1972	S	1978		
Malaysia	1970		1964	S		1970 SA	1972	S			
Maldives	1966[2]					1970 SA					
Mali			S	1968		1970	S	S			
Malta	1970[2]		1964[1]			1970	1971	1975			
Mauritania			1964								
Mauritius	1970[2]		1969[1]	1969[1]		1969 SA	1971	1972			
Mexico	1932		1963	1968	1967[2,8] SA	1969[12] SA	1984[8]	1974[8]		1982	

Monaco	1967									
Mongolia	1968[12]		1963	1967		1969 SA	1971	1972	1978	1982	
Morocco	1970		1966	1967		1970 SA	1971	S	S	S	
Nauru						1982 SA					1986
Nepal	1969		1964	1967		1970 SA	1971	S			
Netherlands	1930[13]	1967	1964	1969	PI: 1971[9]	1975 SA	1976	1981	1983[3]	S	
New Zealand	1930[1]	1960 CP	1963	1968		1969 SA	1972	1972	1984[4]	S	1986
Nicaragua	S		1965	S	1968[2,10] SA[16]	1973 SA	1973	1975	S	S	
Niger	1967[2]		1964	1967			1971	1972			
Nigeria	1968[1]		1967	1967		1968		1973		S	
Niue											1986

State	Geneva Protocol	Antarctic Treaty	Partial Test Ban Treaty	Outer Space Treaty	Treaty of Tlatelolco	Non-Proliferation Treaty	Sea-Bed Treaty	BW Convention	Enmod Convention	'Inhumane Weapons' Convention	Treaty of Rarotonga
Norway	1932	1960 CP	1963	1969		1969 SA	1971	1973	1979	1983	
Pakistan	1960[2]		S	1968				1974	1986	1985	
Panama	1970		1966	S	1971[2] SA	1977	1974	1974			
Papua New Guinea	1981[1]	1981	1980[1]	1980[1]		1982 SA		1980	1980		S
Paraguay	1933[4]		S		1969[2] SA[16]	1970 SA	S	1976			
Peru	1985	1981	1964	1979	1969[2] SA	1970 SA		1985			
Philippines	1973		1965[2]	S		1972 SA		1973		S	
Poland	1929	1961 CP	1963	1968		1969 SA	1971	1973	1978	1983	
Portugal	1930[1]		S			1977 SA	1975	1975	S	S	
Qatar	1976						1974	1975			

Romania	1929[1]	1971[3]	1963	1968		1970 SA	1972	1979	1983	S[4]	
Rwanda	1964[2]		1963	S		1975	1975	1975			
Saint Lucia						1979[1]					
Saint Vincent and the Grenadines						1984[1]					
Samoa, Western			1965			1975 SA					1986
San Marino			1964	1968		1970[9]		1975			
Sao Tome and Principe						1983	1979	1979	1979		
Saudi Arabia	1971			1976			1972	1972			
Senegal	1977		1964			1970 SA	S	1975			
Seychelles			1985	1978		1985	1985	1979			
Sierra Leone	1967		1964	1967		1975	S	1976	S	S	
Singapore			1968[1]	1976		1976 SA	1976	1975			

State	Geneva Protocol	Antarctic Treaty	Partial Test Ban Treaty	Outer Space Treaty	Treaty of Tlatelolco	Non-Proliferation Treaty	Sea-Bed Treaty	BW Convention	Enmod Convention	'Inhumane Weapons' Convention	Treaty of Rarotonga
Solomon Islands						1981[1]	1981[13]	1981[9]	1981[6]		
Somalia			S	S		1970		S			
South Africa	1930[1]	1960 CP	1963	1968			1973	1975			
Spain	1929[15]	1982	1964	1968				1979	1978	S	
Sri Lanka	1954		1964	1986		1979 SA		1986	1978		
Sudan	1980		1966			1973 SA	S			S	
Suriname					1977[2] SA[16]	1976[1] SA					
Swaziland			1969			1969 SA	1971				
Sweden	1930	1984	1963	1967		1970 SA	1972	1976	1984	1982	
Switzerland	1932		1964	1969		1977[11] SA	1976	1976[10]		1982	

Syria	1968[16]		1964	1968[8]		1969[9]		s	S	S	
Taiwan	17		1964	1970[9]		1970	1972[9]	1973[11]			
Tanzania	1963		1964				S	S			
Thailand	1931		1963	1968		1972 SA		1975			
Togo	1971		1964	S		1970	1971	1976		S	
Tonga	1971		1971[1]	1971[1]		1971[1]		1976			
Trinidad and Tobago	1970[2]		1964	S	1970[2]	1986					
Tunisia	1967		1965	1968		1970	1971	1973	1978		
Turkey	1929		1965	1968		1980[13] SA	1972	1974	S[7]	S	
Tuvalu						1979[1]					1986
Uganda	1965		1964	1968		1982			S		
UK	1930[1]	1960 CP	1963[6]	1967	PI: 1969[11] PII: 1969[11]	1968[14] SA[15]	1972[10]	1975[12]	1978		
Ukraine	1963[3]		1963[3]	1967[3]			1971	1975	1978	1982	

State	Geneva Protocol	Antarctic Treaty	Partial Test Ban Treaty	Outer Space Treaty	Treaty of Tlatelolco	Non-Proliferation Treaty	Sea-Bed Treaty	BW Convention	Enmod Convention	'Inhumane Weapons' Convention	Treaty of Rarotonga
United Arab Emirates								S			
Uruguay	1977	1980[4]	1969	1970	1968[2] SA[16]	1970 SA	S	1981			
USA	1975[18]	1960 CP	1963	1967	PI: 1981[12] PII: 1971[13]	1970 SA[16]	1972	1975	1980	S[5]	
USSR	1928[19]	1960 CP	1963	1967	PII: 1979[14]	1970 SA[17]	1972	1975	1978	1982	P2: S[2] P3: S[2]
Venezuela	1928		1965	1970	1970[2,15] SA[16]	1975 SA		1978			
Viet Nam	1980[1]			1980		1982	1980[11]	1980	1980	S	
Yemen Arab Republic	1971		S			1986	S	S	1977		
Yemen, People's Dem. Republic of	1986[20]		1979	1979		1979	1979	1979	1979		
Yugoslavia	1929[21]		1964	S		1970[18] SA	1973[12]	1973		1983	
Zaire			1965	S		1970 SA		1977	S		
Zambia			1965[1]	1973			1972				

The 1925 Geneva Protocol

[1] The Protocol is binding on this state only as regards states which have signed and ratified or acceded to it. The Protocol will cease to be binding on this state in regard to any enemy state whose armed forces or whose allies fail to respect the prohibitions laid down in it.

Australia withdrew its reservation in 1986.

[2] Notification of succession. (In notifying its succession to the obligations contracted in 1930 by the United Kingdom, *Barbados* stated that as far as it was concerned the reservation made by the UK was to be considered as withdrawn.)

[3] In a note of 2 Mar. 1970, submitted at the United Nations, Byelorussia stated that 'it recognizes itself to be a party' to the Protocol.

[4] On 13 July 1952 the People's Republic of China issued a statement recognizing as binding upon it the 1929 accession to the Protocol in the name of China. China considers itself bound by the Protocol on condition of reciprocity on the part of all the other contracting and acceding powers.

[5] Czechoslovakia shall cease to be bound by this Protocol towards any state whose armed forces, or the armed forces of whose allies, fail to respect the prohibitions laid down in the Protocol.

[6] The government of Ireland does not intend to assume, by this accession, any obligation except towards the states having signed and ratified this Protocol or which shall have finally acceded thereto, and should the armed forces or the allies of an enemy state fail to respect the Protocol, the government of Ireland would cease to be bound by the said Protocol in regard to such state. In Feb. 1972, Ireland declared that it had decided to withdraw the above reservations made at the time of accession to the Protocol.

[7] The Protocol is binding on Israel only as regards states which have signed and ratified or acceded to it. The Protocol shall cease to be binding on Israel as regards any enemy state whose armed forces, or the armed forces of whose allies, or the regular or irregular forces, or groups or individuals operating from its territory, fail to respect the prohibitions which are the object of the Protocol.

[8] The accession by Jordan to the Protocol does not in any way imply recognition of Israel. Jordan undertakes to respect the obligations contained in the Protocol with regard to states which have undertaken similar commitments. It is not bound by the Protocol as regards states whose armed forces, regular or irregular, do not respect the provisions of the Protocol.

[9] The accession was made on behalf of the coalition government of Democratic Kampuchea (the government in exile), with a statement that the Protocol will cease to be binding on it in regard to any enemy state whose armed forces or whose allies fail to respect the prohibitions laid down in the Protocol. The French Government declared that as a party to the Geneva Protocol (but not as the depositary) it considers this accession to have no effect. A similar statement was made by the governments of Australia, Bulgaria, Cuba, Czechoslovakia, GDR, Hungary, Mauritius, Netherlands, Poland, Romania, USSR and Viet Nam, which do not recognize the coalition government of Kampuchea.

[10] The accession of Kuwait to the Protocol does not in any way imply recognition of Israel or the establishment of relations with the latter on the basis of the present Protocol. In case of breach of the prohibition laid down in this Protocol by any of the parties, Kuwait will not be bound, with regard to the party committing the breach, to apply the provisions of this Protocol.

[11] The accession to the Protocol does not imply recognition of Israel. The Protocol is binding on Libya only as regards states which are effectively bound by it and will cease to be binding on Libya as regards states whose armed forces, or the armed forces of whose allies, fail to respect the prohibitions which are the object of this Protocol.

[12] In the case of violation of this prohibition by any state in relation to Mongolia or its allies, the government of Mongolia shall not consider itself bound by the obligations of the Protocol towards that state.

[13] As regards the use in war of asphyxiating, poisonous or other gases and of all analogous liquids, materials or devices, this Protocol shall cease to be binding on the Netherlands with regard to any enemy state whose armed forces or whose allies fail to respect the prohibitions laid down in the Protocol.

[14] This is the date of receipt of Paraguay's instrument of accession. The date of the notification by the depositary government 'for the purpose of regularization' is 1969.

[15] Spain declared the Protocol as binding *ipso facto*, without special agreement with respect to any other member or state accepting and observing the same obligation, that is, on condition of reciprocity.

[16] The accession by Syria to the Protocol does not in any case imply recognition of Israel or lead to the establishment of relations with the latter concerning the provisions laid down in the Protocol.

[17] The Protocol, signed in 1929 in the name of China, is taken to be valid for Taiwan which is part of China. However, unlike the People's Republic of China, Taiwan has not reconfirmed its accession to the Protocol.

[18] The Protocol shall cease to be binding on the USA with respect to the use in war of asphyxiating, poisonous or other gases, and of all analogous liquids, materials, or devices, in regard to an enemy state if such state or any of its allies fail to respect the prohibitions laid down in the Protocol.

[19] The Protocol only binds the USSR in relation to the states which have signed and ratified or which have definitely acceded to the Protocol. The Protocol shall cease to be binding on the USSR in regard to any enemy state whose armed forces or whose allies *de jure* or in fact do not respect the prohibitions which are the object of this Protocol.

[20] In case any party fails to observe the prohibition under the Protocol, the People's Democratic Republic of Yemen will consider itself free of its obligation.

[21] The Protocol shall cease to be binding on Yugoslavia in regard to any enemy state whose armed forces or whose allies fail to respect the prohibitions which are the object of the Protocol.

The Antarctic Treaty

[1] The German Democratic Republic stated that in its view Article XIII, paragraph 1 of the Treaty was inconsistent with the principle that all states whose policies are guided by the purposes and principles of the UN Charter have a right to become parties to treaties which affect the interests of all states.

[2] The Federal Republic of Germany stated that the Treaty applies also to Berlin (West).

[3] Romania stated that the provisions of Article XIII, paragraph 1 of the Treaty were not in accordance with the principle according to which multilateral treaties whose object and purposes concern the international community, as a whole, should be open for universal participation.

[4] In acceding to the Treaty, Uruguay proposed the establishment of a general and definitive statute on Antarctica in which the interests of all states involved and of the international community as a whole would be considered equitably. It also declared that it reserved its rights in Antarctica in accordance with international law.

The Partial Test Ban Treaty

[1] Notification of succession.

[2] With a statement that this does not imply the recognition of any territory or regime not recognized by this state.

[3] The United States considers that Byelorussia and Ukraine are already covered by the signature and ratification by the Soviet Union.

[4] The Federal Republic of Germany stated that the Treaty applies also to Berlin (West).

[5] Kuwait stated that its signature and ratification of the Treaty do not in any way imply its recognition of Israel nor oblige it to apply the provisions of the Treaty in respect of the said country.

[6] The United Kingdom stated its view that if a regime is not recognized as the government of a state, neither signature nor the deposit of any instrument by it, nor notification of any of those acts, will bring about recognition of that regime by any other state.

The Outer Space Treaty

[1] Notification of succession.

[2] The Brazilian Government interprets Article X of the Treaty as a specific recognition that the granting of tracking facilities by the parties to the Treaty shall be subject to agreement between the states concerned.

[3] The United States considers that Byelorussia and Ukraine are already covered by the signature and ratification by the Soviet Union.

[4] With a statement that this does not imply the recognition of any territory or regime not recognized by this state.

[5] The Federal Republic of Germany stated that the Treaty applies also to Berlin (West).

[6] Kuwait acceded to the Treaty with the understanding that this does not in any way imply its recognition of Israel and does not oblige it to apply the provisions of the Treaty in respect of the said country.

[7] Madagascar acceded to the Treaty with the understanding that under Article X of the Treaty the state shall retain its freedom of decision with respect to the possible installation of foreign observation bases in its territory and shall continue to possess the right to fix, in each case, the conditions for such installation.

[8] Syria acceded to the Treaty with the understanding that this should not mean in any way the recognition of Israel, nor should it lead to any relationship with Israel that could arise from the Treaty.

[9] The People's Republic of China declared as illegal and null and void the signature and ratification of the Outer Space Treaty by the Taiwan authorities.

The Treaty of Tlatelolco

[1] On signing the Treaty, Argentina stated that it understands Article 18 as recognizing the rights of parties to carry out, by their own means or in association with third parties, explosions of nuclear devices for peaceful purposes, including explosions which involve devices similar to those used in nuclear weapons.

[2] The Treaty is in force for this country due to a declaration, annexed to the instrument of ratification in accordance with Article 28, paragraph 2, which waived the requirements for the entry into force of the Treaty, specified in paragraph 1 of that Article: namely, that all states in the region deposit the instruments of ratification; that Protocol I and Protocol II be signed and ratified by those states to which they apply; and that agreements on safeguards be concluded with the IAEA. (Colombia made this declaration subsequent to the deposit of ratification, as did Nicaragua and Trinidad and Tobago.)

[3] On signing the Treaty, Brazil stated that, according to its interpretation, Article 18 of the Treaty gives the signatories the right to carry out, by their own means or in association with third parties, nuclear explosions for peaceful purposes, including explosions which involve devices similar to those used in nuclear weapons. This statement was reiterated at the ratification. Brazil also stated that it did not waive the requirements for the entry into force of the Treaty laid down in Article 28. The Treaty is therefore not yet in force for Brazil.

[4] Chile has not waived the requirements for the entry into force of the Treaty laid down in Article 28. The Treaty is therefore not yet in force for Chile.

[5] On signing Protocol II, China stated, *inter alia*: China will never use or threaten to use nuclear weapons against non-nuclear Latin American countries and the Latin American nuclear weapon-free zone; nor will China test, manufacture, produce, stockpile, install or deploy nuclear weapons in these countries or in this zone, or send its means of transportation and delivery carrying nuclear weapons to cross the territory, territorial sea or airspace

of Latin American countries. The signing of the Protocol does not imply any change whatsoever in China's stand on the disarmament and nuclear weapons issue and, in particular, does not affect the Chinese Government's stand against the Non-Proliferation Treaty and the Partial Test Ban Treaty.

The Chinese Government holds that, in order that Latin America may truly become a nuclear weapon-free zone, all nuclear countries, and particularly the superpowers, must undertake not to use or threaten to use nuclear weapons against the Latin American countries and the Latin American nuclear weapon-free zone, and implement the following undertakings: (1) dismantle all foreign military bases in Latin America and refrain from establishing new bases there, and (2) prohibit the passage of any means of transportation and delivery carrying nuclear weapons through Latin American territory, territorial sea or airspace.

[6] On signing Protocol I, France made the following reservations and interpretative statements: the Protocol, as well as the provisions of the Treaty to which it refers, will not affect the right of self-defence under Article 51 of the UN Charter; the application of the legislation referred to in Article 3 of the Treaty relates to legislation which is consistent with international law; the obligations under the Protocol shall not apply to transit across the territories of the French Republic situated in the zone of the Treaty, and destined to other territories of the French Republic; the Protocol shall not limit, in any way, the participation of the populations of the French territories in the activities mentioned in Article 1 of the Treaty, and in efforts connected with the national defence of France; the provisions of Articles 1 and 2 of the Protocol apply to the text of the Treaty as it stands at the time when the Protocol is signed by France, and consequently no amendment to the Treaty that might come into force under Article 29 thereof would be binding on the government of France without the latter's express consent.

[7] On signing Protocol II, France stated that it interprets the undertaking contained in Article 3 of the Protocol to mean that it presents no obstacle to the full exercise of the right of self-defence enshrined in Article 51 of the United Nations Charter; it takes note of the interpretation of the Treaty given by the Preparatory Commission for the Denuclearization of Latin America and reproduced in the Final Act, according to which the Treaty does not apply to transit, the granting or denying of which lies within the exclusive competence of each state party in accordance with the pertinent principles and rules of international law; it considers that the application of the legislation referred to in Article 3 of the Treaty relates to legislation which is consistent with international law. The provisions of Articles 1 and 2 of the Protocol apply to the text of the Treaty as it stands at the time when the Protocol is signed by France. Consequently, no amendment to the Treaty that might come into force under the provision of Article 29 would be binding on the government of France without the latter's express consent. If this declaration of interpretation is contested in part or in whole by one or more contracting parties to the Treaty or to Protocol II, these instruments would be null and void as far as relations between the French Republic and the contesting state or states are concerned. On depositing its instrument of ratification of Protocol II, France stated that it did so subject to the statement made on signing the Protocol. On 15 Apr. 1974, France made a supplementary statement to the effect that it was prepared to consider its obligations under Protocol II as applying not only to the signatories of the Treaty, but also to the territories for which the statute of denuclearization was in force in conformity with Article 1 of Protocol I.

[8] On signing the Treaty, Mexico said that if technological progress makes it possible to differentiate between nuclear weapons and nuclear devices for peaceful purposes, it will be necessary to amend the relevant provisions of the Treaty, according to the procedures established therein.

[9] The Netherlands stated that Protocol I shall not be interpreted as prejudicing the position of the Netherlands as regards its recognition or non-recognition of the rights or of claims to sovereignty of the parties to the Treaty, or of the grounds on which such claims are made.

[10] Nicaragua stated that it reserved the right to use nuclear energy for peaceful purposes such as the removal of earth for the construction of canals, irrigation works, power plants, and so on, as well as to allow the transit of atomic material through its territory.

[11] When signing and ratifying Protocol I and Protocol II, the United Kingdom made the following declarations of understanding:

In connection with Article 3 of the Treaty, defining the term 'territory' as including the territorial sea, airspace and any other space over which the state exercises sovereignty in accordance with 'its own legislation', the UK does not regard its signing or ratification of the Protocols as implying recognition of any legislation which does not, in its view, comply with the relevant rules of international law.

The Treaty does not permit the parties to carry out explosions of nuclear devices for peaceful purposes unless and until advances in technology have made possible the development of devices for such explosions which are not capable of being used for weapon purposes.

The signing and ratification by the UK could not be regarded as affecting in any way the legal status of any territory for the international relations of which the UK is responsible, lying within the limits of the geographical zone established by the Treaty.

Should a party to the Treaty carry out any act of aggression with the support of a nuclear weapon state, the UK would be free to reconsider the extent to which it could be regarded as committed by the provisions of Protocol II.

In addition, the UK declared that its undertaking under Article 3 of Protocol II not to use or threaten to use nuclear weapons against the parties to the Treaty extends also to territories in respect of which the undertaking under Article I of Protocol I becomes effective.

[12] The United States ratified Protocol I with the following understandings: The provisions of the Treaty made applicable by this Protocol do not affect the exclusive power and legal competence under international law of a state adhering to this Protocol to grant or deny transit and transport privileges to its own or any other vessels or aircraft irrespective of cargo or armaments; the provisions of the Treaty made applicable by this Protocol do not affect rights under international law of a state adhering to this Protocol regarding the exercise of the freedom of the seas, or regarding passage through or over waters subject to the sovereignty of a state, and the declarations attached by the United States to its ratification of Protocol II apply also to its ratification of Protocol I.

[13] The United States signed and ratified Protocol II with the following declarations and understandings:

In connection with Article 3 of the Treaty, defining the term 'territory' as including the territorial sea, airspace and any other space over which the state exercises sovereignty in accordance with 'its own legislation', the ratification of the Protocol could not be regarded as implying recognition of any legislation which does not, in the view of the USA, comply with the relevant rules of international law.

Each of the parties retains exclusive power and legal competence, unaffected by the terms of the Treaty, to grant or deny non-parties transit and transport privileges.

As regards the undertaking not to use or threaten to use nuclear weapons against the parties, the United States would consider that an armed attack by a party, in which it was assisted by a nuclear weapon state, would be incompatible with the party's obligations under Article 1 of the Treaty.

The definition contained in Article 5 of the Treaty is understood as encompassing all nuclear explosive devices; Articles 1 and 5 of the Treaty restrict accordingly the activities of the parties under paragraph 1 of Article 18.

Article 18, paragraph 4 permits, and US adherence to Protocol II will not prevent, collaboration by the USA with the parties to the Treaty for the purpose of carrying out explosions of nuclear devices for peaceful purposes in a manner consistent with a policy of not contributing to the proliferation of nuclear weapon capabilities.

The United States will act with respect to such territories of Protocol I adherents, as are within the geographical area defined in Article 4, paragraph 2 of the Treaty, in the same manner as Protocol II requires it to act with respect to the territories of the parties.

[14] The Soviet Union signed and ratified Protocol II with the following statement:

The Soviet Union proceeds from the assumption that the effect of Article 1 of the Treaty extends, as specified in Article 5 of the Treaty, to any nuclear explosive device and that, accordingly, the carrying out by any party to the Treaty of explosions of nuclear devices for peaceful purposes would be a violation of its obligations under Article 1 and would be incompatible with its non-nuclear status. For states parties to the Treaty, a solution to the problem of peaceful nuclear explosions can be found in accordance with the provisions of Article V of the Non-Proliferation Treaty and within the framework of the international procedures of the IAEA. The signing of the Protocol by the Soviet Union does not in any way signify recognition of the possibility of the force of the Treaty being extended beyond the territories of the states parties to the Treaty, including airspace and territorial waters as defined in accordance with international law. With regard to the reference in Article 3 of the Treaty to 'its own legislation' in connection with the territorial waters, airspace and any other space over which the states parties to the Treaty exercise sovereignty, the signing of the Protocol by the Soviet Union does not signify recognition of their claims to the exercise of sovereignty which are contrary to generally accepted standards of international law. The Soviet Union takes note of the interpretation of the Treaty given in the Final Act of the Preparatory Commission for the Denuclearization of Latin America to the effect that the transport of nuclear weapons by the parties to the Treaty is covered by the prohibitions in Article 1 of the Treaty. The Soviet Union reaffirms its position that authorizing the transit of nuclear weapons in any form would be contrary to the objectives of the Treaty, according to which, as specially mentioned in the preamble, Latin America must be completely free from nuclear weapons, and that it would be incompatible with the non-nuclear status of the states parties to the Treaty and with their obligations as laid down in Article 1 thereof.

Any actions undertaken by a state or states parties to the Treaty which are not compatible with their non-nuclear status, and also the commission by one or more states parties to the Treaty of an act of aggression with the support of a state which is in possession of nuclear weapons or together with such a state, will be regarded by the Soviet Union as incompatible with the obligations of those countries under the Treaty. In such cases the Soviet Union reserves the right to reconsider its obligations under Protocol II. It further reserves the right to reconsider its attitude to this Protocol in the event of any actions on the part of other states possessing nuclear weapons which are incompatible with their obligations under the said Protocol. The provisions of the articles of Protocol II are applicable to the text of the Treaty for the Prohibition of Nuclear Weapons in Latin America in the wording of the Treaty at the time of the signing of the Protocol by the Soviet Union, due account being taken of the position of the Soviet Union as set out in the present statement. Any amendment to the Treaty entering into force in accordance with the provisions of Articles 29 and 6 of the Treaty without the clearly expressed approval of the Soviet Union shall have no force as far as the Soviet Union is concerned.

In addition, the Soviet Union proceeds from the assumption that the obligations under Protocol II also apply to the territories for which the status of the denuclearized zone is in force in conformity with Protocol I of the Treaty.

[15] Venezuela stated that in view of the existing controversy between Venezuela on the one hand and the United Kingdom and Guyana on the other, Article 25, paragraph 2 of the Treaty should apply to Guyana. This paragraph provides that no political entity should be admitted, part or all of whose territory is the subject of a dispute or claim between an extra-continental country and one or more Latin American states, so long as the dispute has not been settled by peaceful means.

[16] Safeguards under the Non-Proliferation Treaty cover the Treaty of Tlatelolco.

The Non-Proliferation Treaty

[1] Notification of succession.

[2] On the occasion of the deposit of the instrument of ratification, Egypt stated that since it was embarking on the construction of nuclear power reactors, it expected assistance and support from industrialized nations with a developed nuclear industry. It called upon nuclear weapon states to promote research and development of peaceful applications of nuclear explosions in order to overcome all the difficulties at present involved therein. Egypt also appealed to these states to exert their efforts to conclude an agreement prohibiting the use or threat of use of nuclear weapons against any state, and expressed the view that the Middle East should remain completely free of nuclear weapons.

[3] France, not party to the Treaty, declared that it would behave like a state adhering to the Treaty and that it would follow a policy of strengthening appropriate safeguards relating to nuclear equipment, material and

technology. On 12 Sep. 1981 an agreement between France, the European Atomic Energy Community (Euratom) and the IAEA for the application of safeguards in France entered into force. The agreement covers nuclear material and facilities notified to the IAEA by France.

[4] On depositing the instrument of ratification, the Federal Republic of Germany reiterated the declaration made at the time of signing: it reaffirmed its expectation that the nuclear weapon states would intensify their efforts in accordance with the undertakings under Article VI of the Treaty, as well as its understanding that the security of FR Germany continued to be ensured by NATO; it stated that no provision of the Treaty may be interpreted in such a way as to hamper further development of European unification; that research, development and use of nuclear energy for peaceful purposes, as well as international and multinational co-operation in this field, must not be prejudiced by the Treaty; that the application of the Treaty, including the implementation of safeguards, must not lead to discrimination of the nuclear industry of FR Germany in international competition; and that it attached vital importance to the undertaking given by the United States and the United Kingdom concerning the application of safeguards to their peaceful nuclear facilities, hoping that other nuclear weapon states would assume similar obligations.

In a separate note, FR Germany declared that the Treaty will also apply to Berlin (West) without affecting Allied rights and responsibilities, including those relating to demilitarization. In notes of 24 July, 19 Aug. and 25 Nov. 1975, respectively, addressed to the US Department of State, Czechoslovakia, the Soviet Union and the German Democratic Republic stated that this declaration by FR Germany had no legal effect.

[5] On acceding to the Treaty, the Holy See stated, *inter alia*, that the Treaty will attain in full the objectives of security and peace and justify the limitations to which the states party to the Treaty submit, only if it is fully executed in every clause and with all its implications. This concerns not only the obligations to be applied immediately but also those which envisage a process of ulterior commitments. Among the latter, the Holy See considers it suitable to point out the following:

(a) The adoption of appropriate measures to ensure, on a basis of equality, that all non-nuclear weapon states party to the Treaty will have available to them the benefits deriving from peaceful applications of nuclear technology.

(b) The pursuit of negotiations in good faith of effective measures relating to cessation of the nuclear arms race at an early date and to nuclear disarmament, and on a treaty on general and complete disarmament under strict and effective control.

[6] On signing the Treaty, Indonesia stated, *inter alia*, that the government of Indonesia attaches great importance to the declarations of the United States, the United Kingdom and the Soviet Union affirming their intention to provide immediate assistance to any non-nuclear weapon state party to the Treaty that is a victim of an act of aggression in which nuclear weapons are used. Of utmost importance, however, is not the action *after* a nuclear attack has been committed but the guarantees to prevent such an attack. The Indonesian Government trusts that the nuclear weapon states will study further this question of effective measures to ensure the security of the non-nuclear weapon states. On depositing the instrument of ratification, Indonesia expressed the hope that the nuclear countries would be prepared to co-operate with non-nuclear countries in the use of nuclear energy for peaceful purposes and implement the provisions of Article IV of the Treaty without discrimination. It also stated the view that the nuclear weapon states should observe the provisions of Article VI of the Treaty relating to the cessation of the nuclear arms race.

[7] Italy stated that in its belief nothing in the Treaty was an obstacle to the unification of the countries of Western Europe; it noted full compatibility of the Treaty with the existing security agreements; it noted further that when technological progress would allow the development of peaceful explosive devices different from nuclear weapons, the prohibition relating to their manufacture and use shall no longer apply; it interpreted the provisions of Article IX, paragraph 3 of the Treaty, concerning the definition of a nuclear weapon state, in the sense that it referred exclusively to the five countries which had manufactured and exploded a nuclear weapon or other nuclear explosive device prior to 1 Jan. 1967, and stressed that under no circumstance would a claim of pertaining to such category be recognized by the Italian Government for any other state.

[8] On depositing the instrument of ratification, Japan expressed the hope that France and China would accede to the Treaty; it urged a reduction of nuclear armaments and a comprehensive ban on nuclear testing; appealed to all states to refrain from the threat or use of force involving either nuclear or non-nuclear weapons; expressed the view that peaceful nuclear activities in non-nuclear weapon states party to the Treaty should not be hampered and that Japan should not be discriminated against in favour of other parties in any aspect of such activities. It also urged all nuclear weapon states to accept IAEA safeguards on their peaceful nuclear activities.

[9] A statement was made containing a disclaimer regarding the recognition of states party to the Treaty.

[10] On depositing the instrument of ratification, the Republic of Korea took note of the fact that the depositary governments of the three nuclear weapon states had made declarations in June 1968 to take immediate and effective measures to safeguard any non-nuclear weapon state which is a victim of an act or an object of a threat of aggression in which nuclear weapons are used. It recalled that the UN Security Council adopted a resolution to the same effect on 19 June 1968.

[11] On depositing the instruments of accession and ratification, Liechtenstein and Switzerland stated that activities not prohibited under Articles I and II of the Treaty include, in particular, the whole field of energy production and related operations, research and technology concerning future generations of nuclear reactors based on fission or fusion, as well as production of isotopes. Liechtenstein and Switzerland define the term 'source or special fissionable material' in Article III of the Treaty as being in accordance with Article XX of the IAEA Statute, and a modification of this interpretation requires their formal consent; they will accept only such interpretations and definitions of the terms 'equipment or material especially designed or prepared for the processing, use or production of special fissionable material', as mentioned in Article III of the Treaty, that they will expressly approve; and they understand that the application of the Treaty, especially of the control measures, will not lead to discrimination of their industry in international competition.

[12] On signing the Treaty, Mexico stated, *inter alia*, that none of the provisions of the Treaty shall be interpreted as affecting in any way whatsoever the rights and obligations of Mexico as a state party to the Treaty of Tlatelolco.

It is the understanding of Mexico that at the present time any nuclear explosive device is capable of being used as a nuclear weapon and that there is no indication that in the near future it will be possible to manufacture nuclear explosive devices that are not potentially nuclear weapons. However, if technological advances modify this situation, it will be necessary to amend the relevant provisions of the Treaty in accordance with the procedure established therein.

[13] The ratification was accompanied by a statement in which Turkey underlined the non-proliferation obligations of the nuclear weapon states, adding that measures must be taken to meet adequately the security requirements of non-nuclear weapon states. Turkey also stated that measures developed or to be developed at national and international levels to ensure the non-proliferation of nuclear weapons should in no case restrict the non-nuclear weapon states in their option for the application of nuclear energy for peaceful purposes.

[14] The United Kingdom recalled its view that if a regime is not recognized as the government of a state, neither signature nor the deposit of any instrument by it, nor notification of any of those acts, will bring about recognition of that regime by any other state.

[15] This agreement, signed by the United Kingdom, Euratom and the IAEA, provides for the submission of British non-military nuclear installations to safeguards under IAEA supervision.

[16] This agreement provides for safeguards on fissionable material in all facilities within the USA, excluding those associated with activities of direct national security significance.

[17] The agreement provides for the application of IAEA safeguards in Soviet peaceful nuclear facilities designated by the Soviet Union.

[18] In connection with the ratification of the Treaty, Yugoslavia stated, *inter alia*, that it considered a ban on the development, manufacture and use of nuclear weapons and the destruction of all stockpiles of these weapons to be indispensable for the maintenance of a stable peace and international security; it held the view that the chief responsibility for progress in this direction rested with the nuclear weapon powers, and expected these powers to undertake not to use nuclear weapons against the countries which have renounced them as well as against non-nuclear weapon states in general, and to refrain from the threat to use them. It also emphasized the significance it attached to the universality of the efforts relating to the realization of the Non-Proliferation Treaty.

The Sea-Bed Treaty

[1] On signing and ratifying the Treaty, Argentina stated that it interprets the references to the freedom of the high seas as in no way implying a pronouncement of judgement on the different positions relating to questions connected with international maritime law. It understands that the reference to the rights of exploration and exploitation by coastal states over their continental shelves was included solely because those could be the rights most frequently affected by verification procedures. Argentina precludes any possibility of strengthening, through this Treaty, certain positions concerning continental shelves to the detriment of others based on different criteria.

[2] On signing the Treaty, Brazil stated that nothing in the Treaty shall be interpreted as prejudicing in any way the sovereign rights of Brazil in the area of the sea, the sea-bed and the subsoil thereof adjacent to its coasts. It is the understanding of the Brazilian Government that the word 'observation', as it appears in paragraph 1 of Article III of the Treaty, refers only to observation that is incidental to the normal course of navigation in accordance with international law.

[3] In depositing the instrument of ratification, Canada declared: Article I, paragraph 1, cannot be interpreted as indicating that any state has a right to implant or emplace any weapons not prohibited under Article I, paragraph 1, on the sea-bed and ocean floor, and in the subsoil thereof, beyond the limits of national jurisdiction, or as constituting any limitation on the principle that this area of the sea-bed and ocean floor and the subsoil thereof shall be reserved for exclusively peaceful purposes. Articles I, II and III cannot be interpreted as indicating that any state but the coastal state has any right to implant or emplace any weapon not prohibited under Article I, paragraph 1 on the continental shelf, or the subsoil thereof, appertaining to that coastal state, beyond the outer limit of the sea-bed zone referred to in Article I and defined in Article II. Article III cannot be interpreted as indicating any restrictions or limitation upon the rights of the coastal state, consistent with its exclusive sovereign rights with respect to the continental shelf, to verify, inspect or effect the removal of any weapon, structure, installation, facility or device implanted or emplaced on the continental shelf, or the subsoil thereof, appertaining to that coastal state, beyond the outer limit of the sea-bed zone referred to in Article I and defined in Article II. On 12 Apr. 1976, the Federal Republic of Germany stated that the declaration by Canada is not of a nature to confer on the government of this country more far-reaching rights than those to which it is entitled under current international law, and that all rights existing under current international law which are not covered by the prohibitions are left intact by the Treaty.

[4] A statement was made containing a disclaimer regarding recognition of states party to the Treaty.

[5] On ratifying the Treaty, the Federal Republic of Germany declared that the Treaty will apply to Berlin (West).

[6] On the occasion of its accession to the Treaty, the government of India stated that as a coastal state, India has, and always has had, full and exclusive rights over the continental shelf adjoining its territory and beyond its territorial waters and the subsoil thereof. It is the considered view of India that other countries cannot use its continental shelf for military purposes. There cannot, therefore, be any restriction on, or limitation of, the sovereign right of India as a coastal state to verify, inspect, remove or destroy any weapon, device, structure, installation or facility, which might be implanted or emplaced on or beneath its continental shelf by any other country, or to take such other steps as may be considered necessary to safeguard its security. The accession by the government of India to the Treaty is based on this position. In response to the Indian statement, the US

Government expressed the view that, under existing international law, the rights of coastal states over their continental shelves are exclusive only for the purposes of exploration and exploitation of natural resources, and are otherwise limited by the 1958 Convention on the Continental Shelf and other principles of international law. On 12 Apr. 1976, the Federal Republic of Germany stated that the declaration by India is not of a nature to confer on the government of this country more far-reaching rights than those to which it is entitled under current international law, and that all rights existing under current law which are not covered by the prohibitions are left intact by the Treaty.

[7] On signing the Treaty, Italy stated, *inter alia*, that in the case of agreements on further measures in the field of disarmament to prevent an arms race on the sea-bed and ocean floor and in their subsoil, the question of the delimitation of the area within which these measures would find application shall have to be examined and solved in each instance in accordance with the nature of the measures to be adopted. The statement was repeated at the time of ratification.

[8] Mexico declared that in its view no provision of the Treaty can be interpreted to mean that a state has the right to emplace nuclear weapons or other weapons of mass destruction, or arms or military equipment of any type, on the continental shelf of Mexico. It reserves the right to verify, inspect, remove or destroy any weapon, structure, installation, device or equipment placed on its continental shelf, including nuclear weapons or other weapons of mass destruction.

[9] Ratification of the Treaty by Taiwan is considered by Romania as null and void.

[10] The United Kingdom recalled its view that if a regime is not recognized as the government of a state neither signature nor the deposit of any instrument by it, nor notification of any of those acts, will bring about recognition of that regime by any other state.

[11] Viet Nam stated that no provision of the Treaty should be interpreted in a way that would contradict the rights of the coastal states with regard to their continental shelf, including the right to take measures to ensure their security.

[12] On 25 Feb. 1974, the Ambassador of Yugoslavia transmitted to the US Secretary of State a note stating that in the view of the Yugoslav Government, Article III, paragraph 1, of the Treaty should be interpreted in such a way that a state exercising its right under this Article shall be obliged to notify in advance the coastal state, in so far as its observations are to be carried out 'within the stretch of the sea extending above the continental shelf of the said state'. On 16 Jan. 1975 the US Secretary of State presented the view of the United States concerning the Yugoslav note, as follows: In so far as the note is intended to be interpretative of the Treaty, the United States cannot accept it as a valid interpretation. In addition, the United States does not consider that it can have any effect on the existing law of the sea. In so far as the note was intended to be a reservation to the Treaty, the United States placed on record its formal objection to it on the grounds that it was incompatible with the object and purpose of the Treaty. The United States also drew attention to the fact that the note was submitted too late to be .legally effective as a reservation. A similar exchange of notes took place between Yugoslavia and the United Kingdom. On 12 Apr. 1976, the Federal Republic of Germany stated that the declaration by Yugoslavia is not of a nature to confer on the government of this country more far-reaching rights than those to which it is entitled under current international law, and that all rights existing under current international law which are not covered by the prohibitions are left intact by the Treaty.

[13] Notification of succession.

The BW Convention

[1] Considering the obligations resulting from its status as a permanently neutral state, Austria declares a reservation to the effect that its co-operation within the framework of this Convention cannot exceed the limits determined by the status of permanent neutrality and membership with the United Nations.

[2] China stated that the BW Convention has the following defects: it fails explicitly to prohibit the use of biological weapons; it does not provide for 'concrete and effective' measures of supervision and verification; and it lacks measures of sanctions in case of violation of the Convention. The Chinese Government hopes that these defects will be corrected at an appropriate time, and also that a convention for complete prohibition of chemical weapons will soon be concluded. The signature and ratification of the Convention by the Taiwan authorities in the name of China are considered illegal and null and void.

[3] On depositing its instrument of ratification, the Federal Republic of Germany stated that a major shortcoming of the BW Convention is that it does not contain any provisions for verifying compliance with its essential obligations. The Federal Government considers the right to lodge a complaint with the UN Security Council to be an inadequate arrangement. It would welcome the establishment of an independent international committee of experts able to carry out impartial investigations when doubts arise as to whether the Convention is being complied with.

[4] In a statement made on the occasion of the signature of the Convention, India reiterated its understanding that the objective of the Convention is to eliminate biological and toxin weapons, thereby excluding completely the possibility of their use, and that the exemption with regard to biological agents or toxins, which would be permitted for prophylactic, protective or other peaceful purposes, would not in any way create a loophole in regard to the production or retention of biological and toxin weapons. Also any assistance which might be furnished under the terms of the Convention would be of a medical or humanitarian nature and in conformity with the UN Charter. The statement was repeated at the time of the deposit of the instrument of ratification.

[5] Ireland considers that the Convention could be undermined if the reservations made by the parties to the 1925 Geneva Protocol were allowed to stand, as the prohibition of possession is incompatible with the right to retaliate, and that there should be an absolute and universal prohibition of the use of the weapons in question. Ireland notified the depositary government for the Geneva Protocol of the withdrawal of its reservations to the

Protocol, made at the time of accession in 1930. The withdrawal applies to chemical as well as to bacteriological (biological) and toxin agents of warfare.

[6] The Republic of Korea stated that the signing of the Convention does not in any way mean or imply the recognition of any territory or regime which has not been recognized by the Republic of Korea as a state or government.

[7] In the understanding of Kuwait, its ratification of the Convention does not in any way imply its recognition of Israel, nor does it oblige it to apply the provisions of the Conventions in respect of the said country.

[8] Mexico considers that the Convention is only a first step towards an agreement prohibiting also the development, production and stockpiling of all chemical weapons, and notes the fact that the Convention contains an express commitment to continue negotiations in good faith with the aim of arriving at such an agreement.

[9] Notification of succession.

[10] The ratification by Switzerland contains the following reservations:

1. Owing to the fact that the Convention also applies to weapons, equipment or means of delivery designed to use biological agents or toxins, the delimitation of its scope of application can cause difficulties since there are scarcely any weapons, equipment or means of delivery peculiar to such use; therefore, Switzerland reserves the right to decide for itself what auxiliary means fall within that definition.

2. By reason of the obligations resulting from its status as a perpetually neutral state, Switzerland is bound to make the general reservation that its collaboration within the framework of this Convention cannot go beyond the terms prescribed by that status. This reservation refers especially to Article VII of the Convention as well as to any similar clause that could replace or supplement that provision of the Convention.

In a note of 18 Aug. 1976, addressed to the Swiss Ambassador, the US Secretary of State stated the following view of the US Government with regard to the first reservation: The prohibition would apply only to (a) weapons, equipment and means of delivery, the design of which indicated that they could have no other use than that specified, and (b) weapons, equipment and means of delivery, the design of which indicated that they were specifically intended to be capable of the use specified. The government of the United States shares the view of the government of Switzerland that there are few weapons, equipment or means of delivery peculiar to the uses referred to. It does not, however, believe that it would be appropriate, on this ground alone, for states to reserve unilaterally the right to decide which weapons, equipment or means of delivery fell within the definition. Therefore, while acknowledging the entry into force of the Convention between itself and the government of Switzerland, the US Government enters its objection to this reservation.

[11] The deposit of the instrument of ratification by Taiwan is considered by the Soviet Union as an illegal act because the government of the People's Republic of China is regarded by the Soviet Union as the sole representative of China.

[12] The United Kingdom recalled its view that if a regime is not recognized as the government of a state, neither signature nor the deposit of any instrument by it nor notification of any of those acts will bring about recognition of that regime by any other state.

The Enmod Convention

[1] The Federal Republic of Germany declared that the Convention applies also to Berlin (West). The Soviet Union and the German Democratic Republic stated that the West German declaration was 'illegal', while France, the United Kingdom and the United States confirmed its validity.

[2] It is the understanding of the Republic of Korea that any technique for deliberately changing the natural state of rivers falls within the meaning of the term 'environmental modification techniques' as defined in Article II of the Convention. It is further understood that military or any other hostile use of such techniques, which could cause flooding, inundation, reduction in the water-level, drying up, destruction of hydrotechnical installations or other harmful consequences, comes within the scope of the Convention, provided it meets the criteria set out in Article 1 thereof.

[3] Kuwait made the following reservations and understanding: This Convention binds Kuwait only towards states parties thereto; its obligatory character shall *ipso facto* terminate with respect to any hostile state which does not abide by the prohibition contained therein. It is understood that accession to this Convention does not mean in any way recognition of Israel by Kuwait; furthermore, no treaty relation will arise between Kuwait and Israel.

On 23 June 1980, the UN Secretary-General, the depositary of the Convention, received from the government of Israel a communication stating that Israel would adopt towards Kuwait an attitude of complete reciprocity.

[4] The Netherlands accepts the obligation laid down in Article I of the Enmod Convention as extending to states which are not party to the Convention and which act in conformity with Article I of this Convention.

[5] New Zealand declared that, in its interpretation, nothing in the Convention detracts from or limits the obligations of states to refrain from military or any other hostile use of environmental modification techniques which are contrary to international law.

[6] Notification of succession.

[7] On signing the Convention, Turkey declared that the terms 'widespread', 'long-lasting' and 'severe effects' contained in the Convention need to be more clearly defined, and that so long as this clarification was not made, Turkey would be compelled to interpret for itself the terms in question and, consequently, reserved the right to do so as and when required. Turkey also stated its belief that the difference between 'military or any other hostile purposes' and 'peaceful purposes' should be more clearly defined so as to prevent subjective evaluations.

The 'Inhumane Weapons' Convention

1 Upon signature, China stated that the Convention fails to provide for supervision or verification of any violation of its clauses, thus weakening its binding force. The Protocol on mines, booby-traps and other devices fails to lay down strict restrictions on the use of such weapons by the aggressor on the territory of the victim and to provide adequately for the right of a state victim of an aggression to defend itself by all necessary means. The Protocol on incendiary weapons does not stipulate restrictions on the use of such weapons against combat personnel.

2 France stated that it regretted that it had not been possible to reach agreement on the provisions concerning the verification of facts which might be alleged and which might constitute violations of the undertakings subscribed to. It therefore reserved the right to submit, possibly in association with other states, proposals aimed at filling that gap at the first conference to be held pursuant to Article 8 of the Convention and to utilize, as appropriate, procedures that would make it possible to bring before the international community facts and information which, if verified, could constitute violations of the provisions of the Convention and the protocols annexed thereto.

Not being bound by the 1977 Additional Protocol I to the Geneva Conventions of 1949, France considers that the fourth paragraph of the preamble to the Convention on prohibitions or restrictions on the use of certain conventional weapons, which reproduces the provisions of Article 35, paragraph 3, of Additional Protocol I, applies only to states parties to that Protocol. France will apply the provisions of the Convention and its three Protocols to all the armed conflicts referred to in Articles 2 and 3 common to the Geneva Conventions of 1949.

3 Italy stated its regret that no agreement had been reached on provisions that would ensure respect for the obligations under the Convention. Italy intends to undertake efforts to ensure that the problem of the establishment of a mechanism that would make it possible to fill this gap in the Convention is taken up again at the earliest opportunity in every competent forum.

4 Romania stated that the provisions of the Convention and its Protocols have a restricted character and do not ensure adequate protection either to the civilian population or to the combatants as the fundamental principles of international humanitarian law require.

5 The United States stated that it had strongly supported proposals by other countries to include special procedures for dealing with compliance matters, and reserved the right to propose at a later date additional procedures and remedies, should this prove necessary, to deal with such problems.

The Treaty of Rarotonga

· ·1 In signing Protocols 2 and 3 on 10 Feb. 1987, China declared that it respected the status of the South Pacific nuclear-free zone and would neither use nor threaten to use nuclear weapons against the zone nor test nuclear weapons in the region. However, China reserved its right to reconsider its obligations under the Protocols if other nuclear weapon states or the contracting parties to the Treaty took any action in 'gross' violation of the Treaty and the Protocols, thus changing the status of the zone and endangering the security interests of China.

2 In signing Protocols 2 and 3 on 15 Dec. 1986, the Soviet Union stated the view that admission of transit of nuclear weapons or other nuclear explosive devices by any means, as well as of visits by foreign military ships and aircraft with nuclear explosive devices on board, to the ports and airfields within the nuclear-free zone would contradict the aims of the Treaty of Rarotonga and would be inconsistent with the status of the zone. It also warned that in case of action taken by a party or parties violating their major commitments connected with the nuclear-free status of the zone, as well as in case of aggression committed by one or several parties to the Treaty, supported by a nuclear weapon state, or together with it, with the use by such a state of the territory, airspace, territorial sea or archipelagic waters of the parties for visits by nuclear weapon-carrying ships and aircraft or for transit of nuclear weapons, the USSR will have the right to consider itself free of its non-use commitments assumed under Protocol 2.

I. UN member states and year of membership

In the following list of names of the 159 UN member states, the countries marked with an asterisk are also members of the Geneva-based Conference on Disarmament (CD).

Afghanistan, 1946
Albania, 1955
*Algeria, 1962
Angola, 1976
Antigua and Barbuda, 1981
*Argentina, 1945
*Australia, 1945
Austria, 1955
Bahamas, 1973
Bahrain, 1971
Bangladesh, 1974
Barbados, 1966
*Belgium, 1945
Belize, 1981
Benin, 1960
Bhutan, 1971
Bolivia, 1945
Botswana, 1966
*Brazil, 1945
Brunei Darussalam, 1984
*Bulgaria, 1955
Burkina Faso, 1960
*Burma, 1948
Burundi, 1962
Byelorussia, 1945
Cameroon, 1960
*Canada, 1945
Cape Verde, 1975
Central Africa Republic, 1960
Chad, 1960
Chile, 1945
*China, 1945
Colombia, 1945
Comoros, 1975
Congo, 1960
Costa Rica, 1945
Côte d'Ivoire, 1960
*Cuba, 1945
Cyprus, 1960
*Czechoslovakia, 1945
Denmark, 1945
Djibouti, 1977
Dominica, 1978
Dominican Republic, 1945
Ecuador, 1945
*Egypt, 1945
El Salvador, 1945
Equatorial Guinea, 1968
*Ethiopia, 1945
Fiji, 1970
Finland, 1955
*France, 1945
Gabon, 1960
Gambia, 1965
*German Democratic Republic, 1973

*FR Germany, 1973
Ghana, 1957
Greece, 1945
Grenada, 1974
Guatemala, 1945
Guinea, 1958
Guinea-Bissau, 1974
Guyana, 1966
Haiti, 1945
Honduras, 1945
*Hungary, 1955
Iceland, 1946
*India, 1945
*Indonesia, 1950
*Iran, 1945
Iraq, 1945
Ireland, 1955
Israel, 1949
*Italy, 1955
Ivory Coast (see Côte d'Ivoire)
Jamaica, 1962
*Japan, 1956
Jordan, 1955
Kampuchea, 1955
*Kenya, 1963
Kuwait, 1963
Lao People's Democratic
  Republic, 1955
Lebanon, 1945
Lesotho, 1966
Liberia, 1945
Libya, 1955
Luxembourg, 1945
Madagascar, 1960
Malawi, 1964
Malaysia, 1957
Maldives, 1965
Mali, 1960
Malta, 1964
Mauritania, 1961
Mauritius, 1968
*Mexico, 1945
*Mongolia, 1961
*Morocco, 1956
Mozambique, 1975
Nepal, 1955
*Netherlands, 1945
New Zealand, 1945
Nicaragua, 1945
Niger, 1960
*Nigeria, 1960
Norway, 1945
Oman, 1971
*Pakistan, 1947
Panama, 1945

Papua New Guinea, 1975
Paraguay, 1945
*Peru, 1945
Philippines, 1945
*Poland, 1945
Portugal, 1955
Qatar, 1971
*Romania, 1955
Rwanda, 1962
Saint Christopher and Nevis,
  1983
Saint Lucia, 1979
Saint Vincent and the Grenadines,
  1980
Samoa, Western, 1976
Sao Tome and Principe, 1975
Saudi Arabia, 1945
Senegal, 1960
Seychelles, 1976
Sierra Leone, 1961
Singapore, 1965
Solomon Islands, 1978
Somalia, 1960
South Africa, 1945
Spain, 1955
*Sri Lanka, 1955
Sudan, 1956
Suriname, 1975
Swaziland, 1968
*Sweden, 1946
Syria, 1945
Tanzania, 1961
Thailand, 1946
Togo, 1960
Trinidad and Tobago, 1962
Tunisia, 1956
Turkey, 1945
Uganda, 1962
*UK, 1945
Ukraine, 1945
United Arab Emirates, 1971
Uruguay, 1945
*USA, 1945
*USSR, 1945
Vanuatu, 1981
*Venezuela, 1945
Viet Nam, 1977
Yemen Arab Republic, 1947
Yemen, People's Democratic
  Republic of, 1967
*Yugoslavia, 1945
*Zaire, 1960
Zambia, 1964
Zimbabwe, 1980

Errata

World Armaments and Disarmament: SIPRI Yearbook 1986

Table 11A.4, page 240:   In the line for Japan, the figure for 1976 should read 1 488; for 1977, 1 653; and for 1978, 1 822

Page 316, section IV, second paragraph, line 2, should read: 'total of $138 million for the years 1979–82. The OECD puts the figure at $189 million'

INDEX

ABM (Anti-Ballistic Missile) Treaty (1972): interpretation 15, 75; research and 396, 450; Review Conference 75; *see also under* Reykjavik summit meeting
Aérospatiale 33, 93
Afghanistan 165, 169, 174; *see also under* Union of Soviet Socialist Republics
Africa: arms imports 145, 146, 149, 191, 202, 218–19; conflicts in 145, 147, 148, 202, 297, 298, 314–16; debts 145; military aid to 149; military expenditure 145–9, 165–6, 170–1; *see also under names of countries*
Agusta 192
aircraft: *general references:* numbers 6, 7, 18, 20, 30; *individual countries:* China 35; France 3, 29, 32, 301; NATO 13; UK 25, 27–8; USA bombers: Advanced Technology 10, 11; B-1 3, 4, 6, 8, 10, 11; B-52 4, 6, 10, 11, 456; FB-111 4, 11; Stealth 8, 10; USA fighters: F-15 70, 125; F-16 125, 192, 208, 209; F-20 192; F/A-18 125; USSR bombers: Backfire 20; Badger 20; Bear 18, 22; Blackjack 23; Blinder 20; USSR fighters: MiG-23 142; MiG-29 140, 189, 206; *see also* helicopters
aircraft-carriers: France 3, 32; USA 7
Akhromeyev, Marshal Sergei 206
Albania 164, 168
Alfonsín, President Raúl 152
Algeria: arms imports 187, 188, 201, 202; military expenditure 145, 165, 170, 175
America *see* United States of America
AMRAAM missile 125
Angola: arms imports 201, 202; chemical weapons and 106, 111; conflict in 188, 314; military expenditure 165, 170, 175; *see also* UNITA
ANT-52 bomb 32
Antarctic Treaty (1959) 457, 461, 462–76, 478
anti-tank warfare 87–8, 92
ANZUS Treaty 143, 400–1, 452
Apache helicopter 92
Apache missile 91
Aquino, President Corazon 142
Argentina: armed forces, reform 152; arms control and 50, 391, 392; arms imports 194, 199, 201; Brazil and 151; chemical weapons and 111; military, role of in 151; military expenditure 151–3, 167, 172, 177; National Security Law 152–3; *Plan Austral* 152
Ariane rocket 62, 65, 66, 75
armoured fighting vehicles 87, 88
arms control: approaches to, differing 332–3; operational 339, 345, 350–4; practised v. negotiated 336; structural 94, 339, 345, 348, 352, 354; verification, developments in 433–45; *see also under separate topics and treaty names*
arms trade: changes needed 182; commercialization 182, 190; competition 181; controlling 182; demand reduction 181, 190; economic factors 181, 188, 189, 190; exports, values of 220; imports, values of 218–19; modernization and 181, 189; off-set deals 181, 182, 188; political aspects 181, 182, 189; privatization 182; recipient countries 200–9; re-exports 199, 200; SIPRI price system

283–9; SIPRI sources and methods 291–6; supplier countries 181, 183, 186–200; technological transfer 182; upgrading and 181
Army Tactical Missile System 91
artillery, conventional 89–90
artillery, nuclear 4, 7, 12, 20, 24
artillery vehicles 87
AS-3 missile 22
AS-4 missile 22
ASAT (anti-satellite) activities: controlling 394, 395, 397, 433; USA 57, 68, 336, 455; USSR 57, 67–8, 336, 442
ASMP missile 3, 28, 29, 32, 449
ASROC 7, 13
ASW (anti-submarine warfare) systems 7, 14
ATBMs (anti-tactical ballistic missiles) 33, 73, 85
Atlas launcher 59, 61, 62, 75
atomic demolition munitions 7, 12, 20
Australia: chemical weapons and 104, 386; military expenditure 155, 156, 165, 170, 175; nuclear weapon tests 48, 447; seismology and 390; USA and 144
Austria: arms imports 207; military expenditure 134, 155, 156, 168, 173

Bahrain 135, 137, 164, 169, 174
Balkans: chemical weapon-free zone in 447, 448, 454; nuclear weapon-free zone in 454
Bangladesh 165, 169, 174
Basra 302, 305, 309
Battlefield Computing System 89
Belgium: chemical weapons and 101, 385; military expenditure 122, 127, 134, 155, 156, 163, 168, 173; missiles based in 11
Benin 165, 170, 175
Biden, Joseph R. 9, 190
Bigeye bomb 99, 108, 109, 455
Biological Weapons Convention (1972): depositories 409; evaluation 413–14; peaceful uses of biological agents 413; Review Conference 98, 409–14, 452; Review Conference Final Declaration 415–22; scope of 409–10, 459; status of 461, 462–76; strengthening 412–13; verification 409, 411, 414; violations alleged 98, 106
BMD *see* SDI
Bolivia 167, 172, 177
bombs, nuclear: France 32; UK 28; USA 4, 10, 12, 15
Botswana 149, 165, 170, 175
Bradley fighting vehicles 125
Brazil: Argentina and 151; arms exports 188, 198, 199, 220; military, role of in 151; military expenditure 167, 172, 177; South Atlantic peace zone and 405, 406; USA and 199
Britain *see* United Kingdom
Brunei 165, 169, 174
Brussels Club 104
Bulgaria 132, 134, 164, 168, 173
Burkina Faso 165, 170, 175
Burma: chemical weapons 110; conflict in 312–13; military expenditure 165, 169, 174
Burundi 165, 170, 175